THE
DECLINE AND
FALL
OF THE
ROMAN
EMPIRE

VOL 5 & 6

ROYAL

CLASSICS

History of the Decline and Fall of the Roman Empire Vol 5 & 6
Gibbon, Edward 1737 – 1794
First Published by Strahan & Cadell between 1776–1789
Text edits © 2024 Royal Classics
Design © 2024 Royal Classics

Text set in Minion Pro. Chapter headings set in News Gothic Standard.

ISBN: 978-1-77476-987-4

FIRST EDITION / FIRST PRINTING

Many classics were originally published with inconsistent spellings of the same word, spelling errors, and printer errors. The text of our titles have been edited to give readers the best possible reading experience. Sometimes we can make mistakes, which is why we post "first edition" in all of our titles. This is a standard notice that is historically used by publishers. The above edition notice refers to our edition of this title. If changes are made to correct an error in the text, we will change the wording to "second edition." If we change printers but the text remains the same, the wording will change to "second printing."

LIBRARY AND ARCHIVES CANADA CATALOGUING IN PUBLICATION

Library and Archives Canada Cataloguing in Publication

Title: History of the decline and fall of the Roman Empire / Edward Gibbon.

Names: Gibbon, Edward, 1737-1794, author.

Description: First edition. | "First published by Strahan & Cadell between 1776-1789"--Copyright page. | Contents: Vol 5 and 6.

Identifiers: Canadiana 20220472289 | ISBN 9781774769874 (v. 5 & 6 ; hardcover)

Subjects:
LCSH: Rome—History—Empire, 30 B.C.-476 A.D. |
LCSH: Byzantine Empire—History—To 527.

Classification: LCC DG311 .G5 2024 | DDC 937/.06—DC23

THE
DECLINE AND
FALL
OF THE
ROMAN
EMPIRE
VOL 5 & 6

EDWARD GIBBON

VANCOUVER:
ROYAL CLASSICS
2024

CONTENTS

CHAPTER FORTY NINE

Conquest of Italy by the Franks. – Part One

Introduction, Worship, and Persecution of Images. – Revolt of Italy and Rome. – Temporal Dominion of the Popes. – Conquest of Italy by the Franks. – Establishment of Images. – Character and Coronation of Charlemagne. – Restoration and Decay of the Roman Empire in the West. – Independence of Italy. – Constitution of the Germanic Body.

IN THE CONNECTION OF the church and state, I have considered the former as subservient only, and relative, to the latter; a salutary maxim, if in fact, as well as in narrative, it had ever been held sacred. The Oriental philosophy of the Gnostics, the dark abyss of predestination and grace, and the strange transformation of the Eucharist from the sign to the substance of Christ's body, I have purposely abandoned to the curiosity of speculative divines. But I have reviewed, with diligence and pleasure, the objects of ecclesiastical history, by which the decline and fall of the Roman empire were materially affected, the propagation of Christianity, the constitution of the Catholic church, the ruin of Paganism, and the sects that arose from the mysterious controversies concerning the Trinity and incarnation. At the head of this class, we may justly rank the worship of images, so fiercely disputed in the eighth and ninth centuries; since a question of popular superstition produced the revolt of Italy, the temporal power of the popes, and the restoration of the Roman empire in the West.

The primitive Christians were possessed with an unconquerable re-
pugnance to the use and abuse of images; and this aversion may be
ascribed to their descent from the Jews, and their enmity to the Greeks.
The Mosaic law had severely proscribed all representations of the Deity;
and that precept was firmly established in the principles and practice
of the chosen people. The wit of the Christian apologists was pointed
against the foolish idolaters, who bowed before the workmanship of
their own hands; the images of brass and marble, which, had *they* been
endowed with sense and motion, should have started rather from the
pedestal to adore the creative powers of the artist. Perhaps some recent
and imperfect converts of the Gnostic tribe might crown the statues of
Christ and St. Paul with the profane honors which they paid to those of
Aristotle and Pythagoras; but the public religion of the Catholics was
uniformly simple and spiritual; and the first notice of the use of pictures
is in the censure of the council of Illiberis, three hundred years after
the Christian æra. Under the successors of Constantine, in the peace
and luxury of the triumphant church, the more prudent bishops condescended to indulge a visible superstition, for the benefit of the multitude; and, after the ruin of Paganism, they were no longer restrained by
the apprehension of an odious parallel. The first introduction of a sym-
bolic worship was in the veneration of the cross, and of relics. The saints
and martyrs, whose intercession was implored, were seated on the right
hand of God; but the gracious and often supernatural favors, which, in
the popular belief, were showered round their tomb, conveyed an unquestionable sanction of the devout pilgrims, who visited, and touched,
and kissed these lifeless remains, the memorials of their merits and sufferings. But a memorial, more interesting than the skull or the sandals
of a departed worthy, is the faithful copy of his person and features,
delineated by the arts of painting or sculpture. In every age, such copies, so congenial to human feelings, have been cherished by the zeal of
private friendship, or public esteem: the images of the Roman emperors
were adored with civil, and almost religious, honors; a reverence less
ostentatious, but more sincere, was applied to the statues of sages and
patriots; and these profane virtues, these splendid sins, disappeared in
the presence of the holy men, who had died for their celestial and everlasting country. At first, the experiment was made with caution and
scruple; and the venerable pictures were discreetly allowed to instruct
the ignorant, to awaken the cold, and to gratify the prejudices of the
heathen proselytes. By a slow though inevitable progression, the honors of the original were transferred to the copy: the devout Christian
prayed before the image of a saint; and the Pagan rites of genuflec-

tion, luminaries, and incense, again stole into the Catholic church. The scruples of reason, or piety, were silenced by the strong evidence of visions and miracles; and the pictures which speak, and move, and bleed, must be endowed with a divine energy, and may be considered as the proper objects of religious adoration. The most audacious pencil might tremble in the rash attempt of defining, by forms and colors, the infinite Spirit, the eternal Father, who pervades and sustains the universe. But the superstitious mind was more easily reconciled to paint and to worship the angels, and, above all, the Son of God, under the human shape, which, on earth, they have condescended to assume. The second person of the Trinity had been clothed with a real and mortal body; but that body had ascended into heaven: and, had not some similitude been presented to the eyes of his disciples, the spiritual worship of Christ might have been obliterated by the visible relics and representations of the saints. A similar indulgence was requisite and propitious for the Virgin Mary: the place of her burial was unknown; and the assumption of her soul and body into heaven was adopted by the credulity of the Greeks and Latins. The use, and even the worship, of images was firmly established before the end of the sixth century: they were fondly cherished by the warm imagination of the Greeks and Asiatics: the Pantheon and Vatican were adorned with the emblems of a new superstition; but this semblance of idolatry was more coldly entertained by the rude Barbarians and the Arian clergy of the West. The bolder forms of sculpture, in brass or marble, which peopled the temples of antiquity, were offensive to the fancy or conscience of the Christian Greeks: and a smooth surface of colors has ever been esteemed a more decent and harmless mode of imitation.

The merit and effect of a copy depends on its resemblance with the original; but the primitive Christians were ignorant of the genuine features of the Son of God, his mother, and his apostles: the statue of Christ at Paneas in Palestine was more probably that of some temporal savior; the Gnostics and their profane monuments were reprobated; and the fancy of the Christian artists could only be guided by the clandestine imitation of some heathen model. In this distress, a bold and dexterous invention assured at once the likeness of the image and the innocence of the worship. A new super structure of fable was raised on the popular basis of a Syrian legend, on the correspondence of Christ and Abgarus, so famous in the days of Eusebius, so reluctantly deserted by our modern advocates. The bishop of Cæsarea records the epistle, but he most strangely forgets the picture of Christ; the perfect impression of his face on a linen, with which he gratified the faith of the royal stranger who had invoked his healing power, and offered the strong city of Edessa to protect him against the malice of the Jews. The ignorance of the primitive church is explained by the long imprisonment of the image in a niche of the wall, from whence, after an oblivion of five hundred years, it was released by some prudent bishop, and seasonably presented to the devotion of the times. Its first and most glorious exploit was the deliverance of the city from the arms of Chosroes Nushirvan; and it was soon revered as a pledge of the divine promise, that Edessa should never be taken by a foreign enemy. It is true, indeed, that the text of Procopius ascribes the double deliverance of Edessa to the wealth and valor of her citizens, who purchased the absence and repelled the assaults of the Persian monarch. He was ignorant, the profane historian, of the testimony which he is compelled to deliver in the ecclesiastical page of Evagrius, that the Palladium was exposed on the rampart, and that the water which had been sprinkled on the holy face, instead of quenching, added new fuel to the flames of the besieged. After this important service, the image of Edessa was preserved with respect and gratitude; and if the Armenians rejected the legend, the more credulous Greeks adored the similitude, which was not the work of any mortal pencil, but the immediate creation of the divine original. The style and sentiments of a Byzantine hymn will declare how far their worship was removed from the grossest idolatry. "How can we with mortal eyes contemplate this image, whose celestial splendor the host of heaven presumes not to behold? He who dwells in heaven, condescends this day to visit us by his venerable image; He who is seated on the cherubim, visits us this day by a picture, which the Father has delineated with his immaculate hand, which he has formed in an ineffable manner, and which we sanctify by adoring it with fear and love." Before the end of the sixth century, these images, *made without hands,* (in Greek it is a single word,) were propagated in the camps and cities of the Eastern empire: they were the objects of worship, and the instruments of miracles; and in the hour of danger or tumult, their venerable presence could revive the hope, rekindle the courage, or repress the fury, of the Roman legions. Of these pictures, the far greater part, the transcripts of a human pencil, could only pretend to a secondary likeness and improper title: but there were some of higher descent, who derived their resemblance from an immediate contact with the original, endowed, for that purpose, with a miraculous and prolific virtue. The most ambitious aspired from a filial to a fraternal relation with the image of Edessa; and such is the *veronica* of Rome, or Spain, or Jerusalem, which Christ in his agony and bloody sweat applied to his face, and delivered to a holy matron. The fruitful precedent was speedily transferred to the Virgin Mary, and the saints and martyrs. In the church of Diospolis, in Palestine, the features of the Mother of God were deeply inscribed in a marble column; the East and West have been decorated by the pencil of St. Luke; and the Evangelist, who was perhaps a physician, has been forced to exercise the occupation of a painter, so profane and odious in the eyes of the primitive Christians. The Olympian Jove, created by the muse of Homer and the chisel of Phidias, might inspire a philosophic mind with momentary devotion; but these Catholic images were faintly and flatly delineated by monkish artists in the last degeneracy of taste and genius.

The worship of images had stolen into the church by insensible degrees, and each petty step was pleasing to the superstitious mind, as productive of comfort, and innocent of sin. But in the beginning of the eighth century, in the full magnitude of the abuse, the more timorous Greeks were awakened by an apprehension, that under the mask of Christianity, they had restored the religion of their fathers: they heard, with grief and impatience, the name of idolaters; the incessant charge of the Jews and Mahometans, who derived from the Law and the Koran an immortal hatred to graven images and all relative worship. The servitude of the Jews might curb their zeal, and depreciate their authority; but the triumphant Mussulmans, who reigned at Damascus, and threatened Constantinople, cast into the scale of reproach the accumulated weight of truth and victory. The cities of Syria, Palestine, and Egypt had been fortified with the images of Christ, his mother, and his saints; and each city presumed on the hope or promise of miraculous defence. In a rapid conquest of ten years, the Arabs subdued those cities and these images; and, in their opinion, the Lord of Hosts pronounced a decisive judgment between the adoration and contempt of these mute and inanimate idols. For a while Edessa had braved the Persian assaults; but the chosen city, the spouse of Christ, was involved in the common ruin; and his divine resemblance became the slave and trophy of the infidels. After a servitude of three hundred years, the Palladium was yielded to the devotion of Constantinople, for a ransom of twelve thousand pounds of silver, the redemption of two hundred Mussulmans, and a perpetual truce for the territory of Edessa. In this season of distress and dismay, the eloquence of the monks was exercised in the defence of images; and they attempted to prove, that the sin and schism of the greatest part of the Orientals had forfeited the favor, and annihilated the virtue, of these precious symbols. But they were now opposed by the murmurs of many simple or rational Christians, who appealed to the evidence of texts, of facts, and of the primitive times, and secretly desired the reformation of the church. As the worship of images had never been established by any general or positive law, its progress in the Eastern empire had been retarded, or accelerated, by the differences of men and manners, the local degrees of refinement, and the personal characters of the bishops. The splendid devotion was fondly cherished by the levity of the capital, and the inventive genius of the Byzantine clergy; while the rude and remote districts of Asia were strangers to this innovation of sacred luxury. Many large congregations of Gnostics and Arians maintained, after their conversion, the simple worship which had preceded their separation; and the Armenians, the most warlike subjects of Rome, were not reconciled, in the twelfth century, to the sight of images. These various denominations of men afforded a fund of prejudice and aversion, of small account in the villages of Anatolia or Thrace, but which, in the fortune of a soldier, a prelate, or a eunuch, might be often connected with the powers of the church and state.

Of such adventurers, the most fortunate was the emperor Leo the Third, who, from the mountains of Isauria, ascended the throne of the East. He was ignorant of sacred and profane letters; but his education, his reason, perhaps his intercourse with the Jews and Arabs, had inspired the martial peasant with a hatred of images; and it was held to be the duty of a prince to impose on his subjects the dictates of his own conscience. But in the outset of an unsettled reign, during ten years of toil and danger, Leo submitted to the meanness of hypocrisy, bowed before the idols which he despised, and satisfied the Roman pontiff with the annual professions of his orthodoxy and zeal. In the reformation of religion, his first steps were moderate and cautious: he assembled a great council of senators and bishops, and enacted, with their consent, that all the images should be removed from the sanctuary and altar to a proper height in the churches where they might be visible to the eyes, and inaccessible to the superstition, of the people. But it was impossible on either side to check the rapid through adverse impulse of veneration and abhorrence: in their lofty position, the sacred images still edified their votaries, and reproached the tyrant. He was himself provoked by resistance and invective; and his own party accused him of an imperfect discharge of his duty, and urged for his imitation the example of the Jewish king, who had broken without scruple the brazen serpent of the temple. By a second edict, he proscribed the existence as well as the use of religious pictures; the churches of Constantinople and the provinces were cleansed from idolatry; the images of Christ, the Virgin, and the saints, were demolished, or a smooth surface of plaster was spread over the walls of the edifice. The sect of the Iconoclasts was supported by the zeal and despotism of six emperors, and the East and West were involved in a noisy conflict of one hundred and twenty years. It was the design of Leo the Isaurian to pronounce the condemnation of images as an article of faith, and by the authority of a general council: but the convocation of such an assembly was reserved for his son Constantine; and though it is stigmatized by triumphant bigotry as a meeting of fools and atheists, their own partial and mutilated acts betray many symptoms of reason and piety. The debates and decrees of many provincial synods introduced the summons of the general council which met in the suburbs of Constantinople, and was composed of the respectable number of three hundred and thirty-eight bishops of Europe and Anatolia; for the patriarchs of Antioch and Alexandria were the slaves of the caliph, and the Roman pontiff had withdrawn the churches of Italy and the West from the communion of the Greeks. This Byzantine synod assumed the rank and powers of the seventh general council; yet even this title was a recognition of the six preceding assemblies, which had laboriously built the structure of the Catholic faith. After a serious deliberation of six months, the three hundred and thirty-eight bishops pronounced and subscribed a unanimous decree, that all visible symbols of Christ, except in the Eucharist, were either blasphemous or heretical; that image-worship was a corruption of Christianity and a renewal of Paganism; that all such monuments of idolatry should be broken or erased; and that those who should refuse to deliver the objects of their private superstition, were guilty of disobedience to the authority of the church and of the emperor. In their loud and loyal acclamations, they celebrated the merits of their temporal redeemer; and to his zeal and justice they intrusted the execution of their spiritual censures. At Constantinople, as in the former councils, the will of the prince was the rule of episcopal faith; but on this occasion, I am inclined to suspect that a large majority of the prelates sacrificed their secret conscience to the temptations of hope and fear. In the long night of superstition, the Christians had wandered far away from the simplicity of the gospel: nor was it easy for them to discern the clew, and tread back the mazes, of the labyrinth. The worship of images was inseparably blended, at least to a pious fancy, with the Cross, the Virgin, the Saints and their relics; the holy ground was involved in a cloud of miracles and visions; and the nerves of the mind, curiosity and scepticism, were benumbed by the habits of obedience and belief. Constantine himself is accused of indulging a royal license to doubt, or deny, or deride the mysteries of the Catholics, but they were deeply inscribed in the public and private creed of his bishops; and the boldest Iconoclast might assault with a secret horror the monuments of popular devotion, which were consecrated to the honor of his celestial patrons. In the reformation of the sixteenth century, freedom and knowledge had expanded all the faculties of man: the thirst of innovation superseded the reverence of antiquity; and the vigor of Europe could disdain those phantoms which terrified the sickly and servile weakness of the Greeks.

The scandal of an abstract heresy can be only proclaimed to the people by the blast of the ecclesiastical trumpet; but the most ignorant can perceive, the most torpid must feel, the profanation and downfall of their visible deities. The first hostilities of Leo were directed against a lofty Christ on the vestibule, and above the gate, of the palace. A ladder had been planted for the assault, but it was furiously shaken by a crowd of zealots and women: they beheld, with pious transport, the ministers of sacrilege tumbling from on high and dashed against the pavement: and the honors of the ancient martyrs were prostituted to these criminals, who justly suffered for murder and rebellion. The execution of the Imperial edicts was resisted by frequent tumults in Constantinople and the provinces: the person of Leo was endangered, his officers were massacred, and the popular enthusiasm was quelled by the strongest efforts of the civil and military power. Of the Archipelago, or Holy Sea, the numerous islands were filled with images and monks: their votaries abjured, without scruple, the enemy of Christ, his mother, and the saints; they armed a fleet of boats and galleys, displayed their consecrated banners, and boldly steered for the harbor of Constantinople, to place on the throne a new favorite of God and the people. They depended on the succor of a miracle: but their miracles were inefficient against the *Greek fire*; and, after the defeat and conflagration of the fleet, the naked islands were abandoned to the clemency or justice of the conqueror. The son of Leo, in the first year of his reign, had undertaken an expedition against the Saracens: during his absence, the capital, the palace, and the purple, were occupied by his kinsman Artavasdes, the ambitious champion of the orthodox faith. The worship of images was triumphantly restored: the patriarch renounced his dissimulation, or dissembled his sentiments and the righteous claims of the usurper was acknowledged, both in the new, and in ancient, Rome. Constantine flew for refuge to his paternal mountains; but he descended at the head of the bold and affectionate Isaurians; and his final victory confounded the arms and predictions of the fanatics. His long reign was distracted with clamor, sedition, conspiracy, and mutual hatred, and sanguinary revenge; the persecution of images was the motive or pretence, of his adversaries; and, if they missed a temporal diadem, they were rewarded by the Greeks with the crown of martyrdom. In every act of open and clandestine treason, the emperor felt the unforgiving enmity of the monks, the faithful slaves of the superstition to which they owed their riches and influence. They prayed, they preached, they absolved, they inflamed, they conspired; the solitude of Palestine poured forth a torrent of invective; and the pen of St. John Damascenus, the last of the Greek fathers, devoted the tyrant's head, both in this world and the next. I am not at leisure to examine how far the monks provoked, nor how much they have exaggerated, their real and pretended sufferings, nor how many lost their lives or limbs, their eyes or their beards, by the cruelty of the emperor. From the chastisement of individuals, he proceeded to the abolition of the order; and, as it was wealthy and useless, his resentment might be stimulated by avarice, and justified by patriotism. The formidable name and mission of the *Dragon*, his visitor-general, excited the terror and abhorrence of the *black* nation: the religious communities were dissolved, the buildings were converted into magazines, or barracks; the lands, movables, and cattle were confiscated; and our modern precedents will support the charge, that much wanton or malicious havoc was exercised against the relics, and even the books of the monasteries. With the habit and profession of monks, the public and private worship of images was rigorously proscribed; and it should seem, that a solemn abjuration of idolatry was exacted from the subjects, or at least from the clergy, of the Eastern empire.

The patient East abjured, with reluctance, her sacred images; they were fondly cherished, and vigorously defended, by the independent zeal of the Italians. In ecclesiastical rank and jurisdiction, the patriarch of Constantinople and the pope of Rome were nearly equal. But the Greek prelate was a domestic slave under the eye of his master, at whose nod he alternately passed from the convent to the throne, and from the throne to the convent. A distant and dangerous station, amidst the Barbarians of the West, excited the spirit and freedom of the Latin bishops. Their popular election endeared them to the Romans: the public and private indigence was relieved by their ample revenue; and the weakness or neglect of the emperors compelled them to consult, both in peace and war, the temporal safety of the city. In the school of adversity the priest insensibly imbibed the virtues and the ambition of a prince; the same character was assumed, the same policy was adopted, by the Italian, the Greek, or the Syrian, who ascended the chair of St. Peter; and, after the loss of her legions and provinces, the genius and fortune of the popes again restored the supremacy of Rome. It is agreed, that in the eighth century, their dominion was founded on rebellion, and that the rebellion was produced, and justified, by the heresy of the Iconoclasts; but the conduct of the second and third Gregory, in this memorable contest, is variously interpreted by the wishes of their friends and enemies. The Byzantine writers unanimously declare, that, after a fruitless admonition, they pronounced the separation of the East and West, and deprived the sacrilegious tyrant of the revenue and sovereignty of Italy. Their excommunication is still more clearly expressed by the Greeks, who beheld the accomplishment of the papal triumphs; and as they are more strongly attached to their religion than to their country, they praise, instead of blaming, the zeal and orthodoxy of these apostolical men. The modern champions of Rome are eager to accept the praise and the precedent: this great and glorious example of the deposition of royal heretics is celebrated by the cardinals Baronius and Bellarmine; and if they are asked, why the same thunders were not hurled against the Neros and Julians of antiquity, they reply, that the weakness of the primitive church was the sole cause of her patient loyalty. On this occasion the effects of love and hatred are the same; and the zealous Protestants, who seek to kindle the indignation, and to alarm the fears, of princes and magistrates, expatiate on the insolence and treason of the two Gregories against their lawful sovereign. They are defended only by the moderate Catholics, for the most part, of the Gallican church, who respect the saint, without approving the sin. These common advocates of the crown and the mitre circumscribe the truth of facts by the rule of equity, Scripture, and tradition, and appeal to the evidence of the Latins, and the lives and epistles of the popes; themselves.

Conquest of Italy by the Franks. – Part Two

TWO ORIGINAL EPISTLES, from Gregory the Second to the emperor Leo, are still extant; and if they cannot be praised as the most perfect models of eloquence and logic, they exhibit the portrait, or at least the mask, of the founder of the papal monarchy. "During ten pure and fortunate years," says Gregory to the emperor, "we have tasted the annual comfort of your royal letters, subscribed in purple ink, with your own hand, the sacred pledges of your attachment to the orthodox creed of our fathers. How deplorable is the change! how tremendous the scandal! You now accuse the Catholics of idolatry; and, by the accusation, you betray your own impiety and ignorance. To this ignorance we are compelled to adapt the grossness of our style and arguments: the first elements of holy letters are sufficient for your confusion; and were you to enter a grammar-school, and avow yourself the enemy of our worship, the simple and pious children would be provoked to cast their horn-books at your head." After this decent salutation, the pope attempts the usual distinction between the idols of antiquity and the Christian images. The former were the fanciful representations of phantoms or dæmons, at a time when the true God had not manifested his person in any visible likeness. The latter are the genuine forms of Christ, his mother, and his saints, who had approved, by a crowd of miracles, the innocence and merit of this relative worship. He must indeed have trusted to the ignorance of Leo, since he could assert the perpetual use of images, from the apostolic age, and their venerable presence in the six synods of the Catholic church. A more specious argument is drawn from present possession and recent practice the harmony of the Christian world supersedes the demand of a general council; and Gregory frankly confesses, than such assemblies can only be useful under the reign of an orthodox prince. To the impudent and inhuman Leo, more guilty than a heretic, he recommends peace, silence, and implicit obedience to his spiritual guides of Constantinople and Rome. The limits of civil and ecclesiastical powers are defined by the pontiff. To the former he appropriates the body; to the latter, the soul: the sword of justice is in the hands of the magistrate: the more formidable weapon of excommunication is intrusted to the clergy; and in the exercise of their divine commission a zealous son will not spare his offending father: the successor of St. Peter may lawfully chastise the kings of the earth. "You assault us, O tyrant! with a carnal and military hand: unarmed and naked we can only implore the Christ, the prince of the heavenly host, that he will send unto you a devil, for the destruction of your body and the salvation of your soul. You declare, with foolish arrogance, I will despatch my orders to Rome: I will break in pieces the image of St. Peter; and Gregory, like his predecessor Martin, shall be transported in chains, and in exile, to the foot of the Imperial throne. Would to God that I might be permitted to tread in the footsteps of the holy Martin! but may the fate of Constans serve as a warning to the persecutors of the church! After his just condemnation by the bishops of Sicily, the tyrant was cut off, in the fullness of his sins, by a domestic servant: the saint is still adored by the nations of Scythia, among whom he ended his banishment and his life. But it is our duty to live for the edification and support of the faithful people; nor are we reduced to risk our safety on the event of a combat. Incapable as you are of defending your Roman subjects, the maritime situation of the city may perhaps expose it to your depredation but we can remove to the distance of four-and-twenty *stadia*, to the first fortress of the Lombards, and then – you may pursue the winds. Are you ignorant that the popes are the bond of union, the mediators of peace, between the East and West? The eyes of the nations are fixed on our humility; and they revere, as a God upon earth, the apostle St. Peter, whose image you threaten to destroy. The remote and interior kingdoms of the West present their homage to Christ and his vicegerent; and we now prepare to visit one of their most powerful monarchs, who desires to receive from our hands the sacrament of baptism. The Barbarians have submitted to the yoke of the gospel, while you alone are deaf to the voice of the shepherd. These pious Barbarians are kindled into rage: they thirst to avenge the persecution of the East. Abandon your rash and fatal enterprise; reflect, tremble, and repent. If you persist, we are innocent of the blood that will be spilt in the contest; may it fall on your own head!"

The first assault of Leo against the images of Constantinople had been witnessed by a crowd of strangers from Italy and the West, who related with grief and indignation the sacrilege of the emperor. But on the reception of his proscriptive edict, they trembled for their domestic deities: the images of Christ and the Virgin, of the angels, martyrs, and saints, were abolished in all the churches of Italy; and a strong alternative was proposed to the Roman pontiff, the royal favor as the price of his compliance, degradation and exile as the penalty of his disobedience. Neither zeal nor policy allowed him to hesitate; and the haughty strain in which Gregory addressed the emperor displays his confidence in the truth of his doctrine or the powers of resistance. Without depending on prayers or miracles, he boldly armed against the public enemy, and his pastoral letters admonished the Italians of their danger and their duty. At this signal, Ravenna, Venice, and the cities of the Exarchate and Pentapolis, adhered to the cause of religion; their military force by sea and land consisted, for the most part, of the natives; and the spirit of patriotism and zeal was transfused into the mercenary strangers. The Italians swore to live and die in the defence of the pope and the holy images; the Roman people was devoted to their father, and even the Lombards were ambitious to share the merit and advantage of this holy war. The most treasonable act, but the most obvious revenge, was the destruction of the statues of Leo himself: the most effectual and pleasing measure of rebellion, was the withholding the tribute of Italy, and depriving him of a power which he had recently abused by the imposition of a new capitation. A form of administration was preserved by the election of magistrates and governors; and so high was the public indignation, that the Italians were prepared to create an orthodox emperor, and to conduct him with a fleet and army to the palace of Constantinople. In that palace, the Roman bishops, the second and third Gregory, were condemned as the authors of the revolt, and every attempt was made, either by fraud or force, to seize their persons, and to strike at their lives. The city was repeatedly visited or assaulted by captains of the guards, and dukes and exarchs of high dignity or secret trust; they landed with foreign troops, they obtained some domestic aid, and the superstition of Naples may blush that her fathers were attached to the cause of heresy. But these clandestine or open attacks were repelled by the courage and vigilance of the Romans; the Greeks were overthrown and massacred, their leaders suffered an ignominious death, and the popes, however inclined to mercy, refused to intercede for these guilty victims. At Ravenna, the several quarters of the city had long exercised a bloody and hereditary feud; in religious controversy they found a new aliment of faction: but the votaries of images were superior in numbers or spirit, and the exarch, who attempted to stem the torrent, lost his life in a popular sedition. To punish this flagitious deed, and restore his dominion in Italy, the emperor sent a fleet and army into the Adriatic Gulf. After suffering from the winds and waves much loss and delay, the Greeks made their descent in the neighborhood of Ravenna: they threatened to depopulate the guilty capital, and to imitate, perhaps to surpass, the example of Justinian the Second, who had chastised a former rebellion by the choice and execution of fifty of the principal inhabitants. The women and clergy, in sackcloth and ashes, lay prostrate in prayer: the men were in arms for the defence of their country; the common danger had united the factions, and the event of a battle was preferred to the slow miseries of a siege. In a hard-fought day, as the two armies alternately yielded and advanced, a phantom was seen, a voice was heard, and Ravenna was victorious by the assurance of victory. The strangers retreated to their ships, but the populous sea-coast poured forth a multitude of boats; the waters of the Po were so deeply infected with blood, that during six years the public prejudice abstained from the fish of the river; and the institution of an annual feast perpetuated the worship of images, and the abhorrence of the Greek tyrant. Amidst the triumph of the Catholic arms, the Roman pontiff convened a synod of ninety-three bishops against the heresy of the Iconoclasts. With their consent, he pronounced a general excommunication against all who by word or deed should attack the tradition of the fathers and the images of the saints: in this sentence the emperor was tacitly involved, but the vote of a last and hopeless remonstrance may seem to imply that the anathema was yet suspended over his guilty head. No sooner had they confirmed their own safety, the worship of images, and the freedom of Rome and Italy, than the popes appear to have relaxed of their severity, and to have spared the relics of the Byzantine dominion. Their moderate councils delayed and prevented the election of a new emperor, and they exhorted the Italians not to separate from the body of the Roman monarchy. The exarch was permitted to reside within the walls of Ravenna, a captive rather than a master; and till the Imperial coronation of Charlemagne, the government of Rome and Italy was exercised in the name of the successors of Constantine.

The liberty of Rome, which had been oppressed by the arms and arts of Augustus, was rescued, after seven hundred and fifty years of servitude, from the persecution of Leo the Isaurian. By the Cæsars, the triumphs of the consuls had been annihilated: in the decline and fall of the empire, the god Terminus, the sacred boundary, had insensibly receded from the ocean, the Rhine, the Danube, and the Euphrates; and Rome was reduced to her ancient territory from Viterbo to Terracina, and from Narni to the mouth of the Tyber. When the kings were banished, the republic reposed on the firm basis which had been founded by their wisdom and virtue. Their perpetual jurisdiction was divided between two annual magistrates: the senate continued to exercise the powers of administration and counsel; and the legislative authority was distributed in the assemblies of the people, by a well-proportioned scale of property and service. Ignorant of the arts of luxury, the primitive Romans had improved the science of government and war: the will of the community was absolute: the rights of individuals were sacred: one hundred and thirty thousand citizens were armed for defence or conquest; and a band of robbers and outlaws was moulded into a nation deserving of freedom and ambitious of glory. When the sovereignty of the Greek emperors was extinguished, the ruins of Rome presented the sad image of depopulation and decay: her slavery was a habit, her liberty an accident; the effect of superstition, and the object of her own amazement and terror. The last vestige of the substance, or even the forms, of the constitution, was obliterated from the practice and memory of the Romans; and they were devoid of knowledge, or virtue, again to build the fabric of a commonwealth. Their scanty remnant, the offspring of slaves and strangers, was despicable in the eyes of the victorious Barbarians. As often as the Franks or Lombards expressed their most bitter contempt of a foe, they called him a Roman; "and in this name," says the bishop Liutprand, "we include whatever is base, whatever is cowardly, whatever is perfidious, the extremes of avarice and luxury, and every vice that can prostitute the dignity of human nature." By the necessity of their situation, the inhabitants of Rome were cast into the rough model of a republican government: they were compelled to elect some judges in peace, and some leaders in war: the nobles assembled to deliberate, and their resolves could not be executed without the union and consent of the multitude. The style of the Roman senate and people was revived, but the spirit was fled; and their new independence was disgraced by the tumultuous conflict of licentiousness and oppression. The want of laws could only be supplied by the influence of religion, and their foreign and domestic counsels were moderated by the authority of the bishop. His alms, his sermons, his correspondence with the kings and prelates of the West, his recent services, their gratitude, and oath, accustomed the Romans to consider him as the first magistrate or prince of the city. The Christian humility of the popes was not offended by the name of *Dominus*, or Lord; and their face and inscription are still apparent on the most ancient coins. Their temporal dominion is now confirmed by the reverence of a thousand years; and their noblest title is the free choice of a people, whom they had redeemed from slavery.

In the quarrels of ancient Greece, the holy people of Elis enjoyed a perpetual peace, under the protection of Jupiter, and in the exercise of the Olympic games. Happy would it have been for the Romans, if a similar privilege had guarded the patrimony of St. Peter from the calamities of war; if the Christians, who visited the holy threshold, would have sheathed their swords in the presence of the apostle and his successor. But this mystic circle could have been traced only by the wand of a legislator and a sage: this pacific system was incompatible with the zeal and ambition of the popes; the Romans were not addicted, like the inhabitants of Elis, to the innocent and placid labors of agriculture; and the Barbarians of Italy, though softened by the climate, were far below the Grecian states in the institutions of public and private life. A memorable example of repentance and piety was exhibited by Liutprand, king of the Lombards. In arms, at the gate of the Vatican, the conqueror listened to the voice of Gregory the Second, withdrew his troops, resigned his conquests, respectfully visited the church of St. Peter, and after performing his devotions, offered his sword and dagger, his cuirass and mantle, his silver cross, and his crown of gold, on the tomb of the apostle. But this religious fervor was the illusion, perhaps the artifice, of the moment; the sense of interest is strong and lasting; the love of arms and rapine was congenial to the Lombards; and both the prince and people were irresistibly tempted by the disorders of Italy, the nakedness of Rome, and the unwarlike profession of her new chief. On the first edicts of the emperor, they declared themselves the champions of the holy images: Liutprand invaded the province of Romagna, which had already assumed that distinctive appellation; the Catholics of the Exarchate yielded without reluctance to his civil and military power; and a foreign enemy was introduced for the first time into the impregnable fortress of Ravenna. That city and fortress were speedily recovered by the active diligence and maritime forces of the Venetians; and those faithful subjects obeyed the exhortation of Gregory himself, in separating the personal guilt of Leo from the general cause of the Roman empire. The Greeks were less mindful of the service, than the Lombards of the injury: the two nations, hostile in their faith, were reconciled in a dangerous and unnatural alliance: the king and the exarch marched to the conquest of Spoleto and Rome: the storm evaporated without effect, but the policy of Liutprand alarmed Italy with a vexatious alternative of hostility and truce. His successor Astolphus declared himself the equal enemy of the emperor and the pope: Ravenna was subdued by force or treachery, and this final conquest extinguished the series of the exarchs, who had reigned with a subordinate power since the time of Justinian and the ruin of the Gothic kingdom. Rome was summoned to acknowledge the victorious Lombard as her lawful sovereign; the annual tribute of a piece of gold was fixed as the ransom of each citizen, and the sword of destruction was unsheathed to exact the penalty of her disobedience. The Romans hesitated; they entreated; they complained; and the threatening Barbarians were checked by arms and negotiations, till the popes had engaged the friendship of an ally and avenger beyond the Alps.

In his distress, the first Gregory had implored the aid of the hero of the age, of Charles Martel, who governed the French monarchy with the humble title of mayor or duke; and who, by his signal victory over the Saracens, had saved his country, and perhaps Europe, from the Mahometan yoke. The ambassadors of the pope were received by Charles with decent reverence; but the greatness of his occupations, and the shortness of his life, prevented his interference in the affairs of Italy, except by a friendly and ineffectual mediation. His son Pepin, the heir of his power and virtues, assumed the office of champion of the Roman church; and the zeal of the French prince appears to have been prompted by the love of glory and religion. But the danger was on the banks of the Tyber, the succor on those of the Seine, and our sympathy is cold to the relation of distant misery. Amidst the tears of the city, Stephen the Third embraced the generous resolution of visiting in person the courts of Lombardy and France, to deprecate the injustice of his enemy, or to excite the pity and indignation of his friend. After soothing the public despair by litanies and orations, he undertook this laborious journey with the ambassadors of the French monarch and the Greek emperor. The king of the Lombards was inexorable; but his threats could not silence the complaints, nor retard the speed of the Roman pontiff, who traversed the Pennine Alps, reposed in the abbey of St. Maurice, and hastened to grasp the right hand of his protector; a hand which was never lifted in vain, either in war or friendship. Stephen was entertained as the visible successor of the apostle; at the next assembly, the field of March or of May, his injuries were exposed to a devout and warlike nation, and he repassed the Alps, not as a suppliant, but as a conqueror, at the head of a French army, which was led by the king in person. The Lombards, after a weak resistance, obtained an ignominious peace, and swore to restore the possessions, and to respect the sanctity, of the Roman church. But no sooner was Astolphus delivered from the presence of the French arms, than he forgot his promise and resented his disgrace. Rome was again encompassed by his arms; and Stephen, apprehensive of fatiguing the zeal of his Transalpine allies enforced his complaint and request by an eloquent letter in the name and person of St. Peter himself. The apostle assures his adopted sons, the king, the clergy, and the nobles of France, that, dead in the flesh, he is still alive in the spirit; that they now hear, and must obey, the voice of the founder and guardian of the Roman church; that the Virgin, the angels, the saints, and the martyrs, and all the host of heaven, unanimously urge the request, and will confess the obligation; that riches, victory, and paradise, will crown their pious enterprise, and that eternal damnation will be the penalty of their neglect, if they suffer his tomb, his temple, and his people, to fall into the hands of the perfidious Lombards. The second expedition of Pepin was not less rapid and fortunate than the first: St. Peter was satisfied, Rome was again saved, and Astolphus was taught the lessons of justice and sincerity by the scourge of a foreign master. After this double chastisement, the Lombards languished about twenty years in a state of languor and decay. But their minds were not yet humbled to their condition; and instead of affecting the pacific virtues of the feeble, they peevishly harassed the Romans with a repetition of claims, evasions, and inroads, which they undertook without reflection, and terminated without glory. On either side, their expiring monarchy was pressed by the zeal and prudence of Pope Adrian the First, the genius, the fortune, and greatness of Charlemagne, the son of Pepin; these heroes of the church and state were united in public and domestic friendship, and while they trampled on the prostrate, they varnished their proceedings with the fairest colors of equity and moderation. The passes of the Alps, and the walls of Pavia, were the only defence of the Lombards; the former were surprised, the latter were invested, by the son of Pepin; and after a blockade of two years, Desiderius, the last of their native princes, surrendered his sceptre and his capital. Under the dominion of a foreign king, but in the possession of their national laws, the Lombards became the brethren, rather than the subjects, of the Franks; who derived their blood, and manners, and language, from the same Germanic origin.

Conquest of Italy by the Franks. – Part Three

THE MUTUAL OBLIGATIONS OF the popes and the Carlovingian family form the important link of ancient and modern, of civil and ecclesiastical, history. In the conquest of Italy, the champions of the Roman church obtained a favorable occasion, a specious title, the wishes of the people, the prayers and intrigues of the clergy. But the most essential gifts of the popes to the Carlovingian race were the dignities of king of France, and of patrician of Rome. I. Under the sacerdotal monarchy of St. Peter, the nations began to resume the practice of seeking, on the banks of the Tyber, their kings, their laws, and the oracles of their fate. The Franks were perplexed between the name and substance of their government. All the powers of royalty were exercised by Pepin, mayor of the palace; and nothing, except the regal title, was wanting to his ambition. His enemies were crushed by his valor; his friends were multiplied by his liberality; his father had been the savior of Christendom; and the claims of personal merit were repeated and ennobled in a descent of four generations. The name and image of royalty was still preserved in the last descendant of Clovis, the feeble Childeric; but his obsolete right could only be used as an instrument of sedition: the nation was desirous of restoring the simplicity of the constitution; and Pepin, a subject and a prince, was ambitious to ascertain his own rank and the fortune of his family. The mayor and the nobles were bound, by an oath of fidelity, to the royal phantom: the blood of Clovis was pure and sacred in their eyes; and their common ambassadors addressed the Roman pontiff, to dispel their scruples, or to absolve their promise. The interest of Pope Zachary, the successor of the two Gregories, prompted him to decide, and to decide in their favor: he pronounced that the nation might lawfully unite in the same person the title and authority of king; and that the unfortunate Childeric, a victim of the public safety, should be degraded, shaved, and confined in a monastery for the remainder of his days. An answer so agreeable to their wishes was accepted by the Franks as the opinion of a casuist, the sentence of a judge, or the oracle of a prophet: the Merovingian race disappeared from the earth; and Pepin was exalted on a buckler by the suffrage of a free people, accustomed to obey his laws and to march under his standard. His coronation was twice performed, with the sanction of the popes, by their most faithful servant St. Boniface, the apostle of Germany, and by the grateful hands of Stephen the Third, who, in the monastery of St. Denys placed the diadem on the head of his benefactor. The royal unction of the kings of Israel was dexterously applied: the successor of St. Peter assumed the character of a divine ambassador: a German chieftain was transformed into the Lord's anointed; and this Jewish rite has been diffused and maintained by the superstition and vanity of modern Europe. The Franks were absolved from their ancient oath; but a dire anathema was thundered against them and their posterity, if they should dare to renew the same freedom of choice, or to elect a king, except in the holy and meritorious race of the Carlovingian princes. Without apprehending the future danger, these princes gloried in their present security: the secretary of Charlemagne affirms, that the French sceptre was transferred by the authority of the popes; and in their boldest enterprises, they insist, with confidence, on this signal and successful act of temporal jurisdiction.

II. In the change of manners and language the patricians of Rome were far removed from the senate of Romulus, or the palace of Constantine, from the free nobles of the republic, or the fictitious parents of the emperor. After the recovery of Italy and Africa by the arms of Justinian, the importance and danger of those remote provinces required the presence of a supreme magistrate; he was indifferently styled the exarch or the patrician; and these governors of Ravenna, who fill their place in the chronology of princes, extended their jurisdiction over the Roman city. Since the revolt of Italy and the loss of the Exarchate, the distress of the Romans had exacted some sacrifice of their independence. Yet, even in this act, they exercised the right of disposing of themselves; and the decrees of the senate and people successively invested Charles Martel and his posterity with the honors of patrician of Rome. The leaders of a powerful nation would have disdained a servile title and subordinate office; but the reign of the Greek emperors was suspended; and, in the vacancy of the empire, they derived a more glorious commission from the pope and the republic. The Roman ambassadors presented these patricians with the keys of the shrine of St. Peter, as a pledge and symbol of sovereignty; with a holy banner which it was their right and duty to unfurl in the defence of the church and city. In the time of Charles Martel and of Pepin, the interposition of the Lombard kingdom covered the freedom, while it threatened the safety, of Rome; and the *patriciate* represented only the title, the service, the alliance, of these distant protectors. The power and policy of Charlemagne annihilated an enemy, and imposed a master. In his first visit to the capital, he was received with all the honors which had formerly been paid to the exarch, the representative of the emperor; and these honors obtained some new decorations from the joy and gratitude of Pope Adrian the First. No sooner was he informed of the sudden approach of the monarch, than he despatched the magistrates and nobles of Rome to meet him, with the banner, about thirty miles from the city. At the distance of one mile, the Flaminian way was lined with the *schools*, or national communities, of Greeks, Lombards, Saxons, &c.: the Roman youth were under arms; and the children of a more tender age, with palms and olive branches in their hands, chanted the praises of their great deliverer. At the aspect of the holy crosses, and ensigns of the saints, he dismounted from his horse, led the procession of his nobles to the Vatican, and, as he ascended the stairs, devoutly kissed each step of the threshold of the apostles. In the portico, Adrian expected him at the head of his clergy: they embraced, as friends and equals; but in their march to the altar, the king or patrician assumed the right hand of the pope. Nor was the Frank content with these vain and empty demonstrations of respect. In the twenty-six years that elapsed between the conquest of Lombardy and his Imperial coronation, Rome, which had been delivered by the sword, was subject, as his own, to the sceptre of Charlemagne. The people swore allegiance to his person and family: in his name money was coined, and justice was administered; and the election of the popes was examined and confirmed by his authority. Except an original and self-inherent claim of sovereignty, there was not any prerogative remaining, which the title of emperor could add to the patrician of Rome.

The gratitude of the Carlovingians was adequate to these obligations, and their names are consecrated, as the saviors and benefactors of the Roman church. Her ancient patrimony of farms and houses was transformed by their bounty into the temporal dominion of cities and provinces; and the donation of the Exarchate was the first-fruits of the conquests of Pepin. Astolphus with a sigh relinquished his prey; the keys and the hostages of the principal cities were delivered to the French ambassador; and, in his master's name, he presented them before the tomb of St. Peter. The ample measure of the Exarchate might comprise all the provinces of Italy which had obeyed the emperor and his vicegerent; but its strict and proper limits were included in the territories of Ravenna, Bologna, and Ferrara: its inseparable dependency was the Pentapolis, which stretched along the Adriatic from Rimini to Ancona, and advanced into the midland-country as far as the ridges of the Apennine. In this transaction, the ambition and avarice of the popes have been severely condemned. Perhaps the humility of a Christian priest should have rejected an earthly kingdom, which it was not easy for him to govern without renouncing the virtues of his profession. Perhaps a faithful subject, or even a generous enemy, would have been less impatient to divide the spoils of the Barbarian; and if the emperor had intrusted Stephen to solicit in his name the restitution of the Exarchate, I will not absolve the pope from the reproach of treachery and falsehood. But in the rigid interpretation of the laws, every one may accept, without injury, whatever his benefactor can bestow without injustice. The Greek emperor had abdicated, or forfeited, his right to the Exarchate; and the sword of Astolphus was broken by the stronger sword of the Carlovingian. It was not in the cause of the Iconoclast that Pepin has exposed his person and army in a double expedition beyond the Alps: he possessed, and might lawfully alienate, his conquests: and to the importunities of the Greeks he piously replied that no human consideration should tempt him to resume the gift which he had conferred on the Roman Pontiff for the remission of his sins, and the salvation of his soul. The splendid donation was granted in supreme and absolute dominion, and the world beheld for the first time a Christian bishop invested with the prerogatives of a temporal prince; the choice of magistrates, the exercise of justice, the imposition of taxes, and the wealth of the palace of Ravenna. In the dissolution of the Lombard kingdom, the inhabitants of the duchy of Spoleto sought a refuge from the storm, shaved their heads after the Roman fashion, declared themselves the servants and subjects of St. Peter, and completed, by this voluntary surrender, the present circle of the ecclesiastical state. That mysterious circle was enlarged to an indefinite extent, by the verbal or written donation of Charlemagne, who, in the first transports of his victory, despoiled himself and the Greek emperor of the cities and islands which had formerly been annexed to the Exarchate. But, in the cooler moments of absence and reflection, he viewed, with an eye of jealousy and envy, the recent greatness of his ecclesiastical ally. The execution of his own and his father's promises was respectfully eluded: the king of the Franks and Lombards asserted the inalienable rights of the empire; and, in his life and death, Ravenna, as well as Rome, was numbered in the list of his metropolitan cities. The sovereignty of the Exarchate melted away in the hands of the popes; they found in the archbishops of Ravenna a dangerous and domestic rival: the nobles and people disdained the yoke of a priest; and in the disorders of the times, they could only re-tain the memory of an ancient claim, which, in a more prosperous age, they have revived and realized.

Fraud is the resource of weakness and cunning; and the strong, though ignorant, Barbarian was often entangled in the net of sacer-dotal policy. The Vatican and Lateran were an arsenal and manufac-ture, which, according to the occasion, have produced or concealed a various collection of false or genuine, of corrupt or suspicious, acts, as they tended to promote the interest of the Roman church. Before the end of the eighth century, some apostolic scribe, perhaps the notorious Isidore, composed the decretals, and the donation of Constantine, the two magic pillars of the spiritual and temporal monarchy of the popes. This memorable donation was introduced to the world by an epistle of Adrian the First, who exhorts Charlemagne to imitate the liberality, and revive the name, of the great Constantine. According to the legend, the first of the Christian emperors was healed of the leprosy, and puri-fied in the waters of baptism, by St. Silvester, the Roman bishop; and never was physician more gloriously recompensed. His royal proselyte withdrew from the seat and patrimony of St. Peter; declared his resolu-tion of founding a new capital in the East; and resigned to the popes; the free and perpetual sovereignty of Rome, Italy, and the provinces of the West. This fiction was productive of the most beneficial effects. The Greek princes were convicted of the guilt of usurpation; and the revolt of Gregory was the claim of his lawful inheritance. The popes were delivered from their debt of gratitude; and the nominal gifts of the Carlovingians were no more than the just and irrevocable restitution of a scanty portion of the ecclesiastical state. The sovereignty of Rome no longer depended on the choice of a fickle people; and the succes-sors of St. Peter and Constantine were invested with the purple and prerogatives of the Cæsars. So deep was the ignorance and credulity of the times, that the most absurd of fables was received, with equal reverence, in Greece and in France, and is still enrolled among the decrees of the canon law. The emperors, and the Romans, were incapable of discerning a forgery, that subverted their rights and freedom; and the only opposition proceeded from a Sabine monastery, which, in the beginning of the twelfth century, disputed the truth and validity of the donation of Constantine. In the revival of letters and liberty, this fictitious deed was transpierced by the pen of Laurentius Valla, the pen of an eloquent critic and a Roman patriot. His contemporaries of the fifteenth century were astonished at his sacrilegious boldness; yet such is the silent and irresistible progress of reason, that, before the end of the next age, the fable was rejected by the contempt of historians and poets, and the tacit or modest censure of the advocates of the Roman church. The popes themselves have indulged a smile at the credulity of the vulgar; but a false and obsolete title still sanctifies their reign; and, by the same fortune which has attended the decretals and the Sibylline oracles, the edifice has subsisted after the foundations have been undermined.

While the popes established in Italy their freedom and dominion, the images, the first cause of their revolt, were restored in the Eastern empire. Under the reign of Constantine the Fifth, the union of civil and ecclesiastical power had overthrown the tree, without extirpating the root, of superstition. The idols (for such they were now held) were secretly cherished by the order and the sex most prone to devotion; and the fond alliance of the monks and females obtained a final victory over the reason and authority of man. Leo the Fourth maintained with less rigor the religion of his father and grandfather; but his wife, the fair and ambitious Irene, had imbibed the zeal of the Athenians, the heirs of the Idolatry, rather than the philosophy, of their ancestors. During the life of her husband, these sentiments were inflamed by danger and dissimulation, and she could only labor to protect and promote some favorite monks whom she drew from their caverns, and seated on the metropolitan thrones of the East. But as soon as she reigned in her own name and that of her son, Irene more seriously undertook the ruin of the Iconoclasts; and the first step of her future persecution was a general edict for liberty of conscience. In the restoration of the monks, a thousand images were exposed to the public veneration; a thousand legends were inverted of their sufferings and miracles. By the opportunities of death or removal, the episcopal seats were judiciously filled; the most eager competitors for earthly or celestial favor anticipated and flattered the judgment of their sovereign; and the promotion of her secretary Tarasius gave Irene the patriarch of Constantinople, and the command of the Oriental church. But the decrees of a general council could only be repealed by a similar assembly: the Iconoclasts whom she convened were bold in possession, and averse to debate; and the feeble voice of the bishops was reechoed by the more formidable clamor of the soldiers and people of Constantinople. The delay and intrigues of a year, the separation of the disaffected troops, and the choice of Nice for a second orthodox synod, removed these obstacles; and the episcopal conscience was again, after the Greek fashion, in the hands of the prince. No more than eighteen days were allowed for the consummation of this important work: the Iconoclasts appeared, not as judges, but as criminals or penitents: the scene was decorated by the legates of Pope Adrian and the Eastern patriarchs, the decrees were framed by the president Taracius, and ratified by the acclamations and subscriptions of three hundred and fifty bishops. They unanimously pronounced, that the worship of images is agreeable to Scripture and reason, to the fathers and councils of the church: but they hesitate whether that worship be relative or direct; whether the Godhead, and the figure of Christ, be entitled to the same mode of adoration. Of this second Nicene council the acts are still extant; a curious monument of superstition and ignorance, of falsehood and folly. I shall only notice the judgment of the bishops on the comparative merit of image-worship and morality. A monk had concluded a truce with the dæmon of fornication, on condition of interrupting his daily prayers to a picture that hung in his cell. His scruples prompted him to consult the abbot. "Rather than abstain from adoring Christ and his Mother in their holy images, it would be better for you," replied the casuist, "to enter every brothel, and visit every prostitute, in the city." For the honor of orthodoxy, at least the orthodoxy of the Roman church, it is somewhat unfortunate, that the two princes who convened the two councils of Nice are both stained with the blood of their sons. The second of these assemblies was approved and rigorously executed by the despotism of Irene, and she refused her adversaries the toleration which at first she had granted to her friends. During the five succeeding reigns, a period of thirty-eight years, the contest was maintained, with unabated rage and various success, between the worshippers and the breakers of the images; but I am not inclined to pursue with minute diligence the repetition of the same events. Nicephorus allowed a general liberty of speech and practice; and the only virtue of his reign is accused by the monks as the cause of his temporal and eternal perdition. Superstition and weakness formed the character of Michael the First, but the saints and images were incapable of supporting their votary on the throne. In the purple, Leo the Fifth asserted the name and religion of an Armenian; and the idols, with their seditious adherents, were condemned to a second exile. Their applause would have sanctified the murder of an impious tyrant, but his assassin and successor, the second Michael, was tainted from his birth with the Phrygian heresies: he attempted to mediate between the contending parties; and the intractable spirit of the Catholics insensibly cast him into the opposite scale. His moderation was guarded by timidity; but his son Theophilus, alike ignorant of fear and pity, was the last and most cruel of the Iconoclasts. The enthusiasm of the times ran strongly against them; and the emperors who stemmed the torrent were exasperated and punished by the public hatred. After the death of Theophilus, the final victory of the images was achieved by a second female, his widow Theodora, whom he left the guardian of the empire. Her measures were bold and decisive. The fiction of a tardy repentance absolved the fame and the soul of her deceased husband; the sentence of the Iconoclast patriarch was commuted from the loss of his eyes to a whipping of two hundred lashes: the bishops trembled, the monks shouted, and the festival of orthodoxy preserves the annual memory of the triumph of the images. A single question yet remained, whether they are endowed with any proper and inherent sanctity; it was agitated by the Greeks of the eleventh century; and as this opinion has the strongest recommendation of absurdity, I am surprised that it was not more explicitly decided in the affirmative. In the West, Pope Adrian the First accepted and announced the decrees of the Nicene assembly, which is now revered by the Catholics as the seventh in rank of the general councils. Rome and Italy were docile to the voice of their father; but the greatest part of the Latin Christians were far behind in the race of superstition. The churches of France, Germany, England, and Spain, steered a middle course between the adoration and the destruction of images, which they admitted into their temples, not as objects of worship, but as lively and useful memorials of faith and history. An angry book of controversy was composed and published in the name of Charlemagne: under his authority a synod of three hundred bishops was assembled at Frankfort: they blamed the fury of the Iconoclasts, but they pronounced a more severe censure against the superstition of the Greeks, and the decrees of their pretended council, which was long despised by the Barbarians of the West. Among them the worship of images advanced with a silent and insensible progress; but a large atonement is made for their hesitation and delay, by the gross idolatry of the ages which precede the reformation, and of the countries, both in Europe and America, which are still immersed in the gloom of superstition.

Conquest of Italy by the Franks. – Part Four

IT WAS AFTER THE Nicene synod, and under the reign of the pious Irene, that the popes consummated the separation of Rome and Italy, by the translation of the empire to the less orthodox Charlemagne. They were compelled to choose between the rival nations: religion was not the sole motive of their choice; and while they dissembled the failings of their friends, they beheld, with reluctance and suspicion, the Catholic virtues of their foes. The difference of language and manners had perpetuated the enmity of the two capitals; and they were alienated from each other by the hostile opposition of seventy years. In that schism the Romans had tasted of freedom, and the popes of sovereignty: their submission would have exposed them to the revenge of a jealous tyrant; and the revolution of Italy had betrayed the impotence, as well as the tyranny, of the Byzantine court. The Greek emperors had restored the images, but they had not restored the Calabrian estates and the Illyrian diocese, which the Iconoclasts had torn away from the successors of St. Peter; and Pope Adrian threatens them with a sentence of excommunication unless they speedily abjure this practical heresy. The Greeks were now orthodox; but their religion might be tainted by the breath of the reigning monarch: the Franks were now contumacious; but a discerning eye might discern their approaching conversion, from the use, to the adoration, of images. The name of Charlemagne was stained by the polemic acrimony of his scribes; but the conqueror himself conformed, with the temper of a statesman, to the various practice of France and Italy. In his four pilgrimages or visits to the Vatican, he embraced the popes in the communion of friendship and piety; knelt before the tomb, and consequently before the image, of the apostle; and joined, without scruple, in all the prayers and processions of the Roman liturgy. Would prudence or gratitude allow the pontiffs to renounce their benefactor? Had they a right to alienate his gift of the Exarchate? Had they power to abolish his government of Rome? The title of patrician was below the merit and greatness of Charlemagne; and it was only by reviving the Western empire that they could pay their obligations or secure their establishment. By this decisive measure they would finally eradicate the claims of the Greeks; from the debasement of a provincial town, the majesty of Rome would be restored: the Latin Christians would be united, under a supreme head, in their ancient metropolis; and the conquerors of the West would receive their crown from the successors of St. Peter. The Roman church would acquire a zealous and respectable advocate; and, under the shadow of the Carlovingian power, the bishop might exercise, with honor and safety, the government of the city.

Before the ruin of Paganism in Rome, the competition for a wealthy bishopric had often been productive of tumult and bloodshed. The people was less numerous, but the times were more savage, the prize more important, and the chair of St. Peter was fiercely disputed by the leading ecclesiastics who aspired to the rank of sovereign. The reign of Adrian the First surpasses the measure of past or succeeding ages; the walls of Rome, the sacred patrimony, the ruin of the Lombards, and the friendship of Charlemagne, were the trophies of his fame: he secretly edified the throne of his successors, and displayed in a narrow space the virtues of a great prince. His memory was revered; but in the next election, a priest of the Lateran, Leo the Third, was preferred to the nephew and the favorite of Adrian, whom he had promoted to the first dignities of the church. Their acquiescence or repentance disguised, above four years, the blackest intention of revenge, till the day of a procession, when a furious band of conspirators dispersed the unarmed multitude, and assaulted with blows and wounds the sacred person of the pope. But their enterprise on his life or liberty was disappointed, perhaps by their own confusion and remorse. Leo was left for dead on the ground: on his revival from the swoon, the effect of his loss of blood, he recovered his speech and sight; and this natural event was improved to the miraculous restoration of his eyes and tongue, of which he had been deprived, twice deprived, by the knife of the assassins. From his prison he escaped to the Vatican: the duke of Spoleto hastened to his rescue, Charlemagne sympathized in his injury, and in his camp of Paderborn in Westphalia accepted, or solicited, a visit from the Roman pontiff. Leo repassed the Alps with a commission of counts and bishops, the guards of his safety and the judges of his innocence; and it was not without reluctance, that the conqueror of the Saxons delayed till the ensuing year the personal discharge of this pious office. In his fourth and last pilgrimage, he was received at Rome with the due honors of king and patrician: Leo was permitted to purge himself by oath of the crimes imputed to his charge: his enemies were silenced, and the sacrilegious attempt against his life was punished by the mild and insufficient penalty of exile. On the festival of Christmas, the last year of the eighth century, Charlemagne appeared in the church of St. Peter; and, to gratify the vanity of Rome, he had exchanged the simple dress of his country for the habit of a patrician. After the celebration of the holy mysteries, Leo suddenly placed a precious crown on his head, and the dome resounded with the acclamations of the people, "Long life and victory to Charles, the most pious Augustus, crowned by God the great and pacific emperor of the Romans!" The head and body of Charlemagne were consecrated by the royal unction: after the example of the Cæsars, he was saluted or adored by the pontiff: his coronation oath represents a promise to maintain the faith and privileges of the church; and the first-fruits were paid in his rich offerings to the shrine of his apostle. In his familiar conversation, the emperor protested the ignorance of the intentions of Leo, which he would have disappointed by his absence on that memorable day. But the preparations of the ceremony must have disclosed the secret; and the journey of Charlemagne reveals his knowledge and expectation: he had acknowledged that the Imperial title was the object of his ambition, and a Roman synod had pronounced, that it was the only adequate reward of his merit and services.

The appellation of *great* has been often bestowed, and sometimes deserved; but Charlemagne is the only prince in whose favor the title has been indissolubly blended with the name. That name, with the addition of *saint*, is inserted in the Roman calendar; and the saint, by a rare felicity, is crowned with the praises of the historians and philosophers of an enlightened age. His *real* merit is doubtless enhanced by the barbarism of the nation and the times from which he emerged: but the *apparent* magnitude of an object is likewise enlarged by an unequal comparison; and the ruins of Palmyra derive a casual splendor from the nakedness of the surrounding desert. Without injustice to his fame, I may discern some blemishes in the sanctity and greatness of the restorer of the Western empire. Of his moral virtues, chastity is not the most conspicuous: but the public happiness could not be materially injured by his nine wives or concubines, the various indulgence of meaner or more transient amours, the multitude of his bastards whom he bestowed on the church, and the long celibacy and licentious manners of his daughters, whom the father was suspected of loving with too fond a passion. I shall be scarcely permitted to accuse the ambition of a conqueror; but in a day of equal retribution, the sons of his brother Carloman, the Merovingian princes of Aquitain, and the four thousand five hundred Saxons who were beheaded on the same spot, would have something to allege against the justice and humanity of Charlemagne. His treatment of the vanquished Saxons was an abuse of the right of conquest; his laws were not less sanguinary than his arms, and in the discussion of his motives, whatever is subtracted from bigotry must be imputed to temper. The sedentary reader is amazed by his incessant activity of mind and body; and his subjects and enemies were not less astonished at his sudden presence, at the moment when they believed him at the most distant extremity of the empire; neither peace nor war, nor summer nor winter, were a season of repose; and our fancy cannot easily reconcile the annals of his reign with the geography of his expeditions. But this activity was a national, rather than a personal, virtue; the vagrant life of a Frank was spent in the chase, in pilgrimage, in military adventures; and the journeys of Charlemagne were distinguished only by a more numerous train and a more important purpose. His military renown must be tried by the scrutiny of his troops, his enemies, and his actions. Alexander conquered with the arms of Philip, but the *two* heroes who preceded Charlemagne bequeathed him their name, their examples, and the companions of their victories. At the head of his veteran and superior armies, he oppressed the savage or degenerate nations, who were incapable of confederating for their common safety: nor did he ever encounter an equal antagonist in numbers, in discipline, or in arms The science of war has been lost and revived with the arts of peace; but his campaigns are not illustrated by any siege or battle of singular difficulty and success; and he might behold, with envy, the Saracen trophies of his grandfather. After the Spanish expedition, his rear-guard was defeated in the Pyrenæan mountains; and the soldiers, whose situation was irretrievable, and whose valor was useless, might accuse, with their last breath, the want of skill or caution of their general. I touch with reverence the laws of Charlemagne, so highly applauded by a respectable judge. They compose not a system, but a series, of occasional and minute edicts, for the correction of abuses, the reformation of manners, the economy of his farms, the care of his poultry, and even the sale of his eggs. He wished to improve the laws and the character of the Franks; and his attempts, however feeble and imperfect, are deserving of praise: the inveterate evils of the times were suspended or mollified by his government; but in his institutions I can seldom discover the general views and the immortal spirit of a legislator, who survives himself for the benefit of posterity. The union and stability of his empire depended on the life of a single man: he imitated the dangerous practice of dividing his kingdoms among his sons; and after his numerous diets, the whole constitution was left to fluctuate between the disorders of anarchy and despotism. His esteem for the piety and knowledge of the clergy tempted him to intrust that aspiring order with temporal dominion and civil jurisdiction; and his son Lewis, when he was stripped and degraded by the bishops, might accuse, in some measure, the imprudence of his father. His laws enforced the imposition of tithes, because the dæmons had proclaimed in the air that the default of payment had been the cause of the last scarcity. The literary merits of Charlemagne are attested by the foundation of schools, the introduction of arts, the works which were published in his name, and his familiar connection with the subjects and strangers whom he invited to his court to educate both the prince and people. His own studies were tardy, laborious, and imperfect; if he spoke Latin, and understood Greek, he derived the rudiments of knowledge from conversation, rather than from books; and, in his mature age, the emperor strove to acquire the practice of writing, which every peasant now learns in his infancy. The grammar and logic, the music and astronomy, of the times, were only cultivated as the handmaids of superstition; but the curiosity of the human mind must ultimately tend to its improvement, and the encouragement of learning reflects the purest and most pleasing lustre on the character of Charlemagne. The dignity of his person, the length of his reign, the prosperity of his arms, the vigor of his government, and the reverence of distant nations, distinguish him from the royal crowd; and Europe dates a new æra from his restoration of the Western empire.

That empire was not unworthy of its title; and some of the fairest kingdoms of Europe were the patrimony or conquest of a prince, who reigned at the same time in France, Spain, Italy, Germany, and Hungary. I. The Roman province of Gaul had been transformed into the name and monarchy of France; but, in the decay of the Merovingian line, its limits were contracted by the independence of the *Britons* and the revolt of *Aquitain*. Charlemagne pursued, and confined, the Britons on the shores of the ocean; and that ferocious tribe, whose origin and language are so different from the French, was chastised by the imposition of tribute, hostages, and peace. After a long and evasive contest, the rebellion of the dukes of Aquitain was punished by the forfeiture of their province, their liberty, and their lives. Harsh and rigorous would have been such treatment of ambitious governors, who had too faithfully copied the mayors of the palace. But a recent discovery has proved that these unhappy princes were the last and lawful heirs of the blood and sceptre of Clovis, and younger branch, from the brother of Dagobert, of the Merovingian house. Their ancient kingdom was reduced to the duchy of Gascogne, to the counties of Fesenzac and Armagnac, at the foot of the Pyrenees: their race was propagated till the beginning of the sixteenth century; and after surviving their Carlovingian tyrants, they were reserved to feel the injustice, or the favors, of a third dynasty. By the reunion of Aquitain, France was enlarged to its present boundaries, with the additions of the Netherlands and Spain, as far as the Rhine. II. The Saracens had been expelled from France by the grandfather and father of Charlemagne; but they still possessed the greatest part of Spain, from the rock of Gibraltar to the Pyrenees. Amidst their civil divisions, an Arabian emir of Saragossa implored his protection in the diet of Paderborn. Charlemagne undertook the expedition, restored the emir, and, without distinction of faith, impartially crushed the resistance of the Christians, and rewarded the obedience and services of the Mahometans. In his absence he instituted the *Spanish march*, which extended from the Pyrenees to the River Ebro: Barcelona was the residence of the French governor: he possessed the counties of *Rousillon* and *Catalonia*; and the infant kingdoms of *Navarre* and *Arragon* were subject to his jurisdiction. III. As king of the Lombards, and patrician of Rome, he reigned over the greatest part of Italy, a tract of a thousand miles from the Alps to the borders of Calabria. The duchy of *Beneventum*, a Lombard fief, had spread, at the expense of the Greeks, over the modern kingdom of Naples. But Arrechis, the reigning duke, refused to be included in the slavery of his country; assumed the independent title of prince; and opposed his sword to the Carlovingian monarchy. His defence was firm, his submission was not inglorious, and the emperor was content with an easy tribute, the demolition of his fortresses, and the acknowledgment, on his coins, of a supreme lord. The artful flattery of his son Grimoald added the appellation of father, but he asserted his dignity with prudence, and Benventum insensibly escaped from the French yoke. IV. Charlemagne was the first who united Germany under the same sceptre. The name of *Oriental France* is preserved in the circle of *Franconia*; and the people of *Hesse* and *Thuringia* were recently incorporated with the victors, by the conformity of religion and government. The *Alemanni*, so formidable to the Romans, were the faithful vassals and confederates of the Franks; and their country was inscribed within the modern limits of *Alsace*, *Swabia*, and *Switzerland*. The *Bavarians*, with a similar indulgence of their laws and manners, were less patient of a master: the repeated treasons of Tasillo justified the abolition of their hereditary dukes; and their power was shared among the counts, who judged and guarded that important frontier. But the north of Germany, from the Rhine and beyond the Elbe, was still hostile and Pagan; nor was it till after a war of thirty-three years that the Saxons bowed under the yoke of Christ and of Charlemagne. The idols and their votaries were extirpated: the foundation of eight bishoprics, of Munster, Osnaburgh, Paderborn, and Minden, of Bremen, Verden, Hildesheim, and Halberstadt, define, on either side of the Weser, the bounds of ancient Saxony these episcopal seats were the first schools and cities of that savage land; and the religion and humanity of the children atoned, in some degree, for the massacre of the parents. Beyond the Elbe, the *Slavi*, or Sclavonians, of similar manners and various denominations, overspread the modern dominions of Prussia, Poland, and Bohemia, and some transient marks of obedience have tempted the French historian to extend the empire to the Baltic and the Vistula. The conquest or conversion of those countries is of a more recent age; but the first union of *Bohemia* with the Germanic body may be justly ascribed to the arms of Charlemagne. V. He retaliated on the Avars, or Huns of Pannonia, the same calamities which they had inflicted on the nations. Their rings, the wooden fortifications which encircled their districts and villages, were broken down by the triple effort of a French army, that was poured into their country by land and water, through the Carpathian mountains and along the plain of the Danube. After a bloody conflict of eight years, the loss of some French generals was avenged by the slaughter of the most noble Huns: the relics of the nation submitted the royal residence of the chagan was left desolate and unknown; and the treasures, the rapine of two hundred and fifty years, enriched the victorious troops, or decorated the churches of Italy and Gaul. After the reduction of Pannonia, the empire of Charlemagne was bounded only by the conflux of the Danube with the Teyss and the Save: the provinces of Istria, Liburnia, and Dalmatia, were an easy, though unprofitable, accession; and it was an effect of his moderation, that he left the maritime cities under the real or nominal sovereignty of the Greeks. But these distant possessions added more to the reputation than to the power of the Latin emperor; nor did he risk any ecclesiastical foundations to reclaim the Barbarians from their vagrant life and idolatrous worship. Some canals of communication between the rivers, the Saone and the Meuse, the Rhine and the Danube, were faintly attempted. Their execution would have vivified the empire; and more cost and labor were often wasted in the structure of a cathedral.

Conquest of Italy by the Franks. – Part Five

IF WE RETRACE THE outlines of this geographical picture, it will be seen that the empire of the Franks extended, between east and west, from the Ebro to the Elbe or Vistula; between the north and south, from the duchy of Beneventum to the River Eyder, the perpetual boundary of Germany and Denmark. The personal and political importance of Charlemagne was magnified by the distress and division of the rest of Europe. The islands of Great Britain and Ireland were disputed by a crowd of princes of Saxon or Scottish origin: and, after the loss of Spain, the Christian and Gothic kingdom of Alphonso the Chaste was confined to the narrow range of the Asturian mountains. These petty sovereigns revered the power or virtue of the Carlovingian monarch, implored the honor and support of his alliance, and styled him their common parent, the sole and supreme emperor of the West. He maintained a more equal intercourse with the caliph Harun al Rashid, whose dominion stretched from Africa to India, and accepted from his ambassadors a tent, a water-clock, an elephant, and the keys of the Holy Sepulchre. It is not easy to conceive the private friendship of a Frank and an Arab, who were strangers to each other's person, and language, and religion: but their public correspondence was founded on vanity, and their remote situation left no room for a competition of interest. Two thirds of the Western empire of Rome were subject to Charlemagne, and the deficiency was amply supplied by his command of the inaccessible or invincible nations of Germany. But in the choice of his enemies, we may be reasonably surprised that he so often preferred the poverty of the north to the riches of the south. The three-and-thirty campaigns laboriously consumed in the woods and morasses of Germany would have sufficed to assert the amplitude of his title by the expulsion of the Greeks from Italy and the Saracens from Spain. The weakness of the Greeks would have insured an easy victory; and the holy crusade against the Saracens would have been prompted by glory and revenge, and loudly justified by religion and policy. Perhaps, in his expeditions beyond the Rhine and the Elbe, he aspired to save his monarchy from the fate of the Roman empire, to disarm the enemies of civilized society, and to eradicate the seed of future emigrations. But it has been wisely observed, that, in a light of precaution, all conquest must be ineffectual, unless it could be universal, since the increasing circle must be involved in a larger sphere of hostility. The subjugation of Germany withdrew the veil which had so long concealed the continent or islands of Scandinavia from the knowledge of Europe, and awakened the torpid courage of their barbarous natives. The fiercest of the Saxon idolaters escaped from the Christian tyrant to their brethren of the North; the Ocean and Mediterranean were covered with their piratical fleets; and Charlemagne beheld with a sigh the destructive progress of the Normans, who, in less than seventy years, precipitated the fall of his race and monarchy.

Had the pope and the Romans revived the primitive constitution, the titles of emperor and Augustus were conferred on Charlemagne for the term of his life; and his successors, on each vacancy, must have ascended the throne by a formal or tacit election. But the association of his son Lewis the Pious asserts the independent right of monarchy and conquest, and the emperor seems on this occasion to have foreseen and prevented the latent claims of the clergy. The royal youth was commanded to take the crown from the altar, and with his own hands to place it on his head, as a gift which he held from God, his father, and the nation. The same ceremony was repeated, though with less energy, in the subsequent associations of Lothaire and Lewis the Second: the Carlovingian sceptre was transmitted from father to son in a lineal descent of four generations; and the ambition of the popes was reduced to the empty honor of crowning and anointing these hereditary princes, who were already invested with their power and dominions. The pious Lewis survived his brothers, and embraced the whole empire of Charlemagne; but the nations and the nobles, his bishops and his children, quickly discerned that this mighty mass was no longer inspired by the same soul; and the foundations were undermined to the centre, while the external surface was yet fair and entire. After a war, or battle, which consumed one hundred thousand

Franks, the empire was divided by treaty between his three sons, who had violated every filial and fraternal duty. The kingdoms of Germany and France were forever separated; the provinces of Gaul, between the Rhone and the Alps, the Meuse and the Rhine, were assigned, with Italy, to the Imperial dignity of Lothaire. In the partition of his share, Lorraine and Arles, two recent and transitory kingdoms, were bestowed on the younger children; and Lewis the Second, his eldest son, was content with the realm of Italy, the proper and sufficient patrimony of a Roman emperor. On his death without any male issue, the vacant throne was disputed by his uncles and cousins, and the popes most dexterously seized the occasion of judging the claims and merits of the candidates, and of bestowing on the most obsequious, or most liberal, the Imperial office of advocate of the Roman church. The dregs of the Carlovingian race no longer exhibited any symptoms of virtue or power, and the ridiculous epithets of the *bard*, the *stammerer*, the *fat*, and the *simple*, distinguished the tame and uniform features of a crowd of kings alike deserving of oblivion. By the failure of the collateral branches, the whole inheritance devolved to Charles the Fat, the last emperor of his family: his insanity authorized the desertion of Germany, Italy, and France: he was deposed in a diet, and solicited his daily bread from the rebels by whose contempt his life and liberty had been spared. According to the measure of their force, the governors, the bishops, and the lords, usurped the fragments of the falling empire; and some preference was shown to the female or illegitimate blood of Charlemagne. Of the greater part, the title and possession were alike doubtful, and the merit was adequate to the contracted scale of their dominions. Those who could appear with an army at the gates of Rome were crowned emperors in the Vatican; but their modesty was more frequently satisfied with the appellation of kings of Italy: and the whole term of seventy-four years may be deemed a vacancy, from the abdication of Charles the Fat to the establishment of Otho the First.

Otho was of the noble race of the dukes of Saxony; and if he truly descended from Witikind, the adversary and proselyte of Charlemagne, the posterity of a vanquished people was exalted to reign over their conquerors. His father, Henry the Fowler, was elected, by the suffrage of the nation, to save and institute the kingdom of Germany. Its limits were enlarged on every side by his son, the first and greatest of the Othos. A portion of Gaul, to the west of the Rhine, along the banks of the Meuse and the Moselle, was assigned to the Germans, by whose blood and language it has been tinged since the time of Cæsar and Tacitus. Between the Rhine, the Rhone, and the Alps, the successors of Otho acquired a vain supremacy over the broken kingdoms of Burgundy and Arles. In the North, Christianity was propagated by the sword of Otho, the conqueror and apostle of the Slavic nations of the Elbe and Oder: the marches of Brandenburgh and Sleswick were fortified with German colonies; and the king of Denmark, the dukes of Poland and Bohemia, confessed themselves his tributary vassals. At the head of a victorious army, he passed the Alps, subdued the kingdom of Italy, delivered the pope, and forever fixed the Imperial crown in the name and nation of Germany. From that memorable æra, two maxims of public jurisprudence were introduced by force and ratified by time. I. *That* the prince, who was elected in the German diet, acquired, from that instant, the subject kingdoms of Italy and Rome. II. But that he might not legally assume the titles of emperor and Augustus, till he had received the crown from the hands of the Roman pontiff.

The Imperial dignity of Charlemagne was announced to the East by the alteration of his style; and instead of saluting his fathers, the Greek emperors, he presumed to adopt the more equal and familiar appellation of brother. Perhaps in his connection with Irene he aspired to the name of husband: his embassy to Constantinople spoke the language of peace and friendship, and might conceal a treaty of marriage with that ambitious princess, who had renounced the most sacred duties of a mother. The nature, the duration, the probable consequences of such a union between two distant and dissonant empires, it is impossible to conjecture; but the unanimous silence of the Latins may teach us to suspect, that the report was invented by the enemies of Irene, to charge her with the guilt of betraying the church and state to the strangers of the West. The French ambassadors were the spectators, and had nearly been the victims, of the conspiracy of Nicephorus, and the national hatred. Constantinople was exasperated by the treason and sacrilege of ancient Rome: a proverb, "That the Franks were good friends and bad neighbors," was in every one's mouth; but it was dangerous to provoke a neighbor who might be tempted to reiterate, in the church of St. Sophia, the ceremony of his Imperial coronation. After a tedious journey of circuit and delay, the ambassadors of Nicephorus found him in his camp, on the banks of the River Sala; and Charlemagne affected to confound their vanity by displaying, in a Franconian village, the pomp, or at least the pride, of the Byzantine palace. The Greeks were successively led through four halls of audience: in the first they were ready to fall prostrate before a splendid personage in a chair of state, till he informed them that he was only a servant, the constable, or master of the horse, of the emperor. The same mistake, and the same answer, were repeated in the apartments of the count palatine, the steward, and the chamberlain; and their impatience was gradually heightened, till the doors of the presence-chamber were thrown open, and they beheld the genuine monarch, on his throne, enriched with the foreign luxury which he despised, and encircled with the love and reverence of his victorious chiefs. A treaty of peace and alliance was concluded between the two empires, and the limits of the East and West were defined by the right of present possession. But the Greeks soon forgot this humiliating equality, or remembered it only to hate the Barbarians by whom it was extorted. During the short union of virtue and power, they respectfully saluted the *august* Charlemagne, with the acclamations of *basileus*, and emperor of the Romans. As soon as these qualities were separated in the person of his pious son, the Byzantine letters were inscribed, "To the king, or, as he styles himself, the emperor of the Franks and Lombards." When both power and virtue were extinct, they despoiled Lewis the Second of his hereditary title, and with the barbarous appellation of rex or *rega*, degraded him among the crowd of Latin princes. His reply is expressive of his weakness: he proves, with some learning, that, both in sacred and profane history, the name of king is synonymous with the Greek word *basileus*: if, at Constantinople, it were assumed in a more exclusive and imperial sense, he claims from his ancestors, and from the popes, a just participation of the honors of the Roman purple. The same controversy was revived in the reign of the Othos; and their ambassador describes, in lively colors, the insolence of the Byzantine court. The Greeks affected to despise the poverty and ignorance of the Franks and Saxons; and in their last decline refused to prostitute to the kings of Germany the title of Roman emperors.

These emperors, in the election of the popes, continued to exercise the powers which had been assumed by the Gothic and Grecian princes; and the importance of this prerogative increased with the temporal estate and spiritual jurisdiction of the Roman church. In the Christian aristocracy, the principal members of the clergy still formed a senate to assist the administration, and to supply the vacancy, of the bishop. Rome was divided into twenty-eight parishes, and each parish was governed by a cardinal priest, or presbyter, a title which, however common or modest in its origin, has aspired to emulate the purple of kings. Their number was enlarged by the association of the seven deacons of the most considerable hospitals, the seven palatine judges of the Lateran, and some dignitaries of the church. This ecclesiastical senate was directed by the seven cardinal-bishops of the Roman province, who were less occupied in the suburb dioceses of Ostia, Porto, Velitræ, Tusculum, Præneste, Tibur, and the Sabines, than by their weekly service in the Lateran, and their superior share in the honors and authority of the apostolic see. On the death of the pope, these bishops recommended a successor to the suffrage of the college of cardinals, and their choice was ratified or rejected by the applause or clamor of the Roman people. But the election was imperfect; nor could the pontiff be legally consecrated till the emperor, the advocate of the church, had graciously signified his approbation and consent. The royal commissioner examined, on the spot, the form and freedom of the proceedings; nor was it till after a previous scrutiny into the qualifications of the candidates, that he accepted an oath of fidelity, and confirmed the donations which had successively enriched the patrimony of St. Peter. In the frequent schisms, the rival claims were submitted to the sentence of the emperor; and in a synod of bishops he presumed to judge, to condemn, and to punish, the crimes of a guilty pontiff. Otho the First imposed a treaty on the senate and people, who engaged to prefer the candidate most acceptable to his majesty: his successors anticipated or prevented their choice: they bestowed the Roman benefice, like the bishoprics of Cologne or Bamberg, on their chancellors or preceptors; and whatever might be the merit of a Frank or Saxon, his name sufficiently attests the interposition of foreign power. These acts of prerogative were most speciously excused by the vices of a popular election. The competitor who had been excluded by the cardinals appealed to the passions or avarice of the multitude; the Vatican and the Lateran were stained with blood; and the most powerful senators, the marquises of Tuscany and the counts of Tusculum, held the apostolic see in a long and disgraceful servitude. The Roman pontiffs, of the ninth and tenth centuries, were insulted, imprisoned, and murdered, by their tyrants; and such was their indigence, after the loss and usurpation of the ecclesiastical patrimonies, that they could neither support the state of a prince, nor exercise the charity of a priest. The influence of two sister prostitutes, Marozia and Theodora, was founded on their wealth and beauty, their political and amorous intrigues: the most strenuous of their lovers were rewarded with the Roman mitre, and their reign may have suggested to the darker ages the fable of a female pope. The bastard son, the grandson, and the great-grandson of Marozia, a rare genealogy, were seated in the chair of St. Peter, and it was at the age of nineteen years that the second of these became the head of the Latin church. His youth and manhood were of a suitable complexion; and the nations of pilgrims could bear testimony to the charges that were urged against him in a Roman synod, and in

the presence of Otho the Great. As John XII. had renounced the dress
and decencies of his profession, the *soldier* may not perhaps be dishonored by the wine which he drank, the blood that he spilt, the flames
that he kindled, or the licentious pursuits of gaming and hunting. His
open simony might be the consequence of distress; and his blasphemous invocation of Jupiter and Venus, if it be true, could not possibly
be serious. But we read, with some surprise, that the worthy grandson
of Marozia lived in public adultery with the matrons of Rome; that the
Lateran palace was turned into a school for prostitution, and that his
rapes of virgins and widows had deterred the female pilgrims from visiting the tomb of St. Peter, lest, in the devout act, they should be violated by his successor. The Protestants have dwelt with malicious pleasure
on these characters of Antichrist; but to a philosophic eye, the vices of
the clergy are far less dangerous than their virtues. After a long series
of scandal, the apostolic see was reformed and exalted by the austerity and zeal of Gregory VII. That ambitious monk devoted his life to
the execution of two projects. I. To fix in the college of cardinals the
freedom and independence of election, and forever to abolish the right
or usurpation of the emperors and the Roman people. II. To bestow
and resume the Western empire as a fief or benefice of the church, and
to extend his temporal dominion over the kings and kingdoms of the
earth. After a contest of fifty years, the first of these designs was accomplished by the firm support of the ecclesiastical order, whose liberty
was connected with that of their chief. But the second attempt, though
it was crowned with some partial and apparent success, has been vigorously resisted by the secular power, and finally extinguished by the
improvement of human reason.

In the revival of the empire of empire of Rome, neither the bishop nor
the people could bestow on Charlemagne or Otho the provinces which
were lost, as they had been won, by the chance of arms. But the Romans
were free to choose a master for themselves; and the powers which had
been delegated to the patrician, were irrevocably granted to the French
and Saxon emperors of the West. The broken records of the times preserve some remembrance of their palace, their mint, their tribunal,
their edicts, and the sword of justice, which, as late as the thirteenth
century, was derived from Cæsar to the præfect of the city. Between
the arts of the popes and the violence of the people, this supremacy
was crushed and annihilated. Content with the titles of emperor and
Augustus, the successors of Charlemagne neglected to assert this local
jurisdiction. In the hour of prosperity, their ambition was diverted by
more alluring objects; and in the decay and division of the empire, they

were oppressed by the defence of their hereditary provinces. Amidst the ruins of Italy, the famous Marozia invited one of the usurpers to assume the character of her third husband; and Hugh, king of Burgundy was introduced by her faction into the mole of Hadrian or Castle of St. Angelo, which commands the principal bridge and entrance of Rome. Her son by the first marriage, Alberic, was compelled to attend at the nuptial banquet; but his reluctant and ungraceful service was chastised with a blow by his new father. The blow was productive of a revolution. "Romans," exclaimed the youth, "once you were the masters of the world, and these Burgundians the most abject of your slaves. They now reign, these voracious and brutal savages, and my injury is the commencement of your servitude." The alarum bell rang to arms in every quarter of the city: the Burgundians retreated with haste and shame; Marozia was imprisoned by her victorious son, and his brother, Pope John XI., was reduced to the exercise of his spiritual functions. With the title of prince, Alberic possessed above twenty years the government of Rome; and he is said to have gratified the popular prejudice, by restoring the office, or at least the title, of consuls and tribunes. His son and heir Octavian assumed, with the pontificate, the name of John XII.: like his predecessor, he was provoked by the Lombard princes to seek a deliverer for the church and republic; and the services of Otho were rewarded with the Imperial dignity. But the Saxon was imperious, the Romans were impatient, the festival of the coronation was disturbed by the secret conflict of prerogative and freedom, and Otho commanded his sword-bearer not to stir from his person, lest he should be assaulted and murdered at the foot of the altar. Before he repassed the Alps, the emperor chastised the revolt of the people and the ingratitude of John XII. The pope was degraded in a synod; the præfect was mounted on an ass, whipped through the city, and cast into a dungeon; thirteen of the most guilty were hanged, others were mutilated or banished; and this severe process was justified by the ancient laws of Theodosius and Justinian. The voice of fame has accused the second Otho of a perfidious and bloody act, the massacre of the senators, whom he had invited to his table under the fair semblance of hospitality and friendship. In the minority of his son Otho the Third, Rome made a bold attempt to shake off the Saxon yoke, and the consul Crescentius was the Brutus of the republic. From the condition of a subject and an exile, he twice rose to the command of the city, oppressed, expelled, and created the popes, and formed a conspiracy for restoring the authority of the Greek emperors. In the fortress of St. Angelo, he maintained an obstinate siege, till the unfortunate consul was betrayed by a promise of safety: his body was suspended on a gibbet, and his head was exposed on the battlements of the castle. By a reverse of fortune, Otho, after separating his troops, was besieged three days, without food, in his palace; and a disgraceful escape saved him from the justice or fury of the Romans. The senator Ptolemy was the leader of the people, and the widow of Crescentius enjoyed the pleasure or the fame of revenging her husband, by a poison which she administered to her Imperial lover. It was the design of Otho the Third to abandon the ruder countries of the North, to erect his throne in Italy, and to revive the institutions of the Roman monarchy. But his successors only once in their lives appeared on the banks of the Tyber, to receive their crown in the Vatican. Their absence was contemptible, their presence odious and formidable. They descended from the Alps, at the head of their barbarians, who were strangers and enemies to the country; and their transient visit was a scene of tumult and bloodshed. A faint remembrance of their ancestors still tormented the Romans; and they beheld with pious indignation the succession of Saxons, Franks, Swabians, and Bohemians, who usurped the purple and prerogatives of the Cæsars.

Conquest of Italy by the Franks. – Part Six

THERE IS NOTHING PERHAPS more adverse to nature and reason than to hold in obedience remote countries and foreign nations, in opposition to their inclination and interest. A torrent of Barbarians may pass over the earth, but an extensive empire must be supported by a refined system of policy and oppression; in the centre, an absolute power, prompt in action and rich in resources; a swift and easy communication with the extreme parts; fortifications to check the first effort of rebellion; a regular administration to protect and punish; and a well-disciplined army to inspire fear, without provoking discontent and despair. Far different was the situation of the German Cæsars, who were ambitious to enslave the kingdom of Italy. Their patrimonial estates were stretched along the Rhine, or scattered in the provinces; but this ample domain was alienated by the imprudence or distress of successive princes; and their revenue, from minute and vexatious prerogative, was scarcely sufficient for the maintenance of their household. Their troops were formed by the legal or voluntary service of their feudal vassals, who passed the Alps with reluctance, assumed the license of rapine and disorder, and capriciously deserted before the end of the campaign. Whole armies were swept away by the pestilential influence of the climate: the survivors brought back the bones of their princes and nobles, and the effects of their own intemperance were often imputed to the treachery and malice of the Italians, who rejoiced at least in the calamities of the Barbarians. This irregular tyranny might contend on equal terms with the petty tyrants of Italy; nor can the people, or the reader, be much interested in the event of the quarrel. But in the eleventh and twelfth centuries, the Lombards rekindled the flame of industry and freedom; and the generous example was at length imitated by the republics of Tuscany. In the Italian cities a municipal government had never been totally abolished; and their first privileges were granted by the favor and policy of the emperors, who were desirous of erecting a plebeian barrier against the independence of the nobles. But their rapid progress, the daily extension of their power and pretensions, were founded on the numbers and spirit of these rising communities. Each city filled the measure of her diocese or district: the jurisdiction of the counts and bishops, of the marquises and counts, was banished from the land; and the proudest nobles were persuaded or compelled to desert their solitary castles, and to embrace the more honorable character of freemen and magistrates. The legislative authority was inherent in the general assembly; but the executive powers were intrusted to three consuls, annually chosen from the three orders of *captains, valvassors,* and commons, into which the republic was divided. Under the protection of equal law, the labors of agriculture and commerce were gradually revived; but the martial spirit of the Lombards was nourished by the presence of danger; and as often as the bell was rung, or the standard erected, the gates of the city poured forth a numerous and intrepid band, whose zeal in their own cause was soon guided by the use and discipline of arms. At the foot of these popular ramparts, the pride of the Cæsars was overthrown; and the invincible genius of liberty prevailed over the two Frederics, the greatest princes of the middle age; the first, superior perhaps in military prowess; the second, who undoubtedly excelled in the softer accomplishments of peace and learning.

Ambitious of restoring the splendor of the purple, Frederic the First invaded the republics of Lombardy, with the arts of a statesman, the valor of a soldier, and the cruelty of a tyrant. The recent discovery of the Pandects had renewed a science most favorable to despotism; and his venal advocates proclaimed the emperor the absolute master of the lives and properties of his subjects. His royal prerogatives, in a less odious sense, were acknowledged in the diet of Roncaglia; and the revenue of Italy was fixed at thirty thousand pounds of silver, which were multiplied to an indefinite demand by the rapine of the fiscal officers. The obstinate cities were reduced by the terror or the force of his arms: his captives were delivered to the executioner, or shot from his military engines; and after the siege and surrender of Milan, the buildings of that stately capital were razed to the ground, three hundred hostages were sent into Germany, and the inhabitants were dispersed in four villages, under the yoke of the inflexible conqueror. But Milan soon rose from her ashes; and the league of Lombardy was cemented by distress: their cause was espoused by Venice, Pope Alexander the Third, and the Greek emperor: the fabric of oppression was overturned in a day; and in the treaty of Constance, Frederic subscribed, with some reservations, the freedom of four-and-twenty cities. His grandson contended with their vigor and maturity; but Frederic the Second was endowed with some personal and peculiar advantages. His birth and education recommended him to the Italians; and in the implacable discord of the two factions, the Ghibelins were attached to the emperor, while the Guelfs displayed the banner of liberty and the church. The court of Rome had slumbered, when his father Henry the Sixth was permitted to unite with the empire the kingdoms of Naples and Sicily; and from these hereditary realms the son derived an ample and ready supply of troops and treasure. Yet Frederic the Second was finally oppressed by the arms of the Lombards and the thunders of the Vatican: his kingdom was given to a stranger, and the last of his family was beheaded at Naples on a public scaffold. During sixty years, no emperor appeared in Italy, and the name was remembered only by the ignominious sale of the last relics of sovereignty.

The Barbarian conquerors of the West were pleased to decorate their chief with the title of emperor; but it was not their design to invest him with the despotism of Constantine and Justinian. The persons of the Germans were free, their conquests were their own, and their national character was animated by a spirit which scorned the servile jurisprudence of the new or the ancient Rome. It would have been a vain and dangerous attempt to impose a monarch on the armed freemen, who were impatient of a magistrate; on the bold, who refused to obey; on the powerful, who aspired to command. The empire of Charlemagne and Otho was distributed among the dukes of the nations or provinces, the counts of the smaller districts, and the margraves of the marches or frontiers, who all united the civil and military authority as it had been delegated to the lieutenants of the first Cæsars. The Roman governors, who, for the most part, were soldiers of fortune, seduced their mercenary legions, assumed the Imperial purple, and either failed or succeeded in their revolt, without wounding the power and unity of government. If the dukes, margraves, and counts of Germany, were less audacious in their claims, the consequences of their success were more lasting and pernicious to the state. Instead of aiming at the supreme rank, they silently labored to establish and appropriate their provincial independence. Their ambition was seconded by the weight of their estates and vassals, their mutual example and support, the common interest of the subordinate nobility, the change of princes and families, the minorities of Otho the Third and Henry the Fourth, the ambition of the popes, and the vain pursuit of the fugitive crowns of Italy and Rome. All the attributes of regal and territorial jurisdiction were gradually usurped by the commanders of the provinces; the right of peace and war, of life and death, of coinage and taxation, of foreign alliance and domestic economy. Whatever had been seized by violence, was ratified by favor or distress, was granted as the price of a doubtful vote or a voluntary service; whatever had been granted to one could not, without injury, be denied to his successor or equal; and every act of local or temporary possession was insensibly moulded into the constitution of the Germanic kingdom. In every province, the visible presence of the duke or count was interposed between the throne and the nobles; the subjects of the law became the vassals of a private chief; and the standard which *he* received from his sovereign, was often raised against him in the field. The temporal power of the clergy was cherished and exalted by the superstition or policy of the Carlovingian and Saxon dynasties, who blindly depended on their moderation and fidelity; and the bishoprics of Germany were made equal in extent and privilege, superior in wealth and population, to the most ample states of the military order. As long as the emperors retained the prerogative of bestowing on every vacancy these ecclesiastic and secular benefices, their cause was maintained by the gratitude or ambition of their friends and favorites. But in the quarrel of the investitures, they were deprived of their influence over the episcopal chapters; the freedom of election was restored, and the sovereign was reduced, by a solemn mockery, to his *first prayers*, the recommendation, once in his reign, to a single prebend in each church. The secular governors, instead of being recalled at the will of a superior, could be degraded only by the sentence of their peers. In the first age of the monarchy, the appointment of the son to the duchy or county of his father, was solicited as a favor; it was gradually obtained as a custom, and extorted as a right: the lineal succession was often extended to the collateral or female branches; the states of the empire (their popular, and at length their legal, appellation) were divided and alienated by testament and sale; and all idea of a public trust was lost in that of a private and perpetual inheritance. The emperor could not even be enriched by the casualties of forfeiture and extinction: within the term of a year, he was obliged to dispose of the vacant fief; and, in the choice of the candidate, it was his duty to consult either the general or the provincial diet.

After the death of Frederic the Second, Germany was left a monster with a hundred heads. A crowd of princes and prelates disputed the ruins of the empire: the lords of innumerable castles were less prone to obey, than to imitate, their superiors; and, according to the measure of their strength, their incessant hostilities received the names of conquest or robbery. Such anarchy was the inevitable consequence of the laws and manners of Europe; and the kingdoms of France and Italy were shivered into fragments by the violence of the same tempest. But the Italian cities and the French vassals were divided and destroyed, while the union of the Germans has produced, under the name of an empire, a great system of a federative republic. In the frequent and at last the perpetual institution of diets, a national spirit was kept alive, and the powers of a common legislature are still exercised by the three branches or colleges of the electors, the princes, and the free and Imperial cities of Germany. I. Seven of the most powerful feudatories were permitted to assume, with a distinguished name and rank, the exclusive privilege of choosing the Roman emperor; and these electors were the king of Bohemia, the duke of Saxony, the margrave of Brandenburgh, the count palatine of the Rhine, and the three archbishops of Mentz, of Treves, and of Cologne. II. The college of princes and prelates purged themselves of a promiscuous multitude: they reduced to four representative votes the long series of independent counts, and excluded the nobles or equestrian order, sixty thousand of whom, as in the Polish diets, had appeared on horseback in the field of election. III. The pride of birth and dominion, of the sword and the mitre, wisely adopted the commons as the third branch of the legislature, and, in the progress of society, they were introduced about the same æra into the national assemblies of France England, and Germany. The Hanseatic League commanded the trade and navigation of the north: the confederates of the Rhine secured the peace and intercourse of the inland country; the influence of the cities has been adequate to their wealth and policy, and their negative still invalidates the acts of the two superior colleges of electors and princes.

It is in the fourteenth century that we may view in the strongest light the state and contrast of the Roman empire of Germany, which no longer held, except on the borders of the Rhine and Danube, a single province of Trajan or Constantine. Their unworthy successors were the counts of Hapsburgh, of Nassau, of Luxemburgh, and Schwartzenburgh: the emperor Henry the Seventh procured for his son the crown of Bohemia, and his grandson Charles the Fourth was born among a people strange and barbarous in the estimation of the Germans themselves. After the excommunication of Lewis of Bavaria, he received the gift or promise of the vacant empire from the Roman pontiffs, who, in the exile and captivity of Avignon, affected the dominion of the earth. The death of his competitors united the electoral college, and Charles was unanimously saluted king of the Romans, and future emperor; a title which, in the same age, was prostituted to the Cæsars of Germany and Greece. The German emperor was no more than the elective and impotent magistrate of an aristocracy of princes, who had not left him a village that he might call his own. His best prerogative was the right of presiding and proposing in the national senate, which was convened at his summons; and his native kingdom of Bohemia, less opulent than the adjacent city of Nuremberg, was the firmest seat of his power and the richest source of his revenue. The army with which he passed the Alps consisted of three hundred horse. In the cathedral of St. Ambrose, Charles was crowned with the *iron* crown, which tradition ascribed to the Lombard monarchy; but he was admitted only with a peaceful train; the gates of the city were shut upon him; and the king of Italy was held a captive by the arms of the Visconti, whom he confirmed in the sovereignty of Milan. In the Vatican he was again crowned with the *golden* crown of the empire; but, in obedience to a secret treaty, the Roman emperor immediately withdrew, without reposing a single night within the walls of Rome. The eloquent Petrarch, whose fancy revived the visionary glories of the Capitol, deplores and upbraids the ignominious flight of the Bohemian; and even his contemporaries could observe, that the sole exercise of his authority was in the lucrative sale of privileges and titles. The gold of Italy secured the election of his son; but such was the shameful poverty of the Roman emperor, that his person was arrested by a butcher in the streets of Worms, and was detained in the public inn, as a pledge or hostage for the payment of his expenses.

From this humiliating scene, let us turn to the apparent majesty of the same Charles in the diets of the empire. The golden bull, which fixes the Germanic constitution, is promulgated in the style of a sovereign and legislator. A hundred princes bowed before his throne, and exalted their own dignity by the voluntary honors which they yielded to their chief or minister. At the royal banquet, the hereditary great officers, the seven electors, who in rank and title were equal to kings, performed their solemn and domestic service of the palace. The seals of the triple kingdom were borne in state by the archbishops of Mentz, Cologne, and Treves, the perpetual arch-chancellors of Germany, Italy, and Arles. The great marshal, on horseback, exercised his function with a silver measure of oats, which he emptied on the ground, and immediately dismounted to regulate the order of the guests. The great steward, the count palatine of the Rhine, place the dishes on the table. The great chamberlain, the margrave of Brandenburgh, presented, after the repast, the golden ewer and basin, to wash. The king of Bohemia, as great cup-bearer, was represented by the emperor's brother, the duke of Luxemburgh and Brabant; and the procession was closed by the great huntsmen, who introduced a boar and a stag, with a loud chorus of horns and hounds. Nor was the supremacy of the emperor confined to Germany alone: the hereditary monarchs of Europe confessed the preëminence of his rank and dignity: he was the first of the Christian princes, the temporal head of the great republic of the West: to his person the title of majesty was long appropriated; and he disputed with the pope the sublime prerogative of creating kings and assembling councils. The oracle of the civil law, the learned Bartolus, was a pensioner of Charles the Fourth; and his school resounded with the doctrine, that the Roman emperor was the rightful sovereign of the earth, from the rising to the setting sun. The contrary opinion was condemned, not as an error, but as a heresy, since even the gospel had pronounced, "And there went forth a decree from Cæsar Augustus, that *all the world* should be taxed.»

If we annihilate the interval of time and space between Augustus and Charles, strong and striking will be the contrast between the two Cæsars; the Bohemian who concealed his weakness under the mask of ostentation, and the Roman, who disguised his strength under the semblance of modesty. At the head of his victorious legions, in his reign over the sea and land, from the Nile and Euphrates to the Atlantic Ocean, Augustus professed himself the servant of the state and the equal of his fellow-citizens. The conqueror of Rome and her provinces assumed a popular and legal form of a censor, a consul, and a tribune. His will was the law of mankind, but in the declaration of his laws he borrowed the voice of the senate and people; and from their decrees their master accepted and renewed his temporary commission to administer the republic. In his dress, his domestics, his titles, in all the offices of social life, Augustus maintained the character of a private Roman; and his most artful flatterers respected the secret of his absolute and perpetual monarchy.

Description of Arabia and its Inhabitants. – Part One

Description of Arabia and its Inhabitants. – Birth, Character, and Doctrine of Mahomet. – He Preaches at Mecca. – Flies to Medina. – Propagates his Religion by the Sword. – Voluntary or Reluctant Submission of the Arabs. – His Death and Successors. – The Claims and Fortunes of ali and his Descendants.

AFTER PURSUING ABOVE SIX hundred years the fleeting Cæsars of Constantinople and Germany, I now descend, in the reign of Heraclius, on the eastern borders of the Greek monarchy. While the state was exhausted by the Persian war, and the church was distracted by the Nestorian and Monophysite sects, Mahomet, with the sword in one hand and the Koran in the other, erected his throne on the ruins of Christianity and of Rome. The genius of the Arabian prophet, the manners of his nation, and the spirit of his religion, involve the causes of the decline and fall of the Eastern empire; and our eyes are curiously intent on one of the most memorable revolutions, which have impressed a new and lasting character on the nations of the globe.

In the vacant space between Persia, Syria, Egypt, and Æthiopia, the Arabian peninsula may be conceived as a triangle of spacious but irregular dimensions. From the northern point of Beles on the Euphrates, a line of fifteen hundred miles is terminated by the Straits of Bebelmandel and the land of frankincense. About half this length may be allowed for the middle breadth, from east to west, from Bassora to Suez, from the Persian Gulf to the Red Sea. The sides of the triangle are gradually enlarged, and the southern basis presents a front of a thousand miles to the Indian Ocean. The entire surface of the peninsula exceeds in a fourfold proportion that of Germany or France; but the far greater part has been justly stigmatized with the epithets of the *stony* and the *sandy*. Even the wilds of Tartary are decked, by the hand of nature, with lofty trees and luxuriant herbage; and the lonesome traveller derives a sort of comfort and society from the presence of vegetable life. But in the dreary waste of Arabia, a boundless level of sand is intersected by sharp and naked mountains; and the face of the desert, without shade or shelter, is scorched by the direct and intense rays of a tropical sun. Instead of refreshing breezes, the winds, particularly from the south-west, diffuse a noxious and even deadly vapor; the hillocks of sand which they alternately raise and scatter, are compared to the billows of the ocean, and whole caravans, whole armies, have been lost and buried in the whirlwind. The common benefits of water are an object of desire and contest; and such is the scarcity of wood, that some art is requisite to preserve and propagate the element of fire. Arabia is destitute of navigable rivers, which fertilize the soil, and convey its produce to the adjacent regions: the torrents that fall from the hills are imbibed by the thirsty earth: the rare and hardy plants, the tamarind or the acacia, that strike their roots into the clefts of the rocks, are nourished by the dews of the night: a scanty supply of rain is collected in cisterns and aqueducts: the wells and springs are the secret treasure of the desert; and the pilgrim of Mecca, after many a dry and sultry march, is disgusted by the taste of the waters which have rolled over a bed of sulphur or salt. Such is the general and genuine picture of the climate of Arabia. The experience of evil enhances the value of any local or partial enjoyments. A shady grove, a green pasture, a stream of fresh water, are sufficient to attract a colony of sedentary Arabs to the fortunate spots which can afford food and refreshment to themselves and their cattle, and which encourage their industry in the cultivation of the palmtree and the vine. The high lands that border on the Indian Ocean are distinguished by their superior plenty of wood and water; the air is more temperate, the fruits are more delicious, the animals and the human race more numerous: the fertility of the soil invites and rewards the toil of the husbandman; and the peculiar gifts of frankincense and coffee have attracted in different ages the merchants of the world. If it be compared with the rest of the peninsula, this sequestered region may truly deserve the appellation of the *happy*; and the splendid coloring of fancy and fiction has been suggested by contrast, and countenanced by distance. It was for this earthly paradise that Nature had reserved her choicest favors and her most curious workmanship: the incompatible blessings of luxury and innocence were ascribed to the natives: the soil was impregnated with gold and gems, and both the land and sea were taught to exhale the odors of aromatic sweets. This division of the *sandy*, the *stony*, and the *happy*, so familiar to the Greeks and Latins, is unknown to the Arabians themselves; and it is singular enough, that a country, whose language and inhabitants have ever been the same, should scarcely retain a vestige of its ancient geography. The maritime districts of *Bahrein* and *Oman* are opposite to the realm of Persia. The kingdom of *Yemen* displays the limits, or at least the situation, of Arabia Felix: the name of *Neged* is extended over the inland space; and the birth of Mahomet has illustrated the province of *Hejaz* along the coast of the Red Sea.

The measure of population is regulated by the means of subsistence; and the inhabitants of this vast peninsula might be outnumbered by the subjects of a fertile and industrious province. Along the shores of the Persian Gulf, of the ocean, and even of the Red Sea, the *Icthy-ophagi*, or fish eaters, continued to wander in quest of their precarious food. In this primitive and abject state, which ill deserves the name of society, the human brute, without arts or laws, almost without sense or language, is poorly distinguished from the rest of the animal creation. Generations and ages might roll away in silent oblivion, and the helpless savage was restrained from multiplying his race by the wants and pursuits which confined his existence to the narrow margin of the seacoast. But in an early period of antiquity the great body of the Arabs had emerged from this scene of misery; and as the naked wilderness could not maintain a people of hunters, they rose at once to the more secure and plentiful condition of the pastoral life. The same life is uniformly pursued by the roving tribes of the desert; and in the portrait of the modern *Bedoweens*, we may trace the features of their ancestors, who, in the age of Moses or Mahomet, dwelt under similar tents, and conducted their horses, and camels, and sheep, to the same springs and the same pastures. Our toil is lessened, and our wealth is increased, by our dominion over the useful animals; and the Arabian shepherd had acquired the absolute possession of a faithful friend and a laborious slave. Arabia, in the opinion of the naturalist, is the genuine and original country of the *horse*; the climate most propitious, not indeed to the size, but to the spirit and swiftness, of that generous animal. The merit of the Barb, the Spanish, and the English breed, is derived from a mixture of Arabian blood: the Bedoweens preserve, with superstitious care, the honors and the memory of the purest race: the males are sold at a high price, but the females are seldom alienated; and the birth of a noble foal was esteemed among the tribes, as a subject of joy and mutual congratulation. These horses are educated in the tents, among the children of the Arabs, with a tender familiarity, which trains them in the habits of gentleness and attachment. They are accustomed only to walk and to gallop: their sensations are not blunted by the incessant abuse of the spur and the whip: their powers are reserved for the moments of flight and pursuit: but no sooner do they feel the touch of the hand or the stirrup, than they dart away with the swiftness of the wind; and if their friend be dismounted in the rapid career, they instantly stop till he has recovered his seat. In the sands of Africa and Arabia, the *camel* is a sacred and precious gift. That strong and patient beast of burden can perform, without eating or drinking, a journey of several days; and a reservoir of fresh water is preserved in a large bag, a fifth stomach of the animal, whose body is imprinted with the marks of servitude: the larger breed is capable of transporting a weight of a thousand pounds; and the dromedary, of a lighter and more active frame, outstrips the fleetest courser in the race. Alive or dead, almost every part of the camel is serviceable to man: her milk is plentiful and nutritious: the young and tender flesh has the taste of veal: a valuable salt is extracted from the urine: the dung supplies the deficiency of fuel; and the long hair, which falls each year and is renewed, is coarsely manufactured into the garments, the furniture, and the tents of the Bedoweens. In the rainy seasons, they consume the rare and insufficient herbage of the desert: during the heats of summer and the scarcity of winter, they remove their encampments to the sea-coast, the hills of Yemen, or the neighborhood of the Euphrates, and have often extorted the dangerous license of visiting the banks of the Nile, and the villages of Syria and Palestine. The life of a wandering Arab is a life of danger and distress; and though sometimes, by rapine or exchange, he may appropriate the fruits of industry, a private citizen in Europe is in the possession of more solid and pleasing luxury than the proudest emir, who marches in the field at the head of ten thousand horse.

Yet an essential difference may be found between the hordes of Scythia and the Arabian tribes; since many of the latter were collected into towns, and employed in the labors of trade and agriculture. A part of their time and industry was still devoted to the management of their cattle: they mingled, in peace and war, with their brethren of the desert; and the Bedoweens derived from their useful intercourse some supply of their wants, and some rudiments of art and knowledge. Among the forty-two cities of Arabia, enumerated by Abulfeda, the most ancient and populous were situate in the *happy* Yemen: the towers of Saana, and the marvellous reservoir of Merab, were constructed by the kings of the Homerites; but their profane lustre was eclipsed by the prophetic glories of Medina and Mecca, near the Red Sea, and at the distance from each other of two hundred and seventy miles. The last of these holy places was known to the Greeks under the name of Macoraba; and the termination of the word is expressive of its greatness, which has not, indeed, in the most flourishing period, exceeded the size and populousness of Marseilles. Some latent motive, perhaps of superstition, must have impelled the founders, in the choice of a most unpromising situation. They erected their habitations of mud or stone, in a plain about two miles long and one mile broad, at the foot of three barren mountains: the soil is a rock; the water even of the holy well of Zemzem is bitter or brackish; the pastures are remote from the city; and grapes are transported above seventy miles from the gardens of Tayef. The fame and spirit of the Koreishites, who reigned in Mecca, were conspicuous among the Arabian tribes; but their ungrateful soil refused the labors of agriculture, and their position was favorable to the enterprises of trade. By the seaport of Gedda, at the distance only of forty miles, they maintained an easy correspondence with Abyssinia; and that Christian kingdom afforded the first refuge to the disciples of Mahomet. The treasures of Africa were conveyed over the Peninsula to Gerrha or Katif, in the province of Bahrein, a city built, as it is said, of rock-salt, by the Chaldæan exiles; and from thence with the native pearls of the Persian Gulf, they were floated on rafts to the mouth of the Euphrates. Mecca is placed almost at an equal distance, a month›s journey, between Yemen on the right, and Syria on the left hand. The former was the winter, the latter the summer, station of her caravans; and their seasonable arrival relieved the ships of India from the tedious and troublesome navigation of the Red Sea. In the markets of Saana and Merab, in the harbors of Oman and Aden, the camels of the Koreishites were laden with a precious cargo of aromatics; a supply of corn and manufactures was purchased in the fairs of Bostra and Damascus; the lucrative exchange diffused plenty and riches in the streets of Mecca; and the noblest of her sons united the love of arms with the profession of merchandise.

The perpetual independence of the Arabs has been the theme of praise among strangers and natives; and the arts of controversy transform this singular event into a prophecy and a miracle, in favor of the posterity of Ismael. Some exceptions, that can neither be dismissed nor eluded, render this mode of reasoning as indiscreet as it is superfluous;

the kingdom of Yemen has been successively subdued by the Abyssinians, the Persians, the sultans of Egypt, and the Turks; the holy cities of Mecca and Medina have repeatedly bowed under a Scythian tyrant; and the Roman province of Arabia embraced the peculiar wilderness in which Ismael and his sons must have pitched their tents in the face of their brethren. Yet these exceptions are temporary or local; the body of the nation has escaped the yoke of the most powerful monarchies: the arms of Sesostris and Cyrus, of Pompey and Trajan, could never achieve the conquest of Arabia; the present sovereign of the Turks may exercise a shadow of jurisdiction, but his pride is reduced to solicit the friendship of a people, whom it is dangerous to provoke, and fruitless to attack. The obvious causes of their freedom are inscribed on the character and country of the Arabs. Many ages before Mahomet, their intrepid valor had been severely felt by their neighbors in offensive and defensive war. The patient and active virtues of a soldier are insensibly nursed in the habits and discipline of a pastoral life. The care of the sheep and camels is abandoned to the women of the tribe; but the martial youth, under the banner of the emir, is ever on horseback, and in the field, to practise the exercise of the bow, the javelin, and the cimeter. The long memory of their independence is the firmest pledge of its perpetuity and succeeding generations are animated to prove their descent, and to maintain their inheritance. Their domestic feuds are suspended on the approach of a common enemy; and in their last hostilities against the Turks, the caravan of Mecca was attacked and pillaged by fourscore thousand of the confederates. When they advance to battle, the hope of victory is in the front; in the rear, the assurance of a retreat. Their horses and camels, who, in eight or ten days, can perform a march of four or five hundred miles, disappear before the conqueror; the secret waters of the desert elude his search, and his victorious troops are consumed with thirst, hunger, and fatigue, in the pursuit of an invisible foe, who scorns his efforts, and safely reposes in the heart of the burning solitude. The arms and deserts of the Bedoweens are not only the safeguards of their own freedom, but the barriers also of the happy Arabia, whose inhabitants, remote from war, are enervated by the luxury of the soil and climate. The legions of Augustus melted away in disease and lassitude; and it is only by a naval power that the reduction of Yemen has been successfully attempted. When Mahomet erected his holy standard, that kingdom was a province of the Persian empire; yet seven princes of the Homerites still reigned in the mountains; and the vicegerent of Chosroes was tempted to forget his distant country and his unfortunate master. The historians of the age of Justinian represent the state of the independent Arabs, who were divided by interest or affection in the long quarrel of the East: the tribe of *Gassan* was allowed to encamp on the Syrian territory: the princes of *Hira* were permitted to form a city about forty miles to the southward of the ruins of Babylon. Their service in the field was speedy and vigorous; but their friendship was venal, their faith inconstant, their enmity capricious: it was an easier task to excite than to disarm these roving barbarians; and, in the familiar intercourse of war, they learned to see, and to despise, the splendid weakness both of Rome and of Persia. From Mecca to the Euphrates, the Arabian tribes were confounded by the Greeks and Latins, under the general appellation of Saracens, a name which every Christian mouth has been taught to pronounce with terror and abhorrence.

CHAPTER FIFTY

Description of Arabia
and its Inhabitants. – Part Two

THE SLAVES OF DOMESTIC tyranny may vainly exult in their national independence: but the Arab is personally free; and he enjoys, in some degree, the benefits of society, without forfeiting the prerogatives of nature. In every tribe, superstition, or gratitude, or fortune, has exalted a particular family above the heads of their equals. The dignities of sheick and emir invariably descend in this chosen race; but the order of succession is loose and precarious; and the most worthy or aged of the noble kinsmen are preferred to the simple, though important, office of composing disputes by their advice, and guiding valor by their example. Even a female of sense and spirit has been permitted to command the countrymen of Zenobia. The momentary junction of several tribes produces an army: their more lasting union constitutes a nation; and the supreme chief, the emir of emirs, whose banner is displayed at their head, may deserve, in the eyes of strangers, the honors of the kingly name. If the Arabian princes abuse their power, they are quickly punished by the desertion of their subjects, who had been accustomed to a mild and parental jurisdiction. Their spirit is free, their steps are unconfined, the desert is open, and the tribes and families are held together by a mutual and voluntary compact. The softer natives of Yemen supported the pomp and majesty of a monarch; but if he could not leave his palace without endangering his life, the active powers of government must have been devolved on his nobles and magistrates. The cities of Mecca and Medina present, in the heart of Asia, the form, or rather the substance, of a commonwealth. The grandfather of Mahomet, and his lineal ancestors, appear in foreign and domestic transactions as the princes of their country; but they reigned, like Pericles at Athens, or the Medici at Florence, by the opinion of their wisdom and integrity; their influence was divided with their patrimony; and the sceptre was transferred from the uncles of the prophet to a younger branch of the tribe of Koreish. On solemn occasions they convened the assembly of the people; and, since mankind must be either compelled or persuaded to obey, the use and reputation of oratory among the ancient Arabs is the clearest evidence of public freedom. But their simple freedom was of a very different cast from the nice and artificial machinery of the Greek and Roman republics, in which each member possessed an undivided share of the civil and political rights of the community. In the more simple state of the Arabs, the nation is free, because each of her sons disdains a base submission to the will of a master. His breast is fortified by the austere virtues of courage, patience, and sobriety; the love of independence prompts him to exercise the habits of self-command; and the fear of dishonor guards him from the meaner apprehension of pain, of danger, and of death. The gravity and firmness of the mind is conspicuous in his outward demeanor; his speech is low, weighty, and concise; he is seldom provoked to laughter; his only gesture is that of stroking his beard, the venerable symbol of manhood; and the sense of his own importance teaches him to accost his equals without levity, and his superiors without awe. The liberty of the Saracens survived their conquests: the first caliphs indulged the bold and familiar language of their subjects; they ascended the pulpit to persuade and edify the congregation; nor was it before the seat of empire was removed to the Tigris, that the Abbasides adopted the proud and pompous ceremonial of the Persian and Byzantine courts.

In the study of nations and men, we may observe the causes that render them hostile or friendly to each other, that tend to narrow or enlarge, to mollify or exasperate, the social character. The separation of the Arabs from the rest of mankind has accustomed them to confound the ideas of stranger and enemy; and the poverty of the land has introduced a maxim of jurisprudence, which they believe and practise to the present hour. They pretend, that, in the division of the earth, the rich and fertile climates were assigned to the other branches of the human family; and that the posterity of the outlaw Ismael might recover, by fraud or force, the portion of inheritance of which he had been unjustly deprived. According to the remark of Pliny, the Arabian tribes are equally addicted to theft and merchandise; the caravans that traverse the desert are ransomed or pillaged; and their neighbors, since the remote times of Job and Sesostris, have been the victims of their rapacious spirit. If a Bedoween discovers from afar a solitary traveller, he rides furiously against him, crying, with a loud voice, "Undress thyself, thy aunt (*my wife*) is without a garment." A ready submission entitles him to mercy; resistance will provoke the aggressor, and his own blood must expiate the blood which he presumes to shed in legitimate defence. A single robber, or a few associates, are branded with their genuine name; but the exploits of a numerous band assume the character of lawful and honorable war. The temper of a people thus armed against mankind was doubly inflamed by the domestic license of rapine, murder, and revenge. In the constitution of Europe, the right of peace and war is now confined to a small, and the actual exercise to a much smaller, list of respectable potentates; but each Arab, with impunity and renown, might point his javelin against the life of his countrymen. The union of the nation consisted only in a vague resemblance of language and manners; and in each community, the jurisdiction of the magistrate was mute and impotent. Of the time of ignorance which preceded Mahomet, seventeen hundred battles are recorded by tradition: hostility was imbittered with the rancor of civil faction; and the recital, in prose or verse, of an obsolete feud, was sufficient to rekindle the same passions among the descendants of the hostile tribes. In private life every man, at least every family, was the judge and avenger of his own cause. The nice sensibility of honor, which weighs the insult rather than the injury, sheds its deadly venom on the quarrels of the Arabs: the honor of their women, and of their *beards*, is most easily wounded; an indecent action, a contemptuous word, can be expiated only by the blood of the offender; and such is their patient inveteracy, that they expect whole months and years the opportunity of revenge. A fine or compensation for murder is familiar to the Barbarians of every age: but in Arabia the kinsmen of the dead are at liberty to accept the atonement, or to exercise with their own hands the law of retaliation. The refined malice of the Arabs refuses even the head of the murderer, substitutes an innocent for the guilty person, and transfers the penalty to the best and most considerable of the race by whom they have been injured. If he falls by their hands, they are exposed, in their turn, to the danger of reprisals, the interest and principal of the bloody debt are accumulated: the individuals of either family lead a life of malice and suspicion, and fifty years may sometimes elapse before the account of vengeance be finally settled. This sanguinary spirit, ignorant of pity or forgiveness, has been moderated, however, by the maxims of honor, which require in every private encounter some decent equality of age and strength, of numbers and weapons. An annual festival of two, perhaps of four, months, was observed by the Arabs before the time of Mahomet, during which their swords were religiously sheathed both in foreign and domestic hostility; and this partial truce is more strongly expressive of the habits of anarchy and warfare.

But the spirit of rapine and revenge was attempered by the milder influence of trade and literature. The solitary peninsula is encompassed by the most civilized nations of the ancient world; the merchant is the friend of mankind; and the annual caravans imported the first seeds of knowledge and politeness into the cities, and even the camps of the desert. Whatever may be the pedigree of the Arabs, their language is derived from the same original stock with the Hebrew, the Syriac, and the Chaldæan tongues; the independence of the tribes was marked by their peculiar dialects; but each, after their own, allowed a just preference to the pure and perspicuous idiom of Mecca. In Arabia, as well as in Greece, the perfection of language outstripped the refinement of manners; and her speech could diversify the fourscore names of honey, the two hundred of a serpent, the five hundred of a lion, the thousand of a sword, at a time when this copious dictionary was intrusted to the memory of an illiterate people. The monuments of the Homerites were inscribed with an obsolete and mysterious character; but the Cufic letters, the groundwork of the present alphabet, were invented on the banks of the Euphrates; and the recent invention was taught at Mecca by a stranger who settled in that city after the birth of Mahomet. The arts of grammar, of metre, and of rhetoric, were unknown to the freeborn eloquence of the Arabians; but their penetration was sharp, their fancy luxuriant, their wit strong and sententious, and their more elaborate compositions were addressed with energy and effect to the minds of their hearers. The genius and merit of a rising poet was celebrated by the applause of his own and the kindred tribes. A solemn banquet was prepared, and a chorus of women, striking their tymbals, and displaying the pomp of their nuptials, sung in the presence of their sons and husbands the felicity of their native tribe; that a champion had now appeared to vindicate their rights; that a herald had raised his voice to immortalize their renown. The distant or hostile tribes resorted to an annual fair, which was abolished by the fanaticism of the first Moslems; a national assembly that must have contributed to refine and harmonize the Barbarians. Thirty days were employed in the exchange, not only of corn and wine, but of eloquence and poetry. The prize was disputed by the generous emulation of the bards; the victorious performance was deposited in the archives of princes and emirs; and we may read in our own language, the seven original poems which were inscribed in letters of gold, and suspended in the temple of Mecca. The Arabian poets were the historians and moralists of the age; and if they sympathized with the prejudices, they inspired and crowned the virtues, of their countrymen. The indissoluble union of generosity and valor was the darling theme of their song; and when they pointed their keenest satire against a despicable race, they affirmed, in the bitterness of reproach, that the men knew not how to give, nor the women to deny. The same hospitality, which was practised by Abraham, and celebrated by Homer, is still renewed in the camps of the Arabs. The ferocious Bedoweens, the terror of the desert, embrace, without inquiry or hesitation, the stranger who dares to confide in their honor and to enter their tent. His treatment is kind and respectful: he shares the wealth, or the poverty, of his host; and, after a needful repose, he is dismissed on his way, with thanks, with blessings, and perhaps with gifts. The heart and hand are more largely expanded by the wants of a brother or a friend; but the heroic acts that could deserve the public applause, must have surpassed the narrow measure of discretion and experience. A dispute had arisen, who, among the citizens of Mecca, was entitled to the prize of generosity; and a successive application was made to the three who were deemed most worthy of the trial. Abdallah, the son of Abbas, had undertaken a distant journey, and his foot was in the stirrup when he heard the voice of a suppliant, "O son of the uncle of the apostle of God, I am a traveller, and in distress!" He instantly dismounted to present the pilgrim with his camel, her rich caparison, and a purse of four thousand pieces of gold, excepting only the sword, either for its intrinsic value, or as the gift of an honored kinsman. The servant of Kais informed the second suppliant that his master was asleep: but he immediately added, "Here is a purse of seven thousand pieces of gold, (it is all we have in the house,) and here is an order, that will entitle you to a camel and a slave;" the master, as soon as he awoke, praised and enfranchised his faithful steward, with a gentle reproof, that by respecting his slumbers he had stinted his bounty. The third of these heroes, the blind Arabah, at the hour of prayer, was supporting his steps on the shoulders of two slaves. "Alas!" he replied, "my coffers are empty! but these you may sell; if you refuse, I renounce them." At these words, pushing away the youths, he groped along the wall with his staff. The character of Hatem is the perfect model of Arabian virtue: he was brave and liberal, an eloquent poet, and a successful robber; forty camels were roasted at his hospitable feast; and at the prayer of a suppliant enemy he restored both the captives and the spoil. The freedom of his countrymen disdained the laws of justice; they proudly indulged the spontaneous impulse of pity and benevolence.

The religion of the Arabs, as well as of the Indians, consisted in the worship of the sun, the moon, and the fixed stars; a primitive and specious mode of superstition. The bright luminaries of the sky display the visible image of a Deity: their number and distance convey to a philosophic, or even a vulgar, eye, the idea of boundless space: the character of eternity is marked on these solid globes, that seem incapable of corruption or decay: the regularity of their motions may be ascribed to a principle of reason or instinct; and their real, or imaginary, influence encourages the vain belief that the earth and its inhabitants are the object of their peculiar care. The science of astronomy was cultivated at Babylon; but the school of the Arabs was a clear firmament and a naked plain. In their nocturnal marches, they steered by the guidance of the stars: their names, and order, and daily station, were familiar to the curiosity and devotion of the Bedoween; and he was taught by experience to divide, in twenty-eight parts, the zodiac of the moon, and to bless the constellations who refreshed, with salutary rains, the thirst of the desert. The reign of the heavenly orbs could not be extended beyond the visible sphere; and some metaphysical powers were necessary to sustain the transmigration of souls and the resurrection of bodies: a camel was left to perish on the grave, that he might serve his master in another life; and the invocation of departed spirits implies that they were still endowed with consciousness and power. I am ignorant, and I am careless, of the blind mythology of the Barbarians; of the local deities, of the stars, the air, and the earth, of their sex or titles, their attributes or subordination. Each tribe, each family, each independent warrior, created and changed the rites and the object of his fantastic worship; but the nation, in every age, has bowed to the religion, as well as to the language, of Mecca. The genuine antiquity of the Caaba ascends beyond the Christian æra; in describing the coast of the Red Sea, the Greek historian Diodorus has remarked, between the Thamudites and the Sabæans, a famous temple, whose superior sanctity was revered by *all* the Arabians; the linen or silken veil, which is annually renewed by the Turkish emperor, was first offered by a pious king of the Homerites, who reigned seven hundred years before the time of Mahomet. A tent, or a cavern, might suffice for the worship of the savages, but an edifice of stone and clay has been erected in its place; and the art and

power of the monarchs of the East have been confined to the simplicity of the original model. A spacious portico encloses the quadrangle
of the Caaba; a square chapel, twenty-four cubits long, twenty-three
broad, and twenty-seven high: a door and a window admit the light;
the double roof is supported by three pillars of wood; a spout (now
of gold) discharges the rain-water, and the well Zemzem is protected
by a dome from accidental pollution. The tribe of Koreish, by fraud
and force, had acquired the custody of the Caaba: the sacerdotal office devolved through four lineal descents to the grandfather of Mahomet; and the family of the Hashemites, from whence he sprung,
was the most respectable and sacred in the eyes of their country. The
precincts of Mecca enjoyed the rights of sanctuary; and, in the last
month of each year, the city and the temple were crowded with a long
train of pilgrims, who presented their vows and offerings in the house
of God. The same rites which are now accomplished by the faithful
Mussulman, were invented and practised by the superstition of the
idolaters. At an awful distance they cast away their garments: seven
times, with hasty steps, they encircled the Caaba, and kissed the black
stone: seven times they visited and adored the adjacent mountains;
seven times they threw stones into the valley of Mina; and the pilgrimage was achieved, as at the present hour, by a sacrifice of sheep
and camels, and the burial of their hair and nails in the consecrated
ground. Each tribe either found or introduced in the Caaba their domestic worship: the temple was adorned, or defiled, with three hundred and sixty idols of men, eagles, lions, and antelopes; and most
conspicuous was the statue of Hebal, of red agate, holding in his hand
seven arrows, without heads or feathers, the instruments and symbols
of profane divination. But this statue was a monument of Syrian arts:
the devotion of the ruder ages was content with a pillar or a tablet;
and the rocks of the desert were hewn into gods or altars, in imitation
of the black stone of Mecca, which is deeply tainted with the reproach
of an idolatrous origin. From Japan to Peru, the use of sacrifice has
universally prevailed; and the votary has expressed his gratitude, or
fear, by destroying or consuming, in honor of the gods, the dearest
and most precious of their gifts. The life of a man is the most precious oblation to deprecate a public calamity: the altars of Phœnicia
and Egypt, of Rome and Carthage, have been polluted with human
gore: the cruel practice was long preserved among the Arabs; in the
third century, a boy was annually sacrificed by the tribe of the Du-
matians; and a royal captive was piously slaughtered by the prince of
the Saracens, the ally and soldier of the emperor Justinian. A parent

who drags his son to the altar, exhibits the most painful and sublime effort of fanaticism: the deed, or the intention, was sanctified by the example of saints and heroes; and the father of Mahomet himself was devoted by a rash vow, and hardly ransomed for the equivalent of a hundred camels. In the time of ignorance, the Arabs, like the Jews and Egyptians, abstained from the taste of swine›s flesh; they circumcised their children at the age of puberty: the same customs, without the censure or the precept of the Koran, have been silently transmitted to their posterity and proselytes. It has been sagaciously conjectured, that the artful legislator indulged the stubborn prejudices of his coun-trymen. It is more simple to believe that he adhered to the habits and opinions of his youth, without foreseeing that a practice congenial to the climate of Mecca might become useless or inconvenient on the banks of the Danube or the Volga.

Description of Arabia and its Inhabitants. – Part Three

ARABIA WAS FREE: the adjacent kingdoms were shaken by the storms of conquest and tyranny, and the persecuted sects fled to the happy land where they might profess what they thought, and practise what they professed. The religions of the Sabians and Magians, of the Jews and Christians, were disseminated from the Persian Gulf to the Red Sea. In a remote period of antiquity, Sabianism was diffused over Asia by the science of the Chaldæans and the arms of the Assyrians. From the observations of two thousand years, the priests and astronomers of Babylon deduced the eternal laws of nature and providence. They adored the seven gods or angels, who directed the course of the seven planets, and shed their irresistible influence on the earth. The attributes of the seven planets, with the twelve signs of the zodiac, and the twenty-four constellations of the northern and southern hemisphere, were represented by images and talismans; the seven days of the week were dedicated to their respective deities; the Sabians prayed thrice each day; and the temple of the moon at Haran was the term of their pilgrimage. But the flexible genius of their faith was always ready either to teach or to learn: in the tradition of the creation, the deluge, and the patriarchs, they held a singular agreement with their Jewish captives; they appealed to the secret books of Adam, Seth, and Enoch; and a slight infusion of the gospel has transformed the last remnant of the Polytheists into the Christians of St. John, in the territory of Bassora. The altars of Babylon were overturned by the Magians; but the injuries of the Sabians were revenged by the sword of Alexander; Persia groaned above five hundred years under a foreign yoke; and the purest disciples of Zoroaster escaped from the contagion of idolatry, and breathed with their adversaries the freedom of the desert. Seven hundred years before the death of Mahomet, the Jews were settled in Arabia; and a far greater multitude was expelled from the Holy Land in the wars of Titus and Hadrian. The industrious exiles aspired to liberty and power: they erected synagogues in the cities, and castles in the wilderness, and their Gentile converts were confounded with the children of Israel, whom they resembled in the outward mark of circumcision. The Christian missionaries were still more active and successful: the Catholics asserted their universal reign; the sects whom they oppressed, successively retired beyond the limits of the Roman empire; the Marcionites and Manichæans dispersed their *fantastic* opinions and apocryphal gospels; the churches of Yemen, and the princes of Hira and Gassan, were instructed in a purer creed by the Jacobite and Nestorian bishops. The liberty of choice was presented to the tribes: each Arab was free to elect or to compose his private religion: and the rude superstition of his house was mingled with the sublime theology of saints and philosophers. A fundamental article of faith was inculcated by the consent of the learned strangers; the existence of one supreme God who is exalted above the powers of heaven and earth, but who has often revealed himself to mankind by the ministry of his angels and prophets, and whose grace or justice has interrupted, by seasonable miracles, the order of nature. The most rational of the Arabs acknowledged his power, though they neglected his worship; and it was habit rather than conviction that still attached them to the relics of idolatry. The Jews and Christians were the people of the *Book*; the Bible was already translated into the Arabic language, and the volume of the Old Testament was accepted by the concord of these implacable enemies. In the story of the Hebrew patriarchs, the Arabs were pleased to discover the fathers of their nation. They applauded the birth and promises of Ismael; revered the faith and virtue of Abraham; traced his pedigree and their own to the creation of the first man, and imbibed, with equal credulity, the prodigies of the holy text, and the dreams and traditions of the Jewish rabbis.

The base and plebeian origin of Mahomet is an unskilful calumny of the Christians, who exalt instead of degrading the merit of their adversary. His descent from Ismael was a national privilege or fable; but if the first steps of the pedigree are dark and doubtful, he could produce many generations of pure and genuine nobility: he sprung from the tribe of Koreish and the family of Hashem, the most illustrious of the Arabs, the princes of Mecca, and the hereditary guardians of the

Caaba. The grandfather of Mahomet was Abdol Motalleb, the son of Hashem, a wealthy and generous citizen, who relieved the distress of famine with the supplies of commerce. Mecca, which had been fed by the liberality of the father, was saved by the courage of the son. The kingdom of Yemen was subject to the Christian princes of Abyssinia; their vassal Abrahah was provoked by an insult to avenge the honor of the cross; and the holy city was invested by a train of elephants and an army of Africans. A treaty was proposed; and, in the first audience, the grandfather of Mahomet demanded the restitution of his cattle. "And why," said Abrahah, "do you not rather implore my clemency in favor of your temple, which I have threatened to destroy?" "Because," replied the intrepid chief, "the cattle is my own; the Caaba belongs to the gods, and *they* will defend their house from injury and sacrilege.» The want of provisions, or the valor of the Koreish, compelled the Abyssinians to a disgraceful retreat: their discomfiture has been adorned with a miraculous flight of birds, who showered down stones on the heads of the infidels; and the deliverance was long commemorated by the æra of the elephant. The glory of Abdol Motalleb was crowned with domestic happiness; his life was prolonged to the age of one hundred and ten years; and he became the father of six daughters and thirteen sons. His best beloved Abdallah was the most beautiful and modest of the Arabian youth; and in the first night, when he consummated his marriage with Amina, of the noble race of the Zahrites, two hundred virgins are said to have expired of jealousy and despair. Mahomet, or more properly Mohammed, the only son of Abdallah and Amina, was born at Mecca, four years after the death of Justinian, and two months after the defeat of the Abyssinians, whose victory would have introduced into the Caaba the religion of the Christians. In his early infancy, he was deprived of his father, his mother, and his grandfather; his uncles were strong and numerous; and, in the division of the inheritance, the orphan›s share was reduced to five camels and an Æthiopian maid-servant. At home and abroad, in peace and war, Abu Taleb, the most respectable of his uncles, was the guide and guardian of his youth; in his twenty-fifth year, he entered into the service of Cadijah, a rich and noble widow of Mecca, who soon rewarded his fidelity with the gift of her hand and fortune. The marriage contract, in the simple style of antiquity, recites the mutual love of Mahomet and Cadijah; describes him as the most accomplished of the tribe of Koreish; and stipulates a dowry of twelve ounces of gold and twenty camels, which was supplied by the liberality of his uncle. By this alliance, the son of Abdallah was restored to the station of his ancestors;

and the judicious matron was content with his domestic virtues, till, in the fortieth year of his age, he assumed the title of a prophet, and proclaimed the religion of the Koran.

According to the tradition of his companions, Mahomet was distinguished by the beauty of his person, an outward gift which is seldom despised, except by those to whom it has been refused. Before he spoke, the orator engaged on his side the affections of a public or private audience. They applauded his commanding presence, his majestic aspect, his piercing eye, his gracious smile, his flowing beard, his countenance that painted every sensation of the soul, and his gestures that enforced each expression of the tongue. In the familiar offices of life he scrupulously adhered to the grave and ceremonious politeness of his country: his respectful attention to the rich and powerful was dignified by his condescension and affability to the poorest citizens of Mecca: the frankness of his manner concealed the artifice of his views; and the habits of courtesy were imputed to personal friendship or universal benevolence. His memory was capacious and retentive; his wit easy and social; his imagination sublime; his judgment clear, rapid, and decisive. He possessed the courage both of thought and action; and, although his designs might gradually expand with his success, the first idea which he entertained of his divine mission bears the stamp of an original and superior genius. The son of Abdallah was educated in the bosom of the noblest race, in the use of the purest dialect of Arabia; and the fluency of his speech was corrected and enhanced by the practice of discreet and seasonable silence. With these powers of eloquence, Mahomet was an illiterate Barbarian: his youth had never been instructed in the arts of reading and writing; the common ignorance exempted him from shame or reproach, but he was reduced to a narrow circle of existence, and deprived of those faithful mirrors, which reflect to our mind the minds of sages and heroes. Yet the book of nature and of man was open to his view; and some fancy has been indulged in the political and philosophical observations which are ascribed to the Arabian *traveller*. He compares the nations and the regions of the earth; discovers the weakness of the Persian and Roman monarchies; beholds, with pity and indignation, the degeneracy of the times; and resolves to unite under one God and one king the invincible spirit and primitive virtues of the Arabs. Our more accurate inquiry will suggest, that, instead of visiting the courts, the camps, the temples, of the East, the two journeys of Mahomet into Syria were confined to the fairs of Bostra and Damascus; that he was only thirteen years of age when he accompanied the caravan of his uncle; and that his duty compelled him to return as soon as he had disposed of the merchandise of Cadijah. In these hasty and superficial excursions, the eye of genius might discern some objects invisible to his grosser companions; some seeds of knowledge might be cast upon a fruitful soil; but his ignorance of the Syriac language must have checked his curiosity; and I cannot perceive, in the life or writings of Mahomet, that his prospect was far extended beyond the limits of the Arabian world. From every region of that solitary world, the pilgrims of Mecca were annually assembled, by the calls of devotion and commerce: in the free concourse of multitudes, a simple citizen, in his native tongue, might study the political state and character of the tribes, the theory and practice of the Jews and Christians. Some useful strangers might be tempted, or forced, to implore the rights of hospitality; and the enemies of Mahomet have named the Jew, the Persian, and the Syrian monk, whom they accuse of lending their secret aid to the composition of the Koran. Conversation enriches the understanding, but solitude is the school of genius; and the uniformity of a work denotes the hand of a single artist. From his earliest youth Mahomet was addicted to religious contemplation; each year, during the month of Ramadan, he withdrew from the world, and from the arms of Cadijah: in the cave of Hera, three miles from Mecca, he consulted the spirit of fraud or enthusiasm, whose abode is not in the heavens, but in the mind of the prophet. The faith which, under the name of *Islam*, he preached to his family and nation, is compounded of an eternal truth, and a necessary fiction, That there is only one God, and that Mahomet is the apostle of God.

It is the boast of the Jewish apologists, that while the learned nations of antiquity were deluded by the fables of polytheism, their simple ancestors of Palestine preserved the knowledge and worship of the true God. The moral attributes of Jehovah may not easily be reconciled with the standard of *human* virtue: his metaphysical qualities are darkly expressed; but each page of the Pentateuch and the Prophets is an evidence of his power: the unity of his name is inscribed on the first table of the law; and his sanctuary was never defiled by any visible image of the invisible essence. After the ruin of the temple, the faith of the Hebrew exiles was purified, fixed, and enlightened, by the spiritual devotion of the synagogue; and the authority of Mahomet will not justify his perpetual reproach, that the Jews of Mecca or Medina adored Ezra as the son of God. But the children of Israel had ceased to be a people; and the religions of the world were guilty, at least in the eyes of the prophet, of giving sons, or daughters, or companions, to the supreme God. In the rude idolatry of the Arabs, the crime is manifest and audacious: the Sabians are poorly excused by the preëminence of the first planet, or intelligence, in their celestial hierarchy; and in the Magian system the conflict of the two principles betrays the imperfection of the conqueror. The Christians of the seventh century had insensibly relapsed into a semblance of Paganism: their public and private vows were addressed to the relics and images that disgraced the temples of the East: the throne of the Almighty was darkened by a cloud of martyrs, and saints, and angels, the objects of popular veneration; and the Collyridian heretics, who flourished in the fruitful soil of Arabia, invested the Virgin Mary with the name and honors of a goddess. The mysteries of the Trinity and Incarnation *appear* to contradict the principle of the divine unity. In their obvious sense, they introduce three equal deities, and transform the man Jesus into the substance of the Son of God: an orthodox commentary will satisfy only a believing mind: intemperate curiosity and zeal had torn the veil of the sanctuary; and each of the Oriental sects was eager to confess that all, except themselves, deserved the reproach of idolatry and polytheism. The creed of Mahomet is free from suspicion or ambiguity; and the Koran is a glorious testimony to the unity of God. The prophet of Mecca rejected the worship of idols and men, of stars and planets, on the rational principle that whatever rises must set, that whatever is born must die, that whatever is corruptible must decay and perish. In the Author of the universe, his rational enthusiasm confessed and adored an infinite and eternal being, without form or place, without issue or similitude, present to our most secret thoughts, existing by the necessity of his own nature, and deriving from himself all moral and intellectual perfection. These sublime truths, thus announced in the language of the prophet, are firmly held by his disciples, and defined with metaphysical precision by the interpreters of the Koran. A philosophic theist might subscribe the popular creed of the Mahometans; a creed too sublime, perhaps, for our present faculties. What object remains for the fancy, or even the understanding, when we have abstracted from the unknown substance all ideas of time and space, of motion and matter, of sensation and reflection? The first principle of reason and revolution was confirmed by the voice of Mahomet: his proselytes, from India to Morocco, are distinguished by the name of *Unitarians*; and the danger of idolatry has been prevented by the interdiction of images. The doctrine of eternal decrees and absolute predestination is strictly embraced by the Mahometans; and they struggle, with the common difficulties, *how* to reconcile the prescience of God with the freedom and responsibility of man; *how* to explain the permission of evil under the reign of infinite power and infinite goodness.

The God of nature has written his existence on all his works, and his law in the heart of man. To restore the knowledge of the one, and the practice of the other, has been the real or pretended aim of the prophets of every age: the liberality of Mahomet allowed to his predecessors the same credit which he claimed for himself; and the chain of inspiration was prolonged from the fall of Adam to the promulgation of the Koran. During that period, some rays of prophetic light had been imparted to one hundred and twenty-four thousand of the elect, discriminated by their respective measure of virtue and grace; three hundred and thirteen apostles were sent with a special commission to recall their country from idolatry and vice; one hundred and four volumes have been dictated by the Holy Spirit; and six legislators of transcendent brightness have announced to mankind the six successive revelations of various rites, but of one immutable religion. The authority and station of Adam, Noah, Abraham, Moses, Christ, and Mahomet, rise in just gradation above each other; but whosoever hates or rejects any one of the prophets is numbered with the infidels. The writings of the patriarchs were extant only in the apocryphal copies of the Greeks and Syrians: the conduct of Adam had not entitled him to the gratitude or respect of his children; the seven precepts of Noah were observed by an inferior and imperfect class of the proselytes of the synagogue; and the memory of Abraham was obscurely revered by the Sabians in his native land of Chaldæa: of the myriads of prophets, Moses and Christ alone lived and reigned; and the remnant of the inspired writings was comprised in the books of the Old and the New Testament. The miraculous story of Moses is consecrated and embellished in the Koran; and the captive Jews enjoy the secret revenge of imposing their own belief on the nations whose recent creeds they deride. For the author of Christianity, the Mahometans are taught by the prophet to entertain a high and mysterious reverence. "Verily, Christ Jesus, the son of Mary, is the apostle of God, and his word, which he conveyed unto Mary, and a Spirit proceeding from him; honorable in this world, and in the world to come, and one of those who approach near to the presence of God." The wonders of the genuine and apocryphal gospels are profusely heaped on his head; and the Latin church has not disdained to borrow from the Koran the immaculate conception of his virgin mother. Yet Jesus was a mere mortal; and, at the day of judgment, his testimony will serve to condemn both the Jews, who reject him as a prophet, and the Christians, who adore him as the Son of God. The malice of his enemies aspersed his reputation, and conspired against his life; but their intention only was guilty; a phantom or a criminal was substituted on the cross; and the innocent saint was translated to the seventh heaven. During six hundred years the gospel was the way of truth and salvation; but the Christians insensibly forgot both the laws and example of their founder; and Mahomet was instructed by the Gnostics to accuse the church, as well as the synagogue, of corrupting the integrity of the sacred text. The piety of Moses and of Christ rejoiced in the assurance of a future prophet, more illustrious than themselves: the evangelical promise of the *Paraclete*, or Holy Ghost, was prefigured in the name, and accomplished in the person, of Mahomet, the greatest and the last of the apostles of God.

Description of Arabia and its Inhabitants. – Part Four

THE COMMUNICATION OF IDEAS requires a similitude of thought and language: the discourse of a philosopher would vibrate without effect on the ear of a peasant; yet how minute is the distance of *their* understandings, if it be compared with the contact of an infinite and a finite mind, with the word of God expressed by the tongue or the pen of a mortal! The inspiration of the Hebrew prophets, of the apostles and evangelists of Christ, might not be incompatible with the exercise of their reason and memory; and the diversity of their genius is strongly marked in the style and composition of the books of the Old and New Testament. But Mahomet was content with a character, more humble, yet more sublime, of a simple editor; the substance of the Koran, according to himself or his disciples, is uncreated and eternal; subsisting in the essence of the Deity, and inscribed with a pen of light on the table of his everlasting decrees. A paper copy, in a volume of silk and gems, was brought down to the lowest heaven by the angel Gabriel, who, under the Jewish economy, had indeed been despatched on the most important errands; and this trusty messenger successively revealed the chapters and verses to the Arabian prophet. Instead of a perpetual and perfect measure of the divine will, the fragments of the Koran were produced at the discretion of Mahomet; each revelation is suited to the emergencies of his policy or passion; and all contradiction is removed by the saving maxim, that any text of Scripture is abrogated or modified by any subsequent passage. The word of God, and of the apostle, was diligently recorded by his disciples on palm-leaves and the shoulder-bones of mutton; and the pages, without order or connection, were cast into a domestic chest, in the custody of one of his wives. Two years after the death of Mahomet, the sacred volume was collected and published by his friend and successor Abubeker: the work was revised by the caliph Othman, in the thirtieth year of the Hegira; and the various editions of the Koran assert the same miraculous privilege of a uniform and incorruptible text. In the spirit of enthusiasm or vanity, the prophet rests the truth of his mission on the merit of his book; audaciously challenges both men and angels to imitate the beauties of a single page; and presumes to assert that God alone could dictate this incomparable performance. This argument is most powerfully addressed to a devout Arabian, whose mind is attuned to faith and rapture; whose ear is delighted by the music of sounds; and whose ignorance is incapable of comparing the productions of human genius. The harmony and copiousness of style will not reach, in a version, the European infidel: he will peruse with impatience the endless incoherent rhapsody of fable, and precept, and declamation, which seldom excites a sentiment or an idea, which sometimes crawls in the dust, and is sometimes lost in the clouds. The divine attributes exalt the fancy of the Arabian missionary; but his loftiest strains must yield to the sublime simplicity of the book of Job, composed in a remote age, in the same country, and in the same language. If the composition of the Koran exceed the faculties of a man to what superior intelligence should we ascribe the Iliad of Homer, or the Philippics of Demosthenes? In all religions, the life of the founder supplies the silence of his written revelation: the sayings of Mahomet were so many lessons of truth; his actions so many examples of virtue; and the public and private memorials were preserved by his wives and companions. At the end of two hundred years, the Sonna, or oral law, was fixed and consecrated by the labors of Al Bochari, who discriminated seven thousand two hundred and seventy-five genuine traditions, from a mass of three hundred thousand reports, of a more doubtful or spurious character. Each day the pious author prayed in the temple of Mecca, and performed his ablutions with the water of Zemzem: the pages were successively deposited on the pulpit and the sepulchre of the apostle; and the work has been approved by the four orthodox sects of the Sonnites.

The mission of the ancient prophets, of Moses and of Jesus had been confirmed by many splendid prodigies; and Mahomet was repeatedly urged, by the inhabitants of Mecca and Medina, to produce a similar evidence of his divine legation; to call down from heaven the angel or the volume of his revelation, to create a garden in the desert, or to kindle a conflagration in the unbelieving city. As often as he is pressed by the demands of the Koreish, he involves himself in the obscure boast of vision and prophecy, appeals to the internal proofs of his doctrine, and shields himself behind the providence of God, who refuses those signs and wonders that would depreciate the merit of faith, and aggravate the guilt of infidelity But the modest or angry tone of his apologies betrays his weakness and vexation; and these passages of scandal established, beyond suspicion, the integrity of the Koran. The votaries of Mahomet are more assured than himself of his miraculous gifts; and their confidence and credulity increase as they are farther removed from the time and place of his spiritual exploits. They believe or affirm that trees went forth to meet him; that he was saluted by stones; that water gushed from his fingers; that he fed the hungry, cured the sick, and raised the dead; that a beam groaned to him; that a camel complained to him; that a shoulder of mutton informed him of its being poisoned; and that both animate and inanimate nature were equally subject to the apostle of God. His dream of a nocturnal journey is seriously described as a real and corporeal transaction. A mysterious animal, the Borak, conveyed him from the temple of Mecca to that of Jerusalem: with his companion Gabriel he successively ascended the seven heavens, and received and repaid the salutations of the patriarchs, the prophets, and the angels, in their respective mansions. Beyond the seventh heaven, Mahomet alone was permitted to proceed; he passed the veil of unity, approached within two bow-shots of the throne, and felt a cold that pierced him to the heart, when his shoulder was touched by the hand of God. After this familiar, though important conversation, he again descended to Jerusalem, remounted the Borak, returned to Mecca, and performed in the tenth part of a night the journey of many thousand years. According to another legend, the apostle confounded in a national assembly the malicious challenge of the Koreish. His resistless word split asunder the orb of the moon: the obedient planet stooped from her station in the sky, accomplished the seven revolutions round the Caaba, saluted Mahomet in the Arabian tongue, and, suddenly contracting her dimensions, entered at the collar, and issued forth through the sleeve, of his shirt. The vulgar are amused with these marvellous tales; but the gravest of the Mussulman doctors imitate the modesty of their master, and indulge a latitude of faith or interpretation. They might speciously allege, that in preaching the religion it was needless to violate the harmony of nature; that a creed unclouded with mystery may be excused from miracles; and that the sword of Mahomet was not less potent than the rod of Moses.

The polytheist is oppressed and distracted by the variety of superstition: a thousand rites of Egyptian origin were interwoven with the essence of the Mosaic law; and the spirit of the gospel had evaporated in the pageantry of the church. The prophet of Mecca was tempted by prejudice, or policy, or patriotism, to sanctify the rites of the Arabians, and the custom of visiting the holy stone of the Caaba. But the precepts of Mahomet himself inculcates a more simple and rational piety: prayer, fasting, and alms, are the religious duties of a Mussulman; and he is encouraged to hope, that prayer will carry him half way to God, fasting will bring him to the door of his palace, and alms will gain him admittance. I. According to the tradition of the nocturnal journey, the apostle, in his personal conference with the Deity, was commanded to impose on his disciples the daily obligation of fifty prayers. By the advice of Moses, he applied for an alleviation of this intolerable burden; the number was gradually reduced to five; without any dispensation of business or pleasure, or time or place: the devotion of the faithful is repeated at daybreak, at noon, in the afternoon, in the evening, and at the first watch of the night; and in the present decay of religious fervor, our travellers are edified by the profound humility and attention of the Turks and Persians. Cleanliness is the key of prayer: the frequent lustration of the hands, the face, and the body, which was practised of old by the Arabs, is solemnly enjoined by the Koran; and a permission is formally granted to supply with sand the scarcity of water. The words and attitudes of supplication, as it is performed either sitting, or standing, or prostrate on the ground, are prescribed by custom or authority; but the prayer is poured forth in short and fervent ejaculations; the measure of zeal is not exhausted by a tedious liturgy; and each Mussulman for his own person is invested with the character of a priest. Among the theists, who reject the use of images, it has been found necessary to restrain the wanderings of the fancy, by directing the eye and the thought towards a *kebla*, or visible point of the horizon. The prophet was at first inclined to gratify the Jews by the choice of Jerusalem; but he soon returned to a more natural partiality; and five times every day the eyes of the nations at Astracan, at Fez, at Delhi, are devoutly turned to the holy temple of Mecca. Yet every spot for the service of God is equally pure: the Mahometans indifferently pray in their chamber or in the street. As a distinction from the Jews and Christians, the Friday in each week is set apart for the useful institution of public worship: the people is assembled in the mosch; and the imam, some respectable elder, ascends the pulpit, to begin the prayer and pronounce the sermon. But the

Mahometan religion is destitute of priesthood or sacrifice; and the independent spirit of fanaticism looks down with contempt on the ministers and the slaves of superstition. II. The voluntary penance of the ascetics, the torment and glory of their lives, was odious to a prophet who censured in his companions a rash vow of abstaining from flesh, and women, and sleep; and firmly declared, that he would suffer no monks in his religion. Yet he instituted, in each year, a fast of thirty days; and strenuously recommended the observance as a discipline which purifies the soul and subdues the body, as a salutary exercise of obedience to the will of God and his apostle. During the month of Ramadan, from the rising to the setting of the sun, the Mussulman abstains from eating, and drinking, and women, and baths, and perfumes; from all nourishment that can restore his strength, from all pleasure that can gratify his senses. In the revolution of the lunar year, the Ramadan coincides, by turns, with the winter cold and the summer heat; and the patient martyr, without assuaging his thirst with a drop of water, must expect the close of a tedious and sultry day. The interdiction of wine, peculiar to some orders of priests or hermits, is converted by Mahomet alone into a positive and general law; and a considerable portion of the globe has abjured, at his command, the use of that salutary, though dangerous, liquor. These painful restraints are, doubtless, infringed by the libertine, and eluded by the hypocrite; but the legislator, by whom they are enacted, cannot surely be accused of alluring his proselytes by the indulgence of their sensual appetites. III. The charity of the Mahometans descends to the animal creation; and the Koran repeatedly inculcates, not as a merit, but as a strict and indispensable duty, the relief of the indigent and unfortunate. Mahomet, perhaps, is the only lawgiver who has defined the precise measure of charity: the standard may vary with the degree and nature of property, as it consists either in money, in corn or cattle, in fruits or merchandise; but the Mussulman does not accomplish the law, unless he bestows a *tenth* of his revenue; and if his conscience accuses him of fraud or extortion, the tenth, under the idea of restitution, is enlarged to a *fifth*. Benevolence is the foundation of justice, since we are forbid to injure those whom we are bound to assist. A prophet may reveal the secrets of heaven and of futurity; but in his moral precepts he can only repeat the lessons of our own hearts.

The two articles of belief, and the four practical duties, of Islam, are guarded by rewards and punishments; and the faith of the Mussulman is devoutly fixed on the event of the judgment and the last day. The prophet has not presumed to determine the moment of that awful catastrophe, though he darkly announces the signs, both in heaven and earth, which will precede the universal dissolution, when life shall be destroyed, and the order of creation shall be confounded in the primitive chaos. At the blast of the trumpet, new worlds will start into being: angels, genii, and men will arise from the dead, and the human soul will again be united to the body. The doctrine of the resurrection was first entertained by the Egyptians; and their mummies were embalmed, their pyramids were constructed, to preserve the ancient mansion of the soul, during a period of three thousand years. But the attempt is partial and unavailing; and it is with a more philosophic spirit that Mahomet relies on the omnipotence of the Creator, whose word can reanimate the breathless clay, and collect the innumerable atoms, that no longer retain their form or substance. The intermediate state of the soul it is hard to decide; and those who most firmly believe her immaterial nature, are at a loss to understand how she can think or act without the agency of the organs of sense.

The reunion of the soul and body will be followed by the final judgment of mankind; and in his copy of the Magian picture, the prophet has too faithfully represented the forms of proceeding, and even the slow and successive operations, of an earthly tribunal. By his intolerant adversaries he is upbraided for extending, even to themselves, the hope of salvation, for asserting the blackest heresy, that every man who believes in God, and accomplishes good works, may expect in the last day a favorable sentence. Such rational indifference is ill adapted to the character of a fanatic; nor is it probable that a messenger from heaven should depreciate the value and necessity of his own revelation. In the idiom of the Koran, the belief of God is inseparable from that of Mahomet: the good works are those which he has enjoined, and the two qualifications imply the profession of Islam, to which all nations and all sects are equally invited. Their spiritual blindness, though excused by ignorance and crowned with virtue, will be scourged with everlasting torments; and the tears which Mahomet shed over the tomb of his mother for whom he was forbidden to pray, display a striking contrast of humanity and enthusiasm. The doom of the infidels is common: the measure of their guilt and punishment is determined by the degree of evidence which they have rejected, by the magnitude of the errors which they have entertained: the eternal mansions of the Christians, the Jews, the Sabians, the Magians, and idolaters, are sunk below each other in the abyss; and the lowest hell is reserved for the faithless hypocrites who have assumed the mask of religion. After the greater part of mankind has been condemned for their opinions, the true believers only will be judged by their actions. The good and evil of each Mussulman will be accurately weighed in a real or allegorical balance; and a singular mode of compensation will be allowed for the payment of injuries: the aggressor will refund an equivalent of his own good actions, for the benefit of the person whom he has wronged; and if he should be destitute of any moral property, the weight of his sins will be loaded with an adequate share of the demerits of the sufferer. According as the shares of guilt or virtue shall preponderate, the sentence will be pronounced, and all, without distinction, will pass over the sharp and perilous bridge of the abyss; but the innocent, treading in the footsteps of Mahomet, will gloriously enter the gates of paradise, while the guilty will fall into the first and mildest of the seven hells. The term of expiation will vary from nine hundred to seven thousand years; but the prophet has judiciously promised, that all his disciples, whatever may be their sins, shall be saved, by their own faith and his intercession from eternal damnation. It is not surprising that superstition should act most powerfully on the fears of her votaries, since the human fancy can paint with more energy the misery than the bliss of a future life. With the two simple elements of darkness and fire, we create a sensation of pain, which may be aggravated to an infinite degree by the idea of endless duration. But the same idea operates with an opposite effect on the continuity of pleasure; and too much of our present enjoyments is obtained from the relief, or the comparison, of evil. It is natural enough that an Arabian prophet should dwell with rapture on the groves, the fountains, and the rivers of paradise; but instead of inspiring the blessed inhabitants with a liberal taste for harmony and science, conversation and friendship, he idly celebrates the pearls and diamonds, the robes of silk, palaces of marble, dishes of gold, rich wines, artificial dainties, numerous attendants, and the whole train of sensual and costly luxury, which becomes insipid to the owner, even in the short period of this mortal life. Seventy-two *Houris*, or black-eyed girls, of resplendent beauty, blooming youth, virgin purity, and exquisite sensibility, will be created for the use of the meanest believer; a moment of pleasure will be prolonged to a thousand years; and his faculties will be increased a hundred fold, to render him worthy of his felicity. Notwithstanding a vulgar prejudice, the gates of heaven will be open to both sexes; but Mahomet has not specified the male companions of the female elect, lest he should either alarm the jealousy of their former husbands, or disturb their felicity, by the suspicion of an everlasting marriage. This image of a carnal paradise has provoked the indignation, perhaps the envy, of the monks: they declaim against the impure religion of Mahomet;

and his modest apologists are driven to the poor excuse of figures and allegories. But the sounder and more consistent party adhere without shame, to the literal interpretation of the Koran: useless would be the resurrection of the body, unless it were restored to the possession and exercise of its worthiest faculties; and the union of sensual and intellectual enjoyment is requisite to complete the happiness of the double animal, the perfect man. Yet the joys of the Mahometan paradise will not be confined to the indulgence of luxury and appetite; and the prophet has expressly declared that all meaner happiness will be forgotten and despised by the saints and martyrs, who shall be admitted to the beatitude of the divine vision.

The first and most arduous conquests of Mahomet were those of his wife, his servant, his pupil, and his friend; since he presented himself as a prophet to those who were most conversant with his infirmities as a man. Yet Cadijah believed the words, and cherished the glory, of her husband; the obsequious and affectionate Zeid was tempted by the prospect of freedom; the illustrious Ali, the son of Abu Taleb, embraced the sentiments of his cousin with the spirit of a youthful hero; and the wealth, the moderation, the veracity of Abubeker confirmed the religion of the prophet whom he was destined to succeed. By his persuasion, ten of the most respectable citizens of Mecca were introduced to the private lessons of Islam; they yielded to the voice of reason and enthusiasm; they repeated the fundamental creed, "There is but one God, and Mahomet is the apostle of God;" and their faith, even in this life, was rewarded with riches and honors, with the command of armies and the government of kingdoms. Three years were silently employed in the conversion of fourteen proselytes, the first-fruits of his mission; but in the fourth year he assumed the prophetic office, and resolving to impart to his family the light of divine truth, he prepared a banquet, a lamb, as it is said, and a bowl of milk, for the entertainment of forty guests of the race of Hashem. "Friends and kinsmen," said Mahomet to the assembly, "I offer you, and I alone can offer, the most precious of gifts, the treasures of this world and of the world to come. God has commanded me to call you to his service. Who among you will support my burden? Who among you will be my companion and my vizier?" No answer was returned, till the silence of astonishment, and doubt, and contempt, was at length broken by the impatient courage of Ali, a youth in the fourteenth year of his age. "O prophet, I am the man: whosoever rises against thee, I will dash out his teeth, tear out his eyes, break his legs, rip up his belly. O prophet, I will be thy vizier over them." Mahomet accepted his offer with transport, and Abu Taled was ironically exhorted to respect the superior dignity of his son. In a more serious tone, the father of Ali advised his nephew to relinquish his impracticable design. "Spare your remonstrances," replied the intrepid fanatic to his uncle and benefactor; "if they should place the sun on my right hand, and the moon on my left, they should not divert me from my course." He persevered ten years in the exercise of his mission; and the religion which has overspread the East and the West advanced with a slow and painful progress within the walls of Mecca. Yet Mahomet enjoyed the satisfaction of beholding the increase of his infant congregation of Unitarians, who revered him as a prophet, and to whom he seasonably dispensed the spiritual nourishment of the Koran. The number of proselytes may be esteemed by the absence of eighty-three men and eighteen women, who retired to Æthiopia in the seventh year of his mission; and his party was fortified by the timely conversion of his uncle Hamza, and of the fierce and inflexible Omar, who signalized in the cause of Islam the same zeal, which he had exerted for its destruction. Nor was the charity of Mahomet confined to the tribe of Koreish, or the precincts of Mecca: on solemn festivals, in the days of pilgrimage, he frequented the Caaba, accosted the strangers of every tribe, and urged, both in private converse and public discourse, the belief and worship of a sole Deity. Conscious of his reason and of his weakness, he asserted the liberty of conscience, and disclaimed the use of religious violence: but he called the Arabs to repentance, and conjured them to remember the ancient idolaters of Ad and Thamud, whom the divine justice had swept away from the face of the earth.

Description of Arabia and its Inhabitants. – Part Five

THE PEOPLE OF MECCA were hardened in their unbelief by superstition and envy. The elders of the city, the uncles of the prophet, affected to despise the presumption of an orphan, the reformer of his country: the pious orations of Mahomet in the Caaba were answered by the clamors of Abu Taleb. "Citizens and pilgrims, listen not to the tempter, hearken not to his impious novelties. Stand fast in the worship of Al Lâta and Al Uzzah." Yet the son of Abdallah was ever dear to the aged chief: and he protected the fame and person of his nephew against the assaults of the Koreishites, who had long been jealous of the preëminence of the family of Hashem. Their malice was colored with the pretence of religion: in the age of Job, the crime of impiety was punished by the Arabian magistrate; and Mahomet was guilty of deserting and denying the national deities. But so loose was the policy of Mecca, that the leaders of the Koreish, instead of accusing a criminal, were compelled to employ the measures of persuasion or violence. They repeatedly addressed Abu Taleb in the style of reproach and menace. "Thy nephew reviles our religion; he accuses our wise forefathers of ignorance and folly; silence him quickly, lest he kindle tumult and discord in the city. If he persevere, we shall draw our swords against him and his adherents, and thou wilt be responsible for the blood of thy fellow-citizens." The weight and moderation of Abu Taleb eluded the violence of religious faction; the most helpless or timid of the disciples retired to Æthiopia, and the prophet withdrew himself to various places of strength in the town and country. As he was still supported by his family, the rest of the tribe of Koreish engaged themselves to renounce all intercourse with the children of

Hashem, neither to buy nor sell, neither to marry not to give in marriage, but to pursue them with implacable enmity, till they should deliver the person of Mahomet to the justice of the gods. The decree was suspended in the Caaba before the eyes of the nation; the messengers of the Koreish pursued the Mussulman exiles in the heart of Africa: they besieged the prophet and his most faithful followers, intercepted their water, and inflamed their mutual animosity by the retaliation of injuries and insults. A doubtful truce restored the appearances of concord till the death of Abu Taleb abandoned Mahomet to the power of his enemies, at the moment when he was deprived of his domestic comforts by the loss of his faithful and generous Cadijah. Abu Sophian, the chief of the branch of Ommiyah, succeeded to the principality of the republic of Mecca. A zealous votary of the idols, a mortal foe of the line of Hashem, he convened an assembly of the Koreishites and their allies, to decide the fate of the apostle. His imprisonment might provoke the despair of his enthusiasm; and the exile of an eloquent and popular fanatic would diffuse the mischief through the provinces of Arabia. His death was resolved; and they agreed that a sword from each tribe should be buried in his heart, to divide the guilt of his blood, and baffle the vengeance of the Hashemites. An angel or a spy revealed their conspiracy; and flight was the only resource of Mahomet. At the dead of night, accompanied by his friend Abubeker, he silently escaped from his house: the assassins watched at the door; but they were deceived by the figure of Ali, who reposed on the bed, and was covered with the green vestment of the apostle. The Koreish respected the piety of the heroic youth; but some verses of Ali, which are still extant, exhibit an interesting picture of his anxiety, his tenderness, and his religious confidence. Three days Mahomet and his companion were concealed in the cave of Thor, at the distance of a league from Mecca; and in the close of each evening, they received from the son and daughter of Abubeker a secret supply of intelligence and food. The diligence of the Koreish explored every haunt in the neighborhood of the city: they arrived at the entrance of the cavern; but the providential deceit of a spider's web and a pigeon's nest is supposed to convince them that the place was solitary and inviolate. "We are only two," said the trembling Abubeker. "There is a third," replied the prophet; "it is God himself." No sooner was the pursuit abated than the two fugitives issued from the rock, and mounted their camels: on the road to Medina, they were overtaken by the emissaries of the Koreish; they redeemed themselves with prayers and promises from their hands. In this eventful moment, the lance of an Arab might have changed the history of the world. The flight of the prophet from Mecca to Medina has fixed the memorable æra of the *Hegira*, which, at the end of twelve centuries, still discriminates the lunar years of the Mahometan nations.

The religion of the Koran might have perished in its cradle, had not Medina embraced with faith and reverence the holy outcasts of Mecca. Medina, or the *city*, known under the name of Yathreb, before it was sanctified by the throne of the prophet, was divided between the tribes of the Charegites and the Awsites, whose hereditary feud was rekindled by the slightest provocations: two colonies of Jews, who boasted a sacerdotal race, were their humble allies, and without converting the Arabs, they introduced the taste of science and religion, which distinguished Medina as the city of the Book. Some of her noblest citizens, in a pilgrimage to the Caaba, were converted by the preaching of Mahomet; on their return, they diffused the belief of God and his prophet, and the new alliance was ratified by their deputies in two secret and nocturnal interviews on a hill in the suburbs of Mecca. In the first, ten Charegites and two Awsites united in faith and love, protested, in the name of their wives, their children, and their absent brethren, that they would forever profess the creed, and observe the precepts, of the Koran. The second was a political association, the first vital spark of the empire of the Saracens. Seventy-three men and two women of Medina held a solemn conference with Mahomet, his kinsman, and his disciples; and pledged themselves to each other by a mutual oath of fidelity. They promised, in the name of the city, that if he should be banished, they would receive him as a confederate, obey him as a leader, and defend him to the last extremity, like their wives and children. "But if you are recalled by your country," they asked with a flattering anxiety, "will you not abandon your new allies?" "All things," replied Mahomet with a smile, "are now common between us; your blood is as my blood, your ruin as my ruin. We are bound to each other by the ties of honor and interest. I am your friend, and the enemy of your foes." "But if we are killed in your service, what," exclaimed the deputies of Medina, "will be our reward?" "Paradise," replied the prophet. "Stretch forth thy hand." He stretched it forth, and they reiterated the oath of allegiance and fidelity. Their treaty was ratified by the people, who unanimously embraced the profession of Islam; they rejoiced in the exile of the apostle, but they trembled for his safety, and impatiently expected his arrival. After a perilous and rapid journey along the sea-coast, he halted at Koba, two miles from the city, and made his public entry into Medina, sixteen days after his flight from Mecca. Five hundred of the citizens advanced to meet him; he was hailed with acclamations of loyalty and devotion; Mahomet was mounted on a she-camel, an umbrella shaded his head, and a turban was unfurled before him to supply the deficiency of a standard. His bravest disciples, who had been scattered by the storm, assembled round his person; and the equal, though various, merit of the Moslems was distinguished by the names of *Mohagerians* and *Ansars*, the fugitives of Mecca, and the auxiliaries of Medina. To eradicate the seeds of jealousy, Mahomet judiciously coupled his principal followers with the rights and obligations of brethren; and when Ali found himself without a peer, the prophet tenderly declared, that *he* would be the companion and brother of the noble youth. The expedient was crowned with success; the holy fraternity was respected in peace and war, and the two parties vied with each other in a generous emulation of courage and fidelity. Once only the concord was slightly ruffled by an accidental quarrel: a patriot of Medina arraigned the insolence of the strangers, but the hint of their expulsion was heard with abhorrence; and his own son most eagerly offered to lay at the apostle›s feet the head of his father.

From his establishment at Medina, Mahomet assumed the exercise of the regal and sacerdotal office; and it was impious to appeal from a judge whose decrees were inspired by the divine wisdom. A small portion of ground, the patrimony of two orphans, was acquired by gift or purchase; on that chosen spot he built a house and a mosch, more venerable in their rude simplicity than the palaces and temples of the Assyrian caliphs. His seal of gold, or silver, was inscribed with the apostolic title; when he prayed and preached in the weekly assembly, he leaned against the trunk of a palm-tree; and it was long before he indulged himself in the use of a chair or pulpit of rough timber. After a reign of six years, fifteen hundred Moslems, in arms and in the field, renewed their oath of allegiance; and their chief repeated the assurance of protection till the death of the last member, or the final dissolution of the party. It was in the same camp that the deputy of Mecca was astonished by the attention of the faithful to the words and looks of the prophet, by the eagerness with which they collected his spittle, a hair that dropped on the ground, the refuse water of his lustrations, as if they participated in some degree of the prophetic virtue. "I have seen," said he, "the Chosroes of Persia and the Cæsar of Rome, but never did I behold a king among his subjects like Mahomet among his companions." The devout fervor of enthusiasm acts with more energy and truth than the cold and formal servility of courts.

In the state of nature, every man has a right to defend, by force of arms, his person and his possessions; to repel, or even to prevent, the violence of his enemies, and to extend his hostilities to a reasonable measure of satisfaction and retaliation. In the free society of the Arabs, the duties of subject and citizen imposed a feeble restraint; and Mahomet, in the exercise of a peaceful and benevolent mission, had been despoiled and banished by the injustice of his countrymen. The choice of an independent people had exalted the fugitive of Mecca to the rank of a sovereign; and he was invested with the just prerogative of forming alliances, and of waging offensive or defensive war. The imperfection of human rights was supplied and armed by the plenitude of divine power: the prophet of Medina assumed, in his new revelations, a fiercer and more sanguinary tone, which proves that his former moderation was the effect of weakness: the means of persuasion had been tried, the season of forbearance was elapsed, and he was now commanded to propagate his religion by the sword, to destroy the monuments of idolatry, and, without regarding the sanctity of days or months, to pursue the unbelieving nations of the earth. The same bloody precepts, so repeatedly inculcated in the Koran, are ascribed by the author to the Pentateuch and the Gospel. But the mild tenor of the evangelic style may explain an ambiguous text, that Jesus did not bring peace on the earth, but a sword: his patient and humble virtues should not be confounded with the intolerant zeal of princes and bishops, who have disgraced the name of his disciples. In the prosecution of religious war, Mahomet might appeal with more propriety to the example of Moses, of the Judges, and the kings of Israel. The military laws of the Hebrews are still more rigid than those of the Arabian legislator. The Lord of hosts marched in person before the Jews: if a city resisted their summons, the males, without distinction, were put to the sword: the seven nations of Canaan were devoted to destruction; and neither repentance nor conversion, could shield them from the inevitable doom, that no creature within their precincts should be left alive. The fair option of friendship, or submission, or battle, was proposed to the enemies of Mahomet. If they professed the creed of Islam, they were admitted to all the temporal and spiritual benefits of his primitive disciples, and marched under the same banner to extend the religion which they had embraced. The clemency of the prophet was decided by his interest: yet he seldom trampled on a prostrate enemy; and he seems to promise, that on the payment of a tribute, the least guilty of his unbelieving subjects might be indulged in their worship, or at least in their imperfect faith. In the first months of his reign he practised the lessons of holy warfare, and displayed his white banner before the gates of Medina: the martial apostle fought in person at nine battles or sieges; and fifty enterprises of war were achieved in ten years by himself or his lieutenants. The Arab continued to unite the professions of a merchant and a robber; and his petty excursions for the defence or the attack of a caravan insensibly prepared his troops for the conquest of Arabia. The distribution of the spoil was regulated by a divine law: the whole was faithfully collected in one common mass: a fifth of the gold and silver, the prisoners and cattle, the movables and immovables, was reserved by the prophet for pious and charitable uses; the remainder was shared in adequate portions by the soldiers who had obtained the victory or guarded the camp: the rewards of the slain devolved to their widows and orphans; and the increase of cavalry was encouraged by the allotment of a double share to the horse and to the man. From all sides the roving Arabs were allured to the standard of religion and plunder: the apostle sanctified the license of embracing the female captives as their wives or concubines, and the enjoyment of wealth and beauty was a feeble type of the joys of paradise prepared for the valiant martyrs of the faith. "The sword," says Mahomet, "is the key of heaven and of hell; a drop of blood shed in the cause of God, a night spent in arms, is of more avail than two months of fasting or prayer: whosoever falls in battle, his sins are forgiven: at the day of judgment his wounds shall be resplendent as vermilion, and odoriferous as musk; and the loss of his limbs shall be supplied by the wings of angels and cherubim." The intrepid souls of the Arabs were fired with enthusiasm: the picture of the invisible world was strongly painted on their imagination; and the death which they had always despised became an object of hope and desire. The Koran inculcates, in the most absolute sense, the tenets of fate and predestination, which would extinguish both industry and virtue, if the actions of man were governed by his speculative belief. Yet their influence in every age has exalted the courage of the Saracens and Turks. The first companions of Mahomet advanced to battle with a fearless confidence: there is no danger where there is no chance: they were ordained to perish in their beds; or they were safe and invulnerable amidst the darts of the enemy.

Perhaps the Koreish would have been content with the flight of Mahomet, had they not been provoked and alarmed by the vengeance of an enemy, who could intercept their Syrian trade as it passed and repassed through the territory of Medina. Abu Sophian himself, with only thirty or forty followers, conducted a wealthy caravan of a thousand camels; the fortune or dexterity of his march escaped the vigilance of Mahomet; but the chief of the Koreish was informed that the holy robbers were placed in ambush to await his return. He despatched a messenger to his brethren of Mecca, and they were roused, by the fear of losing their merchandise and their provisions, unless they hastened to his relief with the military force of the city. The sacred band of Mahomet was formed of three hundred and thirteen Moslems, of whom seventy-seven were fugitives, and the rest auxiliaries; they mounted by turns a train of seventy camels, (the camels of Yathreb were formidable in war;) but such was the poverty of his first disciples, that only two could appear on horseback in the field. In the fertile and famous vale of Beder, three stations from Medina, he was informed by his scouts of the caravan that approached on one side; of the Koreish, one hundred horse, eight hundred and fifty foot, who advanced on the other. After a short debate, he sacrificed the prospect of wealth to the pursuit of glory and revenge, and a slight intrenchment was formed, to cover his troops, and a stream of fresh water, that glided through the valley. "O God," he exclaimed, as the numbers of the Koreish descended from the hills, "O God, if these are destroyed, by whom wilt thou be worshipped on the earth? – Courage, my children; close your ranks; discharge your arrows, and the day is your own." At these words he placed himself, with Abubeker, on a throne or pulpit, and instantly demanded the succor of Gabriel and three thousand angels. His eye was fixed on the field of battle: the Mussulmans fainted and were pressed: in that decisive moment the prophet started from his throne, mounted his horse, and cast a handful of sand into the air: "Let their faces be covered with confusion." Both armies heard the thunder of his voice: their fancy beheld the angelic warriors: the Koreish trembled and fled: seventy of the bravest were slain; and seventy captives adorned the first victory of the faithful. The dead bodies of the Koreish were despoiled and insulted: two of the most obnoxious prisoners were punished with death; and the ransom of the others, four thousand drams of silver, compensated in some degree the escape of the caravan. But it was in vain that the camels of Abu Sophian explored a new road through the desert and along the Euphrates: they were overtaken by the diligence of the Mussulmans; and wealthy must have been the prize, if twenty thousand drams could be set apart for the fifth of the apostle. The resentment of the public and private loss stimulated Abu Sophian to collect a body of three thousand men, seven hundred of whom were armed with cuirasses, and two hundred were mounted on horseback; three thousand camels attended his march; and his wife Henda, with fifteen matrons of Mecca, incessantly sounded their timbrels to animate the troops, and to magnify the greatness of Hobal, the most popular deity of the Caaba. The standard of God and Mahomet was upheld by nine hundred and fifty believers: the disproportion of numbers was not more alarming than in the field of Beder; and their presumption of victory prevailed against the divine and human sense of the apostle. The second battle was fought on Mount Ohud, six miles to the north of Medina; the Koreish advanced in the form of a crescent; and the right wing of cavalry was led by Caled, the fiercest and most successful of the Arabian warriors. The troops of Mahomet were skilfully posted on the declivity of the hill; and their rear was guarded by a detachment of fifty archers. The weight of their charge impelled and broke the centre of the idolaters: but in the pursuit they lost the advantage of their ground: the archers deserted their station: the Mussulmans were tempted by the spoil, disobeyed their general, and disordered their ranks. The intrepid Caled, wheeling his cavalry on their flank and rear, exclaimed, with a loud voice, that Mahomet was slain. He was indeed wounded in the face with a javelin: two of his teeth were shattered with a stone; yet, in the midst of tumult and dismay, he reproached the infidels with the murder of a prophet; and blessed the friendly hand that stanched his blood, and conveyed him to a place of safety. Seventy martyrs died for the sins of the people; they fell, said the apostle, in pairs, each brother embracing his lifeless companion; their bodies were mangled by the inhuman females of Mecca; and the wife of Abu Sophian tasted the entrails of Hamza, the uncle of Mahomet. They might applaud their superstition, and satiate their fury; but the Mussulmans soon rallied in the field, and the Koreish wanted strength or courage to undertake the siege of Medina. It was attacked the ensuing year by an army of ten thousand enemies; and this third expedition is variously named from the *nations*, which marched under the banner of Abu Sophian, from the *ditch* which was drawn before the city, and a camp of three thousand Mussulmans. The prudence of Mahomet declined a general engagement: the valor of Ali was signalized in single combat; and the war was protracted twenty days, till the final separation of the confederates. A tempest of wind, rain, and hail, overturned their tents: their private quarrels were fomented by an insidious adversary; and the Koreish, deserted by their allies, no longer hoped to subvert the throne, or to check the conquests, of their invincible exile.

Description of Arabia and its Inhabitants. – Part Six

THE CHOICE OF JERUSALEM for the first kebla of prayer discovers the early propensity of Mahomet in favor of the Jews; and happy would it have been for their temporal interest, had they recognized, in the Arabian prophet, the hope of Israel and the promised Messiah. Their obstinacy converted his friendship into implacable hatred, with which he pursued that unfortunate people to the last moment of his life; and in the double character of an apostle and a conqueror, his persecution was extended to both worlds. The Kainoka dwelt at Medina under the protection of the city; he seized the occasion of an accidental tumult, and summoned them to embrace his religion, or contend with him in battle. "Alas!" replied the trembling Jews, "we are ignorant of the use of arms, but we persevere in the faith and worship of our fathers; why wilt thou reduce us to the necessity of a just defence?" The unequal conflict was terminated in fifteen days; and it was with extreme reluctance that Mahomet yielded to the importunity of his allies, and consented to spare the lives of the captives. But their riches were confiscated, their arms became more effectual in the hands of the Mussulmans; and a wretched colony of seven hundred exiles was driven, with their wives and children, to implore a refuge on the confines of Syria. The Nadhirites were more guilty, since they conspired, in a friendly interview, to assassinate the prophet. He besieged their castle, three miles from Medina; but their resolute defence obtained an honorable capitulation; and the garrison, sounding their trumpets and beating their drums, was permitted to depart with the honors of war. The Jews had excited and joined the war of the Koreish: no sooner had the *nations* retired from the *ditch*, than Mahomet, without laying aside his armor, marched on the same day to extirpate the hostile race of the children of Koraidha. After a resistance of twenty-five days, they surrendered at discretion. They trusted to the intercession of their old allies of Medina; they could not be ignorant that fanaticism obliterates the feelings of humanity. A venerable elder, to whose judgment they appealed, pronounced the sentence of their death; seven hundred Jews were dragged in chains to the market-place of the city; they descended alive into the grave prepared for their execution and burial; and the apostle beheld with an inflexible eye the slaughter of his helpless enemies. Their sheep and camels were inherited by the Mussulmans: three hundred cuirasses, five hundred pikes, a thousand lances, composed the most useful portion of the spoil. Six days' journey to the north-east of Medina, the ancient and wealthy town of Chaibar was the seat of the Jewish power in Arabia: the territory, a fertile spot in the desert, was covered with plantations and cattle, and protected by eight castles, some of which were esteemed of impregnable strength. The forces of Mahomet consisted of two hundred horse and fourteen hundred foot: in the succession of eight regular and painful sieges they were exposed to danger, and fatigue, and hunger; and the most undaunted chiefs despaired of the event. The apostle revived their faith and courage by the example of Ali, on whom he bestowed the surname of the Lion of God: perhaps we may believe that a Hebrew champion of gigantic stature was cloven to the chest by his irresistible cimeter; but we cannot praise the modesty of romance, which represents him as tearing from its hinges the gate of a fortress and wielding the ponderous buckler in his left hand. After the reduction of the castles, the town of Chaibar submitted to the yoke. The chief of the tribe was tortured, in the presence of Mahomet, to force a confession of his hidden treasure: the industry of the shepherds and husbandmen was rewarded with a precarious toleration: they were permitted, so long as it should please the conqueror, to improve their patrimony, in equal shares, for *his* emolument and their own. Under the reign of Omar, the Jews of Chaibar were transported to Syria; and the caliph alleged the injunction of his dying master; that one and the true religion should be professed in his native land of Arabia.

Five times each day the eyes of Mahomet were turned towards Mecca, and he was urged by the most sacred and powerful motives to revisit, as a conqueror, the city and the temple from whence he had been driven as an exile. The Caaba was present to his waking and sleeping fancy: an idle dream was translated into vision and prophecy; he unfurled the holy banner; and a rash promise of success too hastily dropped from the lips of the apostle. His march from Medina to Mecca displayed the peaceful and solemn pomp of a pilgrimage: seventy camels, chosen and bedecked for sacrifice, preceded the van; the sacred territory was respected; and the captives were dismissed without ransom to proclaim his clemency and devotion. But no sooner did Mahomet descend into the plain, within a day's journey of the city, than he exclaimed, "They have clothed themselves with the skins of tigers:" the numbers and resolution of the Koreish opposed his progress; and the roving Arabs of the desert might desert or betray a leader whom they had followed for the hopes of spoil. The intrepid fanatic sunk into a cool and cautious politician: he waived in the treaty his title of apostle of God; concluded with the Koreish and their allies a truce of ten years; engaged to restore the fugitives of Mecca who should embrace his religion; and stipulated only, for the ensuing year, the humble privilege of entering the city as a friend, and of remaining three days to accomplish the rites of the pilgrimage. A cloud of shame and sorrow hung on the retreat of the Mussulmans, and their disappointment might justly accuse the failure of a prophet who had so often appealed to the evidence of success. The faith and hope of the pilgrims were rekindled by the prospect of Mecca: their swords were sheathed; seven times in the footsteps of the apostle they encompassed the Caaba: the Koreish had retired to the hills, and Mahomet, after the customary sacrifice, evacuated the city on the fourth day. The people was edified by his devotion; the hostile chiefs were awed, or divided, or seduced; and both Kaled and Amrou, the future conquerors of Syria and Egypt, most seasonably deserted the sinking cause of idolatry. The power of Mahomet was increased by the submission of the Arabian tribes; ten thousand soldiers were assembled for the conquest of Mecca; and the idolaters, the weaker party, were easily convicted of violating the truce. Enthusiasm and discipline impelled the march, and preserved the secret till the blaze of ten thousand fires proclaimed to the astonished Koreish the design, the approach, and the irresistible force of the enemy. The haughty Abu Sophian presented the keys of the city, admired the variety of arms and ensigns that passed before him in review; observed that the son of Abdallah had acquired a mighty kingdom, and confessed, under the cimeter of Omar, that he was the apostle of the true God. The return of Marius and Scylla was stained with the blood of the Romans: the revenge of Mahomet was stimulated by religious zeal, and his injured followers were eager to execute or to prevent the order of a massacre. Instead of indulging their passions and his own, the victorious exile forgave the guilt, and united the factions, of Mecca. His troops, in three divisions, marched into the city: eight-and-twenty of the inhabitants were slain by the sword of Caled; eleven men and six women were proscribed by the sentence of Mahomet; but he blamed the cruelty of his lieutenant; and several of the most obnoxious victims were indebted for their lives to his clemency or contempt. The chiefs of the Koreish were prostrate at his feet. "What mercy can you expect from the man whom you have wronged?" "We confide in the generosity of our kinsman." "And you shall not confide in vain: begone! you are safe, you are free." The people of Mecca deserved their pardon by the profession of Islam; and after an exile of seven years, the fugitive missionary was enthroned as the prince and prophet of his native country. But the three hundred and sixty idols of the Caaba were ignominiously broken: the house of God was purified and adorned: as an example to future times, the apostle again fulfilled the duties of a pilgrim; and a perpetual law was enacted that no unbeliever should dare to set his foot on the territory of the holy city.

The conquest of Mecca determined the faith and obedience of the Arabian tribes; who, according to the vicissitudes of fortune, had obeyed, or disregarded, the eloquence or the arms of the prophet. Indifference for rites and opinions still marks the character of the Bedoweens; and they might accept, as loosely as they hold, the doctrine of the Koran. Yet an obstinate remnant still adhered to the religion and liberty of their ancestors, and the war of Honain derived a proper appellation from the *idols*, whom Mahomet had vowed to destroy, and whom the confederates of Tayef had sworn to defend. Four thousand Pagans advanced with secrecy and speed to surprise the conqueror: they pitied and despised the supine negligence of the Koreish, but they depended on the wishes, and perhaps the aid, of a people who had so lately renounced their gods, and bowed beneath the yoke of their enemy. The banners of Medina and Mecca were displayed by the prophet; a crowd of Bedoweens increased the strength or numbers of the army, and twelve thousand Mussulmans entertained a rash and sinful presumption of their invincible strength. They descended without precaution into the valley of Honain: the heights had been occupied by the archers and slingers of the confederates; their numbers were oppressed, their discipline was confounded, their courage was appalled, and the Koreish smiled at their impending destruction. The prophet, on his white mule, was encompassed by the enemies: he attempted to rush against their spears in search of a glorious death: ten of his faithful companions interposed their weapons and their breasts; three of these fell dead at his feet: "O my brethren," he repeatedly cried, with sorrow and indignation, "I am the son of Abdallah, I am the apostle of truth! O man, stand fast in the faith! O God, send down thy succor!" His uncle Abbas, who, like the heroes of Homer, excelled in the loudness of his voice, made the valley resound with the recital of the gifts and promises of God: the flying Moslems returned from all sides to the holy standard; and Mahomet observed with pleasure that the furnace was again rekindled: his conduct and example restored the battle, and he animated his victorious troops to inflict a merciless revenge on the authors of their shame. From the field of Honain, he marched without delay to the siege of Tayef, sixty miles to the south-east of Mecca, a fortress of strength, whose fertile lands produce the fruits of Syria in the midst of the Arabian desert. A friendly tribe, instructed (I know not how) in the art of sieges, supplied him with a train of battering-rams and military engines, with a body of five hundred artificers. But it was in vain that he offered freedom to the slaves of Tayef; that he violated his own laws by the extirpation of the fruit-trees; that the ground was opened by the miners; that the breach was assaulted by the troops. After a siege of twenty-days, the prophet sounded a retreat; but he retreated with a song of devout triumph, and affected to pray for the repentance and safety of the unbelieving city. The spoils of this fortunate expedition amounted to six thousand captives, twenty-four thousand camels, forty thousand sheep, and four thousand ounces of silver: a tribe who had fought at Honain redeemed their prisoners by the sacrifice of their idols; but Mahomet compensated the loss, by resigning to the soldiers his fifth of the plunder, and wished, for their sake, that he possessed as many head of cattle as there were trees in the province of Tehama. Instead of chastising the disaffection of the Koreish, he endeavored to cut out their tongues, (his own expression,) and to secure their attachment by a superior measure of liberality: Abu Sophian alone was presented with three hundred camels and twenty ounces of silver; and Mecca was sincerely converted to the profitable religion of the Koran.

The *fugitives* and *auxiliaries* complained, that they who had borne the burden were neglected in the season of victory «Alas!» replied their artful leader, «suffer me to conciliate these recent enemies, these doubtful proselytes, by the gift of some perishable goods. To your guard I intrust my life and fortunes. You are the companions of my exile, of my kingdom, of my paradise.» He was followed by the deputies of Tayef, who dreaded the repetition of a siege. «Grant us, O apostle of God! a truce of three years, with the toleration of our ancient worship.» «Not a month, not an hour.» «Excuse us at least from the obligation of prayer.» «Without prayer religion is of no avail.» They submitted in silence: their temples were demolished, and the same sentence of destruction was executed on all the idols of Arabia. His lieutenants, on the shores of the Red Sea, the Ocean, and the Gulf of Persia, were saluted by the acclamations of a faithful people; and the ambassadors, who knelt before the throne of Medina, were as numerous (says the Arabian proverb) as the dates that fall from the maturity of a palm-tree. The nation submitted to the God and the sceptre of Mahomet: the opprobrious name of tribute was abolished: the spontaneous or reluctant oblations of arms and tithes were applied to the service of religion; and one hundred and fourteen thousand Moslems accompanied the last pilgrimage of the apostle.

When Heraclius returned in triumph from the Persian war, he entertained, at Emesa, one of the ambassadors of Mahomet, who invited the princes and nations of the earth to the profession of Islam. On this foundation the zeal of the Arabians has supposed the secret conversion of the Christian emperor: the vanity of the Greeks has feigned a personal visit of the prince of Medina, who accepted from the royal bounty a rich domain, and a secure retreat, in the province of Syria. But the friendship of Heraclius and Mahomet was of short continuance: the new religion had inflamed rather than assuaged the rapacious spirit of the Saracens, and the murder of an envoy afforded a decent pretence for invading, with three thousand soldiers, the territory of Palestine, that extends to the eastward of the Jordan. The holy banner was intrusted to Zeid; and such was the discipline or enthusiasm of the rising sect, that the noblest chiefs served without reluctance under the slave of the prophet. On the event of his decease, Jaafar and Abdallah were successively substituted to the command; and if the three should perish in the war, the troops were authorized to elect their general. The three leaders were slain in the battle of Muta, the first military action, which tried the valor of the Moslems against a foreign enemy. Zeid fell, like a soldier, in the foremost ranks: the death of Jaafar was heroic and memorable: he lost his right hand: he shifted the standard to his left: the left was severed from his body: he embraced the standard with his bleeding stumps, till he was transfixed to the ground with fifty honorable wounds. "Advance," cried Abdallah, who stepped into the vacant place, "advance with confidence: either victory or paradise is our own." The lance of a Roman decided the alternative; but the falling standard was rescued by Caled, the proselyte of Mecca: nine swords were broken in his hand; and his valor withstood and repulsed the superior numbers of the Christians. In the nocturnal council of the camp he was chosen to command: his skilful evolutions of the ensuing day secured either the victory or the retreat of the Saracens; and Caled is renowned among his brethren and his enemies by the glorious appellation of the *Sword of God*. In the pulpit, Mahomet described, with prophetic rapture, the crowns of the blessed martyrs; but in private he betrayed the feelings of human nature: he was surprised as he wept over the daughter of Zeid: "What do I see?" said the astonished votary. "You see," replied the apostle, "a friend who is deploring the loss of his most faithful friend." After the conquest of Mecca, the sovereign of Arabia affected to prevent the hostile preparations of Heraclius; and solemnly proclaimed war against the Romans, without attempting to disguise the hardships and dangers of the enterprise. The Moslems were discouraged: they alleged the want of money, or horses, or provisions; the season of harvest, and the intolerable heat of the summer: "Hell is much hotter," said the indignant prophet. He disdained to compel their service: but on his return he admonished the most guilty, by an excommunication of fifty days. Their desertion enhanced the merit of Abubeker, Othman, and the faithful companions who devoted their lives and fortunes; and Mahomet displayed his banner at the head of ten thousand horse and twenty thousand foot. Painful indeed was the distress of the march: lassitude and thirst were aggravated by the scorching and pestilential winds of the desert: ten men rode by turns on one camel; and they were reduced to the shameful necessity of drinking the water from the belly of that useful animal. In the mid-way, ten days' journey from Medina and Damascus, they reposed near the grove and fountain of Tabuc. Beyond that place Mahomet declined the prosecution of the war: he declared himself satisfied with the peaceful intentions, he was more probably daunted by the martial array, of the emperor of the East. But the active and intrepid Caled spread around the terror of his name; and the prophet received the submission of the tribes and cities, from the Euphrates to Ailah, at the head of the Red Sea. To his Christian subjects, Mahomet readily granted the security of their persons, the freedom of their trade, the property of their goods, and the toleration of their worship. The weakness of their Arabian brethren had restrained them from opposing his ambition; the disciples of Jesus were endeared to the enemy of the Jews; and it was the interest of a conqueror to propose a fair capitulation to the most powerful religion of the earth.

Till the age of sixty-three years, the strength of Mahomet was equal to the temporal and spiritual fatigues of his mission. His epileptic fits, an absurd calumny of the Greeks, would be an object of pity rather than abhorrence; but he seriously believed that he was poisoned at Chaibar by the revenge of a Jewish female. During four years, the health of the prophet declined; his infirmities increased; but his mortal disease was a fever of fourteen days, which deprived him by intervals of the use of reason. As soon as he was conscious of his danger, he edified his brethren by the humility of his virtue or penitence. "If there be any man," said the apostle from the pulpit, "whom I have unjustly scourged, I submit my own back to the lash of retaliation. Have I aspersed the reputation of a Mussulman? let him proclaim *my* thoughts in the face of the congregation. Has any one been despoiled of his goods? the little that I possess shall compensate the principal and the interest of the debt.» «Yes,» replied a voice from the crowd, «I am entitled to three drams of silver.» Mahomet heard the complaint, satisfied the demand, and thanked his creditor for accusing him in this world rather than at the day of judgment. He beheld with temperate firmness the approach of death; enfranchised his slaves (seventeen men, as they are named, and eleven women;) minutely directed the order of his funeral, and moderated the lamentations of his weeping friends, on whom he bestowed the benediction of peace. Till the third day before his death, he regularly performed the function of public prayer: the choice of Abubeker to supply his place, appeared to mark that ancient and faithful friend as his successor in the sacerdotal and regal office; but he prudently declined the risk and envy of a more explicit nomination. At a moment when his faculties were visibly impaired, he called for pen and ink to write, or, more properly, to dictate, a divine book, the sum and accomplishment of all his revelations: a dispute arose in the chamber, whether he should be allowed to supersede the authority of the Koran; and the prophet was forced to reprove the indecent vehemence of his disciples. If the slightest credit may be afforded to the traditions of his wives and companions, he maintained, in the bosom of his family, and to the last moments of his life, the dignity of an apostle, and the faith of an enthusiast; described the visits of Gabriel, who bade an everlasting farewell to the earth, and expressed his lively confidence, not only of the mercy, but of the favor, of the Supreme Being. In a familiar discourse he had mentioned his special prerogative, that the angel of death was not allowed to take his soul till he had respectfully asked the permission of the prophet. The request was granted; and Mahomet immediately fell into the agony of his dissolution: his head was reclined on the lap of Ayesha, the best beloved of all his wives; he fainted with the violence of pain; recovering his spirits, he raised his eyes towards the roof of the house, and, with a steady look, though a faltering voice, uttered the last broken, though articulate, words: «O God!..... pardon my sins....... Yes,...... I come,...... among my fellow-citizens on high;» and thus peaceably expired on a carpet spread upon the floor. An expedition for the conquest of Syria was stopped by this mournful event; the army halted at the gates of Medina; the chiefs were assembled round their dying master. The city, more especially the house, of the prophet, was a scene of clamorous sorrow of silent despair: fanaticism alone could suggest a ray of hope and consolation. «How can he be dead, our witness, our intercessor, our mediator, with God? By God he is not dead: like Moses and Jesus, he is wrapped in a holy trance, and speedily will he return to his faithful people.» The evidence of sense was disregarded; and Omar, unsheathing his cimeter, threatened to strike off the heads of the infidels, who should dare to affirm that the prophet was no more. The tumult was appeased by the weight and moderation of Abubeker. «Is it Mahomet,» said he to Omar and the multitude, «or the God of Mahomet, whom you worship? The God of Mahomet liveth forever; but the apostle was a mortal like ourselves, and according to his own prediction, he has experienced the common fate of mortality.» He was piously interred by the hands of his nearest kinsman, on the same spot on which he expired: Medina has been sanctified by the death and burial of Mahomet; and the innumerable pilgrims of Mecca often turn aside from the way, to bow, in voluntary devotion, before the simple tomb of the prophet.

At the conclusion of the life of Mahomet, it may perhaps be expected, that I should balance his faults and virtues, that I should decide whether the title of enthusiast or impostor more properly belongs to that extraordinary man. Had I been intimately conversant with the son of Abdallah, the task would still be difficult, and the success uncertain: at the distance of twelve centuries, I darkly contemplate his shade through a cloud of religious incense; and could I truly delineate the portrait of an hour, the fleeting resemblance would not equally apply to the solitary of Mount Hera, to the preacher of Mecca, and to the conqueror of Arabia. The author of a mighty revolution appears to have been endowed with a pious and contemplative disposition: so soon as marriage had raised him above the pressure of want, he avoided the paths of ambition and avarice; and till the age of forty he lived with innocence, and would have died without a name. The unity of God is an idea most congenial to nature and reason; and a slight conversation with the Jews and Christians would teach him to despise and detest the idolatry of Mecca. It was the duty of a man and a citizen to impart the doctrine of salvation, to rescue his country from the dominion of sin and error. The energy of a mind incessantly bent on the same object, would convert a general obligation into a particular call; the warm suggestions of the understanding or the fancy would be felt as the inspirations of Heaven; the labor of thought would expire in rapture and vision; and the inward sensation, the invisible monitor, would be described with the form and attributes of an angel of God. From enthusiasm to imposture, the step is perilous and slippery: the dæmon of Socrates affords a memorable instance, how a wise man may deceive himself, how a good man may deceive others, how the conscience may slumber in a mixed and middle state between self-illusion and voluntary fraud. Charity may believe that the original motives of Mahomet were those of pure and genuine benevolence; but a human missionary is incapable of cherishing the obstinate unbelievers who reject his claims despise his arguments, and persecute his life; he might forgive his personal adversaries, he may lawfully hate the enemies of God; the stern passions of pride and revenge were kindled in the bosom of Mahomet, and he sighed, like the prophet of Nineveh, for the destruction of the rebels whom he had condemned. The injustice of Mecca and the choice of Medina, transformed the citizen into a prince, the humble preacher into the leader of armies; but his sword was consecrated by the example of the saints; and the same God who afflicts a sinful world with pestilence and earthquakes, might inspire for their conversion or chastisement the valor of his servants. In the exercise of political government, he was compelled to abate of the stern rigor of fanaticism, to comply in some measure with the prejudices and passions of his followers, and to employ even the vices of mankind as the instruments of their salvation. The use of fraud and perfidy, of cruelty and injustice, were often subservient to the propagation of the faith; and Mahomet commanded or approved the assassination of the Jews and idolaters who had escaped from the field of battle. By the repetition of such acts, the character of Mahomet must have been gradually stained; and the influence of such pernicious habits would be poorly compensated by the practice of the personal and social virtues which are necessary to maintain the reputation of a prophet among his sectaries and friends. Of his last years, ambition was the ruling passion; and a politician will suspect, that he secretly smiled (the victorious impostor!) at the enthusiasm of his youth, and the credulity of his proselytes. A philosopher will observe, that *their* credulity and *his* success would tend more strongly to fortify the assurance of his divine mission, that his interest and religion were inseparably connected, and that his conscience would be soothed by the persuasion, that he alone was absolved by the Deity from the obligation of positive and moral laws. If he retained any vestige of his native innocence, the sins of Mahomet may be allowed as an evidence of his sincerity. In the support of truth, the arts of fraud and fiction may be deemed less criminal; and he would have started at the foulness of the means, had he not been satisfied of the importance and justice of the end. Even in a conqueror or a priest, I can surprise a word or action of unaffected humanity; and the decree of Mahomet, that, in the sale of captives, the mothers should never be separated from their children, may suspend, or moderate, the censure of the historian.

Description of Arabia and its Inhabitants. – Part Seven

THE GOOD SENSE OF Mahomet despised the pomp of royalty: the apostle of God submitted to the menial offices of the family: he kindled the fire, swept the floor, milked the ewes, and mended with his own hands his shoes and his woollen garment. Disdaining the penance and merit of a hermit, he observed, without effort or vanity, the abstemious diet of an Arab and a soldier. On solemn occasions he feasted his companions with rustic and hospitable plenty; but in his domestic life, many weeks would elapse without a fire being kindled on the hearth of the prophet. The interdiction of wine was confirmed by his example; his hunger was appeased with a sparing allowance of barley-bread: he delighted in the taste of milk and honey; but his ordinary food consisted of dates and water. Perfumes and women were the two sensual enjoyments which his nature required, and his religion did not forbid; and Mahomet affirmed, that the fervor of his devotion was increased by these innocent pleasures. The heat of the climate inflames the blood of the Arabs; and their libidinous complexion has been noticed by the writers of antiquity. Their incontinence was regulated by the civil and religious laws of the Koran: their incestuous alliances were blamed; the boundless license of polygamy was reduced to four legitimate wives or concubines; their rights both of bed and of dowry were equitably determined; the freedom of divorce was discouraged, adultery was condemned as a capital offence; and fornication, in either sex, was punished with a hundred stripes. Such were the calm and rational precepts of the legislator: but in his private conduct, Mahomet indulged the appetites of a man, and abused the claims of a prophet. A special revelation dispensed him from the laws which he had imposed on his nation: the female sex, without reserve, was abandoned to his desires; and this singular prerogative excited the envy, rather than the scandal, the veneration, rather than the envy, of the devout Mussulmans. If we remember the seven hundred wives and three hundred concubines of the wise Solomon, we shall applaud the modesty of the Arabian, who espoused no more than seventeen or fifteen wives; eleven are enumerated who occupied at Medina their separate apartments round the house of the apostle, and enjoyed in their turns the favor of his conjugal society. What is singular enough, they were all widows, excepting only Ayesha, the daughter of Abubeker. She was doubtless a virgin, since Mahomet consummated his nuptials (such is the premature ripeness of the climate) when she was only nine years of age. The youth, the beauty, the spirit of Ayesha, gave her a superior ascendant: she was beloved and trusted by the prophet; and, after his death, the daughter of Abubeker was long revered as the mother of the faithful. Her behavior had been ambiguous and indiscreet: in a nocturnal march she was accidentally left behind; and in the morning Ayesha returned to the camp with a man. The temper of Mahomet was inclined to jealousy; but a divine revelation assured him of her innocence: he chastised her accusers, and published a law of domestic peace, that no woman should be condemned unless four male witnesses had seen her in the act of adultery. In his adventures with Zeineb, the wife of Zeid, and with Mary, an Egyptian captive, the amorous prophet forgot the interest of his reputation. At the house of Zeid, his freedman and adopted son, he beheld, in a loose undress, the beauty of Zeineb, and burst forth into an ejaculation of devotion and desire. The servile, or grateful, freedman understood the hint, and yielded without hesitation to the love of his benefactor. But as the filial relation had excited some doubt and scandal, the angel Gabriel descended from heaven to ratify the deed, to annul the adoption, and gently to reprove the apostle for distrusting the indulgence of his God. One of his wives, Hafna, the daughter of Omar, surprised him on her own bed, in the embraces of his Egyptian captive: she promised secrecy and forgiveness, he swore that he would renounce the possession of Mary. Both parties forgot their engagements; and Gabriel again descended with a chapter of the Koran, to absolve him from his oath, and to exhort him freely to enjoy his captives and concubines, without listening to the clamors of his wives. In a solitary retreat of thirty days, he labored, alone with Mary, to fulfil the commands of the angel. When his love and revenge were satiated, he summoned to his presence his eleven wives, reproached their disobedience and indiscretion, and threatened them with a sentence of divorce, both in this world and in the next; a dreadful sentence, since those who had ascended the bed of the prophet were forever excluded from the hope of a second marriage. Perhaps the incontinence of Mahomet may be palliated by the tradition of his natural or preternatural gifts; he united the manly virtue of thirty of the children of Adam: and the apostle might rival the thirteenth labor of the Grecian Hercules. A more serious and decent excuse may be drawn from his fidelity to Cadijah. During the twenty-four years of their marriage, her youthful husband abstained from the right of polygamy, and the pride or tenderness of the venerable matron was never insulted by the society of a rival. After her death, he placed her in the rank of the four perfect women, with the sister of Moses, the mother of Jesus, and Fatima, the best beloved of his daughters. "Was she not old?" said Ayesha, with the insolence of a blooming beauty; "has not God given you a better in her place?" "No, by God," said Mahomet, with an effusion of honest gratitude, "there never can be a better! She believed in me when men despised me; she relieved my wants, when I was poor and persecuted by the world."

In the largest indulgence of polygamy, the founder of a religion and empire might aspire to multiply the chances of a numerous posterity and a lineal succession. The hopes of Mahomet were fatally disappointed. The virgin Ayesha, and his ten widows of mature age and approved fertility, were barren in his potent embraces. The four sons of Cadijah died in their infancy. Mary, his Egyptian concubine, was endeared to him by the birth of Ibrahim. At the end of fifteen months the prophet wept over his grave; but he sustained with firmness the raillery of his enemies, and checked the adulation or credulity of the Moslems, by the assurance that an eclipse of the sun was not occasioned by the death of the infant. Cadijah had likewise given him four daughters, who were married to the most faithful of his disciples: the three eldest died before their father; but Fatima, who possessed his confidence and love, became the wife of her cousin Ali, and the mother of an illustrious progeny. The merit and misfortunes of Ali and his descendants will lead me to anticipate, in this place, the series of the Saracen caliphs, a title which describes the commanders of the faithful as the vicars and successors of the apostle of God.

The birth, the alliance, the character of Ali, which exalted him above the rest of his countrymen, might justify his claim to the vacant throne of Arabia. The son of Abu Taleb was, in his own right, the chief of the family of Hashem, and the hereditary prince or guardian of the city and temple of Mecca. The light of prophecy was extinct; but the husband of Fatima might expect the inheritance and blessing of her father: the Arabs had sometimes been patient of a female reign; and the two grandsons of the prophet had often been fondled in his lap, and shown in his pulpit as the hope of his age, and the chief of the youth of paradise. The first of the true believers might aspire to march before them in this world and in the next; and if some were of a graver and more rigid cast, the zeal and virtue of Ali were never outstripped by any recent proselyte. He united the qualifications of a poet, a soldier, and a saint: his wisdom still breathes in a collection of moral and religious sayings; and every antagonist, in the combats of the tongue or of the sword, was subdued by his eloquence and valor. From the first hour of his mission to the last rites of his funeral, the apostle was never forsaken by a generous friend, whom he delighted to name his brother, his vicegerent, and the faithful Aaron of a second Moses. The son of Abu Taleb was afterwards reproached for neglecting to secure his interest by a solemn declaration of his right, which would have silenced all competition, and sealed his succession by the decrees of Heaven. But the unsuspecting hero confided in himself: the jealousy of empire, and perhaps the fear of opposition, might suspend the resolutions of Mahomet; and the bed of sickness was besieged by the artful Ayesha, the daughter of Abubeker, and the enemy of Ali.

The silence and death of the prophet restored the liberty of the people; and his companions convened an assembly to deliberate on the choice of his successor. The hereditary claim and lofty spirit of Ali were offensive to an aristocracy of elders, desirous of bestowing and resuming the sceptre by a free and frequent election: the Koreish could never be reconciled to the proud preëminence of the line of Hashem; the ancient discord of the tribes was rekindled, the *fugitives* of Mecca and the *auxiliaries* of Medina asserted their respective merits; and the rash proposal of choosing two independent caliphs would have crushed in their infancy the religion and empire of the Saracens. The tumult was appeased by the disinterested resolution of Omar, who, suddenly renouncing his own pretensions, stretched forth his hand, and declared himself the first subject of the mild and venerable Abubeker. The urgency of the moment, and the acquiescence of the people, might excuse this illegal and precipitate measure; but Omar himself confessed from the pulpit, that if any Mussulman should hereafter presume to anticipate the suffrage of his brethren, both the elector and the elected would be worthy of death. After the simple inauguration of Abubeker, he was obeyed in Medina, Mecca, and the provinces of Arabia: the Hashemites alone declined the oath of fidelity; and their chief, in his own house, maintained, above six months, a sullen and independent reserve; without listening to the threats of Omar, who attempted to consume with fire the habitation of the daughter of the apostle. The death of Fatima, and the decline of his party, subdued the indignant spirit of Ali: he condescended to salute the commander of the faithful, accepted his excuse of the necessity of preventing their common enemies, and wisely rejected his courteous offer of abdicating the government of the Arabians. After a reign of two years, the aged caliph was summoned by the angel of death. In his testament, with the tacit approbation of his companions, he bequeathed the sceptre to the firm and intrepid virtue of Omar. «I have no occasion,» said the modest candidate, «for the place.» «But the place has occasion for you,» replied Abubeker; who expired with a fervent prayer, that the God of Mahomet would ratify his choice, and direct the Mussulmans in the way of concord and obedience. The prayer was not ineffectual, since Ali himself, in a life of privacy and prayer, professed to revere the superior worth and dignity of his rival; who comforted him for the loss of empire, by the most flattering marks of confidence and esteem. In the twelfth year of his reign, Omar received a mortal wound from the hand of an assassin: he rejected with equal impartiality the names of his son and of Ali, refused to load his conscience with the sins of his successor, and devolved on six of the most respectable companions the arduous task of electing a commander of the faithful. On this occasion, Ali was again blamed by his friends for submitting his right to the judgment of men, for recognizing their jurisdiction by accepting a place among the six electors. He might have obtained their suffrage, had he deigned to promise a strict and servile conformity, not only to the Koran and tradition, but likewise to the determinations of two *seniors*. With these limitations, Othman, the secretary of Mahomet, accepted the government; nor was it till after the third caliph, twenty-four years after the death of the prophet, that Ali was invested, by the popular choice, with the regal and sacerdotal office. The manners of the Arabians retained their primitive simplicity, and the son of Abu Taleb despised the pomp and vanity of this world. At the hour of prayer, he repaired to the mosch of Medina, clothed in a thin cotton gown, a coarse turban on his head, his slippers in one hand, and his bow in the other, instead of a walking-staff. The companions of the prophet, and the chiefs of the tribes, saluted their new sovereign, and gave him their right hands as a sign of fealty and allegiance.

The mischiefs that flow from the contests of ambition are usually confined to the times and countries in which they have been agitated. But the religious discord of the friends and enemies of Ali has been renewed in every age of the Hegira, and is still maintained in the immortal hatred of the Persians and Turks. The former, who are branded with the appellation of *Shiites* or sectaries, have enriched the Mahometan creed with a new article of faith; and if Mahomet be the apostle, his companion Ali is the vicar, of God. In their private converse, in their public worship, they bitterly execrate the three usurpers who intercepted his indefeasible right to the dignity of Imam and Caliph; and the name of Omar expresses in their tongue the perfect accomplishment of wickedness and impiety. The *Sonnites*, who are supported by the general consent and orthodox tradition of the Mussulmans, entertain a more impartial, or at least a more decent, opinion. They respect the memory of Abubeker, Omar, Othman, and Ali, the holy and legitimate successors of the prophet. But they assign the last and most humble place to the husband of Fatima, in the persuasion that the order of succession was determined by the decrees of sanctity. An historian who balances the four caliphs with a hand unshaken by superstition, will calmly pronounce that their manners were alike pure and exemplary; that their zeal was fervent, and probably sincere; and that, in the midst of riches and power, their lives were devoted to the practice of moral and religious duties. But the public virtues of Abubeker and Omar, the prudence of the first, the severity of the second, maintained the peace and prosperity of their reigns. The feeble temper and declining age of Othman were incapable of sustaining the weight of conquest and empire. He chose, and he was deceived; he trusted, and he was betrayed: the most deserving of the faithful became useless or hostile to his government, and his lavish bounty was productive only of ingratitude and discontent. The spirit of discord went forth in the provinces: their deputies assembled at Medina; and the Charegites, the desperate fanatics who disclaimed the yoke of subordination and reason, were confounded among the free-born Arabs, who demanded the redress of their wrongs and the punishment of their oppressors. From Cufa, from Bassora, from Egypt, from the tribes of the desert, they rose in arms, encamped about a league from Medina, and despatched a haughty mandate to their sovereign, requiring him to execute justice, or to descend from the throne. His repentance began to disarm and disperse the insurgents; but their fury was rekindled by the arts of his enemies; and the forgery of a perfidious secretary was contrived to blast his reputation and precipitate his fall. The caliph had lost the only guard of his predecessors, the esteem and confidence of the Moslems: during a siege of six weeks his water and provisions were intercepted, and the feeble gates of the palace were protected only by the scruples of the more timorous rebels. Forsaken by those who had abused his simplicity, the hopeless and venerable caliph expected the approach of death: the brother of Ayesha marched at the head of the assassins; and Othman, with the Koran in his lap, was pierced with a multitude of wounds. A tumultuous anarchy of five days was appeased by the inauguration of Ali: his refusal would have provoked a general massacre. In this painful situation he supported the becoming pride of the chief of the Hashemites; declared that he had rather serve than reign; rebuked the presumption of the strangers; and required the formal, if not the voluntary, assent of the chiefs of the nation. He has never been accused of prompting the assassin of Omar; though Persia indiscreetly celebrates the festival of that holy martyr. The quarrel between Othman and his subjects was assuaged by the early mediation of Ali; and Hassan, the eldest of his sons, was insulted and wounded in the defence of the caliph. Yet it is doubtful whether the father of Hassan was strenuous and sincere in his opposition to the rebels; and it is certain that he enjoyed the benefit of their crime. The temptation was indeed of such magnitude as might stagger and corrupt the most obdurate virtue. The ambitious candidate no longer aspired to the barren sceptre of Arabia; the Saracens had been victorious in the East and West; and the wealthy kingdoms of Persia, Syria, and Egypt were the patrimony of the commander of the faithful.

Description of Arabia
and its Inhabitants. – Part Eight

A LIFE OF PRAYER and contemplation had not chilled the martial activity of Ali; but in a mature age, after a long experience of mankind, he still betrayed in his conduct the rashness and indiscretion of youth. In the first days of his reign, he neglected to secure, either by gifts or fetters, the doubtful allegiance of Telha and Zobeir, two of the most powerful of the Arabian chiefs. They escaped from Medina to Mecca, and from thence to Bassora; erected the standard of revolt; and usurped the government of Irak, or Assyria, which they had vainly solicited as the reward of their services. The mask of patriotism is allowed to cover the most glaring inconsistencies; and the enemies, perhaps the assassins, of Othman now demanded vengeance for his blood. They were accompanied in their flight by Ayesha, the widow of the prophet, who cherished, to the last hour of her life, an implacable hatred against the husband and the posterity of Fatima. The most reasonable Moslems were scandalized, that the mother of the faithful should expose in a camp her person and character; but the superstitious crowd was confident that her presence would sanctify the justice, and assure the success, of their cause. At the head of twenty thousand of his loyal Arabs, and nine thousand valiant auxiliaries of Cufa, the caliph encountered and defeated the superior numbers of the rebels under the walls of Bassora. Their leaders, Telha and Zobeir, were slain in the first battle that stained with civil blood the arms of the Moslems. After passing through the ranks to animate the troops, Ayesha had chosen her post amidst the dangers of the field. In the heat of the action, seventy men, who held the bridle of her camel, were successively killed or wounded; and the cage or litter, in

which she sat, was stuck with javelins and darts like the quills of a por-
cupine. The venerable captive sustained with firmness the reproaches
of the conqueror, and was speedily dismissed to her proper station at
the tomb of Mahomet, with the respect and tenderness that was still
due to the widow of the apostle. After this victory, which was styled the
Day of the Camel, Ali marched against a more formidable adversary;
against Moawiyah, the son of Abu Sophian, who had assumed the title
of caliph, and whose claim was supported by the forces of Syria and the
interest of the house of Ommiyah. From the passage of Thapsacus, the
plain of Siffin extends along the western bank of the Euphrates. On this
spacious and level theatre, the two competitors waged a desultory war
of one hundred and ten days. In the course of ninety actions or skirmishes, the loss of Ali was estimated at twenty-five, that of Moawiyah
at forty-five, thousand soldiers; and the list of the slain was dignified
with the names of five-and-twenty veterans who had fought at Beder
under the standard of Mahomet. In this sanguinary contest the lawful
caliph displayed a superior character of valor and humanity. His troops
were strictly enjoined to await the first onset of the enemy, to spare their
flying brethren, and to respect the bodies of the dead, and the chastity
of the female captives. He generously proposed to save the blood of the
Moslems by a single combat; but his trembling rival declined the challenge as a sentence of inevitable death. The ranks of the Syrians were
broken by the charge of a hero who was mounted on a piebald horse,
and wielded with irresistible force his ponderous and two-edged sword.
As often as he smote a rebel, he shouted the Allah Acbar, "God is victorious!" and in the tumult of a nocturnal battle, he was heard to repeat four
hundred times that tremendous exclamation. The prince of Damascus
already meditated his flight; but the certain victory was snatched from
the grasp of Ali by the disobedience and enthusiasm of his troops. Their
conscience was awed by the solemn appeal to the books of the Koran
which Moawiyah exposed on the foremost lances; and Ali was compelled to yield to a disgraceful truce and an insidious compromise. He
retreated with sorrow and indignation to Cufa; his party was discouraged; the distant provinces of Persia, of Yemen, and of Egypt, were subdued or seduced by his crafty rival; and the stroke of fanaticism, which
was aimed against the three chiefs of the nation, was fatal only to the
cousin of Mahomet. In the temple of Mecca, three Charegites or enthusiasts discoursed of the disorders of the church and state: they soon
agreed, that the deaths of Ali, of Moawiyah, and of his friend Amrou,
the viceroy of Egypt, would restore the peace and unity of religion. Each
of the assassins chose his victim, poisoned his dagger, devoted his life,

and secretly repaired to the scene of action. Their resolution was equally desperate: but the first mistook the person of Amrou, and stabbed the deputy who occupied his seat; the prince of Damascus was dangerously hurt by the second; the lawful caliph, in the mosch of Cufa, received a mortal wound from the hand of the third. He expired in the sixty-third year of his age, and mercifully recommended to his children, that they would despatch the murderer by a single stroke. The sepulchre of Ali was concealed from the tyrants of the house of Ommiyah; but in the fourth age of the Hegira, a tomb, a temple, a city, arose near the ruins of Cufa. Many thousands of the Shiites repose in holy ground at the feet of the vicar of God; and the desert is vivified by the numerous and annual visits of the Persians, who esteem their devotion not less meritorious than the pilgrimage of Mecca.

The persecutors of Mahomet usurped the inheritance of his children; and the champions of idolatry became the supreme heads of his religion and empire. The opposition of Abu Sophian had been fierce and obstinate; his conversion was tardy and reluctant; his new faith was fortified by necessity and interest; he served, he fought, perhaps he believed; and the sins of the time of ignorance were expiated by the recent merits of the family of Ommiyah. Moawiyah, the son of Abu Sophian, and of the cruel Henda, was dignified, in his early youth, with the office or title of secretary of the prophet: the judgment of Omar intrusted him with the government of Syria; and he administered that important province above forty years, either in a subordinate or supreme rank. Without renouncing the fame of valor and liberality, he affected the reputation of humanity and moderation: a grateful people was attached to their benefactor; and the victorious Moslems were enriched with the spoils of Cyprus and Rhodes. The sacred duty of pursuing the assassins of Othman was the engine and pretence of his ambition. The bloody shirt of the martyr was exposed in the mosch of Damascus: the emir deplored the fate of his injured kinsman; and sixty thousand Syrians were engaged in his service by an oath of fidelity and revenge. Amrou, the conqueror of Egypt, himself an army, was the first who saluted the new monarch, and divulged the dangerous secret, that the Arabian caliphs might be created elsewhere than in the city of the prophet. The policy of Moawiyah eluded the valor of his rival; and, after the death of Ali, he negotiated the abdication of his son Hassan, whose mind was either above or below the government of the world, and who retired without a sigh from the palace of Cufa to an humble cell near the tomb of his grandfather. The aspiring wishes of the caliph were finally crowned by the important change of an elective to an hereditary kingdom. Some murmurs of freedom or fanaticism attested the reluctance of the Arabs, and four citizens of Medina refused the oath of fidelity; but the designs of Moawiyah were conducted with vigor and address; and his son Yezid, a feeble and dissolute youth, was proclaimed as the commander of the faithful and the successor of the apostle of God.

A familiar story is related of the benevolence of one of the sons of Ali. In serving at table, a slave had inadvertently dropped a dish of scalding broth on his master: the heedless wretch fell prostrate, to deprecate his punishment, and repeated a verse of the Koran: "Paradise is for those who command their anger: " – "I am not angry: " – "and for those who pardon offences: " – "I pardon your offence: " – "and for those who return good for evil: " – "I give you your liberty and four hundred pieces of silver." With an equal measure of piety, Hosein, the younger brother of Hassan, inherited a remnant of his father's spirit, and served with honor against the Christians in the siege of Constantinople. The primogeniture of the line of Hashem, and the holy character of grandson of the apostle, had centred in his person, and he was at liberty to prosecute his claim against Yezid, the tyrant of Damascus, whose vices he despised, and whose title he had never deigned to acknowledge. A list was secretly transmitted from Cufa to Medina, of one hundred and forty thousand Moslems, who professed their attachment to his cause, and who were eager to draw their swords so soon as he should appear on the banks of the Euphrates. Against the advice of his wisest friends, he resolved to trust his person and family in the hands of a perfidious people. He traversed the desert of Arabia with a timorous retinue of women and children; but as he approached the confines of Irak he was alarmed by the solitary or hostile face of the country, and suspected either the defection or ruin of his party. His fears were just: Obeidollah, the governor of Cufa, had extinguished the first sparks of an insurrection; and Hosein, in the plain of Kerbela, was encompassed by a body of five thousand horse, who intercepted his communication with the city and the river. He might still have escaped to a fortress in the desert, that had defied the power of Cæsar and Chosroes, and confided in the fidelity of the tribe of Tai, which would have armed ten thousand warriors in his defence. In a conference with the chief of the enemy, he proposed the option of three honorable conditions: that he should be allowed to return to Medina, or be stationed in a frontier garrison against the Turks, or safely conducted to the presence of Yezid. But the commands of the caliph, or his lieutenant, were stern and absolute; and Hosein was informed that he must either submit as a captive and a criminal to the commander of the faithful, or expect the consequences of his rebellion. "Do you think," replied he, "to terrify me with death?" And, during the short respite of a night, he prepared with calm and solemn resignation to encounter his fate. He checked the lamentations of his sister Fatima, who deplored the impending ruin of his house. "Our trust," said Hosein, "is in God alone. All things, both in heaven and earth, must perish and return to their Creator. My brother, my father, my mother, were better than me, and every Mussulman has an example in the prophet." He pressed his friends to consult their safety by a timely flight: they unanimously refused to desert or survive their beloved master: and their courage was fortified by a fervent prayer and the assurance of paradise. On the morning of the fatal day, he mounted on horseback, with his sword in one hand and the Koran in the other: his generous band of martyrs consisted only of thirty-two horse and forty foot; but their flanks and rear were secured by the tent-ropes, and by a deep trench which they had filled with lighted fagots, according to the practice of the Arabs. The enemy advanced with reluctance, and one of their chiefs deserted, with thirty followers, to claim the partnership of inevitable death. In every close onset, or single combat, the despair of the Fatimites was invincible; but the surrounding multitudes galled them from a distance with a cloud of arrows, and the horses and men were successively slain; a truce was allowed on both sides for the hour of prayer; and the battle at length expired by the death of the last companions of Hosein. Alone, weary, and wounded, he seated himself at the door of his tent. As he tasted a drop of water, he was pierced in the mouth with a dart; and his son and nephew, two beautiful youths, were killed in his arms. He lifted his hands to heaven; they were full of blood; and he uttered a funeral prayer for the living and the dead. In a transport of despair his sister issued from the tent, and adjured the general of the Cufians, that he would not suffer Hosein to be murdered before his eyes: a tear trickled down his venerable beard; and the boldest of his soldiers fell back on every side as the dying hero threw himself among them. The remorseless Shamer, a name detested by the faithful, reproached their cowardice; and the grandson of Mahomet was slain with three-and-thirty strokes of lances and swords. After they had trampled on his body, they carried his head to the castle of Cufa, and the inhuman Obeidollah struck him on the mouth with a cane: "Alas," exclaimed an aged Mussulman, "on these lips have I seen the lips of the apostle of God!" In a distant age and climate, the tragic scene of the death of Hosein will awaken the sympathy of the coldest reader. On the annual festival of his martyrdom, in the devout pilgrimage to his sepulchre, his Persian votaries abandon their souls to the religious frenzy of sorrow and indignation.

When the sisters and children of Ali were brought in chains to the throne of Damascus, the caliph was advised to extirpate the enmity of a popular and hostile race, whom he had injured beyond the hope of reconciliation. But Yezid preferred the councils of mercy; and the mourning family was honorably dismissed to mingle their tears with their kindred at Medina. The glory of martyrdom superseded the right of primogeniture; and the twelve imams, or pontiffs, of the Persian creed, are Ali, Hassan, Hosein, and the lineal descendants of Hosein to the ninth generation. Without arms, or treasures, or subjects, they successively enjoyed the veneration of the people, and provoked the jealousy of the reigning caliphs: their tombs, at Mecca or Medina, on the banks of the Euphrates, or in the province of Chorasan, are still visited by the devotion of their sect. Their names were often the pretence of sedition and civil war; but these royal saints despised the pomp of the world: submitted to the will of God and the injustice of man; and devoted their innocent lives to the study and practice of religion. The twelfth and last of the Imams, conspicuous by the title of *Mahadi*, or the Guide, surpassed the solitude and sanctity of his predecessors. He concealed himself in a cavern near Bagdad: the time and place of his death are unknown; and his votaries pretend that he still lives, and will appear before the day of judgment to overthrow the tyranny of Dejal, or the Antichrist. In the lapse of two or three centuries, the posterity of Abbas, the uncle of Mahomet, had multiplied to the number of thirty-three thousand: the race of Ali might be equally prolific: the meanest individual was above the first and greatest of princes; and the most eminent were supposed to excel the perfection of angels. But their adverse fortune, and the wide extent of the Mussulman empire, allowed an ample scope for every bold and artful imposture, who claimed affinity with the holy seed: the sceptre of the Almohades, in Spain and Africa; of the Fatimites, in Egypt and Syria; of the Sultans of Yemen; and of the Sophis of Persia; has been consecrated by this vague and ambiguous title. Under their reigns it might be dangerous to dispute the legitimacy of their birth; and one of the Fatimite caliphs silenced an indiscreet question by drawing his cimeter: "This," said Moez, "is my pedigree; and these," casting a handful of gold to his soldiers, – "and these are my kindred and my children." In the various conditions of princes, or doctors, or nobles, or merchants, or beggars, a swarm of the genuine or fictitious descendants of Mahomet and Ali is honored with the appellation of sheiks, or sherifs, or emirs. In the Ottoman empire they are distinguished by a green turban; receive a stipend from the treasury; are judged only by their chief; and, however debased by fortune or character, still assert the proud preëminence of their birth. A family of three hundred persons, the pure and orthodox branch of the caliph Hassan, is preserved without taint or suspicion in the holy cities of Mecca and Medina, and still retains, after the revolutions of twelve centuries, the custody of the temple, and the sovereignty of their native land. The fame and merit of Mahomet would ennoble a plebeian race, and the ancient blood of the Koreish transcends the recent majesty of the kings of the earth.

The talents of Mahomet are entitled to our applause; but his success has, perhaps, too strongly attracted our admiration. Are we surprised that a multitude of proselytes should embrace the doctrine and the passions of an eloquent fanatic? In the heresies of the church, the same seduction has been tried and repeated from the time of the apostles to that of the reformers. Does it seem incredible that a private citizen should grasp the sword and the sceptre, subdue his native country, and erect a monarchy by his victorious arms? In the moving picture of the dynasties of the East, a hundred fortunate usurpers have arisen from a baser origin, surmounted more formidable obstacles, and filled a larger scope of empire and conquest. Mahomet was alike instructed to preach and to fight; and the union of these opposite qualities, while it enhanced his merit, contributed to his success: the operation of force and persuasion, of enthusiasm and fear, continually acted on each other, till every barrier yielded to their irresistible power. His voice invited the Arabs to freedom and victory, to arms and rapine, to the indulgence of their darling passions in this world and the other: the restraints which he imposed were requisite to establish the credit of the prophet, and to exercise the obedience of the people; and the only objection to his success was his rational creed of the unity and perfections of God. It is not the propagation, but the permanency, of his religion, that deserves our wonder: the same pure and perfect impression which he engraved at Mecca and Medina, is preserved, after the revolutions of twelve centuries, by the Indian, the African, and the Turkish proselytes of the Koran. If the Christian apostles, St. Peter or St. Paul, could return to the Vatican, they might possibly inquire the name of the Deity who is worshipped with such mysterious rites in that magnificent temple: at Oxford or Geneva, they would experience less surprise; but it might still be incumbent on them to peruse the catechism of the church, and to study the orthodox commentators on their own writings and the words of their Master. But the Turkish dome of St. Sophia, with an increase of splendor and size, represents the humble tabernacle erected at Medina by the hands of Mahomet. The Mahometans have uniformly withstood the temptation of reducing the object of their faith and devotion to a level with the senses and imagination of man. "I believe in one God, and Mahomet the apostle of God," is the simple and invariable profession of Islam. The intellectual image of the Deity has never been degraded by any visible idol; the honors of the prophet have never transgressed the measure of human virtue; and his living precepts have restrained the gratitude of his disciples within the bounds of reason and religion. The votaries of Ali have, indeed, consecrated the memory of their hero, his wife, and his children; and some of the Persian doctors pretend that the divine essence was incarnate in the person of the Imams; but their superstition is universally condemned by the Sonnites; and their impiety has afforded a seasonable warning against the worship of saints and martyrs. The metaphysical questions on the attributes of God, and the liberty of man, have been agitated in the schools of the Mahometans, as well as in those of the Christians; but among the former they have never engaged the passions of the people, or disturbed the tranquillity of the state. The cause of this important difference may be found in the separation or union of the regal and sacerdotal characters. It was the interest of the caliphs, the successors of the prophet and commanders of the faithful, to repress and discourage all religious innovations: the order, the discipline, the temporal and spiritual ambition of the clergy, are unknown to the Moslems; and the sages of the law are the guides of their conscience and the oracles of their faith. From the Atlantic to the Ganges, the Koran is acknowledged as the fundamental code, not only of theology, but of civil and criminal jurisprudence; and the laws which regulate the actions and the property of mankind are guarded by the infallible and immutable sanction of the will of God. This religious servitude is attended with some practical disadvantage; the illiterate legislator had been often misled by his own prejudices and those of his country; and the institutions of the Arabian desert may be ill adapted to the wealth and numbers of Ispahan and Constantinople. On these occasions, the Cadhi respectfully places on his head the holy volume, and substitutes a dexterous interpretation more apposite to the principles of equity, and the manners and policy of the times.

His beneficial or pernicious influence on the public happiness is the last consideration in the character of Mahomet. The most bitter or most bigoted of his Christian or Jewish foes will surely allow that he assumed a false commission to inculcate a salutary doctrine, less perfect only than their own. He piously supposed, as the basis of his religion, the truth and sanctity of *their* prior revolutions, the virtues and miracles of their founders. The idols of Arabia were broken before the throne of

God; the blood of human victims was expiated by prayer, and fasting, and alms, the laudable or innocent arts of devotion; and his rewards and punishments of a future life were painted by the images most congenial to an ignorant and carnal generation. Mahomet was, perhaps, incapable of dictating a moral and political system for the use of his countrymen: but he breathed among the faithful a spirit of charity and friendship; recommended the practice of the social virtues; and checked, by his laws and precepts, the thirst of revenge, and the oppression of widows and orphans. The hostile tribes were united in faith and obedience, and the valor which had been idly spent in domestic quarrels was vigorously directed against a foreign enemy. Had the impulse been less powerful, Arabia, free at home and formidable abroad, might have flourished under a succession of her native monarchs. Her sovereignty was lost by the extent and rapidity of conquest. The colonies of the nation were scattered over the East and West, and their blood was mingled with the blood of their converts and captives. After the reign of three caliphs, the throne was transported from Medina to the valley of Damascus and the banks of the Tigris; the holy cities were violated by impious war; Arabia was ruled by the rod of a subject, perhaps of a stranger; and the Bedoweens of the desert, awakening from their dream of dominion, resumed their old and solitary independence.

Conquests by the Arabs. – Part One

The Conquest Of Persia, Syria, Egypt, Africa, And Spain, By The Arabs Or Saracens. – Empire Of The Caliphs, Or Successors Of Mahomet. – State Of The Christians, &c., Under Their Government.

THE REVOLUTION OF ARABIA had not changed the character of the Arabs: the death of Mahomet was the signal of independence; and the hasty structure of his power and religion tottered to its foundations. A small and faithful band of his primitive disciples had listened to his eloquence, and shared his distress; had fled with the apostle from the persecution of Mecca, or had received the fugitive in the walls of Medina. The increasing myriads, who acknowledged Mahomet as their king and prophet, had been compelled by his arms, or allured by his prosperity. The polytheists were confounded by the simple idea of a solitary and invisible God; the pride of the Christians and Jews disdained the yoke of a mortal and contemporary legislator. The habits of faith and obedience were not sufficiently confirmed; and many of the new converts regretted the venerable antiquity of the law of Moses, or the rites and mysteries of the Catholic church; or the idols, the sacrifices, the joyous festivals, of their Pagan ancestors. The jarring interests and hereditary feuds of the Arabian tribes had not yet coalesced in a system of union and subordination; and the Barbarians were impatient of the mildest and most salutary laws that curbed their passions, or violated their customs. They submitted with reluctance to the religious precepts of the Koran, the abstinence from wine, the fast of the Ramadan, and the daily repetition of five prayers; and the alms and tithes, which were collected for the treasury of Medina, could be distinguished only by a name from the payment of a perpetual and ignominious tribute. The example of Mahomet had excited a spirit of fanaticism or imposture, and several of his rivals presumed to imitate the conduct, and defy the authority, of the living prophet. At the head of the *fugitives* and *auxiliaries*, the first caliph was reduced to the cities of Mecca, Medina, and Tayef; and perhaps the Koreish would have restored the idols of the Caaba, if their levity had not been checked by a seasonable reproof. "Ye men of Mecca, will ye be the last to embrace, and the first to abandon, the religion of Islam?" After exhorting the Moslems to confide in the aid of God and his apostle, Abubeker resolved, by a vigorous attack, to prevent the junction of the rebels. The women and children were safely lodged in the cavities of the mountains: the warriors, marching under eleven banners, diffused the terror of their arms; and the appearance of a military force revived and confirmed the loyalty of the faithful. The inconstant tribes accepted, with humble repentance, the duties of prayer, and fasting, and alms; and, after some examples of success and severity, the most daring apostates fell prostrate before the sword of the Lord and of Caled. In the fertile province of Yemanah, between the Red Sea and the Gulf of Persia, in a city not inferior to Medina itself, a powerful chief (his name was Moseilama) had assumed the character of a prophet, and the tribe of Hanifa listened to his voice. A female prophetess was attracted by his reputation; the decencies of words and actions were spurned by these favorites of Heaven; and they employed several days in mystic and amorous converse. An obscure sentence of his Koran, or book, is yet extant; and in the pride of his mission, Moseilama condescended to offer a partition of the earth. The proposal was answered by Mahomet with contempt; but the rapid progress of the impostor awakened the fears of his successor: forty thousand Moslems were assembled under the standard of Caled; and the existence of their faith was resigned to the event of a decisive battle. In the first action they were repulsed by the loss of twelve hundred men; but the skill and perseverance of their general prevailed; their defeat was avenged by the slaughter of ten thousand infidels; and Moseilama himself was pierced by an Æthiopian slave with the same javelin which had mortally wounded the uncle of Mahomet. The various rebels of Arabia without a chief or a cause, were speedily suppressed by the power and discipline of the rising monarchy; and the whole nation again professed, and more steadfastly held, the religion of the Koran. The ambition of the caliphs provided an immediate exercise for the restless spirit of the Saracens: their valor was united in the prosecution of a holy war; and their enthusiasm was equally confirmed by opposition and victory.

From the rapid conquests of the Saracens a presumption will naturally arise, that the caliphs commanded in person the armies of the faithful, and sought the crown of martyrdom in the foremost ranks of the battle. The courage of Abubeker, Omar, and Othman, had indeed been tried in the persecution and wars of the prophet; and the personal assurance of paradise must have taught them to despise the pleasures and dangers of the present world. But they ascended the throne in a venerable or mature age; and esteemed the domestic cares of religion and justice the most important duties of a sovereign. Except the presence of Omar at the siege of Jerusalem, their longest expeditions were the frequent pilgrimage from Medina to Mecca; and they calmly received the tidings of victory as they prayed or preached before the sepulchre of the prophet. The austere and frugal measure of their lives was the effect of virtue or habit, and the pride of their simplicity insulted the vain magnificence of the kings of the earth. When Abubeker assumed the office of caliph, he enjoined his daughter Ayesha to take a strict account of his private patrimony, that it might be evident whether he were enriched or impoverished by the service of the state. He thought himself entitled to a stipend of three pieces of gold, with the sufficient maintenance of a single camel and a black slave; but on the Friday of each week he distributed the residue of his own and the public money, first to the most worthy, and then to the most indigent, of the Moslems. The remains of his wealth, a coarse garment, and five pieces of gold, were delivered to his successor, who lamented with a modest sigh his own inability to equal such an admirable model. Yet the abstinence and humility of Omar were not inferior to the virtues of Abubeker: his food consisted of barley bread or dates; his drink was water; he preached in a gown that was torn or tattered in twelve places; and the Persian satrap, who paid his homage to the conqueror, found him asleep among the beggars on the steps of the mosch of Medina. Economy is the source of liberality, and the increase of the revenue enabled Omar to establish a just and perpetual reward for the past and present services of the faithful. Careless of his own emolument, he assigned to Abbas, the uncle of the prophet, the first and most ample allowance of twenty-five thousand drachms or pieces of silver. Five thousand were allotted to each of the aged warriors, the relics of the field of Beder; and the last and meanest of the companions of Mahomet was distinguished by the annual reward of three thousand pieces. One thousand was the stipend of the veterans who had fought in the first battles against the Greeks and Persians; and the decreasing pay, as low as fifty pieces of silver, was adapted to the respective merit and seniority of the soldiers of Omar.

Under his reign, and that of his predecessor, the conquerors of the East were the trusty servants of God and the people; the mass of the public treasure was consecrated to the expenses of peace and war; a prudent mixture of justice and bounty maintained the discipline of the Saracens, and they united, by a rare felicity, the despatch and execution of despotism with the equal and frugal maxims of a republican government. The heroic courage of Ali, the consummate prudence of Moawiyah, excited the emulation of their subjects; and the talents which had been exercised in the school of civil discord were more usefully applied to propagate the faith and dominion of the prophet. In the sloth and vanity of the palace of Damascus, the succeeding princes of the house of Ommiyah were alike destitute of the qualifications of statesmen and of saints. Yet the spoils of unknown nations were continually laid at the foot of their throne, and the uniform ascent of the Arabian greatness must be ascribed to the spirit of the nation rather than the abilities of their chiefs. A large deduction must be allowed for the weakness of their enemies. The birth of Mahomet was fortunately placed in the most degenerate and disorderly period of the Persians, the Romans, and the Barbarians of Europe: the empires of Trajan, or even of Constantine or Charlemagne, would have repelled the assault of the naked Saracens, and the torrent of fanaticism might have been obscurely lost in the sands of Arabia.

In the victorious days of the Roman republic, it had been the aim of the senate to confine their councils and legions to a single war, and completely to suppress a first enemy before they provoked the hostilities of a second. These timid maxims of policy were disdained by the magnanimity or enthusiasm of the Arabian caliphs. With the same vigor and success they invaded the successors of Augustus and those of Artaxerxes; and the rival monarchies at the same instant became the prey of an enemy whom they had been so long accustomed to despise. In the ten years of the administration of Omar, the Saracens reduced to his obedience thirty-six thousand cities or castles, destroyed four thousand churches or temples of the unbelievers, and edified fourteen hundred moschs for the exercise of the religion of Mahomet. One hundred years after his flight from Mecca, the arms and the reign of his successors extended from India to the Atlantic Ocean, over the various and distant provinces, which may be comprised under the names of, I. Persia; II. Syria; III. Egypt; IV. Africa; and, V. Spain. Under this general division, I shall proceed to unfold these memorable transactions; despatching with brevity the remote and less interesting conquests of the East, and reserving a fuller narrative for those domestic countries which had been included within the pale of the Roman empire. Yet I must excuse my own defects by a just complaint of the blindness and insufficiency of my guides. The Greeks, so loquacious in controversy, have not been anxious to celebrate the triumphs of their enemies. After a century of ignorance, the first annals of the Mussulmans were collected in a great measure from the voice of tradition. Among the numerous productions of Arabic and Persian literature, our interpreters have selected the imperfect sketches of a more recent age. The art and genius of history have ever been unknown to the Asiatics; they are ignorant of the laws of criticism; and our monkish chronicle of the same period may be compared to their most popular works, which are never vivified by the spirit of philosophy and freedom. The *Oriental library* of a Frenchman would instruct the most learned mufti of the East; and perhaps the Arabs might not find in a single historian so clear and comprehensive a narrative of their own exploits as that which will be deduced in the ensuing sheets.

I. In the first year of the first caliph, his lieutenant Caled, the Sword of God, and the scourge of the infidels, advanced to the banks of the Euphrates, and reduced the cities of Anbar and Hira. Westward of the ruins of Babylon, a tribe of sedentary Arabs had fixed themselves on the verge of the desert; and Hira was the seat of a race of kings who had embraced the Christian religion, and reigned above six hundred years under the shadow of the throne of Persia. The last of the Mondars was defeated and slain by Caled; his son was sent a captive to Medina; his nobles bowed before the successor of the prophet; the people was tempted by the example and success of their countrymen; and the caliph accepted as the first-fruits of foreign conquest an annual tribute of seventy thousand pieces of gold. The conquerors, and even their historians, were astonished by the dawn of their future greatness: "In the same year," says Elmacin, "Caled fought many signal battles: an immense multitude of the infidels was slaughtered; and spoils infinite and innumerable were acquired by the victorious Moslems." But the invincible Caled was soon transferred to the Syrian war: the invasion of the Persian frontier was conducted by less active or less prudent commanders: the Saracens were repulsed with loss in the passage of the Euphrates; and, though they chastised the insolent pursuit of the Magians, their remaining forces still hovered in the desert of Babylon.

The indignation and fears of the Persians suspended for a moment their intestine divisions. By the unanimous sentence of the priests and nobles, their queen Arzema was deposed; the sixth of the transient usurpers, who had arisen and vanished in three or four years since the death of Chosroes, and the retreat of Heraclius. Her tiara was placed on the head of Yezdegerd, the grandson of Chosroes; and the same æra, which coincides with an astronomical period, has recorded the fall of the Sassanian dynasty and the religion of Zoroaster. The youth and inexperience of the prince (he was only fifteen years of age) declined a perilous encounter: the royal standard was delivered into the hands of his general Rustam; and a remnant of thirty thousand regular troops was swelled in truth, or in opinion, to one hundred and twenty thousand subjects, or allies, of the great king. The Moslems, whose numbers were reënforced from twelve to thirty thousand, had pitched their camp in the plains of Cadesia: and their line, though it consisted of fewer *men*, could produce more *soldiers*, than the unwieldy host of the infidels. I shall here observe, what I must often repeat, that the charge of the Arabs was not, like that of the Greeks and Romans, the effort of a firm and compact infantry: their military force was chiefly formed of cavalry and archers; and the engagement, which was often interrupted and often renewed by single combats and flying skirmishes, might be protracted without any decisive event to the continuance of several days. The periods of the battle of Cadesia were distinguished by their peculiar appellations. The first, from the well-timed appearance of six thousand of the Syrian brethren, was denominated the day of *succor*. The day of *concussion* might express the disorder of one, or perhaps of both, of the contending armies. The third, a nocturnal tumult, received the whimsical name of the night of *barking*, from the discordant clamors, which were compared to the inarticulate sounds of the fiercest animals. The morning of the succeeding day determined the fate of Persia; and a seasonable whirlwind drove a cloud of dust against the faces of the unbelievers. The clangor of arms was reechoed to the tent of Rustam, who, far unlike the ancient hero of his name, was gently reclining in a cool and tranquil shade, amidst the baggage of his camp, and the train of mules that were laden with gold and silver. On the sound of danger he started from his couch; but his flight was overtaken by a valiant Arab, who caught him by the foot, struck off his head, hoisted it on a lance, and instantly returning to the field of battle, carried slaughter and dismay among the thickest ranks of the Persians. The Saracens confess a loss of seven thousand five hundred men; and the battle of Cadesia is justly described by the epithets of obstinate and atrocious. The standard of the monarchy was overthrown and captured in the field – a leathern apron of a blacksmith, who in ancient times had arisen the deliverer of Persia; but this badge of heroic poverty was disguised, and almost concealed, by a profusion of precious gems. After this victory, the wealthy province of Irak, or Assyria, submitted to the caliph, and his conquests were firmly established by the speedy foundation of Bassora, a place which ever commands the trade and navigation of the Persians. As the distance of fourscore miles from the Gulf, the Euphrates and Tigris unite in a broad and direct current, which is aptly styled the river of the Arabs. In the midway, between the junction and the mouth of these famous streams, the new settlement was planted on the western bank: the first colony was composed of eight hundred Moslems; but the influence of the situation soon reared a flourishing and populous capital. The air, though excessively hot, is pure and healthy: the meadows are filled with palm-trees and cattle; and one of the adjacent valleys has been celebrated among the four paradises or gardens of Asia. Under the first caliphs the jurisdiction of this Arabian colony extended over the southern provinces of Persia: the city has been sanctified by the tombs of the companions and martyrs; and the vessels of Europe still frequent the port of Bassora, as a convenient station and passage of the Indian trade.

CHAPTER FIFTY ONE

Conquests by the Arabs. – Part Two

AFTER THE DEFEAT OF Cadesia, a country intersected by rivers and canals might have opposed an insuperable barrier to the victorious cavalry;
and the walls of Ctesiphon or Madayn, which had resisted the battering-
rams of the Romans, would not have yielded to the darts of the Saracens. But the flying Persians were overcome by the belief, that the last
day of their religion and empire was at hand; the strongest posts were
abandoned by treachery or cowardice; and the king, with a part of his
family and treasures, escaped to Holwan at the foot of the Median hills.
In the third month after the battle, Said, the lieutenant of Omar, passed
the Tigris without opposition; the capital was taken by assault; and the
disorderly resistance of the people gave a keener edge to the sabres of the
Moslems, who shouted with religious transport, "This is the white palace
of Chosroes; this is the promise of the apostle of God!" The naked robbers of the desert were suddenly enriched beyond the measure of their
hope or knowledge. Each chamber revealed a new treasure secreted with
art, or ostentatiously displayed; the gold and silver, the various wardrobes
and precious furniture, surpassed (says Abulfeda) the estimate of fancy
or numbers; and another historian defines the untold and almost infinite
mass, by the fabulous computation of three thousands of thousands of
thousands of pieces of gold. Some minute though curious facts represent the contrast of riches and ignorance. From the remote islands of the
Indian Ocean a large provision of camphire had been imported, which
is employed with a mixture of wax to illuminate the palaces of the East.
Strangers to the name and properties of that odoriferous gum, the Saracens, mistaking it for salt, mingled the camphire in their bread, and were
astonished at the bitterness of the taste. One of the apartments of the
palace was decorated with a carpet of silk, sixty cubits in length, and as

many in breadth: a paradise or garden was depictured on the ground: the flowers, fruits, and shrubs, were imitated by the figures of the gold embroidery, and the colors of the precious stones; and the ample square was encircled by a variegated and verdant border. The Arabian general persuaded his soldiers to relinquish their claim, in the reasonable hope that the eyes of the caliph would be delighted with the splendid workmanship of nature and industry. Regardless of the merit of art, and the pomp of royalty, the rigid Omar divided the prize among his brethren of Medina: the picture was destroyed; but such was the intrinsic value of the materials, that the share of Ali alone was sold for twenty thousand drams. A mule that carried away the tiara and cuirass, the belt and bracelets of Chosroes, was overtaken by the pursuers; the gorgeous trophy was presented to the commander of the faithful; and the gravest of the companions condescended to smile when they beheld the white beard, the hairy arms, and uncouth figure of the veteran, who was invested with the spoils of the Great King. The sack of Ctesiphon was followed by its desertion and gradual decay. The Saracens disliked the air and situation of the place, and Omar was advised by his general to remove the seat of government to the western side of the Euphrates. In every age, the foundation and ruin of the Assyrian cities has been easy and rapid: the country is destitute of stone and timber; and the most solid structures are composed of bricks baked in the sun, and joined by a cement of the native bitumen. The name of *Cufa* describes a habitation of reeds and earth; but the importance of the new capital was supported by the numbers, wealth, and spirit, of a colony of veterans; and their licentiousness was indulged by the wisest caliphs, who were apprehensive of provoking the revolt of a hundred thousand swords: «Ye men of Cufa,» said Ali, who solicited their aid, «you have been always conspicuous by your valor. You conquered the Persian king, and scattered his forces, till you had taken possession of his inheritance.» This mighty conquest was achieved by the battles of Jalula and Nehavend. After the loss of the former, Yezdegerd fled from Holwan, and concealed his shame and despair in the mountains of Farsistan, from whence Cyrus had descended with his equal and valiant companions. The courage of the nation survived that of the monarch: among the hills to the south of Ecbatana or Hamadan, one hundred and fifty thousand Persians made a third and final stand for their religion and country; and the decisive battle of Nehavend was styled by the Arabs the victory of victories. If it be true that the flying general of the Persians was stopped and overtaken in a crowd of mules and camels laden with honey, the incident, however slight and singular, will denote the luxurious impediments of an Oriental army.

The geography of Persia is darkly delineated by the Greeks and Latins; but the most illustrious of her cities appear to be more ancient than the invasion of the Arabs. By the reduction of Hamadan and Ispahan, of Caswin, Tauris, and Rei, they gradually approached the shores of the Caspian Sea: and the orators of Mecca might applaud the success and spirit of the faithful, who had already lost sight of the northern bear, and had almost transcended the bounds of the habitable world. Again, turning towards the West and the Roman empire, they repassed the Tigris over the bridge of Mosul, and, in the captive provinces of Armenia and Mesopotamia, embraced their victorious brethren of the Syrian army. From the palace of Madayn their Eastern progress was not less rapid or extensive. They advanced along the Tigris and the Gulf; penetrated through the passes of the mountains into the valley of Estachar or Persepolis, and profaned the last sanctuary of the Magian empire. The grandson of Chosroes was nearly surprised among the falling columns and mutilated figures; a sad emblem of the past and present fortune of Persia: he fled with accelerated haste over the desert of Kirman, implored the aid of the warlike Segestans, and sought an humble refuge on the verge of the Turkish and Chinese power. But a victorious army is insensible of fatigue: the Arabs divided their forces in the pursuit of a timorous enemy; and the caliph Othman promised the government of Chorasan to the first general who should enter that large and populous country, the kingdom of the ancient Bactrians. The condition was accepted; the prize was deserved; the standard of Mahomet was planted on the walls of Herat, Merou, and Balch; and the successful leader neither halted nor reposed till his foaming cavalry had tasted the waters of the Oxus. In the public anarchy, the independent governors of the cities and castles obtained their separate capitulations: the terms were granted or imposed by the esteem, the prudence, or the compassion, of the victors; and a simple profession of faith established the distinction between a brother and a slave. After a noble defence, Harmozan, the prince or satrap of Ahwaz and Susa, was compelled to surrender his person and his state to the discretion of the caliph; and their interview exhibits a portrait of the Arabian manners. In the presence, and by the command, of Omar, the gay Barbarian was despoiled of his silken robes embroidered with gold, and of his tiara bedecked with rubies and emeralds: "Are you now sensible," said the conqueror to his naked captive – "are you now sensible of the judgment of God, and of the different rewards of infidelity and obedience?" "Alas!" replied Harmozan, "I feel them too deeply. In the days of our common ignorance, we fought with the weapons of the flesh, and my nation was superior. God was then neuter: since he has espoused your quarrel, you have subverted our kingdom and religion." Oppressed by this painful dialogue, the Persian complained of intolerable thirst, but discovered some apprehension lest he should be killed whilst he was drinking a cup of water. "Be of good courage," said the caliph; "your life is safe till you have drunk this water:" the crafty satrap accepted the assurance, and instantly dashed the vase against the ground. Omar would have avenged the deceit, but his companions represented the sanctity of an oath; and the speedy conversion of Harmozan entitled him not only to a free pardon, but even to a stipend of two thousand pieces of gold. The administration of Persia was regulated by an actual survey of the people, the cattle, and the fruits of the earth; and this monument, which attests the vigilance of the caliphs, might have instructed the philosophers of every age.

The flight of Yezdegerd had carried him beyond the Oxus, and as far as the Jaxartes, two rivers of ancient and modern renown, which descend from the mountains of India towards the Caspian Sea. He was hospitably entertained by Tarkhan, prince of Fargana, a fertile province on the Jaxartes: the king of Samarcand, with the Turkish tribes of Sogdiana and Scythia, were moved by the lamentations and promises of the fallen monarch; and he solicited, by a suppliant embassy, the more solid and powerful friendship of the emperor of China. The virtuous Taitsong, the first of the dynasty of the Tang may be justly compared with the Antonines of Rome: his people enjoyed the blessings of prosperity and peace; and his dominion was acknowledged by forty-four hordes of the Barbarians of Tartary. His last garrisons of Cashgar and Khoten maintained a frequent intercourse with their neighbors of the Jaxartes and Oxus; a recent colony of Persians had introduced into China the astronomy of the Magi; and Taitsong might be alarmed by the rapid progress and dangerous vicinity of the Arabs. The influence, and perhaps the supplies, of China revived the hopes of Yezdegerd and the zeal of the worshippers of fire; and he returned with an army of Turks to conquer the inheritance of his fathers. The fortunate Moslems, without unsheathing their swords, were the spectators of his ruin and death. The grandson of Chosroes was betrayed by his servant, insulted by the seditious inhabitants of Merou, and oppressed, defeated, and pursued by his Barbarian allies. He reached the banks of a river, and offered his rings and bracelets for an instant passage in a miller's boat. Ignorant or insensible of royal distress, the rustic replied, that four drams of silver were the daily profit of his mill, and that he would not suspend his work unless the loss were repaid. In this moment of hesitation and delay, the last of the Sassanian kings was overtaken and slaughtered by the

Turkish cavalry, in the nineteenth year of his unhappy reign. His son Firuz, an humble client of the Chinese emperor, accepted the station of captain of his guards; and the Magian worship was long preserved by a colony of loyal exiles in the province of Bucharia. His grandson inherited the regal name; but after a faint and fruitless enterprise, he returned to China, and ended his days in the palace of Sigan. The male line of the Sassanides was extinct; but the female captives, the daughters of Persia, were given to the conquerors in servitude, or marriage; and the race of the caliphs and imams was ennobled by the blood of their royal mothers.

After the fall of the Persian kingdom, the River Oxus divided the territories of the Saracens and of the Turks. This narrow boundary was soon overleaped by the spirit of the Arabs; the governors of Chorasan extended their successive inroads; and one of their triumphs was adorned with the buskin of a Turkish queen, which she dropped in her precipitate flight beyond the hills of Bochara. But the final conquest of Transoxiana, as well as of Spain, was reserved for the glorious reign of the inactive Walid; and the name of Catibah, the camel driver, declares the origin and merit of his successful lieutenant. While one of his colleagues displayed the first Mahometan banner on the banks of the Indus, the spacious regions between the Oxus, the Jaxartes, and the Caspian Sea, were reduced by the arms of Catibah to the obedience of the prophet and of the caliph. A tribute of two millions of pieces of gold was imposed on the infidels; their idols were burnt or broken; the Mussulman chief pronounced a sermon in the new mosch of Carizme; after several battles, the Turkish hordes were driven back to the desert; and the emperors of China solicited the friendship of the victorious Arabs. To their industry, the prosperity of the province, the Sogdiana of the ancients, may in a great measure be ascribed; but the advantages of the soil and climate had been understood and cultivated since the reign of the Macedonian kings. Before the invasion of the Saracens, Carizme, Bochara, and Samarcand were rich and populous under the yoke of the shepherds of the north. These cities were surrounded with a double wall; and the exterior fortification, of a larger circumference, enclosed the fields and gardens of the adjacent district. The mutual wants of India and Europe were supplied by the diligence of the Sogdian merchants; and the inestimable art of transforming linen into paper has been diffused from the manufacture of Samarcand over the western world.

II. No sooner had Abubeker restored the unity of faith and government, than he despatched a circular letter to the Arabian tribes. "In the name of the most merciful God, to the rest of the true believers.

Health and happiness, and the mercy and blessing of God, be upon you. I praise the most high God, and I pray for his prophet Mahomet. This is to acquaint you, that I intend to send the true believers into Syria to take it out of the hands of the infidels. And I would have you know, that the fighting for religion is an act of obedience to God." His messengers returned with the tidings of pious and martial ardor which they had kindled in every province; and the camp of Medina was successively filled with the intrepid bands of the Saracens, who panted for action, complained of the heat of the season and the scarcity of provisions, and accused with impatient murmurs the delays of the caliph. As soon as their numbers were complete, Abubeker ascended the hill, reviewed the men, the horses, and the arms, and poured forth a fervent prayer for the success of their undertaking. In person, and on foot, he accompanied the first day's march; and when the blushing leaders attempted to dismount, the caliph removed their scruples by a declaration, that those who rode, and those who walked, in the service of religion, were equally meritorious. His instructions to the chiefs of the Syrian army were inspired by the warlike fanaticism which advances to seize, and affects to despise, the objects of earthly ambition. "Remember," said the successor of the prophet, "that you are always in the presence of God, on the verge of death, in the assurance of judgment, and the hope of paradise. Avoid injustice and oppression; consult with your brethren, and study to preserve the love and confidence of your troops. When you fight the battles of the Lord, acquit yourselves like men, without turning your backs; but let not your victory be stained with the blood of women or children. Destroy no palm-trees, nor burn any fields of corn. Cut down no fruit-trees, nor do any mischief to cattle, only such as you kill to eat. When you make any covenant or article, stand to it, and be as good as your word. As you go on, you will find some religious persons who live retired in monasteries, and propose to themselves to serve God that way: let them alone, and neither kill them nor destroy their monasteries: And you will find another sort of people, that belong to the synagogue of Satan, who have shaven crowns; be sure you cleave their skulls, and give them no quarter till they either turn Mahometans or pay tribute." All profane or frivolous conversation, all dangerous recollection of ancient quarrels, was severely prohibited among the Arabs: in the tumult of a camp, the exercises of religion were assiduously practised; and the intervals of action were employed in prayer, meditation, and the study of the Koran. The abuse, or even the use, of wine was chastised by fourscore strokes on the soles of the feet, and in the fervor of their primitive zeal, many secret sinners revealed their fault, and solicited their punishment. After some hesitation, the command of the Syrian army was delegated to Abu Obeidah, one of the fugitives of Mecca, and companions of Mahomet; whose zeal and devotion was assuaged, without being abated, by the singular mildness and benevolence of his temper. But in all the emergencies of war, the soldiers demanded the superior genius of Caled; and whoever might be the choice of the prince, the *Sword of God* was both in fact and fame the foremost leader of the Saracens. He obeyed without reluctance; he was consulted without jealousy; and such was the spirit of the man, or rather of the times, that Caled professed his readiness to serve under the banner of the faith, though it were in the hands of a child or an enemy. Glory, and riches, and dominion, were indeed promised to the victorious Mussulman; but he was carefully instructed, that if the goods of this life were his only incitement, *they* likewise would be his only reward.

Conquests by the Arabs. – Part Three

ONE OF THE FIFTEEN provinces of Syria, the cultivated lands to the eastward of the Jordan, had been decorated by Roman vanity with the name of *Arabia*; and the first arms of the Saracens were justified by the semblance of a national right. The country was enriched by the various benefits of trade; by the vigilance of the emperors it was covered with a line of forts; and the populous cities of Gerasa, Philadelphia, and Bosra, were secure, at least from a surprise, by the solid structure of their walls. The last of these cities was the eighteenth station from Medina: the road was familiar to the caravans of Hejaz and Irak, who annually visited this plenteous market of the province and the desert: the perpetual jealousy of the Arabs had trained the inhabitants to arms; and twelve thousand horse could sally from the gates of Bosra, an appellation which signifies, in the Syriac language, a strong tower of defence. Encouraged by their first success against the open towns and flying parties of the borders, a detachment of four thousand Moslems presumed to summon and attack the fortress of Bosra. They were oppressed by the numbers of the Syrians; they were saved by the presence of Caled, with fifteen hundred horse: he blamed the enterprise, restored the battle, and rescued his friend, the venerable Serjabil, who had vainly invoked the unity of God and the promises of the apostle. After a short repose, the Moslems performed their ablutions with sand instead of water; and the morning prayer was recited by Caled before they mounted on horseback. Confident in their strength, the people of Bosra threw open their gates, drew their forces into the plain, and swore to die in the defence of their religion. But a religion of peace was incapable of withstanding the fanatic cry of "Fight, fight! Paradise, paradise!" that reechoed in the ranks of the Saracens; and the uproar of the town, the ringing of bells, and the exclamations of the priests and monks increased the dismay and disorder of the Christians. With the loss of two hundred and thirty men, the Arabs remained masters of the field; and the ramparts of Bosra, in expectation of human or divine aid, were crowded with holy crosses and consecrated banners. The governor Romanus had recommended an early submission: despised by the people, and degraded from his office, he still retained the desire and opportunity of revenge. In a nocturnal interview, he informed the enemy of a subterraneous passage from his house under the wall of the city; the son of the caliph, with a hundred volunteers, were committed to the faith of this new ally, and their successful intrepidity gave an easy entrance to their companions. After Caled had imposed the terms of servitude and tribute, the apostate or convert avowed in the assembly of the people his meritorious treason: "I renounce your society," said Romanus, "both in this world and the world to come. And I deny him that was crucified, and whosoever worships him. And I choose God for my Lord, Islam for my faith, Mecca for my temple, the Moslems for my brethren, and Mahomet for my prophet; who was sent to lead us into the right way, and to exalt the true religion in spite of those who join partners with God."

The conquest of Bosra, four days' journey from Damascus, encouraged the Arabs to besiege the ancient capital of Syria. At some distance from the walls, they encamped among the groves and fountains of that delicious territory, and the usual option of the Mahometan faith, of tribute or of war, was proposed to the resolute citizens, who had been lately strengthened by a reenforcement of five thousand Greeks. In the decline, as in the infancy, of the military art, a hostile defiance was frequently offered and accepted by the generals themselves: many a lance was shivered in the plain of Damascus, and the personal prowess of Caled was signalized in the first sally of the besieged. After an obstinate combat, he had overthrown and made prisoner one of the Christian leaders, a stout and worthy antagonist. He instantly mounted a fresh horse, the gift of the governor of Palmyra, and pushed forwards to the front of the battle. "Repose yourself for a moment," said his friend Derar, "and permit me to supply your place: you are fatigued with fighting with this dog." "O Dear!" replied the indefatigable Saracen, "we shall rest in the world to come. He that labors to-day shall rest to-morrow." With the same unabated ardor, Caled answered, encountered, and vanquished a second champion; and the heads of his two captives who refused to abandon their religion were indignantly hurled into the midst of the city. The event of some general and partial actions reduced the

Damascenes to a closer defence: but a messenger, whom they dropped from the walls, returned with the promise of speedy and powerful succor, and their tumultuous joy conveyed the intelligence to the camp of the Arabs. After some debate, it was resolved by the generals to raise, or rather to suspend, the siege of Damascus, till they had given battle to the forces of the emperor. In the retreat, Caled would have chosen the more perilous station of the rear-guard; he modestly yielded to the wishes of Abu Obeidah. But in the hour of danger he flew to the rescue of his companion, who was rudely pressed by a sally of six thousand horse and ten thousand foot, and few among the Christians could relate at Damascus the circumstances of their defeat. The importance of the contest required the junction of the Saracens, who were dispersed on the frontiers of Syria and Palestine; and I shall transcribe one of the circular mandates which was addressed to Amrou, the future conqueror of Egypt. "In the name of the most merciful God: from Caled to Amrou, health and happiness. Know that thy brethren the Moslems design to march to Aiznadin, where there is an army of seventy thousand Greeks, who purpose to come against us, *that they may extinguish the light of God with their mouths; but God preserveth his light in spite of the infidels.* As soon therefore as this letter of mine shall be delivered to thy hands, come with those that are with thee to Aiznadin, where thou shalt find us if it please the most high God." The summons was cheerfully obeyed, and the forty-five thousand Moslems, who met on the same day, on the same spot ascribed to the blessing of Providence the effects of their activity and zeal.

About four years after the triumph of the Persian war, the repose of Heraclius and the empire was again disturbed by a new enemy, the power of whose religion was more strongly felt, than it was clearly understood, by the Christians of the East. In his palace of Constantinople or Antioch, he was awakened by the invasion of Syria, the loss of Bosra, and the danger of Damascus. An army of seventy thousand veterans, or new levies, was assembled at Hems or Emesa, under the command of his general Werdan: and these troops consisting chiefly of cavalry, might be indifferently styled either Syrians, or Greeks, or Romans: *Syrians*, from the place of their birth or warfare; *Greeks* from the religion and language of their sovereign; and *Romans*, from the proud appellation which was still profaned by the successors of Constantine. On the plain of Aiznadin, as Werdan rode on a white mule decorated with gold chains, and surrounded with ensigns and standards, he was surprised by the near approach of a fierce and naked warrior, who had undertaken to view the state of the enemy. The adventurous valor of Derar was inspired, and has perhaps been adorned, by the enthusiasm of his age and country. The hatred of the Christians, the love of spoil, and the contempt of danger, were the ruling passions of the audacious Saracen; and the prospect of instant death could never shake his religious confidence, or ruffle the calmness of his resolution, or even suspend the frank and martial pleasantry of his humor. In the most hopeless enterprises, he was bold, and prudent, and fortunate: after innumerable hazards, after being thrice a prisoner in the hands of the infidels, he still survived to relate the achievements, and to enjoy the rewards, of the Syrian conquest. On this occasion, his single lance maintained a flying fight against thirty Romans, who were detached by Werdan; and, after killing or unhorsing seventeen of their number, Derar returned in safety to his applauding brethren. When his rashness was mildly censured by the general, he excused himself with the simplicity of a soldier. "Nay," said Derar, "I did not begin first: but they came out to take me, and I was afraid that God should see me turn my back: and indeed I fought in good earnest, and without doubt God assisted me against them; and had I not been apprehensive of disobeying your orders, I should not have come away as I did; and I perceive already that they will fall into our hands." In the presence of both armies, a venerable Greek advanced from the ranks with a liberal offer of peace; and the departure of the Saracens would have been purchased by a gift to each soldier, of a turban, a robe, and a piece of gold; ten robes and a hundred pieces to their leader; one hundred robes and a thousand pieces to the caliph. A smile of indignation expressed the refusal of Caled. "Ye Christian dogs, you know your option; the Koran, the tribute, or the sword. We are a people whose delight is in war, rather than in peace: and we despise your pitiful alms, since we shall be speedily masters of your wealth, your families, and your persons." Notwithstanding this apparent disdain, he was deeply conscious of the public danger: those who had been in Persia, and had seen the armies of Chosroes confessed that they never beheld a more formidable array. From the superiority of the enemy, the artful Saracen derived a fresh incentive of courage: "You see before you," said he, "the united force of the Romans; you cannot hope to escape, but you may conquer Syria in a single day. The event depends on your discipline and patience. Reserve yourselves till the evening. It was in the evening that the Prophet was accustomed to vanquish." During two successive engagements, his temperate firmness sustained the darts of the enemy, and the murmurs of his troops. At length, when the spirits and quivers of the adverse line were almost exhausted, Caled gave the signal of onset and victory. The remains of the Imperial army fled to Antioch, or Cæsarea, or Damascus; and the death of four hundred and seventy Moslems was compensated by the opinion that they had sent to hell above fifty thousand of the infidels. The spoil was inestimable; many banners and crosses of gold and silver, precious stones, silver and gold chains, and innumerable suits of the richest armor and apparel. The general distribution was postponed till Damascus should be taken; but the seasonable supply of arms became the instrument of new victories. The glorious intelligence was transmitted to the throne of the caliph; and the Arabian tribes, the coldest or most hostile to the prophet's mission, were eager and importunate to share the harvest of Syria.

The sad tidings were carried to Damascus by the speed of grief and terror; and the inhabitants beheld from their walls the return of the heroes of Aiznadin. Amrou led the van at the head of nine thousand horse: the bands of the Saracens succeeded each other in formidable review; and the rear was closed by Caled in person, with the standard of the black eagle. To the activity of Derar he intrusted the commission of patrolling round the city with two thousand horse, of scouring the plain, and of intercepting all succor or intelligence. The rest of the Arabian chiefs were fixed in their respective stations before the seven gates of Damascus; and the siege was renewed with fresh vigor and confidence. The art, the labor, the military engines, of the Greeks and Romans are seldom to be found in the simple, though successful, operations of the Saracens: it was sufficient for them to invest a city with arms, rather than with trenches; to repel the allies of the besieged; to attempt a stratagem or an assault; or to expect the progress of famine and discontent. Damascus would have acquiesced in the trial of Aiznadin, as a final and peremptory sentence between the emperor and the caliph; her courage was rekindled by the example and authority of Thomas, a noble Greek, illustrious in a private condition by the alliance of Heraclius. The tumult and illumination of the night proclaimed the design of the morning sally; and the Christian hero, who affected to despise the enthusiasm of the Arabs, employed the resource of a similar superstition. At the principal gate, in the sight of both armies, a lofty crucifix was erected; the bishop, with his clergy, accompanied the march, and laid the volume of the New Testament before the image of Jesus; and the contending parties were scandalized or edified by a prayer that the Son of God would defend his servants and vindicate his truth. The battle raged with incessant fury; and the dexterity of Thomas, an incomparable archer, was fatal to the boldest Saracens, till their death was revenged by a female heroine. The wife of Aban, who had followed him to the holy war, embraced her expiring husband. "Happy," said she, "happy art thou, my dear: thou art gone to thy Lord, who first joined us together, and then parted us asunder. I will revenge thy death, and endeavor to the utmost of my power to come to the place where thou art, because I love thee. Henceforth shall no man ever touch me more, for I have dedicated myself to the service of God." Without a groan, without a tear, she washed the corpse of her husband, and buried him with the usual rites. Then grasping the manly weapons, which in her native land she was accustomed to wield, the intrepid widow of Aban sought the place where his murderer fought in the thickest of the battle. Her first arrow pierced the hand of his standard-bearer; her second wounded Thomas in the eye; and the fainting Christians no longer beheld their ensign or their leader. Yet the generous champion of Damascus refused to withdraw to his palace: his wound was dressed on the rampart; the fight was continued till the evening; and the Syrians rested on their arms. In the silence of the night, the signal was given by a stroke on the great bell; the gates were thrown open, and each gate discharged an impetuous column on the sleeping camp of the Saracens. Caled was the first in arms: at the head of four hundred horse he flew to the post of danger, and the tears trickled down his iron cheeks, as he uttered a fervent ejaculation; "O God, who never sleepest, look upon they servants, and do not deliver them into the hands of their enemies." The valor and victory of Thomas were arrested by the presence of the *Sword of God*; with the knowledge of the peril, the Moslems recovered their ranks, and charged the assailants in the flank and rear. After the loss of thousands, the Christian general retreated with a sigh of despair, and the pursuit of the Saracens was checked by the military engines of the rampart.

After a siege of seventy days, the patience, and perhaps the provisions, of the Damascenes were exhausted; and the bravest of their chiefs submitted to the hard dictates of necessity. In the occurrences of peace and war, they had been taught to dread the fierceness of Caled, and to revere the mild virtues of Abu Obeidah. At the hour of midnight, one hundred chosen deputies of the clergy and people were introduced to the tent of that venerable commander. He received and dismissed them with courtesy. They returned with a written agreement, on the faith of a companion of Mahomet, that all hostilities should cease; that the voluntary emigrants might depart in safety, with as much as they could carry away of their effects; and that the tributary subjects of the caliph should enjoy their lands and houses, with the use and possession of seven churches. On these terms, the most respectable hostages, and the gate nearest to his camp, were delivered into his hands: his soldiers imitated the moderation of their chief; and he enjoyed the submissive gratitude of a people whom he had rescued from destruction. But the success of the treaty had relaxed their vigilance, and in the same moment the opposite quarter of the city was betrayed and taken by assault. A party of a hundred Arabs had opened the eastern gate to a more inexorable foe. "No quarter," cried the rapacious and sanguinary Caled, "no quarter to the enemies of the Lord:" his trumpets sounded, and a torrent of Christian blood was poured down the streets of Damascus. When he reached the church of St. Mary, he was astonished and provoked by the peaceful aspect of his companions; their swords were in the scabbard, and they were surrounded by a multitude of priests and monks. Abu Obeidah saluted the general: "God," said he, "has delivered the city into my hands by way of surrender, and has saved the believers the trouble of fighting." "And am I not," replied the indignant Caled, "am I not the lieutenant of the commander of the faithful? Have I not taken the city by storm? The unbelievers shall perish by the sword. Fall on." The hungry and cruel Arabs would have obeyed the welcome command; and Damascus was lost, if the benevolence of Abu Obeidah had not been supported by a decent and dignified firmness. Throwing himself between the trembling citizens and the most eager of the Barbarians, he adjured them, by the holy name of God, to respect his promise, to suspend their fury, and to wait the determination of their chiefs. The chiefs retired into the church of St. Mary; and after a vehement debate, Caled submitted in some measure to the reason and authority of his colleague; who urged the sanctity of a covenant, the advantage as well as the honor which the Moslems would derive from the punctual performance of their word, and the obstinate resistance which they must encounter from the distrust and despair of the rest of the Syrian cities. It was agreed that the sword should be sheathed, that the part of Damascus which had surrendered to Abu Obeidah, should be immediately entitled to the benefit of his capitulation, and that the final decision should be referred to the justice and wisdom of the caliph. A large majority of the people accepted the terms of toleration and tribute; and Damascus is still peopled by twenty thousand Christians. But the valiant Thomas, and the free-born patriots who had fought under his banner, embraced the alternative of poverty and exile. In the adjacent meadow, a numerous encampment was formed of priests and laymen, of soldiers and citizens, of women and children: they collected, with haste and terror, their most precious movables; and abandoned, with loud lamentations, or silent anguish, their native homes, and the pleasant banks of the Pharpar. The inflexible soul of Caled was not touched by the spectacle of their distress: he disputed with the Damascenes the property of a magazine of corn; endeavored to exclude the garrison from the benefit of the treaty; consented, with reluctance, that each of the fugitives should arm himself with a sword, or a lance, or a bow; and sternly declared, that, after a respite of three days, they might be pursued and treated as the enemies of the Moslems.

The passion of a Syrian youth completed the ruin of the exiles of Damascus. A nobleman of the city, of the name of Jonas, was betrothed to a wealthy maiden; but her parents delayed the consummation of his nuptials, and their daughter was persuaded to escape with the man whom she had chosen. They corrupted the nightly watchmen of the gate Keisan; the lover, who led the way, was encompassed by a squadron of Arabs; but his exclamation in the Greek tongue, "The bird is taken," admonished his mistress to hasten her return. In the presence of Caled, and of death, the unfortunate Jonas professed his belief in one God and his apostle Mahomet; and continued, till the season of his martyrdom, to discharge the duties of a brave and sincere Mussulman. When the city was taken, he flew to the monastery, where Eudocia had taken refuge; but the lover was forgotten; the apostate was scorned; she preferred her religion to her country; and the justice of Caled, though deaf to mercy, refused to detain by force a male or female inhabitant of Damascus. Four days was the general confined to the city by the obligation of the treaty, and the urgent cares of his new conquest. His appetite for blood and rapine would have been extinguished by the hopeless computation of time and distance; but he listened to the importunities of Jonas, who assured him that the weary fugitives might yet be overtaken. At the head of four thousand horse, in the disguise of Christian Arabs, Caled undertook the pursuit. They halted only for the moments of prayer; and their guide had a perfect knowledge of the country. For a long way the footsteps of the Damascenes were plain and conspicuous: they vanished on a sudden; but the Saracens were comforted by the assurance that the caravan had turned aside into the mountains, and must speedily fall into their hands. In traversing the ridges of the Libanus, they endured intolerable hardships, and the sinking spirits of the veteran fanatics were supported and cheered by the unconquerable ardor of a lover. From a peasant of the country, they were informed that the emperor had sent orders to the colony of exiles to pursue without delay the road of the sea-coast, and of Constantinople, apprehensive, perhaps, that the soldiers and people of Antioch might be discouraged by the sight and the story of their sufferings. The Saracens were conducted through the territories of Gabala and Laodicea, at a cautious distance from the walls of the cities; the rain was incessant, the night was dark, a single mountain separated them from the Roman army; and Caled, ever anxious for the safety of his brethren, whispered an ominous dream in the ear of his companion. With the dawn of day, the prospect again cleared, and they saw before them, in a pleasant valley, the tents of Damascus. After a short interval of repose and prayer, Caled divided his cavalry into four squadrons, committing the first to his faithful Derar, and reserving the last for himself. They successively rushed on the promiscuous multitude, insufficiently provided with arms, and already vanquished by sorrow and fatigue. Except a captive, who was pardoned and dismissed, the Arabs enjoyed the satisfaction of believing that not a Christian of either sex escaped the edge of their cimeters. The gold and silver of Damascus was scattered over the camp, and a royal wardrobe of three hundred load of silk might clothe an army of naked Barbarians. In the tumult of the battle, Jonas sought and found the object of his pursuit: but her resentment was inflamed by the last act of his perfidy; and as Eudocia struggled in his hateful embraces, she struck a dagger to her heart. Another female, the widow of Thomas, and the real or supposed daughter of Heraclius, was spared and released without a ransom; but the generosity of Caled was the effect of his contempt; and the haughty Saracen insulted, by a message of defiance, the throne of the Cæsars. Caled had penetrated above a hundred and fifty miles into the heart of the Roman province: he returned to Damascus with the same secrecy and speed On the accession of Omar, the *Sword of God* was removed from the command; but the caliph, who blamed the rashness, was compelled to applaud the vigor and conduct, of the enterprise.

Conquests by the Arabs. – Part Four

ANOTHER EXPEDITION OF THE conquerors of Damascus will equally display their avidity and their contempt for the riches of the present world. They were informed that the produce and manufactures of the country were annually collected in the fair of Abyla, about thirty miles from the city; that the cell of a devout hermit was visited at the same time by a multitude of pilgrims; and that the festival of trade and superstition would be ennobled by the nuptials of the daughter of the governor of Tripoli. Abdallah, the son of Jaafar, a glorious and holy martyr, undertook, with a banner of five hundred horse, the pious and profitable commission of despoiling the infidels. As he approached the fair of Abyla, he was astonished by the report of this mighty concourse of Jews and Christians, Greeks, and Armenians, of natives of Syria and of strangers of Egypt, to the number of ten thousand, besides a guard of five thousand horse that attended the person of the bride. The Saracens paused: "For my own part," said Abdallah, "I *dare not* go back: our foes are many, our danger is great, but our reward is splendid and secure, either in this life or in the life to come. Let every man, according to his inclination, advance or retire.» Not a Mussulman deserted his standard. «Lead the way,» said Abdallah to his Christian guide, «and you shall see what the companions of the prophet can perform.» They charged in five squadrons; but after the first advantage of the surprise, they were encompassed and almost overwhelmed by the multitude of their enemies; and their valiant band is fancifully compared to a white spot in the skin of a black camel. About the hour of sunset, when their weapons dropped from their hands, when they panted on the verge of eternity, they discovered an approaching cloud of dust; they heard the welcome sound of the *tecbir*, and they soon perceived the standard of Caled, who flew to their relief with the utmost speed of his cavalry. The Christians were broken by his attack, and slaughtered in their flight, as far as the river of Tripoli. They left behind them the various riches of the fair; the merchandises that were exposed for sale, the money that was brought for purchase, the gay decorations of the nuptials, and the governor's daughter, with forty of her female attendants. The fruits, provisions, and furniture, the money, plate, and jewels, were diligently laden on the backs of horses, asses, and mules; and the holy robbers returned in triumph to Damascus. The hermit, after a short and angry controversy with Caled, declined the crown of martyrdom, and was left alive in the solitary scene of blood and devastation.

Conquests by the Arabs. – Part Five

SYRIA, ONE OF THE countries that have been improved by the most early cultivation, is not unworthy of the preference. The heat of the climate is tempered by the vicinity of the sea and mountains, by the plenty of wood and water; and the produce of a fertile soil affords the subsistence, and encourages the propagation, of men and animals. From the age of David to that of Heraclius, the country was overspread with ancient and flourishing cities: the inhabitants were numerous and wealthy; and, after the slow ravage of despotism and superstition, after the recent calamities of the Persian war, Syria could still attract and reward the rapacious tribes of the desert. A plain, of ten days' journey, from Damascus to Aleppo and Antioch, is watered, on the western side, by the winding course of the Orontes. The hills of Libanus and Anti-Libanus are planted from north to south, between the Orontes and the Mediterranean; and the epithet of *hollow* (Clesyria) was applied to a long and fruitful valley, which is confined in the same direction, by the two ridges of snowy mountains. Among the cities, which are enumerated by Greek and Oriental names in the geography and conquest of Syria, we may distinguish Emesa or Hems, Heliopolis or Baalbec, the former as the metropolis of the plain, the latter as the capital of the valley. Under the last of the Cæsars, they were strong and populous; the turrets glittered from afar: an ample space was covered with public and private buildings; and the citizens were illustrious by their spirit, or at least by their pride; by their riches, or at least by their luxury. In the days of Paganism, both Emesa and Heliopolis were addicted to the worship of Baal, or the sun; but the decline of their superstition and splendor has been marked by a singular variety of fortune. Not a vestige remains of the temple of Emesa, which was equalled in poetic style to the summits of Mount Libanus, while the ruins of Baalbec, invisible to the writers of antiquity, excite the curiosity and wonder of the European traveller. The measure of the temple is two hundred feet in length, and one hundred in breadth: the front is adorned with a double portico of eight columns; fourteen may be counted on either side; and each column, forty-five feet in height, is composed of three massy blocks of stone or marble. The proportions and ornaments of the Corinthian order express the architecture of the Greeks: but as Baalbec has never been the seat of a monarch, we are at a loss to conceive how the expense of these magnificent structures could be supplied by private or municipal liberality. From the conquest of Damascus the Saracens proceeded to Heliopolis and Emesa: but I shall decline the repetition of the sallies and combats which have been already shown on a larger scale. In the prosecution of the war, their policy was not less effectual than their sword. By short and separate truces they dissolved the union of the enemy; accustomed the Syrians to compare their friendship with their enmity; familiarized the idea of their language, religion, and manners; and exhausted, by clandestine purchase, the magazines and arsenals of the cities which they returned to besiege. They aggravated the ransom of the more wealthy, or the more obstinate; and Chalcis alone was taxed at five thousand ounces of gold, five thousand ounces of silver, two thousand robes of silk, and as many figs and olives as would load five thousand asses. But the terms of truce or capitulation were faithfully observed; and the lieutenant of the caliph, who had promised not to enter the walls of the captive Baalbec, remained tranquil and immovable in his tent till the jarring factions solicited the interposition of a foreign master. The conquest of the plain and valley of Syria was achieved in less than two years. Yet the commander of the faithful reproved the slowness of their progress; and the Saracens, bewailing their fault with tears of rage and repentance, called aloud on their chiefs to lead them forth to fight the battles of the Lord. In a recent action, under the walls of Emesa, an Arabian youth, the cousin of Caled, was heard aloud to exclaim, «Methinks I see the black-eyed girls looking upon me; one of whom, should she appear in this world, all mankind would die for love of her. And I see in the hand of one of them a handkerchief of green silk, and a cap of precious stones, and she beckons me, and calls out, Come hither quickly, for I love thee.» With these words, charging the Christians, he made havoc wherever he went, till, observed at length by the governor of Hems, he was struck through with a javelin.

It was incumbent on the Saracens to exert the full powers of their valor and enthusiasm against the forces of the emperor, who was taught, by repeated losses, that the rovers of the desert had undertaken, and would speedily achieve, a regular and permanent conquest. From the provinces of Europe and Asia, fourscore thousand soldiers were transported by sea and land to Antioch and Cæsarea: the light troops of the army consisted of sixty thousand Christian Arabs of the tribe of Gassan. Under the banner of Jabalah, the last of their princes, they marched in the van; and it was a maxim of the Greeks, that for the purpose of cutting diamond, a diamond was the most effectual. Heraclius withheld his person from the dangers of the field; but his presumption, or perhaps his despondency, suggested a peremptory order, that the fate of the province and the war should be decided by a single battle. The Syrians were attached to the standard of Rome and of the cross: but the noble, the citizen, the peasant, were exasperated by the injustice and cruelty of a licentious host, who oppressed them as subjects, and despised them as strangers and aliens. A report of these mighty preparations was conveyed to the Saracens in their camp of Emesa, and the chiefs, though resolved to fight, assembled a council: the faith of Abu Obeidah would have expected on the same spot the glory of martyrdom; the wisdom of Caled advised an honorable retreat to the skirts of Palestine and Arabia, where they might await the succors of their friends, and the attack of the unbelievers. A speedy messenger soon returned from the throne of Medina, with the blessings of Omar and Ali, the prayers of the widows of the prophet, and a reënforcement of eight thousand Moslems. In their way they overturned a detachment of Greeks, and when they joined at Yermuk the camp of their brethren, they found the pleasing intelligence, that Caled had already defeated and scattered the Christian Arabs of the tribe of Gassan. In the neighborhood of Bosra, the springs of Mount Hermon descend in a torrent to the plain of Decapolis, or ten cities; and the Hieromax, a name which has been corrupted to Yermuk, is lost, after a short course, in the Lake of Tiberias. The banks of this obscure stream were illustrated by a long and bloody encounter. On this momentous occasion, the public voice, and the modesty of Abu Obeidah, restored the command to the most deserving of the Moslems. Caled assumed his station in the front, his colleague was posted in the rear, that the disorder of the fugitive might be checked by his venerable aspect, and the sight of the yellow banner which Mahomet had displayed before the walls of Chaibar. The last line was occupied by the sister of Derar, with the Arabian women who had enlisted in this holy war, who were accustomed to wield the bow and the lance, and who in a moment of captivity had defended, against the uncircumcised ravishers, their chastity and religion. The exhortation of the generals was brief and forcible: "Paradise is before you, the devil and hell-fire in your rear." Yet such was the weight of the Roman cavalry, that the right wing of the Arabs was broken and separated from the main body. Thrice did they retreat in disorder, and thrice were they driven back to the charge by the reproaches and blows of the women. In the intervals of action, Abu Obeidah visited the tents of his brethren, prolonged their repose by repeating at once the prayers of two different hours, bound up their wounds with his own hands, and administered the comfortable reflection, that the infidels partook of their sufferings without partaking of their reward. Four thousand and thirty of the Moslems were buried in the field of battle; and the skill of the Armenian archers enabled seven hundred to boast that they had lost an eye in that meritorious service. The veterans of the Syrian war acknowledged that it was the hardest and most doubtful of the days which they had seen. But it was likewise the most decisive: many thousands of the Greeks and Syrians fell by the swords of the Arabs; many were slaughtered, after the defeat, in the woods and mountains; many, by mistaking the ford, were drowned in the waters of the Yermuk; and however the loss may be magnified, the Christian writers confess and bewail the bloody punishment of their sins. Manuel, the Roman general, was either killed at Damascus, or took refuge in the monastery of Mount Sinai. An exile in the Byzantine court, Jabalah lamented the manners of Arabia, and his unlucky preference of the Christian cause. He had once inclined to the profession of Islam; but in the pilgrimage of Mecca, Jabalah was provoked to strike one of his brethren, and fled with amazement from the stern and equal justice of the caliph. These victorious Saracens enjoyed at Damascus a month of pleasure and repose: the spoil was divided by the discretion of Abu Obeidah: an equal share was allotted to a soldier and to his horse, and a double portion was reserved for the noble coursers of the Arabian breed.

After the battle of Yermuk, the Roman army no longer appeared in the field; and the Saracens might securely choose, among the fortified towns of Syria, the first object of their attack. They consulted the caliph whether they should march to Cæsarea or Jerusalem; and the advice of Ali determined the immediate siege of the latter. To a profane eye, Jerusalem was the first or second capital of Palestine; but after Mecca and Medina, it was revered and visited by the devout Moslems, as the temple of the Holy Land which had been sanctified by the revelation of Moses, of Jesus, and of Mahomet himself. The son of Abu Sophian was sent with five thousand Arabs to try the first experiment of surprise or treaty; but on the eleventh day, the town was invested by the whole force of Abu

Obeidah. He addressed the customary summons to the chief commanders and people of *Ælia*.

"Health and happiness to every one that follows the right way! We require of you to testify that there is but one God, and that Mahomet is his apostle. If you refuse this, consent to pay tribute, and be under us forthwith. Otherwise I shall bring men against you who love death better than you do the drinking of wine or eating hog's flesh. Nor will I ever stir from you, if it please God, till I have destroyed those that fight for you, and made slaves of your children." But the city was defended on every side by deep valleys and steep ascents; since the invasion of Syria, the walls and towers had been anxiously restored; the bravest of the fugitives of Yermuk had stopped in the nearest place of refuge; and in the defence of the sepulchre of Christ, the natives and strangers might feel some sparks of the enthusiasm, which so fiercely glowed in the bosoms of the Saracens. The siege of Jerusalem lasted four months; not a day was lost without some action of sally or assault; the military engines incessantly played from the ramparts; and the inclemency of the winter was still more painful and destructive to the Arabs. The Christians yielded at length to the perseverance of the besiegers. The patriarch Sophronius appeared on the walls, and by the voice of an interpreter demanded a conference. After a vain attempt to dissuade the lieutenant of the caliph from his impious enterprise, he proposed, in the name of the people, a fair capitulation, with this extraordinary clause, that the articles of security should be ratified by the authority and presence of Omar himself. The question was debated in the council of Medina; the sanctity of the place, and the advice of Ali, persuaded the caliph to gratify the wishes of his soldiers and enemies; and the simplicity of his journey is more illustrious than the royal pageants of vanity and oppression. The conqueror of Persia and Syria was mounted on a red camel, which carried, besides his person, a bag of corn, a bag of dates, a wooden dish, and a leathern bottle of water. Wherever he halted, the company, without distinction, was invited to partake of his homely fare, and the repast was consecrated by the prayer and exhortation of the commander of the faithful. But in this expedition or pilgrimage, his power was exercised in the administration of justice: he reformed the licentious polygamy of the Arabs, relieved the tributaries from extortion and cruelty, and chastised the luxury of the Saracens, by despoiling them of their rich silks, and dragging them on their faces in the dirt. When he came within sight of Jerusalem, the caliph cried with a loud voice, "God is victorious. O Lord, give us an easy conquest!" and, pitching his tent of coarse hair, calmly seated himself on the ground. After signing the capitulation, he entered the city without fear or precaution; and courteously discoursed with the patriarch concerning its religious antiquities. Sophronius bowed before his new master, and secretly muttered, in the words of Daniel, "The abomination of desolation is in the holy place." At the hour of prayer they stood together in the church of the resurrection; but the caliph refused to perform his devotions, and contented himself with praying on the steps of the church of Constantine. To the patriarch he disclosed his prudent and honorable motive. "Had I yielded," said Omar, "to your request, the Moslems of a future age would have infringed the treaty under color of imitating my example." By his command the ground of the temple of Solomon was prepared for the foundation of a mosch; and, during a residence of ten days, he regulated the present and future state of his Syrian conquests. Medina might be jealous, lest the caliph should be detained by the sanctity of Jerusalem or the beauty of Damascus; her apprehensions were dispelled by his prompt and voluntary return to the tomb of the apostle.

To achieve what yet remained of the Syrian war the caliph had formed two separate armies; a chosen detachment, under Amrou and Yezid, was left in the camp of Palestine; while the larger division, under the standard of Abu Obeidah and Caled, marched away to the north against Antioch and Aleppo. The latter of these, the Beræa of the Greeks, was not yet illustrious as the capital of a province or a kingdom; and the inhabitants, by anticipating their submission and pleading their poverty, obtained a moderate composition for their lives and religion. But the castle of Aleppo, distinct from the city, stood erect on a lofty artificial mound; the sides were sharpened to a precipice, and faced with free-stone; and the breadth of the ditch might be filled with water from the neighboring springs. After the loss of three thousand men, the garrison was still equal to the defence; and Youkinna, their valiant and hereditary chief, had murdered his brother, a holy monk, for daring to pronounce the name of peace. In a siege of four or five months, the hardest of the Syrian war, great numbers of the Saracens were killed and wounded: their removal to the distance of a mile could not seduce the vigilance of Youkinna; nor could the Christians be terrified by the execution of three hundred captives, whom they beheaded before the castle wall. The silence, and at length the complaints, of Abu Obeidah informed the caliph that their hope and patience were consumed at the foot of this impregnable fortress. "I am variously affected," replied Omar, "by the difference of your success; but I charge you by no means to raise the siege of the castle. Your retreat would diminish the reputation of our arms, and encourage the infidels to fall upon you on all sides. Remain before Aleppo till God shall determine the event, and forage with your horse round the adjacent country." The exhortation of the commander of the faithful was fortified by a supply of volunteers from all the tribes of Arabia, who arrived in the camp on horses or camels. Among these was Dames, of a servile birth, but of gigantic size and intrepid resolution. The forty-seventh day of his service he proposed, with only thirty men, to make an attempt on the castle. The experience and testimony of Caled recommended his offer; and Abu Obeidah admonished his brethren not to despise the baser origin of Dames, since he himself, could he relinquish the public care, would cheerfully serve under the banner of the slave. His design was covered by the appearance of a retreat; and the camp of the Saracens was pitched about a league from Aleppo. The thirty adventurers lay in ambush at the foot of the hill; and Dames at length succeeded in his inquiries, though he was provoked by the ignorance of his Greek captives. "God curse these dogs," said the illiterate Arab; "what a strange barbarous language they speak!" At the darkest hour of the night, he scaled the most accessible height, which he had diligently surveyed, a place where the stones were less entire, or the slope less perpendicular, or the guard less vigilant. Seven of the stoutest Saracens mounted on each other's shoulders, and the weight of the column was sustained on the broad and sinewy back of the gigantic slave. The foremost in this painful ascent could grasp and climb the lowest part of the battlements; they silently stabbed and cast down the sentinels; and the thirty brethren, repeating a pious ejaculation, "O apostle of God, help and deliver us!" were successively drawn up by the long folds of their turbans. With bold and cautious footsteps, Dames explored the palace of the governor, who celebrated, in riotous merriment, the festival of his deliverance. From thence, returning to his companions, he assaulted on the inside the entrance of the castle. They overpowered the guard, unbolted the gate, let down the drawbridge, and defended the narrow pass, till the arrival of Caled, with the dawn of day, relieved their danger and assured their conquest. Youkinna, a formidable foe, became an active and useful proselyte; and the general of the Saracens expressed his regard for the most humble merit, by detaining the army at Aleppo till Dames was cured of his honorable wounds. The capital of Syria was still covered by the castle of Aazaz and the iron bridge of the Orontes. After the loss of those important posts, and the defeat of the last of the Roman armies, the luxury of Antioch trembled and obeyed. Her safety was ransomed with three hundred thousand pieces of gold; but the throne of the successors of Alexander, the seat of the Roman government of the East, which had been decorated by Cæsar with the titles of free, and holy, and inviolate was degraded under the yoke of the caliphs to the secondary rank of a provincial town.

In the life of Heraclius, the glories of the Persian war are clouded on either hand by the disgrace and weakness of his more early and his later days. When the successors of Mahomet unsheathed the sword of war and religion, he was astonished at the boundless prospect of toil and danger; his nature was indolent, nor could the infirm and frigid age of the emperor be kindled to a second effort. The sense of shame, and the importunities of the Syrians, prevented the hasty departure from the scene of action; but the hero was no more; and the loss of Damascus and Jerusalem, the bloody fields of Aiznadin and Yermuk, may be imputed in some degree to the absence or misconduct of the sovereign. Instead of defending the sepulchre of Christ, he involved the church and state in a metaphysical controversy for the unity of his will; and while Heraclius crowned the offspring of his second nuptials, he was tamely stripped of the most valuable part of their inheritance. In the cathedral of Antioch, in the presence of the bishops, at the foot of the crucifix, he bewailed the sins of the prince and people; but his confession instructed the world, that it was vain, and perhaps impious, to resist the judgment of God. The Saracens were invincible in fact, since they were invincible in opinion; and the desertion of Youkinna, his false repentance and repeated perfidy, might justify the suspicion of the emperor, that he was encompassed by traitors and apostates, who conspired to betray his person and their country to the enemies of Christ. In the hour of adversity, his superstition was agitated by the omens and dreams of a falling crown; and after bidding an eternal farewell to Syria, he secretly embarked with a few attendants, and absolved the faith of his subjects. Constantine, his eldest son, had been stationed with forty thousand men at Cæsarea, the civil metropolis of the three provinces of Palestine. But his private interest recalled him to the Byzantine court; and, after the flight of his father, he felt himself an unequal champion to the united force of the caliph. His vanguard was boldly attacked by three hundred Arabs and a thousand black slaves, who, in the depth of winter, had climbed the snowy mountains of Libanus, and who were speedily followed by the victorious squadrons of Caled himself. From the north and south the troops of Antioch and Jerusalem advanced along the seashore till their banners were joined under the walls of the Phœnician cities: Tripoli and Tyre were betrayed; and a fleet of fifty transports, which entered without distrust the captive harbors, brought a seasonable supply of arms and provisions to the camp of the Saracens. Their labors were terminated by the unexpected surrender of Cæsarea: the Roman prince had embarked in the night; and the defenceless citizens solicited their pardon with an offering of two hundred thousand pieces of gold. The remainder of the province, Ramlah, Ptolemais or Acre, Sichem or Neapolis, Gaza, Ascalon, Berytus, Sidon, Gabala, Laodicea, Apamea, Hierapolis, no longer presumed to dispute the will of the conqueror; and Syria bowed under the sceptre of the caliphs seven hundred years after Pompey had despoiled the last of the Macedonian kings.

Conquests by the Arabs. – Part Six

THE SIEGES AND BATTLES of six campaigns had consumed many thousands of the Moslems. They died with the reputation and the cheerfulness of martyrs; and the simplicity of their faith may be expressed in the words of an Arabian youth, when he embraced, for the last time, his sister and mother: "It is not," said he, "the delicacies of Syria, or the fading delights of this world, that have prompted me to devote my life in the cause of religion. But I seek the favor of God and his apostle; and I have heard, from one of the companions of the prophet, that the spirits of the martyrs will be lodged in the crops of green birds, who shall taste the fruits, and drink of the rivers, of paradise. Farewell, we shall meet again among the groves and fountains which God has provided for his elect." The faithful captives might exercise a passive and more arduous resolution; and a cousin of Mahomet is celebrated for refusing, after an abstinence of three days, the wine and pork, the only nourishment that was allowed by the malice of the infidels. The frailty of some weaker brethren exasperated the implacable spirit of fanaticism; and the father of Amer deplored, in pathetic strains, the apostasy and damnation of a son, who had renounced the promises of God, and the intercession of the prophet, to occupy, with the priests and deacons, the lowest mansions of hell. The more fortunate Arabs, who survived the war and persevered in the faith, were restrained by their abstemious leader from the abuse of prosperity. After a refreshment of three days, Abu Obeidah withdrew his troops from the pernicious contagion of the luxury of Antioch, and assured the caliph that their religion and virtue could only be preserved by the hard discipline of poverty and labor. But the virtue of Omar, however rigorous to himself, was kind and liberal to his brethren. After a just tribute of praise and thanksgiving, he dropped a tear of compassion; and sitting down on the ground, wrote an answer, in which he mildly censured the severity of his lieutenant: "God," said the successor of the prophet, "has not forbidden the use of the good things of this world to faithful men, and such as have performed good works. Therefore you ought to have given them leave to rest themselves, and partake freely of those good things which the country affordeth. If any of the Saracens have no family in Arabia, they may marry in Syria; and whosoever of them wants any female slaves, he may purchase as many as he hath occasion for." The conquerors prepared to use, or to abuse, this gracious permission; but the year of their triumph was marked by a mortality of men and cattle; and twenty-five thousand Saracens were snatched away from the possession of Syria. The death of Abu Obeidah might be lamented by the Christians; but his brethren recollected that he was one of the ten elect whom the prophet had named as the heirs of paradise. Caled survived his brethren about three years: and the tomb of the Sword of God is shown in the neighborhood of Emesa. His valor, which founded in Arabia and Syria the empire of the caliphs, was fortified by the opinion of a special providence; and as long as he wore a cap, which had been blessed by Mahomet, he deemed himself invulnerable amidst the darts of the infidels.

The place of the first conquerors was supplied by a new generation of their children and countrymen: Syria became the seat and support of the house of Ommiyah; and the revenue, the soldiers, the ships of that powerful kingdom were consecrated to enlarge on every side the empire of the caliphs. But the Saracens despise a superfluity of fame; and their historians scarcely condescend to mention the subordinate conquests which are lost in the splendor and rapidity of their victorious career. To the *north* of Syria, they passed Mount Taurus, and reduced to their obedience the province of Cilicia, with its capital Tarsus, the ancient monument of the Assyrian kings. Beyond a second ridge of the same mountains, they spread the flame of war, rather than the light of religion, as far as the shores of the Euxine, and the neighborhood of Constantinople. To the *east* they advanced to the banks and sources of the Euphrates and Tigris: the long disputed barrier of Rome and Persia was forever confounded; the walls of Edessa and Amida, of Dara and Nisibis, which had resisted the arms and engines of Sapor or Nushirvan, were levelled in the dust; and the holy city of Abgarus might vainly produce the epistle or the image of Christ to an unbelieving conqueror. To the *west* the Syrian kingdom is bounded by the sea: and the ruin of Aradus, a small island or peninsula on the coast, was postponed during ten years. But the hills of Libanus abounded in timber; the trade of

Phœnicia was populous in mariners; and a fleet of seventeen hundred barks was equipped and manned by the natives of the desert. The Imperial navy of the Romans fled before them from the Pamphylian rocks to the Hellespont; but the spirit of the emperor, a grandson of Heraclius, had been subdued before the combat by a dream and a pun. The Saracens rode masters of the sea; and the islands of Cyprus, Rhodes, and the Cyclades, were successively exposed to their rapacious visits. Three hundred years before the Christian æra, the memorable though fruitless siege of Rhodes by Demetrius had furnished that maritime republic with the materials and the subject of a trophy. A gigantic statue of Apollo, or the sun, seventy cubits in height, was erected at the entrance of the harbor, a monument of the freedom and the arts of Greece. After standing fifty-six years, the colossus of Rhodes was overthrown by an earthquake; but the massy trunk, and huge fragments, lay scattered eight centuries on the ground, and are often described as one of the wonders of the ancient world. They were collected by the diligence of the Saracens, and sold to a Jewish merchant of Edessa, who is said to have laden nine hundred camels with the weight of the brass metal; an enormous weight, though we should include the hundred colossal figures, and the three thousand statues, which adorned the prosperity of the city of the sun.

III. The conquest of Egypt may be explained by the character of the victorious Saracen, one of the first of his nation, in an age when the meanest of the brethren was exalted above his nature by the spirit of enthusiasm. The birth of Amrou was at once base and illustrious; his mother, a notorious prostitute, was unable to decide among five of the Koreish; but the proof of resemblance adjudged the child to Aasi, the oldest of her lovers. The youth of Amrou was impelled by the passions and prejudices of his kindred: his poetic genius was exercised in satirical verses against the person and doctrine of Mahomet; his dexterity was employed by the reigning faction to pursue the religious exiles who had taken refuge in the court of the Æthiopian king. Yet he returned from this embassy a secret proselyte; his reason or his interest determined him to renounce the worship of idols; he escaped from Mecca with his friend Caled; and the prophet of Medina enjoyed at the same moment the satisfaction of embracing the two firmest champions of his cause. The impatience of Amrou to lead the armies of the faithful was checked by the reproof of Omar, who advised him not to seek power and dominion, since he who is a subject to-day, may be a prince to-morrow. Yet his merit was not overlooked by the two first successors of Mahomet; they were indebted to his arms for the conquest of Palestine; and in all the battles and sieges of Syria, he united with the temper of a chief the valor of an adventurous soldier. In a visit to Medina, the caliph expressed a wish to survey the sword which had cut down so many Christian warriors; the son of Aasi unsheathed a short and ordinary cimeter; and as he perceived the surprise of Omar, "Alas," said the modest Saracen, "the sword itself, without the arm of its master, is neither sharper nor more weighty than the sword of Pharezdak the poet." After the conquest of Egypt, he was recalled by the jealousy of the caliph Othman; but in the subsequent troubles, the ambition of a soldier, a statesman, and an orator, emerged from a private station. His powerful support, both in council and in the field, established the throne of the Ommiades; the administration and revenue of Egypt were restored by the gratitude of Moawiyah to a faithful friend who had raised himself above the rank of a subject; and Amrou ended his days in the palace and city which he had founded on the banks of the Nile. His dying speech to his children is celebrated by the Arabians as a model of eloquence and wisdom: he deplored the errors of his youth but if the penitent was still infected by the vanity of a poet, he might exaggerate the venom and mischief of his impious compositions.

From his camp in Palestine, Amrou had surprised or anticipated the caliph's leave for the invasion of Egypt. The magnanimous Omar trusted in his God and his sword, which had shaken the thrones of Chosroes and Cæsar: but when he compared the slender force of the Moslems with the greatness of the enterprise, he condemned his own rashness, and listened to his timid companions. The pride and the greatness of Pharaoh were familiar to the readers of the Koran; and a tenfold repetition of prodigies had been scarcely sufficient to effect, not the victory, but the flight, of six hundred thousand of the children of Israel: the cities of Egypt were many and populous; their architecture was strong and solid; the Nile, with its numerous branches, was alone an insuperable barrier; and the granary of the Imperial city would be obstinately defended by the Roman powers. In this perplexity, the commander of the faithful resigned himself to the decision of chance, or, in his opinion, of Providence. At the head of only four thousand Arabs, the intrepid Amrou had marched away from his station of Gaza when he was overtaken by the messenger of Omar. "If you are still in Syria," said the ambiguous mandate, "retreat without delay; but if, at the receipt of this epistle, you have already reached the frontiers of Egypt, advance with confidence, and depend on the succor of God and of your brethren." The experience, perhaps the secret intelligence, of Amrou had taught him to suspect the mutability of courts; and he continued his march till his tents were unquestionably pitched on Egyptian ground. He there assembled his officers, broke the seal, perused the epistle, gravely inquired the name and situation of the place, and declared his ready obedience to the commands of the caliph. After a siege of thirty days, he took possession of Farmah or Pelusium; and that key of Egypt, as it has been justly named, unlocked the entrance of the country as far as the ruins of Heliopolis and the neighborhood of the modern Cairo.

On the Western side of the Nile, at a small distance to the east of the Pyramids, at a small distance to the south of the Delta, Memphis, one hundred and fifty furlongs in circumference, displayed the magnificence of ancient kings. Under the reign of the Ptolemies and Cæsars, the seat of government was removed to the sea-coast; the ancient capital was eclipsed by the arts and opulence of Alexandria; the palaces, and at length the temples, were reduced to a desolate and ruinous condition: yet, in the age of Augustus, and even in that of Constantine, Memphis was still numbered among the greatest and most populous of the provincial cities. The banks of the Nile, in this place of the breadth of three thousand feet, were united by two bridges of sixty and of thirty boats, connected in the middle stream by the small island of Rouda, which was covered with gardens and habitations. The eastern extremity of the bridge was terminated by the town of Babylon and the camp of a Roman legion, which protected the passage of the river and the second capital of Egypt. This important fortress, which might fairly be described as a part of Memphis or *Misrah*, was invested by the arms of the lieutenant of Omar: a reënforcement of four thousand Saracens soon arrived in his camp; and the military engines, which battered the walls, may be imputed to the art and labor of his Syrian allies. Yet the siege was protracted to seven months; and the rash invaders were encompassed and threatened by the inundation of the Nile. Their last assault was bold and successful: they passed the ditch, which had been fortified with iron spikes, applied their scaling ladders, entered the fortress with the shout of "God is victorious!" and drove the remnant of the Greeks to their boats and the Isle of Rouda. The spot was afterwards recommended to the conqueror by the easy communication with the gulf and the peninsula of Arabia; the remains of Memphis were deserted; the tents of the Arabs were converted into permanent habitations; and the first mosch was blessed by the presence of fourscore companions of Mahomet. A new city arose in their camp, on the eastward bank of the Nile; and the contiguous quarters of Babylon and Fostat are confounded in their present decay by the appellation of old Misrah, or Cairo, of which they form an extensive suburb. But the name of Cairo, the town of victory, more strictly belongs to the modern capital, which was founded in the tenth century by the Fatimite caliphs. It has gradually receded from the river; but the continuity of buildings may be traced by an attentive eye from the monuments of Sesostris to those of Saladin.

Yet the Arabs, after a glorious and profitable enterprise, must have retreated to the desert, had they not found a powerful alliance in the heart of the country. The rapid conquest of Alexander was assisted by the superstition and revolt of the natives: they abhorred their Persian oppressors, the disciples of the Magi, who had burnt the temples of Egypt, and feasted with sacrilegious appetite on the flesh of the god Apis. After a period of ten centuries, the same revolution was renewed by a similar cause; and in the support of an incomprehensible creed, the zeal of the Coptic Christians was equally ardent. I have already explained the origin and progress of the Monophysite controversy, and the persecution of the emperors, which converted a sect into a nation, and alienated Egypt from their religion and government. The Saracens were received as the deliverers of the Jacobite church; and a secret and effectual treaty was opened during the siege of Memphis between a victorious army and a people of slaves. A rich and noble Egyptian, of the name of Mokawkas, had dissembled his faith to obtain the administration of his province: in the disorders of the Persian war he aspired to independence: the embassy of Mahomet ranked him among princes; but he declined, with rich gifts and ambiguous compliments, the proposal of a new religion. The abuse of his trust exposed him to the resentment of Heraclius: his submission was delayed by arrogance and fear; and his conscience was prompted by interest to throw himself on the favor of the nation and the support of the Saracens. In his first conference with Amrou, he heard without indignation the usual option of the Koran, the tribute, or the sword. "The Greeks," replied Mokawkas, "are determined to abide the determination of the sword; but with the Greeks I desire no communion, either in this world or in the next, and I abjure forever the Byzantine tyrant, his synod of Chalcedon, and his Melchite slaves. For myself and my brethren, we are resolved to live and die in the profession of the gospel and unity of Christ. It is impossible for us to embrace the revelations of your prophet; but we are desirous of peace, and cheerfully submit to pay tribute and obedience to his temporal successors." The tribute was ascertained at two pieces of gold for the head of every Christian; but old men, monks, women, and children, of both sexes, under sixteen years of age, were exempted from this personal assessment: the Copts above and below Memphis swore allegiance to the caliph, and promised a hospitable entertainment of three days to every Mussulman who should travel through their country. By this charter of security, the ecclesiastical and civil tyranny of the Melchites was destroyed: the anathemas of St. Cyril were thundered from every pulpit; and the sacred edifices, with the patrimony of the church, were restored to the national communion of the Jacobites, who enjoyed without moderation the moment of triumph and revenge. At the pressing summons of Amrou, their patriarch Benjamin emerged from his desert; and after the first interview, the courteous Arab affected to declare that he had never conversed with a Christian priest of more innocent manners and a more venerable aspect. In the march from Memphis to Alexandria, the lieutenant of Omar intrusted his safety to the zeal and gratitude of the Egyptians: the roads and bridges were diligently repaired; and in every step of his progress, he could depend on a constant supply of provisions and intelligence. The Greeks of Egypt, whose numbers could scarcely equal a tenth of the natives, were overwhelmed by the universal defection: they had ever been hated, they were no longer feared: the magistrate fled from his tribunal, the bishop from his altar; and the distant garrisons were surprised or starved by the surrounding multitudes. Had not the Nile afforded a safe and ready conveyance to the sea, not an individual could have escaped, who by birth, or language, or office, or religion, was connected with their odious name.

By the retreat of the Greeks from the provinces of Upper Egypt, a considerable force was collected in the Island of Delta; the natural and artificial channels of the Nile afforded a succession of strong and defensible posts; and the road to Alexandria was laboriously cleared by the victory of the Saracens in two-and-twenty days of general or partial combat. In their annals of conquest, the siege of Alexandria is perhaps the most arduous and important enterprise. The first trading city in the world was abundantly replenished with the means of subsistence and defence. Her numerous inhabitants fought for the dearest of human rights, religion and property; and the enmity of the natives seemed to exclude them from the common benefit of peace and toleration. The sea was continually open; and if Heraclius had been awake to the public distress, fresh armies of Romans and Barbarians might have been poured into the harbor to save the second capital of the empire. A circumference of ten miles would have scattered the forces of the Greeks, and favored the stratagems of an active enemy; but the two sides of an oblong square were covered by the sea and the Lake Maræotis, and each of the narrow ends exposed a front of no more than ten furlongs. The efforts of the Arabs were not inadequate to the difficulty of the attempt and the value of the prize.

From the throne of Medina, the eyes of Omar were fixed on the camp and city: his voice excited to arms the Arabian tribes and the veterans of Syria; and the merit of a holy war was recommended by the peculiar fame and fertility of Egypt. Anxious for the ruin or expulsion of their tyrants, the faithful natives devoted their labors to the service of Amrou: some sparks of martial spirit were perhaps rekindled by the example of their allies; and the sanguine hopes of Mokawkas had fixed his sepulchre in the church of St. John of Alexandria. Eutychius the patriarch observes, that the Saracens fought with the courage of lions: they repulsed the frequent and almost daily sallies of the besieged, and soon assaulted in their turn the walls and towers of the city. In every attack, the sword, the banner of Amrou, glittered in the van of the Moslems. On a memorable day, he was betrayed by his imprudent valor: his followers who had entered the citadel were driven back; and the general, with a friend and slave, remained a prisoner in the hands of the Christians. When Amrou was conducted before the præfect, he remembered his dignity, and forgot his situation: a lofty demeanor, and resolute language, revealed the lieutenant of the caliph, and the battle-axe of a soldier was already raised to strike off the head of the audacious captive. His life was saved by the readiness of his slave, who instantly gave his master a blow on the face, and commanded him, with an angry tone, to be silent in the presence of his superiors. The credulous Greek was deceived: he listened to the offer of a treaty, and his prisoners were dismissed in the hope of a more respectable embassy, till the joyful acclamations of the camp announced the return of their general, and insulted the folly of the infidels. At length, after a siege of fourteen months, and the loss of three-and-twenty thousand men, the Saracens prevailed: the Greeks embarked their dispirited and diminished numbers, and the standard of Mahomet was planted on the walls of the capital of Egypt. "I have taken," said Amrou to the caliph, "the great city of the West. It is impossible for me to enumerate the variety of its riches and beauty; and I shall content myself with observing, that it contains four thousand palaces, four thousand baths, four hundred theatres or places of amusement, twelve thousand shops for the sale of vegetable food, and forty thousand tributary Jews. The town has been subdued by force of arms, without treaty or capitulation, and the Moslems are impatient to seize the fruits of their victory." The commander of the faithful rejected with firmness the idea of pillage, and directed his lieutenant to reserve the wealth and revenue of Alexandria for the public service and the propagation of the faith: the inhabitants were numbered; a tribute was imposed, the zeal and resentment of the Jacobites were curbed, and the Melchites who submitted to the Arabian yoke were indulged in the obscure but tranquil exercise of their worship. The intelligence of this disgraceful and calamitous event afflicted the declining health of the emperor; and Heraclius died of a dropsy about seven weeks after the loss of Alexandria. Under the minority of his grandson, the clamors of a people, deprived of their daily sustenance, compelled the Byzantine court to undertake the recovery of the capital of Egypt. In the space of four years, the harbor and fortifications of Alexandria were twice occupied by a fleet and army of Romans. They were twice expelled by the valor of Amrou, who was recalled by the domestic peril from the distant wars of Tripoli and Nubia. But the facility of the attempt, the repetition of the insult, and the obstinacy of the resistance, provoked him to swear, that if a third time he drove the infidels into the sea, he would render Alexandria as accessible on all sides as the house of a prostitute. Faithful to his promise, he dismantled several parts of the walls and towers; but the people was spared in the chastisement of the city, and the mosch of *Mercy* was erected on the spot where the victorious general had stopped the fury of his troops.

Conquests by the Arabs. – Part Seven

I SHOULD DECEIVE THE expectation of the reader, if I passed in silence the fate of the Alexandrian library, as it is described by the learned Abulpharagius. The spirit of Amrou was more curious and liberal than that of his brethren, and in his leisure hours, the Arabian chief was pleased with the conversation of John, the last disciple of Ammonius, and who derived the surname of *Philoponus* from his laborious studies of grammar and philosophy. Emboldened by this familiar intercourse, Philoponus presumed to solicit a gift, inestimable in *his* opinion, contemptible in that of the Barbarians – the royal library, which alone, among the spoils of Alexandria, had not been appropriated by the visit and the seal of the conqueror. Amrou was inclined to gratify the wish of the grammarian, but his rigid integrity refused to alienate the minutest object without the consent of the caliph; and the well-known answer of Omar was inspired by the ignorance of a fanatic. «If these writings of the Greeks agree with the book of God, they are useless, and need not be preserved: if they disagree, they are pernicious, and ought to be destroyed.» The sentence was executed with blind obedience: the volumes of paper or parchment were distributed to the four thousand baths of the city; and such was their incredible multitude, that six months were barely sufficient for the consumption of this precious fuel. Since the Dynasties of Abulpharagius have been given to the world in a Latin version, the tale has been repeatedly transcribed; and every scholar, with pious indignation, has deplored the irreparable shipwreck of the learning, the arts, and the genius, of antiquity. For my own part, I am strongly tempted to deny both the fact and the consequences. The fact is indeed marvellous. «Read and wonder!» says the historian himself: and the solitary report of a stranger who wrote at the end of six hundred years on the confines of Media, is overbalanced by the silence of two annalist of a more early date, both Christians, both natives of Egypt, and the most ancient of whom, the patriarch Eutychius, has amply described the conquest of Alexandria. The rigid sentence of Omar is repugnant to the sound and orthodox precept of the Mahometan casuists they expressly declare, that the religious books of the Jews and Christians, which are acquired by the right of war, should never be committed to the flames; and that the works of profane science, historians or poets, physicians or philosophers, may be lawfully applied to the use of the faithful. A more destructive zeal may perhaps be attributed to the first successors of Mahomet; yet in this instance, the conflagration would have speedily expired in the deficiency of materials. I should not recapitulate the disasters of the Alexandrian library, the involuntary flame that was kindled by Cæsar in his own defence, or the mischievous bigotry of the Christians, who studied to destroy the monuments of idolatry. But if we gradually descend from the age of the Antonines to that of Theodosius, we shall learn from a chain of contemporary witnesses, that the royal palace and the temple of Serapis no longer contained the four, or the seven, hundred thousand volumes, which had been assembled by the curiosity and magnificence of the Ptolemies. Perhaps the church and seat of the patriarchs might be enriched with a repository of books; but if the ponderous mass of Arian and Monophysite controversy were indeed consumed in the public baths, a philosopher may allow, with a smile, that it was ultimately devoted to the benefit of mankind. I sincerely regret the more valuable libraries which have been involved in the ruin of the Roman empire; but when I seriously compute the lapse of ages, the waste of ignorance, and the calamities of war, our treasures, rather than our losses, are the objects of my surprise. Many curious and interesting facts are buried in oblivion: the three great historians of Rome have been transmitted to our hands in a mutilated state, and we are deprived of many pleasing compositions of the lyric, iambic, and dramatic poetry of the Greeks. Yet we should gratefully remember, that the mischances of time and accident have spared the classic works to which the suffrage of antiquity had adjudged the first place of genius and glory: the teachers of ancient knowledge, who are still extant, had perused and compared the writings of their predecessors; nor can it fairly be presumed that any important truth, any useful discovery in art or nature, has been snatched away from the curiosity of modern ages.

In the administration of Egypt, Amrou balanced the demands of justice and policy; the interest of the people of the law, who were defended by God; and of the people of the alliance, who were protected by man. In the recent tumult of conquest and deliverance, the tongue of the Copts and the sword of the Arabs were most adverse to the tranquillity of the province. To the former, Amrou declared, that faction and falsehood would be doubly chastised; by the punishment of the accusers, whom he should detest as his personal enemies, and by the promotion of their innocent brethren, whom their envy had labored to injure and supplant. He excited the latter by the motives of religion and honor to sustain the dignity of their character, to endear themselves by a modest and temperate conduct to God and the caliph, to spare and protect a people who had trusted to their faith, and to content themselves with the legitimate and splendid rewards of their victory. In the management of the revenue, he disapproved the simple but oppressive mode of a capitation, and preferred with reason a proportion of taxes deducted on every branch from the clear profits of agriculture and commerce. A third part of the tribute was appropriated to the annual repairs of the dikes and canals, so essential to the public welfare. Under his administration, the fertility of Egypt supplied the dearth of Arabia; and a string of camels, laden with corn and provisions, covered almost without an interval the long road from Memphis to Medina. But the genius of Amrou soon renewed the maritime communication which had been attempted or achieved by the Pharaohs the Ptolemies, or the Cæsars; and a canal, at least eighty miles in length, was opened from the Nile to the Red Sea. This inland navigation, which would have joined the Mediterranean and the Indian Ocean, was soon discontinued as useless and dangerous: the throne was removed from Medina to Damascus, and the Grecian fleets might have explored a passage to the holy cities of Arabia.

Of his new conquest, the caliph Omar had an imperfect knowledge from the voice of fame and the legends of the Koran. He requested that his lieutenant would place before his eyes the realm of Pharaoh and the Amalekites; and the answer of Amrou exhibits a lively and not unfaithful picture of that singular country. "O commander of the faithful, Egypt is a compound of black earth and green plants, between a pulverized mountain and a red sand. The distance from Syene to the sea is a month's journey for a horseman. Along the valley descends a river, on which the blessing of the Most High reposes both in the evening and morning, and which rises and falls with the revolutions of the sun and moon. When the annual dispensation of Providence unlocks the springs and fountains that nourish the earth, the Nile rolls his swelling and sounding waters through the realm of Egypt: the fields are overspread by the salutary flood; and the villages communicate with each other in their painted barks. The retreat of the inundation deposits a fertilizing mud for the reception of the various seeds: the crowds of husbandmen who blacken the land may be compared to a swarm of industrious ants; and their native indolence is quickened by the lash of the task-master, and the promise of the flowers and fruits of a plentiful increase. Their hope is seldom deceived; but the riches which they extract from the wheat, the barley, and the rice, the legumes, the fruit-trees, and the cattle, are unequally shared between those who labor and those who possess. According to the vicissitudes of the seasons, the face of the country is adorned with a *silver* wave, a verdant *emerald*, and the deep yellow of a *golden* harvest.» Yet this beneficial order is sometimes interrupted; and the long delay and sudden swell of the river in the first year of the conquest might afford some color to an edifying fable. It is said, that the annual sacrifice of a virgin had been interdicted by the piety of Omar; and that the Nile lay sullen and inactive in his shallow bed, till the mandate of the caliph was cast into the obedient stream, which rose in a single night to the height of sixteen cubits. The admiration of the Arabs for their new conquest encouraged the license of their romantic spirit. We may read, in the gravest authors, that Egypt was crowded with twenty thousand cities or villages: *that*, exclusive of the Greeks and Arabs, the Copts alone were found, on the assessment, six millions of tributary subjects, or twenty millions of either sex, and of every age: *that* three hundred millions of gold or silver were annually paid to the treasury of the caliphs. Our reason must be startled by these extravagant assertions; and they will become more palpable, if we assume the compass and measure the extent of habitable ground: a valley from the tropic to Memphis seldom broader than twelve miles, and the triangle of the Delta, a flat surface of two thousand one hundred square leagues, compose a twelfth part of the magnitude of France. A more accurate research will justify a more reasonable estimate. The three hundred millions, created by the error of a scribe, are reduced to the decent revenue of four millions three hundred thousand pieces of gold, of which nine hundred thousand were consumed by the pay of the soldiers. Two authentic lists, of the present and of the twelfth century, are circumscribed within the respectable number of two thousand seven hundred villages and towns. After a long residence at Cairo, a French consul has ventured to assign about four millions of Mahometans, Christians, and Jews, for the ample, though not incredible, scope of the population of Egypt.

IV. The conquest of Africa, from the Nile to the Atlantic Ocean, was first attempted by the arms of the caliph Othman. The pious design was approved by the companions of Mahomet and the chiefs of the tribes; and twenty thousand Arabs marched from Medina, with the gifts and the blessing of the commander of the faithful. They were joined in the camp of Memphis by twenty thousand of their countrymen; and the conduct of the war was intrusted to Abdallah, the son of Said and the foster-brother of the caliph, who had lately supplanted the conqueror and lieutenant of Egypt. Yet the favor of the prince, and the merit of his favorite, could not obliterate the guilt of his apostasy. The early conversion of Abdallah, and his skilful pen, had recommended him to the important office of transcribing the sheets of the Koran: he betrayed his trust, corrupted the text, derided the errors which he had made, and fled to Mecca to escape the justice, and expose the ignorance, of the apostle. After the conquest of Mecca, he fell prostrate at the feet of Mahomet; his tears, and the entreaties of Othman, extorted a reluctant pardon; but the prophet declared that he had so long hesitated, to allow time for some zealous disciple to avenge his injury in the blood of the apostate. With apparent fidelity and effective merit, he served the religion which it was no longer his interest to desert: his birth and talents gave him an honorable rank among the Koreish; and, in a nation of cavalry, Abdallah was renowned as the boldest and most dexterous horseman of Arabia. At the head of forty thousand Moslems, he advanced from Egypt into the unknown countries of the West. The sands of Barca might be impervious to a Roman legion but the Arabs were attended by their faithful camels; and the natives of the desert beheld without terror the familiar aspect of the soil and climate. After a painful march, they pitched their tents before the walls of Tripoli, a maritime city in which the name, the wealth, and the inhabitants of the province had gradually centred, and which now maintains the third rank among the states of Barbary. A reënforcement of Greeks was surprised and cut in pieces on the sea-shore; but the fortifications of Tripoli resisted the first assaults; and the Saracens were tempted by the approach of the præfect Gregory to relinquish the labors of the siege for the perils and the hopes of a decisive action. If his standard was followed by one hundred and twenty thousand men, the regular bands of the empire must have been lost in the naked and disorderly crowd of Africans and Moors, who formed the strength, or rather the numbers, of his host. He rejected with indignation the option of the Koran or the tribute; and during several days the two armies were fiercely engaged from the dawn of light to the hour of noon, when their fatigue and the excessive heat compelled them to seek shelter and refreshment in their respective camps. The daughter of Gregory, a maid of incomparable beauty and spirit, is said to have fought by his side:

from her earliest youth she was trained to mount on horseback, to draw the bow, and to wield the cimeter; and the richness of her arms and apparel were conspicuous in the foremost ranks of the battle. Her hand, with a hundred thousand pieces of gold, was offered for the head of the Arabian general, and the youths of Africa were excited by the prospect of the glorious prize. At the pressing solicitation of his brethren, Abdallah withdrew his person from the field; but the Saracens were discouraged by the retreat of their leader, and the repetition of these equal or unsuccessful conflicts.

A noble Arabian, who afterwards became the adversary of Ali, and the father of a caliph, had signalized his valor in Egypt, and Zobeir was the first who planted the scaling-ladder against the walls of Babylon. In the African war he was detached from the standard of Abdallah. On the news of the battle, Zobeir, with twelve companions, cut his way through the camp of the Greeks, and pressed forwards, without tasting either food or repose, to partake of the dangers of his brethren. He cast his eyes round the field: "Where," said he, "is our general?" "In his tent." "Is the tent a station for the general of the Moslems?" Abdallah represented with a blush the importance of his own life, and the temptation that was held forth by the Roman præfect. "Retort," said Zobeir, "on the infidels their ungenerous attempt. Proclaim through the ranks that the head of Gregory shall be repaid with his captive daughter, and the equal sum of one hundred thousand pieces of gold." To the courage and discretion of Zobeir the lieutenant of the caliph intrusted the execution of his own stratagem, which inclined the long-disputed balance in favor of the Saracens. Supplying by activity and artifice the deficiency of numbers, a part of their forces lay concealed in their tents, while the remainder prolonged an irregular skirmish with the enemy till the sun was high in the heavens. On both sides they retired with fainting steps: their horses were unbridled, their armor was laid aside, and the hostile nations prepared, or seemed to prepare, for the refreshment of the evening, and the encounter of the ensuing day. On a sudden the charge was sounded; the Arabian camp poured forth a swarm of fresh and intrepid warriors; and the long line of the Greeks and Africans was surprised, assaulted, overturned, by new squadrons of the faithful, who, to the eye of fanaticism, might appear as a band of angels descending from the sky. The præfect himself was slain by the hand of Zobeir: his daughter, who sought revenge and death, was surrounded and made prisoner; and the fugitives involved in their disaster the town of Sufetula, to which they escaped from the sabres and lances of the Arabs. Sufetula was built one hundred and fifty miles to the south of Carthage: a gentle declivity is watered by a running stream, and shaded by a grove of juniper-trees; and, in the ruins of a triumphal arch, a portico, and three temples of the Corinthian order, curiosity may yet admire the magnificence of the Romans. After the fall of this opulent city, the provincials and Barbarians implored on all sides the mercy of the conqueror. His vanity or his zeal might be flattered by offers of tribute or professions of faith: but his losses, his fatigues, and the progress of an epidemical disease, prevented a solid establishment; and the Saracens, after a campaign of fifteen months, retreated to the confines of Egypt, with the captives and the wealth of their African expedition. The caliph's fifth was granted to a favorite, on the nominal payment of five hundred thousand pieces of gold; but the state was doubly injured by this fallacious transaction, if each foot-soldier had shared one thousand, and each horseman three thousand, pieces, in the real division of the plunder. The author of the death of Gregory was expected to have claimed the most precious reward of the victory: from his silence it might be presumed that he had fallen in the battle, till the tears and exclamations of the præfect's daughter at the sight of Zobeir revealed the valor and modesty of that gallant soldier. The unfortunate virgin was offered, and almost rejected as a slave, by her father's murderer, who coolly declared that his sword was consecrated to the service of religion; and that he labored for a recompense far above the charms of mortal beauty, or the riches of this transitory life. A reward congenial to his temper was the honorable commission of announcing to the caliph Othman the success of his arms. The companions the chiefs, and the people, were assembled in the mosch of Medina, to hear the interesting narrative of Zobeir; and as the orator forgot nothing except the merit of his own counsels and actions, the name of Abdallah was joined by the Arabians with the heroic names of Caled and Amrou.

Conquests by the Arabs. – Part Eight

THE WESTERN CONQUESTS OF the Saracens were suspended near twenty years, till their dissensions were composed by the establishment of the house of Ommiyah; and the caliph Moawiyah was invited by the cries of the Africans themselves. The successors of Heraclius had been informed of the tribute which they had been compelled to stipulate with the Arabs, but instead of being moved to pity and relieve their distress, they imposed, as an equivalent or a fine, a second tribute of a similar amount. The ears of the Byzantine ministers were shut against the complaints of their poverty and ruin: their despair was reduced to prefer the dominion of a single master; and the extortions of the patriarch of Carthage, who was invested with civil and military power, provoked the sectaries, and even the Catholics of the Roman province, to abjure the religion as well as the authority of their tyrants. The first lieutenant of Moawiyah acquired a just renown, subdued an important city, defeated an army of thirty thousand Greeks, swept away fourscore thousand captives, and enriched with their spoils the bold adventures of Syria and Egypt. But the title of conqueror of Africa is more justly due to his successor Akbah. He marched from Damascus at the head of ten thousand of the bravest Arabs; and the genuine force of the Moslems was enlarged by the doubtful aid and conversion of many thousand Barbarians. It would be difficult, nor is it necessary, to trace the accurate line of the progress of Akbah. The interior regions have been peopled by the Orientals with fictitious armies and imaginary citadels. In the warlike province of Zab, or Numidia, fourscore thousand of the natives might assemble in arms; but the number of three hundred and sixty towns is incompatible with the ignorance or decay of husbandry; and a circumference of three leagues will not be justified by the ruins of Erbe or Lambesa, the ancient metropolis of that inland country. As we approach the sea-coast, the well-known cities of Bugia and Tangier define the more certain limits of the Saracen victories. A remnant of trade still adheres to the commodious harbor of Bugia which, in a more prosperous age, is said to have contained about twenty thousand houses; and the plenty of iron which is dug from the adjacent mountains might have supplied a braver people with the instruments of defence. The remote position and venerable antiquity of Tingi, or Tangier, have been decorated by the Greek and Arabian fables; but the figurative expressions of the latter, that the walls were constructed of brass, and that the roofs were covered with gold and silver, may be interpreted as the emblems of strength and opulence. The provinces of Mauritania Tingitana, which assumed the name of the capital, had been imperfectly discovered and settled by the Romans; the five colonies were confined to a narrow pale, and the more southern parts were seldom explored except by the agents of luxury, who searched the forests for ivory and the citron-wood, and the shores of the ocean for the purple shell-fish. The fearless Akbah plunged into the heart of the country, traversed the wilderness in which his successors erected the splendid capitals of Fez and Morocco, and at length penetrated to the verge of the Atlantic and the great desert. The river Sus descends from the western sides of Mount Atlas, fertilizes, like the Nile, the adjacent soil, and falls into the sea at a moderate distance from the Canary, or Fortunate Islands. Its banks were inhabited by the last of the Moors, a race of savages, without laws, or discipline, or religion; they were astonished by the strange and irresistible terrors of the Oriental arms; and as they possessed neither gold nor silver, the riches spoil was the beauty of the female captives, some of whom were afterwards sold for a thousand pieces of gold. The career, though not the zeal, of Akbah was checked by the prospect of a boundless ocean. He spurred his horse into the waves, and raising his eyes to heaven, exclaimed with a tone of a fanatic, "Great God! if my course were not stopped by this sea, I would still go on, to the unknown kingdoms of the West, preaching the unity of thy holy name, and putting to the sword the rebellious nations who worship any other Gods than thee." Yet this Mahometan Alexander, who sighed for new worlds, was unable to preserve his recent conquests. By the universal defection of the Greeks and Africans, he was recalled from the shores of the Atlantic, and the surrounding multitudes left him only the resource of an honorable death. The last scene was dignified by an example of national virtue. An ambitious chief, who had disputed the command and failed in the attempt, was led about as a prisoner in the camp of the Arabian general. The insurgents had trusted to his discontent and revenge; he disdained their offers, and revealed their designs. In the hour of danger, the grateful Akbah unlocked his fetters, and advised him to retire; he chose to die under the banner of his rival. Embracing as friends and martyrs, they unsheathed their cimeters, broke their scabbards, and maintained an obstinate combat, till they fell by each other's side on the last of their slaughtered countrymen. The third general or governor of Africa, Zuheir, avenged and encountered the fate of his predecessor. He vanquished the natives in many battles; he was overthrown by a powerful army, which Constantinople had sent to the relief of Carthage.

It had been the frequent practice of the Moorish tribes to join the invaders, to share the plunder, to profess the faith, and to revolt to their savage state of independence and idolatry, on the first retreat or misfortune of the Moslems. The prudence of Akbah had proposed to found an Arabian colony in the heart of Africa; a citadel that might curb the levity of the Barbarians, a place of refuge to secure, against the accidents of war, the wealth and the families of the Saracens. With this view, and under the modest title of the station of a caravan, he planted this colony in the fiftieth year of the Hegira. In the present decay, Cairoan still holds the second rank in the kingdom of Tunis, from which it is distant about fifty miles to the south: its inland situation, twelve miles westward of the sea, has protected the city from the Greek and Sicilian fleets. When the wild beasts and serpents were extirpated, when the forest, or rather wilderness, was cleared, the vestiges of a Roman town were discovered in a sandy plain: the vegetable food of Cairoan is brought from afar; and the scarcity of springs constrains the inhabitants to collect in cisterns and reservoirs a precarious supply of rain-water. These obstacles were subdued by the industry of Akbah; he traced a circumference of three thousand and six hundred paces, which he encompassed with a brick wall; in the space of five years, the governor's palace was surrounded with a sufficient number of private habitations; a spacious mosch was supported by five hundred columns of granite, porphyry, and Numidian marble; and Cairoan became the seat of learning as well as of empire. But these were the glories of a later age; the new colony was shaken by the successive defeats of Akbah and Zuheir, and the western expeditions were again interrupted by the civil discord of the Arabian monarchy. The son of the valiant Zobeir maintained a war of twelve years, a siege of seven months against the house of Ommiyah. Abdallah was said to unite the fierceness of the lion with the subtlety of the fox; but if he inherited the courage, he was devoid of the generosity, of his father.

The return of domestic peace allowed the caliph Abdalmalek to resume the conquest of Africa; the standard was delivered to Hassan, governor of Egypt, and the revenue of that kingdom, with an army of forty thousand men, was consecrated to the important service. In the vicissitudes of war, the interior provinces had been alternately won and lost by the Saracens. But the sea-coast still remained in the hands of the Greeks; the predecessors of Hassan had respected the name and fortifications of Carthage; and the number of its defenders was recruited by the fugitives of Cabes and Tripoli. The arms of Hassan, were bolder and more fortunate: he reduced and pillaged the metropolis of Africa; and the mention of scaling-ladders may justify the suspicion that he anticipated, by a sudden assault, the more tedious operations of a regular siege. But the joy of the conquerors was soon disturbed by the appearance of the Christian succors. The præfect and patrician John, a general of experience and renown, embarked at Constantinople the forces of the Eastern empire; they were joined by the ships and soldiers of Sicily, and a powerful reenforcement of Goths was obtained from the fears and religion of the Spanish monarch. The weight of the confederate navy broke the chain that guarded the entrance of the harbor; the Arabs retired to Cairoan, or Tripoli; the Christians landed; the citizens hailed the ensign of the cross, and the winter was idly wasted in the dream of victory or deliverance. But Africa was irrecoverably lost; the zeal and resentment of the commander of the faithful prepared in the ensuing spring a more numerous armament by sea and land; and the patrician in his turn was compelled to evacuate the post and fortifications of Carthage. A second battle was fought in the neighborhood of Utica: the Greeks and Goths were again defeated; and their timely embarkation saved them from the sword of Hassan, who had invested the slight and insufficient rampart of their camp. Whatever yet remained of Carthage was delivered to the flames, and the colony of Dido and Cæsar lay desolate above two hundred years, till a part, perhaps a twentieth, of the old circumference was repeopled by the first of the Fatimite caliphs. In the beginning of the sixteenth century, the second capital of the West was represented by a mosch, a college without students, twenty-five or thirty shops, and the huts of five hundred peasants, who, in their abject poverty, displayed the arrogance of the Punic senators. Even that paltry village was swept away by the Spaniards whom Charles the Fifth had stationed in the fortress of the Goletta. The ruins of Carthage have perished; and the place might be unknown if some broken arches of an aqueduct did not guide the footsteps of the inquisitive traveller.

The Greeks were expelled, but the Arabians were not yet masters of the country. In the interior provinces the Moors or *Berbers*, so feeble under the first Cæsars, so formidable to the Byzantine princes, maintained a disorderly resistance to the religion and power of the successors of Mahomet. Under the standard of their queen Cahina, the independent tribes acquired some degree of union and discipline; and as the Moors respected in their females the character of a prophetess, they attacked the invaders with an enthusiasm similar to their own. The veteran bands of Hassan were inadequate to the defence of Africa: the conquests of an age were lost in a single day; and the Arabian chief, overwhelmed by the torrent, retired to the confines of Egypt, and expected, five years, the promised succors of the caliph. After the retreat of the Saracens, the victorious prophetess assembled the Moorish chiefs, and recommended a measure of strange and savage policy. "Our cities," said she, "and the gold and silver which they contain, perpetually attract the arms of the Arabs. These vile metals are not the objects of our ambition; we content ourselves with the simple productions of the earth. Let us destroy these cities; let us bury in their ruins those pernicious treasures; and when the avarice of our foes shall be destitute of temptation, perhaps they will cease to disturb the tranquillity of a warlike people." The proposal was accepted with unanimous applause. From Tangier to Tripoli, the buildings, or at least the fortifications, were demolished, the fruit-trees were cut down, the means of subsistence were extirpated, a fertile and populous garden was changed into a desert, and the historians of a more recent period could discern the frequent traces of the prosperity and devastation of their ancestors. Such is the tale of the modern Arabians. Yet I strongly suspect that their ignorance of antiquity, the love of the marvellous, and the fashion of extolling the philosophy of Barbarians, has induced them to describe, as one voluntary act, the calamities of three hundred years since the first fury of the Donatists and Vandals. In the progress of the revolt, Cahina had most probably contributed her share of destruction; and the alarm of universal ruin might terrify and alienate the cities that had reluctantly yielded to her unworthy yoke. They no longer hoped, perhaps they no longer wished, the return of their Byzantine sovereigns: their present servitude was not alleviated by the benefits of order and justice; and the most zealous Catholic must prefer the imperfect truths of the Koran to the blind and rude idolatry of the Moors. The general of the Saracens was again received as the savior of the province: the friends of civil society conspired against the savages of the land; and the royal prophetess was slain, in the first battle, which overturned the baseless fabric of her superstition and empire. The same spirit revived under the successor of Hassan: it was finally quelled by the activity of Musa and his two sons; but the number of the rebels may be presumed from that of three hundred thousand captives; sixty thousand of whom, the caliph's fifth, were sold for the profit of the public treasury. Thirty thousand of the Barbarian youth were enlisted in the troops; and the pious labors of Musa, to inculcate the knowledge and practice of the Koran, accustomed the Africans to obey the apostle of God and the commander of the faithful. In their climate and government, their diet and habitation, the wandering Moors resembled the Bedoweens of the desert. With the religion they were proud to adopt the language, name, and origin, of Arabs: the blood of the strangers and natives was insensibly mingled; and from the Euphrates to the Atlantic, the same nation might seem to be diffused over the sandy plains of Asia and Africa. Yet I will not deny that fifty thousand tents of pure Arabians might be transported over the Nile, and scattered through the Libyan desert: and I am not ignorant that five of the Moorish tribes still retain their *barbarous* idiom, with the appellation and character of *white* Africans.

V. In the progress of conquest from the north and south, the Goths and the Saracens encountered each other on the confines of Europe and Africa. In the opinion of the latter, the difference of religion is a reasonable ground of enmity and warfare.

As early as the time of Othman, their piratical squadrons had ravaged the coast of Andalusia; nor had they forgotten the relief of Carthage by the Gothic succors. In that age, as well as in the present, the kings of Spain were possessed of the fortress of Ceuta; one of the columns of Hercules, which is divided by a narrow strait from the opposite pillar or point of Europe. A small portion of Mauritania was still wanting to the African conquest; but Musa, in the pride of victory, was repulsed from the walls of Ceuta, by the vigilance and courage of Count Julian, the general of the Goths. From his disappointment and perplexity, Musa was relieved by an unexpected message of the Christian chief, who offered his place, his person, and his sword, to the successors of Mahomet, and solicited the disgraceful honor of introducing their arms into the heart of Spain. If we inquire into the cause of his treachery, the Spaniards will repeat the popular story of his daughter Cava; of a virgin who was seduced, or ravished, by her sovereign; of a father who sacrificed his religion and country to the thirst of revenge. The passions of princes have often been licentious and destructive; but this well-known tale, romantic in itself, is indifferently supported by external evidence; and the history of Spain will suggest some motive of interest and policy more congenial to the breast of a veteran statesman. After the decease or deposition of Witiza, his two sons were supplanted by the ambition of Roderic, a noble Goth, whose father, the duke or governor of a province, had fallen a victim to the preceding tyranny. The monarchy was still elective; but the sons of Witiza, educated on the steps of the throne, were impatient of a private station. Their resentment was the more dangerous, as it was varnished with the dissimulation of courts: their followers were excited by the remembrance of favors and the promise of a revolution; and their uncle Oppas, archbishop of Toledo and Seville, was the first person in the church, and the second in the state. It is probable that Julian was involved in the disgrace of the unsuccessful faction; that he had little to hope and much to fear from the new reign; and that the imprudent king could not forget or forgive the injuries which Roderic and his family had sustained. The merit and influence of the count rendered him a useful or formidable subject: his estates were ample, his followers bold and numerous; and it was too fatally shown, that, by his Andalusian and Mauritanian commands, he held in his hand the keys of the Spanish monarchy. Too feeble, however, to meet his sovereign in arms, he sought the aid of a foreign power; and his rash invitation of the Moors and Arabs produced the calamities of eight hundred years. In his epistles, or in a personal interview, he revealed the wealth and nakedness of his country; the weakness of an unpopular prince; the degeneracy of an effeminate people. The Goths were no longer the victorious Barbarians, who had humbled the pride of Rome, despoiled the queen of nations, and penetrated from the Danube to the Atlantic Ocean. Secluded from the world by the Pyrenæan mountains, the successors of Alaric had slumbered in a long peace: the walls of the cities were mouldered into dust: the youth had abandoned the exercise of arms; and the presumption of their ancient renown would expose them in a field of battle to the first assault of the invaders. The ambitious Saracen was fired by the ease and importance of the attempt; but the execution was delayed till he had consulted the commander of the faithful; and his messenger returned with the permission of Walid to annex the unknown kingdoms of the West to the religion and throne of the caliphs. In his residence of Tangier, Musa, with secrecy and caution, continued his correspondence and hastened his preparations. But the remorse of the conspirators was soothed by the fallacious assurance that he should content himself with the glory and spoil, without aspiring to establish the Moslems beyond the sea that separates Africa from Europe.

Before Musa would trust an army of the faithful to the traitors and infidels of a foreign land, he made a less dangerous trial of their strength and veracity. One hundred Arabs, and four hundred Africans, passed over, in four vessels, from Tangier or Ceuta: the place of their descent on the opposite shore of the strait is marked by the name of Tarif their chief; and the date of this memorable event is fixed to the month of Ramadan, of the ninety-first year of the Hegira, to the month of July, seven hundred and forty-eight years from the Spanish æra of Cæsar, seven hundred and ten after the birth of Christ. From their first station, they marched eighteen miles through a hilly country to the castle and town of Julian: on which (it is still called Algezire) they bestowed the name of the Green Island, from a verdant cape that advances into the sea. Their hospitable entertainment, the Christians who joined their standard, their inroad into a fertile and unguarded province, the richness of their spoil, and the safety of their return, announced to their brethren the most favorable omens of victory. In the ensuing spring, five thousand veterans and volunteers were embarked under the command of Tarik, a dauntless and skilful soldier, who surpassed the expectation of his chief; and the necessary transports were provided by the industry of their too faithful ally. The Saracens landed at the pillar or point of Europe; the corrupt and familiar appellation of Gibraltar (*Gebel al Tarik*) describes the mountain of Tarik; and the intrenchments of his camp were the first outline of those fortifications, which, in the hands of our countrymen, have resisted the art and power of the house of Bourbon. The adjacent governors informed the court of Toledo of the descent and progress of the Arabs; and the defeat of his lieutenant Edeco, who had been commanded to seize and bind the presumptuous strangers, admonished Roderic of the magnitude of the danger. At the royal summons, the dukes and counts, the bishops and nobles of the Gothic monarchy, assembled at the head of their followers; and the title of King of the Romans, which is employed by an Arabic historian, may be excused by the close affinity of language, religion, and manners, between the nations of Spain. His army consisted of ninety or a hundred thousand men; a formidable power, if their fidelity and discipline had been adequate to their numbers. The troops of Tarik had been augmented to twelve thousand Saracens; but the Christian malcontents were attracted by the influence of Julian, and a crowd of Africans most greedily tasted the temporal blessings of the Koran. In the neighborhood of Cadiz, the town of Xeres has been illustrated by the encounter which determined the fate of the kingdom; the stream of the Guadalete, which falls into the bay, divided the two camps, and marked the advancing and retreating skirmishes of three successive and bloody days. On the fourth day, the two armies joined a more serious and decisive issue; but Alaric would have blushed at the sight of his unworthy successor, sustaining on his head a diadem of pearls, encumbered with a flowing robe of gold and silken embroidery, and reclining on a litter or car of ivory drawn by two white mules. Notwithstanding the valor of the Saracens, they fainted under the weight of multitudes, and the plain of Xeres was overspread with sixteen thousand of their dead bodies. "My brethren," said Tarik to his surviving companions, "the enemy is before you, the sea is behind; whither would ye fly? Follow your general I am resolved either to lose my life, or to trample on the prostrate king of the Romans." Besides the resource of despair, he confided in the secret correspondence and nocturnal interviews of Count Julian with the sons and the brother of Witiza. The two princes and the archbishop of Toledo occupied the most important post: their well-timed defection broke the ranks of the Christians; each warrior was prompted by fear or suspicion to consult his personal safety; and the remains of the Gothic army were scattered or destroyed in the flight and pursuit of the three following days. Amidst the general disorder, Roderic started from his car, and mounted Orelia, the fleetest of his horses; but he escaped from a soldier's death to perish more ignobly in the waters of the Bætis or Guadalquivir. His diadem, his robes, and his courser, were found on the bank; but as the body of the Gothic prince was lost in the waves, the pride and ignorance of the caliph must have been gratified with some meaner head, which was exposed in triumph before the palace of Damascus. "And such," continues a valiant historian of the Arabs, "is the fate of those kings who withdraw themselves from a field of battle."

Count Julian had plunged so deep into guilt and infamy, that his only hope was in the ruin of his country. After the battle of Xeres, he recommended the most effectual measures to the victorious Saracen. "The king of the Goths is slain; their princes have fled before you, the army is routed, the nation is astonished. Secure with sufficient detachments the cities of Bætica; but in person, and without delay, march to the royal city of Toledo, and allow not the distracted Christians either time or tranquillity for the election of a new monarch." Tarik listened to his advice. A Roman captive and proselyte, who had been enfranchised by the caliph himself, assaulted Cordova with seven hundred horse: he swam the river, surprised the town, and drove the Christians into the great church, where they defended themselves above three months. Another detachment reduced the sea-coast of Bætica, which in the last period of the Moorish power has comprised in a narrow space the populous kingdom of Grenada. The march of Tarik from the Bætis to the Tagus was directed through the Sierra Morena, that separates Andalusia and Castille, till he appeared in arms under the walls of Toledo. The most zealous of the Catholics had escaped with the relics of their saints; and if the gates were shut, it was only till the victor had subscribed a fair and reasonable capitulation. The voluntary exiles were allowed to depart with their effects; seven churches were appropriated to the Christian worship; the archbishop and his clergy were at liberty to exercise their functions, the monks to practise or neglect their penance; and the Goths and Romans were left in all civil and criminal cases to the subordinate jurisdiction of their own laws and magistrates. But if the justice of Tarik protected the Christians, his gratitude and policy rewarded the Jews, to whose secret or open aid he was indebted for his most important acquisitions. Persecuted by the kings and synods of Spain, who had often pressed the alternative of banishment or baptism, that outcast nation embraced the moment of revenge: the comparison of their past and present state was the pledge of their fidelity; and the alliance between the disciples of Moses and of Mahomet was maintained till the final æra of their common expulsion. From the royal seat of Toledo, the Arabian leader spread his conquests to the north, over the modern realms of Castille and Leon; but it is needless to enumerate the cities that yielded on his approach, or again to describe the table of emerald, transported from the East by the Romans, acquired by the Goths among the spoils of Rome, and presented by the Arabs to the throne of Damascus. Beyond the Asturian mountains, the maritime town of Gijon was the term of the lieutenant of Musa, who had performed, with the speed of a traveller, his victorious march, of seven hundred miles, from the rock of Gibraltar to the Bay of Biscay. The failure of land compelled him to retreat; and he was recalled to Toledo, to excuse his presumption of subduing a kingdom in the absence of his general. Spain, which, in a more savage and disorderly state, had resisted, two hundred years, the arms of the Romans, was overrun in a few months by those of the Saracens; and such was the eagerness of submission and treaty, that the governor of Cordova is recorded as the only chief who fell, without conditions, a prisoner into their hands. The cause of the Goths had been irrevocably judged in the field of Xeres; and, in the national dismay, each part of the monarchy declined a contest with the antagonist who had vanquished the united strength of the whole. That strength had been wasted by two successive seasons of famine and pestilence; and the governors, who were impatient to surrender, might exaggerate the difficulty of collecting the provisions of a siege. To disarm the Christians, superstition likewise contributed her terrors: and the subtle Arab encouraged the report of dreams, omens, and prophecies, and of the portraits of the destined conquerors of Spain, that were discovered on breaking open an apartment of the royal palace. Yet a spark of the vital flame was still alive: some invincible fugitives preferred a life of poverty and freedom in the Asturian valleys; the hardy mountaineers repulsed the slaves of the caliph; and the sword of Pelagius has been transformed into the sceptre of the Catholic kings.

Conquests by the Arabs. – Part Nine

ON THE INTELLIGENCE OF this rapid success, the applause of Musa degenerated into envy; and he began, not to complain, but to fear, that Tarik would leave him nothing to subdue. At the head of ten thousand Arabs and eight thousand Africans, he passed over in person from Mauritania to Spain: the first of his companions were the noblest of the Koreish; his eldest son was left in the command of Africa; the three younger brethren were of an age and spirit to second the boldest enterprises of their father. At his landing in Algezire, he was respectfully entertained by Count Julian, who stifled his inward remorse, and testified, both in words and actions, that the victory of the Arabs had not impaired his attachment to their cause. Some enemies yet remained for the sword of Musa. The tardy repentance of the Goths had compared their own numbers and those of the invaders; the cities from which the march of Tarik had declined considered themselves as impregnable; and the bravest patriots defended the fortifications of Seville and Merida. They were successively besieged and reduced by the labor of Musa, who transported his camp from the Bætis to the Anas, from the Guadalquivir to the Guadiana. When he beheld the works of Roman magnificence, the bridge, the aqueducts, the triumphal arches, and the theatre, of the ancient metropolis of Lusitania, "I should imagine," said he to his four companions, "that the human race must have united their art and power in the foundation of this city: happy is the man who shall become its master!" He aspired to that happiness, but the *Emeritans* sustained on this occasion the honor of their descent from the veteran legionaries of Augustus. Disdaining the confinement of their walls, they gave battle to the Arabs on the plain; but an ambuscade rising from the shelter of a quarry, or a ruin, chastised their indiscretion, and intercepted their return. The wooden turrets of assault were rolled forwards to the foot of the rampart; but the defence of Merida was obstinate and long; and the *castle of the martyrs* was a perpetual testimony of the losses of the Moslems. The constancy of the besieged was at length subdued by famine and despair; and the prudent victor disguised his impatience under the names of clemency and esteem. The alternative of exile or tribute was allowed; the churches were divided between the two religions; and the wealth of those who had fallen in the siege, or retired to Gallicia, was confiscated as the reward of the faithful. In the midway between Merida and Toledo, the lieutenant of Musa saluted the vicegerent of the caliph, and conducted him to the palace of the Gothic kings. Their first interview was cold and formal: a rigid account was exacted of the treasures of Spain: the character of Tarik was exposed to suspicion and obloquy; and the hero was imprisoned, reviled, and ignominiously scourged by the hand, or the command, of Musa. Yet so strict was the discipline, so pure the zeal, or so tame the spirit, of the primitive Moslems, that, after this public indignity, Tarik could serve and be trusted in the reduction of the Tarragonest province. A mosch was erected at Saragossa, by the liberality of the Koreish: the port of Barcelona was opened to the vessels of Syria; and the Goths were pursued beyond the Pyrenæan mountains into their Gallic province of Septimania or Languedoc. In the church of St. Mary at Carcassone, Musa found, but it is improbable that he left, seven equestrian statues of massy silver; and from his *ter* or column of Narbonne, he returned on his footsteps to the Gallician and Lusitanian shores of the ocean. During the absence of the father, his son Abdelaziz chastised the insurgents of Seville, and reduced, from Malaga to Valentia, the sea-coast of the Mediterranean: his original treaty with the discreet and valiant Theodemir will represent the manners and policy of the times. «*The conditions of peace agreed and sworn between Abdelaziz, the son of Musa, the son of Nassir, and Theodemir prince of the Goths.* In the name of the most merciful God, Abdelaziz makes peace on these conditions: *that* Theodemir shall not be disturbed in his principality; nor any injury be offered to the life or property, the wives and children, the religion and temples, of the Christians: *that* Theodemir shall freely deliver his seven cities, Orihuela, Valentola, Alicanti Mola, Vacasora, Bigerra, (now Bejar,) Ora, (or Opta,) and Lorca: *that* he shall not assist or entertain the enemies of the caliph, but shall faithfully communicate his knowledge of their hostile designs: *that* himself, and each of the Gothic nobles, shall annually pay one piece of gold, four measures of wheat, as many of barley, with a certain proportion of honey, oil, and vinegar; and that each of their vassals shall be taxed at one moiety of the said imposition. Given the fourth of Regeb, in the year of the Hegira ninety-four, and subscribed with the names of four Mussulman witnesses.» Theodemir and his subjects were treated with uncommon lenity; but the rate of tribute appears to have fluctuated from a tenth to a fifth, according to the submission or obstinacy of the Christians. In this revolution, many partial calamities were inflicted by the carnal or religious passions of the enthusiasts: some churches were profaned by the new worship: some relics or images were confounded with idols: the rebels were put to the sword; and one town (an obscure place between Cordova and Seville) was razed to its foundations. Yet if we compare the invasion of Spain by the Goths, or its recovery by the kings of Castile and Arragon, we must applaud the moderation and discipline of the Arabian conquerors.

The exploits of Musa were performed in the evening of life, though he affected to disguise his age by coloring with a red powder the whiteness of his beard. But in the love of action and glory, his breast was still fired with the ardor of youth; and the possession of Spain was considered only as the first step to the monarchy of Europe. With a powerful armament by sea and land, he was preparing to repass the Pyrenees, to extinguish in Gaul and Italy the declining kingdoms of the Franks and Lombards, and to preach the unity of God on the altar of the Vatican. From thence, subduing the Barbarians of Germany, he proposed to follow the course of the Danube from its source to the Euxine Sea, to overthrow the Greek or Roman empire of Constantinople, and returning from Europe to Asia, to unite his new acquisitions with Antioch and the provinces of Syria. But his vast enterprise, perhaps of easy execution, must have seemed extravagant to vulgar minds; and the visionary conqueror was soon reminded of his dependence and servitude. The friends of Tarik had effectually stated his services and wrongs: at the court of Damascus, the proceedings of Musa were blamed, his intentions were suspected, and his delay in complying with the first invitation was chastised by a harsher and more peremptory summons. An intrepid messenger of the caliph entered his camp at Lugo in Gallicia, and in the presence of the Saracens and Christians arrested the bridle of his horse. His own loyalty, or that of his troops, inculcated the duty of obedience: and his disgrace was alleviated by the recall of his rival, and the permission of investing with his two governments his two sons, Abdallah and Abdelaziz. His long triumph from Ceuta to Damascus displayed the spoils of Africa and the treasures of Spain: four hundred Gothic nobles, with gold coronets and girdles, were distinguished in his train; and the number of male and female captives, selected for their birth or beauty, was computed at eighteen, or even at thirty, thousand persons. As soon as he reached Tiberias in Palestine, he was apprised of the sickness and danger of the caliph, by a private message from Soliman, his brother and presumptive heir; who wished to reserve for his own reign the spectacle of victory. Had Walid recovered, the delay of Musa would have been criminal: he pursued his march, and found an enemy on the throne. In his trial before a partial judge against a popular antagonist, he was convicted of vanity and falsehood; and a fine of two hundred thousand pieces of gold either exhausted his poverty or proved his rapaciousness. The unworthy treatment of Tarik was revenged by a similar indignity; and the veteran commander, after a public whipping, stood a whole day in the sun before the palace gate, till he obtained a decent exile, under the pious name of a pilgrimage to Mecca. The resentment of the caliph might have been satiated with the ruin of Musa; but his fears demanded the extirpation of a potent and injured family. A sentence of death was intimated with secrecy and speed to the trusty servants of the throne both in Africa and Spain; and the forms, if not the substance, of justice were superseded in this bloody execution. In the mosch or palace of Cordova, Abdelaziz was slain by the swords of the conspirators; they accused their governor of claiming the honors of royalty; and his scandalous marriage with Egilona, the widow of Roderic, offended the prejudices both of the Christians and Moslems. By a refinement of cruelty, the head of the son was presented to the father, with an insulting question, whether he acknowledged the features of the rebel? "I know his features," he exclaimed with indignation: "I assert his innocence; and I imprecate the same, a juster fate, against the authors of his death." The age and despair of Musa raised him above the power of kings; and he expired at Mecca of the anguish of a broken heart. His rival was more favorably treated: his services were forgiven; and Tarik was permitted to mingle with the crowd of slaves. I am ignorant whether Count Julian was rewarded with the death which he deserved indeed, though not from the hands of the Saracens; but the tale of their ingratitude to the sons of Witiza is disproved by the most unquestionable evidence. The two royal youths were reinstated in the private patrimony of their father; but on the decease of Eba, the elder, his daughter was unjustly despoiled of her portion by the violence of her uncle Sigebut. The Gothic maid pleaded her cause before the caliph Hashem, and obtained the restitution of her inheritance; but she was given in marriage to a noble Arabian, and their two sons, Isaac and Ibrahim, were received in Spain with the consideration that was due to their origin and riches.

A province is assimilated to the victorious state by the introduction of strangers and the imitative spirit of the natives; and Spain, which had been successively tinctured with Punic, and Roman, and Gothic blood, imbibed, in a few generations, the name and manners of the Arabs. The first conquerors, and the twenty successive lieutenants of the caliphs, were attended by a numerous train of civil and military followers, who preferred a distant fortune to a narrow home: the private and public interest was promoted by the establishment of faithful colonies; and the cities of Spain were proud to commemorate the tribe or country of their Eastern progenitors. The victorious though motley bands of Tarik and Musa asserted, by the name of *Spaniards*, their original claim of conquest; yet they allowed their brethren of Egypt to share their establishments of Murcia and Lisbon. The royal legion of Damascus was planted at Cordova; that of Emesa at Seville; that of Kinnisrin or Chalcis at Jaen; that of Palestine at Algezire and Medina Sidonia. The natives of Yemen and Persia were scattered round Toledo and the inland country, and the fertile seats of Grenada were bestowed on ten thousand horsemen of Syria and Irak, the children of the purest and most noble of the Arabian tribes. A spirit of emulation, sometimes beneficial, more frequently dangerous, was nourished by these hereditary factions. Ten years after the conquest, a map of the province was presented to the caliph: the seas, the rivers, and the harbors, the inhabitants and cities, the climate, the soil, and the mineral productions of the earth. In the space of two centuries, the gifts of nature were improved by the agriculture, the manufactures, and the commerce, of an industrious people; and the effects of their diligence have been magnified by the idleness of their fancy. The first of the Ommiades who reigned in Spain solicited the support of the Christians; and in his edict of peace and protection, he contents himself with a modest imposition of ten thousand ounces of gold, ten thousand pounds of silver, ten thousand horses, as many mules, one thousand cuirasses, with an equal number of helmets and lances. The most powerful of his successors derived from the same kingdom the annual tribute of twelve millions and forty-five thousand dinars or pieces of gold, about six millions of sterling money; a sum which, in the tenth century, most probably surpassed the united revenues of the Christians monarchs. His royal seat of Cordova contained six hundred moschs, nine hundred baths, and two hundred thousand houses; he gave laws to eighty cities of the first, to three hundred of the second and third order; and the fertile banks of the Guadalquivir were adorned with twelve thousand villages and hamlets. The Arabs might exaggerate the truth, but they created and they describe the most prosperous æra of the riches, the cultivation, and the populousness of Spain.

The wars of the Moslems were sanctified by the prophet; but among the various precepts and examples of his life, the caliphs selected the lessons of toleration that might tend to disarm the resistance of the unbelievers. Arabia was the temple and patrimony of the God of Mahomet; but he beheld with less jealousy and affection the nations of the earth. The polytheists and idolaters, who were ignorant of his name, might be lawfully extirpated by his votaries; but a wise policy supplied the obligation of justice; and after some acts of intolerant zeal, the Mahometan conquerors of Hindostan have spared the pagodas of that devout and populous country. The disciples of Abraham, of Moses, and of Jesus, were solemnly invited to accept the more *perfect* revelation of Mahomet; but if they preferred the payment of a moderate tribute, they were entitled to the freedom of conscience and religious worship. In a field of battle the forfeit lives of the prisoners were redeemed by the profession of *Islam*; the females were bound to embrace the religion of their masters, and a race of sincere proselytes was gradually multiplied by the education of the infant captives. But the millions of African and Asiatic converts, who swelled the native band of the faithful Arabs, must have been allured, rather than constrained, to declare their belief in one God and the apostle of God. By the repetition of a sentence and the loss of a foreskin, the subject or the slave, the captive or the criminal, arose in a moment the free and equal companion of the victorious Moslems. Every sin was expiated, every engagement was dissolved: the vow of celibacy was superseded by the indulgence of nature; the active spirits who slept in the cloister were awakened by the trumpet of the Saracens; and in the convulsion of the world, every member of a new society ascended to the natural level of his capacity and courage. The minds of the multitude were tempted by the invisible as well as temporal blessings of the Arabian prophet; and charity will hope that many of his proselytes entertained a serious conviction of the truth and sanctity of his revelation. In the eyes of an inquisitive polytheist, it must appear worthy of the human and the divine nature. More pure than the system of Zoroaster, more liberal than the law of Moses, the religion of Mahomet might seem less inconsistent with reason than the creed of mystery and superstition, which, in the seventh century, disgraced the simplicity of the gospel.

In the extensive provinces of Persia and Africa, the national religion has been eradicated by the Mahometan faith. The ambiguous theology of the Magi stood alone among the sects of the East; but the profane writings of Zoroaster might, under the reverend name of Abraham, be dexterously connected with the chain of divine revelation. Their evil principle, the dæmon Ahriman, might be represented as the rival, or as the creature, of the God of light. The temples of Persia were devoid of images; but the worship of the sun and of fire might be stigmatized as a gross and criminal idolatry. The milder sentiment was consecrated by the practice of Mahomet and the prudence of the caliphs; the Magians or Ghebers were ranked with the Jews and Christians among the people of the written law; and as late as the third century of the Hegira, the city of Herat will afford a lively contrast of private zeal and public toleration. Under the payment of an annual tribute, the Mahometan law secured to the Ghebers of Herat their civil and religious liberties: but the recent and humble mosch was overshadowed by the antique splendor of the adjoining temple of fire. A fanatic Imam deplored, in his sermons, the scandalous neighborhood, and accused the weakness or indifference of the faithful. Excited by his voice, the people assembled in tumult; the two houses of prayer were consumed by the flames, but the vacant ground was immediately occupied by the foundations of a new mosch. The injured Magi appealed to the sovereign of Chorasan; he promised justice and relief; when, behold! four thousand citizens of Herat, of a grave character and mature age, unanimously swore that the idolatrous fane had *never* existed; the inquisition was silenced and their conscience was satisfied (says the historian Mirchond) with this holy and meritorious perjury. But the greatest part of the temples of Persia were ruined by the insensible and general desertion of their votaries. It was *insensible*, since it is not accompanied with any memorial of time or place, of persecution or resistance. It was *general*, since the whole realm, from Shiraz to Samarcand, imbibed the faith of the Koran; and the preservation of the native tongue reveals the descent of the Mahometans of Persia. In the mountains and deserts, an obstinate race of unbelievers adhered to the superstition of their fathers; and a faint tradition of the Magian theology is kept alive in the province of Kirman, along the banks of the Indus, among the exiles of Surat, and in the colony which, in the last century, was planted by Shaw Abbas at the gates of Ispahan. The chief pontiff has retired to Mount Elbourz, eighteen leagues from the city of Yezd: the perpetual fire (if it continues to burn) is inaccessible to the profane; but his residence is the school, the oracle, and the pilgrimage of the Ghebers, whose hard and uniform features attest the unmingled purity of their blood. Under the jurisdiction of their elders, eighty thousand families maintain an innocent and industrious life: their subsistence is derived from some curious manufactures and mechanic trades;

and they cultivate the earth with the fervor of a religious duty. Their ignorance withstood the despotism of Shaw Abbas, who demanded with threats and tortures the prophetic books of Zoroaster; and this obscure remnant of the Magians is spared by the moderation or contempt of their present sovereigns.

The Northern coast of Africa is the only land in which the light of the gospel, after a long and perfect establishment, has been totally extinguished. The arts, which had been taught by Carthage and Rome, were involved in a cloud of ignorance; the doctrine of Cyprian and Augustin was no longer studied. Five hundred episcopal churches were overturned by the hostile fury of the Donatists, the Vandals, and the Moors. The zeal and numbers of the clergy declined; and the people, without discipline, or knowledge, or hope, submissively sunk under the yoke of the Arabian prophet. Within fifty years after the expulsion of the Greeks, a lieutenant of Africa informed the caliph that the tribute of the infidels was abolished by their conversion; and, though he sought to disguise his fraud and rebellion, his specious pretence was drawn from the rapid and extensive progress of the Mahometan faith. In the next age, an extraordinary mission of five bishops was detached from Alexandria to Cairoan. They were ordained by the Jacobite patriarch to cherish and revive the dying embers of Christianity: but the interposition of a foreign prelate, a stranger to the Latins, an enemy to the Catholics, supposes the decay and dissolution of the African hierarchy. It was no longer the time when the successor of St. Cyprian, at the head of a numerous synod, could maintain an equal contest with the ambition of the Roman pontiff. In the eleventh century, the unfortunate priest who was seated on the ruins of Carthage implored the arms and the protection of the Vatican; and he bitterly complains that his naked body had been scourged by the Saracens, and that his authority was disputed by the four suffragans, the tottering pillars of his throne. Two epistles of Gregory the Seventh are destined to soothe the distress of the Catholics and the pride of a Moorish prince. The pope assures the sultan that they both worship the same God, and may hope to meet in the bosom of Abraham; but the complaint that three bishops could no longer be found to consecrate a brother, announces the speedy and inevitable ruin of the episcopal order. The Christians of Africa and Spain had long since submitted to the practice of circumcision and the legal abstinence from wine and pork; and the name of *Mozarabe* (adoptive Arabs) was applied to their civil or religious conformity. About the middle of the twelfth century, the worship of Christ and the succession of pastors were abolished along the coast of Barbary, and in the kingdoms

of Cordova and Seville, of Valencia and Grenada. The throne of the Almohades, or Unitarians, was founded on the blindest fanaticism, and
their extraordinary rigor might be provoked or justified by the recent
victories and intolerant zeal of the princes of Sicily and Castille, of Arragon and Portugal. The faith of the Mozarabes was occasionally revived
by the papal missionaries; and, on the landing of Charles the Fifth, some
families of Latin Christians were encouraged to rear their heads at Tunis
and Algiers. But the seed of the gospel was quickly eradicated, and the
long province from Tripoli to the Atlantic has lost all memory of the
language and religion of Rome.

After the revolution of eleven centuries, the Jews and Christians of
the Turkish empire enjoy the liberty of conscience which was granted
by the Arabian caliphs. During the first age of the conquest, they suspected the loyalty of the Catholics, whose name of Melchites betrayed
their secret attachment to the Greek emperor, while the Nestorians and
Jacobites, his inveterate enemies, approved themselves the sincere and
voluntary friends of the Mahometan government. Yet this partial jealousy was healed by time and submission; the churches of Egypt were
shared with the Catholics; and all the Oriental sects were included in
the common benefits of toleration. The rank, the immunities, the domestic jurisdiction of the patriarchs, the bishops, and the clergy, were
protected by the civil magistrate: the learning of individuals recommended them to the employments of secretaries and physicians: they
were enriched by the lucrative collection of the revenue; and their merit
was sometimes raised to the command of cities and provinces. A caliph
of the house of Abbas was heard to declare that the Christians were
most worthy of trust in the administration of Persia. "The Moslems,"
said he, "will abuse their present fortune; the Magians regret their fallen
greatness; and the Jews are impatient for their approaching deliverance."
But the slaves of despotism are exposed to the alternatives of favor and
disgrace. The captive churches of the East have been afflicted in every
age by the avarice or bigotry of their rulers; and the ordinary and legal
restraints must be offensive to the pride, or the zeal, of the Christians.
About two hundred years after Mahomet, they were separated from
their fellow-subjects by a turban or girdle of a less honorable color; instead of horses or mules, they were condemned to ride on asses, in the
attitude of women. Their public and private building were measured
by a diminutive standard; in the streets or the baths it is their duty to
give way or bow down before the meanest of the people; and their testimony is rejected, if it may tend to the prejudice of a true believer. The
pomp of processions, the sound of bells or of psalmody, is interdicted

in their worship; a decent reverence for the national faith is imposed on their sermons and conversations; and the sacrilegious attempt to enter a mosch, or to seduce a Mussulman, will not be suffered to escape with impunity. In a time, however, of tranquillity and justice, the Christians have never been compelled to renounce the Gospel, or to embrace the Koran; but the punishment of death is inflicted upon the apostates who have professed and deserted the law of Mahomet. The martyrs of Cordova provoked the sentence of the cadhi, by the public confession of their inconstancy, or their passionate invectives against the person and religion of the prophet.

At the end of the first century of the Hegira, the caliphs were the most potent and absolute monarchs of the globe. Their prerogative was not circumscribed, either in right or in fact, by the power of the nobles, the freedom of the commons, the privileges of the church, the votes of a senate, or the memory of a free constitution. The authority of the companions of Mahomet expired with their lives; and the chiefs or emirs of the Arabian tribes left behind, in the desert, the spirit of equality and independence. The regal and sacerdotal characters were united in the successors of Mahomet; and if the Koran was the rule of their actions, they were the supreme judges and interpreters of that divine book. They reigned by the right of conquest over the nations of the East, to whom the name of liberty was unknown, and who were accustomed to applaud in their tyrants the acts of violence and severity that were exercised at their own expense. Under the last of the Ommiades, the Arabian empire extended two hundred days' journey from east to west, from the confines of Tartary and India to the shores of the Atlantic Ocean. And if we retrench the sleeve of the robe, as it is styled by their writers, the long and narrow province of Africa, the solid and compact dominion from Fargana to Aden, from Tarsus to Surat, will spread on every side to the measure of four or five months of the march of a caravan. We should vainly seek the indissoluble union and easy obedience that pervaded the government of Augustus and the Antonines; but the progress of the Mahometan religion diffused over this ample space a general resemblance of manners and opinions. The language and laws of the Koran were studied with equal devotion at Samarcand and Seville: the Moor and the Indian embraced as countrymen and brothers in the pilgrimage of Mecca; and the Arabian language was adopted as the popular idiom in all the provinces to the westward of the Tigris.

More Conquests by the Arabs.
– Part One

The Two Sieges of Constantinople by the Ar-
abs. – Their Invasion of France, and Defeat by
Charles Martel. – Civil War of the Ommiades
and Abbassides. – Learning of the Arabs. –
Luxury of the Caliphs. – Naval Enterprises on
Crete, Sicily, and Rome. – Decay and Division
of the Empire of the Caliphs. – Defeats and
Victories of the Greek Emperors.

WHEN THE ARABS FIRST issued from the desert, they must have been surprised at the ease and rapidity of their own success. But when they advanced in the career of victory to the banks of the Indus and the summit of the Pyrenees; when they had repeatedly tried the edge of their cimeters and the energy of their faith, they might be equally astonished that any nation could resist their invincible arms; that any boundary should confine the dominion of the successor of the prophet. The confidence of soldiers and fanatics may indeed be excused, since the calm historian of the present hour, who strives to follow the rapid course of the Saracens, must study to explain by what means the church and state were saved from this impending, and, as it should seem, from this inevitable, danger. The deserts of Scythia and Sarmatia might be guarded by their extent, their climate, their poverty, and the courage of the northern shepherds; China was remote and inaccessible; but the greatest part of the temperate zone was subject to the Mahometan conquerors, the Greeks were exhausted by the calamities of war and the loss of their fairest provinces, and the Barbarians of Europe might justly tremble at the precipitate fall of the Gothic monarchy. In this inquiry I shall unfold the events that rescued our ancestors of Britain, and our neighbors of Gaul, from the civil and religious yoke of the Koran; that protected the majesty of Rome, and delayed the servitude of Constantinople; that invigorated the defence of the Christians, and scattered among their enemies the seeds of division and decay.

Forty-six years after the flight of Mahomet from Mecca, his disciples appeared in arms under the walls of Constantinople. They were animated by a genuine or fictitious saying of the prophet, that, to the first army which besieged the city of the Cæsars, their sins were forgiven: the long series of Roman triumphs would be meritoriously transferred to the conquerors of New Rome; and the wealth of nations was deposited in this well-chosen seat of royalty and commerce. No sooner had the caliph Moawiyah suppressed his rivals and established his throne, than he aspired to expiate the guilt of civil blood, by the success and glory of this holy expedition; his preparations by sea and land were adequate to the importance of the object; his standard was intrusted to Sophian, a veteran warrior, but the troops were encouraged by the example and presence of Yezid, the son and presumptive heir of the commander of the faithful. The Greeks had little to hope, nor had their enemies any reason of fear, from the courage and vigilance of the reigning emperor, who disgraced the name of Constantine, and imitated only the inglorious years of his grandfather Heraclius. Without delay or opposition, the naval forces of the Saracens passed through the unguarded channel of the Hellespont, which even now, under the feeble and disorderly government of the Turks, is maintained as the natural bulwark of the capital. The Arabian fleet cast anchor, and the troops were disembarked near the palace of Hebdomon, seven miles from the city. During many days, from the dawn of light to the evening, the line of assault was extended from the golden gate to the eastern promontory and the foremost warriors were impelled by the weight and effort of the succeeding columns. But the besiegers had formed an insufficient estimate of the strength and resources of Constantinople. The solid and lofty walls were guarded by numbers and discipline: the spirit of the Romans was rekindled by the last danger of their religion and empire: the fugitives from the conquered provinces more successfully renewed the defence of Damascus and Alexandria; and the Saracens were dismayed by the strange and prodigious effects of artificial fire. This firm and effectual resistance diverted their arms to the more easy attempt of plundering the European and Asiatic coasts of the Propontis; and, after keeping the sea from the month of April to that of September, on the approach of winter they retreated fourscore miles from the capital, to the Isle of Cyzicus, in which they had established their magazine of spoil and provisions. So patient was their perseverance, or so languid were their operations, that they repeated in the six following summers the same attack and retreat, with a gradual abatement of hope and vigor, till the mischances of shipwreck and disease, of the sword and of fire, compelled them to relinquish the fruitless enterprise. They might bewail the loss, or commemorate the martyrdom, of thirty thousand Moslems, who fell in the siege of Constantinople; and the solemn funeral of Abu Ayub, or Job, excited the curiosity of the Christians themselves. That venerable Arab, one of the last of the companions of Mahomet, was numbered among the *ansars*, or auxiliaries, of Medina, who sheltered the head of the flying prophet. In his youth he fought, at Beder and Ohud, under the holy standard: in his mature age he was the friend and follower of Ali; and the last remnant of his strength and life was consumed in a distant and dangerous war against the enemies of the Koran. His memory was revered; but the place of his burial was neglected and unknown, during a period of seven hundred and eighty years, till the conquest of Constantinople by Mahomet the Second. A seasonable vision (for such are the manufacture of every religion) revealed the holy spot at the foot of the walls and the bottom of the harbor; and the mosch of Ayub has been deservedly chosen for the simple and martial inauguration of the Turkish sultans.

The event of the siege revived, both in the East and West, the reputation of the Roman arms, and cast a momentary shade over the glories of the Saracens. The Greek ambassador was favorably received at Damascus, a general council of the emirs or Koreish: a peace, or truce, of thirty years was ratified between the two empires; and the stipulation of an annual tribute, fifty horses of a noble breed, fifty slaves, and three thousand pieces of gold, degraded the majesty of the commander of the faithful. The aged caliph was desirous of possessing his dominions, and ending his days in tranquillity and repose: while the Moors and Indians trembled at his name, his palace and city of Damascus was insulted by the Mardaites, or Maronites, of Mount Libanus, the firmest barrier of the empire, till they were disarmed and transplanted by the suspicious policy of the Greeks. After the revolt of Arabia and Persia, the house of Ommiyah was reduced to the kingdoms of Syria and Egypt: their distress and fear enforced their compliance with the pressing demands of the Christians; and the tribute was increased to a slave, a horse, and a thousand pieces of gold, for each of the three hundred and sixty-five days of the solar year. But as soon as the empire was again united by the arms and policy of Abdalmalek, he disclaimed a badge of servitude not less injurious to his conscience than to his pride; he discontinued the payment of the tribute; and the resentment of the Greeks was disabled from action by the mad tyranny of the second Justinian, the just rebellion of his subjects, and the frequent change of his antagonists and successors. Till the reign of Abdalmalek, the Saracens had been content with the free possession of the Persian and Roman treasures, in the coins of Chosroes and Cæsar. By the command of that caliph, a national mint was established, both for silver and gold, and the inscription of the Dinar, though it might be censured by some timorous casuists, proclaimed the unity of the God of Mahomet. Under the reign of the caliph Walid, the Greek language and characters were excluded from the accounts of the public revenue. If this change was productive of the invention or familiar use of our present numerals, the Arabic or Indian ciphers, as they are commonly styled, a regulation of office has promoted the most important discoveries of arithmetic, algebra, and the mathematical sciences.

Whilst the caliph Walid sat idle on the throne of Damascus, whilst his lieutenants achieved the conquest of Transoxiana and Spain, a third army of Saracens overspread the provinces of Asia Minor, and approached the borders of the Byzantine capital. But the attempt and disgrace of the second siege was reserved for his brother Soliman, whose ambition appears to have been quickened by a more active and martial spirit. In the revolutions of the Greek empire, after the tyrant Justinian had been punished and avenged, an humble secretary, Anastasius or Artemius, was promoted by chance or merit to the vacant purple. He was alarmed by the sound of war; and his ambassador returned from Damascus with the tremendous news, that the Saracens were preparing an armament by sea and land, such as would transcend the experience of the past, or the belief of the present age. The precautions of Anastasius were not unworthy of his station, or of the impending danger. He issued a peremptory mandate, that all persons who were not provided with the means of subsistence for a three years' siege should evacuate the city: the public granaries and arsenals were abundantly replenished; the walls were restored and strengthened; and the engines for casting stones, or darts, or fire, were stationed along the ramparts, or in the brigantines of war, of which an additional number was hastily constructed. To prevent is safer, as well as more honorable, than to repel, an attack; and a design was meditated, above the usual spirit of the Greeks, of burning the naval stores of the enemy, the cypress timber that had been hewn in Mount Libanus, and was piled along the sea-shore of Phœnicia, for the service of the Egyptian fleet. This generous enterprise was defeated by the cowardice or treachery of the troops, who, in the new language of the empire, were styled of the *Obsequian Theme*. They murdered their chief, deserted their standard in the Isle of Rhodes, dispersed themselves over the adjacent continent, and deserved pardon or reward by investing with the purple a simple officer of the revenue. The name of Theodosius might recommend him to the senate and people; but, after some months, he sunk into a cloister, and resigned, to the firmer hand of Leo the Isaurian, the urgent defence of the capital and empire. The most formidable of the Saracens, Moslemah, the brother of the caliph, was advancing at the head of one hundred and twenty thousand Arabs and Persians, the greater part mounted on horses or camels; and the successful sieges of Tyana, Amorium, and Pergamus, were of sufficient duration to exercise their skill and to elevate their hopes. At the well-known passage of Abydus, on the Hellespont, the Mahometan arms were transported, for the first time, from Asia to Europe. From thence, wheeling round the Thracian cities of the Propontis, Moslemah invested Constantinople on the land side, surrounded his camp with a ditch and rampart, prepared and planted his engines of assault, and declared, by words and actions, a patient resolution of expecting the return of seed-time and harvest, should the obstinacy of the besieged prove equal to his own. The Greeks would gladly have ransomed their religion and empire, by a fine or assessment of a piece of gold on the head of each inhabitant of the city; but the liberal offer was rejected with disdain, and the presumption of Moslemah was exalted by the speedy approach and invincible force of the natives of Egypt and Syria. They are said to have amounted to eighteen hundred ships: the number betrays their inconsiderable size; and of the twenty stout and capacious vessels, whose magnitude impeded their progress, each was manned with no more than one hundred heavy-armed soldiers. This huge armada proceeded on a smooth sea, and with a gentle gale, towards the mouth of the Bosphorus; the surface of the strait was overshadowed, in the language of the Greeks, with a moving forest, and the same fatal night had been fixed by the Saracen chief for a general assault by sea and land. To allure the confidence of the enemy, the emperor had thrown aside the chain that usually guarded the entrance of the harbor; but while they hesitated whether they should seize the opportunity, or apprehend the snare, the ministers of destruction were at hand. The fire-ships of the Greeks were launched against them; the Arabs, their arms, and vessels, were involved in the same flames; the disorderly fugitives were dashed against each other or overwhelmed in the waves; and I no longer find a vestige of the fleet, that had threatened to extirpate the Roman name. A still more fatal and irreparable loss was that of the caliph Soliman, who died of an indigestion, in his camp near Kinnisrin or Chalcis in Syria, as he was preparing to lead against Constantinople the remaining forces of the East. The brother of Moslemah was succeeded by a kinsman and an enemy; and the throne of an active and able prince was degraded by the useless and pernicious virtues of a bigot. While he started and satisfied the scruples of a blind conscience, the siege was continued through the winter by the neglect, rather than by the resolution of the caliph Omar. The winter proved uncommonly rigorous: above a hundred days the ground was covered with deep snow, and the natives of the sultry climes of Egypt and Arabia lay torpid and almost lifeless in their frozen camp. They revived on the return of spring; a second effort had been made in their favor; and their distress was relieved by the arrival of two numerous fleets, laden with corn, and arms, and soldiers; the first from Alexandria, of four hundred transports and galleys; the second of three hundred and sixty vessels from the ports of Africa. But the Greek fires were again kindled; and if the destruction was less complete, it was owing to the experience which had taught the Moslems to remain at a safe distance, or to the perfidy of the Egyptian mariners, who deserted with their ships to the emperor of the Christians. The trade and navigation of the capital were restored; and the produce of the fisheries supplied the wants, and even the luxury, of the inhabitants. But the calamities of famine and disease were soon felt by the troops of Moslemah, and as the former was miserably assuaged, so the latter was dreadfully propagated, by the pernicious nutriment which hunger compelled them to extract from the most unclean or unnatural food. The spirit of conquest, and even of enthusiasm, was extinct: the Saracens could no longer struggle, beyond their lines, either single or in small parties, without exposing themselves to the merciless retaliation of the Thracian peasants. An army of Bulgarians was attracted from the Danube by the gifts and promises of Leo; and these savage auxiliaries made some atonement for the evils which they had inflicted on the empire, by the defeat and slaughter of twenty-two thousand Asiatics. A report was dexterously scattered, that the Franks, the unknown nations of the Latin world, were arming by sea and land in the defence of the Christian cause, and their formidable aid was expected with far different sensations in the camp and city. At length, after a siege of thirteen months, the hopeless Moslemah received from the caliph the welcome permission of retreat. * The march of the Arabian cavalry over the Hellespont and through the provinces of Asia, was executed without delay or molestation; but an army of their brethren had been cut in pieces on the side of Bithynia, and the remains of the fleet were so repeatedly damaged by tempest and fire, that only five galleys entered the port of Alexandria to relate the tale of their various and almost incredible disasters.

In the two sieges, the deliverance of Constantinople may be chiefly ascribed to the novelty, the terrors, and the real efficacy of the *Greek fire*. The important secret of compounding and directing this artificial flame was imparted by Callinicus, a native of Heliopolis in Syria, who deserted from the service of the caliph to that of the emperor. The skill of a chemist and engineer was equivalent to the succor of fleets and armies; and this discovery or improvement of the military art was fortunately reserved for the distressful period, when the degenerate Romans of the East were incapable of contending with the warlike enthusiasm and youthful vigor of the Saracens. The historian who presumes to analyze this extraordinary composition should suspect his own ignorance and that of his Byzantine guides, so prone to the marvellous, so careless, and, in this instance, so jealous of the truth. From their obscure, and perhaps fallacious, hints it should seem that the principal ingredient of the Greek fire was the *naphtha*, or liquid bitumen, a light, tenacious, and inflammable oil, which springs from the earth, and catches fire as soon as it comes in contact with the air. The naphtha was mingled, I know not by what methods or in what proportions, with sulphur and with the pitch that is extracted from evergreen firs. From this mixture, which produced a thick smoke and a loud explosion, proceeded a fierce and obstinate flame, which not only rose in perpendicular ascent, but likewise burnt with equal vehemence in descent or lateral progress; instead of being extinguished, it was nourished and quickened by the element of water; and sand, urine, or vinegar, were the only remedies that could damp the fury of this powerful agent, which was justly denominated by the Greeks the *liquid*, or the *maritime*, fire. For the annoyance of the enemy, it was employed with equal effect, by sea and land, in battles or in sieges. It was either poured from the rampart in large boilers, or launched in red-hot balls of stone and iron, or darted in arrows and javelins, twisted round with flax and tow, which had deeply imbibed the inflammable oil; sometimes it was deposited in fire-ships, the victims and instruments of a more ample revenge, and was most commonly blown through long tubes of copper which were planted on the prow of a galley, and fancifully shaped into the mouths of savage monsters, that seemed to vomit a stream of liquid and consuming fire. This important art was preserved at Constantinople, as the palladium of the state: the galleys and *artillery* might occasionally be lent to the allies of Rome; but the composition of the Greek fire was concealed with the most jealous scruple, and the terror of the enemies was increased and prolonged by their ignorance and surprise. In the treaties of the administration of the empire, the royal author suggests the answers and excuses that might best elude the indiscreet curiosity and importunate demands of the Barbarians. They should be told that the mystery of the Greek fire had been revealed by an angel to the first and greatest of the Constantines, with a sacred injunction, that this gift of Heaven, this peculiar blessing of the Romans, should never be communicated to any foreign nation; that the prince and the subject were alike bound to religious silence under the temporal and spiritual penalties of treason and sacrilege; and that the impious attempt would provoke the sudden and supernatural vengeance of the God of the Christians. By these precautions, the secret was confined, above four hundred years, to the Romans of the East; and at the end of the eleventh century, the Pisans, to whom every sea and every art were familiar, suffered the effects, without understanding the composition, of the Greek fire. It was at length either discovered or stolen by the Mahometans; and, in the holy wars of Syria and Egypt, they retorted an invention, contrived against themselves, on the heads of the Christians. A knight, who despised the swords and lances of the Saracens, relates, with heartfelt sincerity, his own fears, and those of his companions, at the sight and sound of the mischievous engine that discharged a torrent of the Greek fire, the *feu Gregeois*, as it is styled by the more early of the French writers. It came flying through the air, says Joinville, like a winged long-tailed dragon, about the thickness of a hogshead, with the report of thunder and the velocity of lightning; and the darkness of the night was dispelled by this deadly illumination. The use of the Greek, or, as it might now be called, of the Saracen fire, was continued to the middle of the fourteenth century, when the scientific or casual compound of nitre, sulphur, and charcoal, effected a new revolution in the art of war and the history of mankind.

More Conquests by the Arabs. – Part Two

CONSTANTINOPLE AND THE GREEK fire might exclude the Arabs from the eastern entrance of Europe; but in the West, on the side of the Pyrenees, the provinces of Gaul were threatened and invaded by the conquerors of Spain. The decline of the French monarchy invited the attack of these insatiate fanatics. The descendants of Clovis had lost the inheritance of his martial and ferocious spirit; and their misfortune or demerit has affixed the epithet of *lazy* to the last kings of the Merovingian race. They ascended the throne without power, and sunk into the grave without a name. A country palace, in the neighborhood of Compiegne was allotted for their residence or prison: but each year, in the month of March or May, they were conducted in a wagon drawn by oxen to the assembly of the Franks, to give audience to foreign ambassadors, and to ratify the acts of the mayor of the palace. That domestic officer was become the minister of the nation and the master of the prince. A public employment was converted into the patrimony of a private family: the elder Pepin left a king of mature years under the guardianship of his own widow and her child; and these feeble regents were forcibly dispossessed by the most active of his bastards. A government, half savage and half corrupt, was almost dissolved; and the tributary dukes, and provincial counts, and the territorial lords, were tempted to despise the weakness of the monarch, and to imitate the ambition of the mayor. Among these independent chiefs, one of the boldest and most successful was Eudes, duke of Aquitain, who in the southern provinces of Gaul usurped the authority, and even the title of king. The Goths, the Gascons, and the Franks, assembled under the standard of this Christian hero: he repelled the first invasion of the Saracens; and Zama, lieutenant of the caliph, lost his army and his life under the walls of Thoulouse. The ambition of his successors was stimulated by revenge; they repassed the Pyrenees with the means and the resolution of conquest. The advantageous situation which had recommended Narbonne as the first Roman colony, was again chosen by the Moslems: they claimed the province of Septimania or Languedoc as a just dependence of the Spanish monarchy: the vineyards of Gascony and the city of Bourdeaux were possessed by the sovereign of Damascus and Samarcand; and the south of France, from the mouth of the Garonne to that of the Rhone, assumed the manners and religion of Arabia.

But these narrow limits were scorned by the spirit of Abdalraman, or Abderame, who had been restored by the caliph Hashem to the wishes of the soldiers and people of Spain. That veteran and daring commander adjudged to the obedience of the prophet whatever yet remained of France or of Europe; and prepared to execute the sentence, at the head of a formidable host, in the full confidence of surmounting all opposition either of nature or of man. His first care was to suppress a domestic rebel, who commanded the most important passes of the Pyrenees: Manuza, a Moorish chief, had accepted the alliance of the duke of Aquitain; and Eudes, from a motive of private or public interest, devoted his beauteous daughter to the embraces of the African misbeliever. But the strongest fortresses of Cerdagne were invested by a superior force; the rebel was overtaken and slain in the mountains; and his widow was sent a captive to Damascus, to gratify the desires, or more probably the vanity, of the commander of the faithful. From the Pyrenees, Abderame proceeded without delay to the passage of the Rhone and the siege of Arles. An army of Christians attempted the relief of the city: the tombs of their leaders were yet visible in the thirteenth century; and many thousands of their dead bodies were carried down the rapid stream into the Mediterranean Sea. The arms of Abderame were not less successful on the side of the ocean. He passed without opposition the Garonne and Dordogne, which unite their waters in the Gulf of Bourdeaux; but he found, beyond those rivers, the camp of the intrepid Eudes, who had formed a second army and sustained a second defeat, so fatal to the Christians, that, according to their sad confession, God alone could reckon the number of the slain. The victorious Saracen overran the provinces of Aquitain, whose Gallic names are disguised, rather than lost, in the modern appellations of Perigord, Saintonge, and Poitou: his standards were planted on the walls, or at least before the gates, of Tours and of Sens; and his detachments overspread the kingdom of Burgundy as far as the well-known cities of Lyons and Besancon. The memory of these devastations (for Abderame did not spare the country or the people) was long preserved by tradition; and the invasion of France by the Moors or Mahometans affords the groundwork of those fables, which have been so wildly disfigured in the romances of chivalry, and so elegantly adorned by the Italian muse. In the decline of society and art, the deserted cities could supply a slender booty to the Saracens; their richest spoil was found in the churches and monasteries, which they stripped of their ornaments and delivered to the flames: and the tutelar saints, both Hilary of Poitiers and Martin of Tours, forgot their miraculous powers in the defence of their own sepulchres. A victorious line of march had been prolonged above a thousand miles from the rock of Gibraltar to the banks of the Loire; the repetition of an equal space would have carried the Saracens to the confines of Poland and the Highlands of Scotland; the Rhine is not more impassable than the Nile or Euphrates, and the Arabian fleet might have sailed without a naval combat into the mouth of the Thames. Perhaps the interpretation of the Koran would now be taught in the schools of Oxford, and her pulpits might demonstrate to a circumcised people the sanctity and truth of the revelation of Mahomet.

From such calamities was Christendom delivered by the genius and fortune of one man. Charles, the illegitimate son of the elder Pepin, was content with the titles of mayor or duke of the Franks; but he deserved to become the father of a line of kings. In a laborious administration of twenty-four years, he restored and supported the dignity of the throne, and the rebels of Germany and Gaul were successively crushed by the activity of a warrior, who, in the same campaign, could display his banner on the Elbe, the Rhone, and the shores of the ocean. In the public danger he was summoned by the voice of his country; and his rival, the duke of Aquitain, was reduced to appear among the fugitives and suppliants. "Alas!" exclaimed the Franks, "what a misfortune! what an indignity! We have long heard of the name and conquests of the Arabs: we were apprehensive of their attack from the East; they have now conquered Spain, and invade our country on the side of the West. Yet their numbers, and (since they have no buckler) their arms, are inferior to our own." "If you follow my advice," replied the prudent mayor of the palace, "you will not interrupt their march, nor precipitate your attack. They are like a torrent, which it is dangerous to stem in its career. The thirst of riches, and the consciousness of success, redouble their valor, and valor is of more avail than arms or numbers. Be patient till they have loaded themselves with the encumbrance of wealth. The possession of wealth will divide their councils and assure your victory." This subtile policy is perhaps a refinement of the Arabian writers; and the situation of Charles will suggest a more narrow and selfish motive of procrastination – the secret desire of humbling the pride and wasting the provinces of the rebel duke of Aquitain. It is yet more probable, that the delays of Charles were inevitable and reluctant. A standing army was unknown under the first and second race; more than half the kingdom was now in the hands of the Saracens: according to their respective situation, the Franks of Neustria and Austrasia were to conscious or too careless of the impending danger; and the voluntary aids of the Gepidæ and Germans were separated by a long interval from the standard of the Christian general. No sooner had he collected his forces, than he sought and found the enemy in the centre of France, between Tours and Poitiers. His well-conducted march was covered with a range of hills, and Abderame appears to have been surprised by his unexpected presence. The nations of Asia, Africa, and Europe, advanced with equal ardor to an encounter which would change the history of the world. In the six first days of desultory combat, the horsemen and archers of the East maintained their advantage: but in the closer onset of the seventh day, the Orientals were oppressed by the strength and stature of the Germans, who, with stout hearts and *iron* hands, asserted the civil and religious freedom of their posterity. The epithet of *Martel*, the *Hammer*, which has been added to the name of Charles, is expressive of his weighty and irresistible strokes: the valor of Eudes was excited by resentment and emulation; and their companions, in the eye of history, are the true Peers and Paladins of French chivalry. After a bloody field, in which Abderame was slain, the Saracens, in the close of the evening, retired to their camp. In the disorder and despair of the night, the various tribes of Yemen and Damascus, of Africa and Spain, were provoked to turn their arms against each other: the remains of their host were suddenly dissolved, and each *emir* consulted his safety by a hasty and separate retreat. At the dawn of the day, the stillness of a hostile camp was suspected by the victorious Christians: on the report of their spies, they ventured to explore the riches of the vacant tents; but if we except some celebrated relics, a small portion of the spoil was restored to the innocent and lawful owners. The joyful tidings were soon diffused over the Catholic world, and the monks of Italy could affirm and believe that three hundred and fifty, or three hundred and seventy-five, thousand of the Mahometans had been crushed by the hammer of Charles, while no more than fifteen hundred Christians were slain in the field of Tours. But this incredible tale is sufficiently disproved by the caution of the

French general, who apprehended the snares and accidents of a pursuit, and dismissed his German allies to their native forests. The inactivity of a conqueror betrays the loss of strength and blood, and the most cruel execution is inflicted, not in the ranks of battle, but on the backs of a flying enemy. Yet the victory of the Franks was complete and final; Aquitain was recovered by the arms of Eudes; the Arabs never resumed the conquest of Gaul, and they were soon driven beyond the Pyrenees by Charles Martel and his valiant race. It might have been expected that the savior of Christendom would have been canonized, or at least applauded, by the gratitude of the clergy, who are indebted to his sword for their present existence. But in the public distress, the mayor of the palace had been compelled to apply the riches, or at least the revenues, of the bishops and abbots, to the relief of the state and the reward of the soldiers. His merits were forgotten, his sacrilege alone was remembered, and, in an epistle to a Carlovingian prince, a Gallic synod presumes to declare that his ancestor was damned; that on the opening of his tomb, the spectators were affrighted by a smell of fire and the aspect of a horrid dragon; and that a saint of the times was indulged with a pleasant vision of the soul and body of Charles Martel, burning, to all eternity, in the abyss of hell.

The loss of an army, or a province, in the Western world, was less painful to the court of Damascus, than the rise and progress of a domestic competitor. Except among the Syrians, the caliphs of the house of Ommiyah had never been the objects of the public favor. The life of Mahomet recorded their perseverance in idolatry and rebellion: their conversion had been reluctant, their elevation irregular and factious, and their throne was cemented with the most holy and noble blood of Arabia. The best of their race, the pious Omar, was dissatisfied with his own title: their personal virtues were insufficient to justify a departure from the order of succession; and the eyes and wishes of the faithful were turned towards the line of Hashem, and the kindred of the apostle of God. Of these the Fatimites were either rash or pusillanimous; but the descendants of Abbas cherished, with courage and discretion, the hopes of their rising fortunes. From an obscure residence in Syria, they secretly despatched their agents and missionaries, who preached in the Eastern provinces their hereditary indefeasible right; and Mohammed, the son of Ali, the son of Abdallah, the son of Abbas, the uncle of the prophet, gave audience to the deputies of Chorasan, and accepted their free gift of four hundred thousand pieces of gold. After the death of Mohammed, the oath of allegiance was administered in the name of his son Ibrahim to a numerous band of votaries, who expected only a signal and a leader; and the governor of Chorasan continued to deplore his fruitless admonitions and the deadly slumber of the caliphs of Damascus, till he himself, with all his adherents, was driven from the city and palace of Meru, by the rebellious arms of Abu Moslem. That maker of kings, the author, as he is named, of the *call* of the Abbassides, was at length rewarded for his presumption of merit with the usual gratitude of courts. A mean, perhaps a foreign, extraction could not repress the aspiring energy of Abu Moslem. Jealous of his wives, liberal of his wealth, prodigal of his own blood and of that of others, he could boast with pleasure, and possibly with truth, that he had destroyed six hundred thousand of his enemies; and such was the intrepid gravity of his mind and countenance, that he was never seen to smile except on a day of battle. In the visible separation of parties, the *green* was consecrated to the Fatimites; the Ommiades were distinguished by the *white*; and the *black*, as the most adverse, was naturally adopted by the Abbassides. Their turbans and garments were stained with that gloomy color: two black standards, on pike staves nine cubits long, were borne aloft in the van of Abu Moslem; and their allegorical names of the night and the shadow obscurely represented the indissoluble union and perpetual succession of the line of Hashem. From the Indus to the Euphrates, the East was convulsed by the quarrel of the white and the black factions: the Abbassides were most frequently victorious; but their public success was clouded by the personal misfortune of their chief. The court of Damascus, awakening from a long slumber, resolved to prevent the pilgrimage of Mecca, which Ibrahim had undertaken with a splendid retinue, to recommend himself at once to the favor of the prophet and of the people. A detachment of cavalry intercepted his march and arrested his person; and the unhappy Ibrahim, snatched away from the promise of untasted royalty, expired in iron fetters in the dungeons of Haran. His two younger brothers, Saffah * and Almansor, eluded the search of the tyrant, and lay concealed at Cufa, till the zeal of the people and the approach of his Eastern friends allowed them to expose their persons to the impatient public. On Friday, in the dress of a caliph, in the colors of the sect, Saffah proceeded with religious and military pomp to the mosch: ascending the pulpit, he prayed and preached as the lawful successor of Mahomet; and after his departure, his kinsmen bound a willing people by an oath of fidelity. But it was on the banks of the Zab, and not in the mosch of Cufa, that this important controversy was determined. Every advantage appeared to be on the side of the white faction: the authority of established government; an army of a hundred and twenty thousand soldiers, against a sixth part of that number; and the presence and merit of the caliph Mervan, the fourteenth and last of the house of Ommiyah. Before his accession to the throne, he had deserved, by his Georgian warfare, the honorable epithet of the ass of Mesopotamia; and he might have been ranked amongst the greatest princes, had not, says Abulfeda, the eternal order decreed that moment for the ruin of his family; a decree against which all human fortitude and prudence must struggle in vain. The orders of Mervan were mistaken, or disobeyed: the return of his horse, from which he had dismounted on a necessary occasion, impressed the belief of his death; and the enthusiasm of the black squadrons was ably conducted by Abdallah, the uncle of his competitor. After an irretrievable defeat, the caliph escaped to Mosul; but the colors of the Abbassides were displayed from the rampart; he suddenly repassed the Tigris, cast a melancholy look on his palace of Haran, crossed the Euphrates, abandoned the fortifications of Damascus, and, without halting in Palestine, pitched his last and fatal camp at Busir, on the banks of the Nile. His speed was urged by the incessant diligence of Abdallah, who in every step of the pursuit acquired strength and reputation: the remains of the white faction were finally vanquished in Egypt; and the lance, which terminated the life and anxiety of Mervan, was not less welcome perhaps to the unfortunate than to the victorious chief. The merciless inquisition of the conqueror eradicated the most distant branches of the hostile race: their bones were scattered, their memory was accursed, and the martyrdom of Hossein was abundantly revenged on the posterity of his tyrants. Fourscore of the Ommiades, who had yielded to the faith or clemency of their foes, were invited to a banquet at Damascus. The laws of hospitality were violated by a promiscuous massacre: the board was spread over their fallen bodies; and the festivity of the guests was enlivened by the music of their dying groans. By the event of the civil war, the dynasty of the Abbassides was firmly established; but the Christians only could triumph in the mutual hatred and common loss of the disciples of Mahomet.

Yet the thousands who were swept away by the sword of war might have been speedily retrieved in the succeeding generation, if the consequences of the revolution had not tended to dissolve the power and unity of the empire of the Saracens. In the proscription of the Ommiades, a royal youth of the name of Abdalrahman alone escaped the rage of his enemies, who hunted the wandering exile from the banks of the Euphrates to the valleys of Mount Atlas. His presence in the neighborhood of Spain revived the zeal of the white faction. The name and cause of the Abbassides had been first vindicated by the Persians: the West had been pure from civil arms; and the servants of the abdicated family still held, by a precarious tenure, the inheritance of their lands and the offices of government. Strongly prompted by gratitude, indignation, and fear, they invited the grandson of the caliph Hashem to ascend the throne of his ancestors; and, in his desperate condition, the extremes of rashness and prudence were almost the same. The acclamations of the people saluted his landing on the coast of Andalusia: and, after a successful struggle, Abdalrahman established the throne of Cordova, and was the father of the Ommiades of Spain, who reigned above two hundred and fifty years from the Atlantic to the Pyrenees. He slew in battle a lieutenant of the Abbassides, who had invaded his dominions with a fleet and army: the head of Ala, in salt and camphire, was suspended by a daring messenger before the palace of Mecca; and the caliph Almansor rejoiced in his safety, that he was removed by seas and lands from such a formidable adversary. Their mutual designs or declarations of offensive war evaporated without effect; but instead of opening a door to the conquest of Europe, Spain was dissevered from the trunk of the monarchy, engaged in perpetual hostility with the East, and inclined to peace and friendship with the Christian sovereigns of Constantinople and France. The example of the Ommiades was imitated by the real or fictitious progeny of Ali, the Edrissites of Mauritania, and the more powerful Fatimites of Africa and Egypt. In the tenth century, the chair of Mahomet was disputed by three caliphs or commanders of the faithful, who reigned at Bagdad, Cairoan, and Cordova, excommunicating each other, and agreed only in a principle of discord, that a sectary is more odious and criminal than an unbeliever.

Mecca was the patrimony of the line of Hashem, yet the Abbassides were never tempted to reside either in the birthplace or the city of the prophet. Damascus was disgraced by the choice, and polluted with the blood, of the Ommiades; and, after some hesitation, Almansor, the brother and successor of Saffah, laid the foundations of Bagdad, the Imperial seat of his posterity during a reign of five hundred years. The chosen spot is on the eastern bank of the Tigris, about fifteen miles above the ruins of Modain: the double wall was of a circular form; and such was the rapid increase of a capital, now dwindled to a provincial town, that the funeral of a popular saint might be attended by eight hundred thousand men and sixty thousand women of Bagdad and the adjacent villages. In this *city of peace*, amidst the riches of the East, the Abbassides soon disdained the abstinence and frugality of the first caliphs, and aspired to emulate the magnificence of the Persian kings. After his wars and buildings, Almansor left behind him in gold and silver about thirty millions sterling: and this treasure was exhausted in a few years by the vices or virtues of his children. His son Mahadi, in a single pilgrimage to Mecca, expended six millions of dinars of gold. A pious and charitable motive may sanctify the foundation of cisterns and caravanseras, which he distributed along a measured road of seven hundred miles; but his train of camels, laden with snow, could serve only to astonish the natives of Arabia, and to refresh the fruits and liquors of the royal banquet. The courtiers would surely praise the liberality of his grandson Almamon, who gave away four fifths of the income of a province, a sum of two millions four hundred thousand gold dinars, before he drew his foot from the stirrup. At the nuptials of the same prince, a thousand pearls of the largest size were showered on the head of the bride, and a lottery of lands and houses displayed the capricious bounty of fortune. The glories of the court were brightened, rather than impaired, in the decline of the empire, and a Greek ambassador might admire, or pity, the magnificence of the feeble Moctader. "The caliph's whole army," says the historian Abulfeda, "both horse and foot, was under arms, which together made a body of one hundred and sixty thousand men. His state officers, the favorite slaves, stood near him in splendid apparel, their belts glittering with gold and gems. Near them were seven thousand eunuchs, four thousand of them white, the remainder black. The porters or door-keepers were in number seven hundred. Barges and boats, with the most superb decorations, were seen swimming upon the Tigris. Nor was the palace itself less splendid, in which were hung up thirty-eight thousand pieces of tapestry, twelve thousand five hundred of which were of silk embroidered with gold. The carpets on the floor were twenty-two thousand. A hundred lions were brought out, with a keeper to each lion. Among the other spectacles of rare and stupendous luxury was a tree of gold and silver spreading into eighteen large branches, on which, and on the lesser boughs, sat a variety of birds made of the same precious metals, as well as the leaves of the tree. While the machinery affected spontaneous motions, the several birds warbled their natural harmony. Through this scene of magnificence, the Greek ambassador was led by the vizier to the foot of the caliph's throne." In the West, the Ommiades of Spain supported, with equal pomp, the title of commander of the faithful. Three miles from Cordova, in honor of his favorite sultana, the third and greatest of the Abdalrahmans constructed the city, palace, and gardens of Zehra. Twenty-five years, and above three millions sterling, were employed by the founder: his liberal taste invited the artists of Constantinople, the most skilful sculptors and architects of the age; and the buildings were sustained or adorned by twelve hundred columns of Spanish and African, of Greek and Italian marble. The hall of audience was incrusted with gold and pearls, and a great basin in the centre was surrounded with the curious and costly figures of birds and quadrupeds. In a lofty pavilion of the gardens, one of these basins and fountains, so delightful in a sultry climate, was replenished not with water, but with the purest quicksilver. The seraglio of Abdalrahman, his wives, concubines, and black eunuchs, amounted to six thousand three hundred persons: and he was attended to the field by a guard of twelve thousand horse, whose belts and cimeters were studded with gold.

More Conquests by the Arabs.
– Part Three

IN A PRIVATE CONDITION, our desires are perpetually repressed by poverty and subordination; but the lives and labors of millions are devoted to the service of a despotic prince, whose laws are blindly obeyed, and whose wishes are instantly gratified. Our imagination is dazzled by the splendid picture; and whatever may be the cool dictates of reason, there are few among us who would obstinately refuse a trial of the comforts and the cares of royalty. It may therefore be of some use to borrow the experience of the same Abdalrahman, whose magnificence has perhaps excited our admiration and envy, and to transcribe an authentic memorial which was found in the closet of the deceased caliph. "I have now reigned above fifty years in victory or peace; beloved by my subjects, dreaded by my enemies, and respected by my allies. Riches and honors, power and pleasure, have waited on my call, nor does any earthly blessing appear to have been wanting to my felicity. In this situation, I have diligently numbered the days of pure and genuine happiness which have fallen to my lot: they amount to Fourteen: – O man! place not thy confidence in this present world!" The luxury of the caliphs, so useless to their private happiness, relaxed the nerves, and terminated the progress, of the Arabian empire. Temporal and spiritual conquest had been the sole occupation of the first successors of Mahomet; and after supplying themselves with the necessaries of life, the whole revenue was scrupulously devoted to that salutary work. The Abbassides were impoverished by the multitude of their wants, and their contempt of economy. Instead of pursuing the great object of ambition, their leisure, their affections, the powers of their mind, were diverted by pomp and pleasure: the rewards of valor were embezzled by women and eunuchs, and the royal camp was encumbered by the luxury of the palace. A similar temper was diffused among the subjects of the caliph. Their stern enthusiasm was softened by time and prosperity. They sought riches in the occupations of industry, fame in the pursuits of literature, and happiness in the tranquillity of domestic life. War was no longer the passion of the Saracens; and the increase of pay, the repetition of donatives, were insufficient to allure the posterity of those voluntary champions who had crowded to the standard of Abubeker and Omar for the hopes of spoil and of paradise.

Under the reign of the Ommiades, the studies of the Moslems were confined to the interpretation of the Koran, and the eloquence and poetry of their native tongue. A people continually exposed to the dangers of the field must esteem the healing powers of medicine, or rather of surgery; but the starving physicians of Arabia murmured a complaint that exercise and temperance deprived them of the greatest part of their practice. After their civil and domestic wars, the subjects of the Abbassides, awakening from this mental lethargy, found leisure and felt curiosity for the acquisition of profane science. This spirit was first encouraged by the caliph Almansor, who, besides his knowledge of the Mahometan law, had applied himself with success to the study of astronomy. But when the sceptre devolved to Almamon, the seventh of the Abbassides, he completed the designs of his grandfather, and invited the muses from their ancient seats. His ambassadors at Constantinople, his agents in Armenia, Syria, and Egypt, collected the volumes of Grecian science; at his command they were translated by the most skilful interpreters into the Arabic language: his subjects were exhorted assiduously to peruse these instructive writings; and the successor of Mahomet assisted with pleasure and modesty at the assemblies and disputations of the learned. "He was not ignorant," says Abulpharagius, "that they are the elect of God, his best and most useful servants, whose lives are devoted to the improvement of their rational faculties. The mean ambition of the Chinese or the Turks may glory in the industry of their hands or the indulgence of their brutal appetites. Yet these dexterous artists must view, with hopeless emulation, the hexagons and pyramids of the cells of a beehive: these fortitudinous heroes are awed by the superior fierceness of the lions and tigers; and in their amorous enjoyments they are much inferior to the vigor of the grossest and most sordid quadrupeds. The teachers of wisdom are the true luminaries and legislators of a world, which, without their aid, would again sink in ignorance and barbarism." The zeal and curiosity of Almamon were imitated by succeeding princes of the line of Abbas: their rivals, the Fatimites of Africa and the Ommiades of Spain, were the patrons of the learned, as well as the commanders of the faithful; the same royal prerogative was claimed by their independent emirs of the provinces; and their emulation diffused the taste and the rewards of science from Samarcand and Bochara to Fez and Cordova. The vizier of a sultan consecrated a sum of two hundred thousand pieces of gold to the foundation of a college at Bagdad, which he endowed with an annual revenue of fifteen thousand dinars. The fruits of instruction were communicated, perhaps at different times, to six thousand disciples of every degree, from the son of the noble to that of the mechanic: a sufficient allowance was provided for the indigent scholars; and the merit or industry of the professors was repaid with adequate stipends. In every city the productions of Arabic literature were copied and collected by the curiosity of the studious and the vanity of the rich. A private doctor refused the invitation of the sultan of Bochara, because the carriage of his books would have required four hundred camels. The royal library of the Fatimites consisted of one hundred thousand manuscripts, elegantly transcribed and splendidly bound, which were lent, without jealousy or avarice, to the students of Cairo. Yet this collection must appear moderate, if we can believe that the Ommiades of Spain had formed a library of six hundred thousand volumes, forty-four of which were employed in the mere catalogue. Their capital, Cordova, with the adjacent towns of Malaga, Almeria, and Murcia, had given birth to more than three hundred writers, and above seventy public libraries were opened in the cities of the Andalusian kingdom. The age of Arabian learning continued about five hundred years, till the great eruption of the Moguls, and was coeval with the darkest and most slothful period of European annals; but since the sun of science has arisen in the West, it should seem that the Oriental studies have languished and declined.

In the libraries of the Arabians, as in those of Europe, the far greater part of the innumerable volumes were possessed only of local value or imaginary merit. The shelves were crowded with orators and poets, whose style was adapted to the taste and manners of their countrymen; with general and partial histories, which each revolving generation supplied with a new harvest of persons and events; with codes and commentaries of jurisprudence, which derived their authority from the law of the prophet; with the interpreters of the Koran, and orthodox tradition; and with the whole theological tribe, polemics, mystics, scholastics, and moralists, the first or the last of writers, according to the different estimates of sceptics or believers. The works of speculation or science may be reduced to the four classes of philosophy, mathematics, astronomy, and physic. The sages of Greece were translated and illustrated in the Arabic language, and some treatises, now lost in the original, have been recovered in the versions of the East, which possessed and studied the writings of Aristotle and Plato, of Euclid and Apollonius, of Ptolemy, Hippocrates, and Galen. Among the ideal systems which have varied with the fashion of the times, the Arabians adopted the philosophy of the Stagirite, alike intelligible or alike obscure for the readers of every age. Plato wrote for the Athenians, and his allegorical genius is too closely blended with the language and religion of Greece. After the fall of that religion, the Peripatetics, emerging from their obscurity, prevailed in the controversies of the Oriental sects, and their founder was long afterwards restored by the Mahometans of Spain to the Latin schools. The physics, both of the Academy and the Lycæum, as they are built, not on observation, but on argument, have retarded the progress of real knowledge. The metaphysics of infinite, or finite, spirit, have too often been enlisted in the service of superstition. But the human faculties are fortified by the art and practice of dialectics; the ten predicaments of Aristotle collect and methodize our ideas, and his syllogism is the keenest weapon of dispute. It was dexterously wielded in the schools of the Saracens, but as it is more effectual for the detection of error than for the investigation of truth, it is not surprising that new generations of masters and disciples should still revolve in the same circle of logical argument. The mathematics are distinguished by a peculiar privilege, that, in the course of ages, they may always advance, and can never recede. But the ancient geometry, if I am not misinformed, was resumed in the same state by the Italians of the fifteenth century; and whatever may be the origin of the name, the science of algebra is ascribed to the Grecian Diophantus by the modest testimony of the Arabs themselves. They cultivated with more success the sublime science of astronomy, which elevates the mind of man to disdain his diminutive planet and momentary existence. The costly instruments of observation were supplied by the caliph Almamon, and the land of the Chaldæans still afforded the same spacious level, the same unclouded horizon. In the plains of Sinaar, and a second time in those of Cufa, his mathematicians accurately measured a degree of the great circle of the earth, and determined at twenty-four thousand miles the entire circumference of our globe. From the reign of the Abbassides to that of the grandchildren of Tamerlane, the stars, without the aid of glasses, were diligently observed; and the astronomical tables of Bagdad, Spain, and Samarcand, correct some minute errors, without daring to renounce the hypothesis of Ptolemy, without advancing a step towards the discovery of the solar system. In the Eastern courts, the truths of science could be recommended only by ignorance and folly, and the astronomer would have been disregarded, had he not debased his wisdom or honesty by the vain predictions of astrology. But in the science of medicine, the Arabians have been deservedly applauded. The names of Mesua and Geber, of Razis and Avicenna, are ranked with the Grecian masters; in the city of Bagdad, eight hundred and sixty physicians were licensed to exercise their lucrative profession: in Spain, the life of the Catholic princes was intrusted to the skill of the Saracens, and the school of Salerno, their legitimate offspring, revived in Italy and Europe the precepts of the healing art. The success of each professor must have been influenced by personal and accidental causes; but we may form a less fanciful estimate of their general knowledge of anatomy, botany, and chemistry, the threefold basis of their theory and practice. A superstitious reverence for the dead confined both the Greeks and the Arabians to the dissection of apes and quadrupeds; the more solid and visible parts were known in the time of Galen, and the finer scrutiny of the human frame was reserved for the microscope and the injections of modern artists. Botany is an active science, and the discoveries of the torrid zone might enrich the herbal of Dioscorides with two thousand plants. Some traditional knowledge might be secreted in the temples and monasteries of Egypt; much useful experience had been acquired in the practice of arts and manufactures; but the *science* of chemistry owes its origin and improvement to the industry of the Saracens. They first invented and named the alembic for the purposes of distillation, analyzed the substances of the three kingdoms of nature, tried the distinction and affinities of alcalis and acids, and converted the poisonous minerals into soft and salutary medicines. But the most eager search of Arabian chemistry was the transmutation of metals, and the elixir of immortal health: the reason and the fortunes of thousands were evaporated in the crucibles of alchemy, and the consummation of the great work was promoted by the worthy aid of mystery, fable, and superstition.

But the Moslems deprived themselves of the principal benefits of a familiar intercourse with Greece and Rome, the knowledge of antiquity, the purity of taste, and the freedom of thought. Confident in the riches of their native tongue, the Arabians disdained the study of any foreign idiom. The Greek interpreters were chosen among their Christian subjects; they formed their translations, sometimes on the original text, more frequently perhaps on a Syriac version; and in the crowd of astronomers and physicians, there is no example of a poet, an orator, or even an historian, being taught to speak the language of the Saracens. The mythology of Homer would have provoked the abhorrence of those stern fanatics: they possessed in lazy ignorance the colonies of the Macedonians, and the provinces of Carthage and Rome: the heroes of Plutarch and Livy were buried in oblivion; and the history of the world before Mahomet was reduced to a short legend of the patriarchs, the prophets, and the Persian kings. Our education in the Greek and Latin schools may have fixed in our minds a standard of exclusive taste; and I am not forward to condemn the literature and judgment of nations, of whose language I am ignorant. Yet I *know* that the classics have much to teach, and I *believe* that the Orientals have much to learn; the temperate dignity of style, the graceful proportions of art, the forms of visible and intellectual beauty, the just delineation of character and passion, the rhetoric of narrative and argument, the regular fabric of epic and dramatic poetry. The influence of truth and reason is of a less ambiguous complexion. The philosophers of Athens and Rome enjoyed the blessings, and asserted the rights, of civil and religious freedom. Their moral and political writings might have gradually unlocked the fetters of Eastern despotism, diffused a liberal spirit of inquiry and toleration, and encouraged the Arabian sages to suspect that their caliph was a tyrant, and their prophet an impostor. The instinct of superstition was alarmed by the introduction even of the abstract sciences; and the more rigid doctors of the law condemned the rash and pernicious curiosity of Almamon. To the thirst of martyrdom, the vision of paradise, and the belief of predestination, we must ascribe the invincible enthusiasm of the prince and people. And the sword of the Saracens became less formidable when their youth was drawn away from the camp to the college, when the armies of the faithful presumed to read and to reflect. Yet the foolish vanity of the Greeks was jealous of their studies, and reluctantly imparted the sacred fire to the Barbarians of the East.

In the bloody conflict of the Ommiades and Abbassides, the Greeks had stolen the opportunity of avenging their wrongs and enlarging their limits. But a severe retribution was exacted by Mohadi, the third caliph of the new dynasty, who seized, in his turn, the favorable opportunity, while a woman and a child, Irene and Constantine, were seated on the Byzantine throne. An army of ninety-five thousand Persians and Arabs was sent from the Tigris to the Thracian Bosphorus, under the command of Harun, or Aaron, the second son of the commander of the faithful. His encampment on the opposite heights of Chrysopolis, or Scutari, informed Irene, in her palace of Constantinople, of the loss of her troops and provinces. With the consent or connivance of their sovereign, her ministers subscribed an ignominious peace; and the exchange of some royal gifts could not disguise the annual tribute of seventy thousand dinars of gold, which was imposed on the Roman empire. The Saracens had too rashly advanced into the midst of a distant and hostile land: their retreat was solicited by the promise of faithful guides and plentiful markets; and not a Greek had courage to whisper, that their weary forces might be surrounded and destroyed in their necessary passage between a slippery mountain and the River Sangarius. Five years after this expedition, Harun ascended the throne of his father and his elder brother; the most powerful and vigorous monarch of his race, illustrious in the West, as the ally of Charlemagne, and familiar to the most childish readers, as the perpetual hero of the Arabian tales. His title to the name of *Al Rashid* (the *Just*) is sullied by the extirpation of the generous, perhaps the innocent, Barmecides; yet he could listen to the complaint of a poor widow who had been pillaged by his troops, and who dared, in a passage of the Koran, to threaten the inattentive despot with the judgment of God and posterity. His court was adorned with luxury and science; but, in a reign of three-and-twenty years, Harun repeatedly visited his provinces from Chorasan to Egypt; nine times he performed the pilgrimage of Mecca; eight times he invaded the territories of the Romans; and as often as they declined the payment of the tribute, they were taught to feel that a month of depredation was more costly than a year of submission. But when the unnatural mother of Constantine was deposed and banished, her successor, Nicephorus, resolved to obliterate this badge of servitude and disgrace. The epistle of the emperor to the caliph was pointed with an allusion to the game of chess, which had already spread from Persia to Greece. "The queen (he spoke of Irene) considered you as a rook, and herself as a pawn. That pusillanimous female submitted to pay a tribute, the double of which she ought to have exacted from the Barbarians. Restore therefore the fruits of your injustice, or abide the determination of the sword." At these words the ambassadors cast a bundle of swords before the foot of the throne. The caliph smiled at the menace, and drawing his cimeter, *samsamah*, a weapon of historic or fabulous renown, he cut asunder the feeble arms of the Greeks, without turning the edge, or endangering the temper, of his blade. He then dictated an epistle of tremendous brevity: "In the name of the most merciful God, Harun al Rashid, commander of the faithful, to Nicephorus, the Roman dog. I have read thy letter, O thou son of an unbelieving mother. Thou shalt not hear, thou shalt behold, my reply." It was written in characters of blood and fire on the plains of Phrygia; and the warlike celerity of the Arabs could only be checked by the arts of deceit and the show of repentance. The triumphant caliph retired, after the fatigues of the campaign, to his favorite palace of Racca on the Euphrates: but the distance of five hundred miles, and the inclemency of the season, encouraged his adversary to violate the peace. Nicephorus was astonished by the bold and rapid march of the commander of the faithful, who repassed, in the depth of winter, the snows of Mount Taurus: his stratagems of policy and war were exhausted; and the perfidious Greek escaped with three wounds from a field of battle overspread with forty thousand of his subjects. Yet the emperor was ashamed of submission, and the caliph was resolved on victory. One hundred and thirty-five thousand regular soldiers received pay, and were inscribed in the military roll; and above three hundred thousand persons of every denomination marched under the black standard of the Abbassides. They swept the surface of Asia Minor far beyond Tyana and Ancyra, and invested the Pontic Heraclea, once a flourishing state, now a paltry town; at that time capable of sustaining, in her antique walls, a month's siege against the forces of the East. The ruin was complete, the spoil was ample; but if Harun had been conversant with Grecian story, he would have regretted the statue of Hercules, whose attributes, the club, the bow, the quiver, and the lion's hide, were sculptured in massy gold. The progress of desolation by sea and land, from the Euxine to the Isle of Cyprus, compelled the emperor Nicephorus to retract his haughty defiance. In the new treaty, the ruins of Heraclea were left forever as a lesson and a trophy; and the coin of the tribute was marked with the image and superscription of Harun and his three sons. Yet this plurality of lords might contribute to remove the dishonor of the Roman name. After the death of their father, the heirs of the caliph were involved in civil discord, and the conqueror, the liberal Almamon, was sufficiently engaged in the restoration of domestic peace and the introduction of foreign science.

More Conquests by the Arabs.
– Part Four

UNDER THE REIGN OF Almamon at Bagdad, of Michael the Stammerer at Constantinople, the islands of Crete and Sicily were subdued by the Arabs. The former of these conquests is disdained by their own writers, who were ignorant of the fame of Jupiter and Minos, but it has not been overlooked by the Byzantine historians, who now begin to cast a clearer light on the affairs of their own times. A band of Andalusian volunteers, discontented with the climate or government of Spain, explored the adventures of the sea; but as they sailed in no more than ten or twenty galleys, their warfare must be branded with the name of piracy. As the subjects and sectaries of the *white* party, they might lawfully invade the dominions of the *black* caliphs. A rebellious faction introduced them into Alexandria; they cut in pieces both friends and foes, pillaged the churches and the moschs, sold above six thousand Christian captives, and maintained their station in the capital of Egypt, till they were oppressed by the forces and the presence of Almamon himself. From the mouth of the Nile to the Hellespont, the islands and sea-coasts both of the Greeks and Moslems were exposed to their depredations; they saw, they envied, they tasted the fertility of Crete, and soon returned with forty galleys to a more serious attack. The Andalusians wandered over the land fearless and unmolested; but when they descended with their plunder to the sea-shore, their vessels were in flames, and their chief, Abu Caab, confessed himself the author of the mischief. Their clamors accused his madness or treachery. «Of what do you complain?» replied the crafty emir. «I have brought you to a land flowing with milk and honey. Here is your true country; repose from your toils, and forget the barren place of your nativity.» «And our wives and children?» «Your beauteous captives will supply the place of your wives, and in their embraces you will soon become the fathers of a new progeny.» The first habitation was their camp, with a ditch and rampart, in the Bay of Suda; but an apostate monk led them to a more desirable position in the eastern parts; and the name of Candax, their fortress and colony, has been extended to the whole island, under the corrupt and modern appellation of *Candia*. The hundred cities of the age of Minos were diminished to thirty; and of these, only one, most probably Cydonia, had courage to retain the substance of freedom and the profession of Christianity. The Saracens of Crete soon repaired the loss of their navy; and the timbers of Mount Ida were launched into the main. During a hostile period of one hundred and thirty-eight years, the princes of Constantinople attacked these licentious corsairs with fruitless curses and ineffectual arms.

The loss of Sicily was occasioned by an act of superstitious rigor. An amorous youth, who had stolen a nun from her cloister, was sentenced by the emperor to the amputation of his tongue. Euphemius appealed to the reason and policy of the Saracens of Africa; and soon returned with the Imperial purple, a fleet of one hundred ships, and an army of seven hundred horse and ten thousand foot. They landed at Mazara near the ruins of the ancient Selinus; but after some partial victories, Syracuse was delivered by the Greeks, the apostate was slain before her walls, and his African friends were reduced to the necessity of feeding on the flesh of their own horses. In their turn they were relieved by a powerful reënforcement of their brethren of Andalusia; the largest and western part of the island was gradually reduced, and the commodious harbor of Palermo was chosen for the seat of the naval and military power of the Saracens. Syracuse preserved about fifty years the faith which she had sworn to Christ and to Cæsar. In the last and fatal siege, her citizens displayed some remnant of the spirit which had formerly resisted the powers of Athens and Carthage. They stood above twenty days against the battering-rams and *catapult*, the mines and tortoises of the besiegers; and the place might have been relieved, if the mariners of the Imperial fleet had not been detained at Constantinople in building a church to the Virgin Mary. The deacon Theodosius, with the bishop and clergy, was dragged in chains from the altar to Palermo, cast into a subterraneous dungeon, and exposed to the hourly peril of death or apostasy. His pathetic, and not inelegant, complaint may be read as the epitaph of his country. From the Roman conquest to this final calamity, Syracuse, now dwindled to the primitive Isle of Ortygea, had insensibly declined. Yet the relics were still precious; the plate of the cathedral weighed five thousand pounds of silver; the entire spoil was computed at one million of pieces of gold, (about four hundred thousand pounds sterling,) and the captives must outnumber the seventeen thousand Christians, who were transported from the sack of Tauromenium into African servitude. In Sicily, the religion and language of the Greeks were eradicated; and such was the docility of the rising generation, that fifteen thousand boys were circumcised and clothed on the same day with the son of the Fatimite caliph. The Arabian squadrons issued from the harbors of Palermo, Biserta, and Tunis; a hundred and fifty towns of Calabria and Campania were attacked and pillaged; nor could the suburbs of Rome be defended by the name of the Cæsars and apostles. Had the Mahometans been united, Italy must have fallen an easy and glorious accession to the empire of the prophet. But the caliphs of Bagdad had lost their authority in the West; the Aglabites and Fatimites usurped the provinces of Africa, their emirs of Sicily aspired to independence; and the design of conquest and dominion was degraded to a repetition of predatory inroads.

In the sufferings of prostrate Italy, the name of Rome awakens a solemn and mournful recollection. A fleet of Saracens from the African coast presumed to enter the mouth of the Tyber, and to approach a city which even yet, in her fallen state, was revered as the metropolis of the Christian world. The gates and ramparts were guarded by a trembling people; but the tombs and temples of St. Peter and St. Paul were left exposed in the suburbs of the Vatican and of the Ostian way. Their invisible sanctity had protected them against the Goths, the Vandals, and the Lombards; but the Arabs disdained both the gospel and the legend; and their rapacious spirit was approved and animated by the precepts of the Koran. The Christian *idols* were stripped of their costly offerings; a silver altar was torn away from the shrine of St. Peter; and if the bodies or the buildings were left entire, their deliverance must be imputed to the haste, rather than the scruples, of the Saracens. In their course along the Appian way, they pillaged Fundi and besieged Gayeta; but they had turned aside from the walls of Rome, and by their divisions, the Capitol was saved from the yoke of the prophet of Mecca. The same danger still impended on the heads of the Roman people; and their domestic force was unequal to the assault of an African emir. They claimed the protection of their Latin sovereign; but the Carlovingian standard was overthrown by a detachment of the Barbarians: they meditated the restoration of the Greek emperors; but the attempt was treasonable, and the succor remote and precarious. Their distress appeared to receive some aggravation from the death of their spiritual and temporal chief; but the pressing emergency superseded the forms and intrigues of an election; and the unanimous choice of Pope Leo the Fourth was the safety of the church and city. This pontiff was born a Roman; the courage of the first ages of the republic glowed in his breast; and, amidst the ruins of his country, he stood erect, like one of the firm and lofty columns that rear their heads above the fragments of the Roman forum. The first days of his reign were consecrated to the purification and removal of relics, to prayers and processions, and to all the solemn offices of religion, which served at least to heal the imagination, and restore the hopes, of the multitude. The public defence had been long neglected, not from the presumption of peace, but from the distress and poverty of the times. As far as the scantiness of his means and the shortness of his leisure would allow, the ancient walls were repaired by the command of Leo; fifteen towers, in the most accessible stations, were built or renewed; two of these commanded on either side of the Tyber; and an iron chain was drawn across the stream to impede the ascent of a hostile navy. The Romans were assured of a short respite by the welcome news, that the siege of Gayeta had been raised, and that a part of the enemy, with their sacrilegious plunder, had perished in the waves.

But the storm, which had been delayed, soon burst upon them with redoubled violence. The Aglabite, who reigned in Africa, had inherited from his father a treasure and an army: a fleet of Arabs and Moors, after a short refreshment in the harbors of Sardinia, cast anchor before the mouth of the Tyber, sixteen miles from the city: and their discipline and numbers appeared to threaten, not a transient inroad, but a serious design of conquest and dominion. But the vigilance of Leo had formed an alliance with the vassals of the Greek empire, the free and maritime states of Gayeta, Naples, and Amalfi; and in the hour of danger, their galleys appeared in the port of Ostia under the command of Cæsarius, the son of the Neapolitan duke, a noble and valiant youth, who had already vanquished the fleets of the Saracens. With his principal companions, Cæsarius was invited to the Lateran palace, and the dexterous pontiff affected to inquire their errand, and to accept with joy and surprise their providential succor. The city bands, in arms, attended their father to Ostia, where he reviewed and blessed his generous deliverers. They kissed his feet, received the communion with martial devotion, and listened to the prayer of Leo, that the same God who had supported St. Peter and St. Paul on the waves of the sea, would strengthen the hands of his champions against the adversaries of his holy name. After a similar prayer, and with equal resolution, the Moslems advanced to the attack of the Christian galleys, which preserved their advantageous station along the coast. The victory inclined to the side of the allies, when it was less gloriously decided in their favor by a sudden tempest, which confounded the skill and courage of the stoutest mariners. The Christians were sheltered in a friendly harbor, while the Africans were scattered and dashed in pieces among the rocks and islands of a hostile shore. Those who escaped from shipwreck and hunger neither found, nor deserved, mercy at the hands of their implacable pursuers. The sword and the gibbet reduced the dangerous multitude of captives; and the remainder was more usefully employed, to restore the sacred edifices which they had attempted to subvert. The pontiff, at the head of the citizens and allies, paid his grateful devotion at the shrines of the apostles; and, among the spoils of this naval victory, thirteen Arabian bows of pure and massy silver were suspended round the altar of the fishermen of Galilee. The reign of Leo the Fourth was employed in the defence and ornament of the Roman state. The churches were renewed and embellished: near four thousand pounds of silver were consecrated to repair the losses of St. Peter; and his sanctuary was decorated with a plate of gold of the weight of two hundred and sixteen pounds, embossed with the portraits of the pope and emperor, and encircled with a string of pearls. Yet this vain magnificence reflects less glory on the character of Leo than the paternal care with which he rebuilt the walls of Horta and Ameria; and transported the wandering inhabitants of Centumcellæ to his new foundation of Leopolis, twelve miles from the sea-shore. By his liberality, a colony of Corsicans, with their wives and children, was planted in the station of Porto, at the mouth of the Tyber: the falling city was restored for their use, the fields and vineyards were divided among the new settlers: their first efforts were assisted by a gift of horses and cattle; and the hardy exiles, who breathed revenge against the Saracens, swore to live and die under the standard of St. Peter. The nations of the West and North who visited the threshold of the apostles had gradually formed the large and populous suburb of the Vatican, and their various habitations were distinguished, in the language of the times, as the schools of the Greeks and Goths, of the Lombards and Saxons. But this venerable spot was still open to sacrilegious insult: the design of enclosing it with walls and towers exhausted all that authority could command, or charity would supply: and the pious labor of four years was animated in every season, and at every hour, by the presence of the indefatigable pontiff. The love of fame, a generous but worldly passion, may be detected in the name of the *Leonine city*, which he bestowed on the Vatican; yet the pride of the dedication was tempered with Christian penance and humility. The boundary was trod by the bishop and his clergy, barefoot, in sackcloth and ashes; the songs of triumph were modulated to psalms and litanies; the walls were besprinkled with holy water; and the ceremony was concluded with a prayer, that, under the guardian care of the apostles and the angelic host, both the old and the new Rome might ever be preserved pure, prosperous, and impregnable.

The emperor Theophilus, son of Michael the Stammerer, was one of the most active and high-spirited princes who reigned at Constantinople during the middle age. In offensive or defensive war, he marched in person five times against the Saracens, formidable in his attack, esteemed by the enemy in his losses and defeats. In the last of these expeditions he penetrated into Syria, and besieged the obscure town of Sozopetra; the casual birthplace of the caliph Motassem, whose father Harun was attended in peace or war by the most favored of his wives and concubines. The revolt of a Persian impostor employed at that moment the arms of the Saracen, and he could only intercede in favor of a place for which he felt and acknowledged some degree of filial affection. These solicitations determined the emperor to wound his pride in so sensible a part. Sozopetra was levelled with the ground, the Syrian prisoners were marked or mutilated with ignominious cruelty, and a thousand female captives were forced away from the adjacent territory. Among these a matron of the house of Abbas invoked, in an agony of despair, the name of Motassem; and the insults of the Greeks engaged the honor of her kinsman to avenge his indignity, and to answer her appeal. Under the reign of the two elder brothers, the inheritance of the youngest had been confined to Anatolia, Armenia, Georgia, and Circassia; this frontier station had exercised his military talents; and among his accidental claims to the name of *Octonary*, the most meritorious are the *eight* battles which he gained or fought against the enemies of the Koran. In this personal quarrel, the troops of Irak, Syria, and Egypt, were recruited from the tribes of Arabia and the Turkish hordes; his cavalry might be numerous, though we should deduct some myriads from the hundred and thirty thousand horses of the royal stables; and the expense of the armament was computed at four millions sterling, or one hundred thousand pounds of gold. From Tarsus, the place of assembly, the Saracens advanced in three divisions along the high road of Constantinople: Motassem himself commanded the centre, and the vanguard was given to his son Abbas, who, in the trial of the first adventures, might succeed with the more glory, or fail with the least reproach. In the revenge of his injury, the caliph prepared to retaliate a similar affront. The father of Theophilus was a native of Amorium in Phrygia: the original seat of the Imperial house had been adorned with privileges and monuments; and, whatever might be the indifference of the people, Constantinople itself was scarcely of more value in the eyes of the sovereign and his court. The name of Amorium was inscribed on the shields of the Saracens; and their three armies were again united under the walls of the devoted city. It had been proposed by the wisest counsellors, to evacuate Amorium, to remove the inhabitants, and to abandon the empty structures to the vain resentment of the Barbarians. The emperor embraced the more generous resolution of defending, in a siege and battle, the country of his ancestors. When the armies drew near, the front of the Mahometan line appeared to a Roman eye more closely planted with spears and javelins; but the event of the action was not glorious on either side to the national troops. The Arabs were broken, but it was by the swords of thirty thousand Persians, who had obtained service and settlement in the Byzantine empire. The Greeks were repulsed and vanquished, but it was by the arrows of the Turkish cavalry; and had not their bowstrings been damped and relaxed by the evening rain, very few of the Christians could have escaped with the emperor from the field of battle. They breathed at Dorylæum, at the distance of three days; and Theophilus, reviewing his trembling squadrons, forgave the common flight both of the prince and people. After this discovery of his weakness, he vainly hoped to deprecate the fate of Amorium: the inexorable caliph rejected with contempt his prayers and promises; and detained the Roman ambassadors to be the witnesses of his great revenge. They had nearly been the witnesses of his shame. The vigorous assaults of fifty-five days were encountered by a faithful governor, a veteran garrison, and a desperate people; and the Saracens must have raised the siege, if a domestic traitor had not pointed to the weakest part of the wall, a place which was decorated with the statues of a lion and a bull. The vow of Motassem was accomplished with unrelenting rigor: tired, rather than satiated, with destruction, he returned to his new palace of Samara, in the neighborhood of Bagdad, while the *unfortunate* Theophilus implored the tardy and doubtful aid of his Western rival the emperor of the Franks. Yet in the siege of Amorium about seventy thousand Moslems had perished: their loss had been revenged by the slaughter of thirty thousand Christians, and the sufferings of an equal number of captives, who were treated as the most atrocious criminals. Mutual necessity could sometimes extort the exchange or ransom of prisoners: but in the national and religious conflict of the two empires, peace was without confidence, and war without mercy. Quarter was seldom given in the field; those who escaped the edge of the sword were condemned to hopeless servitude, or exquisite torture; and a Catholic emperor relates, with visible satisfaction, the execution of the Saracens of Crete, who were flayed alive, or plunged into caldrons of boiling oil. To a point of honor Motassem had sacrificed a flourishing city, two hundred thousand lives, and the property of millions. The same caliph descended from his horse, and dirtied his robe, to relieve the distress of a decrepit old man, who, with his laden ass, had tumbled into a ditch. On which of these actions did he reflect with the most pleasure, when he was summoned by the angel of death?

With Motassem, the eighth of the Abbassides, the glory of his family and nation expired. When the Arabian conquerors had spread themselves over the East, and were mingled with the servile crowds of Persia, Syria, and Egypt, they insensibly lost the freeborn and martial virtues of the desert. The courage of the South is the artificial fruit of discipline and prejudice; the active power of enthusiasm had decayed, and the mercenary forces of the caliphs were recruited in those climates of the North, of which valor is the hardy and spontaneous production. Of the Turks who dwelt beyond the Oxus and Jaxartes, the robust youths, either taken in war or purchased in trade, were educated in the exercises of the field, and the profession of the Mahometan faith. The Turkish guards stood in arms round the throne of their benefactor, and their chiefs usurped the dominion of the palace and the provinces. Motassem, the first author of this dangerous example, introduced into the capital above fifty thousand Turks: their licentious conduct provoked the public indignation, and the quarrels of the soldiers and people induced the caliph to retire from Bagdad, and establish his own residence and the camp of his Barbarian favorites at Samara on the Tigris, about twelve leagues above the city of Peace. His son Motawakkel was a jealous and cruel tyrant: odious to his subjects, he cast himself on the fidelity of the strangers, and these strangers, ambitious and apprehensive, were tempted by the rich promise of a revolution. At the instigation, or at least in the cause of his son, they burst into his apartment at the hour of supper, and the caliph was cut into seven pieces by the same swords which he had recently distributed among the guards of his life and throne. To this throne, yet streaming with a father's blood, Montasser was triumphantly led; but in a reign of six months, he found only the pangs of a guilty conscience. If he wept at the sight of an old tapestry which represented the crime and punishment of the son of Chosroes, if his days were abridged by grief and remorse, we may allow some pity to a parricide, who exclaimed, in the bitterness of death, that he had lost both this world and the world to come. After this act of treason, the ensigns of royalty, the garment and walking-staff of Mahomet, were given and torn away by the foreign mercenaries, who in four years created, deposed, and murdered, three commanders of the faithful. As often as the Turks were inflamed by fear, or rage, or avarice, these caliphs were dragged by the feet, exposed naked to the scorching sun, beaten with iron clubs, and compelled to purchase, by the abdication of their dignity, a short reprieve of inevitable fate. At length, however, the fury of the tempest was spent or diverted: the Abbassides returned to the less turbulent residence of Bagdad; the insolence of the Turks was curbed with a firmer and more skilful hand, and their numbers were divided and destroyed in foreign warfare. But the nations of the East had been taught to trample on the successors of the prophet; and the blessings of domestic peace were obtained by the relaxation of strength and discipline. So uniform are the mischiefs of military despotism, that I seem to repeat the story of the prætorians of Rome.

While the flame of enthusiasm was damped by the business, the pleasure, and the knowledge, of the age, it burnt with concentrated heat in the breasts of the chosen few, the congenial spirits, who were ambitious of reigning either in this world or in the next. How carefully soever the book of prophecy had been sealed by the apostle of Mecca, the wishes, and (if we may profane the word) even the reason, of fanaticism might believe that, after the successive missions of Adam, Noah, Abraham, Moses, Jesus, and Mahomet, the same God, in the fulness of time, would reveal a still more perfect and permanent law. In the two hundred and seventy-seventh year of the Hegira, and in the neighborhood of Cufa, an Arabian preacher, of the name of Carmath, assumed the lofty and incomprehensible style of the Guide, the Director, the Demonstration, the Word, the Holy Ghost, the Camel, the Herald of the Messiah, who had conversed with him in a human shape, and the representative of Mohammed the son of Ali, of St. John the Baptist, and of the angel Gabriel. In his mystic volume, the precepts of the Koran were refined to a more spiritual sense: he relaxed the duties of ablution, fasting, and pilgrimage; allowed the indiscriminate use of wine and forbidden food; and nourished the fervor of his disciples by the daily repetition of fifty prayers. The idleness and ferment of the rustic crowd awakened the attention of the magistrates of Cufa; a timid persecution assisted the progress of the new sect; and the name of the prophet became more revered after his person had been withdrawn from the world. His twelve apostles dispersed themselves among the Bedoweens, "a race of men," says Abulfeda, "equally devoid of reason and of religion;" and the success of their preaching seemed to threaten Arabia with a new revolution. The Carmathians were ripe for rebellion, since they disclaimed the title of the house of Abbas, and abhorred the worldly pomp of the caliphs of Bagdad. They were susceptible of discipline, since they vowed a blind and absolute submission to their Imam, who was called to the prophetic office by the voice of God and the people. Instead of the legal tithes, he claimed the fifth of their substance and spoil; the most flagitious sins were no more than the type of disobedience; and the brethren were united and concealed by an oath of secrecy. After a bloody conflict, they prevailed in the province of Bahrein, along the Persian Gulf: far and wide, the tribes of the desert were subject to the sceptre, or rather to the sword of Abu Said and his son Abu Taher; and these rebellious imams could muster in the field a hundred and seven thousand fanatics. The mercenaries of the caliph were dismayed at the approach of an enemy who neither asked nor accepted quarter; and the difference between, them in fortitude and patience, is expressive of the change which three centuries of prosperity had effected in the character of the Arabians. Such troops were discomfited in every action; the cities of Racca and Baalbec, of Cufa and Bassora, were taken and pillaged; Bagdad was filled with consternation; and the caliph trembled behind the veils of his palace. In a daring inroad beyond the Tigris, Abu Taher advanced to the gates of the capital with no more than five hundred horse. By the special order of Moctader, the bridges had been broken down, and the person or head of the rebel was expected every hour by the commander of the faithful. His lieutenant, from a motive of fear or pity, apprised Abu Taher of his danger, and recommended a speedy escape. "Your master," said the intrepid Carmathian to the messenger, "is at the head of thirty thousand soldiers: three such men as these are wanting in his host:" at the same instant, turning to three of his companions, he commanded the first to plunge a dagger into his breast, the second to leap into the Tigris, and the third to cast himself headlong down a precipice. They obeyed without a murmur. "Relate," continued the imam, "what you have seen: before the evening your general shall be chained among my dogs." Before the evening, the camp was surprised, and the menace was executed. The rapine of the Carmathians was sanctified by their aversion to the worship of Mecca: they robbed a caravan of pilgrims, and twenty thousand devout Moslems were abandoned on the burning sands to a death of hunger and thirst. Another year they suffered the pilgrims to proceed without interruption; but, in the festival of devotion, Abu Taher stormed the holy city, and trampled on the most venerable relics of the Mahometan faith. Thirty thousand citizens and strangers were put to the sword; the sacred precincts were polluted by the burial of three thousand dead bodies; the well of Zemzem overflowed with blood; the golden spout was forced from its place; the veil of the Caaba was divided among these impious sectaries; and the black stone, the first monument of the nation, was borne away in triumph to their capital. After this deed of sacrilege and cruelty, they continued to infest the confines of Irak, Syria, and Egypt: but the vital principle of enthusiasm had withered at the root. Their scruples, or their avarice, again opened the pilgrimage of Mecca, and restored the black stone of the Caaba; and it is needless to inquire into what factions they were broken, or by whose swords they were finally extirpated. The sect of the Carmathians may be considered as the second visible cause of the decline and fall of the empire of the caliphs.

More Conquests by the Arabs.
– Part Five

THE THIRD AND MOST obvious cause was the weight and magnitude of the empire itself. The caliph Almamon might proudly assert, that it was easier for him to rule the East and the West, than to manage a chessboard of two feet square: yet I suspect that in both those games he was guilty of many fatal mistakes; and I perceive, that in the distant provinces the authority of the first and most powerful of the Abbassides was already impaired. The analogy of despotism invests the representative with the full majesty of the prince; the division and balance of powers might relax the habits of obedience, might encourage the passive subject to inquire into the origin and administration of civil government. He who is born in the purple is seldom worthy to reign; but the elevation of a private man, of a peasant, perhaps, or a slave, affords a strong presumption of his courage and capacity. The viceroy of a remote kingdom aspires to secure the property and inheritance of his precarious trust; the nations must rejoice in the presence of their sovereign; and the command of armies and treasures are at once the object and the instrument of his ambition. A change was scarcely visible as long as the lieutenants of the caliph were content with their vicarious title; while they solicited for themselves or their sons a renewal of the Imperial grant, and still maintained on the coin and in the public prayers the name and prerogative of the commander of the faithful. But in the long and hereditary exercise of power, they assumed the pride and attributes of royalty; the alternative of peace or war, of reward or punishment, depended solely on their will; and the revenues of their government were reserved for local services or private magnificence. Instead of a regular supply of men and money, the successors of the prophet were flattered with the osten-tatious gift of an elephant, or a cast of hawks, a suit of silk hangings, or some pounds of musk and amber.

After the revolt of Spain from the temporal and spiritual supremacy of the Abbassides, the first symptoms of disobedience broke forth in the province of Africa. Ibrahim, the son of Aglab, the lieutenant of the vigilant and rigid Harun, bequeathed to the dynasty of the *Agla-bite* the inheritance of his name and power. The indolence or policy of the caliphs dissembled the injury and loss, and pursued only with poison the founder of the *Edrisites*, who erected the kingdom and city of Fez on the shores of the Western ocean. In the East, the first dynasty was that of the *Taherites*; the posterity of the valiant Taher, who, in the civil wars of the sons of Harun, had served with too much zeal and success the cause of Almamon, the younger brother. He was sent into honorable exile, to command on the banks of the Oxus; and the in-dependence of his successors, who reigned in Chorasan till the fourth generation, was palliated by their modest and respectful demeanor, the happiness of their subjects and the security of their frontier. They were supplanted by one of those adventures so frequent in the annals of the East, who left his trade of a brazier (from whence the name of *Soffarides*) for the profession of a robber. In a nocturnal visit to the treasure of the prince of Sistan, Jacob, the son of Leith, stumbled over a lump of salt, which he unwarily tasted with his tongue. Salt, among the Orientals, is the symbol of hospitality, and the pious robber immediately retired without spoil or damage. The discovery of this honorable behavior recommended Jacob to pardon and trust; he led an army at first for his benefactor, at last for himself, subdued Persia, and threatened the residence of the Abbassides. On his march towards Bagdad, the conqueror was arrested by a fever. He gave audience in bed to the ambassador of the caliph; and beside him on a table were exposed a naked cimeter, a crust of brown bread, and a bunch of on-ions. "If I die," said he, "your master is delivered from his fears. If I live, *this* must determine between us. If I am vanquished, I can return without reluctance to the homely fare of my youth.» From the height where he stood, the descent would not have been so soft or harmless: a timely death secured his own repose and that of the caliph, who paid with the most lavish concessions the retreat of his brother Amrou to the palaces of Shiraz and Ispahan. The Abbassides were too feeble to contend, too proud to forgive: they invited the powerful dynasty of the *Samanides*, who passed the Oxus with ten thousand horse so poor, that their stirrups were of wood: so brave, that they vanquished the Soffarian army, eight times more numerous than their own. The captive Amrou was sent in chains, a grateful offering to the court of Bagdad; and as the victor was content with the inheritance of Transoxiana and Chorasan, the realms of Persia returned for a while to the allegiance of the caliphs. The provinces of Syria and Egypt were twice dismembered by their Turkish slaves of the race of *Toulon* and *Ilkshid*. These Barbarians, in religion and manners the countrymen of Mahomet, emerged from the bloody factions of the palace to a provincial command and an independent throne: their names became famous and formidable in their time; but the founders of these two potent dynasties confessed, either in words or actions, the vanity of ambition. The first on his death-bed implored the mercy of God to a sinner, ignorant of the limits of his own power: the second, in the midst of four hundred thousand soldiers and eight thousand slaves, concealed from every human eye the chamber where he attempted to sleep. Their sons were educated in the vices of kings; and both Egypt and Syria were recovered and possessed by the Abbassides during an interval of thirty years. In the decline of their empire, Mesopotamia, with the important cities of Mosul and Aleppo, was occupied by the Arabian princes of the tribe of *Hamadan*. The poets of their court could repeat without a blush, that nature had formed their countenances for beauty, their tongues for eloquence, and their hands for liberality and valor: but the genuine tale of the elevation and reign of the *Hamadanites* exhibits a scene of treachery, murder, and parricide. At the same fatal period, the Persian kingdom was again usurped by the dynasty of the *Bowides*, by the sword of three brothers, who, under various names, were styled the support and columns of the state, and who, from the Caspian Sea to the ocean, would suffer no tyrants but themselves. Under their reign, the language and genius of Persia revived, and the Arabs, three hundred and four years after the death of Mahomet, were deprived of the sceptre of the East.

Rahadi, the twentieth of the Abbassides, and the thirty-ninth of the successors of Mahomet, was the last who deserved the title of commander of the faithful; the last (says Abulfeda) who spoke to the people, or conversed with the learned; the last who, in the expense of his household, represented the wealth and magnificence of the ancient caliphs. After him, the lords of the Eastern world were reduced to the most abject misery, and exposed to the blows and insults of a servile condition. The revolt of the provinces circumscribed their dominions within the walls of Bagdad: but that capital still contained an innumerable multitude, vain of their past fortune, discontented with their present state, and oppressed by the demands of a treasury which had formerly been replenished by the spoil and tribute of nations. Their idleness was exercised by faction and controversy. Under the mask of piety, the rigid followers of Hanbal invaded the pleasures of domestic life, burst into the houses of plebeians and princes, the wine, broke the instruments, beat the musicians, and dishonored, with infamous suspicions, the associates of every handsome youth. In each profession, which allowed room for two persons, the one was a votary, the other an antagonist, of Ali; and the Abbassides were awakened by the clamorous grief of the sectaries, who denied their title, and cursed their progenitors. A turbulent people could only be repressed by a military force; but who could satisfy the avarice or assert the discipline of the mercenaries themselves? The African and the Turkish guards drew their swords against each other, and the chief commanders, the emirs al Omra, imprisoned or deposed their sovereigns, and violated the sanctuary of the mosch and harem. If the caliphs escaped to the camp or court of any neighboring prince, their deliverance was a change of servitude, till they were prompted by despair to invite the Bowides, the sultans of Persia, who silenced the factions of Bagdad by their irresistible arms. The civil and military powers were assumed by Moezaldowlat, the second of the three brothers, and a stipend of sixty thousand pounds sterling was assigned by his generosity for the private expense of the commander of the faithful. But on the fortieth day, at the audience of the ambassadors of Chorasan, and in the presence of a trembling multitude, the caliph was dragged from his throne to a dungeon, by the command of the stranger, and the rude hands of his Dilemites. His palace was pillaged, his eyes were put out, and the mean ambition of the Abbassides aspired to the vacant station of danger and disgrace. In the school of adversity, the luxurious caliphs resumed the grave and abstemious virtues of the primitive times. Despoiled of their armor and silken robes, they fasted, they prayed, they studied the Koran and the tradition of the Sonnites: they performed, with zeal and knowledge, the functions of their ecclesiastical character. The respect of nations still waited on the successors of the apostle, the oracles of the law and conscience of the faithful; and the weakness or division of their tyrants sometimes restored the Abbassides to the sovereignty of Bagdad. But their misfortunes had been imbittered by the triumph of the Fatimites, the real or spurious progeny of Ali. Arising from the extremity of Africa, these successful rivals extinguished, in Egypt and Syria, both the spiritual and temporal authority of the Abbassides; and the monarch of the Nile insulted the humble pontiff on the banks of the Tigris.

In the declining age of the caliphs, in the century which elapsed after the war of Theophilus and Motassem, the hostile transactions of the two nations were confined to some inroads by sea and land, the fruits of their close vicinity and indelible hatred. But when the Eastern world was convulsed and broken, the Greeks were roused from their lethargy by the hopes of conquest and revenge. The Byzantine empire, since the accession of the Basilian race, had reposed in peace and dignity; and they might encounter with their entire strength the front of some petty emir, whose rear was assaulted and threatened by his national foes of the Mahometan faith. The lofty titles of the morning star, and the death of the Saracens, were applied in the public acclamations to Nicephorus Phocas, a prince as renowned in the camp, as he was unpopular in the city. In the subordinate station of great domestic, or general of the East, he reduced the Island of Crete, and extirpated the nest of pirates who had so long defied, with impunity, the majesty of the empire. His military genius was displayed in the conduct and success of the enterprise, which had so often failed with loss and dishonor. The Saracens were confounded by the landing of his troops on safe and level bridges, which he cast from the vessels to the shore. Seven months were consumed in the siege of Candia; the despair of the native Cretans was stimulated by the frequent aid of their brethren of Africa and Spain; and after the massy wall and double ditch had been stormed by the Greeks a hopeless conflict was still maintained in the streets and houses of the city. The whole island was subdued in the capital, and a submissive people accepted, without resistance, the baptism of the conqueror. Constantinople applauded the long-forgotten pomp of a triumph; but the Imperial diadem was the sole reward that could repay the services, or satisfy the ambition, of Nicephorus.

After the death of the younger Romanus, the fourth in lineal descent of the Basilian race, his widow Theophania successively married Nicephorus Phocas and his assassin John Zimisces, the two heroes of the age. They reigned as the guardians and colleagues of her infant sons; and the twelve years of their military command form the most splendid period of the Byzantine annals. The subjects and confederates, whom they led to war, appeared, at least in the eyes of an enemy, two hundred thousand strong; and of these about thirty thousand were armed with cuirasses: a train of four thousand mules attended their march; and their evening camp was regularly fortified with an enclosure of iron spikes. A series of bloody and undecisive combats is nothing more than an anticipation of what would have been effected in a few years by the course of nature; but I shall briefly prosecute the conquests of the two emperors from the hills of Cappadocia to the desert of Bagdad. The sieges of Mopsuestia and Tarsus, in Cilicia, first exercised the skill and perseverance of their troops, on whom, at this moment, I shall not hesitate to bestow the name of Romans. In the double city of Mopsuestia, which is divided by the River Sarus, two hundred thousand Moslems were predestined to death or slavery, a surprising degree of population, which must at least include the inhabitants of the dependent districts. They were surrounded and taken by assault; but Tarsus was reduced by the slow progress of famine; and no sooner had the Saracens yielded on honorable terms than they were mortified by the distant and unprofitable view of the naval succors of Egypt. They were dismissed with a safe-conduct to the confines of Syria: a part of the old Christians had quietly lived under their dominion; and the vacant habitations were replenished by a new colony. But the mosch was converted into a stable; the pulpit was delivered to the flames; many rich crosses of gold and gems, the spoils of Asiatic churches, were made a grateful offering to the piety or avarice of the emperor; and he transported the gates of Mopsuestia and Tarsus, which were fixed in the walls of Constantinople, an eternal monument of his victory. After they had forced and secured the narrow passes of Mount Amanus, the two Roman princes repeatedly carried their arms into the heart of Syria. Yet, instead of assaulting the walls of Antioch, the humanity or superstition of Nicephorus appeared to respect the ancient metropolis of the East: he contented himself with drawing round the city a line of circumvallation; left a stationary army; and instructed his lieutenant to expect, without impatience, the return of spring. But in the depth of winter, in a dark and rainy night, an adventurous subaltern, with three hundred soldiers, approached the rampart, applied his scaling-ladders, occupied two adjacent towers, stood firm against the pressure of multitudes, and bravely maintained his post till he was relieved by the tardy, though effectual, support of his reluctant chief. The first tumult of slaughter and rapine subsided; the reign of Cæsar and of Christ was restored; and the efforts of a hundred thousand Saracens, of the armies of Syria and the fleets of Africa, were consumed without effect before the walls of Antioch. The royal city of Aleppo was subject to Seifeddowlat, of the dynasty of Hamadan, who clouded his past glory by the precipitate retreat which abandoned his kingdom and capital to the Roman invaders. In his stately palace, that stood without the walls of Aleppo, they joyfully seized a well-furnished magazine of arms, a stable of fourteen hundred mules, and three hundred bags of silver and gold. But the walls of the city withstood the strokes of their battering-rams: and the besiegers pitched their tents on the neighboring mountain of Jaushan. Their retreat exasperated the quarrel of the townsmen and mercenaries; the guard of the gates and ramparts was deserted; and while they furiously charged each other in the marketplace, they were surprised and destroyed by the sword of a common enemy. The male sex was exterminated by the sword; ten thousand youths were led into captivity; the weight of the precious spoil exceeded the strength and number of the beasts of burden; the superfluous remainder was burnt; and, after a licentious possession of ten days, the Romans marched away from the naked and bleeding city. In their Syrian inroads they commanded the husbandmen to cultivate their lands, that they themselves, in the ensuing season, might reap the benefit; more than a hundred cities were reduced to obedience; and eighteen pulpits of the principal moschs were committed to the flames to expiate the sacrilege of the disciples of Mahomet. The classic names of Hierapolis, Apamea, and Emesa, revive for a moment in the list of conquest: the emperor Zimisces encamped in the paradise of Damascus, and accepted the ransom of a submissive people; and the torrent was only stopped by the impregnable fortress of Tripoli, on the sea-coast of Phœnicia. Since the days of Heraclius, the Euphrates, below the passage of Mount Taurus, had been impervious, and almost invisible, to the Greeks. The river yielded a free passage to the victorious Zimisces; and the historian may imitate the speed with which he overran the once famous cities of Samosata, Edessa, Martyropolis, Amida, and Nisibis, the ancient limit of the empire in the neighborhood of the Tigris. His ardor was quickened by the desire of grasping the virgin treasures of Ecbatana, a well-known name, under which the Byzantine writer has concealed the capital of the Abbassides. The consternation of the fugitives had already diffused the terror of his name; but the fancied riches of Bagdad had already been dissipated by the avarice and prodigality of domestic tyrants. The prayers of the people, and the stern demands of the lieutenant of the Bowides, required the caliph to provide for the defence of the city. The helpless Mothi replied, that his arms, his revenues, and his provinces, had been torn from his hands, and that he was ready to abdicate a dignity which he was unable to support. The emir was inexorable; the furniture of the palace was sold; and the paltry price of forty thousand pieces of gold was instantly consumed in private luxury. But the apprehensions of Bagdad were relieved by the retreat of the Greeks: thirst and hunger guarded the desert of Mesopotamia; and the emperor, satiated with glory, and laden with Oriental spoils, returned to Constantinople, and displayed, in his triumph, the silk, the aromatics, and three hundred myriads of gold and silver. Yet the powers of the East had been bent, not broken, by this transient hurricane. After the departure of the Greeks, the fugitive princes returned to their capitals; the subjects disclaimed their involuntary oaths of allegiance; the Moslems again purified their temples, and overturned the idols of the saints and martyrs; the Nestorians and Jacobites preferred a Saracen to an orthodox master; and the numbers and spirit of the Melchites were inadequate to the support of the church and state. Of these extensive conquests, Antioch, with the cities of Cilicia and the Isle of Cyprus, was alone restored, a permanent and useful accession to the Roman empire.

Fate of the Eastern Empire.
– Part One

Fate of the Eastern Empire in the Tenth Century. – Extent and Division. – Wealth and Revenue. – Palace of Constantinople. – Titles and Offices. – Pride and Power of the Emperors. – Tactics of the Greeks, Arabs, and Franks. – Loss of the Latin Tongue. – Studies and Solitude of the Greeks.

A RAY OF HISTORIC light seems to beam from the darkness of the tenth century. We open with curiosity and respect the royal volumes of Constantine Porphyrogenitus, which he composed at a mature age for the instruction of his son, and which promise to unfold the state of the eastern empire, both in peace and war, both at home and abroad. In the first of these works he minutely describes the pompous ceremonies of the church and palace of Constantinople, according to his own practice, and that of his predecessors. In the second, he attempts an accurate survey of the provinces, the *themes*, as they were then denominated, both of Europe and Asia. The system of Roman tactics, the discipline and order of the troops, and the military operations by land and sea, are explained in the third of these didactic collections, which may be ascribed to Constantine or his father Leo. In the fourth, of the administration of the empire, he reveals the secrets of the Byzantine policy, in friendly or hostile intercourse with the nations of the earth. The literary labors of the age, the practical systems of law, agriculture, and history, might redound to the benefit of the subject and the honor of the Macedonian princes. The sixty books of the *Basilics*, the code and pandects of civil jurisprudence, were gradually framed in the three first reigns of that prosperous dynasty. The art of agriculture had amused the leisure, and exercised the pens, of the best and wisest of the ancients; and their chosen precepts are comprised in the twenty books of the *Geoponics* of Constantine. At his command, the historical examples of vice and virtue were methodized in fifty-three books, and every citizen might apply, to his contemporaries or himself, the lesson or the warning of past times. From the august character of a legislator, the sovereign of the East descends to the more humble office of a teacher and a scribe; and if his successors and subjects were regardless of his paternal cares, *we* may inherit and enjoy the everlasting legacy.

A closer survey will indeed reduce the value of the gift, and the gratitude of posterity: in the possession of these Imperial treasures we may still deplore our poverty and ignorance; and the fading glories of their authors will be obliterated by indifference or contempt. The Basilics will sink to a broken copy, a partial and mutilated version, in the Greek language, of the laws of Justinian; but the sense of the old civilians is often superseded by the influence of bigotry: and the absolute prohibition of divorce, concubinage, and interest for money, enslaves the freedom of trade and the happiness of private life. In the historical book, a subject of Constantine might admire the inimitable virtues of Greece and Rome: he might learn to what a pitch of energy and elevation the human character had formerly aspired. But a contrary effect must have been produced by a new edition of the lives of the saints, which the great logothete, or chancellor of the empire, was directed to prepare; and the dark fund of superstition was enriched by the fabulous and florid legends of Simon the *Metaphrast*. The merits and miracles of the whole calendar are of less account in the eyes of a sage, than the toil of a single husbandman, who multiplies the gifts of the Creator, and supplies the food of his brethren. Yet the royal authors of the *Geoponics* were more seriously employed in expounding the precepts of the destroying art, which had been taught since the days of Xenophon, as the art of heroes and kings. But the *Tactics* of Leo and Constantine are mingled with the baser alloy of the age in which they lived. It was destitute of original genius; they implicitly transcribe the rules and maxims which had been confirmed by victories. It was unskilled in the propriety of style and method; they blindly confound the most distant and discordant institutions, the phalanx of Sparta and that of Macedon, the legions of Cato and Trajan, of Augustus and Theodosius. Even the use, or at least the importance, of these military rudiments may be fairly questioned: their general theory is dictated by reason; but the merit, as well as difficulty, consists in the application. The discipline of a soldier is formed by exercise rather than by study: the talents of a commander are appropriated to those calm, though rapid, minds, which nature produces to decide the fate of armies and nations: the former is the habit of a life, the latter the glance of a moment; and the battles won by lessons of tactics may be numbered with the epic poems created from the rules of criticism. The book of ceremonies is a recital, tedious yet imperfect, of the despicable pageantry which had infected the church and state since the gradual decay of the purity of the one and the power of the other. A review of the themes or provinces might promise such authentic and useful information, as the curiosity of government only can obtain, instead of traditionary fables on the origin of the cities, and malicious epigrams on the vices of their inhabitants. Such information the historian would have been pleased to record; nor should his silence be condemned if the most interesting objects, the population of the capital and provinces, the amount of the taxes and revenues, the numbers of subjects and strangers who served under the Imperial standard, have been unnoticed by Leo the philosopher, and his son Constantine. His treatise of the public administration is stained with the same blemishes; yet it is discriminated by peculiar merit; the antiquities of the nations may be doubtful or fabulous; but the geography and manners of the Barbaric world are delineated with curious accuracy. Of these nations, the Franks alone were qualified to observe in their turn, and to describe, the metropolis of the East. The ambassador of the great Otho, a bishop of Cremona, has painted the state of Constantinople about the middle of the tenth century: his style is glowing, his narrative lively, his observation keen; and even the prejudices and passions of Liutprand are stamped with an original character of freedom and genius. From this scanty fund of foreign and domestic materials, I shall investigate the form and substance of the Byzantine empire; the provinces and wealth, the civil government and military force, the character and literature, of the Greeks in a period of six hundred years, from the reign of Heraclius to his successful invasion of the Franks or Latins.

After the final division between the sons of Theodosius, the swarms of Barbarians from Scythia and Germany over-spread the provinces and extinguished the empire of ancient Rome. The weakness of Constantinople was concealed by extent of dominion: her limits were inviolate, or at least entire; and the kingdom of Justinian was enlarged by the splendid acquisition of Africa and Italy. But the possession of these new conquests was transient and precarious; and almost a moiety of the Eastern empire was torn away by the arms of the Saracens. Syria and Egypt were oppressed by the Arabian caliphs;

and, after the reduction of Africa, their lieutenants invaded and subdued the Roman province which had been changed into the Gothic
monarchy of Spain. The islands of the Mediterranean were not inaccessible to their naval powers; and it was from their extreme stations,
the harbors of Crete and the fortresses of Cilicia, that the faithful or
rebel emirs insulted the majesty of the throne and capital. The remaining provinces, under the obedience of the emperors, were cast
into a new mould; and the jurisdiction of the presidents, the consul-
ars, and the counts were superseded by the institution of the *themes*,
or military governments, which prevailed under the successors of
Heraclius, and are described by the pen of the royal author. Of the
twenty-nine themes, twelve in Europe and seventeen in Asia, the origin is obscure, the etymology doubtful or capricious: the limits were
arbitrary and fluctuating; but some particular names, that sound the
most strangely to our ear, were derived from the character and attributes of the troops that were maintained at the expense, and for
the guard, of the respective divisions. The vanity of the Greek princes
most eagerly grasped the shadow of conquest and the memory of lost
dominion. A new Mesopotamia was created on the western side of
the Euphrates: the appellation and prætor of Sicily were transferred
to a narrow slip of Calabria; and a fragment of the duchy of Beneventum was promoted to the style and title of the theme of Lombardy.
In the decline of the Arabian empire, the successors of Constantine
might indulge their pride in more solid advantages. The victories of
Nicephorus, John Zimisces, and Basil the Second, revived the fame,
and enlarged the boundaries, of the Roman name: the province of
Cilicia, the metropolis of Antioch, the islands of Crete and Cyprus,
were restored to the allegiance of Christ and Cæsar: one third of Italy was annexed to the throne of Constantinople: the kingdom of
Bulgaria was destroyed; and the last sovereigns of the Macedonian
dynasty extended their sway from the sources of the Tigris to the
neighborhood of Rome. In the eleventh century, the prospect was
again clouded by new enemies and new misfortunes: the relics of
Italy were swept away by the Norman adventures; and almost all the
Asiatic branches were dissevered from the Roman trunk by the Turkish conquerors. After these losses, the emperors of the Comnenian
family continued to reign from the Danube to Peloponnesus, and
from Belgrade to Nice, Trebizond, and the winding stream of the
Meander. The spacious provinces of Thrace, Macedonia, and Greece,
were obedient to their sceptre; the possession of Cyprus, Rhodes,
and Crete, was accompanied by the fifty islands of the Ægean or Holy

Sea; and the remnant of their empire transcends the measure of the largest of the European kingdoms.

The same princes might assert, with dignity and truth, that of all the monarchs of Christendom they possessed the greatest city, the most ample revenue, the most flourishing and populous state. With the decline and fall of the empire, the cities of the West had decayed and fallen; nor could the ruins of Rome, or the mud walls, wooden hovels, and narrow precincts of Paris and London, prepare the Latin stranger to contemplate the situation and extent of Constantinople, her stately palaces and churches, and the arts and luxury of an innumerable people. Her treasures might attract, but her virgin strength had repelled, and still promised to repel, the audacious invasion of the Persian and Bulgarian, the Arab and the Russian. The provinces were less fortunate and impregnable; and few districts, few cities, could be discovered which had not been violated by some fierce Barbarian, impatient to despoil, because he was hopeless to possess. From the age of Justinian the Eastern empire was sinking below its former level; the powers of destruction were more active than those of improvement; and the calamities of war were imbittered by the more permanent evils of civil and ecclesiastical tyranny. The captive who had escaped from the Barbarians was often stripped and imprisoned by the ministers of his sovereign: the Greek superstition relaxed the mind by prayer, and emaciated the body by fasting; and the multitude of convents and festivals diverted many hands and many days from the temporal service of mankind. Yet the subjects of the Byzantine empire were still the most dexterous and diligent of nations; their country was blessed by nature with every advantage of soil, climate, and situation; and, in the support and restoration of the arts, their patient and peaceful temper was more useful than the warlike spirit and feudal anarchy of Europe. The provinces that still adhered to the empire were repeopled and enriched by the misfortunes of those which were irrecoverably lost. From the yoke of the caliphs, the Catholics of Syria, Egypt, and Africa retired to the allegiance of their prince, to the society of their brethren: the movable wealth, which eludes the search of oppression, accompanied and alleviated their exile, and Constantinople received into her bosom the fugitive trade of Alexandria and Tyre. The chiefs of Armenia and Scythia, who fled from hostile or religious persecution, were hospitably entertained: their followers were encouraged to build new cities and to cultivate waste lands; and many spots, both in Europe and Asia, preserved the name, the manners, or at least the memory, of these national colonies. Even the tribes of

Barbarians, who had seated themselves in arms on the territory of the empire, were gradually reclaimed to the laws of the church and state; and as long as they were separated from the Greeks, their posterity supplied a race of faithful and obedient soldiers. Did we possess sufficient materials to survey the twenty-nine themes of the Byzantine monarchy, our curiosity might be satisfied with a chosen example: it is fortunate enough that the clearest light should be thrown on the most interesting province, and the name of Peloponnesus will awaken the attention of the classic reader.

As early as the eighth century, in the troubled reign of the Iconoclasts, Greece, and even Peloponnesus, were overrun by some Sclavonian bands who outstripped the royal standard of Bulgaria. The strangers of old, Cadmus, and Danaus, and Pelops, had planted in that fruitful soil the seeds of policy and learning; but the savages of the north eradicated what yet remained of their sickly and withered roots. In this irruption, the country and the inhabitants were transformed; the Grecian blood was contaminated; and the proudest nobles of Peloponnesus were branded with the names of foreigners and *slaves*. By the diligence of succeeding princes, the land was in some measure purified from the Barbarians; and the humble remnant was bound by an oath of obedience, tribute, and military service, which they often renewed and often violated. The siege of Patras was formed by a singular concurrence of the Sclavonians of Peloponnesus and the Saracens of Africa. In their last distress, a pious fiction of the approach of the prætor of Corinth revived the courage of the citizens. Their sally was bold and successful; the strangers embarked, the rebels submitted, and the glory of the day was ascribed to a phantom or a stranger, who fought in the foremost ranks under the character of St. Andrew the Apostle. The shrine which contained his relics was decorated with the trophies of victory, and the captive race was forever devoted to the service and vassalage of the metropolitan church of Patras. By the revolt of two Sclavonian tribes, in the neighborhood of Helos and Lacedæmon, the peace of the peninsula was often disturbed. They sometimes insulted the weakness, and sometimes resisted the oppression, of the Byzantine government, till at length the approach of their hostile brethren extorted a golden bull to define the rites and obligations of the Ezzerites and Milengi, whose annual tribute was defined at twelve hundred pieces of gold. From these strangers the Imperial geographer has accurately distinguished a domestic, and perhaps original, race, who, in some degree, might derive their blood from the much-injured Helots. The liberality of the Romans, and especially of Augustus, had enfranchised the maritime cities from the dominion of Sparta; and the continuance of the same benefit ennobled them with the title of *Eleuthero*, or Free-Laconians. In the time of Constantine Porphyrogenitus, they had acquired the name of *Mainotes*, under which they dishonor the claim of liberty by the inhuman pillage of all that is shipwrecked on their rocky shores. Their territory, barren of corn, but fruitful of olives, extended to the Cape of Malea: they accepted a chief or prince from the Byzantine prætor, and a light tribute of four hundred pieces of gold was the badge of their immunity, rather than of their dependence. The freemen of Laconia assumed the character of Romans, and long adhered to the religion of the Greeks. By the zeal of the emperor Basil, they were baptized in the faith of Christ: but the altars of Venus and Neptune had been crowned by these rustic votaries five hundred years after they were proscribed in the Roman world. In the theme of Peloponnesus, forty cities were still numbered, and the declining state of Sparta, Argos, and Corinth, may be suspended in the tenth century, at an equal distance, perhaps, between their antique splendor and their present desolation. The duty of military service, either in person or by substitute, was imposed on the lands or benefices of the province; a sum of five pieces of gold was assessed on each of the substantial tenants; and the same capitation was shared among several heads of inferior value. On the proclamation of an Italian war, the Peloponnesians excused themselves by a voluntary oblation of one hundred pounds of gold, (four thousand pounds sterling,) and a thousand horses with their arms and trappings. The churches and monasteries furnished their contingent; a sacrilegious profit was extorted from the sale of ecclesiastical honors; and the indigent bishop of Leucadia was made responsible for a pension of one hundred pieces of gold.

But the wealth of the province, and the trust of the revenue, were founded on the fair and plentiful produce of trade and manufacturers; and some symptoms of liberal policy may be traced in a law which exempts from all personal taxes the mariners of Peloponnesus, and the workmen in parchment and purple. This denomination may be fairly applied or extended to the manufacturers of linen, woollen, and more especially of silk: the two former of which had flourished in Greece since the days of Homer; and the last was introduced perhaps as early as the reign of Justinian. These arts, which were exercised at Corinth, Thebes, and Argos, afforded food and occupation to a numerous people: the men, women, and children were distributed according to their age and strength; and, if many of these were domestic slaves, their masters, who directed the work and enjoyed the profit, were of a free and honorable condition. The gifts which a rich and generous matron of Peloponnesus presented to the emperor Basil, her adopted son, were doubtless fabricated in the Grecian looms. Danielis bestowed a carpet of fine wool, of a pattern which imitated the spots of a peacock's tail, of a magnitude to overspread the floor of a new church, erected in the triple name of Christ, of Michael the archangel, and of the prophet Elijah. She gave six hundred pieces of silk and linen, of various use and denomination: the silk was painted with the Tyrian dye, and adorned by the labors of the needle; and the linen was so exquisitely fine, that an entire piece might be rolled in the hollow of a cane. In his description of the Greek manufactures, an historian of Sicily discriminates their price, according to the weight and quality of the silk, the closeness of the texture, the beauty of the colors, and the taste and materials of the embroidery. A single, or even a double or treble thread was thought sufficient for ordinary sale; but the union of six threads composed a piece of stronger and more costly workmanship. Among the colors, he celebrates, with affectation of eloquence, the fiery blaze of the scarlet, and the softer lustre of the green. The embroidery was raised either in silk or gold: the more simple ornament of stripes or circles was surpassed by the nicer imitation of flowers: the vestments that were fabricated for the palace or the altar often glittered with precious stones; and the figures were delineated in strings of Oriental pearls. Till the twelfth century, Greece alone, of all the countries of Christendom, was possessed of the insect who is taught by nature, and of the workmen who are instructed by art, to prepare this elegant luxury. But the secret had been stolen by the dexterity and diligence of the Arabs: the caliphs of the East and West scorned to borrow from the unbelievers their furniture and apparel; and two cities of Spain, Almeria and Lisbon, were famous for the manufacture, the use, and, perhaps, the exportation, of silk. It was first introduced into Sicily by the Normans; and this emigration of trade distinguishes the victory of Roger from the uniform and fruitless hostilities of every age. After the sack of Corinth, Athens, and Thebes, his lieutenant embarked with a captive train of weavers and artificers of both sexes, a trophy glorious to their master, and disgraceful to the Greek emperor. The king of Sicily was not insensible of the value of the present; and, in the restitution of the prisoners, he excepted only the male and female manufacturers of Thebes and Corinth, who labor, says the Byzantine historian, under a barbarous lord, like the old Eretrians in the service of Darius. A stately edifice, in the palace of Palermo, was erected for the use of this industrious colony; and the art was propagated by their children and disciples to satisfy the increasing demand of the western world. The decay of the looms of Sicily may be ascribed to the troubles of the island, and the competition of the Italian cities. In the year thirteen hundred and fourteen, Lucca alone, among her sister republics, enjoyed the lucrative monopoly. A domestic revolution dispersed the manufacturers to Florence, Bologna, Venice, Milan, and even the countries beyond the Alps; and thirteen years after this event the statutes of Modena enjoin the planting of mulberry-trees, and regulate the duties on raw silk. The northern climates are less propitious to the education of the silkworm; but the industry of France and England is supplied and enriched by the productions of Italy and China.

Fate of the Eastern Empire.
– Part Two

I MUST REPEAT THE complaint that the vague and scanty memorials of the times will not afford any just estimate of the taxes, the revenue, and the resources of the Greek empire. From every province of Europe and Asia the rivulets of gold and silver discharged into the Imperial reservoir a copious and perennial stream. The separation of the branches from the trunk increased the relative magnitude of Constantinople; and the maxims of despotism contracted the state to the capital, the capital to the palace, and the palace to the royal person. A Jewish traveller, who visited the East in the twelfth century, is lost in his admiration of the Byzantine riches. "It is here," says Benjamin of Tudela, "in the queen of cities, that the tributes of the Greek empire are annually deposited and the lofty towers are filled with precious magazines of silk, purple, and gold. It is said, that Constantinople pays each day to her sovereign twenty thousand pieces of gold; which are levied on the shops, taverns, and markets, on the merchants of Persia and Egypt, of Russia and Hungary, of Italy and Spain, who frequent the capital by sea and land." In all pecuniary matters, the authority of a Jew is doubtless respectable; but as the three hundred and sixty-five days would produce a yearly income exceeding seven millions sterling, I am tempted to retrench at least the numerous festivals of the Greek calendar. The mass of treasure that was saved by Theodora and Basil the Second will suggest a splendid, though indefinite, idea of their supplies and resources. The mother of Michael, before she retired to a cloister, attempted to check or expose the prodigality of her ungrateful son, by a free and faithful account of the wealth which he inherited; one hundred and nine thousand pounds of gold, and three hundred thousand of silver, the fruits of her own economy and that of her deceased husband. The avarice of Basil is not less renowned than his valor and fortune: his victorious armies were paid and rewarded without breaking into the mass of two hundred thousand pounds of gold, (about eight millions sterling,) which he had buried in the subterraneous vaults of the palace. Such accumulation of treasure is rejected by the theory and practice of modern policy; and we are more apt to compute the national riches by the use and abuse of the public credit. Yet the maxims of antiquity are still embraced by a monarch formidable to his enemies; by a republic respectable to her allies; and both have attained their respective ends of military power and domestic tranquillity.

Whatever might be consumed for the present wants, or reserved for the future use, of the state, the first and most sacred demand was for the pomp and pleasure of the emperor, and his discretion only could define the measure of his private expense. The princes of Constantinople were far removed from the simplicity of nature; yet, with the revolving seasons, they were led by taste or fashion to withdraw to a purer air, from the smoke and tumult of the capital. They enjoyed, or affected to enjoy, the rustic festival of the vintage: their leisure was amused by the exercise of the chase and the calmer occupation of fishing, and in the summer heats, they were shaded from the sun, and refreshed by the cooling breezes from the sea. The coasts and islands of Asia and Europe were covered with their magnificent villas; but, instead of the modest art which secretly strives to hide itself and to decorate the scenery of nature, the marble structure of their gardens served only to expose the riches of the lord, and the labors of the architect. The successive casualties of inheritance and forfeiture had rendered the sovereign proprietor of many stately houses in the city and suburbs, of which twelve were appropriated to the ministers of state; but the great palace, the centre of the Imperial residence, was fixed during eleven centuries to the same position, between the hippodrome, the cathedral of St. Sophia, and the gardens, which descended by many a terrace to the shores of the Propontis. The primitive edifice of the first Constantine was a copy, or rival, of ancient Rome; the gradual improvements of his successors aspired to emulate the wonders of the old world, and in the tenth century, the Byzantine palace excited the admiration, at least of the Latins, by an unquestionable preëminence of strength, size, and magnificence. But the toil and treasure of so many ages had produced a vast and irregular pile: each separate building was marked with the character of the times and of the founder; and the want of space might excuse the reigning monarch, who demolished, perhaps with secret satisfaction, the works of his predecessors. The economy of the emperor Theophilus allowed a more free and ample scope for his domestic luxury and splendor. A favorite ambassador, who had astonished the Abbassides themselves by his pride and liberality, presented on his return the model of a palace, which the caliph of Bagdad had recently constructed on the banks of the Tigris. The model was instantly copied and surpassed: the new buildings of Theophilus were accompanied with gardens, and with five churches, one of which was conspicuous for size and beauty: it was crowned with three domes, the roof of gilt brass reposed on columns of Italian marble, and the walls were incrusted with marbles of various colors. In the face of the church, a semicircular portico, of the figure and name of the Greek *sigma*, was supported by fifteen columns of Phrygian marble, and the subterraneous vaults were of a similar construction. The square before the sigma was decorated with a fountain, and the margin of the basin was lined and encompassed with plates of silver. In the beginning of each season, the basin, instead of water, was replenished with the most exquisite fruits, which were abandoned to the populace for the entertainment of the prince. He enjoyed this tumultuous spectacle from a throne resplendent with gold and gems, which was raised by a marble staircase to the height of a lofty terrace. Below the throne were seated the officers of his guards, the magistrates, the chiefs of the factions of the circus; the inferior steps were occupied by the people, and the place below was covered with troops of dancers, singers, and pantomimes. The square was surrounded by the hall of justice, the arsenal, and the various offices of business and pleasure; and the *purple* chamber was named from the annual distribution of robes of scarlet and purple by the hand of the empress herself. The long series of the apartments was adapted to the seasons, and decorated with marble and porphyry, with painting, sculpture, and mosaics, with a profusion of gold, silver, and precious stones. His fanciful magnificence employed the skill and patience of such artists as the times could afford: but the taste of Athens would have despised their frivolous and costly labors; a golden tree, with its leaves and branches, which sheltered a multitude of birds warbling their artificial notes, and two lions of massy gold, and of natural size, who looked and roared like their brethren of the forest. The successors of Theophilus, of the Basilian and Comnenian dynasties, were not less ambitious of leaving some memorial of their residence; and the portion of the palace most splendid and august was dignified with the title of the golden *triclinium*. With becoming modesty, the rich and noble Greeks aspired to imitate their sovereign, and when they passed through the streets on horseback, in their robes of silk and embroidery, they were mistaken by the children for kings. A matron of Peloponnesus, who had cherished the infant fortunes of Basil the Macedonian, was excited by tenderness or vanity to visit the greatness of her adopted son. In a journey of five hundred miles from Patras to Constantinople, her age or indolence declined the fatigue of a horse or carriage: the soft litter or bed of Danielis was transported on the shoulders of ten robust slaves; and as they were relieved at easy distances, a band of three hundred were selected for the performance of this service. She was entertained in the Byzantine palace with filial reverence, and the honors of a queen; and whatever might be the origin of her wealth, her gifts were not unworthy of the regal dignity. I have already described the fine and curious manufactures of Peloponnesus, of linen, silk, and woollen; but the most acceptable of her presents consisted in three hundred beautiful youths, of whom one hundred were eunuchs; "for she was not ignorant," says the historian, "that the air of the palace is more congenial to such insects, than a shepherd's dairy to the flies of the summer." During her lifetime, she bestowed the greater part of her estates in Peloponnesus, and her testament instituted Leo, the son of Basil, her universal heir. After the payment of the legacies, fourscore villas or farms were added to the Imperial domain; and three thousand slaves of Danielis were enfranchised by their new lord, and transplanted as a colony to the Italian coast. From this example of a private matron, we may estimate the wealth and magnificence of the emperors. Yet our enjoyments are confined by a narrow circle; and, whatsoever may be its value, the luxury of life is possessed with more innocence and safety by the master of his own, than by the steward of the public, fortune.

In an absolute government, which levels the distinctions of noble and plebeian birth, the sovereign is the sole fountain of honor; and the rank, both in the palace and the empire, depends on the titles and offices which are bestowed and resumed by his arbitrary will. Above a thousand years, from Vespasian to Alexius Comnenus, the *Cæsar* was the second person, or at least the second degree, after the supreme title of *Augustus* was more freely communicated to the sons and brothers of the reigning monarch. To elude without violating his promise to a powerful associate, the husband of his sister, and, without giving himself an equal, to reward the piety of his brother Isaac, the crafty Alexius interposed a new and supereminent dignity. The happy flexibility of the Greek tongue allowed him to compound the names of Augustus and Emperor (Sebastos and Autocrator,) and the union produces the sonorous title of *Sebastocrator*. He was exalted above the Cæsar on the first step of the throne: the public acclamations repeated his name; and he was only distinguished from the sovereign by some peculiar ornaments of the head and feet. The emperor alone could assume the purple or red buskins, and the close diadem or tiara, which imitated the fashion of the Persian kings. It was a high pyramidal cap of cloth or silk, almost concealed by a profusion of pearls and jewels: the crown was formed by a horizontal circle and two arches of gold: at the summit, the point of their intersection, was placed a globe or cross, and two strings or lappets of pearl depended on either cheek. Instead of red, the buskins of the Sebastocrator and Cæsar were green; and on their *open* coronets or crowns, the precious gems were more sparingly distributed. Beside and below the Cæsar the fancy of Alexius created the *Panhypersebasto* and the *Protosebastos*, whose sound and signification will satisfy a Grecian ear. They imply a superiority and a priority above the simple name of Augustus; and this sacred and primitive title of the Roman prince was degraded to the kinsmen and servants of the Byzantine court. The daughter of Alexius applauds, with fond complacency, this artful gradation of hopes and honors; but the science of words is accessible to the meanest capacity; and this vain dictionary was easily enriched by the pride of his successors. To their favorite sons or brothers, they imparted the more lofty appellation of Lord or *Despot*, which was illustrated with new ornaments, and prerogatives, and placed immediately after the person of the emperor himself. The five titles of, 1. *Despot*; 2. *Sebastocrator*; 3. *Cæsar*; 4. *Panhypersebastos*; and, 5. *Protosebastos*; were usually confined to the princes of his blood: they were the emanations of his majesty; but as they exercised no regular functions, their existence was useless, and their authority precarious.

But in every monarchy the substantial powers of government must be divided and exercised by the ministers of the palace and treasury, the fleet and army. The titles alone can differ; and in the revolution of ages, the counts and præfects, the prætor and quæstor, insensibly descended, while their servants rose above their heads to the first honors of the state. 1. In a monarchy, which refers every object to the person of the prince, the care and ceremonies of the palace form the most respectable department. The *Curopalata*, so illustrious in the age of Justinian, was supplanted by the *Protovestiare*, whose primitive functions were limited to the custody of the wardrobe. From thence his jurisdiction was extended over the numerous menials of pomp and luxury; and he presided with his silver wand at the public and private audience. 2. In the ancient system of Constantine, the name of *Logothete*, or accountant, was applied to the receivers of the finances: the principal officers were distinguished as the Logothetes of the domain, of the posts, the army, the private and public treasure; and the *great Logothete*, the supreme guardian of the laws and revenues, is compared with the chancellor of the Latin monarchies. His discerning eye pervaded the civil administration; and he was assisted, in due subordination, by the eparch or præfect of the city, the first secretary, and the keepers of the privy seal, the archives, and the red or purple ink which was reserved for the sacred signature of the emperor alone. The introductor and interpreter of foreign ambassadors were the great *Chiauss* and the *Dragoman*, two names of Turkish origin, and which are still familiar to the Sublime Porte. 3. From the humble style and service of guards, the *Domestics* insensibly rose to the station of generals; the military themes of the East and West, the legions of Europe and Asia, were often divided, till the great Domestic was finally invested with the universal and absolute command of the land forces. The *Protostrator*, in his original functions, was the assistant of the emperor when he mounted on horseback: he gradually became the lieutenant of the great Domestic in the field; and his jurisdiction extended over the stables, the cavalry, and the royal train of hunting and hawking. The *Stratopedarch* was the great judge of the camp: the *Protospathaire* commanded the guards; the *Constable*, the *great Æteriarch*, and the *Acolyth*, were the separate chiefs of the Franks, the Barbarians, and the Varangi, or English, the mercenary strangers, who, at the decay of the national spirit, formed the nerve of the Byzantine armies. 4. The naval powers were under the command of the *great Duke*; in his absence they obeyed the *great Drungaire* of the fleet; and, in *his* place, the *Emir*, or *Admiral*, a name of Saracen extraction, but which has been naturalized in all the modern languages of Europe. Of these officers, and of many more whom it would be useless to enumerate, the civil and military hierarchy was framed. Their honors and emoluments, their dress and titles, their mutual salutations and respective preëminence, were balanced with more exquisite labor than would have fixed the constitution of a free people; and the code was almost perfect when this baseless fabric, the monument of pride and servitude, was forever buried in the ruins of the empire.

CHAPTER FIFTY THREE
Fate of the Eastern Empire.
– Part Three

THE MOST LOFTY TITLES, and the most humble postures, which devotion has applied to the Supreme Being, have been prostituted by flattery and fear to creatures of the same nature with ourselves. The mode of *adoration*, of falling prostrate on the ground, and kissing the feet of the emperor, was borrowed by Diocletian from Persian servitude; but it was continued and aggravated till the last age of the Greek monarchy. Excepting only on Sundays, when it was waived, from a motive of religious pride, this humiliating reverence was exacted from all who entered the royal presence, from the princes invested with the diadem and purple, and from the ambassadors who represented their independent sovereigns, the caliphs of Asia, Egypt, or Spain, the kings of France and Italy, and the Latin emperors of ancient Rome. In his transactions of business, Liutprand, bishop of Cremona, asserted the free spirit of a Frank and the dignity of his master Otho. Yet his sincerity cannot disguise the abasement of his first audience. When he approached the throne, the birds of the golden tree began to warble their notes, which were accompanied by the roarings of the two lions of gold. With his two companions Liutprand was compelled to bow and to fall prostrate; and thrice to touch the ground with his forehead. He arose, but in the short interval, the throne had been hoisted from the floor to the ceiling, the Imperial figure appeared in new and more gorgeous apparel, and the interview was concluded in haughty and majestic silence. In this honest and curious narrative, the Bishop of Cremona represents the ceremonies of the Byzantine court, which are still practised in the Sublime Porte, and which were preserved in the last age by the dukes of Muscovy or Russia. After a long journey by sea and land, from Venice to Constantinople, the ambassador halted at the golden gate, till he was conducted by the formal officers to the hospitable palace prepared for his reception; but this palace was a prison, and his jealous keepers prohibited all social intercourse either with strangers or natives. At his first audience, he offered the gifts of his master, slaves, and golden vases, and costly armor. The ostentatious payment of the officers and troops displayed before his eyes the riches of the empire: he was entertained at a royal banquet, in which the ambassadors of the nations were marshalled by the esteem or contempt of the Greeks: from his own table, the emperor, as the most signal favor, sent the plates which he had tasted; and his favorites were dismissed with a robe of honor. In the morning and evening of each day, his civil and military servants attended their duty in the palace; their labors were repaid by the sight, perhaps by the smile, of their lord; his commands were signified by a nod or a sign: but all earthly greatness *stood* silent and submissive in his presence. In his regular or extraordinary processions through the capital, he unveiled his person to the public view: the rites of policy were connected with those of religion, and his visits to the principal churches were regulated by the festivals of the Greek calendar. On the eve of these processions, the gracious or devout intention of the monarch was proclaimed by the heralds. The streets were cleared and purified; the pavement was strewed with flowers; the most precious furniture, the gold and silver plate, and silken hangings, were displayed from the windows and balconies, and a severe discipline restrained and silenced the tumult of the populace. The march was opened by the military officers at the head of their troops: they were followed in long order by the magistrates and ministers of the civil government: the person of the emperor was guarded by his eunuchs and domestics, and at the church door he was solemnly received by the patriarch and his clergy. The task of applause was not abandoned to the rude and spontaneous voices of the crowd. The most convenient stations were occupied by the bands of the blue and green factions of the circus; and their furious conflicts, which had shaken the capital, were insensibly sunk to an emulation of servitude. From either side they echoed in responsive melody the praises of the emperor; their poets and musicians directed the choir, and long life and victory were the burden of every song. The same acclamations were performed at the audience, the banquet, and the church; and as an evidence of boundless sway, they were repeated in the Latin, Gothic, Persian, French, and even English language, by the mercenaries who sustained the real or fictitious character of those nations. By the pen of Constantine Porphyrogenitus, this science of form and flattery has been reduced into a pompous and trifling volume, which the vanity of succeeding times might enrich with an ample supplement. Yet the calmer reflection of a prince would surely suggest that the same acclamations were applied to every character and every reign: and if he had risen from a private rank, he might remember, that his own voice had been the loudest and most eager in applause, at the very moment when he envied the fortune, or conspired against the life, of his predecessor.

The princes of the North, of the nations, says Constantine, without faith or fame, were ambitious of mingling their blood with the blood of the Cæsars, by their marriage with a royal virgin, or by the nuptials of their daughters with a Roman prince. The aged monarch, in his instructions to his son, reveals the secret maxims of policy and pride; and suggests the most decent reasons for refusing these insolent and unreasonable demands. Every animal, says the discreet emperor, is prompted by the distinction of language, religion, and manners. A just regard to the purity of descent preserves the harmony of public and private life; but the mixture of foreign blood is the fruitful source of disorder and discord. Such had ever been the opinion and practice of the sage Romans: their jurisprudence proscribed the marriage of a citizen and a stranger: in the days of freedom and virtue, a senator would have scorned to match his daughter with a king: the glory of Mark Antony was sullied by an Egyptian wife: and the emperor Titus was compelled, by popular censure, to dismiss with reluctance the reluctant Berenice. This perpetual interdict was ratified by the fabulous sanction of the great Constantine. The ambassadors of the nations, more especially of the unbelieving nations, were solemnly admonished, that such strange alliances had been condemned by the founder of the church and city. The irrevocable law was inscribed on the altar of St. Sophia; and the impious prince who should stain the majesty of the purple was excluded from the civil and ecclesiastical communion of the Romans. If the ambassadors were instructed by any false brethren in the Byzantine history, they might produce three memorable examples of the violation of this imaginary law: the marriage of Leo, or rather of his father Constantine the Fourth, with the daughter of the king of the Chozars, the nuptials of the granddaughter of Romanus with a Bulgarian prince, and the union of Bertha of France or Italy with young Romanus, the son of Constantine Porphyrogenitus himself. To these objections three answers were prepared, which solved the difficulty and established the law. I. The deed and the guilt of Constantine Copronymus were acknowledged. The Isaurian heretic, who sullied the baptismal font, and declared war against the holy images, had indeed embraced a Barbarian wife. By this impious alliance he accomplished the measure of his crimes, and was devoted to the just censure of the church and of posterity. II. Romanus could not be alleged as a legitimate emperor; he was a plebeian usurper, ignorant of the laws, and regardless of the honor, of the monarchy. His son Christopher, the father of the bride, was the third in rank in the college of princes, at once the subject and the accomplice of a rebellious parent. The Bulgarians were sincere and devout Christians; and the safety of the empire, with the redemption of many thousand captives, depended on this preposterous alliance. Yet no consideration could dispense from the law of Constantine: the clergy, the senate, and the people, disapproved the conduct of Romanus; and he was reproached, both in his life and death, as the author of the public disgrace. III. For the marriage of his own son with the daughter of Hugo, king of Italy, a more honorable defence is contrived by the wise Porphyrogenitus. Constantine, the great and holy, esteemed the fidelity and valor of the Franks; and his prophetic spirit beheld the vision of their future greatness. They alone were excepted from the general prohibition: Hugo, king of France, was the lineal descendant of Charlemagne; and his daughter Bertha inherited the prerogatives of her family and nation. The voice of truth and malice insensibly betrayed the fraud or error of the Imperial court. The patrimonial estate of Hugo was reduced from the monarchy of France to the simple county of Arles; though it was not denied, that, in the confusion of the times, he had usurped the sovereignty of Provence, and invaded the kingdom of Italy. His father was a private noble; and if Bertha derived her female descent from the Carlovingian line, every step was polluted with illegitimacy or vice. The grandmother of Hugo was the famous Valdrada, the concubine, rather than the wife, of the second Lothair; whose adultery, divorce, and second nuptials, had provoked against him the thunders of the Vatican. His mother, as she was styled, the great Bertha, was successively the wife of the count of Arles and of the marquis of Tuscany: France and Italy were scandalized by her gallantries; and, till the age of threescore, her lovers, of every degree, were the zealous servants of her ambition. The example of maternal incontinence was copied by the king of Italy; and the three favorite concubines of Hugo were decorated with the classic names of Venus, Juno, and Semele. The daughter of Venus was granted to the solicitations of the Byzantine court: her name of Bertha was changed to that of Eudoxia; and she was wedded, or rather betrothed, to young Romanus, the future heir of the empire of the East. The consummation of this foreign alliance was suspended by the tender age of the two parties; and, at the end of five years, the union was dissolved by the death of the virgin spouse. The second wife of the emperor Romanus was a maiden of plebeian, but of Roman, birth; and their two daughters, Theophano and Anne, were given in marriage to the princes of the earth. The eldest was bestowed, as the pledge of peace, on the eldest son of the great Otho, who had solicited this alliance with arms and embassies. It might legally be questioned how far a Saxon was entitled to the privilege of the French nation; but every scruple was silenced by the fame and piety of a hero who had restored the empire of the West. After the death of her father-in-law and husband, Theophano governed Rome, Italy, and Germany, during the minority of her son, the third Otho; and the Latins have praised the virtues of an empress, who sacrificed to a superior duty the remembrance of her country. In the nuptials of her sister Anne, every prejudice was lost, and every consideration of dignity was superseded, by the stronger argument of necessity and fear. A Pagan of the North, Wolodomir, great prince of Russia, aspired to a daughter of the Roman purple; and his claim was enforced by the threats of war, the promise of conversion, and the offer of a powerful succor against a domestic rebel. A victim of her religion and country, the Grecian princess was torn from the palace of her fathers, and condemned to a savage reign, and a hopeless exile on the banks of the Borysthenes, or in the neighborhood of the Polar circle. Yet the marriage of Anne was fortunate and fruitful: the daughter of her grandson Joroslaus was recommended by her Imperial descent; and the king of France, Henry I., sought a wife on the last borders of Europe and Christendom.

In the Byzantine palace, the emperor was the first slave of the ceremonies which he imposed, of the rigid forms which regulated each word and gesture, besieged him in the palace, and violated the leisure of his rural solitude. But the lives and fortunes of millions hung on his arbitrary will; and the firmest minds, superior to the allurements of pomp and luxury, may be seduced by the more active pleasure of commanding their equals. The legislative and executive powers were centred in the person of the monarch, and the last remains of the authority of the senate were finally eradicated by Leo the philosopher. A lethargy of servitude had benumbed the minds of the Greeks: in the wildest tumults of rebellion they never aspired to the idea of a free constitution; and the private character of the prince was the only source and measure of their public happiness. Superstition rivetted their chains; in the church of St. Sophia he was solemnly crowned by the patriarch; at the foot of the altar, they pledged their passive and unconditional obedience to his government and family. On his side he engaged to abstain as much as possible from the capital punishments of death and mutilation; his orthodox creed was subscribed with his own hand, and he promised to obey the decrees of the seven synods, and the canons of the holy church. But the assurance of mercy was loose and indefinite: he swore, not to his people, but to an invisible judge; and except in the inexpiable guilt of heresy, the ministers of heaven were always prepared to preach the indefeasible right, and to absolve the venial transgressions, of their sovereign. The Greek ecclesiastics were themselves the subjects of the civil magistrate: at the nod of a tyrant, the bishops were created, or transferred, or deposed, or punished with an ignominious death: whatever might be their wealth or influence, they could never succeed like the Latin clergy in the establishment of an independent republic; and the patriarch of Constantinople condemned, what he secretly envied, the temporal greatness of his Roman brother. Yet the exercise of boundless despotism is happily checked by the laws of nature and necessity. In proportion to his wisdom and virtue, the master of an empire is confined to the path of his sacred and laborious duty. In proportion to his vice and folly, he drops the sceptre too weighty for his hands; and the motions of the royal image are ruled by the imperceptible thread of some minister or favorite, who undertakes for his private interest to exercise the task of the public oppression. In some fatal moment, the most absolute monarch may dread the reason or the caprice of a nation of slaves; and experience has proved, that whatever is gained in the extent, is lost in the safety and solidity, of regal power.

Whatever titles a despot may assume, whatever claims he may assert, it is on the sword that he must ultimately depend to guard him against his foreign and domestic enemies. From the age of Charlemagne to that of the Crusades, the world (for I overlook the remote monarchy of China) was occupied and disputed by the three great empires or nations of the Greeks, the Saracens, and the Franks. Their military strength may be ascertained by a comparison of their courage, their arts and riches, and their obedience to a supreme head, who might call into action all the energies of the state. The Greeks, far inferior to their rivals in the first, were superior to the Franks, and at least equal to the Saracens, in the second and third of these warlike qualifications.

The wealth of the Greeks enabled them to purchase the service of the poorer nations, and to maintain a naval power for the protection of their coasts and the annoyance of their enemies. A commerce of mutual benefit exchanged the gold of Constantinople for the blood of Sclavonians and Turks, the Bulgarians and Russians: their valor contributed to the victories of Nicephorus and Zimisces; and if a hostile people pressed too closely on the frontier, they were recalled to the defence of their country, and the desire of peace, by the well-managed attack of a more distant tribe. The command of the Mediterranean, from the mouth of the Tanais to the columns of Hercules, was always claimed, and often possessed, by the successors of Constantine. Their capital was filled with naval stores and dexterous artificers: the situation of Greece and Asia, the long coasts, deep gulfs, and numerous islands, accustomed their subjects to the exercise of navigation; and the trade of Venice and Amalfi supplied a nursery of seamen to the Imperial fleet. Since the time of the Peloponnesian and Punic wars, the sphere of action had not been enlarged; and the science of naval architecture appears to have declined. The art of constructing those stupendous machines which displayed three, or six, or ten, ranges of oars, rising above, or falling behind, each other, was unknown to the ship-builders of Constantinople, as well as to the mechanicians of modern days. The *Dromones*, or light galleys of the Byzantine empire, were content with two tier of oars; each tier was composed of five-and-twenty benches; and two rowers were seated on each bench, who plied their oars on either side of the vessel. To these we must add the captain or centurion, who, in time of action, stood erect with his armor-bearer on the poop, two steersmen at the helm, and two officers at the prow, the one to manage the anchor, the other to point and play against the enemy the tube of liquid fire. The whole crew, as in the infancy of the art, performed the double service of mariners and soldiers; they were provided with defensive and offensive arms, with bows and arrows, which they used from the upper deck, with long pikes, which they pushed through the portholes of the lower tier. Sometimes, indeed, the ships of war were of a larger and more solid construction; and the labors of combat and navigation were more regularly divided between seventy soldiers and two hundred and thirty mariners. But for the most part they were of the light and manageable size; and as the Cape of Malea in Peloponnesus was still clothed with its ancient terrors, an Imperial fleet was transported five miles over land across the Isthmus of Corinth. The principles of maritime tactics had not undergone any change since the time of Thucydides: a squadron of galleys still advanced in a crescent, charged to the front, and strove to impel their sharp beaks against the feeble sides of their antagonists. A machine for casting stones and darts was built of strong timbers, in the midst of the deck; and the operation of boarding was effected by a crane that hoisted baskets of armed men. The language of signals, so clear and copious in the naval grammar of the moderns, was imperfectly expressed by the various positions and colors of a commanding flag. In the darkness of the night, the same orders to chase, to attack, to halt, to retreat, to break, to form, were conveyed by the lights of the leading galley. By land, the fire-signals were repeated from one mountain to another; a chain of eight stations commanded a space of five hundred miles; and Constantinople in a few hours was apprised of the hostile motions of the Saracens of Tarsus. Some estimate may be formed of the power of the Greek emperors, by the curious and minute detail of the armament which was prepared for the reduction of Crete. A fleet of one hundred and twelve galleys, and seventy-five vessels of the Pamphylian style, was equipped in the capital, the islands of the Ægean Sea, and the seaports of Asia, Macedonia, and Greece. It carried thirty-four thousand mariners, seven thousand three hundred and forty soldiers, seven hundred Russians, and five thousand and eighty-seven Mardaites, whose fathers had been transplanted from the mountains of Libanus. Their pay, most probably of a month, was computed at thirty-four centenaries of gold, about one hundred and thirty-six thousand pounds sterling. Our fancy is bewildered by the endless recapitulation of arms and engines, of clothes and linen, of bread for the men and forage for the horses, and of stores and utensils of every description, inadequate to the conquest of a petty island, but amply sufficient for the establishment of a flourishing colony.

The invention of the Greek fire did not, like that of gun powder, produce a total revolution in the art of war. To these liquid combustibles the city and empire of Constantine owed their deliverance; and they were employed in sieges and sea-fights with terrible effect. But they were either less improved, or less susceptible of improvement: the engines of antiquity, the catapultæ, balistæ, and battering-rams, were still of most frequent and powerful use in the attack and defence of fortifications; nor was the decision of battles reduced to the quick and heavy *fire* of a line of infantry, whom it were fruitless to protect with armor against a similar fire of their enemies. Steel and iron were still the common instruments of destruction and safety; and the helmets, cuirasses, and shields, of the tenth century did not, either in form or substance, essentially differ from those which had covered the companions of Alexander or Achilles. But instead of accustoming the modern Greeks, like the legionaries of old, to the constant and easy use of this salutary weight, their armor was laid aside in light chariots, which followed the march, till, on the approach of an enemy, they resumed with haste and reluctance the unusual encumbrance. Their offensive weapons consisted of swords, battle-axes, and spears; but the Macedonian pike was shortened a fourth of its length, and reduced to the more convenient measure of twelve cubits or feet. The sharpness of the Scythian and Arabian arrows had been severely felt; and the emperors lament the decay of archery as a cause of the public misfortunes, and recommend, as an advice and a command, that the military youth, till the age of forty, should assiduously practise the exercise of the bow. The *bands*, or regiments, were usually three hundred strong; and, as a medium between the extremes of four and sixteen, the foot soldiers of Leo and Constantine were formed eight deep; but the cavalry charged in four ranks, from the reasonable consideration, that the weight of the front could not be increased by any pressure of the hindmost horses. If the ranks of the infantry or cavalry were sometimes doubled, this cautious array betrayed a secret distrust of the courage of the troops, whose numbers might swell the appearance of the line, but of whom only a chosen band would dare to encounter the spears and swords of the Barbarians. The order of battle must have varied according to the ground, the object, and the adversary; but their ordinary disposition, in two lines and a reserve, presented a succession of hopes and resources most agreeable to the temper as well as the judgment of the Greeks. In case of a repulse, the first line fell back into the intervals of the second; and the reserve, breaking into two divisions, wheeled round the flanks to improve the victory or cover the retreat. Whatever authority could enact was accomplished, at least in theory, by the camps and marches, the exercises and evolutions, the edicts and books, of the Byzantine monarch. Whatever art could produce from the forge, the loom, or the laboratory, was abundantly supplied by the riches of the prince, and the industry of his numerous workmen. But neither authority nor art could frame the most important machine, the soldier himself; and if the *ceremonies* of Constantine always suppose the safe and triumphal return of the emperor, his *tactics* seldom soar above the means of escaping a defeat, and procrastinating the war. Notwithstanding some transient success, the Greeks were sunk in their own esteem and that of their neighbors. A cold hand and a loquacious tongue was the vulgar description of the nation: the author of the tactics was besieged in his capital; and the last of the Barbarians, who trembled at the name of the Saracens, or Franks, could proudly exhibit the medals of gold and silver which they had extorted from the feeble sovereign of Constantinople. What spirit their government and character denied, might have been inspired in some degree by the influence of religion; but the religion of the Greeks could only teach them to suffer and to yield. The emperor Nicephorus, who restored for a moment the discipline and glory of the Roman name, was desirous of bestowing the honors of martyrdom on the Christians who lost their lives in a holy war against the infidels. But this political law was defeated by the opposition of the patriarch, the bishops, and the principal senators; and they strenuously urged the canons of St. Basil, that all who were polluted by the bloody trade of a soldier should be separated, during three years, from the communion of the faithful.

These scruples of the Greeks have been compared with the tears of the primitive Moslems when they were held back from battle; and this contrast of base superstition and high-spirited enthusiasm, unfolds to a philosophic eye the history of the rival nations. The subjects of the last caliphs had undoubtedly degenerated from the zeal and faith of the companions of the prophet. Yet their martial creed still represented the Deity as the author of war: the vital though latent spark of fanaticism still glowed in the heart of their religion, and among the Saracens, who dwelt on the Christian borders, it was frequently rekindled to a lively and active flame. Their regular force was formed of the valiant slaves who had been educated to guard the person and accompany the standard of their lord: but the Mussulman people of Syria and Cilicia, of Africa and Spain, was awakened by the trumpet which proclaimed a holy war against the infidels. The rich were ambitious of death or victory in the cause of God; the poor were allured by the hopes of plunder; and the old, the infirm, and the women, assumed their share of meritorious service by sending their substitutes, with arms and horses, into the field. These offensive and defensive arms were similar in strength and temper to those of the Romans, whom they far excelled in the management of the horse and the bow: the massy silver of their belts, their bridles, and their swords, displayed the magnificence of a prosperous nation; and except some black archers of the South, the Arabs disdained the naked bravery of their ancestors. Instead of wagons, they were attended by a long train of camels, mules, and asses: the multitude of these animals, whom they bedecked with flags and streamers, appeared to swell the pomp and magnitude of their host; and the horses of the enemy were often disordered by the uncouth figure and odious smell of the camels of the East. Invincible by their patience of thirst and heat, their spirits were frozen by a winter's cold, and the consciousness of their propensity to sleep exacted the most rigorous precautions against the surprises of the night. Their order of battle was a long square of two deep and solid lines; the first of archers, the second of cavalry. In their engagements by sea and land, they sustained with patient firmness the fury of the attack, and seldom advanced to the charge till they could discern and oppress the lassitude of their foes. But if they were repulsed and broken, they knew not how to rally or renew the combat; and their dismay was heightened by the superstitious prejudice, that God had declared himself on the side of their enemies. The decline and fall of the caliphs countenanced this fearful opinion; nor were there wanting, among the Mahometans and Christians, some obscure prophecies which prognosticated their alternate defeats. The unity of the Arabian empire was dissolved, but the independent fragments were equal to populous and powerful kingdoms; and in their naval and military armaments, an emir of Aleppo or Tunis might command no despicable fund of skill, and industry, and treasure. In their transactions of peace and war with the Saracens, the princes of Constantinople too often felt that these Barbarians had nothing barbarous in their discipline; and that if they were destitute of original genius, they had been endowed with a quick spirit of curiosity and imitation. The model was indeed more perfect than the copy; their ships, and engines, and fortifications, were of a less skilful construction; and they confess, without shame, that the same God who has given a tongue to the Arabians, had more nicely fashioned the hands of the Chinese, and the heads of the Greeks.

Fate of the Eastern Empire.
– Part Four

A NAME OF SOME German tribes between the Rhine and the Weser had spread its victorious influence over the greatest part of Gaul, Germany, and Italy; and the common appellation of Franks was applied by the Greeks and Arabians to the Christians of the Latin church, the nations of the West, who stretched beyond *their* knowledge to the shores of the Atlantic Ocean. The vast body had been inspired and united by the soul of Charlemagne; but the division and degeneracy of his race soon annihilated the Imperial power, which would have rivalled the Cæsars of Byzantium, and revenged the indignities of the Christian name. The enemies no longer feared, nor could the subjects any longer trust, the application of a public revenue, the labors of trade and manufactures in the military service, the mutual aid of provinces and armies, and the naval squadrons which were regularly stationed from the mouth of the Elbe to that of the Tyber. In the beginning of the tenth century, the family of Charlemagne had almost disappeared; his monarchy was broken into many hostile and independent states; the regal title was assumed by the most ambitious chiefs; their revolt was imitated in a long subordination of anarchy and discord, and the nobles of every province disobeyed their sovereign, oppressed their vassals, and exercised perpetual hostilities against their equals and neighbors. Their private wars, which overturned the fabric of government, fomented the martial spirit of the nation. In the system of modern Europe, the power of the sword is possessed, at least in fact, by five or six mighty potentates; their operations are conducted on a distant frontier, by an order of men who devote their lives to the study and practice of the military art: the rest of the country and community enjoys in the midst of war the tranquillity of peace, and is only made sensible of the change by the aggravation or decrease of the public taxes. In the disorders of the tenth and eleventh centuries, every peasant was a soldier, and every village a fortification; each wood or valley was a scene of murder and rapine; and the lords of each castle were compelled to assume the character of princes and warriors. To their own courage and policy they boldly trusted for the safety of their family, the protection of their lands, and the revenge of their injuries; and, like the conquerors of a larger size, they were too apt to transgress the privilege of defensive war. The powers of the mind and body were hardened by the presence of danger and necessity of resolution: the same spirit refused to desert a friend and to forgive an enemy; and, instead of sleeping under the guardian care of a magistrate, they proudly disdained the authority of the laws. In the days of feudal anarchy, the instruments of agriculture and art were converted into the weapons of bloodshed: the peaceful occupations of civil and ecclesiastical society were abolished or corrupted; and the bishop who exchanged his mitre for a helmet, was more forcibly urged by the manners of the times than by the obligation of his tenure.

The love of freedom and of arms was felt, with conscious pride, by the Franks themselves, and is observed by the Greeks with some degree of amazement and terror. "The Franks," says the emperor Constantine, "are bold and valiant to the verge of temerity; and their dauntless spirit is supported by the contempt of danger and death. In the field and in close onset, they press to the front, and rush headlong against the enemy, without deigning to compute either his numbers or their own. Their ranks are formed by the firm connections of consanguinity and friendship; and their martial deeds are prompted by the desire of saving or revenging their dearest companions. In their eyes, a retreat is a shameful flight; and flight is indelible infamy." A nation endowed with such high and intrepid spirit, must have been secure of victory if these advantages had not been counter-balanced by many weighty defects. The decay of their naval power left the Greeks and Saracens in possession of the sea, for every purpose of annoyance and supply. In the age which preceded the institution of knighthood, the Franks were rude and unskilful in the service of cavalry; and in all perilous emergencies, their warriors were so conscious of their ignorance, that they chose to dismount from their horses and fight on foot. Unpractised in the use of pikes, or of missile weapons, they were encumbered by the length of their swords, the weight of their armor, the magnitude of their shields, and, if I may repeat the satire of the meagre Greeks, by their unwieldy intemperance. Their independent spirit disdained the yoke of subordination, and abandoned the standard of their chief, if he attempted to keep the field beyond the term of their stipulation or service. On all sides they were open to the snares of an enemy less brave but more artful than themselves. They might be bribed, for the Barbarians were venal; or surprised in the night, for they neglected the precautions of a close encampment or vigilant sentinels. The fatigues of a summer's campaign exhausted their strength and patience, and they sunk in despair if their voracious appetite was disappointed of a plentiful supply of wine and of food. This general character of the Franks was marked with some national and local shades, which I should ascribe to accident rather than to climate, but which were visible both to natives and to foreigners. An ambassador of the great Otho declared, in the palace of Constantinople, that the Saxons could dispute with swords better than with pens, and that they preferred inevitable death to the dishonor of turning their backs to an enemy. It was the glory of the nobles of France, that, in their humble dwellings, war and rapine were the only pleasure, the sole occupation, of their lives. They affected to deride the palaces, the banquets, the polished manner of the Italians, who in the estimate of the Greeks themselves had degenerated from the liberty and valor of the ancient Lombards.

By the well-known edict of Caracalla, his subjects, from Britain to Egypt, were entitled to the name and privileges of Romans, and their national sovereign might fix his occasional or permanent residence in any province of their common country. In the division of the East and West, an ideal unity was scrupulously observed, and in their titles, laws, and statutes, the successors of Arcadius and Honorius announced themselves as the inseparable colleagues of the same office, as the joint sovereigns of the Roman world and city, which were bounded by the same limits. After the fall of the Western monarchy, the majesty of the purple resided solely in the princes of Constantinople; and of these, Justinian was the first who, after a divorce of sixty years, regained the dominion of ancient Rome, and asserted, by the right of conquest, the august title of Emperor of the Romans. A motive of vanity or discontent solicited one of his successors, Constans the Second, to abandon the Thracian Bosphorus, and to restore the pristine honors of the Tyber: an extravagant project, (exclaims the malicious Byzantine,) as if he had despoiled a beautiful and blooming virgin, to enrich, or rather to expose, the deformity of a wrinkled and decrepit matron. But the sword of the Lombards opposed his settlement in Italy: he entered Rome not as a conqueror, but as a fugitive, and, after a visit of twelve days, he pillaged, and forever deserted, the ancient capital of the world. The final revolt and separation of Italy was accomplished about two centuries after the conquests of Justinian, and from his reign we may date the gradual oblivion of the Latin tongue. That legislator had composed his Institutes, his Code, and his Pandects, in a language which he celebrates as the proper and public style of the Roman government, the consecrated idiom of the palace and senate of Constantinople, of the campus and tribunals of the East. But this foreign dialect was unknown to the people and soldiers of the Asiatic provinces, it was imperfectly understood by the greater part of the interpreters of the laws and the ministers of the state. After a short conflict, nature and habit prevailed over the obsolete institutions of human power: for the general benefit of his subjects, Justinian promulgated his novels in the two languages: the several parts of his voluminous jurisprudence were successively translated; the original was forgotten, the version was studied, and the Greek, whose intrinsic merit deserved indeed the preference, obtained a legal, as well as popular establishment in the Byzantine monarchy. The birth and residence of succeeding princes estranged them from the Roman idiom: Tiberius by the Arabs, and Maurice by the Italians, are distinguished as the first of the Greek Cæsars, as the founders of a new dynasty and empire: the silent revolution was accomplished before the death of Heraclius; and the ruins of the Latin speech were darkly preserved in the terms of jurisprudence and the acclamations of the palace. After the restoration of the Western empire by Charlemagne and the Othos, the names of Franks and Latins acquired an equal signification and extent; and these haughty Barbarians asserted, with some justice, their superior claim to the language and dominion of Rome. They insulted the alien of the East who had renounced the dress and idiom of Romans; and their reasonable practice will justify the frequent appellation of Greeks. But this contemptuous appellation was indignantly rejected by the prince and people to whom it was applied. Whatsoever changes had been introduced by the lapse of ages, they alleged a lineal and unbroken succession from Augustus and Constantine; and, in the lowest period of degeneracy and decay, the name of Romans adhered to the last fragments of the empire of Constantinople.

While the government of the East was transacted in Latin, the Greek was the language of literature and philosophy; nor could the masters of this rich and perfect idiom be tempted to envy the borrowed learning and imitative taste of their Roman disciples. After the fall of Paganism, the loss of Syria and Egypt, and the extinction of the schools of Alexandria and Athens, the studies of the Greeks insensibly retired to some regular monasteries, and above all, to the royal college of Constantinople, which was burnt in the reign of Leo the Isaurian. In the pompous style of the age, the president of that foundation was named the Sun of Science: his twelve associates, the professors in the different arts and faculties, were the twelve signs of the zodiac; a library of thirty-six thousand five hundred volumes was open to their inquiries; and they could show an ancient manuscript of Homer, on a roll of parchment one hundred and twenty feet in length, the intestines, as it was fabled, of a prodigious serpent. But the seventh and eight centuries were a period of discord and darkness: the library was burnt, the college was abolished, the Iconoclasts are represented as the foes of antiquity; and a savage ignorance and contempt of letters has disgraced the princes of the Heraclean and Isaurian dynasties.

In the ninth century we trace the first dawnings of the restoration of science. After the fanaticism of the Arabs had subsided, the caliphs aspired to conquer the arts, rather than the provinces, of the empire: their liberal curiosity rekindled the emulation of the Greeks, brushed away the dust from their ancient libraries, and taught them to know and reward the philosophers, whose labors had been hitherto repaid by the pleasure of study and the pursuit of truth. The Cæsar Bardas, the uncle of Michael the Third, was the generous protector of letters, a title which alone has preserved his memory and excused his ambition. A particle of the treasures of his nephew was sometimes diverted from the indulgence of vice and folly; a school was opened in the palace of Magnaura; and the presence of Bardas excited the emulation of the masters and students. At their head was the philosopher Leo, archbishop of Thessalonica: his profound skill in astronomy and the mathematics was admired by the strangers of the East; and this occult science was magnified by vulgar credulity, which modestly supposes that all knowledge superior to its own must be the effect of inspiration or magic. At the pressing entreaty of the Cæsar, his friend, the celebrated Photius, renounced the freedom of a secular and studious life, ascended the patriarchal throne, and was alternately excommunicated and absolved by the synods of the East and West. By the confession even of priestly hatred, no art or science, except poetry, was foreign to this universal scholar, who was deep in thought, indefatigable in reading, and eloquent in diction. Whilst he exercised the office of protospathaire or captain of the guards, Photius was sent ambassador to the caliph of Bagdad. The tedious hours of exile, perhaps of confinement, were beguiled by the hasty composition of his *Library*, a living monument of erudition and criticism. Two hundred and fourscore writers, historians, orators, philosophers, theologians, are reviewed without any regular method: he abridges their narrative or doctrine, appreciates their style and character, and judges even the fathers of the church with a discreet freedom, which often breaks through the superstition of the times. The emperor Basil, who lamented the defects of his own education, intrusted to the care of Photius his son and successor, Leo the philosopher; and the reign of that prince and of his son Constantine Porphyrogenitus forms one of the most prosperous æras of the Byzantine literature. By their munificence the treasures of antiquity were deposited in the Imperial library; by their pens, or those of their associates, they were imparted in such extracts and abridgments as might amuse the curiosity, without oppressing the indolence, of the public. Besides the *Basilics*, or code of laws, the arts of husbandry and war, of feeding or destroying the human species, were propagated with equal diligence; and the history of Greece and Rome was digested into fifty-three heads or titles, of which two only (of embassies, and of virtues and vices) have escaped the injuries of time. In every station, the reader might contemplate the image of the past world, apply the lesson or warning of each page, and learn to admire, perhaps to imitate, the examples of a brighter period. I shall not expatiate on the works of the Byzantine Greeks, who, by the assiduous study of the ancients, have deserved, in some measure, the remembrance and gratitude of the moderns. The scholars of the present age may still enjoy the benefit of the philosophical commonplace book of Stobæus, the grammatical and historical lexicon of Suidas, the Chiliads of Tzetzes, which comprise six hundred narratives in twelve thousand verses, and the commentaries on Homer of Eustathius, archbishop of Thessalonica, who, from his horn of plenty, has poured the names and authorities of four hundred writers. From these originals, and from the numerous tribe of scholiasts and critics, some estimate may be formed of the literary wealth of the twelfth century: Constantinople was enlightened by the genius of Homer and Demosthenes, of Aristotle and Plato: and in the enjoyment or neglect of our present riches, we must envy the generation that could still peruse the history of Theopompus, the orations of Hyperides, the comedies of Menander, and the odes of Alcæus and Sappho. The frequent labor of illustration attests not only the existence, but the popularity, of the Grecian classics: the general knowledge of the age may be deduced from the example of two learned females, the empress Eudocia, and the princess Anna Comnena, who cultivated, in the purple, the arts of rhetoric and philosophy. The vulgar dialect of the city was gross and barbarous: a more correct and elaborate style distinguished the discourse, or at least the compositions, of the church and palace, which sometimes affected to copy the purity of the Attic models.

In our modern education, the painful though necessary attainment of two languages, which are no longer living, may consume the time and damp the ardor of the youthful student. The poets and orators were long imprisoned in the barbarous dialects of our Western ancestors, devoid of harmony or grace; and their genius, without precept or example, was abandoned to the rule and native powers of their judgment and fancy. But the Greeks of Constantinople, after purging away the impurities of their vulgar speech, acquired the free use of their ancient language, the most happy composition of human art, and a familiar knowledge of the sublime masters who had pleased or instructed the first of nations. But these advantages only tend to aggravate the reproach and shame of a degenerate people. They held in their lifeless hands the riches of their fathers, without inheriting the spirit which had created and improved that sacred patrimony: they read, they praised, they compiled, but their languid souls seemed alike incapable of thought and action. In the revolution of ten centuries, not a single discovery was made to exalt the dignity or promote the happiness of mankind. Not a single idea has been added to the speculative systems of antiquity, and a succession of patient disciples became in their turn the dogmatic teachers of the next servile generation. Not a single composition of history, philosophy, or literature, has been saved from oblivion by the intrinsic beauties of style or sentiment, of original fancy, or even of successful imitation. In prose, the least offensive of the Byzantine writers are absolved from censure by their naked and unpresuming simplicity: but the orators, most eloquent in their own conceit, are the farthest removed from the models whom they affect to emulate. In every page our taste and reason are wounded by the choice of gigantic and obsolete words, a stiff and intricate phraseology, the discord of images, the childish play of false or unseasonable ornament, and the painful attempt to elevate themselves, to astonish the reader, and to involve a trivial meaning in the smoke of obscurity and exaggeration. Their prose is soaring to the vicious affectation of poetry: their poetry is sinking below the flatness and insipidity of prose. The tragic, epic, and lyric muses, were silent and inglorious: the bards of Constantinople seldom rose above a riddle or epigram, a panegyric or tale; they forgot even the rules of prosody; and with the melody of Homer yet sounding in their ears, they confound all measure of feet and syllables in the impotent strains which have received the name of *political* or city verses. The minds of the Greek were bound in the fetters of a base and imperious superstition which extends her dominion round the circle of profane science. Their understandings were bewildered in metaphysical controversy: in the belief of visions and miracles, they had lost all principles of moral evidence, and their taste was vitiated by the homilies of the monks, an absurd medley of declamation and Scripture. Even these contemptible studies were no longer dignified by the abuse of superior talents: the leaders of the Greek church were humbly content to admire and copy the oracles of antiquity, nor did the schools of pulpit produce any rivals of the fame of Athanasius and Chrysostom.

In all the pursuits of active and speculative life, the emulation of states and individuals is the most powerful spring of the efforts and improvements of mankind. The cities of ancient Greece were cast in the happy mixture of union and independence, which is repeated on a larger scale, but in a looser form, by the nations of modern Europe; the union of language, religion, and manners, which renders them the spectators and judges of each other's merit; the independence of government and interest, which asserts their separate freedom, and excites them to strive for preëminence in the career of glory. The situation of the Romans was less favorable; yet in the early ages of the republic, which fixed the national character, a similar emulation was kindled among the states of Latium and Italy; and in the arts and sciences, they aspired to equal or surpass their Grecian masters. The empire of the Cæsars undoubtedly checked the activity and progress of the human mind; its magnitude might indeed allow some scope for domestic competition; but when it was gradually reduced, at first to the East and at last to Greece and Constantinople, the Byzantine subjects were degraded to an abject and languid temper, the natural effect of their solitary and insulated state. From the North they were oppressed by nameless tribes of Barbarians, to whom they scarcely imparted the appellation of men. The language and religion of the more polished Arabs were an insurmountable bar to all social intercourse. The conquerors of Europe were their brethren in the Christian faith; but the speech of the Franks or Latins was unknown, their manners were rude, and they were rarely connected, in peace or war, with the successors of Heraclius. Alone in the universe, the self-satisfied pride of the Greeks was not disturbed by the comparison of foreign merit; and it is no wonder if they fainted in the race, since they had neither competitors to urge their speed, nor judges to crown their victory. The nations of Europe and Asia were mingled by the expeditions to the Holy Land; and it is under the Comnenian dynasty that a faint emulation of knowledge and military virtue was rekindled in the Byzantine empire.

Origin and Doctrine
of the Paulicians. – Part One

Origin and Doctrine of the Paulicians. – Their Persecution by the Greek Emperors. – Revolt in Armenia &c. – Transplantation into Thrace. – Propagation in the West. – The Seeds, Character, and Consequences of the Reformation.

IN THE PROFESSION OF Christianity, the variety of national characters may be clearly distinguished. The natives of Syria and Egypt abandoned their lives to lazy and contemplative devotion: Rome again aspired to the dominion of the world; and the wit of the lively and loquacious Greeks was consumed in the disputes of metaphysical theology. The incomprehensible mysteries of the Trinity and Incarnation, instead of commanding their silent submission, were agitated in vehement and subtile controversies, which enlarged their faith at the expense, perhaps, of their charity and reason. From the council of Nice to the end of the seventh century, the peace and unity of the church was invaded by these spiritual wars; and so deeply did they affect the decline and fall of the empire, that the historian has too often been compelled to attend the synods, to explore the creeds, and to enumerate the sects, of this busy period of ecclesiastical annals. From the beginning of the eighth century to the last ages of the Byzantine empire, the sound of controversy was seldom heard: curiosity was exhausted, zeal was fatigued, and, in the decrees of six councils, the articles of the Catholic faith had been irrevocably defined. The spirit of dispute, however vain and pernicious, requires some energy and exercise of the mental faculties; and the prostrate Greeks were content to fast, to pray, and to believe in blind obedience to the patriarch and his clergy. During a long dream of superstition, the Virgin and the Saints, their visions and miracles, their relics and images, were preached by the monks, and worshipped by the people; and the appellation of people might be extended, without injustice, to the first ranks of civil society. At an unseasonable moment, the Isaurian emperors attempted somewhat rudely to awaken their subjects: under their influence reason might obtain some proselytes, a far greater number was swayed by interest or fear; but the Eastern world embraced or deplored their visible deities, and the restoration of images was celebrated as the feast of orthodoxy. In this passive and unanimous state the ecclesiastical rulers were relieved from the toil, or deprived of the pleasure, of persecution. The Pagans had disappeared; the Jews were silent and obscure; the disputes with the Latins were rare and remote hostilities against a national enemy; and the sects of Egypt and Syria enjoyed a free toleration under the shadow of the Arabian caliphs. About the middle of the seventh century, a branch of Manichæans was selected as the victims of spiritual tyranny; their patience was at length exasperated to despair and rebellion; and their exile has scattered over the West the seeds of reformation. These important events will justify some inquiry into the doctrine and story of the Paulicians; and, as they cannot plead for themselves, our candid criticism will magnify the *good*, and abate or suspect the *evil*, that is reported by their adversaries.

The Gnostics, who had distracted the infancy, were oppressed by the greatness and authority, of the church. Instead of emulating or surpassing the wealth, learning, and numbers of the Catholics, their obscure remnant was driven from the capitals of the East and West, and confined to the villages and mountains along the borders of the Euphrates. Some vestige of the Marcionites may be detected in the fifth century; but the numerous sects were finally lost in the odious name of the Manichæans; and these heretics, who presumed to reconcile the doctrines of Zoroaster and Christ, were pursued by the two religions with equal and unrelenting hatred. Under the grandson of Heraclius, in the neighborhood of Samosata, more famous for the birth of Lucian than for the title of a Syrian kingdom, a reformer arose, esteemed by the *Paulicians* as the chosen messenger of truth. In his humble dwelling of Mananalis, Constantine entertained a deacon, who returned from Syrian captivity, and received the inestimable gift of the New Testament, which was already concealed from the vulgar by the prudence of the Greek, and perhaps of the Gnostic, clergy. These books became the measure of his studies and the rule of his faith; and the Catholics, who dispute his interpretation, acknowledge that his text was genuine and sincere. But he attached himself with peculiar devotion to the writings and character of St. Paul: the name of the Paulicians is derived by their enemies from some unknown and domestic teacher; but I am confident that they gloried in their affinity to the apostle of the Gentiles. His disciples, Titus, Timothy, Sylvanus, Tychicus, were represented by Constantine and his fellow-laborers: the names of the apostolic churches were applied to the congregations which they assembled in Armenia and Cappadocia; and this innocent allegory revived the example and memory of the first ages. In the Gospel, and the Epistles of St. Paul, his faithful follower investigated the Creed of primitive Christianity; and, whatever might be the success, a Protestant reader will applaud the spirit, of the inquiry. But if the Scriptures of the Paulicians were pure, they were not perfect. Their founders rejected the two Epistles of St. Peter, the apostle of the circumcision, whose dispute with their favorite for the observance of the law could not easily be forgiven. They agreed with their Gnostic brethren in the universal contempt for the Old Testament, the books of Moses and the prophets, which have been consecrated by the decrees of the Catholic church. With equal boldness, and doubtless with more reason, Constantine, the new Sylvanus, disclaimed the visions, which, in so many bulky and splendid volumes, had been published by the Oriental sects; the fabulous productions of the Hebrew patriarchs and the sages of the East; the spurious gospels, epistles, and acts, which in the first age had overwhelmed the orthodox code; the theology of Manes, and the authors of the kindred heresies; and the thirty generations, or æons, which had been created by the fruitful fancy of Valentine. The Paulicians sincerely condemned the memory and opinions of the Manichæan sect, and complained of the injustice which impressed that invidious name on the simple votaries of St. Paul and of Christ.

Of the ecclesiastical chain, many links had been broken by the Paulician reformers; and their liberty was enlarged, as they reduced the number of masters, at whose voice profane reason must bow to mystery and miracle. The early separation of the Gnostics had preceded the establishment of the Catholic worship; and against the gradual innovations of discipline and doctrine they were as strongly guarded by habit and aversion, as by the silence of St. Paul and the evangelists. The objects which had been transformed by the magic of superstition, appeared to the eyes of the Paulicians in their genuine and naked colors. An image made without hands was the common workmanship of a mortal artist, to whose skill alone the wood and canvas must be indebted for their merit or value. The miraculous relics were a heap of bones and ashes, destitute of life or virtue, or of any relation, perhaps, with the person to whom they were ascribed. The true and vivifying cross was a piece of sound or rotten timber, the body and blood of Christ, a loaf of bread and a cup of wine, the gifts of nature and the symbols of grace. The mother of God was degraded from her celestial honors and immaculate virginity; and the saints and angels were no longer solicited to exercise the laborious office of mediation in heaven, and ministry upon earth. In the practice, or at least in the theory, of the sacraments, the Paulicians were inclined to abolish all visible objects of worship, and the words of the gospel were, in their judgment, the baptism and communion of the faithful. They indulged a convenient latitude for the interpretation of Scripture: and as often as they were pressed by the literal sense, they could escape to the intricate mazes of figure and allegory. Their utmost diligence must have been employed to dissolve the connection between the Old and the New Testament; since they adored the latter as the oracles of God, and abhorred the former as the fabulous and absurd invention of men or dæmons. We cannot be surprised, that they should have found in the Gospel the orthodox mystery of the Trinity: but, instead of confessing the human nature and substantial sufferings of Christ, they amused their fancy with a celestial body that passed through the virgin like water through a pipe; with a fantastic crucifixion, that eluded the vain and important malice of the Jews. A creed thus simple and spiritual was not adapted to the genius of the times; and the rational Christian, who might have been contented with the light yoke and easy burden of Jesus and his apostles, was justly offended, that the Paulicians should dare to violate the unity of God, the first article of natural and revealed religion. Their belief and their trust was in the Father, of Christ, of the human soul, and of the invisible world. But they likewise held the eternity of matter; a stubborn and rebellious substance, the origin of a second principle of an active being, who has created this visible world, and exercises his temporal reign till the final consummation of death and sin. The appearances of moral and physical evil had established the two principles in the ancient philosophy and religion of the East; from whence this doctrine was transfused to the various swarms of the Gnostics. A thousand shades may be devised in the nature and character of *Ahriman*, from a rival god to a subordinate dæmon, from passion and frailty to pure and perfect malevolence: but, in spite of our efforts, the goodness, and the power, of Ormusd are placed at the opposite extremities of the line; and every step that approaches the one must recede in equal proportion from the other.

The apostolic labors of Constantine Sylvanus soon multiplied the number of his disciples, the secret recompense of spiritual ambition. The remnant of the Gnostic sects, and especially the Manichæans of Armenia, were united under his standard; many Catholics were converted or seduced by his arguments; and he preached with success in the regions of Pontus and Cappadocia, which had long since imbibed the religion of Zoroaster. The Paulician teachers were distinguished only by their Scriptural names, by the modest title of Fellow-pilgrims, by the austerity of their lives, their zeal or knowledge, and the credit of some extraordinary gifts of the Holy Spirit. But they were incapable of desiring, or at least of obtaining, the wealth and honors of the Catholic prelacy; such anti-Christian pride they bitterly censured; and even the rank of elders or presbyters was condemned as an institution of the Jewish synagogue. The new sect was loosely spread over the provinces of Asia Minor to the westward of the Euphrates; six of their principal congregations represented the churches to which St. Paul had addressed his epistles; and their founder chose his residence in the neighborhood of Colonia, in the same district of Pontus which had been celebrated by the altars of Bellona and the miracles of Gregory. After a mission of twenty-seven years, Sylvanus, who had retired from the tolerating government of the Arabs, fell a sacrifice to Roman persecution. The laws of the pious emperors, which seldom touched the lives of less odious heretics, proscribed without mercy or disguise the tenets, the books, and the persons of the Montanists and Manichæans: the books were delivered to the flames; and all who should presume to secrete such writings, or to profess such opinions, were devoted to an ignominious death. A Greek minister, armed with legal and military powers, appeared at Colonia to strike the shepherd, and to reclaim, if possible, the lost sheep. By a refinement of cruelty, Simeon placed the unfortunate Sylvanus before a line of his disciples, who were commanded, as the price of their pardon and the proof of their repentance, to massacre their spiritual father. They turned aside from the impious office; the stones dropped from their filial hands, and of the whole number, only one executioner could be found, a new David, as he is styled by the Catholics, who boldly overthrew the giant of heresy. This apostate (Justin was his name) again deceived and betrayed his unsuspecting brethren, and a new conformity to the acts of St. Paul may be found in the conversion of Simeon: like the apostle, he embraced the doctrine which he had been sent to persecute, renounced his honors and fortunes, and required among the Paulicians the fame of a missionary and a martyr. They were not ambitious of martyrdom, but in a calamitous period of one hundred and fifty years, their patience sustained whatever zeal could inflict; and power was insufficient to eradicate the obstinate vegetation of fanaticism and reason. From the blood and ashes of the first victims, a succession of teachers and congregations repeatedly arose: amidst their foreign hostilities, they found leisure for domestic quarrels: they preached, they disputed, they suffered; and the virtues, the apparent virtues, of Sergius, in a pilgrimage of thirty-three years, are reluctantly confessed by the orthodox historians. The native cruelty of Justinian the Second was stimulated by a pious cause; and he vainly hoped to extinguish, in a single conflagration, the name and memory of the Paulicians. By their primitive simplicity, their abhorrence of popular superstition, the Iconoclast princes might have been reconciled to some erroneous doctrines; but they themselves were exposed to the calumnies of the monks, and they chose to be the tyrants, lest they should be accused as the accomplices, of the Manichæans. Such a reproach has sullied the clemency of Nicephorus, who relaxed in their favor the severity of the penal statutes, nor will his character sustain the honor of a more liberal motive. The feeble Michael the First, the rigid Leo the Armenian, were foremost in the race of persecution; but the prize must doubtless be adjudged to the sanguinary devotion of Theodora, who restored the images to the Oriental church. Her inquisitors explored the cities and mountains of the Lesser Asia, and the flatterers of the empress have affirmed that, in a short reign, one hundred thousand Paulicians were extirpated by the sword, the gibbet, or the flames. Her guilt or merit has perhaps been stretched beyond the measure of truth: but if the account be allowed, it must be presumed that many simple Iconoclasts were punished under a more odious name; and that some who were driven from the church, unwillingly took refuge in the bosom of heresy.

The most furious and desperate of rebels are the sectaries of a religion long persecuted, and at length provoked. In a holy cause they are no longer susceptible of fear or remorse: the justice of their arms hardens them against the feelings of humanity; and they revenge their fathers' wrongs on the children of their tyrants. Such have been the Hussites of Bohemia and the Calvinists of France, and such, in the ninth century, were the Paulicians of Armenia and the adjacent provinces. They were first awakened to the massacre of a governor and bishop, who exercised the Imperial mandate of converting or destroying the heretics; and the deepest recesses of Mount Argæus protected their independence and revenge. A more dangerous and consuming flame was kindled by the persecution of Theodora, and the revolt of Carbeas, a valiant Paulician, who commanded the guards of the general of the East. His father had been impaled by the Catholic inquisitors; and religion, or at least nature, might justify his desertion and revenge. Five thousand of his brethren were united by the same motives; they renounced the allegiance of anti-Christian Rome; a Saracen emir introduced Carbeas to the caliph; and the commander of the faithful extended his sceptre to the implacable enemy of the Greeks. In the mountains between Siwas and Trebizond he founded or fortified the city of Tephrice, which is still occupied by a fierce or licentious people, and the neighboring hills were covered with the Paulician fugitives, who now reconciled the use of the Bible and the sword. During more than thirty years, Asia was afflicted by the calamities of foreign and domestic war; in their hostile inroads, the disciples of St. Paul were joined with those of Mahomet; and the peaceful Christians, the aged parent and tender virgin, who were delivered into barbarous servitude, might justly accuse the intolerant spirit of their sovereign. So urgent was the mischief, so intolerable the shame, that even the dissolute Michael, the son of Theodora, was compelled to march in person against the Paulicians: he was defeated under the walls of Samosata; and the Roman emperor fled before the heretics whom his mother had condemned to the flames. The Saracens fought under the same banners, but the victory was ascribed to Carbeas; and the captive generals, with more than a hundred tribunes, were either released by his avarice, or tortured by his fanaticism. The valor and ambition of Chrysocheir, his successor, embraced a wider circle of rapine and revenge. In alliance with his faithful Moslems, he boldly penetrated into the heart of Asia; the troops of the frontier and the palace were repeatedly overthrown; the edicts of persecution were answered by the pillage of Nice and Nicomedia, of Ancyra and Ephesus; nor could the apostle St. John protect from violation his city and sepulchre. The cathedral of Ephesus was turned into a stable for mules and horses; and the Paulicians vied with the Saracens in their contempt and abhorrence of images and relics. It is not unpleasing to observe the triumph of rebellion over the same despotism which had disdained the prayers of an injured people. The emperor Basil, the Macedonian, was reduced to sue for peace, to offer a ransom for the captives, and to request, in the language of moderation and charity, that Chrysocheir would spare his fellow-Christians, and content himself with a royal donative of gold and silver and silk garments. "If the emperor," replied the insolent fanatic, "be desirous of peace, let him abdicate the East, and reign without molestation in the West. If he refuse, the servants of the Lord will precipitate him from the throne." The reluctant Basil suspended the treaty, accepted the defiance, and led his army into the land of heresy, which he wasted with fire and sword. The open country of the Paulicians was exposed to the same calamities which they had inflicted; but when he had explored the strength of Tephrice, the multitude of the Barbarians, and the ample magazines of arms and provisions, he desisted with a sigh from the hopeless siege. On his return to Constantinople, he labored, by the foundation of convents and churches, to secure the aid of his celestial patrons, of Michael the archangel and the prophet Elijah; and it was his daily prayer that he might live to transpierce, with three arrows, the head of his impious adversary. Beyond his expectations, the wish was accomplished: after a successful inroad, Chrysocheir was surprised and slain in his retreat; and the rebel's head was triumphantly presented at the foot of the throne. On the reception of this welcome trophy, Basil instantly called for his bow, discharged three arrows with unerring aim, and accepted the applause of the court, who hailed the victory of the royal archer. With Chrysocheir, the glory of the Paulicians faded and withered: on the second expedition of the emperor, the impregnable Tephrice, was deserted by the heretics, who sued for mercy or escaped to the borders. The city was ruined, but the spirit of independence survived in the mountains: the Paulicians defended, above a century, their religion and liberty, infested the Roman limits, and maintained their perpetual alliance with the enemies of the empire and the gospel.

Origin and Doctrine
of the Paulicians. – Part Two

ABOUT THE MIDDLE OF the eight century, Constantine, surnamed Copronymus by the worshippers of images, had made an expedition into Armenia, and found, in the cities of Melitene and Theodosiopolis, a great number of Paulicians, his kindred heretics. As a favor, or punishment, he transplanted them from the banks of the Euphrates to Constantinople and Thrace; and by this emigration their doctrine was introduced and diffused in Europe. If the sectaries of the metropolis were soon mingled with the promiscuous mass, those of the country struck a deep root in a foreign soil. The Paulicians of Thrace resisted the storms of persecution, maintained a secret correspondence with their Armenian brethren, and gave aid and comfort to their preachers, who solicited, not without success, the infant faith of the Bulgarians. In the tenth century, they were restored and multiplied by a more powerful colony, which John Zimisces transported from the Chalybian hills to the valleys of Mount Hæmus. The Oriental clergy who would have preferred the destruction, impatiently sighed for the absence, of the Manichæans: the warlike emperor had felt and esteemed their valor: their attachment to the Saracens was pregnant with mischief; but, on the side of the Danube, against the Barbarians of Scythia, their service might be useful, and their loss would be desirable. Their exile in a distant land was softened by a free toleration: the Paulicians held the city of Philippopolis and the keys of Thrace; the Catholics were their subjects; the Jacobite emigrants their associates: they occupied a line of villages and castles in Macedonia and Epirus; and many native Bulgarians were associated to the communion of arms and heresy. As long as they were awed by power and treated with moderation, their voluntary bands were distinguished in the armies of the empire; and the courage of these *dogs*, ever greedy of war, ever thirsty of human blood, is noticed with astonishment, and almost with reproach, by the pusillanimous Greeks. The same spirit rendered them arrogant and contumacious: they were easily provoked by caprice or injury; and their privileges were often violated by the faithless bigotry of the government and clergy. In the midst of the Norman war, two thousand five hundred Manichæans deserted the standard of Alexius Comnenus, and retired to their native homes. He dissembled till the moment of revenge; invited the chiefs to a friendly conference; and punished the innocent and guilty by imprisonment, confiscation, and baptism. In an interval of peace, the emperor undertook the pious office of reconciling them to the church and state: his winter quarters were fixed at Philippopolis; and the thirteenth apostle, as he is styled by his pious daughter, consumed whole days and nights in theological controversy. His arguments were fortified, their obstinacy was melted, by the honors and rewards which he bestowed on the most eminent proselytes; and a new city, surrounded with gardens, enriched with immunities, and dignified with his own name, was founded by Alexius for the residence of his vulgar converts. The important station of Philippopolis was wrested from their hands; the contumacious leaders were secured in a dungeon, or banished from their country; and their lives were spared by the prudence, rather than the mercy, of an emperor, at whose command a poor and solitary heretic was burnt alive before the church of St. Sophia. But the proud hope of eradicating the prejudices of a nation was speedily overturned by the invincible zeal of the Paulicians, who ceased to dissemble or refused to obey. After the departure and death of Alexius, they soon resumed their civil and religious laws. In the beginning of the thirteenth century, their pope or primate (a manifest corruption) resided on the confines of Bulgaria, Croatia, and Dalmatia, and governed, by his vicars, the filial congregations of Italy and France. From that æra, a minute scrutiny might prolong and perpetuate the chain of tradition. At the end of the last age, the sect or colony still inhabited the valleys of Mount Hæmus, where their ignorance and poverty were more frequently tormented by the Greek clergy than by the Turkish government. The modern Paulicians have lost all memory of their origin; and their religion is disgraced by the worship of the cross, and the practice of bloody sacrifice, which some captives have imported from the wilds of Tartary.

In the West, the first teachers of the Manichæan theology had been repulsed by the people, or suppressed by the prince. The favor and success of the Paulicians in the eleventh and twelfth centuries must be imputed to the strong, though secret, discontent which armed the most pious Christians against the church of Rome. Her avarice was oppressive, her despotism odious; less degenerate perhaps than the Greeks in the worship of saints and images, her innovations were more rapid and scandalous: she had rigorously defined and imposed the doctrine of transubstantiation: the lives of the Latin clergy were more corrupt, and the Eastern bishops might pass for the successors of the apostles, if they were compared with the lordly prelates, who wielded by turns the crosier, the sceptre, and the sword. Three different roads might introduce the Paulicians into the heart of Europe. After the conversion of Hungary, the pilgrims who visited Jerusalem might safely follow the course of the Danube: in their journey and return they passed through Philippopolis; and the sectaries, disguising their name and heresy, might accompany the French or German caravans to their respective countries. The trade and dominion of Venice pervaded the coast of the Adriatic, and the hospitable republic opened her bosom to foreigners of every climate and religion. Under the Byzantine standard, the Paulicians were often transported to the Greek provinces of Italy and Sicily: in peace and war, they freely conversed with strangers and natives, and their opinions were silently propagated in Rome, Milan, and the kingdoms beyond the Alps. It was soon discovered, that many thousand Catholics of every rank, and of either sex, had embraced the Manichæan heresy; and the flames which consumed twelve canons of Orleans was the first act and signal of persecution. The Bulgarians, a name so innocent in its origin, so odious in its application, spread their branches over the face of Europe. United in common hatred of idolatry and Rome, they were connected by a form of episcopal and presbyterian government; their various sects were discriminated by some fainter or darker shades of theology; but they generally agreed in the two principles, the contempt of the Old Testament and the denial of the body of Christ, either on the cross or in the eucharist. A confession of simple worship and blameless manners is extorted from their enemies; and so high was their standard of perfection, that the increasing congregations were divided into two classes of disciples, of those who practised, and of those who aspired. It was in the country of the Albigeois, in the southern provinces of France, that the Paulicians were most deeply implanted; and the same vicissitudes of martyrdom and revenge which had been displayed in the neighborhood of the Euphrates, were repeated in the thirteenth century on the banks of the Rhone. The laws of the Eastern emperors were revived by Frederic the Second. The insurgents of Tephrice were represented by the barons and cities of Languedoc: Pope Innocent III. surpassed the sanguinary fame of Theodora. It was in cruelty alone that her soldiers could equal the heroes of the Crusades, and the cruelty of her priests was far excelled by the founders of the Inquisition; an office more adapted to confirm, than to refute, the belief of an evil principle. The visible assemblies of the Paulicians, or Albigeois, were extirpated by fire and sword; and the bleeding remnant escaped by flight, conceal-ment, or Catholic conformity. But the invincible spirit which they had kindled still lived and breathed in the Western world. In the state, in the church, and even in the cloister, a latent succession was preserved of the disciples of St. Paul; who protested against the tyranny of Rome, em-braced the Bible as the rule of faith, and purified their creed from all the visions of the Gnostic theology. The struggles of Wickliff in England, of Huss in Bohemia, were premature and ineffectual; but the names of Zuinglius, Luther, and Calvin, are pronounced with gratitude as the deliverers of nations.

A philosopher, who calculates the degree of their merit and the value of their reformation, will prudently ask from what articles of faith, *above* or *against* our reason, they have enfranchised the Chris-tians; for such enfranchisement is doubtless a benefit so far as it may be compatible with truth and piety. After a fair discussion, we shall rather be surprised by the timidity, than scandalized by the freedom, of our first reformers. With the Jews, they adopted the belief and defence of all the Hebrew Scriptures, with all their prodigies, from the garden of Eden to the visions of the prophet Daniel; and they were bound, like the Catholics, to justify against the Jews the abolition of a divine law. In the great mysteries of the Trinity and Incarnation the reformers were severely orthodox: they freely adopted the theology of the four, or the six first councils; and with the Athanasian creed, they pronounced the eternal damnation of all who did not believe the Catholic faith. Tran-substantiation, the invisible change of the bread and wine into the body and blood of Christ, is a tenet that may defy the power of argument and pleasantry; but instead of consulting the evidence of their senses, of their sight, their feeling, and their taste, the first Protestants were en-tangled in their own scruples, and awed by the words of Jesus in the institution of the sacrament. Luther maintained a *corporeal*, and Calvin a *real*, presence of Christ in the eucharist; and the opinion of Zuinglius, that it is no more than a spiritual communion, a simple memorial, has slowly prevailed in the reformed churches. But the loss of one mystery was amply compensated by the stupendous doctrines of original sin, redemption, faith, grace, and predestination, which have been strained from the epistles of St. Paul. These subtile questions had most assuredly been prepared by the fathers and schoolmen; but the final improvement and popular use may be attributed to the first reformers, who enforced them as the absolute and essential terms of salvation. Hitherto the weight of supernatural belief inclines against the Protestants; and many a sober Christian would rather admit that a wafer is God, than that God is a cruel and capricious tyrant.

Yet the services of Luther and his rivals are solid and important; and the philosopher must own his obligations to these fearless enthusiasts. I. By their hands the lofty fabric of superstition, from the abuse of indulgences to the intercession of the Virgin, has been levelled with the ground. Myriads of both sexes of the monastic profession were restored to the liberty and labors of social life. A hierarchy of saints and angels, of imperfect and subordinate deities, were stripped of their temporal power, and reduced to the enjoyment of celestial happiness; their images and relics were banished from the church; and the credulity of the people was no longer nourished with the daily repetition of miracles and visions. The imitation of Paganism was supplied by a pure and spiritual worship of prayer and thanksgiving, the most worthy of man, the least unworthy of the Deity. It only remains to observe, whether such sublime simplicity be consistent with popular devotion; whether the vulgar, in the absence of all visible objects, will not be inflamed by enthusiasm, or insensibly subside in languor and indifference. II. The chain of authority was broken, which restrains the bigot from thinking as he pleases, and the slave from speaking as he thinks: the popes, fathers, and councils, were no longer the supreme and infallible judges of the world; and each Christian was taught to acknowledge no law but the Scriptures, no interpreter but his own conscience. This freedom, however, was the consequence, rather than the design, of the Reformation. The patriot reformers were ambitious of succeeding the tyrants whom they had dethroned. They imposed with equal rigor their creeds and confessions; they asserted the right of the magistrate to punish heretics with death. The pious or personal animosity of Calvin proscribed in Servetus the guilt of his own rebellion; and the flames of Smithfield, in which he was afterwards consumed, had been kindled for the Anabaptists by the zeal of Cranmer. The nature of the tiger was the same, but he was gradually deprived of his teeth and fangs. A spiritual and temporal kingdom was possessed by the Roman pontiff; the Protestant doctors were subjects of an humble rank, without revenue or jurisdiction. *His* decrees were consecrated by the antiquity of the Catholic church: *their* arguments and disputes were submitted to the people; and their appeal to private judgment was accepted beyond their wishes, by curiosity and enthusiasm. Since the days of Luther and Calvin, a secret reformation has been silently working in the bosom of the reformed churches; many weeds of prejudice were eradicated; and the disciples of Erasmus diffused a spirit of freedom and moderation. The liberty of conscience has been claimed as a common benefit, an inalienable right: the free governments of Holland and England introduced the practice of toleration; and the narrow allowance of the laws has been enlarged by the prudence and humanity of the times. In the exercise, the mind has understood the limits of its powers, and the words and shadows that might amuse the child can no longer satisfy his manly reason. The volumes of controversy are overspread with cobwebs: the doctrine of a Protestant church is far removed from the knowledge or belief of its private members; and the forms of orthodoxy, the articles of faith, are subscribed with a sigh, or a smile, by the modern clergy. Yet the friends of Christianity are alarmed at the boundless impulse of inquiry and scepticism. The predictions of the Catholics are accomplished: the web of mystery is unravelled by the Arminians, Arians, and Socinians, whose number must not be computed from their separate congregations; and the pillars of Revelation are shaken by those men who preserve the name without the substance of religion, who indulge the license without the temper of philosophy.

CHAPTER FIFTY FIVE

The Bulgarians, The Hungarians and The Russians. – Part One

The Bulgarians. – Origin, Migrations, and Settlement of the Hungarians. – Their Inroads in the East and West. – The Monarchy of Russia. – Geography and Trade. – Wars of the Russians against the Greek Empire. – Conversion of the Barbarians.

UNDER THE REIGN OF Constantine the grandson of Heraclius, the ancient barrier of the Danube, so often violated and so often restored, was irretrievably swept away by a new deluge of Barbarians. Their progress was favored by the caliphs, their unknown and accidental auxiliaries: the Roman legions were occupied in Asia; and after the loss of Syria, Egypt, and Africa, the Cæsars were twice reduced to the danger and disgrace of defending their capital against the Saracens. If, in the account of this interesting people, I have deviated from the strict and original line of my undertaking, the merit of the subject will hide my transgression, or solicit my excuse. In the East, in the West, in war, in religion, in science, in their prosperity, and in their decay, the Arabians press themselves on our curiosity: the first overthrow of the church and empire of the Greeks may be imputed to their arms; and the disciples of Mahomet still hold the civil and religious sceptre of the Oriental world. But the same labor would be unworthily bestowed on the swarms of savages, who, between the seventh and the twelfth century, descended from the plains of Scythia, in transient inroad or perpetual emigration. Their names are uncouth, their origins doubtful, their actions obscure, their superstition was blind, their valor brutal, and the uniformity of their public and private lives was neither softened by innocence nor

refined by policy. The majesty of the Byzantine throne repelled and survived their disorderly attacks; the greater part of these Barbarians has
disappeared without leaving any memorial of their existence, and the
despicable remnant continues, and may long continue, to groan under
the dominion of a foreign tyrant. From the antiquities of, I. *Bulgarians*,
II. *Hungarians*, and, III. *Russians*, I shall content myself with selecting
such facts as yet deserve to be remembered. The conquests of the, IV.
Normans, and the monarchy of the, V. Turks, will naturally terminate
in the memorable Crusades to the Holy Land, and the double fall of the
city and empire of Constantine.

I. In his march to Italy, Theodoric the Ostrogoth had trampled on
the arms of the Bulgarians. After this defeat, the name and the nation
are lost during a century and a half; and it may be suspected that the
same or a similar appellation was revived by strange colonies from the
Borysthenes, the Tanais, or the Volga. A king of the ancient Bulgaria
bequeathed to his five sons a last lesson of moderation and concord. It
was received as youth has ever received the counsels of age and experience: the five princes buried their father; divided his subjects and cattle;
forgot his advice; separated from each other; and wandered in quest of
fortune till we find the most adventurous in the heart of Italy, under the
protection of the exarch of Ravenna. But the stream of emigration was
directed or impelled towards the capital. The modern Bulgaria, along
the southern banks of the Danube, was stamped with the name and image which it has retained to the present hour: the new conquerors successively acquired, by war or treaty, the Roman provinces of Dardania,
Thessaly, and the two Epirus; the ecclesiastical supremacy was translated from the native city of Justinian; and, in their prosperous age, the
obscure town of Lychnidus, or Achrida, was honored with the throne of
a king and a patriarch. The unquestionable evidence of language attests
the descent of the Bulgarians from the original stock of the Sclavonian,
or more properly Slavonian, race; and the kindred bands of Servians,
Bosnians, Rascians, Croatians, Walachians, &c., followed either the
standard or the example of the leading tribe. From the Euxine to the
Adriatic, in the state of captives, or subjects, or allies, or enemies, of the
Greek empire, they overspread the land; and the national appellation of
the slaves has been degraded by chance or malice from the signification
of glory to that of servitude. Among these colonies, the Chrobatians,
or Croats, who now attend the motions of an Austrian army, are the
descendants of a mighty people, the conquerors and sovereigns of Dalmatia. The maritime cities, and of these the infant republic of Ragusa,
implored the aid and instructions of the Byzantine court: they were ad-

vised by the magnanimous Basil to reserve a small acknowledgment of their fidelity to the Roman empire, and to appease, by an annual tribute, the wrath of these irresistible Barbarians. The kingdom of Croatia was shared by eleven *Zoupans*, or feudatory lords; and their united forces were numbered at sixty thousand horse and one hundred thousand foot. A long sea-coast, indented with capacious harbors, covered with a string of islands, and almost in sight of the Italian shores, disposed both the natives and strangers to the practice of navigation. The boats or brigantines of the Croats were constructed after the fashion of the old Liburnians: one hundred and eighty vessels may excite the idea of a respectable navy; but our seamen will smile at the allowance of ten, or twenty, or forty, men for each of these ships of war. They were gradually converted to the more honorable service of commerce; yet the Sclavonian pirates were still frequent and dangerous; and it was not before the close of the tenth century that the freedom and sovereignty of the Gulf were effectually vindicated by the Venetian republic. The ancestors of these Dalmatian kings were equally removed from the use and abuse of navigation: they dwelt in the White Croatia, in the inland regions of Silesia and Little Poland, thirty days' journey, according to the Greek computation, from the sea of darkness.

The glory of the Bulgarians was confined to a narrow scope both of time and place. In the ninth and tenth centuries, they reigned to the south of the Danube; but the more powerful nations that had followed their emigration repelled all return to the north and all progress to the west. Yet in the obscure catalogue of their exploits, they might boast an honor which had hitherto been appropriated to the Goths: that of slaying in battle one of the successors of Augustus and Constantine. The emperor Nicephorus had lost his fame in the Arabian, he lost his life in the Sclavonian, war. In his first operations he advanced with boldness and success into the centre of Bulgaria, and burnt the *royal court*, which was probably no more than an edifice and village of timber. But while he searched the spoil and refused all offers of treaty, his enemies collected their spirits and their forces: the passes of retreat were insuperably barred; and the trembling Nicephorus was heard to exclaim, "Alas, alas! unless we could assume the wings of birds, we cannot hope to escape." Two days he waited his fate in the inactivity of despair; but, on the morning of the third, the Bulgarians surprised the camp, and the Roman prince, with the great officers of the empire, were slaughtered in their tents. The body of Valens had been saved from insult; but the head of Nicephorus was exposed on a spear, and his skull, enchased with gold, was often replenished in the feasts of victory. The Greeks bewailed the dishonor of the throne; but they acknowledged the just punishment of avarice and cruelty. This savage cup was deeply tinctured with the manners of the Scythian wilderness; but they were softened before the end of the same century by a peaceful intercourse with the Greeks, the possession of a cultivated region, and the introduction of the Christian worship. The nobles of Bulgaria were educated in the schools and palace of Constantinople; and Simeon, a youth of the royal line, was instructed in the rhetoric of Demosthenes and the logic of Aristotle. He relinquished the profession of a monk for that of a king and warrior; and in his reign of more than forty years, Bulgaria assumed a rank among the civilized powers of the earth. The Greeks, whom he repeatedly attacked, derived a faint consolation from indulging themselves in the reproaches of perfidy and sacrilege. They purchased the aid of the Pagan Turks; but Simeon, in a second battle, redeemed the loss of the first, at a time when it was esteemed a victory to elude the arms of that formidable nation. The Servians were overthrown, made captive and dispersed; and those who visited the country before their restoration could discover no more than fifty vagrants, without women or children, who extorted a precarious subsistence from the chase. On classic ground, on the banks of Achelöus, the Greeks were defeated; their horn was broken by the strength of the Barbaric Hercules. He formed the siege of Constantinople; and, in a personal conference with the emperor, Simeon imposed the conditions of peace. They met with the most jealous precautions: the royal gallery was drawn close to an artificial and well-fortified platform; and the majesty of the purple was emulated by the pomp of the Bulgarian. "Are you a Christian?" said the humble Romanus: "it is your duty to abstain from the blood of your fellow-Christians. Has the thirst of riches seduced you from the blessings of peace? Sheathe your sword, open your hand, and I will satiate the utmost measure of your desires." The reconciliation was sealed by a domestic alliance; the freedom of trade was granted or restored; the first honors of the court were secured to the friends of Bulgaria, above the ambassadors of enemies or strangers; and her princes were dignified with the high and invidious title of *Basileus*, or emperor. But this friendship was soon disturbed: after the death of Simeon, the nations were again in arms; his feeble successors were divided and extinguished; and, in the beginning of the eleventh century, the second Basil, who was born in the purple, deserved the appellation of conqueror of the Bulgarians. His avarice was in some measure gratified by a treasure of four hundred thousand pounds sterling, (ten thousand pounds' weight of gold,) which he found in the palace of Lychnidus.

His cruelty inflicted a cool and exquisite vengeance on fifteen thousand captives who had been guilty of the defence of their country. They were deprived of sight; but to one of each hundred a single eye was left, that he might conduct his blind century to the presence of their king. Their king is said to have expired of grief and horror; the nation was awed by this terrible example; the Bulgarians were swept away from their settlements, and circumscribed within a narrow province; the surviving chiefs bequeathed to their children the advice of patience and the duty of revenge.

II. When the black swarm of Hungarians first hung over Europe, above nine hundred years after the Christian æra, they were mistaken by fear and superstition for the Gog and Magog of the Scriptures, the signs and forerunners of the end of the world. Since the introduction of letters, they have explored their own antiquities with a strong and laudable impulse of patriotic curiosity. Their rational criticism can no longer be amused with a vain pedigree of Attila and the Huns; but they complain that their primitive records have perished in the Tartar war; that the truth or fiction of their rustic songs is long since forgotten; and that the fragments of a rude chronicle must be painfully reconciled with the contemporary though foreign intelligence of the imperial geographer. *Magiar* is the national and oriental denomination of the Hungarians; but, among the tribes of Scythia, they are distinguished by the Greeks under the proper and peculiar name of *Turks*, as the descendants of that mighty people who had conquered and reigned from China to the Volga. The Pannonian colony preserved a correspondence of trade and amity with the eastern Turks on the confines of Persia and after a separation of three hundred and fifty years, the missionaries of the king of Hungary discovered and visited their ancient country near the banks of the Volga. They were hospitably entertained by a people of Pagans and Savages who still bore the name of Hungarians; conversed in their native tongue, recollected a tradition of their long-lost brethren, and listened with amazement to the marvellous tale of their new kingdom and religion. The zeal of conversion was animated by the interest of consanguinity; and one of the greatest of their princes had formed the generous, though fruitless, design of replenishing the solitude of Pannonia by this domestic colony from the heart of Tartary. From this primitive country they were driven to the West by the tide of war and emigration, by the weight of the more distant tribes, who at the same time were fugitives and conquerors. Reason or fortune directed their course towards the frontiers of the Roman empire: they halted in the usual stations along the banks of the great rivers; and in the territories of Moscow, Kiow, and Moldavia, some vestiges have been discovered of their temporary residence. In this long and various peregrination, they could not always escape the dominion of the stronger; and the purity of their blood was improved or sullied by the mixture of a foreign race: from a motive of compulsion, or choice, several tribes of the Chazars were associated to the standard of their ancient vassals; introduced the use of a second language; and obtained by their superior renown the most honorable place in the front of battle. The military force of the Turks and their allies marched in seven equal and artificial divisions; each division was formed of thirty thousand eight hundred and fifty-seven warriors, and the proportion of women, children, and servants, supposes and requires at least a million of emigrants. Their public counsels were directed by seven *vayvods*, or hereditary chiefs; but the experience of discord and weakness recommended the more simple and vigorous administration of a single person. The sceptre, which had been declined by the modest Lebedias, was granted to the birth or merit of Almus and his son Arpad, and the authority of the supreme khan of the Chazars confirmed the engagement of the prince and people; of the people to obey his commands, of the prince to consult their happiness and glory.

With this narrative we might be reasonably content, if the penetration of modern learning had not opened a new and larger prospect of the antiquities of nations. The Hungarian language stands alone, and as it were insulated, among the Sclavonian dialects; but it bears a close and clear affinity to the idioms of the Fennic race, of an obsolete and savage race, which formerly occupied the northern regions of Asia and Europe. The genuine appellation of *Ugri* or *Igours* is found on the western confines of China; their migration to the banks of the Irtish is attested by Tartar evidence; a similar name and language are detected in the southern parts of Siberia; and the remains of the Fennic tribes are widely, though thinly scattered from the sources of the Oby to the shores of Lapland. The consanguinity of the Hungarians and Laplanders would display the powerful energy of climate on the children of a common parent; the lively contrast between the bold adventurers who are intoxicated with the wines of the Danube, and the wretched fugitives who are immersed beneath the snows of the polar circle. Arms and freedom have ever been the ruling, though too often the unsuccessful, passion of the Hungarians, who are endowed by nature with a vigorous constitution of soul and body. Extreme cold has diminished the stature and congealed the faculties of the Laplanders; and the arctic tribes, alone among the sons of men, are ignorant of war, and unconscious of human blood; a happy ignorance, if reason and virtue were the guardians of their peace!

The Bulgarians, The Hungarians and The Russians. – Part Two

It is the observation of the Imperial author of the Tactics, that all the Scythian hordes resembled each other in their pastoral and military life, that they all practised the same means of subsistence, and employed the same instruments of destruction. But he adds, that the two nations of Bulgarians and Hungarians were superior to their brethren, and similar to each other in the improvements, however rude, of their discipline and government: their visible likeness determines Leo to confound his friends and enemies in one common description; and the picture may be heightened by some strokes from their contemporaries of the tenth century. Except the merit and fame of military prowess, all that is valued by mankind appeared vile and contemptible to these Barbarians, whose native fierceness was stimulated by the consciousness of numbers and freedom. The tents of the Hungarians were of leather, their garments of fur; they shaved their hair, and scarified their faces: in speech they were slow, in action prompt, in treaty perfidious; and they shared the common reproach of Barbarians, too ignorant to conceive the importance of truth, too proud to deny or palliate the breach of their most solemn engagements. Their simplicity has been praised; yet they abstained only from the luxury they had never known; whatever they saw they coveted; their desires were insatiate, and their sole industry was the hand of violence and rapine. By the definition of a pastoral nation, I have recalled a long description of the economy, the warfare, and the government that prevail in that state of society; I may add, that to fishing, as well as to the chase, the Hungarians were indebted for a part of their subsistence; and since they *seldom* cultivated the ground, they must, at least in their new settlements, have sometimes practised a slight and unskilful husbandry. In their emigrations, perhaps in their expeditions, the host was accompanied by thousands of sheep and oxen which increased the cloud of formidable dust, and afforded a constant and wholesale supply of milk and animal food. A plentiful command of forage was the first care of the general, and if the flocks and herds were secure of their pastures, the hardy warrior was alike insensible of danger and fatigue. The confusion of men and cattle that overspread the country exposed their camp to a nocturnal surprise, had not a still wider circuit been occupied by their light cavalry, perpetually in motion to discover and delay the approach of the enemy. After some experience of the Roman tactics, they adopted the use of the sword and spear, the helmet of the soldier, and the iron breastplate of his steed: but their native and deadly weapon was the Tartar bow: from the earliest infancy their children and servants were exercised in the double science of archery and horsemanship; their arm was strong; their aim was sure; and in the most rapid career, they were taught to throw themselves backwards, and to shoot a volley of arrows into the air. In open combat, in secret ambush, in flight, or pursuit, they were equally formidable; an appearance of order was maintained in the foremost ranks, but their charge was driven forwards by the impatient pressure of succeeding crowds. They pursued, headlong and rash, with loosened reins and horrific outcries; but, if they fled, with real or dissembled fear, the ardor of a pursuing foe was checked and chastised by the same habits of irregular speed and sudden evolution. In the abuse of victory, they astonished Europe, yet smarting from the wounds of the Saracen and the Dane: mercy they rarely asked, and more rarely bestowed: both sexes if accused is equally inaccessible to pity, and their appetite for raw flesh might countenance the popular tale, that they drank the blood, and feasted on the hearts of the slain. Yet the Hungarians were not devoid of those principles of justice and humanity, which nature has implanted in every bosom. The license of public and private injuries was restrained by laws and punishments; and in the security of an open camp, theft is the most tempting and most dangerous offence. Among the Barbarians there were many, whose spontaneous virtue supplied their laws and corrected their manners, who performed the duties, and sympathized with the affections, of social life.

After a long pilgrimage of flight or victory, the Turkish hordes approached the common limits of the French and Byzantine empires. Their first conquests and final settlements extended on either side of the Danube above Vienna, below Belgrade, and beyond the measure of the Roman province of Pannonia, or the modern kingdom of Hungary. That ample and fertile land was loosely occupied by the Moravians, a Sclavonian name and tribe, which were driven by the invaders into the compass of a narrow province. Charlemagne had stretched a vague and nominal empire as far as the edge of Transylvania; but, after the failure of his legitimate line, the dukes of Moravia forgot their obedience and tribute to the monarchs of Oriental France. The bastard Arnulph was provoked to invite the arms of the Turks: they rushed through the real or figurative wall, which his indiscretion had thrown open; and the king of Germany has been justly reproached as a traitor to the civil and ecclesiastical society of the Christians. During the life of Arnulph, the Hungarians were checked by gratitude or fear; but in the infancy of his son Lewis they discovered and invaded Bavaria; and such was their Scythian speed, that in a single day a circuit of fifty miles was stripped and consumed. In the battle of Augsburgh the Christians maintained their advantage till the seventh hour of the day, they were deceived and vanquished by the flying stratagems of the Turkish cavalry. The conflagration spread over the provinces of Bavaria, Swabia, and Franconia; and the Hungarians promoted the reign of anarchy, by forcing the stoutest barons to discipline their vassals and fortify their castles. The origin of walled towns is ascribed to this calamitous period; nor could any distance be secure against an enemy, who, almost at the same instant, laid in ashes the Helvetian monastery of St. Gall, and the city of Bremen, on the shores of the northern ocean. Above thirty years the Germanic empire, or kingdom, was subject to the ignominy of tribute; and resistance was disarmed by the menace, the serious and effectual menace of dragging the women and children into captivity, and of slaughtering the males above the age of ten years. I have neither power nor inclination to follow the Hungarians beyond the Rhine; but I must observe with surprise, that the southern provinces of France were blasted by the tempest, and that Spain, behind her Pyrenees, was astonished at the approach of these formidable strangers. The vicinity of Italy had tempted their early inroads; but from their camp on the Brenta, they beheld with some terror the apparent strength and populousness of the new discovered country. They requested leave to retire; their request was proudly rejected by the Italian king; and the lives of twenty thousand Christians paid the forfeit of his obstinacy and rashness. Among the cities of the West, the royal Pavia was conspicuous in fame and splendor; and the preëminence of Rome itself was only derived from the relics of the apostles. The Hungarians appeared; Pavia was in flames; forty-three churches were consumed; and, after the massacre of the people, they spared about two hundred wretches who had gathered some bushels of gold and silver (a vague exaggeration) from the smoking ruins of their country. In these annual excursions from the Alps to the neighborhood of Rome and Capua, the churches, that yet escaped, resounded with a fearful litany: "O, save and deliver us from the arrows of the Hungarians!" But the saints were deaf or inexorable; and the torrent rolled forwards, till it was stopped by the extreme land of Calabria. A composition was offered and accepted for the head of each Italian subject; and ten bushels of silver were poured forth in the Turkish camp. But falsehood is the natural antagonist of violence; and the robbers were defrauded both in the numbers of the assessment and the standard of the metal. On the side of the East, the Hungarians were opposed in doubtful conflict by the equal arms of the Bulgarians, whose faith forbade an alliance with the Pagans, and whose situation formed the barrier of the Byzantine empire. The barrier was overturned; the emperor of Constantinople beheld the waving banners of the Turks; and one of their boldest warriors presumed to strike a battle-axe into the golden gate. The arts and treasures of the Greeks diverted the assault; but the Hungarians might boast, in their retreat, that they had imposed a tribute on the spirit of Bulgaria and the majesty of the Cæsars. The remote and rapid operations of the same campaign appear to magnify the power and numbers of the Turks; but their courage is most deserving of praise, since a light troop of three or four hundred horse would often attempt and execute the most daring inroads to the gates of Thessalonica and Constantinople. At this disastrous æra of the ninth and tenth centuries, Europe was afflicted by a triple scourge from the North, the East, and the South: the Norman, the Hungarian, and the Saracen, sometimes trod the same ground of desolation; and these savage foes might have been compared by Homer to the two lions growling over the carcass of a mangled stag.

The deliverance of Germany and Christendom was achieved by the Saxon princes, Henry the Fowler and Otho the Great, who, in two memorable battles, forever broke the power of the Hungarians. The valiant Henry was roused from a bed of sickness by the invasion of his country; but his mind was vigorous and his prudence successful. "My companions," said he, on the morning of the combat, "maintain your ranks, receive on your bucklers the first arrows of the Pagans, and prevent their second discharge by the equal and rapid career of your lances." They obeyed and conquered: and the historical picture of the castle of Merseburgh expressed the features, or at least the character, of Henry, who, in an age of ignorance, intrusted to the finer arts the perpetuity of his name. At the end of twenty years, the children of the Turks who had fallen by his sword invaded the empire of his son; and their force is defined, in the lowest estimate, at one hundred thousand horse. They were invited by domestic faction; the gates of Germany were treacherously unlocked; and they spread, far beyond the Rhine and the Meuse, into the heart of Flanders. But the vigor and prudence of Otho dispelled the conspiracy; the princes were made sensible that unless they were true to each other, their religion and country were irrecoverably lost; and the national powers were reviewed in the plains of Augsburgh. They marched and fought in eight legions, according to the division of provinces and tribes; the first, second, and third, were composed of Bavarians; the fourth, of Franconians; the fifth, of Saxons, under the immediate command of the monarch; the sixth and seventh consisted of Swabians; and the eighth legion, of a thousand Bohemians, closed the rear of the host. The resources of discipline and valor were fortified by the arts of superstition, which, on this occasion, may deserve the epithets of generous and salutary. The soldiers were purified with a fast; the camp was blessed with the relics of saints and martyrs; and the Christian hero girded on his side the sword of Constantine, grasped the invincible spear of Charlemagne, and waved the banner of St. Maurice, the præfect of the Thebæan legion. But his firmest confidence was placed in the holy lance, whose point was fashioned of the nails of the cross, and which his father had extorted from the king of Burgundy, by the threats of war, and the gift of a province. The Hungarians were expected in the front; they secretly passed the Lech, a river of Bavaria that falls into the Danube; turned the rear of the Christian army; plundered the baggage, and disordered the legion of Bohemia and Swabia. The battle was restored by the Franconians, whose duke, the valiant Conrad, was pierced with an arrow as he rested from his fatigues: the Saxons fought under the eyes of their king; and his victory surpassed, in merit and importance, the triumphs of the last two hundred years. The loss of the Hungarians was still greater in the flight than in the action; they were encompassed by the rivers of Bavaria; and their past cruelties excluded them from the hope of mercy. Three captive princes were hanged at Ratisbon, the multitude of prisoners was slain or mutilated, and the fugitives, who presumed to appear in the face of their country, were condemned to everlasting poverty and disgrace. Yet the spirit of the nation was humbled, and the most accessible passes of Hungary were fortified with a ditch and rampart. Adversity suggested the counsels of moderation and peace: the robbers of the West acquiesced in a sedentary life; and the next generation was taught, by a discerning prince, that far more might be gained by multiplying and exchanging the produce of a fruitful soil. The native race, the Turkish or Fennic blood, was mingled with new colonies of Scythian or Sclavonian origin; many thousands of robust and industrious captives had been imported from all the countries of Europe; and after the marriage of Geisa with a Bavarian princess, he bestowed honors and estates on the nobles of Germany. The son of Geisa was invested with the regal title, and the house of Arpad reigned three hundred years in the kingdom of Hungary. But the freeborn Barbarians were not dazzled by the lustre of the diadem, and the people asserted their indefeasible right of choosing, deposing, and punishing the hereditary servant of the state.

III. The name of Russians was first divulged, in the ninth century, by an embassy of Theophilus, emperor of the East, to the emperor of the West, Lewis, the son of Charlemagne. The Greeks were accompanied by the envoys of the great duke, or chagan, or *czar*, of the Russians. In their journey to Constantinople, they had traversed many hostile nations; and they hoped to escape the dangers of their return, by requesting the French monarch to transport them by sea to their native country. A closer examination detected their origin: they were the brethren of the Swedes and Normans, whose name was already odious and formidable in France; and it might justly be apprehended, that these Russian strangers were not the messengers of peace, but the emissaries of war. They were detained, while the Greeks were dismissed; and Lewis expected a more satisfactory account, that he might obey the laws of hospitality or prudence, according to the interest of both empires. This Scandinavian origin of the people, or at least the princes, of Russia, may be confirmed and illustrated by the national annals and the general history of the North. The Normans, who had so long been concealed by a veil of impenetrable darkness, suddenly burst forth in the spirit of naval and military enterprise. The vast, and, as it is said, the populous regions of Denmark, Sweden, and Norway, were crowded with independent chieftains and desperate adventurers, who sighed in the laziness of peace, and smiled in the agonies of death. Piracy was the exercise, the trade, the glory, and the virtue, of the Scandinavian youth. Impatient of a bleak climate and narrow limits, they started from the banquet, grasped their arms, sounded their horn, ascended their vessels, and explored every coast that promised either spoil or settlement. The Baltic was the first scene of their naval achievements they visited the eastern shores, the silent residence of Fennic and Sclavonic tribes, and the primitive Russians of the Lake Ladoga paid a tribute, the skins of white squirrels, to these strangers, whom they saluted with the title of *Varan-*

gians or Corsairs. Their superiority in arms, discipline, and renown, commanded the fear and reverence of the natives. In their wars against the more inland savages, the Varangians condescended to serve as friends and auxiliaries, and gradually, by choice or conquest, obtained the dominion of a people whom they were qualified to protect. Their tyranny was expelled, their valor was again recalled, till at length Ruric, a Scandinavian chief, became the father of a dynasty which reigned above seven hundred years. His brothers extended his influence: the example of service and usurpation was imitated by his companions in the southern provinces of Russia; and their establishments, by the usual methods of war and assassination, were cemented into the fabric of a powerful monarchy.

As long as the descendants of Ruric were considered as aliens and conquerors, they ruled by the sword of the Varangians, distributed estates and subjects to their faithful captains, and supplied their numbers with fresh streams of adventurers from the Baltic coast. But when the Scandinavian chiefs had struck a deep and permanent root into the soil, they mingled with the Russians in blood, religion, and language, and the first Waladimir had the merit of delivering his country from these foreign mercenaries. They had seated him on the throne; his riches were insufficient to satisfy their demands; but they listened to his pleasing advice, that they should seek, not a more grateful, but a more wealthy, master; that they should embark for Greece, where, instead of the skins of squirrels, silk and gold would be the recompense of their service. At the same time, the Russian prince admonished his Byzantine ally to disperse and employ, to recompense and restrain, these impetuous children of the North. Contemporary writers have recorded the introduction, name, and character, of the *Varangians*: each day they rose in confidence and esteem; the whole body was assembled at Constantinople to perform the duty of guards; and their strength was recruited by a numerous band of their countrymen from the Island of Thule. On this occasion, the vague appellation of Thule is applied to England; and the new Varangians were a colony of English and Danes who fled from the yoke of the Norman conqueror. The habits of pilgrimage and piracy had approximated the countries of the earth; these exiles were entertained in the Byzantine court; and they preserved, till the last age of the empire, the inheritance of spotless loyalty, and the use of the Danish or English tongue. With their broad and double-edged battle-axes on their shoulders, they attended the Greek emperor to the temple, the senate, and the hippodrome; he slept and feasted under their trusty guard; and the keys of the palace, the treasury, and the capital, were held by the firm and faithful hands of the Varangians.

In the tenth century, the geography of Scythia was extended far beyond the limits of ancient knowledge; and the monarchy of the Russians obtains a vast and conspicuous place in the map of Constantine. The sons of Ruric were masters of the spacious province of Wolodomir, or Moscow; and, if they were confined on that side by the hordes of the East, their western frontier in those early days was enlarged to the Baltic Sea and the country of the Prussians. Their northern reign ascended above the sixtieth degree of latitude over the Hyperborean regions, which fancy had peopled with monsters, or clouded with eternal darkness. To the south they followed the course of the Borysthenes, and approached with that river the neighborhood of the Euxine Sea. The tribes that dwelt, or wandered, in this ample circuit were obedient to the same conqueror, and insensibly blended into the same nation. The language of Russia is a dialect of the Sclavonian; but in the tenth century, these two modes of speech were different from each other; and, as the Sclavonian prevailed in the South, it may be presumed that the original Russians of the North, the primitive subjects of the Varangian chief, were a portion of the Fennic race. With the emigration, union, or dissolution, of the wandering tribes, the loose and indefinite picture of the Scythian desert has continually shifted. But the most ancient map of Russia affords some places which still retain their name and position; and the two capitals, Novogorod and Kiow, are coeval with the first age of the monarchy. Novogorod had not yet deserved the epithet of great, nor the alliance of the Hanseatic League, which diffused the streams of opulence and the principles of freedom. Kiow could not yet boast of three hundred churches, an innumerable people, and a degree of greatness and splendor which was compared with Constantinople by those who had never seen the residence of the Cæsars. In their origin, the two cities were no more than camps or fairs, the most convenient stations in which the Barbarians might assemble for the occasional business of war or trade. Yet even these assemblies announce some progress in the arts of society; a new breed of cattle was imported from the southern provinces; and the spirit of commercial enterprise pervaded the sea and land, from the Baltic to the Euxine, from the mouth of the Oder to the port of Constantinople. In the days of idolatry and barbarism, the Sclavonic city of Julin was frequented and enriched by the Normans, who had prudently secured a free mart of purchase and exchange. From this harbor, at the entrance of the Oder, the corsair, or merchant, sailed in forty-three days to the eastern shores of the Baltic, the most distant nations were intermingled, and the holy groves of Curland *are said* to have been decorated with *Grecian* and Spanish gold. Between the sea and Novogorod an easy intercourse was discovered; in the summer, through a gulf, a lake, and a navigable river; in the winter season, over the hard and level surface of boundless snows. From the neighborhood of that city, the Russians descended the streams that fall into the Borysthenes; their canoes, of a single tree, were laden with slaves of every age, furs of every species, the spoil of their beehives, and the hides of their cattle; and the whole produce of the North was collected and discharged in the magazines of Kiow. The month of June was the ordinary season of the departure of the fleet: the timber of the canoes was framed into the oars and benches of more solid and capacious boats; and they proceeded without obstacle down the Borysthenes, as far as the seven or thirteen ridges of rocks, which traverse the bed, and precipitate the waters, of the river. At the more shallow falls it was sufficient to lighten the vessels; but the deeper cataracts were impassable; and the mariners, who dragged their vessels and their slaves six miles over land, were exposed in this toilsome journey to the robbers of the desert. At the first island below the falls, the Russians celebrated the festival of their escape: at a second, near the mouth of the river, they repaired their shattered vessels for the longer and more perilous voyage of the Black Sea. If they steered along the coast, the Danube was accessible; with a fair wind they could reach in thirty-six or forty hours the opposite shores of Anatolia; and Constantinople admitted the annual visit of the strangers of the North. They returned at the stated season with a rich cargo of corn, wine, and oil, the manufactures of Greece, and the spices of India. Some of their countrymen resided in the capital and provinces; and the national treaties protected the persons, effects, and privileges, of the Russian merchant.

CHAPTER FIFTY FIVE

The Bulgarians, The Hungarians and The Russians. – Part Three

BUT THE SAME COMMUNICATION which had been opened for the benefit, was soon abused for the injury, of mankind. In a period of one hundred and ninety years, the Russians made four attempts to plunder the treasures of Constantinople: the event was various, but the motive, the means, and the object, were the same in these naval expeditions. The Russian traders had seen the magnificence, and tasted the luxury of the city of the Cæsars. A marvellous tale, and a scanty supply, excited the desires of their savage countrymen: they envied the gifts of nature which their climate denied; they coveted the works of art, which they were too lazy to imitate and too indigent to purchase; the Varangian princes unfurled the banners of piratical adventure, and their bravest soldiers were drawn from the nations that dwelt in the northern isles of the ocean. The image of their naval armaments was revived in the last century, in the fleets of the Cossacks, which issued from the Borysthenes, to navigate the same seas for a similar purpose. The Greek appellation of *monoxyla*, or single canoes, might justly be applied to the bottom of their vessels. It was scooped out of the long stem of a beech or willow, but the slight and narrow foundation was raised and continued on either side with planks, till it attained the length of sixty, and the height of about twelve, feet. These boats were built without a deck, but with two rudders and a mast; to move with sails and oars; and to contain from forty to seventy men, with their arms, and provisions of fresh water and salt fish. The first trial of the Russians was made with two hundred boats; but when the national force was exerted, they might arm against Constantinople a thousand or twelve hundred vessels. Their fleet was not much inferior to the royal navy of Agamemnon, but it was magnified in the eyes of fear to ten or fifteen times the real proportion of its strength and numbers. Had the Greek emperors been endowed with foresight to discern, and vigor to prevent, perhaps they might have sealed with a maritime force the mouth of the Borysthenes. Their indolence abandoned the coast of Anatolia to the calamities of a piratical war, which, after an interval of six hundred years, again infested the Euxine; but as long as the capital was respected, the sufferings of a distant province escaped the notice both of the prince and the historian. The storm which had swept along from the Phasis and Trebizond, at length burst on the Bosphorus of Thrace; a strait of fifteen miles, in which the rude vessels of the Russians might have been stopped and destroyed by a more skilful adversary. In their first enterprise under the princes of Kiow, they passed without opposition, and occupied the port of Constantinople in the absence of the emperor Michael, the son of Theophilus. Through a crowd of perils, he landed at the palace-stairs, and immediately repaired to a church of the Virgin Mary. By the advice of the patriarch, her garment, a precious relic, was drawn from the sanctuary and dipped in the sea; and a seasonable tempest, which determined the retreat of the Russians, was devoutly ascribed to the mother of God. The silence of the Greeks may inspire some doubt of the truth, or at least of the importance, of the second attempt by Oleg, the guardian of the sons of Ruric. A strong barrier of arms and fortifications defended the Bosphorus: they were eluded by the usual expedient of drawing the boats over the isthmus; and this simple operation is described in the national chronicles, as if the Russian fleet had sailed over dry land with a brisk and favorable gale. The leader of the third armament, Igor, the son of Ruric, had chosen a moment of weakness and decay, when the naval powers of the empire were employed against the Saracens. But if courage be not wanting, the instruments of defence are seldom deficient. Fifteen broken and decayed galleys were boldly launched against the enemy; but instead of the single tube of Greek fire usually planted on the prow, the sides and stern of each vessel were abundantly supplied with that liquid combustible. The engineers were dexterous; the weather was propitious; many thousand Russians, who chose rather to be drowned than burnt, leaped into the sea; and those who escaped to the Thracian shore were inhumanly slaughtered by the peasants and soldiers. Yet one third of the canoes escaped into shallow water; and the next spring Igor was again prepared to retrieve his disgrace and claim his revenge. After a long peace, Jaroslaus, the great grandson of Igor, resumed the same project of a naval invasion. A fleet, under the command of his son, was repulsed at the entrance of the Bosphorus by the same artificial flames. But in the rashness of pursuit, the vanguard of the Greeks was encompassed by an irresistible multitude of boats and men; their provision of fire was probably exhausted; and twenty-four galleys were either taken, sunk, or destroyed.

Yet the threats or calamities of a Russian war were more frequently diverted by treaty than by arms. In these naval hostilities, every disadvantage was on the side of the Greeks; their savage enemy afforded no mercy: his poverty promised no spoil; his impenetrable retreat deprived the conqueror of the hopes of revenge; and the pride or weakness of empire indulged an opinion, that no honor could be gained or lost in the intercourse with Barbarians. At first their demands were high and inadmissible, three pounds of gold for each soldier or mariner of the fleet: the Russian youth adhered to the design of conquest and glory; but the counsels of moderation were recommended by the hoary sages. "Be content," they said, "with the liberal offers of Cæsar; is it not far better to obtain without a combat the possession of gold, silver, silks, and all the objects of our desires? Are we sure of victory? Can we conclude a treaty with the sea? We do not tread on the land; we float on the abyss of water, and a common death hangs over our heads." The memory of these Arctic fleets that seemed to descend from the polar circle left deep impression of terror on the Imperial city. By the vulgar of every rank, it was asserted and believed, that an equestrian statue in the square of Taurus was secretly inscribed with a prophecy, how the Russians, in the last days, should become masters of Constantinople. In our own time, a Russian armament, instead of sailing from the Borysthenes, has circumnavigated the continent of Europe; and the Turkish capital has been threatened by a squadron of strong and lofty ships of war, each of which, with its naval science and thundering artillery, could have sunk or scattered a hundred canoes, such as those of their ancestors. Perhaps the present generation may yet behold the accomplishment of the prediction, of a rare prediction, of which the style is unambiguous and the date unquestionable.

By land the Russians were less formidable than by sea; and as they fought for the most part on foot, their irregular legions must often have been broken and overthrown by the cavalry of the Scythian hordes. Yet their growing towns, however slight and imperfect, presented a shelter to the subject, and a barrier to the enemy: the monarchy of Kiow, till a fatal partition, assumed the dominion of the North; and the nations from the Volga to the Danube were subdued or repelled by the arms of Swatoslaus, the son of Igor, the son of Oleg, the son of Ruric. The vigor of his mind and body was fortified by the hardships of a military and savage life. Wrapped in a bear-skin, Swatoslaus usually slept on the ground, his head reclining on a saddle; his diet was coarse and frugal, and, like the heroes of Homer, his meat (it was often horse-flesh) was broiled or roasted on the coals. The exercise of war gave stability and discipline to his army; and it may be presumed, that no soldier was permitted to transcend the luxury of his chief. By an embassy from Nicephorus, the Greek emperor, he was moved to undertake the conquest of Bulgaria; and a gift of fifteen hundred pounds of gold was laid at his feet to defray the expense, or reward the toils, of the expedition. An army of sixty thousand men was assembled and embarked; they sailed from the Borysthenes to the Danube; their landing was effected on the Mæsian shore; and, after a sharp encounter, the swords of the Russians prevailed against the arrows of the Bulgarian horse. The vanquished king sunk into the grave; his children were made captive; and his dominions, as far as Mount Hæmus, were subdued or ravaged by the northern invaders. But instead of relinquishing his prey, and performing his engagements, the Varangian prince was more disposed to advance than to retire; and, had his ambition been crowned with success, the seat of empire in that early period might have been transferred to a more temperate and fruitful climate. Swatoslaus enjoyed and acknowledged the advantages of his new position, in which he could unite, by exchange or rapine, the various productions of the earth. By an easy navigation he might draw from Russia the native commodities of furs, wax, and hydromel: Hungary supplied him with a breed of horses and the spoils of the West; and Greece abounded with gold, silver, and the foreign luxuries, which his poverty had affected to disdain. The bands of Patzinacites, Chozars, and Turks, repaired to the standard of victory; and the ambassador of Nicephorus betrayed his trust, assumed the purple, and promised to share with his new allies the treasures of the Eastern world. From the banks of the Danube the Russian prince pursued his march as far as Adrianople; a formal summons to evacuate the Roman province was dismissed with contempt; and Swatoslaus fiercely replied, that Constantinople might soon expect the presence of an enemy and a master.

Nicephorus could no longer expel the mischief which he had introduced; but his throne and wife were inherited by John Zimisces, who, in a diminutive body, possessed the spirit and abilities of a hero. The first victory of his lieutenants deprived the Russians of their foreign allies, twenty thousand of whom were either destroyed by the sword, or provoked to revolt, or tempted to desert. Thrace was delivered, but seventy thousand Barbarians were still in arms; and the legions that had been recalled from the new conquests of Syria, prepared, with the return of the spring, to march under the banners of a warlike prince, who declared himself the friend and avenger of the injured Bulgaria. The passes of Mount Hæmus had been left unguarded; they were instantly occupied; the Roman vanguard was formed of the *immortals*, (a proud imitation of the Persian style;) the emperor led the main body of ten thousand five hundred foot; and the rest of his forces followed in slow and cautious array, with the baggage and military engines. The first exploit of Zimisces was the reduction of Marcianopolis, or Peristhlaba, in two days; the trumpets sounded; the walls were scaled; eight thousand five hundred Russians were put to the sword; and the sons of the Bulgarian king were rescued from an ignominious prison, and invested with a nominal diadem. After these repeated losses, Swatoslaus retired to the strong post of Drista, on the banks of the Danube, and was pursued by an enemy who alternately employed the arms of celerity and delay. The Byzantine galleys ascended the river, the legions completed a line of circumvallation; and the Russian prince was encompassed, assaulted, and famished, in the fortifications of the camp and city. Many deeds of valor were performed; several desperate sallies were attempted; nor was it till after a siege of sixty-five days that Swatoslaus yielded to his adverse fortune. The liberal terms which he obtained announce the prudence of the victor, who respected the valor, and apprehended the despair, of an unconquered mind. The great duke of Russia bound himself, by solemn imprecations, to relinquish all hostile designs; a safe passage was opened for his return; the liberty of trade and navigation was restored; a measure of corn was distributed to each of his soldiers; and the allowance of twenty-two thousand measures attests the loss and the remnant of the Barbarians. After a painful voyage, they again reached the mouth of the Borysthenes; but their provisions were exhausted; the season was unfavorable; they passed the winter on the ice; and, before they could prosecute their march, Swatoslaus was surprised and oppressed by the neighboring tribes with whom the Greeks entertained a perpetual and useful correspondence. Far different was the return of Zimisces, who was received in his capital like Camillus or Marius, the saviors of ancient Rome. But the merit of the victory was attributed by the pious emperor to the mother of God; and the image of the Virgin Mary, with the divine infant in her arms, was placed on a triumphal car, adorned with the spoils of war, and the ensigns of Bulgarian royalty. Zimisces made his public entry on horseback; the diadem on his head, a crown of laurel in his hand; and Constantinople was astonished to applaud the martial virtues of her sovereign.

Photius of Constantinople, a patriarch, whose ambition was equal to his curiosity, congratulates himself and the Greek church on the conversion of the Russians. Those fierce and bloody Barbarians had been persuaded, by the voice of reason and religion, to acknowledge Jesus for their God, the Christian missionaries for their teachers, and the Romans for their friends and brethren. His triumph was transient and premature. In the various fortune of their piratical adventures, some Russian chiefs might allow themselves to be sprinkled with the waters of baptism; and a Greek bishop, with the name of metropolitan, might administer the sacraments in the church of Kiow, to a congregation of slaves and natives. But the seed of the gospel was sown on a barren soil: many were the apostates, the converts were few; and the baptism of Olga may be fixed as the æra of Russian Christianity. A female, perhaps of the basest origin, who could revenge the death, and assume the sceptre, of her husband Igor, must have been endowed with those active virtues which command the fear and obedience of Barbarians. In a moment of foreign and domestic peace, she sailed from Kiow to Constantinople; and the emperor Constantine Porphyrogenitus has described, with minute diligence, the ceremonial of her reception in his capital and palace. The steps, the titles, the salutations, the banquet, the presents, were exquisitely adjusted to gratify the vanity of the stranger, with due reverence to the superior majesty of the purple. In the sacrament of baptism, she received the venerable name of the empress Helena; and her conversion might be preceded or followed by her uncle, two interpreters, sixteen damsels of a higher, and eighteen of a lower rank, twenty-two domestics or ministers, and forty-four Russian merchants, who composed the retinue of the great princess Olga. After her return to Kiow and Novogorod, she firmly persisted in her new religion; but her labors in the propagation of the gospel were not crowned with success; and both her family and nation adhered with obstinacy or indifference to the gods of their fathers. Her son Swatoslaus was apprehensive of the scorn and ridicule of his companions; and her grandson Wolodomir devoted his youthful zeal to multiply and decorate the monuments of ancient worship. The savage deities of the North were still propitiated with human sacrifices: in the choice of the victim, a citizen was preferred to a stranger, a Christian to an idolater; and the father, who defended his son from the sacerdotal knife, was involved in the same doom by the rage of a fanatic tumult. Yet the lessons and example of the pious Olga had made a deep, though secret, impression in the minds of the prince and people: the Greek missionaries continued to preach, to dispute, and to baptize: and the ambassadors or merchants of Russia compared the idolatry of the woods with the elegant superstition of Constantinople. They had gazed with admiration on the dome of St. Sophia: the lively pictures of saints and martyrs, the riches of the altar, the number and vestments of the priests, the pomp and order of the ceremonies; they were edified by the alternate succession of devout silence and harmonious song; nor was it difficult to persuade them, that a choir of angels descended each day from heaven to join in the devotion of the Christians. But the conversion of Wolodomir was determined, or hastened, by his desire of a Roman bride. At the same time, and in the city of Cherson, the rites of baptism and marriage were celebrated by the Christian pontiff: the city he restored to the emperor Basil, the brother of his spouse; but the brazen gates were transported, as it is said, to Novogorod, and erected before the first church as a trophy of his victory and faith. At his despotic command, Peround, the god of thunder, whom he had so long adored, was dragged through the streets of Kiow; and twelve sturdy Barbarians battered with clubs the misshapen image, which was indignantly cast into the waters of the Borysthenes. The edict of Wolodomir had proclaimed, that all who should refuse the rites of baptism would be treated as the enemies of God and their prince; and the rivers were instantly filled with many thousands of obedient Russians, who acquiesced in the truth and excellence of a doctrine which had been embraced by the great duke and his boyars. In the next generation, the relics of Paganism were finally extirpated; but as the two brothers of Wolodomir had died without baptism, their bones were taken from the grave, and sanctified by an irregular and posthumous sacrament.

In the ninth, tenth, and eleventh centuries of the Christian æra, the reign of the gospel and of the church was extended over Bulgaria, Hungary, Bohemia, Saxony, Denmark, Norway, Sweden, Poland, and Russia. The triumphs of apostolic zeal were repeated in the iron age of Christianity; and the northern and eastern regions of Europe submitted to a religion, more different in theory than in practice, from the worship of their native idols. A laudable ambition excited the monks both of Germany and Greece, to visit the tents and huts of the Barbarians: poverty, hardships, and dangers, were the lot of the first missionaries; their courage was active and patient; their motive pure and meritorious; their present reward consisted in the testimony of their conscience and the respect of a grateful people; but the fruitful harvest of their toils was inherited and enjoyed by the proud and wealthy prelates of succeeding times. The first conversions were free and spontaneous: a holy life and an eloquent tongue were the only arms of the missionaries; but the domestic fables of the Pagans were silenced by the miracles and visions of the strangers; and the favorable temper of the chiefs was accelerated by the dictates of vanity and interest. The leaders of nations, who were saluted with the titles of kings and saints, held it lawful and pious to impose the Catholic faith on their subjects and neighbors; the coast of the Baltic, from Holstein to the Gulf of Finland, was invaded under the standard of the cross; and the reign of idolatry was closed by the conversion of Lithuania in the fourteenth century. Yet truth and candor must acknowledge, that the conversion of the North imparted many temporal benefits both to the old and the new Christians. The rage of war, inherent to the human species, could not be healed by the evangelic precepts of charity and peace; and the ambition of Catholic princes has renewed in every age the calamities of hostile contention. But the admission of the Barbarians into the pale of civil and ecclesiastical society delivered Europe from the depredations, by sea and land, of the Normans, the Hungarians, and the Russians, who learned to spare their brethren and cultivate their possessions. The establishment of law and order was promoted by the influence of the clergy; and the rudiments of art and science were introduced into the savage countries of the globe. The liberal piety of the Russian princes engaged in their service the most skilful of the Greeks, to decorate the cities and instruct the inhabitants: the dome and the paintings of St. Sophia were rudely copied in the churches of Kiow and Novogorod: the writings of the fathers were translated into the Sclavonic idiom; and three hundred noble youths were invited or compelled to attend the lessons of the college of Jaroslaus. It should appear that Russia might have derived an early and rapid improvement from her peculiar connection with the church and state of Constantinople, which at that age so justly despised the ignorance of the Latins. But the Byzantine nation was servile, solitary, and verging to a hasty decline: after the fall of Kiow, the navigation of the Borysthenes was forgotten; the great princes of Wolodomir and Moscow were separated from the sea and Christendom; and the divided monarchy was oppressed by the ignominy and blindness of Tartar servitude. The Sclavonic and Scandinavian kingdoms, which had been converted by the Latin missionaries, were exposed, it is true, to the spiritual jurisdiction and temporal claims of the popes; but they were united in language and religious worship, with each other, and with Rome; they imbibed the free and generous spirit of the European republic, and gradually shared the light of knowledge which arose on the western world.

The Saracens, The Franks and The Normans. – Part One

*The Saracens, Franks, and Greeks, in Italy. –
First Adventures and Settlement of the Nor-
mans. – Character and Conquest of Robert
Guiscard, Duke of Apulia – Deliverance of
Sicily by his Brother Roger. – Victories of Rob-
ert over the Emperors of the East and West.
– Roger, King of Sicily, Invades Africa and
Greece. – The Emperor Manuel Comnenus.
– Wars of the Greeks and Normans. – Extinc-
tion of the Normans.*

THE THREE GREAT NATIONS of the world, the Greeks, the Saracens, and
the Franks, encountered each other on the theatre of Italy. The southern
provinces, which now compose the kingdom of Naples, were subject,
for the most part, to the Lombard dukes and princes of Beneventum;
so powerful in war, that they checked for a moment the genius of Charlemagne; so liberal in peace, that they maintained in their capital an
academy of thirty-two philosophers and grammarians. The division
of this flourishing state produced the rival principalities of Benevento,
Salerno, and Capua; and the thoughtless ambition or revenge of the
competitors invited the Saracens to the ruin of their common inheritance. During a calamitous period of two hundred years, Italy was exposed to a repetition of wounds, which the invaders were not capable
of healing by the union and tranquility of a perfect conquest. Their frequent and almost annual squadrons issued from the port of Palermo,
and were entertained with too much indulgence by the Christians of
Naples: the more formidable fleets were prepared on the African coast;

and even the Arabs of Andalusia were sometimes tempted to assist or oppose the Moslems of an adverse sect. In the revolution of human events, a new ambuscade was concealed in the Caudine Forks, the fields of Cannæ were bedewed a second time with the blood of the Africans, and the sovereign of Rome again attacked or defended the walls of Capua and Tarentum. A colony of Saracens had been planted at Bari, which commands the entrance of the Adriatic Gulf; and their impartial depredations provoked the resentment, and conciliated the union of the two emperors. An offensive alliance was concluded between Basil the Macedonian, the first of his race, and Lewis the great-grandson of Charlemagne; and each party supplied the deficiencies of his associate. It would have been imprudent in the Byzantine monarch to transport his stationary troops of Asia to an Italian campaign; and the Latin arms would have been insufficient if his superior navy had not occupied the mouth of the Gulf. The fortress of Bari was invested by the infantry of the Franks, and by the cavalry and galleys of the Greeks; and, after a defence of four years, the Arabian emir submitted to the clemency of Lewis, who commanded in person the operations of the siege. This important conquest had been achieved by the concord of the East and West; but their recent amity was soon imbittered by the mutual complaints of jealousy and pride. The Greeks assumed as their own the merit of the conquest and the pomp of the triumph; extolled the greatness of their powers, and affected to deride the intemperance and sloth of the handful of Barbarians who appeared under the banners of the Carlovingian prince. His reply is expressed with the eloquence of indignation and truth: "We confess the magnitude of your preparation," says the great-grandson of Charlemagne. "Your armies were indeed as numerous as a cloud of summer locusts, who darken the day, flap their wings, and, after a short flight, tumble weary and breathless to the ground. Like them, ye sunk after a feeble effort; ye were vanquished by your own cowardice; and withdrew from the scene of action to injure and despoil our Christian subjects of the Sclavonian coast. We were few in number, and why were we few? Because, after a tedious expectation of your arrival, I had dismissed my host, and retained only a chosen band of warriors to continue the blockade of the city. If they indulged their hospitable feasts in the face of danger and death, did these feasts abate the vigor of their enterprise? Is it by your fasting that the walls of Bari have been overturned? Did not these valiant Franks, diminished as they were by languor and fatigue, intercept and vanish the three most powerful emirs of the Saracens? and did not their defeat precipitate the fall of the city? Bari is now fallen; Tarentum trembles; Calabria will be delivered;

and, if we command the sea, the Island of Sicily may be rescued from the hands of the infidels. My brother," accelerate (a name most offensive to the vanity of the Greek,) "accelerate your naval succors, respect your allies, and distrust your flatterers."

These lofty hopes were soon extinguished by the death of Lewis, and the decay of the Carlovingian house; and whoever might deserve the honor, the Greek emperors, Basil, and his son Leo, secured the advantage, of the reduction of Bari. The Italians of Apulia and Calabria were persuaded or compelled to acknowledge their supremacy, and an ideal line from Mount Garganus to the Bay of Salerno, leaves the far greater part of the kingdom of Naples under the dominion of the Eastern empire. Beyond that line, the dukes or republics of Amalfi and Naples, who had never forfeited their voluntary allegiance, rejoiced in the neighborhood of their lawful sovereign; and Amalfi was enriched by supplying Europe with the produce and manufactures of Asia. But the Lombard princes of Benevento, Salerno, and Capua, were reluctantly torn from the communion of the Latin world, and too often violated their oaths of servitude and tribute. The city of Bari rose to dignity and wealth, as the metropolis of the new theme or province of Lombardy: the title of patrician, and afterwards the singular name of *Catapan*, was assigned to the supreme governor; and the policy both of the church and state was modelled in exact subordination to the throne of Constantinople. As long as the sceptre was disputed by the princes of Italy, their efforts were feeble and adverse; and the Greeks resisted or eluded the forces of Germany, which descended from the Alps under the Imperial standard of the Othos. The first and greatest of those Saxon princes was compelled to relinquish the siege of Bari: the second, after the loss of his stoutest bishops and barons, escaped with honor from the bloody field of Crotona. On that day the scale of war was turned against the Franks by the valor of the Saracens. These corsairs had indeed been driven by the Byzantine fleets from the fortresses and coasts of Italy; but a sense of interest was more prevalent than superstition or resentment, and the caliph of Egypt had transported forty thousand Moslems to the aid of his Christian ally. The successors of Basil amused themselves with the belief, that the conquest of Lombardy had been achieved, and was still preserved by the justice of their laws, the virtues of their ministers, and the gratitude of a people whom they had rescued from anarchy and oppression. A series of rebellions might dart a ray of truth into the palace of Constantinople; and the illusions of flattery were dispelled by the easy and rapid success of the Norman adventurers.

The revolution of human affairs had produced in Apulia and Calabria a melancholy contrast between the age of Pythagoras and the tenth century of the Christian æra. At the former period, the coast of Great Greece (as it was then styled) was planted with free and opulent cities: these cities were peopled with soldiers, artists, and philosophers; and the military strength of Tarentum; Sybaris, or Crotona, was not inferior to that of a powerful kingdom. At the second æra, these once flourishing provinces were clouded with ignorance impoverished by tyranny, and depopulated by Barbarian war; nor can we severely accuse the exaggeration of a contemporary, that a fair and ample district was reduced to the same desolation which had covered the earth after the general deluge. Among the hostilities of the Arabs, the Franks, and the Greeks, in the southern Italy, I shall select two or three anecdotes expressive of their national manners. 1. It was the amusement of the Saracens to profane, as well as to pillage, the monasteries and churches. At the siege of Salerno, a Mussulman chief spread his couch on the communion-table, and on that altar sacrificed each night the virginity of a Christian nun. As he wrestled with a reluctant maid, a beam in the roof was accidentally or dexterously thrown down on his head; and the death of the lustful emir was imputed to the wrath of Christ, which was at length awakened to the defence of his faithful spouse. 2. The Saracens besieged the cities of Beneventum and Capua: after a vain appeal to the successors of Charlemagne, the Lombards implored the clemency and aid of the Greek emperor. A fearless citizen dropped from the walls, passed the intrenchments, accomplished his commission, and fell into the hands of the Barbarians as he was returning with the welcome news. They commanded him to assist their enterprise, and deceive his countrymen, with the assurance that wealth and honors should be the reward of his falsehood, and that his sincerity would be punished with immediate death. He affected to yield, but as soon as he was conducted within hearing of the Christians on the rampart, «Friends and brethren,» he cried with a loud voice, «be bold and patient, maintain the city; your sovereign is informed of your distress, and your deliverers are at hand. I know my doom, and commit my wife and children to your gratitude.» The rage of the Arabs confirmed his evidence; and the self-devoted patriot was transpierced with a hundred spears. He deserves to live in the memory of the virtuous, but the repetition of the same story in ancient and modern times, may sprinkle some doubts on the reality of this generous deed. 3. The recital of a third incident may provoke a smile amidst the horrors of war. Theobald, marquis of Camerino and Spoleto, supported the rebels of Beneventum; and his wanton cruelty was not incompatible in that age with the character of a hero. His captives of the Greek nation or party were castrated without mercy, and the outrage was aggravated by a cruel jest, that he wished to present the emperor with a supply of eunuchs, the most precious ornaments of the Byzantine court. The garrison of a castle had been defeated in a sally, and the prisoners were sentenced to the customary operation. But the sacrifice was disturbed by the intrusion of a frantic female, who, with bleeding cheeks dishevelled hair, and importunate clamors, compelled the marquis to listen to her complaint. «Is it thus,» she cried, «ye magnanimous heroes, that ye wage war against women, against women who have never injured ye, and whose only arms are the distaff and the loom?» Theobald denied the charge, and protested that, since the Amazons, he had never heard of a female war. «And how,» she furiously exclaimed, «can you attack us more directly, how can you wound us in a more vital part, than by robbing our husbands of what we most dearly cherish, the source of our joys, and the hope of our posterity? The plunder of our flocks and herds I have endured without a murmur, but this fatal injury, this irreparable loss, subdues my patience, and calls aloud on the justice of heaven and earth.» A general laugh applauded her eloquence; the savage Franks, inaccessible to pity, were moved by her ridiculous, yet rational despair; and with the deliverance of the captives, she obtained the restitution of her effects. As she returned in triumph to the castle, she was overtaken by a messenger, to inquire, in the name of Theobald, what punishment should be inflicted on her husband, were he again taken in arms. «Should such,» she answered without hesitation, «be his guilt and misfortune, he has eyes, and a nose, and hands, and feet. These are his own, and these he may deserve to forfeit by his personal offences. But let my lord be pleased to spare what his little handmaid presumes to claim as her peculiar and lawful property.»

The establishment of the Normans in the kingdoms of Naples and Sicily is an event most romantic in its origin, and in its consequences most important both to Italy and the Eastern empire. The broken provinces of the Greeks, Lombards, and Saracens, were exposed to every invader, and every sea and land were invaded by the adventurous spirit of the Scandinavian pirates. After a long indulgence of rapine and slaughter, a fair and ample territory was accepted, occupied, and named, by the Normans of France: they renounced their gods for the God of the Christians; and the dukes of Normandy acknowledged themselves the vassals of the successors of Charlemagne and Capet.

The savage fierceness which they had brought from the snowy mountains of Norway was refined, without being corrupted, in a warmer climate; the companions of Rollo insensibly mingled with the natives; they imbibed the manners, language, and gallantry, of the French nation; and in a martial age, the Normans might claim the palm of valor and glorious achievements. Of the fashionable superstitions, they embraced with ardor the pilgrimages of Rome, Italy, and the Holy Land. In this active devotion, the minds and bodies were invigorated by exercise: danger was the incentive, novelty the recompense; and the prospect of the world was decorated by wonder, credulity, and ambitious hope. They confederated for their mutual defence; and the robbers of the Alps, who had been allured by the garb of a pilgrim, were often chastised by the arm of a warrior. In one of these pious visits to the cavern of Mount Garganus in Apulia, which had been sanctified by the apparition of the archangel Michael, they were accosted by a stranger in the Greek habit, but who soon revealed himself as a rebel, a fugitive, and a mortal foe of the Greek empire. His name was Melo; a noble citizen of Bari, who, after an unsuccessful revolt, was compelled to seek new allies and avengers of his country. The bold appearance of the Normans revived his hopes and solicited his confidence: they listened to the complaints, and still more to the promises, of the patriot. The assurance of wealth demonstrated the justice of his cause; and they viewed, as the inheritance of the brave, the fruitful land which was oppressed by effeminate tyrants. On their return to Normandy, they kindled a spark of enterprise, and a small but intrepid band was freely associated for the deliverance of Apulia. They passed the Alps by separate roads, and in the disguise of pilgrims; but in the neighborhood of Rome they were saluted by the chief of Bari, who supplied the more indigent with arms and horses, and instantly led them to the field of action. In the first conflict, their valor prevailed; but in the second engagement they were overwhelmed by the numbers and military engines of the Greeks, and indignantly retreated with their faces to the enemy. The unfortunate Melo ended his life a suppliant at the court of Germany: his Norman followers, excluded from their native and their promised land, wandered among the hills and valleys of Italy, and earned their daily subsistence by the sword. To that formidable sword the princes of Capua, Beneventum, Salerno, and Naples, alternately appealed in their domestic quarrels; the superior spirit and discipline of the Normans gave victory to the side which they espoused; and their cautious policy observed the balance of power, lest the preponderance of any rival state should render their aid less important, and their service less profitable. Their first asylum was a strong camp in the depth of the marshes of Campania: but they were soon endowed by the liberality of the duke of Naples with a more plentiful and permanent seat. Eight miles from his residence, as a bulwark against Capua, the town of Aversa was built and fortified for their use; and they enjoyed as their own the corn and fruits, the meadows and groves, of that fertile district. The report of their success attracted every year new swarms of pilgrims and soldiers: the poor were urged by necessity; the rich were excited by hope; and the brave and active spirits of Normandy were impatient of ease and ambitious of renown. The independent standard of Aversa afforded shelter and encouragement to the outlaws of the province, to every fugitive who had escaped from the injustice or justice of his superiors; and these foreign associates were quickly assimilated in manners and language to the Gallic colony. The first leader of the Normans was Count Rainulf; and, in the origin of society, preëminence of rank is the reward and the proof of superior merit.

Since the conquest of Sicily by the Arabs, the Grecian emperors had been anxious to regain that valuable possession; but their efforts, however strenuous, had been opposed by the distance and the sea. Their costly armaments, after a gleam of success, added new pages of calamity and disgrace to the Byzantine annals: twenty thousand of their best troops were lost in a single expedition; and the victorious Moslems derided the policy of a nation which intrusted eunuchs not only with the custody of their women, but with the command of their men. After a reign of two hundred years, the Saracens were ruined by their divisions. The emir disclaimed the authority of the king of Tunis; the people rose against the emir; the cities were usurped by the chiefs; each meaner rebel was independent in his village or castle; and the weaker of two rival brothers implored the friendship of the Christians. In every service of danger the Normans were prompt and useful; and five hundred *knights*, or warriors on horseback, were enrolled by Arduin, the agent and interpreter of the Greeks, under the standard of Maniaces, governor of Lombardy. Before their landing, the brothers were reconciled; the union of Sicily and Africa was restored; and the island was guarded to the water's edge. The Normans led the van and the Arabs of Messina felt the valor of an untried foe. In a second action the emir of Syracuse was unhorsed and transpierced by the *iron arm* of William of Hauteville. In a third engagement, his intrepid companions discomfited the host of sixty thousand Saracens, and left the Greeks no more than the labor of the pursuit: a splendid victory; but of which the pen of the historian may divide the merit with the lance of the Normans. It is, however, true, that they essentially promoted the success of Maniaces, who reduced thirteen cities, and the greater part of Sicily, under the obedience of the emperor. But his military fame was sullied by ingratitude and tyranny. In the division of the spoils, the deserts of his brave auxiliaries were forgotten; and neither their avarice nor their pride could brook this injurious treatment. They complained by the mouth of their interpreter: their complaint was disregarded; their interpreter was scourged; the sufferings were *his*; the insult and resentment belonged to *those* whose sentiments he had delivered. Yet they dissembled till they had obtained, or stolen, a safe passage to the Italian continent: their brethren of Aversa sympathized in their indignation, and the province of Apulia was invaded as the forfeit of the debt. Above twenty years after the first emigration, the Normans took the field with no more than seven hundred horse and five hundred foot; and after the recall of the Byzantine legions from the Sicilian war, their numbers are magnified to the amount of threescore thousand men. Their herald proposed the option of battle or retreat; «of battle,» was the unanimous cry of the Normans; and one of their stoutest warriors, with a stroke of his fist, felled to the ground the horse of the Greek messenger. He was dismissed with a fresh horse; the insult was concealed from the Imperial troops; but in two successive battles they were more fatally instructed of the prowess of their adversaries. In the plains of Cannæ, the Asiatics fled before the adventurers of France; the duke of Lombardy was made prisoner; the Apulians acquiesced in a new dominion; and the four places of Bari, Otranto, Brundusium, and Tarentum, were alone saved in the shipwreck of the Grecian fortunes. From this æra we may date the establishment of the Norman power, which soon eclipsed the infant colony of Aversa. Twelve counts were chosen by the popular suffrage; and age, birth, and merit, were the motives of their choice. The tributes of their peculiar districts were appropriated to their use; and each count erected a fortress in the midst of his lands, and at the head of his vassals. In the centre of the province, the common habitation of Melphi was reserved as the metropolis and citadel of the republic; a house and separate quarter was allotted to each of the twelve counts: and the national concerns were regulated by this military senate. The first of his peers, their president and general, was entitled count of Apulia; and this dignity was conferred on William of the iron arm, who, in the language of the age, is styled a lion in battle, a lamb in society, and an angel in council. The manners of his countrymen are fairly delineated by a contemporary and national historian. «The Normans,» says Malaterra, «are a cunning and revengeful people; eloquence and dissimulation appear to be their hereditary qualities: they can stoop to flatter; but unless they are curbed by the restraint of law, they indulge the licentiousness of nature and passion. Their princes affect the praises of popular munificence; the people observe the medium, or rather blond the extremes, of avarice and prodigality; and in their eager thirst of wealth and dominion, they despise whatever they possess, and hope whatever they desire. Arms and horses, the luxury of dress, the exercises of hunting and hawking are the delight of the Normans; but, on pressing occasions, they can endure with incredible patience the inclemency of every climate, and the toil and absence of a military life.»

The Saracens, The Franks and The Normans. – Part Two

THE NORMANS OF APULIA were seated on the verge of the two empires; and, according to the policy of the hour, they accepted the investiture of their lands, from the sovereigns of Germany or Constantinople. But the firmest title of these adventurers was the right of conquest: they neither loved nor trusted; they were neither trusted nor beloved: the contempt of the princes was mixed with fear, and the fear of the natives was mingled with hatred and resentment. Every object of desire, a horse, a woman, a garden, tempted and gratified the rapaciousness of the strangers; and the avarice of their chiefs was only colored by the more specious names of ambition and glory. The twelve counts were sometimes joined in the league of injustice: in their domestic quarrels they disputed the spoils of the people: the virtues of William were buried in his grave; and Drogo, his brother and successor, was better qualified to lead the valor, than to restrain the violence, of his peers. Under the reign of Constantine Monomachus, the policy, rather than benevolence, of the Byzantine court, attempted to relieve Italy from this adherent mischief, more grievous than a flight of Barbarians; and Argyrus, the son of Melo, was invested for this purpose with the most lofty titles and the most ample commission. The memory of his father might recommend him to the Normans; and he had already engaged their voluntary service to quell the revolt of Maniaces, and to avenge their own and the public injury. It was the design of Constantine to transplant the warlike colony from the Italian provinces to the Persian war; and the son of Melo distributed among the chiefs the gold and manufactures of Greece, as the first-fruits of the Imperial bounty. But his arts were baffled by the sense and spirit of the conquerors of Apulia: his gifts, or at least his proposals, were rejected; and they unanimously refused to relinquish their possessions and their hopes for the distant prospect of Asiatic fortune. After the means of persuasion had failed, Argyrus resolved to compel or to destroy: the Latin powers were solicited against the common enemy; and an offensive alliance was formed of the pope and the two emperors of the East and West. The throne of St. Peter was occupied by Leo the Ninth, a simple saint, of a temper most apt to deceive himself and the world, and whose venerable character would consecrate with the name of piety the measures least compatible with the practice of religion. His humanity was affected by the complaints, perhaps the calumnies, of an injured people: the impious Normans had interrupted the payment of tithes; and the temporal sword might be lawfully unsheathed against the sacrilegious robbers, who were deaf to the censures of the church. As a German of noble birth and royal kindred, Leo had free access to the court and confidence of the emperor Henry the Third; and in search of arms and allies, his ardent zeal transported him from Apulia to Saxony, from the Elbe to the Tyber. During these hostile preparations, Argyrus indulged himself in the use of secret and guilty weapons: a crowd of Normans became the victims of public or private revenge; and the valiant Drogo was murdered in a church. But his spirit survived in his brother Humphrey, the third count of Apulia. The assassins were chastised; and the son of Melo, overthrown and wounded, was driven from the field, to hide his shame behind the walls of Bari, and to await the tardy succor of his allies.

But the power of Constantine was distracted by a Turkish war; the mind of Henry was feeble and irresolute; and the pope, instead of repassing the Alps with a German army, was accompanied only by a guard of seven hundred Swabians and some volunteers of Lorraine. In his long progress from Mantua to Beneventum, a vile and promiscuous multitude of Italians was enlisted under the holy standard: the priest and the robber slept in the same tent; the pikes and crosses were intermingled in the front; and the martial saint repeated the lessons of his youth in the order of march, of encampment, and of combat. The Normans of Apulia could muster in the field no more than three thousand horse, with a handful of infantry: the defection of the natives intercepted their provisions and retreat; and their spirit, incapable of fear, was chilled for a moment by superstitious awe. On the hostile approach of Leo, they knelt without disgrace or reluctance before their spiritual father. But the pope was inexorable; his lofty Germans affected to deride the diminutive stature of their adversaries; and the Normans were informed that death or exile was their only alternative. Flight they disdained, and, as many of them had been three days without tasting food, they embraced the assurance of a more easy and honorable death. They climbed the hill of Civitella, descended into the plain, and charged in three divisions the army of the pope. On the left, and in the centre, Richard count of Aversa, and Robert the famous Guiscard, attacked, broke, routed, and pursued the Italian multitudes, who fought without discipline, and fled without shame. A harder trial was reserved for the valor of Count Humphrey, who led the cavalry of the right wing. The Germans have been described as unskillful in the management of the horse and the lance, but on foot they formed a strong and impenetrable phalanx; and neither man, nor steed, nor armor, could resist the weight of their long and two-handed swords. After a severe conflict, they were encompassed by the squadrons returning from the pursuit; and died in the ranks with the esteem of their foes, and the satisfaction of revenge. The gates of Civitella were shut against the flying pope, and he was overtaken by the pious conquerors, who kissed his feet, to implore his blessing and the absolution of their sinful victory. The soldiers beheld in their enemy and captive the vicar of Christ; and, though we may suppose the policy of the chiefs, it is probable that they were infected by the popular superstition. In the calm of retirement, the well-meaning pope deplored the effusion of Christian blood, which must be imputed to his account: he felt, that he had been the author of sin and scandal; and as his undertaking had failed, the indecency of his military character was universally condemned. With these dispositions, he listened to the offers of a beneficial treaty; deserted an alliance which he had preached as the cause of God; and ratified the past and future conquests of the Normans. By whatever hands they had been usurped, the provinces of Apulia and Calabria were a part of the donation of Constantine and the patrimony of St. Peter: the grant and the acceptance confirmed the mutual claims of the pontiff and the adventurers. They promised to support each other with spiritual and temporal arms; a tribute or quitrent of twelve pence was afterwards stipulated for every ploughland; and since this memorable transaction, the kingdom of Naples has remained above seven hundred years a fief of the Holy See.

The pedigree of Robert of Guiscard is variously deduced from the peasants and the dukes of Normandy: from the peasants, by the pride and ignorance of a Grecian princess; from the dukes, by the ignorance and flattery of the Italian subjects. His genuine descent may be ascribed to the second or middle order of private nobility. He sprang from a race of *valvassors* or *bannerets*, of the diocese of Coutances, in the Lower Normandy: the castle of Hauteville was their honorable seat: his father Tancred was conspicuous in the court and army of the duke; and his military service was furnished by ten soldiers or knights. Two marriages, of a rank not unworthy of his own, made him the father of twelve sons, who were educated at home by the impartial tenderness of his second wife. But a narrow patrimony was insufficient for this numerous and daring progeny; they saw around the neighborhood the mischiefs of poverty and discord, and resolved to seek in foreign wars a more glorious inheritance. Two only remained to perpetuate the race, and cherish their father's age: their ten brothers, as they successfully attained the vigor of manhood, departed from the castle, passed the Alps, and joined the Apulian camp of the Normans. The elder were prompted by native spirit; their success encouraged their younger brethren, and the three first in seniority, William, Drogo, and Humphrey, deserved to be the chiefs of their nation and the founders of the new republic. Robert was the eldest of the seven sons of the second marriage; and even the reluctant praise of his foes has endowed him with the heroic qualities of a soldier and a statesman. His lofty stature surpassed the tallest of his army: his limbs were cast in the true proportion of strength and gracefulness; and to the decline of life, he maintained the patient vigor of health and the commanding dignity of his form. His complexion was ruddy, his shoulders were broad, his hair and beard were long and of a flaxen color, his eyes sparkled with fire, and his voice, like that of Achilles, could impress obedience and terror amidst the tumult of battle. In the ruder ages of chivalry, such qualifications are not below the notice of the poet or historians: they may observe that Robert, at once, and with equal dexterity, could wield in the right hand his sword, his lance in the left; that in the battle of Civitella he was thrice unhorsed; and that in the close of that memorable day he was adjudged to have borne away the prize of valor from the warriors of the two armies. His boundless ambition was founded on the consciousness of superior worth: in the pursuit of greatness, he was never arrested by the scruples of justice, and seldom moved by the feelings of humanity: though not insensible of fame, the choice of open or clandestine means was determined only by his present advantage. The surname of *Guiscard* was applied to this master of political wisdom, which is too often confounded with the practice of dissimulation and deceit; and Robert is praised by the Apulian poet for excelling the cunning of Ulysses and the eloquence of Cicero. Yet these arts were disguised by an appearance of military frankness: in his highest fortune, he was accessible and courteous to his fellow-soldiers; and while he indulged the prejudices of his new subjects, he affected in his dress and manners to maintain the ancient fashion of his country. He grasped with a rapacious, that he might distribute with a liberal, hand: his primitive indigence had taught the habits of frugality; the gain of a merchant was not below his attention; and his prisoners were tortured with slow and unfeeling cruelty, to force a discovery of their secret treasure. According to the Greeks, he departed from Normandy with only five followers on horseback and thirty on foot; yet even this allowance appears too bountiful: the sixth son of Tancred of Hauteville passed the Alps as a pilgrim; and his first military band was levied among the adventurers of Italy. His brothers and countrymen had divided the fertile lands of Apulia; but they guarded their shares with the jealousy of avarice; the aspiring youth was driven forwards to the mountains of Calabria, and in his first exploits against the Greeks and the natives, it is not easy to discriminate the hero from the robber. To surprise a castle or a convent, to ensnare a wealthy citizen, to plunder the adjacent villages for necessary food, were the obscure labors which formed and exercised the powers of his mind and body. The volunteers of Normandy adhered to his standard; and, under his command, the peasants of Calabria assumed the name and character of Normans.

As the genius of Robert expanded with his fortune, he awakened the jealousy of his elder brother, by whom, in a transient quarrel, his life was threatened and his liberty restrained. After the death of Humphrey, the tender age of his sons excluded them from the command; they were reduced to a private estate, by the ambition of their guardian and uncle; and Guiscard was exalted on a buckler, and saluted count of Apulia and general of the republic. With an increase of authority and of force, he resumed the conquest of Calabria, and soon aspired to a rank that should raise him forever above the heads of his equals. By some acts of rapine or sacrilege, he had incurred a papal excommunication; but Nicholas the Second was easily persuaded that the divisions of friends could terminate only in their mutual prejudice; that the Normans were the faithful champions of the Holy See; and it was safer to trust the alliance of a prince than the caprice of an aristocracy. A synod of one hundred bishops was convened at Melphi; and the count interrupted an important enterprise to guard the person and execute the decrees of the Roman pontiff. His gratitude and policy conferred on Robert and his posterity the ducal title, with the investiture of Apulia, Calabria, and all the lands, both in Italy and Sicily, which his sword could rescue from the schismatic Greeks and the unbelieving Saracens. This apostolic sanction might justify his arms; but the obedience of a free and victorious people could not be transferred without their consent; and Guiscard dissembled his elevation till the ensuing campaign had been illustrated by the conquest of Consenza and Reggio. In the hour of triumph, he assembled his troops, and solicited the Normans to confirm by their suffrage the judgment of the vicar of Christ: the soldiers hailed with joyful acclamations their valiant duke; and the counts, his former equals, pronounced the oath of fidelity with hollow smiles and secret indignation. After this inauguration, Robert styled himself, "By the grace of God and St. Peter, duke of Apulia, Calabria, and hereafter of Sicily;" and it was the labor of twenty years to deserve and realize these lofty appellations. Such tardy progress, in a narrow space, may seem unworthy of the abilities of the chief and the spirit of the nation; but the Normans were few in number; their resources were scanty; their service was voluntary and precarious. The bravest designs of the duke were sometimes opposed by the free voice of his parliament of barons: the twelve counts of popular election conspired against his authority; and against their perfidious uncle, the sons of Humphrey demanded justice and revenge. By his policy and vigor, Guiscard discovered their plots, suppressed their rebellions, and punished the guilty with death or exile: but in these domestic feuds, his years, and the national strength, were unprofitably consumed. After the defeat of his foreign enemies, the Greeks, Lombards, and Saracens, their broken forces retreated to the strong and populous cities of the sea-coast. They excelled in the arts of fortification and defence; the Normans were accustomed to serve on horseback in the field, and their rude attempts could only succeed by the efforts of persevering courage. The resistance of Salerno was maintained above eight months; the siege or blockade of Bari lasted near four years. In these actions the Norman duke was the foremost in every danger; in every fatigue the last and most patient. As he pressed the citadel of Salerno, a huge stone from the rampart shattered one of his military engines; and by a splinter he was wounded in the breast. Before the gates of Bari, he lodged in a miserable hut or barrack, composed of dry branches, and thatched with straw; a perilous station, on all sides open to the inclemency of the winter and the spears of the enemy.

The Italian conquests of Robert correspond with the limits of the present kingdom of Naples; and the countries united by his arms have not been dissevered by the revolutions of seven hundred years. The monarchy has been composed of the Greek provinces of Calabria and Apulia, of the Lombard principality of Salerno, the republic of Amalphi, and the inland dependencies of the large and ancient duchy of Beneventum. Three districts only were exempted from the common law of subjection; the first forever, the two last till the middle of the succeeding century. The city and immediate territory of Benevento had been transferred, by gift or exchange, from the German emperor to the Roman pontiff; and although this holy land was sometimes invaded, the name of St. Peter was finally more potent than the sword of the Normans. Their first colony of Aversa subdued and held the state of Capua; and her princes were reduced to beg their bread before the palace of their fathers. The dukes of Naples, the present metropolis, maintained the popular freedom, under the shadow of the Byzantine empire. Among the new acquisitions of Guiscard, the science of Salerno, and the trade of Amalphi, may detain for a moment the curiosity of the reader. I. Of the learned faculties, jurisprudence implies the previous establishment of laws and property; and theology may perhaps be superseded by the full light of religion and reason. But the savage and the sage must alike implore the assistance of physic; and, if our diseases are inflamed by luxury, the mischiefs of blows and wounds would be more frequent in the ruder ages of society. The treasures of Grecian medicine had been communicated to the Arabian colonies of Africa, Spain, and Sicily; and in the intercourse of peace and war, a spark of knowledge had been kindled and cherished at Salerno, an illustrious city, in which the men were honest and the women beautiful. A school, the first that arose in the darkness of Europe, was consecrated to the healing art: the conscience of monks and bishops was reconciled to that salutary and lucrative profession; and a crowd of patients, of the most eminent rank, and most distant climates, invited or visited the physicians of Salerno. They were protected by the Norman conquerors; and Guiscard, though bred in arms, could discern the merit and value of a philosopher. After a pilgrimage of thirty-nine years, Constantine, an African Christian, returned from Bagdad, a master of the language and learning of the Arabians; and Salerno was enriched by the practice, the lessons, and the writings of the pupil of Avicenna. The school of medicine has long slept in the name of a university; but her precepts are abridged in a string of aphorisms, bound together in the Leonine verses, or Latin rhymes, of the twelfth century. II. Seven miles to the west of Salerno, and thirty to the south of Naples, the obscure town of Amalphi displayed the power and rewards of industry. The land, however fertile, was of narrow extent; but the sea was accessible and open: the inhabitants first assumed the office of supplying the western world with the manufactures and productions of the East; and this useful traffic was the source of their opulence and freedom. The government was popular, under the administration of a duke and the supremacy of the Greek emperor. Fifty thousand citizens were numbered in the walls of Amalphi; nor was any city more abundantly provided with gold, silver, and the objects of precious luxury. The mariners who swarmed in her port, excelled in the theory and practice of navigation and astronomy: and the discovery of the compass, which has opened the globe, is owing to their ingenuity or good fortune. Their trade was extended to the coasts, or at least to the commodities, of Africa, Arabia, and India: and their settlements in Constantinople, Antioch, Jerusalem, and Alexandria, acquired the privileges of independent colonies. After three hundred years of prosperity, Amalphi was oppressed by the arms of the Normans, and sacked by the jealousy of Pisa; but the poverty of one thousand fisherman is yet dignified by the remains of an arsenal, a cathedral, and the palaces of royal merchants.

The Saracens, The Franks and The Normans. – Part Three

ROGER, THE TWELFTH AND last of the sons of Tancred, had been long detained in Normandy by his own and his father's age. He accepted the welcome summons; hastened to the Apulian camp; and deserved at first the esteem, and afterwards the envy, of his elder brother. Their valor and ambition were equal; but the youth, the beauty, the elegant manners, of Roger engaged the disinterested love of the soldiers and people. So scanty was his allowance for himself and forty followers, that he descended from conquest to robbery, and from robbery to domestic theft; and so loose were the notions of property, that, by his own historian, at his special command, he is accused of stealing horses from a stable at Melphi. His spirit emerged from poverty and disgrace: from these base practices he rose to the merit and glory of a holy war; and the invasion of Sicily was seconded by the zeal and policy of his brother Guiscard. After the retreat of the Greeks, the *idolaters*, a most audacious reproach of the Catholics, had retrieved their losses and possessions; but the deliverance of the island, so vainly undertaken by the forces of the Eastern empire, was achieved by a small and private band of adventurers. In the first attempt, Roger braved, in an open boat, the real and fabulous dangers of Scylla and Charybdis; landed with only sixty soldiers on a hostile shore; drove the Saracens to the gates of Messina and safely returned with the spoils of the adjacent country. In the fortress of Trani, his active and patient courage were equally conspicuous. In his old age he related with pleasure, that, by the distress of the siege, himself, and the countess his wife, had been reduced to a single cloak or mantle, which they wore alternately; that in a sally his horse had been slain, and he was dragged away by the Saracens; but that he owed his rescue to his good sword, and had retreated with his saddle on his back, lest the meanest trophy might be left in the hands of the miscreants. In the siege of Trani, three hundred Normans withstood and repulsed the forces of the island. In the field of Ceramio, fifty thousand horse and foot were overthrown by one hundred and thirty-six Christian soldiers, without reckoning St. George, who fought on horseback in the foremost ranks. The captive banners, with four camels, were reserved for the successor of St. Peter; and had these barbaric spoils been exposed, not in the Vatican, but in the Capitol, they might have revived the memory of the Punic triumphs. These insufficient numbers of the Normans most probably denote their knights, the soldiers of honorable and equestrian rank, each of whom was attended by five or six followers in the field; yet, with the aid of this interpretation, and after every fair allowance on the side of valor, arms, and reputation, the discomfiture of so many myriads will reduce the prudent reader to the alternative of a miracle or a fable. The Arabs of Sicily derived a frequent and powerful succor from their countrymen of Africa: in the siege of Palermo, the Norman cavalry was assisted by the galleys of Pisa; and, in the hour of action, the envy of the two brothers was sublimed to a generous and invincible emulation. After a war of thirty years, Roger, with the title of great count, obtained the sovereignty of the largest and most fruitful island of the Mediterranean; and his administration displays a liberal and enlightened mind, above the limits of his age and education. The Moslems were maintained in the free enjoyment of their religion and property: a philosopher and physician of Mazara, of the race of Mahomet, harangued the conqueror, and was invited to court; his geography of the seven climates was translated into Latin; and Roger, after a diligent perusal, preferred the work of the Arabian to the writings of the Grecian Ptolemy. A remnant of Christian natives had promoted the success of the Normans: they were rewarded by the triumph of the cross. The island was restored to the jurisdiction of the Roman pontiff; new bishops were planted in the principal cities; and the clergy was satisfied by a liberal endowment of churches and monasteries. Yet the Catholic hero asserted the rights of the civil magistrate. Instead of resigning the investiture of benefices, he dexterously applied to his own profit the papal claims: the supremacy of the crown was secured and enlarged, by the singular bull, which declares the princes of Sicily hereditary and perpetual legates of the Holy See.

To Robert Guiscard, the conquest of Sicily was more glorious than beneficial: the possession of Apulia and Calabria was inadequate to his ambition; and he resolved to embrace or create the first occasion of invading, perhaps of subduing, the Roman empire of the East. From his first wife, the partner of his humble fortune, he had been divorced under the pretence of consanguinity; and her son Bohemond was destined to imitate, rather than to succeed, his illustrious father. The second wife of Guiscard was the daughter of the princes of Salerno; the Lombards acquiesced in the lineal succession of their son Roger; their five daughters were given in honorable nuptials, and one of them was betrothed, in a tender age, to Constantine, a beautiful youth, the son and heir of the emperor Michael. But the throne of Constantinople was shaken by a revolution: the Imperial family of Ducas was confined to the palace or the cloister; and Robert deplored, and resented, the disgrace of his daughter and the expulsion of his ally. A Greek, who styled himself the father of Constantine, soon appeared at Salerno, and related the adventures of his fall and flight. That unfortunate friend was acknowledged by the duke, and adorned with the pomp and titles of Imperial dignity: in his triumphal progress through Apulia and Calabria, Michael was saluted with the tears and acclamations of the people; and Pope Gregory the Seventh exhorted the bishops to preach, and the Catholics to fight, in the pious work of his restoration. His conversations with Robert were frequent and familiar; and their mutual promises were justified by the valor of the Normans and the treasures of the East. Yet this Michael, by the confession of the Greeks and Latins, was a pageant and an impostor; a monk who had fled from his convent, or a domestic who had served in the palace. The fraud had been contrived by the subtle Guiscard; and he trusted, that after this pretender had given a decent color to his arms, he would sink, at the nod of the conqueror, into his primitive obscurity. But victory was the only argument that could determine the belief of the Greeks; and the ardor of the Latins was much inferior to their credulity: the Norman veterans wished to enjoy the harvest of their toils, and the unwarlike Italians trembled at the known and unknown dangers of a transmarine expedition. In his new levies, Robert exerted the influence of gifts and promises, the terrors of civil and ecclesiastical authority; and some acts of violence might justify the reproach, that age and infancy were pressed without distinction into the service of their unrelenting prince. After two years' incessant preparations the land and naval forces were assembled at Otranto, at the heel, or extreme promontory, of Italy; and Robert was accompanied by his wife, who fought by his side, his son Bohemond, and the representative of the emperor Michael. Thirteen hundred knights of Norman race or discipline, formed the sinews of the army, which might be swelled to thirty thousand followers of every denomination. The men, the horses, the arms, the engines, the wooden towers, covered with raw hides, were embarked on board one hundred and fifty vessels: the transports had been built in the ports of Italy, and the galleys were supplied by the alliance of the republic of Ragusa.

At the mouth of the Adriatic Gulf, the shores of Italy and Epirus incline towards each other. The space between Brundusium and Durazzo, the Roman passage, is no more than one hundred miles; at the last station of Otranto, it is contracted to fifty; and this narrow distance had suggested to Pyrrhus and Pompey the sublime or extravagant idea of a bridge. Before the general embarkation, the Norman duke despatched Bohemond with fifteen galleys to seize or threaten the Isle of Corfu, to survey the opposite coast, and to secure a harbor in the neighborhood of Vallona for the landing of the troops. They passed and landed without perceiving an enemy; and this successful experiment displayed the neglect and decay of the naval power of the Greeks. The islands of Epirus and the maritime towns were subdued by the arms or the name of Robert, who led his fleet and army from Corfu (I use the modern appellation) to the siege of Durazzo. That city, the western key of the empire, was guarded by ancient renown, and recent fortifications, by George Palæologus, a patrician, victorious in the Oriental wars, and a numerous garrison of Albanians and Macedonians, who, in every age, have maintained the character of soldiers. In the prosecution of his enterprise, the courage of Guiscard was assailed by every form of danger and mischance. In the most propitious season of the year, as his fleet passed along the coast, a storm of wind and snow unexpectedly arose: the Adriatic was swelled by the raging blast of the south, and a new shipwreck confirmed the old infamy of the Acroceraunian rocks. The sails, the masts, and the oars, were shattered or torn away; the sea and shore were covered with the fragments of vessels, with arms and dead bodies; and the greatest part of the provisions were either drowned or damaged. The ducal galley was laboriously rescued from the waves, and Robert halted seven days on the adjacent cape, to collect the relics of his loss, and revive the drooping spirits of his soldiers. The Normans were no longer the bold and experienced mariners who had explored the ocean from Greenland to Mount Atlas, and who smiled at the petty dangers of the Mediterranean. They had wept during the tempest; they were alarmed by the hostile approach of the Venetians, who had been solicited by the prayers and promises of the Byzantine court. The first day's action was not disadvantageous to Bohemond, a beardless youth, who led the naval powers of his father. All night the galleys of the republic lay on their anchors in the form of a crescent; and the victory of the second day was decided by the dexterity of their evolutions, the station of their archers, the weight of their javelins, and the borrowed aid of the Greek fire. The Apulian and Ragusian vessels fled to the shore, several were cut from their cables, and dragged away by the conqueror; and a sally from the town carried slaughter and dismay to the tents of the Norman duke. A seasonable relief was poured into Durazzo, and as soon as the besiegers had lost the command of the sea, the islands and maritime towns withdrew from the camp the supply of tribute and provision. That camp was soon afflicted with a pestilential disease; five hundred knights perished by an inglorious death; and the list of burials (if all could obtain a decent burial) amounted to ten thousand persons. Under these calamities, the mind of Guiscard alone was firm and invincible; and while he collected new forces from Apulia and Sicily, he battered, or scaled, or sapped, the walls of Durazzo. But his industry and valor were encountered by equal valor and more perfect industry. A movable turret, of a size and capacity to contain five hundred soldiers, had been rolled forwards to the foot of the rampart: but the descent of the door or drawbridge was checked by an enormous beam, and the wooden structure was constantly consumed by artificial flames.

While the Roman empire was attacked by the Turks in the East, east, and the Normans in the West, the aged successor of Michael surrendered the sceptre to the hands of Alexius, an illustrious captain, and the founder of the Comnenian dynasty. The princess Anne, his daughter and historian, observes, in her affected style, that even Hercules was unequal to a double combat; and, on this principle, she approves a hasty peace with the Turks, which allowed her father to undertake in person the relief of Durazzo. On his accession, Alexius found the camp without soldiers, and the treasury without money; yet such were the vigor and activity of his measures, that in six months he assembled an army of seventy thousand men, and performed a march of five hundred miles. His troops were levied in Europe and Asia, from Peloponnesus to the Black Sea; his majesty was displayed in the silver arms and rich trappings of the companies of Horse-guards; and the emperor was attended by a train of nobles and princes, some of whom, in rapid succession, had been clothed with the purple, and were indulged by the lenity of the times in a life of affluence and dignity. Their youthful ardor might animate the multitude; but their love of pleasure and contempt of subordination were pregnant with disorder and mischief; and their importunate clamors for speedy and decisive action disconcerted the prudence of Alexius, who might have surrounded and starved the besieging army. The enumeration of provinces recalls a sad comparison of the past and present limits of the Roman world: the raw levies were drawn together in haste and terror; and the garrisons of Anatolia, or Asia Minor, had been purchased by the evacuation of the cities which were immediately occupied by the Turks. The strength of the Greek army consisted in the Varangians, the Scandinavian guards, whose numbers were recently augmented by a colony of exiles and volunteers from the British Island of Thule. Under the yoke of the Norman conqueror, the Danes and English were oppressed and united; a band of adventurous youths resolved to desert a land of slavery; the sea was open to their escape; and, in their long pilgrimage, they visited every coast that afforded any hope of liberty and revenge. They were entertained in the service of the Greek emperor; and their first station was in a new city on the Asiatic shore: but Alexius soon recalled them to the defence of his person and palace; and bequeathed to his successors the inheritance of their faith and valor. The name of a Norman invader revived the memory of their wrongs: they marched with alacrity against the national foe, and panted to regain in Epirus the glory which they had lost in the battle of Hastings. The Varangians were supported by some companies of Franks or Latins; and the rebels, who had fled to Constantinople from the tyranny of Guiscard, were eager to signalize their zeal and gratify their revenge. In this emergency, the emperor had not disdained the impure aid of the Paulicians or Manichæans of Thrace and Bulgaria; and these heretics united with the patience of martyrdom the spirit and discipline of active valor. The treaty with the sultan had procured a supply of some thousand Turks; and the arrows of the Scythian horse were opposed to the lances of the Norman cavalry. On the report and distant prospect of these formidable numbers, Robert assembled a council of his principal officers. "You behold," said he, "your danger: it is urgent and inevitable. The hills are covered with arms and standards; and the emperor of the Greeks is accustomed to wars and triumphs. Obedience and union are our only safety; and I am ready to yield the command to a more worthy leader." The vote and acclamation even of his secret enemies, assured him, in that perilous moment, of their esteem and confidence; and the duke thus continued: "Let us trust in the rewards of victory, and deprive cowardice of the means of escape. Let us burn our vessels and our baggage, and give battle on this spot, as if it were the place of our nativity and our burial." The resolution was unanimously approved; and, without confining himself to his lines, Guiscard awaited in battle-array the nearer approach of the enemy. His rear was covered by a small river; his right wing extended to the sea; his left to the hills: nor was he conscious, perhaps, that on the same ground Cæsar and Pompey had formerly disputed the empire of the world.

Against the advice of his wisest captains, Alexius resolved to risk the event of a general action, and exhorted the garrison of Durazzo to assist their own deliverance by a well-timed sally from the town. He marched in two columns to surprise the Normans before daybreak on two different sides: his light cavalry was scattered over the plain; the archers formed the second line; and the Varangians claimed the honors of the vanguard. In the first onset, the battle-axes of the strangers made a deep and bloody impression on the army of Guiscard, which was now reduced to fifteen thousand men. The Lombards and Calabrians ignominiously turned their backs; they fled towards the river and the sea; but the bridge had been broken down to check the sally of the garrison, and the coast was lined with the Venetian galleys, who played their engines among the disorderly throng. On the verge of ruin, they were saved by the spirit and conduct of their chiefs. Gaita, the wife of Robert, is painted by the Greeks as a warlike Amazon, a second Pallas; less skilful in arts, but not less terrible in arms, than the Athenian goddess: though wounded by an arrow, she stood her ground, and strove, by her exhortation and example, to rally the flying troops. Her female voice was seconded by the more powerful voice and arm of the Norman duke, as calm in action as he was magnanimous in council: "Whither," he cried aloud, "whither do ye fly? Your enemy is implacable; and death is less grievous than servitude." The moment was decisive: as the Varangians advanced before the line, they discovered the nakedness of their flanks: the main battle of the duke, of eight hundred knights, stood firm and entire; they couched their lances, and the Greeks deplore the furious and irresistible shock of the French cavalry. Alexius was not deficient in the duties of a soldier or a general; but he no sooner beheld the slaughter of the Varangians, and the flight of the Turks, than he despised his subjects, and despaired of his fortune. The princess Anne, who drops a tear on this melancholy event, is reduced to praise the strength and swiftness of her father's horse, and his vigorous struggle when he was almost overthrown by the stroke of a lance, which had shivered the Imperial helmet. His desperate valor broke through a squadron of Franks who opposed his flight; and after wandering two days and as many nights in the mountains, he found some repose, of body, though not of mind, in the walls of Lychnidus. The victorious Robert reproached the tardy and feeble pursuit which had suffered the escape of so illustrious a prize: but he consoled his disappointment by the trophies and standards of the field, the wealth and luxury of the Byzantine camp, and the glory of defeating an army five times more numerous than his own. A multitude of Italians had been the victims of their own fears; but only thirty of his knights were slain in this memorable day. In the Roman host, the loss of Greeks, Turks, and English, amounted to five or six thousand: the plain of Durazzo was stained with noble and royal blood; and the end of the impostor Michael was more honorable than his life.

It is more than probable that Guiscard was not afflicted by the loss of a costly pageant, which had merited only the contempt and derision of the Greeks. After their defeat, they still persevered in the defence of Durazzo; and a Venetian commander supplied the place of George Palæologus, who had been imprudently called away from his station. The tents of the besiegers were converted into barracks, to sustain the inclemency of the winter; and in answer to the defiance of the garrison, Robert insinuated, that his patience was at least equal to their obstinacy. Perhaps he already trusted to his secret correspondence with a Venetian noble, who sold the city for a rich and honorable marriage. At the dead of night, several rope-ladders were dropped from the walls; the light Calabrians ascended in silence; and the Greeks were awakened by the name and trumpets of the conqueror. Yet they defended the streets three days against an enemy already master of the rampart; and near seven months elapsed between the first investment and the final surrender of the place. From Durazzo, the Norman duke advanced into the heart of Epirus or Albania; traversed the first mountains of Thessaly; surprised three hundred English in the city of Castoria; approached Thessalonica; and made Constantinople tremble. A more pressing duty suspended the prosecution of his ambitious designs. By shipwreck, pestilence, and the sword, his army was reduced to a third of the original numbers; and instead of being recruited from Italy, he was informed, by plaintive epistles, of the mischiefs and dangers which had been produced by his absence: the revolt of the cities and barons of Apulia; the distress of the pope; and the approach or invasion of Henry king of Germany. Highly presuming that his person was sufficient for the public safety, he repassed the sea in a single brigantine, and left the remains of the army under the command of his son and the Norman counts, exhorting Bohemond to respect the freedom of his peers, and the counts to obey the authority of their leader. The son of Guiscard trod in the footsteps of his father; and the two destroyers are compared, by the Greeks, to the caterpillar and the locust, the last of whom devours whatever has escaped the teeth of the former. After winning two battles against the emperor, he descended into the plain of Thessaly, and besieged Larissa, the fabulous realm of Achilles, which contained the treasure and magazines of the Byzantine camp. Yet a just praise must not be refused to the fortitude and prudence of Alexius, who bravely struggled with the calamities of the times. In the poverty of the state, he presumed to borrow the superfluous ornaments of the churches: the desertion of the Manichæans was supplied by some tribes of Moldavia: a reënforcement of seven thousand Turks replaced and revenged the loss of their brethren; and the Greek soldiers were exercised to ride, to draw the bow, and to the daily practice of ambuscades and evolutions. Alexius had been taught by experience, that the formidable cavalry of the Franks on foot was unfit for action, and almost incapable of motion; his archers were directed to aim their arrows at the horse rather than the man; and a variety of spikes and snares were scattered over the ground on which he might expect an attack. In the neighborhood of Larissa the events of war were protracted and balanced. The courage of Bohemond was always conspicuous, and often successful; but his camp was pillaged by a stratagem of the Greeks; the city was impregnable; and the venal or discontented counts deserted his standard, betrayed their trusts, and enlisted in the service of the emperor. Alexius returned to Constantinople with the advantage, rather than the honor, of victory. After evacuating the conquests which he could no longer defend, the son of Guiscard embarked for Italy, and was embraced by a father who esteemed his merit, and sympathized in his misfortune.

The Saracens, The Franks and The Normans. – Part Four

OF THE LATIN PRINCES, the allies of Alexius and enemies of Robert, the most prompt and powerful was Henry the Third or Fourth, king of Germany and Italy, and future emperor of the West. The epistle of the Greek monarch to his brother is filled with the warmest professions of friendship, and the most lively desire of strengthening their alliance by every public and private tie. He congratulates Henry on his success in a just and pious war; and complains that the prosperity of his own empire is disturbed by the audacious enterprises of the Norman Robert. The lists of his presents expresses the manners of the age – a radiated crown of gold, a cross set with pearls to hang on the breast, a case of relics, with the names and titles of the saints, a vase of crystal, a vase of sardonyx, some balm, most probably of Mecca, and one hundred pieces of purple. To these he added a more solid present, of one hundred and forty-four thousand Byzantines of gold, with a further assurance of two hundred and sixteen thousand, so soon as Henry should have entered in arms the Apulian territories, and confirmed by an oath the league against the common enemy. The German, who was already in Lombardy at the head of an army and a faction, accepted these liberal offers, and marched towards the south: his speed was checked by the sound of the battle of Durazzo; but the influence of his arms, or name, in the hasty return of Robert, was a full equivalent for the Grecian bribe. Henry was the severe adversary of the Normans, the allies and vassals of Gregory the Seventh, his implacable foe. The long quarrel of the throne and mitre had been recently kindled by the zeal and ambition of that haughty priest: the king and the pope had degraded each other; and each had seated a rival on the temporal or spiritual throne of his antagonist. After the defeat and death of his Swabian rebel, Henry descended into Italy, to assume the Imperial crown, and to drive from the Vatican the tyrant of the church. But the Roman people adhered to the cause of Gregory: their resolution was fortified by supplies of men and money from Apulia; and the city was thrice ineffectually besieged by the king of Germany. In the fourth year he corrupted, as it is said, with Byzantine gold, the nobles of Rome, whose estates and castles had been ruined by the war. The gates, the bridges, and fifty hostages, were delivered into his hands: the anti-pope, Clement the Third, was consecrated in the Lateran: the grateful pontiff crowned his protector in the Vatican; and the emperor Henry fixed his residence in the Capitol, as the lawful successor of Augustus and Charlemagne. The ruins of the Septizonium were still defended by the nephew of Gregory: the pope himself was invested in the castle of St. Angelo; and his last hope was in the courage and fidelity of his Norman vassal. Their friendship had been interrupted by some reciprocal injuries and complaints; but, on this pressing occasion, Guiscard was urged by the obligation of his oath, by his interest, more potent than oaths, by the love of fame, and his enmity to the two emperors. Unfurling the holy banner, he resolved to fly to the relief of the prince of the apostles: the most numerous of his armies, six thousand horse, and thirty thousand foot, was instantly assembled; and his march from Salerno to Rome was animated by the public applause and the promise of the divine favor. Henry, invincible in sixty-six battles, trembled at his approach; recollected some indispensable affairs that required his presence in Lombardy; exhorted the Romans to persevere in their allegiance; and hastily retreated three days before the entrance of the Normans. In less than three years, the son of Tancred of Hauteville enjoyed the glory of delivering the pope, and of compelling the two emperors, of the East and West, to fly before his victorious arms. But the triumph of Robert was clouded by the calamities of Rome. By the aid of the friends of Gregory, the walls had been perforated or scaled; but the Imperial faction was still powerful and active; on the third day, the people rose in a furious tumult; and a hasty word of the conqueror, in his defence or revenge, was the signal of fire and pillage. The Saracens of Sicily, the subjects of Roger, and auxiliaries of his brother, embraced this fair occasion of rifling and profaning the holy city of the Christians: many thousands of the citizens, in the sight, and by the allies, of their spiritual father were exposed to violation, captivity, or death; and a spacious quarter of the city, from the Lateran to the Coliseum, was consumed by the flames, and devoted to perpetual solitude. From a city, where he was now hated, and might be no longer feared, Gregory retired to end his days in the palace of Salerno. The artful pontiff might flatter the vanity of Guiscard with the hope of a Roman or Imperial crown; but this dangerous measure, which would have inflamed the ambition of the Norman, must forever have alienated the most faithful princes of Germany.

The deliverer and scourge of Rome might have indulged himself in a season of repose; but in the same year of the flight of the German emperor, the indefatigable Robert resumed the design of his eastern conquests. The zeal or gratitude of Gregory had promised to his valor the kingdoms of Greece and Asia; his troops were assembled in arms, flushed with success, and eager for action. Their numbers, in the language of Homer, are compared by Anna to a swarm of bees; yet the utmost and moderate limits of the powers of Guiscard have been already defined; they were contained on this second occasion in one hundred and twenty vessels; and as the season was far advanced, the harbor of Brundusium was preferred to the open road of Otranto. Alexius, apprehensive of a second attack, had assiduously labored to restore the naval forces of the empire; and obtained from the republic of Venice an important succor of thirty-six transports, fourteen galleys, and nine galiots or ships of extra-ordinary strength and magnitude. Their services were liberally paid by the license or monopoly of trade, a profitable gift of many shops and houses in the port of Constantinople, and a tribute to St. Mark, the more acceptable, as it was the produce of a tax on their rivals at Amalphi. By the union of the Greeks and Venetians, the Adriatic was covered with a hostile fleet; but their own neglect, or the vigilance of Robert, the change of a wind, or the shelter of a mist, opened a free passage; and the Norman troops were safely disembarked on the coast of Epirus. With twenty strong and well-appointed galleys, their intrepid duke immediately sought the enemy, and though more accustomed to fight on horseback, he trusted his own life, and the lives of his brother and two sons, to the event of a naval combat. The dominion of the sea was disputed in three engagements, in sight of the Isle of Corfu: in the two former, the skill and numbers of the allies were superior; but in the third, the Normans obtained a final and complete victory. The light brigantines of the Greeks were scattered in ignominious flight: the nine castles of the Venetians maintained a more obstinate conflict; seven were sunk, two were taken; two thousand five hundred captives implored in vain the mercy of the victor; and the daughter of Alexius deplores the loss of thirteen thousand of his subjects or allies. The want of experience had been supplied by the genius of Guiscard;

and each evening, when he had sounded a retreat, he calmly explored the causes of his repulse, and invented new methods how to remedy his own defects, and to baffle the advantages of the enemy. The winter season suspended his progress: with the return of spring he again aspired to the conquest of Constantinople; but, instead of traversing the hills of Epirus, he turned his arms against Greece and the islands, where the spoils would repay the labor, and where the land and sea forces might pursue their joint operations with vigor and effect. But, in the Isle of Cephalonia, his projects were fatally blasted by an epidemical disease: Robert himself, in the seventieth year of his age, expired in his tent; and a suspicion of poison was imputed, by public rumor, to his wife, or to the Greek emperor. This premature death might allow a boundless scope for the imagination of his future exploits; and the event sufficiently declares, that the Norman greatness was founded on his life. Without the appearance of an enemy, a victorious army dispersed or retreated in disorder and consternation; and Alexius, who had trembled for his empire, rejoiced in his deliverance. The galley which transported the remains of Guiscard was ship-wrecked on the Italian shore; but the duke's body was recovered from the sea, and deposited in the sepulchre of Venusia, a place more illustrious for the birth of Horace than for the burial of the Norman heroes. Roger, his second son and successor, immediately sunk to the humble station of a duke of Apulia: the esteem or partiality of his father left the valiant Bohemond to the inheritance of his sword. The national tranquillity was disturbed by his claims, till the first crusade against the infidels of the East opened a more splendid field of glory and conquest.

Of human life, the most glorious or humble prospects are alike and soon bounded by the sepulchre. The male line of Robert Guiscard was extinguished, both in Apulia and at Antioch, in the second generation; but his younger brother became the father of a line of kings; and the son of the great count was endowed with the name, the conquests, and the spirit, of the first Roger. The heir of that Norman adventurer was born in Sicily; and, at the age of only four years, he succeeded to the sovereignty of the island, a lot which reason might envy, could she indulge for a moment the visionary, though virtuous wish of dominion. Had Roger been content with his fruitful patrimony, a happy and grateful people might have blessed their benefactor; and if a wise administration could have restored the prosperous times of the Greek colonies, the opulence and power of Sicily alone might have equalled the widest scope that could be acquired and desolated by the sword of war. But the ambition of the great count was ignorant of these noble pursuits;

it was gratified by the vulgar means of violence and artifice. He sought to obtain the undivided possession of Palermo, of which one moiety had been ceded to the elder branch; struggled to enlarge his Calabrian limits beyond the measure of former treaties; and impatiently watched the declining health of his cousin William of Apulia, the grandson of Robert. On the first intelligence of his premature death, Roger sailed from Palermo with seven galleys, cast anchor in the Bay of Salerno, received, after ten days' negotiation, an oath of fidelity from the Norman capital, commanded the submission of the barons, and extorted a legal investiture from the reluctant popes, who could not long endure either the friendship or enmity of a powerful vassal. The sacred spot of Benevento was respectfully spared, as the patrimony of St. Peter; but the reduction of Capua and Naples completed the design of his uncle Guiscard; and the sole inheritance of the Norman conquests was possessed by the victorious Roger. A conscious superiority of power and merit prompted him to disdain the titles of duke and of count; and the Isle of Sicily, with a third perhaps of the continent of Italy, might form the basis of a kingdom which would only yield to the monarchies of France and England. The chiefs of the nation who attended his coronation at Palermo might doubtless pronounce under what name he should reign over them; but the example of a Greek tyrant or a Saracen emir was insufficient to justify his regal character; and the nine kings of the Latin world might disclaim their new associate, unless he were consecrated by the authority of the supreme pontiff. The pride of Anacletus was pleased to confer a title, which the pride of the Norman had stooped to solicit; but his own legitimacy was attacked by the adverse election of Innocent the Second; and while Anacletus sat in the Vatican, the successful fugitive was acknowledged by the nations of Europe. The infant monarchy of Roger was shaken, and almost overthrown, by the unlucky choice of an ecclesiastical patron; and the sword of Lothaire the Second of Germany, the excommunications of Innocent, the fleets of Pisa, and the zeal of St. Bernard, were united for the ruin of the Sicilian robber. After a gallant resistance, the Norman prince was driven from the continent of Italy: a new duke of Apulia was invested by the pope and the emperor, each of whom held one end of the *gonfanon*, or flagstaff, as a token that they asserted their right, and suspended their quarrel. But such jealous friendship was of short and precarious duration: the German armies soon vanished in disease and desertion: the Apulian duke, with all his adherents, was exterminated by a conqueror who seldom forgave either the dead or the living; like his predecessor Leo the Ninth, the feeble though haughty pontiff became the captive and friend of the Normans; and their reconciliation was celebrated by the eloquence of Bernard, who now revered the title and virtues of the king of Sicily.

As a penance for his impious war against the successor of St. Peter, that monarch might have promised to display the banner of the cross, and he accomplished with ardor a vow so propitious to his interest and revenge. The recent injuries of Sicily might provoke a just retaliation on the heads of the Saracens: the Normans, whose blood had been mingled with so many subject streams, were encouraged to remember and emulate the naval trophies of their fathers, and in the maturity of their strength they contended with the decline of an African power. When the Fatimite caliph departed for the conquest of Egypt, he rewarded the real merit and apparent fidelity of his servant Joseph with a gift of his royal mantle, and forty Arabian horses, his palace with its sumptuous furniture, and the government of the kingdoms of Tunis and Algiers. The Zeirides, the descendants of Joseph, forgot their allegiance and gratitude to a distant benefactor, grasped and abused the fruits of prosperity; and after running the little course of an Oriental dynasty, were now fainting in their own weakness. On the side of the land, they were pressed by the Almohades, the fanatic princes of Morocco, while the sea-coast was open to the enterprises of the Greeks and Franks, who, before the close of the eleventh century, had extorted a ransom of two hundred thousand pieces of gold. By the first arms of Roger, the island or rock of Malta, which has been since ennobled by a military and religious colony, was inseparably annexed to the crown of Sicily. Tripoli, a strong and maritime city, was the next object of his attack; and the slaughter of the males, the captivity of the females, might be justified by the frequent practice of the Moslems themselves. The capital of the Zeirides was named Africa from the country, and Mahadia from the Arabian founder: it is strongly built on a neck of land, but the imperfection of the harbor is not compensated by the fertility of the adjacent plain. Mahadia was besieged by George the Sicilian admiral, with a fleet of one hundred and fifty galleys, amply provided with men and the instruments of mischief: the sovereign had fled, the Moorish governor refused to capitulate, declined the last and irresistible assault, and secretly escaping with the Moslem inhabitants abandoned the place and its treasures to the rapacious Franks. In successive expeditions, the king of Sicily or his lieutenants reduced the cities of Tunis, Safax, Capsia, Bona, and a long tract of the sea-coast; the fortresses were garrisoned, the country was tributary, and a boast that it held Africa in subjection might be inscribed with some flattery on the sword of Roger. After his death, that sword was broken; and these transmarine possessions were neglected, evacuated, or lost, under the troubled reign of his successor. The triumphs of Scipio and Belisarius have proved, that the African continent is neither inaccessible nor invincible; yet the great princes and powers of Christendom have repeatedly failed in their armaments against the Moors, who may still glory in the easy conquest and long servitude of Spain.

Since the decease of Robert Guiscard, the Normans had relinquished, above sixty years, their hostile designs against the empire of the East. The policy of Roger solicited a public and private union with the Greek princes, whose alliance would dignify his regal character: he demanded in marriage a daughter of the Comnenian family, and the first steps of the treaty seemed to promise a favorable event. But the contemptuous treatment of his ambassadors exasperated the vanity of the new monarch; and the insolence of the Byzantine court was expiated, according to the laws of nations, by the sufferings of a guiltless people. With the fleet of seventy galleys, George, the admiral of Sicily, appeared before Corfu; and both the island and city were delivered into his hands by the disaffected inhabitants, who had yet to learn that a siege is still more calamitous than a tribute. In this invasion, of some moment in the annals of commerce, the Normans spread themselves by sea, and over the provinces of Greece; and the venerable age of Athens, Thebes, and Corinth, was violated by rapine and cruelty. Of the wrongs of Athens, no memorial remains. The ancient walls, which encompassed, without guarding, the opulence of Thebes, were scaled by the Latin Christians; but their sole use of the gospel was to sanctify an oath, that the lawful owners had not secreted any relic of their inheritance or industry. On the approach of the Normans, the lower town of Corinth was evacuated; the Greeks retired to the citadel, which was seated on a lofty eminence, abundantly watered by the classic fountain of Pirene; an impregnable fortress, if the want of courage could be balanced by any advantages of art or nature. As soon as the besiegers had surmounted the labor (their sole labor) of climbing the hill, their general, from the commanding eminence, admired his own victory, and testified his gratitude to Heaven, by tearing from the altar the precious image of Theodore, the tutelary saint. The silk weavers of both sexes, whom George transported to Sicily, composed the most valuable part of the spoil; and in comparing the skilful industry of the mechanic with the sloth and cowardice of the soldier, he was heard to exclaim that the distaff and loom were the only weapons which the Greeks were capable of using. The progress of this naval armament was marked by two conspicuous events, the rescue of the king of France, and the insult of the Byzantine capital. In his return by sea from an unfortunate crusade, Louis the Seventh was intercepted by the Greeks, who basely violated the laws of honor and religion. The fortunate encounter of the Norman fleet delivered the royal captive; and after a free and honorable entertainment in the court of Sicily, Louis continued his journey to Rome and Paris. In the absence of the emperor, Constantinople and the Hellespont were left without defence and without the suspicion of danger. The clergy and people (for the soldiers had followed the standard of Manuel) were astonished and dismayed at the hostile appearance of a line of galleys, which boldly cast anchor in the front of the Imperial city. The forces of the Sicilian admiral were inadequate to the siege or assault of an immense and populous metropolis; but George enjoyed the glory of humbling the Greek arrogance, and of marking the path of conquest to the navies of the West. He landed some soldiers to rifle the fruits of the royal gardens, and pointed with silver, or most probably with fire, the arrows which he discharged against the palace of the Cæsars. This playful outrage of the pirates of Sicily, who had surprised an unguarded moment, Manuel affected to despise, while his martial spirit, and the forces of the empire, were awakened to revenge. The Archipelago and Ionian Sea were covered with his squadrons and those of Venice; but I know not by what favorable allowance of transports, victuallers, and pinnaces, our reason, or even our fancy, can be reconciled to the stupendous account of fifteen hundred vessels, which is proposed by a Byzantine historian. These operations were directed with prudence and energy: in his homeward voyage George lost nineteen of his galleys, which were separated and taken: after an obstinate defence, Corfu implored the clemency of her lawful sovereign; nor could a ship, a soldier, of the Norman prince, be found, unless as a captive, within the limits of the Eastern empire. The prosperity and the health of Roger were already in a declining state: while he listened in his palace of Palermo to the messengers of victory or defeat, the invincible Manuel, the foremost in every assault, was celebrated by the Greeks and Latins as the Alexander or the Hercules of the age.

The Saracens, The Franks and The Normans. – Part Five

A PRINCE OF SUCH a temper could not be satisfied with having repelled the insolence of a Barbarian. It was the right and duty, it might be the interest and glory, of Manuel to restore the ancient majesty of the empire, to recover the provinces of Italy and Sicily, and to chastise this pretended king, the grandson of a Norman vassal. The natives of Calabria were still attached to the Greek language and worship, which had been inexorably proscribed by the Latin clergy: after the loss of her dukes, Apulia was chained as a servile appendage to the crown of Sicily; the founder of the monarchy had ruled by the sword; and his death had abated the fear, without healing the discontent, of his subjects: the feudal government was always pregnant with the seeds of rebellion; and a nephew of Roger himself invited the enemies of his family and nation. The majesty of the purple, and a series of Hungarian and Turkish wars, prevented Manuel from embarking his person in the Italian expedition. To the brave and noble Palæologus, his lieutenant, the Greek monarch intrusted a fleet and army: the siege of Bari was his first exploit; and, in every operation, gold as well as steel was the instrument of victory. Salerno, and some places along the western coast, maintained their fidelity to the Norman king; but he lost in two campaigns the greater part of his continental possessions; and the modest emperor, disdaining all flattery and falsehood, was content with the reduction of three hundred cities or villages of Apulia and Calabria, whose names and titles were inscribed on all the walls of the palace. The prejudices of the Latins were gratified by a genuine or fictitious donation under the seal of the German Cæsars; but the successor of Constantine soon renounced this ignominious pretence, claimed the indefeasible dominion of Italy, and professed his design of chasing the Barbarians beyond the Alps. By the artful speeches, liberal gifts, and unbounded promises, of their Eastern ally, the free cities were encouraged to persevere in their generous struggle against the despotism of Frederic Barbarossa: the walls of Milan were rebuilt by the contributions of Manuel; and he poured, says the historian, a river of gold into the bosom of Ancona, whose attachment to the Greeks was fortified by the jealous enmity of the Venetians. The situation and trade of Ancona rendered it an important garrison in the heart of Italy: it was twice besieged by the arms of Frederic; the imperial forces were twice repulsed by the spirit of freedom; that spirit was animated by the ambassador of Constantinople; and the most intrepid patriots, the most faithful servants, were rewarded by the wealth and honors of the Byzantine court. The pride of Manuel disdained and rejected a Barbarian colleague; his ambition was excited by the hope of stripping the purple from the German usurpers, and of establishing, in the West, as in the East, his lawful title of sole emperor of the Romans. With this view, he solicited the alliance of the people and the bishop of Rome. Several of the nobles embraced the cause of the Greek monarch; the splendid nuptials of his niece with Odo Frangipani secured the support of that powerful family, and his royal standard or image was entertained with due reverence in the ancient metropolis. During the quarrel between Frederic and Alexander the Third, the pope twice received in the Vatican the ambassadors of Constantinople. They flattered his piety by the long-promised union of the two churches, tempted the avarice of his venal court, and exhorted the Roman pontiff to seize the just provocation, the favorable moment, to humble the savage insolence of the Alemanni and to acknowledge the true representative of Constantine and Augustus.

But these Italian conquests, this universal reign, soon escaped from the hand of the Greek emperor. His first demands were eluded by the prudence of Alexander the Third, who paused on this deep and momentous revolution; nor could the pope be seduced by a personal dispute to renounce the perpetual inheritance of the Latin name. After the reunion with Frederic, he spoke a more peremptory language, confirmed the acts of his predecessors, excommunicated the adherents of Manuel, and pronounced the final separation of the churches, or at least the empires, of Constantinople and Rome. The free cities of Lombardy no longer remembered their foreign benefactor, and without preserving the friendship of Ancona, he soon incurred the enmity of Venice. By his own avarice, or the complaints of his subjects, the Greek emperor was provoked to arrest the persons, and confiscate the effects, of the Venetian merchants. This violation of the public faith exasperated a free and commercial people: one hundred galleys were launched and armed in as many days; they swept the coasts of Dalmatia and Greece: but after some mutual wounds, the war was terminated by an agreement, inglorious to the empire, insufficient for the republic; and a complete vengeance of these and of fresh injuries was reserved for the succeeding generation. The lieutenant of Manuel had informed his sovereign that he was strong enough to quell any domestic revolt of Apulia and Calabria; but that his forces were inadequate to resist the impending attack of the king of Sicily. His prophecy was soon verified: the death of Palæologus devolved the command on several chiefs, alike eminent in rank, alike defective in military talents; the Greeks were oppressed by land and sea; and a captive remnant that escaped the swords of the Normans and Saracens, abjured all future hostility against the person or dominions of their conqueror. Yet the king of Sicily esteemed the courage and constancy of Manuel, who had landed a second army on the Italian shore; he respectfully addressed the new Justinian; solicited a peace or truce of thirty years, accepted as a gift the regal title; and acknowledged himself the military vassal of the Roman empire. The Byzantine Cæsars acquiesced in this shadow of dominion, without expecting, perhaps without desiring, the service of a Norman army; and the truce of thirty years was not disturbed by any hostilities between Sicily and Constantinople. About the end of that period, the throne of Manuel was usurped by an inhuman tyrant, who had deserved the abhorrence of his country and mankind: the sword of William the Second, the grandson of Roger, was drawn by a fugitive of the Comnenian race; and the subjects of Andronicus might salute the strangers as friends, since they detested their sovereign as the worst of enemies. The Latin historians expatiate on the rapid progress of the four counts who invaded Romania with a fleet and army, and reduced many castles and cities to the obedience of the king of Sicily. The Greeks accuse and magnify the wanton and sacrilegious cruelties that were perpetrated in the sack of Thessalonica, the second city of the empire. The former deplore the fate of those invincible but unsuspecting warriors who were destroyed by the arts of a vanquished foe. The latter applaud, in songs of triumph, the repeated victories of their countrymen on the Sea of Marmora or Propontis, on the banks of the Strymon, and under the walls of Durazzo. A revolution which punished the crimes of Andronicus, had united against the Franks the zeal and courage of the successful insurgents: ten thousand were slain in battle, and Isaac Angelus, the new emperor, might indulge his vanity or vengeance in the treatment of four thousand captives. Such was the event of the last contest between the Greeks and Normans: before the expiration of twenty years, the rival nations were lost or degraded in foreign servitude; and the successors of Constantine did not long survive to insult the fall of the Sicilian monarchy.

The sceptre of Roger successively devolved to his son and grandson: they might be confounded under the name of William: they are strongly discriminated by the epithets of the *bad* and the *good*; but these epithets, which appear to describe the perfection of vice and virtue, cannot strictly be applied to either of the Norman princes. When he was roused to arms by danger and shame, the first William did not degenerate from the valor of his race; but his temper was slothful; his manners were dissolute; his passions headstrong and mischievous; and the monarch is responsible, not only for his personal vices, but for those of Majo, the great admiral, who abused the confidence, and conspired against the life, of his benefactor. From the Arabian conquest, Sicily had imbibed a deep tincture of Oriental manners; the despotism, the pomp, and even the harem, of a sultan; and a Christian people was oppressed and insulted by the ascendant of the eunuchs, who openly professed, or secretly cherished, the religion of Mahomet. An eloquent historian of the times has delineated the misfortunes of his country: the ambition and fall of the ungrateful Majo; the revolt and punishment of his assassins; the imprisonment and deliverance of the king himself; the private feuds that arose from the public confusion; and the various forms of calamity and discord which afflicted Palermo, the island, and the continent, during the reign of William the First, and the minority of his son. The youth, innocence, and beauty of William the Second, endeared him to the nation: the factions were reconciled; the laws were revived; and from the manhood to the premature death of that amiable prince, Sicily enjoyed a short season of peace, justice, and happiness, whose value was enhanced by the remembrance of the past and the dread of futurity. The legitimate male posterity of Tancred of Hauteville was extinct in the person of the second William; but his aunt, the daughter of Roger, had married the most powerful prince of the age; and Henry the Sixth, the son of Frederic Barbarossa, descended from the Alps to claim the Imperial crown and the inheritance of his wife. Against the unanimous wish of a free people, this inheritance could only be acquired by arms; and I am pleased to transcribe the style and sense of the historian Falcandus, who writes at the moment, and on the spot, with the feelings of a patriot, and the prophetic eye of a statesman. "Constantia, the daughter of Sicily, nursed from her cradle in the pleasures and plenty, and educated in the arts and manners, of this fortunate isle, departed long since to enrich the Barbarians with our treasures, and now returns, with her savage allies, to contaminate the beauties of her venerable parent. Already I behold the swarms of angry Barbarians: our opulent cities, the places flourishing in a long peace, are shaken with fear, desolated by slaughter, consumed by rapine, and polluted by intemperance and lust. I see the massacre or captivity of our citizens, the rapes of our virgins and matrons. In this extremity (he interrogates a friend) how must the Sicilians act? By the unanimous election of a king of valor and experience, Sicily and Calabria might yet be preserved; for in the levity of the Apulians, ever eager for new revolutions, I can repose neither confidence nor hope. Should Calabria be lost, the lofty towers, the numerous youth, and the naval strength, of Messina, might guard the passage against a foreign invader. If the savage Germans coalesce with the pirates of Messina; if they destroy with fire the fruitful region, so often wasted by the fires of Mount Ætna, what resource will be left for the interior parts of the island, these noble cities which should never be violated by the hostile footsteps of a Barbarian? Catana has again been overwhelmed by an earthquake: the ancient virtue of Syracuse expires in poverty and solitude; but Palermo is still crowned with a diadem, and her triple walls enclose the active multitudes of Christians and Saracens. If the two nations, under one king, can unite for their common safety, they may rush on the Barbarians with invincible arms. But if the Saracens, fatigued by a repetition of injuries, should now retire and rebel; if they should occupy the castles of the mountains and sea-coast, the unfortunate Christians, exposed to a double attack, and placed as it were between the hammer and the anvil, must resign themselves to hopeless and inevitable servitude." We must not forget, that a priest here prefers his country to his religion; and that the Moslems, whose alliance he seeks, were still numerous and powerful in the state of Sicily.

The hopes, or at least the wishes, of Falcandus were at first gratified by the free and unanimous election of Tancred, the grandson of the first king, whose birth was illegitimate, but whose civil and military virtues shone without a blemish. During four years, the term of his life and reign, he stood in arms on the farthest verge of the Apulian frontier, against the powers of Germany; and the restitution of a royal captive, of Constantia herself, without injury or ransom, may appear to surpass the most liberal measure of policy or reason. After his decease, the kingdom of his widow and infant son fell without a struggle; and Henry pursued his victorious march from Capua to Palermo. The political balance of Italy was destroyed by his success; and if the pope and the free cities had consulted their obvious and real interest, they would have combined the powers of earth and heaven to prevent the dangerous union of the German empire with the kingdom of Sicily. But the subtle policy, for which the Vatican has so often been praised or arraigned, was on this occasion blind and inactive; and if it were true that Celestine the Third had kicked away the Imperial crown from the head of the prostrate Henry, such an act of impotent pride could serve only to cancel an obligation and provoke an enemy. The Genoese, who enjoyed a beneficial trade and establishment in Sicily, listened to the promise of his boundless gratitude and speedy departure: their fleet commanded the straits of Messina, and opened the harbor of Palermo; and the first act of his government was to abolish the privileges, and to seize the property, of these imprudent allies. The last hope of Falcandus was defeated by the discord of the Christians and Mahometans: they fought in the capital; several thousands of the latter were slain; but their surviving brethren fortified the mountains, and disturbed above thirty years the peace of the island. By the policy of Frederic the Second, sixty thousand Saracens were transplanted to Nocera in Apulia. In their wars against the Roman church, the emperor and his son Mainfroy were strengthened and disgraced by the service of the enemies of Christ; and this national colony maintained their religion and manners in the heart of Italy, till they were extirpated, at the end of the thirteenth century, by the zeal and revenge of the house of Anjou. All the calamities which the prophetic orator had deplored were surpassed by the cruelty and avarice of the German conqueror. He violated the royal sepulchres, and explored the secret treasures of the palace, Palermo, and the whole kingdom: the pearls and jewels, however precious, might be easily removed; but one hundred and sixty horses were laden with the gold and silver of Sicily. The young king, his mother and sisters, and the nobles of both sexes, were separately confined in the fortresses of the Alps; and, on the slightest rumor of rebellion, the captives were deprived of life, of their eyes, or of the hope of posterity. Constantia herself was touched with sympathy for the miseries of her country; and the heiress of the Norman line might struggle to check her despotic husband, and to save the patrimony of her new-born son, of an emperor so famous in the next age under the name of Frederic the Second. Ten years after this revolution, the French monarchs annexed to their crown the duchy of Normandy: the sceptre of her ancient dukes had been transmitted, by a granddaughter of William the Conqueror, to the house of Plantagenet; and the adventurous Normans, who had raised so many trophies in France, England, and Ireland, in Apulia, Sicily, and the East, were lost, either in victory or servitude, among the vanquished nations.

The Turks. – Part One

The Turks of the House of Seljuk. – Their Revolt against Mahmud Conqueror of Hindostan. – Togrul Subdues Persia, and Protects the Caliphs. – Defeat and Captivity of the Emperor Romanus Diogenes by Alp Arslan. – Power and Magnificence of Malek Shah. – Conquest of Asia Minor and Syria. – State and Oppression of Jerusalem. – Pilgrimages to the Holy Sepulchre.

FROM THE ISLE OF Sicily, the reader must transport himself beyond the Caspian Sea, to the original seat of the Turks or Turkmans, against whom the first crusade was principally directed. Their Scythian empire of the sixth century was long since dissolved; but the name was still famous among the Greeks and Orientals; and the fragments of the nation, each a powerful and independent people, were scattered over the desert from China to the Oxus and the Danube: the colony of Hungarians was admitted into the republic of Europe, and the thrones of Asia were occupied by slaves and soldiers of Turkish extraction. While Apulia and Sicily were subdued by the Norman lance, a swarm of these northern shepherds overspread the kingdoms of Persia; their princes of the race of Seljuk erected a splendid and solid empire from Samarcand to the confines of Greece and Egypt; and the Turks have maintained their dominion in Asia Minor, till the victorious crescent has been planted on the dome of St. Sophia.

One of the greatest of the Turkish princes was Mahmood or Mahmud, the Gaznevide, who reigned in the eastern provinces of Persia, one thousand years after the birth of Christ. His father Sebectagi was the slave of the slave of the slave of the commander of the faithful. But in this descent of servitude, the first degree was merely titular, since it was filled by the sovereign of Transoxiana and Chorasan, who still paid a nominal allegiance to the caliph of Bagdad. The second rank was that of a minister of state, a lieutenant of the Samanides, who broke, by his revolt, the bonds of political slavery. But the third step was a state of real and domestic servitude in the family of that rebel; from which Sebectagi, by his courage and dexterity, ascended to the supreme command of the city and provinces of Gazna, as the son-in-law and successor of his grateful master. The falling dynasty of the Samanides was at first protected, and at last overthrown, by their servants; and, in the public disorders, the fortune of Mahmud continually increased. From him the title of *Sultan* was first invented; and his kingdom was enlarged from Transoxiana to the neighborhood of Ispahan, from the shores of the Caspian to the mouth of the Indus. But the principal source of his fame and riches was the holy war which he waged against the Gentoos of Hindostan. In this foreign narrative I may not consume a page; and a volume would scarcely suffice to recapitulate the battles and sieges of his twelve expeditions. Never was the Mussulman hero dismayed by the inclemency of the seasons, the height of the mountains, the breadth of the rivers, the barrenness of the desert, the multitudes of the enemy, or the formidable array of their elephants of war. The sultan of Gazna surpassed the limits of the conquests of Alexander: after a march of three months, over the hills of Cashmir and Thibet, he reached the famous city of Kinnoge, on the Upper Ganges; and, in a naval combat on one of the branches of the Indus, he fought and vanquished four thousand boats of the natives. Delhi, Lahor, and Multan, were compelled to open their gates: the fertile kingdom of Guzarat attracted his ambition and tempted his stay; and his avarice indulged the fruitless project of discovering the golden and aromatic isles of the Southern Ocean. On the payment of a tribute, the *rajahs* preserved their dominions; the people, their lives and fortunes; but to the religion of Hindostan the zealous Mussulman was cruel and inexorable: many hundred temples, or pagodas, were levelled with the ground; many thousand idols were demolished; and the servants of the prophet were stimulated and rewarded by the precious materials of which they were composed. The pagoda of Sumnat was situate on the promontory of Guzarat, in the neighborhood of Diu, one of the last remaining possessions of the Portuguese. It was endowed with the revenue of two thousand villages; two thousand Brahmins were consecrated to the service of the Deity, whom they washed each morning and evening in water from the distant Ganges: the subordinate ministers consisted of three hundred musicians, three hundred barbers, and five hundred dancing girls, conspicuous for their birth or beauty. Three sides of the temple were protected by the ocean, the narrow isthmus was fortified by a natural or artificial precipice; and the city and adjacent country were peopled by a nation of fanatics. They confessed the sins and the punishment of Kinnoge and Delhi; but if the impious stranger should presume to approach *their* holy precincts, he would surely be overwhelmed by a blast of the divine vengeance. By this challenge, the faith of Mahmud was animated to a personal trial of the strength of this Indian deity. Fifty thousand of his worshippers were pierced by the spear of the Moslems; the walls were scaled; the sanctuary was profaned; and the conqueror aimed a blow of his iron mace at the head of the idol. The trembling Brahmins are said to have offered ten millions sterling for his ransom; and it was urged by the wisest counsellors, that the destruction of a stone image would not change the hearts of the Gentoos; and that such a sum might be dedicated to the relief of the true believers. «Your reasons,» replied the sultan, «are specious and strong; but never in the eyes of posterity shall Mahmud appear as a merchant of idols.» He repeated his blows, and a treasure of pearls and rubies, concealed in the belly of the statue, explained in some degree the devout prodigality of the Brahmins. The fragments of the idol were distributed to Gazna, Mecca, and Medina. Bagdad listened to the edifying tale; and Mahmud was saluted by the caliph with the title of guardian of the fortune and faith of Mahomet.

From the paths of blood (and such is the history of nations) I cannot refuse to turn aside to gather some flowers of science or virtue. The name of Mahmud the Gaznevide is still venerable in the East: his subjects enjoyed the blessings of prosperity and peace; his vices were concealed by the veil of religion; and two familiar examples will testify his justice and magnanimity. I. As he sat in the Divan, an unhappy subject bowed before the throne to accuse the insolence of a Turkish soldier who had driven him from his house and bed. "Suspend your clamors," said Mahmud; "inform me of his next visit, and ourself in person will judge and punish the offender." The sultan followed his guide, invested the house with his guards, and extinguishing the torches, pronounced the death of the criminal, who had been seized in the act of rapine and adultery. After the execution of his sentence, the lights were rekindled, Mahmud fell prostrate in prayer, and rising from the ground, demanded some homely fare, which he devoured with the voraciousness of hunger. The poor man, whose injury he had avenged, was unable to suppress his astonishment and curiosity; and the courteous monarch condescended to explain the motives of this singular behavior. "I had reason to suspect that none, except one of my sons, could dare to perpetrate such an outrage; and I extinguished the lights, that my justice might be blind and inexorable. My prayer was a thanksgiving on the discovery of the offender; and so painful was my anxiety, that I had passed three days without food since the first moment of your complaint." II. The sultan of Gazna had declared war against the dynasty of the Bowides, the sovereigns of the western Persia: he was disarmed by an epistle of the sultana mother, and delayed his invasion till the manhood of her son. "During the life of my husband," said the artful regent, "I was ever apprehensive of your ambition: he was a prince and a soldier worthy of your arms. He is now no more; his sceptre has passed to a woman and a child, and you *dare not* attack their infancy and weakness. How inglorious would be your conquest, how shameful your defeat! and yet the event of war is in the hand of the Almighty.» Avarice was the only defect that tarnished the illustrious character of Mahmud; and never has that passion been more richly satiated. The Orientals exceed the measure of credibility in the account of millions of gold and silver, such as the avidity of man has never accumulated; in the magnitude of pearls, diamonds, and rubies, such as have never been produced by the workmanship of nature. Yet the soil of Hindostan is impregnated with precious minerals: her trade, in every age, has attracted the gold and silver of the world; and her virgin spoils were rifled by the first of the Mahometan conquerors. His behavior, in the last days of his life, evinces the vanity of these possessions, so laboriously won, so dangerously held, and so inevitably lost. He surveyed the vast and various chambers of the treasury of Gazna, burst into tears, and again closed the doors, without bestowing any portion of the wealth which he could no longer hope to preserve. The following day he reviewed the state of his military force; one hundred thousand foot, fifty-five thousand horse, and thirteen hundred elephants of battle. He again wept the instability of human greatness; and his grief was imbittered by the hostile progress of the Turkmans, whom he had introduced into the heart of his Persian kingdom.

In the modern depopulation of Asia, the regular operation of government and agriculture is confined to the neighborhood of cities; and the distant country is abandoned to the pastoral tribes of Arabs, Curds, and *Turkmans*. Of the last-mentioned people, two considerable branches extend on either side of the Caspian Sea: the western colony can muster forty thousand soldiers; the eastern, less obvious to the traveller, but more strong and populous, has increased to the number of one hundred thousand families. In the midst of civilized nations, they preserve the manners of the Scythian desert, remove their encampments with a change of seasons, and feed their cattle among the ruins of palaces and temples. Their flocks and herds are their only riches; their tents, either black or white, according to the color of the banner, are covered with felt, and of a circular form; their winter apparel is a sheepskin; a robe of cloth or cotton their summer garment: the features of the men are harsh and ferocious; the countenance of their women is soft and pleasing. Their wandering life maintains the spirit and exercise of arms; they fight on horseback; and their courage is displayed in frequent contests with each other and with their neighbors. For the license of pasture they pay a slight tribute to the sovereign of the land; but the domestic jurisdiction is in the hands of the chiefs and elders. The first emigration of the Eastern Turkmans, the most ancient of the race, may be ascribed to the tenth century of the Christian æra. In the decline of the caliphs, and the weakness of their lieutenants, the barrier of the Jaxartes was often violated; in each invasion, after the victory or retreat of their countrymen, some wandering tribe, embracing the Mahometan faith, obtained a free encampment in the spacious plains and pleasant climate of Transoxiana and Carizme. The Turkish slaves who aspired to the throne encouraged these emigrations which recruited their armies, awed their subjects and rivals, and protected the frontier against the wilder natives of Turkestan; and this policy was abused by Mahmud the Gaznevide beyond the example of former times. He was admonished of his error by the chief of the race of Seljuk, who dwelt in the territory of Bochara. The sultan had inquired what supply of men he could furnish for military service. "If you send," replied Ismael, "one of these arrows into our camp, fifty thousand of your servants will mount on horseback." – "And if that number," continued Mahmud, "should not be sufficient?" – "Send this second arrow to the horde of Balik, and you will find fifty thousand more." – "But," said the Gaznevide, dissembling his anxiety, "if I should stand in need of the whole force of your kindred tribes?" – "Despatch my bow," was the last reply of Ismael, "and as it is circulated around, the summons will be obeyed by two hundred thousand horse." The apprehension of such formidable friendship induced Mahmud to transport the most obnoxious tribes into the heart of Chorasan, where they would be separated from their brethren of the River Oxus, and enclosed on all sides by the walls of obedient cities. But the face of the country was an object of temptation rather than terror; and the vigor of government was relaxed by the absence and death of the sultan of Gazna. The shepherds were converted into robbers; the bands of robbers were collected into an army of conquerors: as far as

Ispahan and the Tigris, Persia was afflicted by their predatory inroads; and the Turkmans were not ashamed or afraid to measure their courage and numbers with the proudest sovereigns of Asia. Massoud, the son and successor of Mahmud, had too long neglected the advice of his wisest Omrahs. "Your enemies," they repeatedly urged, "were in their origin a swarm of ants; they are now little snakes; and, unless they be instantly crushed, they will acquire the venom and magnitude of serpents." After some alternatives of truce and hostility, after the repulse or partial success of his lieutenants, the sultan marched in person against the Turkmans, who attacked him on all sides with barbarous shouts and irregular onset. "Massoud," says the Persian historian, "plunged singly to oppose the torrent of gleaming arms, exhibiting such acts of gigantic force and valor as never king had before displayed. A few of his friends, roused by his words and actions, and that innate honor which inspires the brave, seconded their lord so well, that wheresoever he turned his fatal sword, the enemies were mowed down, or retreated before him. But now, when victory seemed to blow on his standard, misfortune was active behind it; for when he looked round, he beheld almost his whole army, excepting that body he commanded in person, devouring the paths of flight." The Gaznevide was abandoned by the cowardice or treachery of some generals of Turkish race; and this memorable day of Zendecan founded in Persia the dynasty of the shepherd kings.

The victorious Turkmans immediately proceeded to the election of a king; and, if the probable tale of a Latin historian deserves any credit, they determined by lot the choice of their new master. A number of arrows were successively inscribed with the name of a tribe, a family, and a candidate; they were drawn from the bundle by the hand of a child; and the important prize was obtained by Togrul Beg, the son of Michael the son of Seljuk, whose surname was immortalized in the greatness of his posterity. The sultan Mahmud, who valued himself on his skill in national genealogy, professed his ignorance of the family of Seljuk; yet the father of that race appears to have been a chief of power and renown. For a daring intrusion into the harem of his prince, Seljuk was banished from Turkestan: with a numerous tribe of his friends and vassals, he passed the Jaxartes, encamped in the neighborhood of Samarcand, embraced the religion of Mahomet, and acquired the crown of martyrdom in a war against the infidels. His age, of a hundred and seven years, surpassed the life of his son, and Seljuk adopted the care of his two grandsons, Togrul and Jaafar; the eldest of whom, at the age of forty-five, was invested with the title of Sultan, in the royal city of Nishabur. The blind determination of chance was justified by the virtues of the successful candidate. It would be superfluous to praise the valor of a Turk; and the ambition of Togrul was equal to his valor. By his arms, the Gasnevides were expelled from the eastern kingdoms of Persia, and gradually driven to the banks of the Indus, in search of a softer and more wealthy conquest. In the West he annihilated the dynasty of the Bowides; and the sceptre of Irak passed from the Persian to the Turkish nation. The princes who had felt, or who feared, the Seljukian arrows, bowed their heads in the dust; by the conquest of Aderbijan, or Media, he approached the Roman confines; and the shepherd presumed to despatch an ambassador, or herald, to demand the tribute and obedience of the emperor of Constantinople. In his own dominions, Togrul was the father of his soldiers and people; by a firm and equal administration, Persia was relieved from the evils of anarchy; and the same hands which had been imbrued in blood became the guardians of justice and the public peace. The more rustic, perhaps the wisest, portion of the Turkmans continued to dwell in the tents of their ancestors; and, from the Oxus to the Euphrates, these military colonies were protected and propagated by their native princes. But the Turks of the court and city were refined by business and softened by pleasure: they imitated the dress, language, and manners of Persia; and the royal palaces of Nishabur and Rei displayed the order and magnificence of a great monarchy. The most deserving of the Arabians and Persians were promoted to the honors of the state; and the whole body of the Turkish nation embraced, with fervor and sincerity, the religion of Mahomet. The northern swarms of Barbarians, who overspread both Europe and Asia, have been irreconcilably separated by the consequences of a similar conduct. Among the Moslems, as among the Christians, their vague and local traditions have yielded to the reason and authority of the prevailing system, to the fame of antiquity, and the consent of nations. But the triumph of the Koran is more pure and meritorious, as it was not assisted by any visible splendor of worship which might allure the Pagans by some resemblance of idolatry. The first of the Seljukian sultans was conspicuous by his zeal and faith: each day he repeated the five prayers which are enjoined to the true believers; of each week, the two first days were consecrated by an extraordinary fast; and in every city a mosch was completed, before Togrul presumed to lay the foundations of a palace.

With the belief of the Koran, the son of Seljuk imbibed a lively reverence for the successor of the prophet. But that sublime character was still disputed by the caliphs of Bagdad and Egypt, and each of the rivals was solicitous to prove his title in the judgment of the strong, though illiterate Barbarians. Mahmud the Gaznevide had declared himself in favor of the line of Abbas; and had treated with indignity the robe of honor which was presented by the Fatimite ambassador. Yet the ungrateful Hashemite had changed with the change of fortune; he applauded the victory of Zendecan, and named the Seljukian sultan his temporal vicegerent over the Moslem world. As Togrul executed and enlarged this important trust, he was called to the deliverance of the caliph Cayem, and obeyed the holy summons, which gave a new kingdom to his arms. In the palace of Bagdad, the commander of the faithful still slumbered, a venerable phantom. His servant or master, the prince of the Bowides, could no longer protect him from the insolence of meaner tyrants; and the Euphrates and Tigris were oppressed by the revolt of the Turkish and Arabian emirs. The presence of a conqueror was implored as a blessing; and the transient mischiefs of fire and sword were excused as the sharp but salutary remedies which alone could restore the health of the republic. At the head of an irresistible force, the sultan of Persia marched from Hamadan: the proud were crushed, the prostrate were spared; the prince of the Bowides disappeared; the heads of the most obstinate rebels were laid at the feet of Togrul; and he inflicted a lesson of obedience on the people of Mosul and Bagdad. After the chastisement of the guilty, and the restoration of peace, the royal shepherd accepted the reward of his labors; and a solemn comedy represented the triumph of religious prejudice over Barbarian power. The Turkish sultan embarked on the Tigris, landed at the gate of Racca, and made his public entry on horseback. At the palace-gate he respectfully dismounted, and walked on foot, preceded by his emirs without arms. The caliph was seated behind his black veil: the black garment of the Abbassides was cast over his shoulders, and he held in his hand the staff of the apostle of God. The conqueror of the East kissed the ground, stood some time in a modest posture, and was led towards the throne by the vizier and interpreter. After Togrul had seated himself on another throne, his commission was publicly read, which declared him the temporal lieutenant of the vicar of the prophet. He was successively invested with seven robes of honor, and presented with seven slaves, the natives of the seven climates of the Arabian empire. His mystic veil was perfumed with musk; two crowns were placed on his head; two cimeters were girded to his side, as the symbols of a double reign over the East and West. After this inauguration, the sultan was prevented from prostrating himself a second time; but he twice kissed the hand of the commander of the faithful, and his titles were proclaimed by the voice of heralds and the applause of the Moslems. In a second visit to Bagdad, the Seljukian prince again rescued the caliph from his enemies and devoutly, on foot, led the bridle of his mule from the prison to the palace. Their alliance was cemented by the marriage of Togrul's sister with the successor of the prophet. Without reluctance he had introduced a Turkish virgin into his harem; but Cayem proudly refused his daughter to the sultan, disdained to mingle the blood of the Hashemites with the blood of a Scythian shepherd; and protracted the negotiation many months, till the gradual diminution of his revenue admonished him that he was still in the hands of a master. The royal nuptials were followed by the death of Togrul himself; as he left no children, his nephew Alp Arslan succeeded to the title and prerogatives of sultan; and his name, after that of the caliph, was pronounced in the public prayers of the Moslems. Yet in this revolution, the Abbassides acquired a larger measure of liberty and power. On the throne of Asia, the Turkish monarchs were less jealous of the domestic administration of Bagdad; and the commanders of the faithful were relieved from the ignominious vexations to which they had been exposed by the presence and poverty of the Persian dynasty.

CHAPTER FIFTY SEVEN

The Turks. – Part Two

Since the fall of the caliphs, the discord and degeneracy of the Saracens respected the Asiatic provinces of Rome; which, by the victories of Nicephorus, Zimisces, and Basil, had been extended as far as Antioch and the eastern boundaries of Armenia. Twenty-five years after the death of Basil, his successors were suddenly assaulted by an unknown race of Barbarians, who united the Scythian valor with the fanaticism of new proselytes, and the art and riches of a powerful monarchy. The myriads of Turkish horse overspread a frontier of six hundred miles from Tauris to Arzeroum, and the blood of one hundred and thirty thousand Christians was a grateful sacrifice to the Arabian prophet. Yet the arms of Togrul did not make any deep or lasting impression on the Greek empire. The torrent rolled away from the open country; the sultan retired without glory or success from the siege of an Armenian city; the obscure hostilities were continued or suspended with a vicissitude of events; and the bravery of the Macedonian legions renewed the fame of the conqueror of Asia. The name of Alp Arslan, the valiant lion, is expressive of the popular idea of the perfection of man; and the successor of Togrul displayed the fierceness and generosity of the royal animal. He passed the Euphrates at the head of the Turkish cavalry, and entered Cæsarea, the metropolis of Cappadocia, to which he had been attracted by the fame and wealth of the temple of St. Basil. The solid structure resisted the destroyer: but he carried away the doors of the shrine incrusted with gold and pearls, and profaned the relics of the tutelar saint, whose mortal frailties were now covered by the venerable rust of antiquity. The final conquest of Armenia and Georgia was achieved by Alp Arslan. In Armenia, the title of a kingdom, and the spirit of a nation, were annihilated: the artificial fortifications were yielded by the mercenaries of Constantinople; by strangers without faith, veterans without pay or arms, and recruits without experience or discipline. The loss of this important frontier was the news of a day; and the Catholics were neither surprised nor displeased, that a people so deeply infected with the Nestorian and Eutychian errors had been delivered by Christ and his mother into the hands of the infidels. The woods and valleys of Mount Caucasus were more strenuously defended by the native Georgians or Iberians; but the Turkish sultan and his son Malek were indefatigable in this holy war: their captives were compelled to promise a spiritual, as well as temporal, obedience; and, instead of their collars and bracelets, an iron horseshoe, a badge of ignominy, was imposed on the infidels who still adhered to the worship of their fathers. The change, however, was not sincere or universal; and, through ages of servitude, the Georgians have maintained the succession of their princes and bishops. But a race of men, whom nature has cast in her most perfect mould, is degraded by poverty, ignorance, and vice; their profession, and still more their practice, of Christianity is an empty name; and if they have emerged from heresy, it is only because they are too illiterate to remember a metaphysical creed.

The false or genuine magnanimity of Mahmud the Gaznevide was not imitated by Alp Arslan; and he attacked without scruple the Greek empress Eudocia and her children. His alarming progress compelled her to give herself and her sceptre to the hand of a soldier; and Romanus Diogenes was invested with the Imperial purple. His patriotism, and perhaps his pride, urged him from Constantinople within two months after his accession; and the next campaign he most scandalously took the field during the holy festival of Easter. In the palace, Diogenes was no more than the husband of Eudocia: in the camp, he was the emperor of the Romans, and he sustained that character with feeble resources and invincible courage. By his spirit and success the soldiers were taught to act, the subjects to hope, and the enemies to fear. The Turks had penetrated into the heart of Phrygia; but the sultan himself had resigned to his emirs the prosecution of the war; and their numerous detachments were scattered over Asia in the security of conquest. Laden with spoil, and careless of discipline, they were separately surprised and defeated by the Greeks: the activity of the emperor seemed to multiply his presence: and while they heard of his expedition to Antioch, the enemy felt his sword on the hills of Trebizond. In three laborious campaigns, the Turks were driven beyond the Euphrates; in the fourth and last, Romanus undertook the deliverance of Armenia. The desolation of the land obliged him to transport a supply of two months' provisions;

and he marched forwards to the siege of Malazkerd, an important fortress in the midway between the modern cities of Arzeroum and Van. His army amounted, at the least, to one hundred thousand men. The troops of Constantinople were reënforced by the disorderly multitudes of Phrygia and Cappadocia; but the real strength was composed of the subjects and allies of Europe, the legions of Macedonia, and the squadrons of Bulgaria; the Uzi, a Moldavian horde, who were themselves of the Turkish race; and, above all, the mercenary and adventurous bands of French and Normans. Their lances were commanded by the valiant Ursel of Baliol, the kinsman or father of the Scottish kings, and were allowed to excel in the exercise of arms, or, according to the Greek style, in the practice of the Pyrrhic dance.

On the report of this bold invasion, which threatened his hereditary dominions, Alp Arslan flew to the scene of action at the head of forty thousand horse. His rapid and skilful evolutions distressed and dismayed the superior numbers of the Greeks; and in the defeat of Basilacius, one of their principal generals, he displayed the first example of his valor and clemency. The imprudence of the emperor had separated his forces after the reduction of Malazkerd. It was in vain that he attempted to recall the mercenary Franks: they refused to obey his summons; he disdained to await their return: the desertion of the Uzi filled his mind with anxiety and suspicion; and against the most salutary advice he rushed forwards to speedy and decisive action. Had he listened to the fair proposals of the sultan, Romanus might have secured a retreat, perhaps a peace; but in these overtures he supposed the fear or weakness of the enemy, and his answer was conceived in the tone of insult and defiance. "If the Barbarian wishes for peace, let him evacuate the ground which he occupies for the encampment of the Romans, and surrender his city and palace of Rei as a pledge of his sincerity." Alp Arslan smiled at the vanity of the demand, but he wept the death of so many faithful Moslems; and, after a devout prayer, proclaimed a free permission to all who were desirous of retiring from the field. With his own hands he tied up his horse's tail, exchanged his bow and arrows for a mace and cimeter, clothed himself in a white garment, perfumed his body with musk, and declared that if he were vanquished, that spot should be the place of his burial. The sultan himself had affected to cast away his missile weapons: but his hopes of victory were placed in the arrows of the Turkish cavalry, whose squadrons were loosely distributed in the form of a crescent. Instead of the successive lines and reserves of the Grecian tactics, Romulus led his army in a single and solid phalanx, and pressed with vigor and impatience the artful and yielding resistance of the Barbarians. In this desultory and fruitless combat he spent the greater part of a summer's day, till prudence and fatigue compelled him to return to his camp. But a retreat is always perilous in the face of an active foe; and no sooner had the standard been turned to the rear than the phalanx was broken by the base cowardice, or the baser jealousy, of Andronicus, a rival prince, who disgraced his birth and the purple of the Cæsars. The Turkish squadrons poured a cloud of arrows on this moment of confusion and lassitude; and the horns of their formidable crescent were closed in the rear of the Greeks. In the destruction of the army and pillage of the camp, it would be needless to mention the number of the slain or captives. The Byzantine writers deplore the loss of an inestimable pearl: they forgot to mention, that in this fatal day the Asiatic provinces of Rome were irretrievably sacrificed.

As long as a hope survived, Romanus attempted to rally and save the relics of his army. When the centre, the Imperial station, was left naked on all sides, and encompassed by the victorious Turks, he still, with desperate courage, maintained the fight till the close of day, at the head of the brave and faithful subjects who adhered to his standard. They fell around him; his horse was slain; the emperor was wounded; yet he stood alone and intrepid, till he was oppressed and bound by the strength of multitudes. The glory of this illustrious prize was disputed by a slave and a soldier; a slave who had seen him on the throne of Constantinople, and a soldier whose extreme deformity had been excused on the promise of some signal service. Despoiled of his arms, his jewels, and his purple, Romanus spent a dreary and perilous night on the field of battle, amidst a disorderly crowd of the meaner Barbarians. In the morning the royal captive was presented to Alp Arslan, who doubted of his fortune, till the identity of the person was ascertained by the report of his ambassadors, and by the more pathetic evidence of Basilacius, who embraced with tears the feet of his unhappy sovereign. The successor of Constantine, in a plebeian habit, was led into the Turkish divan, and commanded to kiss the ground before the lord of Asia. He reluctantly obeyed; and Alp Arslan, starting from his throne, is said to have planted his foot on the neck of the Roman emperor. But the fact is doubtful; and if, in this moment of insolence, the sultan complied with the national custom, the rest of his conduct has extorted the praise of his bigoted foes, and may afford a lesson to the most civilized ages. He instantly raised the royal captive from the ground; and thrice clasping his hand with tender sympathy, assured him, that his life and dignity should be inviolate in the hands of a prince who had learned to respect the majesty of his equals and the vicissitudes of fortune. From the divan, Romanus was conducted to an adjacent tent, where he was served with pomp and reverence by the officers of the sultan, who, twice each day, seated him in the place of honor at his own table. In a free and familiar conversation of eight days, not a word, not a look, of insult escaped from the conqueror; but he severely censured the unworthy subjects who had deserted their valiant prince in the hour of danger, and gently admonished his antagonist of some errors which he had committed in the management of the war. In the preliminaries of negotiation, Alp Arslan asked him what treatment he expected to receive, and the calm indifference of the emperor displays the freedom of his mind. "If you are cruel," said he, "you will take my life; if you listen to pride, you will drag me at your chariot-wheels; if you consult your interest, you will accept a ransom, and restore me to my country." "And what," continued the sultan, "would have been your own behavior, had fortune smiled on your arms?" The reply of the Greek betrays a sentiment, which prudence, and even gratitude, should have taught him to suppress. "Had I vanquished," he fiercely said, "I would have inflicted on thy body many a stripe." The Turkish conqueror smiled at the insolence of his captive; observed that the Christian law inculcated the love of enemies and forgiveness of injuries; and nobly declared, that he would not imitate an example which he condemned. After mature deliberation, Alp Arslan dictated the terms of liberty and peace, a ransom of a million, an annual tribute of three hundred and sixty thousand pieces of gold, the marriage of the royal children, and the deliverance of all the Moslems, who were in the power of the Greeks. Romanus, with a sigh, subscribed this treaty, so disgraceful to the majesty of the empire; he was immediately invested with a Turkish robe of honor; his nobles and patricians were restored to their sovereign; and the sultan, after a courteous embrace, dismissed him with rich presents and a military guard. No sooner did he reach the confines of the empire, than he was informed that the palace and provinces had disclaimed their allegiance to a captive: a sum of two hundred thousand pieces was painfully collected; and the fallen monarch transmitted this part of his ransom, with a sad confession of his impotence and disgrace. The generosity, or perhaps the ambition, of the sultan, prepared to espouse the cause of his ally; but his designs were prevented by the defeat, imprisonment, and death, of Romanus Diogenes.

In the treaty of peace, it does not appear that Alp Arslan extorted any province or city from the captive emperor; and his revenge was satisfied with the trophies of his victory, and the spoils of Anatolia, from Antioch to the Black Sea. The fairest part of Asia was subject to his laws: twelve hundred princes, or the sons of princes, stood before his throne; and two hundred thousand soldiers marched under his banners. The sultan disdained to pursue the fugitive Greeks; but he meditated the more glorious conquest of Turkestan, the original seat of the house of Seljuk. He moved from Bagdad to the banks of the Oxus; a bridge was thrown over the river; and twenty days were consumed in the passage of his troops. But the progress of the great king was retarded by the governor of Berzem; and Joseph the Carizmian presumed to defend his fortress against the powers of the East. When he was produced a captive in the royal tent, the sultan, instead of praising his valor, severely reproached his obstinate folly: and the insolent replies of the rebel provoked a sentence, that he should be fastened to four stakes, and left to expire in that painful situation. At this command, the desperate Carizmian, drawing a dagger, rushed headlong towards the throne: the guards raised their battle-axes; their zeal was checked by Alp Arslan, the most skilful archer of the age: he drew his bow, but his foot slipped, the arrow glanced aside, and he received in his breast the dagger of Joseph, who was instantly cut in pieces. The wound was mortal; and the Turkish prince bequeathed a dying admonition to the pride of kings. "In my youth," said Alp Arslan, "I was advised by a sage to humble myself before God; to distrust my own strength; and never to despise the most contemptible foe. I have neglected these lessons; and my neglect has been deservedly punished. Yesterday, as from an eminence I beheld the numbers, the discipline, and the spirit, of my armies, the earth seemed to tremble under my feet; and I said in my heart, Surely thou art the king of the world, the greatest and most invincible of warriors. These armies are no longer mine; and, in the confidence of my personal strength, I now fall by the hand of an assassin." Alp Arslan possessed the virtues of a Turk and a Mussulman; his voice and stature commanded the reverence of mankind; his face was shaded with long whiskers; and his ample turban was fashioned in the shape of a crown. The remains of the sultan were deposited in the tomb of the Seljukian dynasty; and the passenger might read and meditate this useful inscription: "O ye who have seen the glory of Alp Arslan exalted to the heavens, repair to Maru, and you will behold it buried in the dust." The annihilation of the inscription, and the tomb itself, more forcibly proclaims the instability of human greatness.

During the life of Alp Arslan, his eldest son had been acknowledged as the future sultan of the Turks. On his father's death the inheritance was disputed by an uncle, a cousin, and a brother: they drew their cimeters, and assembled their followers; and the triple victory of Malek Shah established his own reputation and the right of primogeniture. In every age, and more especially in Asia, the thirst of power has inspired the same passions, and occasioned the same disorders; but, from the long series of civil war, it would not be easy to extract a sentiment more pure and magnanimous than is contained in the saying of the Turkish prince. On the eve of the battle, he performed his devotions at Thous, before the tomb of the Imam Riza. As the sultan rose from the ground, he asked his vizier Nizam, who had knelt beside him, what had been the object of his secret petition: "That your arms may be crowned with victory," was the prudent, and most probably the sincere, answer of the minister. "For my part," replied the generous Malek, "I implored the Lord of Hosts that he would take from me my life and crown, if my brother be more worthy than myself to reign over the Moslems." The favorable judgment of heaven was ratified by the caliph; and for the first time, the sacred title of Commander of the Faithful was communicated to a Barbarian. But this Barbarian, by his personal merit, and the extent of his empire, was the greatest prince of his age. After the settlement of Persia and Syria, he marched at the head of innumerable armies to achieve the conquest of Turkestan, which had been undertaken by his father. In his passage of the Oxus, the boatmen, who had been employed in transporting some troops, complained, that their payment was assigned on the revenues of Antioch. The sultan frowned at this preposterous choice; but he smiled at the artful flattery of his vizier. "It was not to postpone their reward, that I selected those remote places, but to leave a memorial to posterity, that, under your reign, Antioch and the Oxus were subject to the same sovereign." But this description of his limits was unjust and parsimonious: beyond the Oxus, he reduced to his obedience the cities of Bochara, Carizme, and Samarcand, and crushed each rebellious slave, or independent savage, who dared to resist. Malek passed the Sihon or Jaxartes, the last boundary of Persian civilization: the hordes of Turkestan yielded to his supremacy: his name was inserted on the coins, and in the prayers of Cashgar, a Tartar kingdom on the extreme borders of China. From the Chinese frontier, he stretched his immediate jurisdiction or feudatory sway to the west and south, as far as the mountains of Georgia, the neighborhood of Constantinople, the holy city of Jerusalem, and the spicy groves of Arabia Felix. Instead of resigning himself to the luxury of his harem, the shepherd king, both in peace and war, was in action and in the field. By the perpetual motion of the royal camp, each province was successively blessed with his presence; and he is said to have perambulated twelve times the wide extent of his dominions, which surpassed the *Asiatic* reign of Cyrus and the caliphs. Of these expeditions, the most pious and splendid was the pilgrimage of Mecca: the freedom and safety of the caravans were protected by his arms; the citizens and pilgrims were enriched by the profusion of his alms; and the desert was cheered by the places of relief and refreshment, which he instituted for the use of his brethren. Hunting was the pleasure, and even the passion, of the sultan, and his train consisted of forty-seven thousand horses; but after the massacre of a Turkish chase, for each piece of game, he bestowed a piece of gold on the poor, a slight atonement, at the expense of the people, for the cost and mischief of the amusement of kings. In the peaceful prosperity of his reign, the cities of Asia were adorned with palaces and hospitals with moschs and colleges; few departed from his Divan without reward, and none without justice. The language and literature of Persia revived under the house of Seljuk; and if Malek emulated the liberality of a Turk less potent than himself, his palace might resound with the songs of a hundred poets. The sultan bestowed a more serious and learned care on the reformation of the calendar, which was effected by a general assembly of the astronomers of the East. By a law of the prophet, the Moslems are confined to the irregular course of the lunar months; in Persia, since the age of Zoroaster, the revolution of the sun has been known and celebrated as an annual festival; but after the fall of the Magian empire, the intercalation had been neglected; the fractions of minutes and hours were multiplied into days; and the date of the springs was removed from the sign of Aries to that of Pisces. The reign of Malek was illustrated by the *Gelalan* æra; and all errors, either past or future, were corrected by a computation of time, which surpasses the Julian, and approaches the accuracy of the Gregorian, style.

In a period when Europe was plunged in the deepest barbarism, the light and splendor of Asia may be ascribed to the docility rather than the knowledge of the Turkish conquerors. An ample share of their wisdom and virtue is due to a Persian vizier, who ruled the empire under the reigns of Alp Arslan and his son. Nizam, one of the most illustrious ministers of the East, was honored by the caliph as an oracle of religion and science; he was trusted by the sultan as the faithful vicegerent of his power and justice. After an administration of thirty years, the fame of the vizier, his wealth, and even his services, were transformed into crimes. He was overthrown by the insidious arts of a woman and a rival; and his fall was hastened by a rash declaration, that his cap and ink-horn, the badges of his office, were connected by the divine decree with the throne and diadem of the sultan. At the age of ninety-three years, the venerable statesman was dismissed by his master, accused by his enemies, and murdered by a fanatic: the last words of Nizam attested his innocence, and the remainder of Malek's life was short and inglorious. From Ispahan, the scene of this disgraceful transaction, the sultan moved to Bagdad, with the design of transplanting the caliph, and of fixing his own residence in the capital of the Moslem world. The feeble successor of Mahomet obtained a respite of ten days; and before the expiration of the term, the Barbarian was summoned by the angel of death. His ambassadors at Constantinople had asked in marriage a Roman princess; but the proposal was decently eluded; and the daughter of Alexius, who might herself have been the victim, expresses her abhorrence of his unnatural conjunction. The daughter of the sultan was bestowed on the caliph Moctadi, with the imperious condition, that, renouncing the society of his wives and concubines, he should forever confine himself to this honorable alliance.

CHAPTER FIFTY SEVEN

The Turks. – Part Three

THE GREATNESS AND UNITY of the Turkish empire expired in the person of Malek Shah. His vacant throne was disputed by his brother and his four sons; and, after a series of civil wars, the treaty which reconciled the surviving candidates confirmed a lasting separation in the *Persia* dynasty, the eldest and principal branch of the house of Seljuk. The three younger dynasties were those of *Kerman*, of *Syria*, and of *Roum*: the first of these commanded an extensive, though obscure, dominion on the shores of the Indian Ocean: the second expelled the Arabian princes of Aleppo and Damascus; and the third, our peculiar care, invaded the Roman provinces of Asia Minor. The generous policy of Malek contributed to their elevation: he allowed the princes of his blood, even those whom he had vanquished in the field, to seek new kingdoms worthy of their ambition; nor was he displeased that they should draw away the more ardent spirits, who might have disturbed the tranquillity of his reign. As the supreme head of his family and nation, the great sultan of Persia commanded the obedience and tribute of his royal brethren: the thrones of Kerman and Nice, of Aleppo and Damascus; the Atabeks, and emirs of Syria and Mesopotamia, erected their standards under the shadow of his sceptre: and the hordes of Turkmans overspread the plains of the Western Asia. After the death of Malek, the bands of union and subordination were relaxed and finally dissolved: the indulgence of the house of Seljuk invested their slaves with the inheritance of kingdoms; and, in the Oriental style, a crowd of princes arose from the dust of their feet.

A prince of the royal line, Cutulmish, the son of Izrail, the son of Seljuk, had fallen in a battle against Alp Arslan and the humane victor had dropped a tear over his grave. His five sons, strong in arms, ambitious of power, and eager for revenge, unsheathed their cimeters against the son of Alp Arslan. The two armies expected the signal when the caliph, forgetful of the majesty which secluded him from vulgar eyes, interposed his venerable mediation. "Instead of shedding the blood of your brethren, your brethren both in descent and faith, unite your forces in a holy war against the Greeks, the enemies of God and his apostle." They listened to his voice; the sultan embraced his rebellious kinsmen; and the eldest, the valiant Soliman, accepted the royal standard, which gave him the free conquest and hereditary command of the provinces of the Roman empire, from Arzeroum to Constantinople, and the unknown regions of the West. Accompanied by his four brothers, he passed the Euphrates; the Turkish camp was soon seated in the neighborhood of Kutaieh in Phrygia; and his flying cavalry laid waste the country as far as the Hellespont and the Black Sea. Since the decline of the empire, the peninsula of Asia Minor had been exposed to the transient, though destructive, inroads of the Persians and Saracens; but the fruits of a lasting conquest were reserved for the Turkish sultan; and his arms were introduced by the Greeks, who aspired to reign on the ruins of their country. Since the captivity of Romanus, six years the feeble son of Eudocia had trembled under the weight of the Imperial crown, till the provinces of the East and West were lost in the same month by a double rebellion: of either chief Nicephorus was the common name; but the surnames of Bryennius and Botoniates distinguish the European and Asiatic candidates. Their reasons, or rather their promises, were weighed in the Divan; and, after some hesitation, Soliman declared himself in favor of Botoniates, opened a free passage to his troops in their march from Antioch to Nice, and joined the banner of the Crescent to that of the Cross. After his ally had ascended the throne of Constantinople, the sultan was hospitably entertained in the suburb of Chrysopolis or Scutari; and a body of two thousand Turks was transported into Europe, to whose dexterity and courage the new emperor was indebted for the defeat and captivity of his rival, Bryennius. But the conquest of Europe was dearly purchased by the sacrifice of Asia: Constantinople was deprived of the obedience and revenue of the provinces beyond the Bosphorus and Hellespont; and the regular progress of the Turks, who fortified the passes of the rivers and mountains, left not a hope of their retreat or expulsion. Another candidate implored the aid of the sultan: Melissenus, in his purple robes and red buskins, attended the motions of the Turkish camp; and the desponding cities were tempted by the summons of a Roman prince, who immediately surrendered them into the hands of the Barbarians. These acquisitions were confirmed by a treaty of peace with the emperor Alexius: his fear of Robert compelled him to seek the friendship of Soliman; and it was not till after the sultan's death that he extended as far as Nicomedia, about sixty miles from Constantinople, the eastern boundary of the Roman world. Trebizond alone, defended on either side by the sea and mountains, preserved at the extremity of the Euxine the ancient character of a Greek colony, and the future destiny of a Christian empire.

Since the first conquests of the caliphs, the establishment of the Turks in Anatolia or Asia Minor was the most deplorable loss which the church and empire had sustained. By the propagation of the Moslem faith, Soliman deserved the name of *Gazi*, a holy champion; and his new kingdoms, of the Romans, or of *Roum*, was added to the tables of Oriental geography. It is described as extending from the Euphrates to Constantinople, from the Black Sea to the confines of Syria; pregnant with mines of silver and iron, of alum and copper, fruitful in corn and wine, and productive of cattle and excellent horses. The wealth of Lydia, the arts of the Greeks, the splendor of the Augustan age, existed only in books and ruins, which were equally obscure in the eyes of the Scythian conquerors. Yet, in the present decay, Anatolia still contains *some* wealthy and populous cities; and, under the Byzantine empire, they were far more flourishing in numbers, size, and opulence. By the choice of the sultan, Nice, the metropolis of Bithynia, was preferred for his palace and fortress: the seat of the Seljukian dynasty of Roum was planted one hundred miles from Constantinople; and the divinity of Christ was denied and derided in the same temple in which it had been pronounced by the first general synod of the Catholics. The unity of God, and the mission of Mahomet, were preached in the moschs; the Arabian learning was taught in the schools; the Cadhis judged according to the law of the Koran; the Turkish manners and language prevailed in the cities; and Turkman camps were scattered over the plains and mountains of Anatolia. On the hard conditions of tribute and servitude, the Greek Christians might enjoy the exercise of their religion; but their most holy churches were profaned; their priests and bishops were insulted; they were compelled to suffer the triumph of the *Pagans*, and the apostasy of their brethren; many thousand children were marked by the knife of circumcision; and many thousand captives were devoted to the service or the pleasures of their masters. After the loss of Asia, Antioch still maintained her primitive allegiance to Christ and Cæsar; but the solitary province was separated from all Roman aid, and surrounded on all sides by the Mahometan powers. The despair of Philaretus the governor prepared the sacrifice of his religion and loyalty, had not his guilt been prevented by his son, who hastened to the Nicene palace, and offered to deliver this valuable prize into the hands of Soliman. The ambitious sultan mounted on horseback, and in twelve nights (for he reposed in the day) performed a march of six hundred miles. Antioch was oppressed by the speed and secrecy of his enterprise; and the dependent cities, as far as Laodicea and the confines of Aleppo, obeyed the example of the metropolis. From Laodicea to the Thracian Bosphorus, or arm of St. George, the conquests and reign of Soliman extended thirty days' journey in length, and in breadth about ten or fifteen, between the rocks of Lycia and the Black Sea. The Turkish ignorance of navigation protected, for a while, the inglorious safety of the emperor; but no sooner had a fleet of two hundred ships been constructed by the hands of the captive Greeks, than Alexius trembled behind the walls of his capital. His plaintive epistles were dispersed over Europe, to excite the compassion of the Latins, and to paint the danger, the weakness, and the riches of the city of Constantine.

But the most interesting conquest of the Seljukian Turks was that of Jerusalem, which soon became the theatre of nations. In their capitulation with Omar, the inhabitants had stipulated the assurance of their religion and property; but the articles were interpreted by a master against whom it was dangerous to dispute; and in the four hundred years of the reign of the caliphs, the political climate of Jerusalem was exposed to the vicissitudes of storm and sunshine. By the increase of proselytes and population, the Mahometans might excuse the usurpation of three fourths of the city: but a peculiar quarter was resolved for the patriarch with his clergy and people; a tribute of two pieces of gold was the price of protection; and the sepulchre of Christ, with the church of the Resurrection, was still left in the hands of his votaries. Of these votaries, the most numerous and respectable portion were strangers to Jerusalem: the pilgrimages to the Holy Land had been stimulated, rather than suppressed, by the conquest of the Arabs; and the enthusiasm which had always prompted these perilous journeys, was nourished by the congenial passions of grief and indignation. A crowd of pilgrims from the East and West continued to visit the holy sepulchre, and the adjacent sanctuaries, more especially at the festival of Easter; and the Greeks and Latins, the Nestorians and Jacobites, the Copts and Abyssinians, the Armenians and Georgians, maintained the chapels, the clergy, and the poor of their respective communions. The harmony of prayer in so many various tongues, the worship of so many nations in the common temple of their religion, might have afforded a spectacle of edification and peace; but the zeal of the Christian sects was imbittered by hatred and revenge; and in the kingdom of a suffering Messiah, who had pardoned his enemies, they aspired to command and persecute their spiritual brethren. The preëminence was asserted by the spirit and numbers of the Franks; and the greatness of Charlemagne protected both the Latin pilgrims and the Catholics of the East. The poverty of Carthage, Alexandria, and Jerusalem, was relieved by the alms of that pious emperor; and many monasteries of Palestine were founded or restored by his liberal devotion. Harun Alrashid, the greatest of the Abbassides, esteemed in his Christian brother a similar supremacy of genius and power: their friendship was cemented by a frequent intercourse of gifts and embassies; and the caliph, without resigning the substantial dominion, presented the emperor with the keys of the holy sepulchre, and perhaps of the city of Jerusalem. In the decline of the Carlovingian monarchy, the republic of Amalphi promoted the interest of trade and religion in the East. Her vessels transported the Latin pilgrims to the coasts of Egypt and Palestine, and deserved, by their useful imports, the favor and alliance of the Fatimite caliphs: an annual fair was instituted on Mount Calvary: and the Italian merchants founded the convent and hospital of St. John of Jerusalem, the cradle of the monastic and military order, which has since reigned in the isles of Rhodes and of Malta. Had the Christian pilgrims been content to revere the tomb of a prophet, the disciples of Mahomet, instead of blaming, would have imitated, their piety: but these rigid *Unitarians* were scandalized by a worship which represents the birth, death, and resurrection, of a God; the Catholic images were branded with the name of idols; and the Moslems smiled with indignation at the miraculous flame which was kindled on the eve of Easter in the holy sepulchre. This pious fraud, first devised in the ninth century, was devoutly cherished by the Latin crusaders, and is annually repeated by the clergy of the Greek, Armenian, and Coptic sects, who impose on the credulous spectators for their own benefit, and that of their tyrants. In every age, a principle of toleration has been fortified by a sense of interest: and the revenue of the prince and his emir was increased each year, by the expense and tribute of so many thousand strangers.

The revolution which transferred the sceptre from the Abbassides to the Fatimites was a benefit, rather than an injury, to the Holy Land. A sovereign resident in Egypt was more sensible of the importance of Christian trade; and the emirs of Palestine were less remote from the justice and power of the throne. But the third of these Fatimite caliphs was the famous Hakem, a frantic youth, who was delivered by his impiety and despotism from the fear either of God or man; and whose reign was a wild mixture of vice and folly. Regardless of the most ancient customs of Egypt, he imposed on the women an absolute confinement; the restraint excited the clamors of both sexes; their clamors provoked his fury; a part of Old Cairo was delivered to the flames and the guards and citizens were engaged many days in a bloody conflict. At first the caliph declared himself a zealous Mussulman, the founder or benefactor of moschs and colleges: twelve hundred and ninety copies of the Koran were transcribed at his expense in letters of gold; and his edict extirpated the vineyards of the Upper Egypt. But his vanity was soon flattered by the hope of introducing a new religion; he aspired above the fame of a prophet, and styled himself the visible image of the Most High God, who, after nine apparitions on earth, was at length manifest in his royal person. At the name of Hakem, the lord of the living and the dead, every knee was bent in religious adoration: his mysteries were performed on a mountain near Cairo: sixteen thousand converts had signed his profession of faith; and at the present hour, a free and warlike people, the Druses of Mount Libanus, are persuaded of the life and divinity of a madman and tyrant. In his divine character, Hakem hated the Jews and Christians, as the servants of his rivals; while some remains of prejudice or prudence still pleaded in favor of the law of Mahomet. Both in Egypt and Palestine, his cruel and wanton persecution made some martyrs and many apostles: the common rights and special privileges of the sectaries were equally disregarded; and a general interdict was laid on the devotion of strangers and natives. The temple of the Christian world, the church of the Resurrection, was demolished to its foundations; the luminous prodigy of Easter was interrupted, and much profane labor was exhausted to destroy the cave in the rock which properly constitutes the holy sepulchre. At the report of this sacrilege, the nations of Europe were astonished and afflicted: but instead of arming in the defence of the Holy Land, they contented themselves with burning, or banishing, the Jews, as the secret advisers of the impious Barbarian. Yet the calamities of Jerusalem were in some measure alleviated by the inconstancy or repentance of Hakem himself; and the royal mandate was sealed for the restitution of the churches, when the tyrant was assassinated by the emissaries of his sister. The succeeding caliphs resumed the maxims of religion and policy: a free toleration was again granted; with the pious aid of the emperor of Constantinople, the holy sepulchre arose from its ruins; and, after a short abstinence, the pilgrims returned with an increase of appetite to the spiritual feast. In the sea-voyage of Palestine, the dangers were frequent, and the opportunities rare: but the conversion of Hungary opened a safe communication between Germany and Greece. The charity of St. Stephen, the apostle of his kingdom, relieved and conducted his itinerant brethren; and from Belgrade to Antioch, they traversed fifteen hundred miles of a Christian empire. Among the Franks, the zeal of pilgrimage prevailed beyond the example of former times: and the roads were covered with multitudes of either sex, and of every rank, who professed their contempt of life, so soon as they should have kissed the tomb of their Redeemer. Princes and prelates abandoned the care of their dominions; and the numbers of these pious caravans were a prelude to the armies which marched in the ensuing age under the banner of the cross. About thirty years before the first crusade, the arch bishop of Mentz, with the bishops of Utrecht, Bamberg, and Ratisbon, undertook this laborious journey from the Rhine to the Jordan; and the multitude of their followers amounted to seven thousand persons. At Constantinople, they were hospitably entertained by the emperor; but the ostentation of their wealth provoked the assault of the wild Arabs: they drew their swords with scrupulous reluctance, and sustained siege in the village of Capernaum, till they were rescued by the venal protection of the Fatimite emir. After visiting the holy places, they embarked for Italy, but only a remnant of two thousand arrived in safety in their native land. Ingulphus, a secretary of William the Conqueror, was a companion of this pilgrimage: he observes that they sailed from Normandy, thirty stout and well-appointed horsemen; but that they repassed the Alps, twenty miserable palmers, with the staff in their hand, and the wallet at their back.

After the defeat of the Romans, the tranquillity of the Fatimite caliphs was invaded by the Turks. One of the lieutenants of Malek Shah, Atsiz the Carizmian, marched into Syria at the head of a powerful army, and reduced Damascus by famine and the sword. Hems, and the other cities of the province, acknowledged the caliph of Bagdad and the sultan of Persia; and the victorious emir advanced without resistance to the banks of the Nile: the Fatimite was preparing to fly into the heart of Africa; but the negroes of his guard and the inhabitants of Cairo made a desperate sally, and repulsed the Turk from the confines of Egypt. In his retreat he indulged the license of slaughter and rapine: the judge and notaries of Jerusalem were invited to his camp; and their execution was followed by the massacre of three thousand citizens. The cruelty or the defeat of Atsiz was soon punished by the sultan Toucush, the brother of Malek Shah, who, with a higher title and more formidable powers, asserted the dominion of Syria and Palestine.

The house of Seljuk reigned about twenty years in Jerusalem; but the hereditary command of the holy city and territory was intrusted or abandoned to the emir Ortok, the chief of a tribe of Turkmans, whose children, after their expulsion from Palestine, formed two dynasties on the borders of Armenia and Assyria. The Oriental Christians and the Latin pilgrims deplored a revolution, which, instead of the regular government and old alliance of the caliphs, imposed on their necks the iron yoke of the strangers of the North. In his court and camp the great sultan had adopted in some degree the arts and manners of Persia; but the body of the Turkish nation, and more especially the pastoral tribes, still breathed the fierceness of the desert. From Nice to Jerusalem, the western countries of Asia were a scene of foreign and domestic hostility; and the shepherds of Palestine, who held a precarious sway on a doubtful frontier, had neither leisure nor capacity to await the slow profits of commercial and religious freedom. The pilgrims, who, through innumerable perils, had reached the gates of Jerusalem, were the victims of private rapine or public oppression, and often sunk under the pressure of famine and disease, before they were permitted to salute the holy sepulchre. A spirit of native barbarism, or recent zeal, prompted the Turkmans to insult the clergy of every sect: the patriarch was dragged by the hair along the pavement, and cast into a dungeon, to extort a ransom from the sympathy of his flock; and the divine worship in the church of the Resurrection was often disturbed by the savage rudeness of its masters. The pathetic tale excited the millions of the West to march under the standard of the cross to the relief of the Holy Land; and yet how trifling is the sum of these accumulated evils, if compared with the single act of the sacrilege of Hakem, which had been so patiently endured by the Latin Christians! A slighter provocation inflamed the more irascible temper of their descendants: a new spirit had arisen of religious chivalry and papal dominion; a nerve was touched of exquisite feeling; and the sensation vibrated to the heart of Europe.

The First Crusade. – Part One

Origin and Numbers of the First Crusade. – Characters of the Latin Princes. – Their March to Constantinople. – Policy of the Greek Emperor Alexius. – Conquest of Nice, Antioch, and Jerusalem, by the Franks. – Deliverance of the Holy Sepulchre. – Godfrey of Bouillon, First King of Jerusalem. – Institutions of the French or Latin Kingdom.

ABOUT TWENTY YEARS AFTER the conquest of Jerusalem by the Turks, the holy sepulchre was visited by a hermit of the name of Peter, a native of Amiens, in the province of Picardy in France. His resentment and sympathy were excited by his own injuries and the oppression of the Christian name; he mingled his tears with those of the patriarch, and earnestly inquired, if no hopes of relief could be entertained from the Greek emperors of the East. The patriarch exposed the vices and weakness of the successors of Constantine. "I will rouse," exclaimed the hermit, "the martial nations of Europe in your cause;" and Europe was obedient to the call of the hermit. The astonished patriarch dismissed him with epistles of credit and complaint; and no sooner did he land at Bari, than Peter hastened to kiss the feet of the Roman pontiff. His stature was small, his appearance contemptible; but his eye was keen and lively; and he possessed that vehemence of speech, which seldom fails to impart the persuasion of the soul. He was born of a gentleman's family, (for we must now adopt a modern idiom,) and his military service was under the neighboring counts of Boulogne, the heroes of the first crusade. But he soon relinquished the sword and the world; and if it be true, that his wife, however noble, was aged and ugly, he might withdraw, with the less reluctance, from her bed to a convent, and at length to a hermitage. * In this austere solitude, his body was emaciated, his fancy was inflamed; whatever he wished, he believed; whatever he believed, he saw in dreams and revelations. From Jerusalem the pilgrim returned an accomplished fanatic; but as he excelled in the popular madness of the times, Pope Urban the Second received him as a prophet, applauded his glorious design, promised to support it in a general council, and encouraged him to proclaim the deliverance of the Holy Land. Invigorated by the approbation of the pontiff, his zealous missionary traversed. with speed and success, the provinces of Italy and France. His diet was abstemious, his prayers long and fervent, and the alms which he received with one hand, he distributed with the other: his head was bare, his feet naked, his meagre body was wrapped in a coarse garment; he bore and displayed a weighty crucifix; and the ass on which he rode was sanctified, in the public eye, by the service of the man of God. He preached to innumerable crowds in the churches, the streets, and the highways: the hermit entered with equal confidence the palace and the cottage; and the people (for all was people) was impetuously moved by his call to repentance and arms. When he painted the sufferings of the natives and pilgrims of Palestine, every heart was melted to compassion; every breast glowed with indignation, when he challenged the warriors of the age to defend their brethren, and rescue their Savior: his ignorance of art and language was compensated by sighs, and tears, and ejaculations; and Peter supplied the deficiency of reason by loud and frequent appeals to Christ and his mother, to the saints and angels of paradise, with whom he had personally conversed. The most perfect orator of Athens might have envied the success of his eloquence; the rustic enthusiast inspired the passions which he felt, and Christendom expected with impatience the counsels and decrees of the supreme pontiff.

The magnanimous spirit of Gregory the Seventh had already embraced the design of arming Europe against Asia; the ardor of his zeal and ambition still breathes in his epistles: from either side of the Alps, fifty thousand Catholics had enlisted under the banner of St. Peter; and his successor reveals his intention of marching at their head against the impious sectaries of Mahomet. But the glory or reproach of executing, though not in person, this holy enterprise, was reserved for Urban the Second, the most faithful of his disciples. He undertook the conquest of the East, whilst the larger portion of Rome was possessed and fortified by his rival Guibert of Ravenna, who contended with Urban for the name and honors of the pontificate. He attempted to unite the powers of the West, at a time when the princes were separated from the church, and the people from their princes, by the excommunication which himself and his predecessors had thundered against the emperor and the king of France. Philip the First, of France, supported with patience the censures which he had provoked by his scandalous life and adulterous marriage. Henry the Fourth, of Germany, asserted the right of investitures, the prerogative of confirming his bishops by the delivery of the ring and crosier. But the emperor's party was crushed in Italy by the arms of the Normans and the Countess Mathilda; and the long quarrel had been recently envenomed by the revolt of his son Conrad and the shame of his wife, who, in the synods of Constance and Placentia, confessed the manifold prostitutions to which she had been exposed by a husband regardless of her honor and his own. So popular was the cause of Urban, so weighty was his influence, that the council which he summoned at Placentia was composed of two hundred bishops of Italy, France, Burgandy, Swabia, and Bavaria. Four thousand of the clergy, and thirty thousand of the laity, attended this important meeting; and, as the most spacious cathedral would have been inadequate to the multitude, the session of seven days was held in a plain adjacent to the city. The ambassadors of the Greek emperor, Alexius Comnenus, were introduced to plead the distress of their sovereign, and the danger of Constantinople, which was divided only by a narrow sea from the victorious Turks, the common enemies of the Christian name. In their suppliant address they flattered the pride of the Latin princes; and, appealing at once to their policy and religion, exhorted them to repel the Barbarians on the confines of Asia, rather than to expect them in the heart of Europe. At the sad tale of the misery and perils of their Eastern brethren, the assembly burst into tears; the most eager champions declared their readiness to march; and the Greek ambassadors were dismissed with the assurance of a speedy and powerful succor. The relief of Constantinople was included in the larger and most distant project of the deliverance of Jerusalem; but the prudent Urban adjourned the final decision to a second synod, which he proposed to celebrate in some city of France in the autumn of the same year. The short delay would propagate the flame of enthusiasm; and his firmest hope was in a nation of soldiers still proud of the preëminence of their name, and ambitious to emulate their hero Charlemagne, who, in the popular romance of Turpin, had achieved the conquest of the Holy Land. A latent motive of affection or vanity might influence the choice of Urban: he was himself a native of France, a monk of Clugny, and the first of his countrymen who ascended the throne of St. Peter. The pope had illustrated his family and province; nor is there perhaps a more exquisite gratification than to revisit, in a conspicuous dignity, the humble and laborious scenes of our youth.

It may occasion some surprise that the Roman pontiff should erect, in the heart of France, the tribunal from whence he hurled his anathemas against the king; but our surprise will vanish so soon as we form a just estimate of a king of France of the eleventh century. Philip the First was the great-grandson of Hugh Capet, the founder of the present race, who, in the decline of Charlemagne's posterity, added the regal title to his patrimonial estates of Paris and Orleans. In this narrow compass, he was possessed of wealth and jurisdiction; but in the rest of France, Hugh and his first descendants were no more than the feudal lords of about sixty dukes and counts, of independent and hereditary power, who disdained the control of laws and legal assemblies, and whose disregard of their sovereign was revenged by the disobedience of their inferior vassals. At Clermont, in the territories of the count of Auvergne, the pope might brave with impunity the resentment of Philip; and the council which he convened in that city was not less numerous or respectable than the synod of Placentia. Besides his court and council of Roman cardinals, he was supported by thirteen archbishops and two hundred and twenty-five bishops: the number of mitred prelates was computed at four hundred; and the fathers of the church were blessed by the saints and enlightened by the doctors of the age. From the adjacent kingdoms, a martial train of lords and knights of power and renown attended the council, in high expectation of its resolves; and such was the ardor of zeal and curiosity, that the city was filled, and many thousands, in the month of November, erected their tents or huts in the open field. A session of eight days produced some useful or edifying canons for the reformation of manners; a severe censure was pronounced against the license of private war; the Truce of God was confirmed, a suspension of hostilities during four days of the week; women and priests were placed under the safeguard of the church; and a protection of three years was extended to husbandmen and merchants, the defenceless victims of military rapine. But a law, however venerable be the sanction, cannot suddenly transform the temper of the times; and the benevolent efforts of Urban deserve the less praise, since he labored to appease some domestic quarrels that he might spread the flames of war from the Atlantic to the Euphrates. From the synod of Placentia, the rumor of his great design had gone forth among the nations: the clergy on their return had preached in every diocese the merit and glory of the deliverance of the Holy Land; and when the pope ascended a lofty scaffold in the market-place of Clermont, his eloquence was addressed to a well-prepared and impatient audience. His topics were obvious, his exhortation was vehement, his success inevitable. The orator was interrupted by the shout of thousands, who with one voice, and in their rustic idiom, exclaimed aloud, "God wills it, God wills it." "It is indeed the will of God," replied the pope; "and let this memorable word, the inspiration surely of the Holy Spirit, be forever adopted as your cry of battle, to animate the devotion and courage of the champions of Christ. His cross is the symbol of your salvation; wear it, a red, a bloody cross, as an external mark, on your breasts or shoulders, as a pledge of your sacred and irrevocable engagement." The proposal was joyfully accepted; great numbers, both of the clergy and laity, impressed on their garments the sign of the cross, and solicited the pope to march at their head. This dangerous honor was declined by the more prudent successor of Gregory, who alleged the schism of the church, and the duties of his pastoral office, recommending to the faithful, who were disqualified by sex or profession, by age or infirmity, to aid, with their prayers and alms, the personal service of their robust brethren. The name and powers of his legate he devolved on Adhemar bishop of Puy, the first who had received the cross at his hands. The foremost of the temporal chiefs was Raymond count of Thoulouse, whose ambassadors in the council excused the absence, and pledged the honor, of their master. After the confession and absolution of their sins, the champions of the cross were dismissed with a superfluous admonition to invite their countrymen and friends; and their departure for the Holy Land was fixed to the festival of the Assumption, the fifteenth of August, of the ensuing year.

So familiar, and as it were so natural to man, is the practice of violence, that our indulgence allows the slightest provocation, the most disputable right, as a sufficient ground of national hostility. But the name and nature of a *holy war* demands a more rigorous scrutiny; nor can we hastily believe, that the servants of the Prince of Peace would unsheathe the sword of destruction, unless the motive were pure, the quarrel legitimate, and the necessity inevitable. The policy of an action may be determined from the tardy lessons of experience; but, before we act, our conscience should be satisfied of the justice and propriety of our enterprise. In the age of the crusades, the Christians, both of the East and West, were persuaded of their lawfulness and merit; their arguments are clouded by the perpetual abuse of Scripture and rhetoric; but they seem to insist on the right of natural and religious defence, their peculiar title to the Holy Land, and the impiety of their Pagan and Mahometan foes. I. The right of a just defence may fairly include our civil and spiritual allies: it depends on the existence of danger; and that danger must be estimated by the twofold consideration of the malice, and the power, of our enemies. A pernicious tenet has been imputed to the Mahometans, the duty of *extirpating* all other religions by the sword. This charge of ignorance and bigotry is refuted by the Koran, by the history of the Mussulman conquerors, and by their public and legal toleration of the Christian worship. But it cannot be denied, that the Oriental churches are depressed under their iron yoke; that, in peace and war, they assert a divine and indefeasible claim of universal empire; and that, in their orthodox creed, the unbelieving nations are continually threatened with the loss of religion or liberty. In the eleventh century, the victorious arms of the Turks presented a real and urgent apprehension of these losses. They had subdued, in less than thirty years, the kingdoms of Asia, as far as Jerusalem and the Hellespont; and the Greek empire tottered on the verge of destruction. Besides an honest sympathy for their brethren, the Latins had a right and interest in the support of Constantinople, the most important barrier of the West; and the privilege of defence must reach to prevent, as well as to repel, an impending assault. But this salutary purpose might have been accomplished by a moderate succor; and our calmer reason must disclaim the innumerable hosts, and remote operations, which overwhelmed Asia and depopulated Europe. II. Palestine could add nothing to the strength or safety of the Latins; and fanaticism alone could pretend to justify the conquest of that distant and narrow province. The Christians affirmed that their inalienable title to the promised land had been sealed by the blood of their divine Savior; it was their right and duty to rescue their inheritance from the unjust possessors, who profaned his sepulchre, and oppressed the pilgrimage of his disciples. Vainly would it be alleged that the preëminence of Jerusalem, and the sanctity of Palestine, have been abolished with the Mosaic law; that the God of the Christians is not a local deity, and that the recovery of Bethlem or Calvary, his cradle or his tomb, will not atone for the violation of the moral precepts of the gospel. Such arguments glance aside from the leaden shield of superstition; and the religious mind will not easily relinquish its hold on the sacred ground of mystery and miracle. III. But the holy wars which have been waged in every climate of the globe, from Egypt to Livonia, and from Peru to Hindostan, require the support of some more general and flexible tenet. It has been often supposed, and sometimes affirmed, that a difference of religion is a worthy cause of hostility; that obstinate unbelievers may be slain or subdued by the champions of the cross; and that grace is the sole fountain of dominion as well as of mercy. Above four hundred years before the first crusade, the eastern and western provinces of the Roman empire had been acquired about the same time, and in the same manner, by the Barbarians of Germany and Arabia. Time and treaties had legitimated the conquest of the *Christian* Franks; but in the eyes of their subjects and neighbors, the Mahometan princes were still tyrants and usurpers, who, by the arms of war or rebellion, might be lawfully driven from their unlawful possession.

As the manners of the Christians were relaxed, their discipline of penance was enforced; and with the multiplication of sins, the remedies were multiplied. In the primitive church, a voluntary and open confession prepared the work of atonement. In the middle ages, the bishops and priests interrogated the criminal; compelled him to account for his thoughts, words, and actions; and prescribed the terms of his reconciliation with God. But as this discretionary power might alternately be abused by indulgence and tyranny, a rule of discipline was framed, to inform and regulate the spiritual judges. This mode of legislation was invented by the Greeks; their *penitentials* were translated, or imitated, in the Latin church; and, in the time of Charlemagne, the clergy of every diocese were provided with a code, which they prudently concealed from the knowledge of the vulgar. In this dangerous estimate of crimes and punishments, each case was supposed, each difference was remarked, by the experience or penetration of the monks; some sins are enumerated which innocence could not have suspected, and others which reason cannot believe; and the more ordinary offences of fornication and adultery, of perjury and sacrilege, of rapine and murder, were expiated by a penance, which, according to the various circumstances, was prolonged from forty days to seven years. During this term of mortification, the patient was healed, the criminal was absolved, by a salutary regimen of fasts and prayers: the disorder of his dress was expressive of grief and remorse; and he humbly abstained from all the business and pleasure of social life. But the rigid execution of these laws would have depopulated the palace, the camp, and the city; the Barbarians of the West believed and trembled; but nature often rebelled against principle; and the magistrate labored without effect to enforce the jurisdiction of the priest. A literal accomplishment of penance was indeed impracticable: the guilt of adultery was multiplied by daily repetition; that of homicide might involve the massacre of a whole people; each act was separately numbered; and, in those times of anarchy and vice, a modest sinner might easily incur a debt of three hundred years. His insolvency was relieved by a commutation, or *indulgence*: a year of penance was appreciated at twenty-six *solidi* of silver, about four pounds sterling, for the rich; at three solidi, or nine shillings, for the indigent: and these alms were soon appropriated to the use of the church, which derived, from the redemption of sins, an inexhaustible source of opulence and dominion. A debt of three hundred years, or twelve hundred pounds, was enough to impoverish a plentiful fortune; the scarcity of gold and silver was supplied by the alienation of land; and the princely donations of Pepin and Charlemagne are expressly given for the *remedy* of their soul. It is a maxim of the civil law, that whosoever cannot pay with his purse, must pay with his body; and the practice of flagellation was adopted by the monks, a cheap, though painful equivalent. By a fantastic arithmetic, a year of penance was taxed at three thousand lashes; and such was the skill and patience of a famous hermit, St. Dominic of the iron Cuirass, that in six days he could discharge an entire century, by a whipping of three hundred thousand stripes. His example was followed by many penitents of both sexes; and, as a vicarious sacrifice was accepted, a sturdy disciplinarian might expiate on his own back the sins of his benefactors. These compensations of the purse and the person introduced, in the eleventh century, a more honorable mode of satisfaction. The merit of military service against the Saracens of Africa and Spain had been allowed by the predecessors of Urban the Second. In the council of Clermont, that pope proclaimed a *plenary indulgence* to those who should enlist under the banner of the cross; the absolution of all their sins, and a full receipt for *all* that might be due of canonical penance. The cold philosophy of modern times is incapable of feeling the impression that was made on a sinful and fanatic world. At the voice of their pastor, the robber, the incendiary, the homicide, arose by thousands to redeem their souls, by repeating on the infidels the same deeds which they had exercised against their Christian brethren; and the terms of atonement were eagerly embraced by offenders of every rank and denomination. None were pure; none were exempt from the guilt and penalty of sin; and those who were the least amenable to the justice of God and the church were the best entitled to the temporal and eternal recompense of their pious courage. If they fell, the spirit of the Latin clergy did not hesitate to adorn their tomb with the crown of martyrdom; and should they survive, they could expect without impatience the delay and increase of their heavenly reward. They offered their blood to the Son of God, who had laid down his life for their salvation: they took up the cross, and entered with confidence into the way of the Lord. His providence would watch over their safety; perhaps his visible and miraculous power would smooth the difficulties of their holy enterprise. The cloud and pillar of Jehovah had marched before the Israelites into the promised land. Might not the Christians more reasonably hope that the rivers would open for their passage; that the walls of their strongest cities would fall at the sound of their trumpets; and that the sun would be arrested in his mid career, to allow them time for the destruction of the infidels?

The First Crusade. – Part Two

OF THE CHIEFS AND soldiers who marched to the holy sepulchre, I will dare to affirm, that *all* were prompted by the spirit of enthusiasm; the belief of merit, the hope of reward, and the assurance of divine aid. But I am equally persuaded, that in many it was not the sole, that in *some* it was not the leading, principle of action. The use and abuse of religion are feeble to stem, they are strong and irresistible to impel, the stream of national manners. Against the private wars of the Barbarians, their bloody tournaments, licentious love, and judicial duels, the popes and synods might ineffectually thunder. It is a more easy task to provoke the metaphysical disputes of the Greeks, to drive into the cloister the victims of anarchy or despotism, to sanctify the patience of slaves and cowards, or to assume the merit of the humanity and benevolence of modern Christians. War and exercise were the reigning passions of the Franks or Latins; they were enjoined, as a penance, to gratify those passions, to visit distant lands, and to draw their swords against the nation of the East. Their victory, or even their attempt, would immortalize the names of the intrepid heroes of the cross; and the purest piety could not be insensible to the most splendid prospect of military glory. In the petty quarrels of Europe, they shed the blood of their friends and countrymen, for the acquisition perhaps of a castle or a village. They could march with alacrity against the distant and hostile nations who were devoted to their arms; their fancy already grasped the golden sceptres of Asia; and the conquest of Apulia and Sicily by the Normans might exalt to royalty the hopes of the most private adventurer. Christendom, in her rudest state, must have yielded to the climate and cultivation of the Mahometan countries; and their natural and artificial wealth had been magnified by the tales of pilgrims, and the gifts of an imperfect commerce. The vulgar, both the great and small, were taught to believe every wonder, of lands flowing with milk and honey, of mines and treasures, of gold and diamonds, of palaces of marble and jasper, and of odoriferous groves of cinnamon and frankincense. In this earthly paradise, each warrior depended on his sword to carve a plenteous and honorable establishment, which he measured only by the extent of his wishes. Their vassals and soldiers trusted their fortunes to God and their master: the spoils of a Turkish emir might enrich the meanest follower of the camp; and the flavor of the wines, the beauty of the Grecian women, were temptations more adapted to the nature, than to the profession, of the champions of the cross. The love of freedom was a powerful incitement to the multitudes who were oppressed by feudal or ecclesiastical tyranny. Under this holy sign, the peasants and burghers, who were attached to the servitude of the glebe, might escape from a haughty lord, and transplant themselves and their families to a land of liberty. The monk might release himself from the discipline of his convent: the debtor might suspend the accumulation of usury, and the pursuit of his creditors; and outlaws and malefactors of every cast might continue to brave the laws and elude the punishment of their crimes.

These motives were potent and numerous: when we have singly computed their weight on the mind of each individual, we must add the infinite series, the multiplying powers, of example and fashion. The first proselytes became the warmest and most effectual missionaries of the cross: among their friends and countrymen they preached the duty, the merit, and the recompense, of their holy vow; and the most reluctant hearers were insensibly drawn within the whirlpool of persuasion and authority. The martial youths were fired by the reproach or suspicion of cowardice; the opportunity of visiting with an army the sepulchre of Christ was embraced by the old and infirm, by women and children, who consulted rather their zeal than their strength; and those who in the evening had derided the folly of their companions, were the most eager, the ensuing day, to tread in their footsteps. The ignorance, which magnified the hopes, diminished the perils, of the enterprise. Since the Turkish conquest, the paths of pilgrimage were obliterated; the chiefs themselves had an imperfect notion of the length of the way and the state of their enemies; and such was the stupidity of the people, that, at the sight of the first city or castle beyond the limits of their knowledge, they were ready to ask whether that was not the Jerusalem, the term and object of their labors. Yet the more prudent of the crusaders, who were not sure that they should be fed from heaven with a shower of quails or manna, provided themselves with those precious metals, which, in every country, are the representatives of every commodity. To defray, according to their rank, the expenses of the road, princes alienated their provinces, nobles their lands and castles, peasants their cattle and the instruments of husbandry. The value of property was depreciated by the eager competition of multitudes; while the price of arms and horses was raised to an exorbitant height by the wants and impatience of the buyers. Those who remained at home, with sense and money, were enriched by the epidemical disease: the sovereigns acquired at a cheap rate the domains of their vassals; and the ecclesiastical purchasers completed the payment by the assurance of their prayers. The cross, which was commonly sewed on the garment, in cloth or silk, was inscribed by some zealots on their skin: a hot iron, or indelible liquor, was applied to perpetuate the mark; and a crafty monk, who showed the miraculous impression on his breast was repaid with the popular veneration and the richest benefices of Palestine.

The fifteenth of August had been fixed in the council of Clermont for the departure of the pilgrims; but the day was anticipated by the thoughtless and needy crowd of plebeians, and I shall briefly despatch the calamities which they inflicted and suffered, before I enter on the more serious and successful enterprise of the chiefs. Early in the spring, from the confines of France and Lorraine, above sixty thousand of the populace of both sexes flocked round the first missionary of the crusade, and pressed him with clamorous importunity to lead them to the holy sepulchre. The hermit, assuming the character, without the talents or authority, of a general, impelled or obeyed the forward impulse of his votaries along the banks of the Rhine and Danube. Their wants and numbers soon compelled them to separate, and his lieutenant, Walter the Penniless, a valiant though needy soldier, conducted a van guard of pilgrims, whose condition may be determined from the proportion of eight horsemen to fifteen thousand foot. The example and footsteps of Peter were closely pursued by another fanatic, the monk Godescal, whose sermons had swept away fifteen or twenty thousand peasants from the villages of Germany. Their rear was again pressed by a herd of two hundred thousand, the most stupid and savage refuse of the people, who mingled with their devotion a brutal license of rapine, prostitution, and drunkenness. Some counts and gentlemen, at the head of three thousand horse, attended the motions of the multitude to partake in the spoil; but their genuine leaders (may we credit such folly?) were a goose and a goat, who were carried in the front, and to whom these worthy Christians ascribed an infusion of the divine spirit. Of these, and of other bands of enthusiasts, the first and most easy warfare was against the Jews, the murderers of the Son of God. In the trading cities of the Moselle and the Rhine, their colonies were numerous and rich; and they enjoyed, under the protection of the emperor and the bishops, the free exercise of their religion. At Verdun, Treves, Mentz, Spires, Worms, many thousands of that unhappy people were pillaged and massacred: nor had they felt a more bloody stroke since the persecution of Hadrian. A remnant was saved by the firmness of their bishops, who accepted a feigned and transient conversion; but the more obstinate Jews opposed their fanaticism to the fanaticism of the Christians, barricadoed their houses, and precipitating themselves, their families, and their wealth, into the rivers or the flames, disappointed the malice, or at least the avarice, of their implacable foes.

Between the frontiers of Austria and the seat of the Byzantine monarchy, the crusaders were compelled to traverse as interval of six hundred miles; the wild and desolate countries of Hungary and Bulgaria. The soil is fruitful, and intersected with rivers; but it was then covered with morasses and forests, which spread to a boundless extent, whenever man has ceased to exercise his dominion over the earth. Both nations had imbibed the rudiments of Christianity; the Hungarians were ruled by their native princes; the Bulgarians by a lieutenant of the Greek emperor; but, on the slightest provocation, their ferocious nature was rekindled, and ample provocation was afforded by the disorders of the first pilgrims Agriculture must have been unskilful and languid among a people, whose cities were built of reeds and timber, which were deserted in the summer season for the tents of hunters and shepherds. A scanty supply of provisions was rudely demanded, forcibly seized, and greedily consumed; and on the first quarrel, the crusaders gave a loose to indignation and revenge. But their ignorance of the country, of war, and of discipline, exposed them to every snare. The Greek præfect of Bulgaria commanded a regular force; at the trumpet of the Hungarian king, the eighth or the tenth of his martial subjects bent their bows and mounted on horseback; their policy was insidious, and their retaliation on these pious robbers was unrelenting and bloody. About a third of the naked fugitives (and the hermit Peter was of the number) escaped to the Thracian mountains; and the emperor, who respected the pilgrimage and succor of the Latins, conducted them by secure and easy journeys to Constantinople, and advised them to await the arrival of their brethren. For a while they remembered their faults and losses; but no sooner were they revived by the hospitable entertainment, than their venom was again inflamed; they stung their benefactor, and neither gardens, nor palaces, nor churches, were safe from their depredations. For his own safety, Alexius allured them to pass over to the Asiatic side of the Bosphorus; but their blind impetuosity soon urged them to desert the station which he had assigned, and to rush headlong against the Turks, who occupied the road to Jerusalem. The hermit, conscious of his shame, had withdrawn from the camp to Constantinople; and his lieutenant, Walter the Penniless, who was worthy of a better command, attempted without success to introduce some order and prudence among the herd of savages. They separated in quest of prey, and themselves fell an easy prey to the arts of the sultan. By a rumor that their foremost companions were rioting in the spoils of his capital, Soliman tempted the main body to descend into the plain of Nice: they were overwhelmed by the Turkish arrows; and a pyramid of bones informed their companions of the place of their defeat. Of the first crusaders, three hundred thousand had already perished, before a single city was rescued from the infidels, before their graver and more noble brethren had completed the preparations of their enterprise.

"To save time and space, I shall represent, in a short table, the particular references to the great events of the first crusade."

[See Table 1.: Events Of The First Crusade.]

None of the great sovereigns of Europe embarked their persons in the first crusade. The emperor Henry the Fourth was not disposed to obey the summons of the pope: Philip the First of France was occupied by his pleasures; William Rufus of England by a recent conquest; the kings of Spain were engaged in a domestic war against the Moors; and the northern monarchs of Scotland, Denmark, Sweden, and Poland, were yet strangers to the passions and interests of the South. The religious ardor was more strongly felt by the princes of the second order, who held an important place in the feudal system. Their situation will naturally cast under four distinct heads the review of their names and characters; but I may escape some needless repetition, by observing at once, that courage and the exercise of arms are the common attribute of these Christian adventurers. I. The first rank both in war and council is justly due to Godfrey of Bouillon; and happy would it have been for the crusaders, if they had trusted themselves to the sole conduct of that accomplished hero, a worthy representative of Charlemagne, from whom he was descended in the female line. His father was of the noble race of the counts of Boulogne: Brabant, the lower province of Lorraine, was the inheritance of his mother; and by the emperor's bounty he was himself invested with that ducal title, which has been improperly transferred to his lordship of Bouillon in the Ardennes. In the service of Henry the Fourth, he bore the great standard of the empire, and pierced with his lance the breast of Rodolph, the rebel king: Godfrey was the first who ascended the walls of Rome; and his sickness, his vow, perhaps his remorse for bearing arms against the pope, confirmed an early resolution of visiting the holy sepulchre, not as a pilgrim, but a deliverer. His valor was matured by prudence and moderation; his piety, though blind, was sincere; and, in the tumult of a camp, he practised the real and fictitious virtues of a convent. Superior to the private factions of the chiefs, he reserved his enmity for the enemies of Christ; and though he gained a kingdom by the attempt, his pure and disinterested zeal was acknowledged by his rivals. Godfrey of Bouillon was accompanied by his two brothers, by Eustace the elder, who had succeeded to the county of Boulogne, and by the younger, Baldwin, a character of more ambiguous virtue. The duke of Lorraine, was alike celebrated on either side of the Rhine: from his birth and education, he was equally conversant with the French and Teutonic languages: the barons of France, Germany, and Lorraine, assembled their vassals; and the confederate force that marched under his banner was composed of fourscore thousand foot and about ten thousand horse. II. In the parliament that was held at Paris, in the king's presence, about two months after the council of Clermont, Hugh, count of Vermandois, was the most conspicuous of the princes who assumed the cross. But the appellation of *the Great* was applied, not so much to his merit or possessions, (though neither were contemptible,) as to the royal birth of the brother of the king of France. Robert, duke of Normandy, was the eldest son of William the Conqueror; but on his father's death he was deprived of the kingdom of England, by his own indolence and the activity of his brother Rufus. The worth of Robert was degraded by an excessive levity and easiness of temper: his cheerfulness seduced him to the indulgence of pleasure; his profuse liberality impoverished the prince and people; his indiscriminate clemency multiplied the number of offenders; and the amiable qualities of a private man became the essential defects of a sovereign. For the trifling sum of ten thousand marks, he mortgaged Normandy during his absence to the English usurper; but his engagement and behavior in the holy war announced in Robert a reformation of manners, and restored him in some degree to the public esteem. Another Robert was count of Flanders, a royal province, which, in this century, gave three queens to the thrones of France, England, and Denmark: he was surnamed the Sword and Lance of the Christians; but in the exploits of a soldier he sometimes forgot the duties of a general. Stephen, count of Chartres, of Blois, and of Troyes, was one of the richest princes of the age; and the number of his castles has been compared to the three hundred and sixty-five days of the year. His mind was improved by literature; and, in the council of the chiefs, the eloquent Stephen was chosen to discharge the office of their president. These four were the principal leaders of the French, the Normans, and the pilgrims of the British isles: but the list of the barons who were possessed of three or four towns would exceed, says a contemporary, the catalogue of the Trojan war. III. In the south of France, the command was assumed by Adhemar bishop of Puy, the pope legate, and by Raymond count of St. Giles and Thoulouse who added the prouder titles of duke of Narbonne and marquis of Provence. The former was a respectable prelate, alike qualified for this world and the next. The latter was a veteran warrior, who had fought against the Saracens of Spain, and who consecrated his declining age, not only to the deliverance, but to the perpetual service, of the holy sepulchre. His experience and riches gave him a strong ascendant in the Christian camp, whose distress he was often able, and sometimes willing, to relieve. But it was easier for him to extort the praise of the Infidels, than to preserve the love of his subjects and associates. His eminent qualities were clouded by a temper haughty, envious, and obstinate; and, though he resigned an ample patrimony for the cause of God, his piety, in the public opinion, was not exempt from avarice and ambition. A mercantile, rather than a martial, spirit prevailed among his *provincials*, a common name, which included the natives of Auvergne and Languedoc, the vassals of the kingdom of Burgundy or Arles. From the adjacent frontier of Spain he drew a band of hardy adventurers; as he marched through Lombardy, a crowd of Italians flocked to his standard, and his united force consisted of one hundred thousand horse and foot. If Raymond was the first to enlist and the last to depart, the delay may be excused by the greatness of his preparation and the promise of an everlasting farewell. IV. The name of Bohemond, the son of Robert Guiscard, was already famous by his double victory over the Greek emperor; but his father's will had reduced him to the principality of Tarentum, and the remembrance of his Eastern trophies, till he was awakened by the rumor and passage of the French pilgrims. It is in the person of this Norman chief that we may seek for the coolest policy and ambition, with a small allay of religious fanaticism. His conduct may justify a belief that he had secretly directed the design of the pope, which he affected to second with astonishment and zeal: at the siege of Amalphi, his example and discourse inflamed the passions of a confederate army; he instantly tore his garment to supply crosses for the numerous candidates, and prepared to visit Constantinople and Asia at the head of ten thousand horse and twenty thousand foot. Several princes of the Norman race accompanied this veteran general; and his cousin Tancred was the partner, rather than the servant, of the war. In the accomplished character of Tancred we discover all the virtues of a perfect knight, the true spirit of chivalry, which inspired the generous sentiments and social offices of man far better than the base philosophy, or the baser religion, of the times.

The First Crusade. – Part Three

BETWEEN THE AGE OF Charlemagne and that of the crusades, a revolution had taken place among the Spaniards, the Normans, and the
French, which was gradually extended to the rest of Europe. The service
of the infantry was degraded to the plebeians; the cavalry formed the
strength of the armies, and the honorable name of *miles*, or soldier, was
confined to the gentlemen who served on horseback, and were invested with the character of knighthood. The dukes and counts, who had
usurped the rights of sovereignty, divided the provinces among their
faithful barons: the barons distributed among their vassals the fiefs or
benefices of their jurisdiction; and these military tenants, the peers of
each other and of their lord, composed the noble or equestrian order,
which disdained to conceive the peasant or burgher as of the same species with themselves. The dignity of their birth was preserved by pure
and equal alliances; their sons alone, who could produce four quarters
or lines of ancestry without spot or reproach, might legally pretend to
the honor of knighthood; but a valiant plebeian was sometimes enriched and ennobled by the sword, and became the father of a new race.
A single knight could impart, according to his judgment, the character which he received; and the warlike sovereigns of Europe derived
more glory from this personal distinction than from the lustre of their
diadem. This ceremony, of which some traces may be found in Tacitus
and the woods of Germany, was in its origin simple and profane; the
candidate, after some previous trial, was invested with the sword and
spurs; and his cheek or shoulder was touched with a slight blow, as an
emblem of the last affront which it was lawful for him to endure. But
superstition mingled in every public and private action of life: in the
holy wars, it sanctified the profession of arms; and the order of chiv-

alry was assimilated in its rights and privileges to the sacred orders of priesthood. The bath and white garment of the novice were an indecent copy of the regeneration of baptism: his sword, which he offered on the altar, was blessed by the ministers of religion: his solemn reception was preceded by fasts and vigils; and he was created a knight in the name of God, of St. George, and of St. Michael the archangel. He swore to accomplish the duties of his profession; and education, example, and the public opinion, were the inviolable guardians of his oath. As the champion of God and the ladies, (I blush to unite such discordant names,) he devoted himself to speak the truth; to maintain the right; to protect the distressed; to practise *courtesy*, a virtue less familiar to the ancients; to pursue the infidels; to despise the allurements of ease and safety; and to vindicate in every perilous adventure the honor of his character. The abuse of the same spirit provoked the illiterate knight to disdain the arts of industry and peace; to esteem himself the sole judge and avenger of his own injuries; and proudly to neglect the laws of civil society and military discipline. Yet the benefits of this institution, to refine the temper of Barbarians, and to infuse some principles of faith, justice, and humanity, were strongly felt, and have been often observed. The asperity of national prejudice was softened; and the community of religion and arms spread a similar color and generous emulation over the face of Christendom. Abroad in enterprise and pilgrimage, at home in martial exercise, the warriors of every country were perpetually associated; and impartial taste must prefer a Gothic tournament to the Olympic games of classic antiquity. Instead of the naked spectacles which corrupted the manners of the Greeks, and banished from the stadium the virgins and matrons, the pompous decoration of the lists was crowned with the presence of chaste and high-born beauty, from whose hands the conqueror received the prize of his dexterity and courage. The skill and strength that were exerted in wrestling and boxing bear a distant and doubtful relation to the merit of a soldier; but the tournaments, as they were invented in France, and eagerly adopted both in the East and West, presented a lively image of the business of the field. The single combats, the general skirmish, the defence of a pass, or castle, were rehearsed as in actual service; and the contest, both in real and mimic war, was decided by the superior management of the horse and lance. The lance was the proper and peculiar weapon of the knight: his horse was of a large and heavy breed; but this charger, till he was roused by the approaching danger, was usually led by an attendant, and he quietly rode a pad or palfrey of a more easy pace. His helmet and sword, his greaves and buckler, it would be superfluous to describe; but I may remark, that, at the period of the crusades, the armor was less ponderous than in later times; and that, instead of a massy cuirass, his breast was defended by a hauberk or coat of mail. When their long lances were fixed in the rest, the warriors furiously spurred their horses against the foe; and the light cavalry of the Turks and Arabs could seldom stand against the direct and impetuous weight of their charge. Each knight was attended to the field by his faithful squire, a youth of equal birth and similar hopes; he was followed by his archers and men at arms, and four, or five, or six soldiers were computed as the furniture of a complete *lance*. In the expeditions to the neighboring kingdoms or the Holy Land, the duties of the feudal tenure no longer subsisted; the voluntary service of the knights and their followers were either prompted by zeal or attachment, or purchased with rewards and promises; and the numbers of each squadron were measured by the power, the wealth, and the fame, of each independent chieftain. They were distinguished by his banner, his armorial coat, and his cry of war; and the most ancient families of Europe must seek in these achievements the origin and proof of their nobility. In this rapid portrait of chivalry I have been urged to anticipate on the story of the crusades, at once an effect and a cause, of this memorable institution.

Such were the troops, and such the leaders, who assumed the cross for the deliverance of the holy sepulchre. As soon as they were relieved by the absence of the plebeian multitude, they encouraged each other, by interviews and messages, to accomplish their vow, and hasten their departure. Their wives and sisters were desirous of partaking the danger and merit of the pilgrimage: their portable treasures were conveyed in bars of silver and gold; and the princes and barons were attended by their equipage of hounds and hawks to amuse their leisure and to supply their table. The difficulty of procuring subsistence for so many myriads of men and horses engaged them to separate their forces: their choice or situation determined the road; and it was agreed to meet in the neighborhood of Constantinople, and from thence to begin their operations against the Turks. From the banks of the Meuse and the Moselle, Godfrey of Bouillon followed the direct way of Germany, Hungary, and Bulgaria; and, as long as he exercised the sole command every step afforded some proof of his prudence and virtue. On the confines of Hungary he was stopped three weeks by a Christian people, to whom the name, or at least the abuse, of the cross was justly odious. The Hungarians still smarted with the wounds which they had received from the first pilgrims: in their turn they had abused the right of defence and retaliation; and they had reason to apprehend a severe revenge from a hero of the same nation, and who was engaged in the same cause. But, after weighing the motives and the events, the virtuous duke was content to pity the crimes and misfortunes of his worthless brethren; and his twelve deputies, the messengers of peace, requested in his name a free passage and an equal market. To remove their suspicions, Godfrey trusted himself, and afterwards his brother, to the faith of Carloman, king of Hungary, who treated them with a simple but hospitable entertainment: the treaty was sanctified by their common gospel; and a proclamation, under pain of death, restrained the animosity and license of the Latin soldiers. From Austria to Belgrade, they traversed the plains of Hungary, without enduring or offering an injury; and the proximity of Carloman, who hovered on their flanks with his numerous cavalry, was a precaution not less useful for their safety than for his own. They reached the banks of the Save; and no sooner had they passed the river, than the king of Hungary restored the hostages, and saluted their departure with the fairest wishes for the success of their enterprise. With the same conduct and discipline, Godfrey pervaded the woods of Bulgaria and the frontiers of Thrace; and might congratulate himself that he had almost reached the first term of his pilgrimage, without drawing his sword against a Christian adversary. After an easy and pleasant journey through Lombardy, from Turin to Aquileia, Raymond and his provincials marched forty days through the savage country of Dalmatia and Sclavonia. The weather was a perpetual fog; the land was mountainous and desolate; the natives were either fugitive or hostile: loose in their religion and government, they refused to furnish provisions or guides; murdered the stragglers; and exercised by night and day the vigilance of the count, who derived more security from the punishment of some captive robbers than from his interview and treaty with the prince of Scodra. His march between Durazzo and Constantinople was harassed, without being stopped, by the peasants and soldiers of the Greek emperor; and the same faint and ambiguous hostility was prepared for the remaining chiefs, who passed the Adriatic from the coast of Italy. Bohemond had arms and vessels, and foresight and discipline; and his name was not forgotten in the provinces of Epirus and Thessaly. Whatever obstacles he encountered were surmounted by his military conduct and the valor of Tancred; and if the Norman prince affected to spare the Greeks, he gorged his soldiers with the full plunder of an heretical castle. The nobles of France pressed forwards with the vain and thoughtless ardor of which their nation has been sometimes accused. From the Alps to Apulia the march of Hugh the Great, of the two Roberts, and of Stephen of Chartres, through a wealthy country, and amidst the applauding Catholics, was a devout or triumphant progress: they kissed the feet of the Roman pontiff; and the golden standard of St. Peter was delivered to the brother of the French monarch. But in this visit of piety and pleasure, they neglected to secure the season, and the means of their embarkation: the winter was insensibly lost: their troops were scattered and corrupted in the towns of Italy. They separately accomplished their passage, regardless of safety or dignity; and within nine months from the feast of the Assumption, the day appointed by Urban, all the Latin princes had reached Constantinople. But the count of Vermandois was produced as a captive; his foremost vessels were scattered by a tempest; and his person, against the law of nations, was detained by the lieutenants of Alexius. Yet the arrival of Hugh had been announced by four-and-twenty knights in golden armor, who commanded the emperor to revere the general of the Latin Christians, the brother of the king of kings.

In some oriental tale I have read the fable of a shepherd, who was ruined by the accomplishment of his own wishes: he had prayed for water; the Ganges was turned into his grounds, and his flock and cottage were swept away by the inundation. Such was the fortune, or at least the apprehension of the Greek emperor Alexius Comnenus, whose name has already appeared in this history, and whose conduct is so differently represented by his daughter Anne, and by the Latin writers. In the council of Placentia, his ambassadors had solicited a moderate succor, perhaps of ten thousand soldiers, but he was astonished by the approach of so many potent chiefs and fanatic nations. The emperor fluctuated between hope and fear, between timidity and courage; but in the crooked policy which he mistook for wisdom, I cannot believe, I cannot discern, that he maliciously conspired against the life or honor of the French heroes. The promiscuous multitudes of Peter the Hermit were savage beasts, alike destitute of humanity and reason: nor was it possible for Alexius to prevent or deplore their destruction. The troops of Godfrey and his peers were less contemptible, but not less suspicious, to the Greek emperor. Their motives *might* be pure and pious: but he was equally alarmed by his knowledge of the ambitious Bohemond, and his ignorance of the Transalpine chiefs: the courage of the French was blind and headstrong; they might be tempted by the luxury and wealth of Greece, and elated by the view and opinion of their invincible strength: and Jerusalem might be forgotten in the prospect of Constantinople. After a long march and painful abstinence, the troops of Godfrey encamped in the plains of Thrace; they heard with indignation, that their brother, the count of Vermandois, was imprisoned by the Greeks; and their reluctant duke was compelled to indulge them in some freedom of retaliation and rapine. They were appeased by the submission of Alexius: he promised to supply their camp; and as they refused, in the midst of winter, to pass the Bosphorus, their quarters were assigned among the gardens and palaces on the shores of that narrow sea. But an incurable jealousy still rankled in the minds of the two nations, who despised each other as slaves and Barbarians. Ignorance is the ground of suspicion, and suspicion was inflamed into daily provocations: prejudice is blind, hunger is deaf; and Alexius is accused of a design to starve or assault the Latins in a dangerous post, on all sides encompassed with the waters. Godfrey sounded his trumpets, burst the net, overspread the plain, and insulted the suburbs; but the gates of Constantinople were strongly fortified; the ramparts were lined with archers; and, after a doubtful conflict, both parties listened to the voice of peace and religion. The gifts and promises of the emperor insensibly soothed the fierce spirit of the western strangers; as a Christian warrior, he rekindled their zeal for the prosecution of their holy enterprise, which he engaged to second with his troops and treasures. On the return of spring, Godfrey was persuaded to occupy a pleasant and plentiful camp in Asia; and no sooner had he passed the Bosphorus, than the Greek vessels were suddenly recalled to the opposite shore. The same policy was repeated with the succeeding chiefs, who were swayed by the example, and weakened by the departure, of their foremost companions. By his skill and diligence, Alexius prevented the union of any two of the confederate armies at the same moment under the walls of Constantinople; and before the feast of the Pentecost not a Latin pilgrim was left on the coast of Europe.

The same arms which threatened Europe might deliver Asia, and repel the Turks from the neighboring shores of the Bosphorus and Hellespont. The fair provinces from Nice to Antioch were the recent patrimony of the Roman emperor; and his ancient and perpetual claim still embraced the kingdoms of Syria and Egypt. In his enthusiasm, Alexius indulged, or affected, the ambitious hope of leading his new allies to subvert the thrones of the East; but the calmer dictates of reason and temper dissuaded him from exposing his royal person to the faith of unknown and lawless Barbarians. His prudence, or his pride, was content with extorting from the French princes an oath of homage and fidelity, and a solemn promise, that they would either restore, or hold, their Asiatic conquests as the humble and loyal vassals of the Roman empire. Their independent spirit was fired at the mention of this foreign and voluntary servitude: they successively yielded to the dexterous application of gifts and flattery; and the first proselytes became the most eloquent and effectual missionaries to multiply the companions of their shame. The pride of Hugh of Vermandois was soothed by the honors of his captivity; and in the brother of the French king, the example of submission was prevalent and weighty. In the mind of Godfrey of Bouillon every human consideration was subordinate to the glory of God and the success of the crusade. He had firmly resisted the temptations of Bohemond and Raymond, who urged the attack and conquest of Constantinople. Alexius esteemed his virtues, deservedly named him the champion of the empire, and dignified his homage with the filial name and the rights of adoption. The hateful Bohemond was received as a true and ancient ally; and if the emperor reminded him of former hostilities, it was only to praise the valor that he had displayed, and the glory that he had acquired, in the fields of Durazzo and Larissa. The son of Guiscard was lodged and entertained, and served with Imperial pomp: one day, as he passed through the gallery of the palace, a door was carelessly left open to expose a pile of gold and silver, of silk and gems, of curious and costly furniture, that was heaped, in seeming disorder, from the floor to the roof of the chamber. "What conquests," exclaimed the ambitious miser, "might not be achieved by the possession of such a treasure!" – "It is your own," replied a Greek attendant, who watched the motions of his soul; and Bohemond, after some hesitation, condescended to accept this magnificent present. The Norman was flattered by the assurance of an independent principality; and Alexius eluded, rather than denied, his daring demand of the office of great domestic, or general of the East. The two Roberts, the son of the conqueror of England, and the kinsmen of three queens, bowed in their turn before the Byzantine throne. A private letter of Stephen of Chartres attests his admiration of the emperor, the most excellent and liberal of men, who taught him to believe that he was a favorite, and promised to educate and establish his youngest son. In his southern province, the count of St. Giles and Thoulouse faintly recognized the supremacy of the king of France, a prince of a foreign nation and language. At the head of a hundred thousand men, he declared that he was the soldier and servant of Christ alone, and that the Greek might be satisfied with an equal treaty of alliance and friendship. His obstinate resistance enhanced the value and the price of his submission; and he shone, says the princess Anne, among the Barbarians, as the sun amidst the stars of heaven. His disgust of the noise and insolence of the French, his suspicions of the designs of Bohemond, the emperor imparted to his faithful Raymond; and that aged statesman might clearly discern, that however false in friendship, he was sincere in his enmity. The spirit of chivalry was last subdued in the person of Tancred; and none could deem themselves dishonored by the imitation of that gallant knight. He disdained the gold and flattery of the Greek monarch; assaulted in his presence an insolent patrician; escaped to Asia in the habit of a private soldier; and yielded with a sigh to the authority of Bohemond, and the interest of the Christian cause. The best and most ostensible reason was the impossibility of passing the sea and accomplishing their vow, without the license and the vessels of Alexius; but they cherished a secret hope, that as soon as they trod the continent of Asia, their swords would obliterate their shame, and dissolve the engagement, which on his side might not be very faithfully performed. The ceremony of their homage was grateful to a people who had long since considered pride as the substitute of power. High on his throne, the emperor sat mute and immovable: his majesty was adored by the Latin princes; and they submitted to kiss either his feet or his knees, an indignity which their own writers are ashamed to confess and unable to deny.

Private or public interest suppressed the murmurs of the dukes and counts; but a French baron (he is supposed to be Robert of Paris) presumed to ascend the throne, and to place himself by the side of Alexius. The sage reproof of Baldwin provoked him to exclaim, in his barbarous idiom, "Who is this rustic, that keeps his seat, while so many valiant captains are standing round him?" The emperor maintained his silence, dissembled his indignation, and questioned his interpreter concerning the meaning of the words, which he partly suspected from the universal language of gesture and countenance. Before the departure of the pilgrims, he endeavored to learn the name and condition of the audacious baron. "I am a Frenchman," replied Robert, "of the purest and most ancient nobility of my country. All that I know is, that there is a church in my neighborhood, the resort of those who are desirous of approving their valor in single combat. Till an enemy appears, they address their prayers to God and his saints. That church I have frequently visited. But never have I found an antagonist who dared to accept my defiance." Alexius dismissed the challenger with some prudent advice for his conduct in the Turkish warfare; and history repeats with pleasure this lively example of the manners of his age and country.

The conquest of Asia was undertaken and achieved by Alexander, with thirty-five thousand Macedonians and Greeks; and his best hope was in the strength and discipline of his phalanx of infantry. The principal force of the crusaders consisted in their cavalry; and when that force was mustered in the plains of Bithynia, the knights and their martial attendants on horseback amounted to one hundred thousand fighting men, completely armed with the helmet and coat of mail. The value of these soldiers deserved a strict and authentic account; and the flower of European chivalry might furnish, in a first effort, this formidable body of heavy horse. A part of the infantry might be enrolled for the service of scouts, pioneers, and archers; but the promiscuous crowd were lost in their own disorder; and we depend not on the eyes and knowledge, but on the belief and fancy, of a chaplain of Count Baldwin, in the estimate of six hundred thousand pilgrims able to bear arms, besides the priests and monks, the women and children of the Latin camp. The reader starts; and before he is recovered from his surprise, I shall add, on the same testimony, that if all who took the cross had accomplished their vow, above six millions would have migrated from Europe to Asia. Under this oppression of faith, I derive some relief from a more sagacious and thinking writer, who, after the same review of the cavalry, accuses the credulity of the priest of Chartres, and even doubts whether the *Cisalpine* regions (in the geography of a Frenchman) were sufficient to produce and pour forth such incredible multitudes. The coolest scepticism will remember, that of these religious volunteers great numbers never beheld Constantinople and Nice. Of enthusiasm the influence is irregular and transient: many were detained at home by reason or cowardice, by poverty or weakness; and many were repulsed by the obstacles of the way, the more insuperable as they were unforeseen, to these ignorant fanatics. The savage countries of Hungary and Bulgaria were whitened with their bones: their vanguard was cut in pieces by the Turkish sultan; and the loss of the first adventure, by the sword, or climate, or fatigue, has already been stated at three hundred thousand men. Yet the myriads that survived, that marched, that pressed forwards on the holy pilgrimage, were a subject of astonishment to themselves and to the Greeks. The copious energy of her language sinks under the efforts of the princess Anne: the images of locusts, of leaves and flowers, of the sands of the sea, or the stars of heaven, imperfectly represent what she had seen and heard; and the daughter of Alexius exclaims, that Europe was loosened from its foundations, and hurled against Asia. The ancient hosts of Darius and Xerxes labor under the same doubt of a vague and indefinite magnitude; but I am inclined to believe, that a larger number has never been contained within the lines of a single camp, than at the siege of Nice, the first operation of the Latin princes. Their motives, their characters, and their arms, have been already displayed. Of their troops the most numerous portion were natives of France: the Low Countries, the banks of the Rhine, and Apulia, sent a powerful reënforcement: some bands of adventurers were drawn from Spain, Lombardy, and England; and from the distant bogs and mountains of Ireland or Scotland issued some naked and savage fanatics, ferocious at home but unwarlike abroad. Had not superstition condemned the sacrilegious prudence of depriving the poorest or weakest Christian of the merit of the pilgrimage, the useless crowd, with mouths but without hands, might have been stationed in the Greek empire, till their companions had opened and secured the way of the Lord. A small remnant of the pilgrims, who passed the Bosphorus, was permitted to visit the holy sepulchre. Their northern constitution was scorched by the rays, and infected by the vapors, of a Syrian sun. They consumed, with heedless prodigality, their stores of water and provision: their numbers exhausted the inland country: the sea was remote, the Greeks were unfriendly, and the Christians of every sect fled before the voracious and cruel rapine of their brethren. In the dire necessity of famine, they sometimes roasted and devoured the flesh of their infant or adult captives. Among the Turks and Saracens, the idolaters of Europe were rendered more odious by the name and reputation of Cannibals; the spies, who introduced themselves into the kitchen of Bohemond, were shown several human bodies turning on the spit: and the artful Norman encouraged a report, which increased at the same time the abhorrence and the terror of the infidels.

The First Crusade. – Part Four

I HAVE EXPIATED WITH pleasure on the first steps of the crusaders, as they paint the manners and character of Europe: but I shall abridge the tedious and uniform narrative of their blind achievements, which were performed by strength and are described by ignorance. From their first station in the neighborhood of Nicomedia, they advanced in successive divisions; passed the contracted limit of the Greek empire; opened a road through the hills, and commenced, by the siege of his capital, their pious warfare against the Turkish sultan. His kingdom of Roum extended from the Hellespont to the confines of Syria, and barred the pilgrimage of Jerusalem, his name was Kilidge-Arslan, or Soliman, of the race of Seljuk, and son of the first conqueror; and in the defence of a land which the Turks considered as their own, he deserved the praise of his enemies, by whom alone he is known to posterity. Yielding to the first impulse of the torrent, he deposited his family and treasure in Nice; retired to the mountains with fifty thousand horse; and twice descended to assault the camps or quarters of the Christian besiegers, which formed an imperfect circle of above six miles. The lofty and solid walls of Nice were covered by a deep ditch, and flanked by three hundred and seventy towers; and on the verge of Christendom, the Moslems were trained in arms, and inflamed by religion. Before this city, the French princes occupied their stations, and prosecuted their attacks without correspondence or subordination: emulation prompted their valor; but their valor was sullied by cruelty, and their emulation degenerated into envy and civil discord. In the siege of Nice, the arts and engines of antiquity were employed by the Latins; the mine and the battering-ram, the tortoise, and the belfrey or movable turret, artificial fire, and the *catapult* and *balist*, the sling, and the crossbow for the casting of stones and darts. In the space of seven weeks much labor and blood were expended, and some progress, especially by Count Raymond, was made on the side of the besiegers. But the Turks could protract their resistance and secure their escape, as long as they were masters of the Lake Ascanius, which stretches several miles to the westward of the city. The means of conquest were supplied by the prudence and industry of Alexius; a great number of boats was transported on sledges from the sea to the lake; they were filled with the most dexterous of his archers; the flight of the sultana was intercepted; Nice was invested by land and water; and a Greek emissary persuaded the inhabitants to accept his master's protection, and to save themselves, by a timely surrender, from the rage of the savages of Europe. In the moment of victory, or at least of hope, the crusaders, thirsting for blood and plunder, were awed by the Imperial banner that streamed from the citadel; and Alexius guarded with jealous vigilance this important conquest. The murmurs of the chiefs were stifled by honor or interest; and after a halt of nine days, they directed their march towards Phrygia under the guidance of a Greek general, whom they suspected of a secret connivance with the sultan. The consort and the principal servants of Soliman had been honorably restored without ransom; and the emperor's generosity to the *miscreants* was interpreted as treason to the Christian cause.

Soliman was rather provoked than dismayed by the loss of his capital: he admonished his subjects and allies of this strange invasion of the Western Barbarians; the Turkish emirs obeyed the call of loyalty or religion; the Turkman hordes encamped round his standard; and his whole force is loosely stated by the Christians at two hundred, or even three hundred and sixty thousand horse. Yet he patiently waited till they had left behind them the sea and the Greek frontier; and hovering on the flanks, observed their careless and confident progress in two columns beyond the view of each other. Some miles before they could reach Dorylæum in Phrygia, the left, and least numerous, division was surprised, and attacked, and almost oppressed, by the Turkish cavalry. The heat of the weather, the clouds of arrows, and the barbarous onset, overwhelmed the crusaders; they lost their order and confidence, and the fainting fight was sustained by the personal valor, rather than by the military conduct, of Bohemond, Tancred, and Robert of Normandy. They were revived by the welcome banners of Duke Godfrey, who flew to their succor, with the count of Vermandois, and sixty thousand horse; and was followed by Raymond of Tholouse, the bishop of Puy, and the remainder of the sacred army. Without a moment's pause, they formed in new order, and advanced to a second battle. They were received with equal resolution; and, in their common disdain for the unwarlike people of Greece and Asia, it was confessed on both sides, that the Turks and the Franks were the only nations entitled to the appellation of soldiers. Their encounter was varied, and balanced by the contrast of arms and discipline; of the direct charge, and wheeling evolutions; of the couched lance, and the brandished javelin; of a weighty broadsword, and a crooked sabre; of cumbrous armor, and thin flowing robes; and of the long Tartar bow, and the *arbalist* or crossbow, a deadly weapon, yet unknown to the Orientals. As long as the horses were fresh, and the quivers full, Soliman maintained the advantage of the day; and four thousand Christians were pierced by the Turkish arrows. In the evening, swiftness yielded to strength: on either side, the numbers were equal or at least as great as any ground could hold, or any generals could manage; but in turning the hills, the last division of Raymond and his *provincials* was led, perhaps without design on the rear of an exhausted enemy; and the long contest was determined. Besides a nameless and unaccounted multitude, three thousand *Pagan* knights were slain in the battle and pursuit; the camp of Soliman was pillaged; and in the variety of precious spoil, the curiosity of the Latins was amused with foreign arms and apparel, and the new aspect of dromedaries and camels. The importance of the victory was proved by the hasty retreat of the sultan: reserving ten thousand guards of the relics of his army, Soliman evacuated the kingdom of Roum, and hastened to implore the aid, and kindle the resentment, of his Eastern brethren. In a march of five hundred miles, the crusaders traversed the Lesser Asia, through a wasted land and deserted towns, without finding either a friend or an enemy. The geographer may trace the position of Dorylæum, Antioch of Pisidia, Iconium, Archelais, and Germanicia, and may compare those classic appellations with the modern names of Eskishehr the old city, Akshehr the white city, Cogni, Erekli, and Marash. As the pilgrims passed over a desert, where a draught of water is exchanged for silver, they were tormented by intolerable thirst; and on the banks of the first rivulet, their haste and intemperance were still more pernicious to the disorderly throng. They climbed with toil and danger the steep and slippery sides of Mount Taurus; many of the soldiers cast away their arms to secure their footsteps; and had not terror preceded their van, the long and trembling file might have been driven down the precipice by a handful of resolute enemies. Two of their most respectable chiefs, the duke of Lorraine and the count of Tholouse, were carried in litters: Raymond was raised, as it is said by miracle, from a hopeless malady;

and Godfrey had been torn by a bear, as he pursued that rough and perilous chase in the mountains of Pisidia.

To improve the general consternation, the cousin of Bohemond and the brother of Godfrey were detached from the main army with their respective squadrons of five, and of seven, hundred knights. They overran in a rapid career the hills and sea-coast of Cilicia, from Cogni to the Syrian gates: the Norman standard was first planted on the walls of Tarsus and Malmistra; but the proud injustice of Baldwin at length provoked the patient and generous Italian; and they turned their consecrated swords against each other in a private and profane quarrel. Honor was the motive, and fame the reward, of Tancred; but fortune smiled on the more selfish enterprise of his rival. He was called to the assistance of a Greek or Armenian tyrant, who had been suffered under the Turkish yoke to reign over the Christians of Edessa. Baldwin accepted the character of his son and champion: but no sooner was he introduced into the city, than he inflamed the people to the massacre of his father, occupied the throne and treasure, extended his conquests over the hills of Armenia and the plain of Mesopotamia, and founded the first principality of the Franks or Latins, which subsisted fifty-four years beyond the Euphrates.

Before the Franks could enter Syria, the summer, and even the autumn, were completely wasted: the siege of Antioch, or the separation and repose of the army during the winter season, was strongly debated in their council: the love of arms and the holy sepulchre urged them to advance; and reason perhaps was on the side of resolution, since every hour of delay abates the fame and force of the invader, and multiplies the resources of defensive war. The capital of Syria was protected by the River Orontes; and the *iron bridge*, of nine arches, derives its name from the massy gates of the two towers which are constructed at either end. They were opened by the sword of the duke of Normandy: his victory gave entrance to three hundred thousand crusaders, an account which may allow some scope for losses and desertion, but which clearly detects much exaggeration in the review of Nice. In the description of Antioch, it is not easy to define a middle term between her ancient magnificence, under the successors of Alexander and Augustus, and the modern aspect of Turkish desolation. The Tetrapolis, or four cities, if they retained their name and position, must have left a large vacuity in a circumference of twelve miles; and that measure, as well as the number of four hundred towers, are not perfectly consistent with the five gates, so often mentioned in the history of the siege. Yet Antioch must have still flourished as a great and populous capital. At the head of the Turkish emirs, Baghisian, a veteran chief, commanded in the place: his garrison was composed of six or seven thousand horse, and fifteen or twenty thousand foot: one hundred thousand Moslems are said to have fallen by the sword; and their numbers were probably inferior to the Greeks, Armenians, and Syrians, who had been no more than fourteen years the slaves of the house of Seljuk. From the remains of a solid and stately wall, it appears to have arisen to the height of threescore feet in the valleys; and wherever less art and labor had been applied, the ground was supposed to be defended by the river, the morass, and the mountains. Notwithstanding these fortifications, the city had been repeatedly taken by the Persians, the Arabs, the Greeks, and the Turks; so large a circuit must have yielded many pervious points of attack; and in a siege that was formed about the middle of October, the vigor of the execution could alone justify the boldness of the attempt. Whatever strength and valor could perform in the field was abundantly discharged by the champions of the cross: in the frequent occasions of sallies, of forage, of the attack and defence of convoys, they were often victorious; and we can only complain, that their exploits are sometimes enlarged beyond the scale of probability and truth. The sword of Godfrey divided a Turk from the shoulder to the haunch; and one half of the infidel fell to the ground, while the other was transported by his horse to the city gate. As Robert of Normandy rode against his antagonist, "I devote thy head," he piously exclaimed, "to the dæmons of hell;" and that head was instantly cloven to the breast by the resistless stroke of his descending falchion. But the reality or the report of such gigantic prowess must have taught the Moslems to keep within their walls: and against those walls of earth or stone, the sword and the lance were unavailing weapons. In the slow and successive labors of a siege, the crusaders were supine and ignorant, without skill to contrive, or money to purchase, or industry to use, the artificial engines and implements of assault. In the conquest of Nice, they had been powerfully assisted by the wealth and knowledge of the Greek emperor: his absence was poorly supplied by some Genoese and Pisan vessels, that were attracted by religion or trade to the coast of Syria: the stores were scanty, the return precarious, and the communication difficult and dangerous. Indolence or weakness had prevented the Franks from investing the entire circuit; and the perpetual freedom of two gates relieved the wants and recruited the garrison of the city. At the end of seven months, after the ruin of their cavalry, and an enormous loss by famine, desertion and fatigue, the progress of the crusaders was imperceptible, and their success remote, if the Latin Ulysses, the artful and ambitious Bohemond, had not employed the arms of cunning and deceit. The Christians of Antioch were numerous and discontented: Phirouz, a Syrian renegado, had acquired the favor of the emir and the command of three towers; and the merit of his repentance disguised to the Latins, and perhaps to himself, the foul design of perfidy and treason. A secret correspondence, for their mutual interest, was soon established between Phirouz and the prince of Tarento; and Bohemond declared in the council of the chiefs, that he could deliver the city into their hands. But he claimed the sovereignty of Antioch as the reward of his service; and the proposal which had been rejected by the envy, was at length extorted from the distress, of his equals. The nocturnal surprise was executed by the French and Norman princes, who ascended in person the scaling-ladders that were thrown from the walls: their new proselyte, after the murder of his too scrupulous brother, embraced and introduced the servants of Christ; the army rushed through the gates; and the Moslems soon found, that although mercy was hopeless, resistance was impotent. But the citadel still refused to surrender; and the victims themselves were speedily encompassed and besieged by the innumerable forces of Kerboga, prince of Mosul, who, with twenty-eight Turkish emirs, advanced to the deliverance of Antioch. Five-and-twenty days the Christians spent on the verge of destruction; and the proud lieutenant of the caliph and the sultan left them only the choice of servitude or death. In this extremity they collected the relics of their strength, sallied from the town, and in a single memorable day, annihilated or dispersed the host of Turks and Arabians, which they might safely report to have consisted of six hundred thousand men. Their supernatural allies I shall proceed to consider: the human causes of the victory of Antioch were the fearless despair of the Franks; and the surprise, the discord, perhaps the errors, of their unskilful and presumptuous adversaries. The battle is described with as much disorder as it was fought; but we may observe the tent of Kerboga, a movable and spacious palace, enriched with the luxury of Asia, and capable of holding above two thousand persons; we may distinguish his three thousand guards, who were cased, the horse as well as the men, in complete steel.

In the eventful period of the siege and defence of Antioch, the crusaders were alternately exalted by victory or sunk in despair; either swelled with plenty or emaciated with hunger. A speculative reasoner might suppose, that their faith had a strong and serious influence on their practice; and that the soldiers of the cross, the deliverers of the holy sepulchre, prepared themselves by a sober and virtuous life for the daily contemplation of martyrdom. Experience blows away this charitable illusion; and seldom does the history of profane war display such scenes of intemperance and prostitution as were exhibited under the walls of Antioch. The grove of Daphne no longer flourished; but the Syrian air was still impregnated with the same vices; the Christians were seduced by every temptation that nature either prompts or reprobates; the authority of the chiefs was despised; and sermons and edicts were alike fruitless against those scandalous disorders, not less pernicious to military discipline, than repugnant to evangelic purity. In the first days of the siege and the possession of Antioch, the Franks consumed with wanton and thoughtless prodigality the frugal subsistence of weeks and months: the desolate country no longer yielded a supply; and from that country they were at length excluded by the arms of the besieging Turks. Disease, the faithful companion of want, was envenomed by the rains of the winter, the summer heats, unwholesome food, and the close imprisonment of multitudes. The pictures of famine and pestilence are always the same, and always disgustful; and our imagination may suggest the nature of their sufferings and their resources. The remains of treasure or spoil were eagerly lavished in the purchase of the vilest nourishment; and dreadful must have been the calamities of the poor, since, after paying three marks of silver for a goat and fifteen for a lean camel, the count of Flanders was reduced to beg a dinner, and Duke Godfrey to borrow a horse. Sixty thousand horse had been reviewed in the camp: before the end of the siege they were diminished to two thousand, and scarcely two hundred fit for service could be mustered on the day of battle. Weakness of body and terror of mind extinguished the ardent enthusiasm of the pilgrims; and every motive of honor and religion was subdued by the desire of life. Among the chiefs, three heroes may be found without fear or reproach: Godfrey of Bouillon was supported by his magnanimous piety; Bohemond by ambition and interest; and Tancred declared, in the true spirit of chivalry, that as long as he was at the head of forty knights, he would never relinquish the enterprise of Palestine. But the count of Tholouse and Provence was suspected of a voluntary indisposition; the duke of Normandy was recalled from the sea-shore by the censures of the church: Hugh the Great, though he led the vanguard of the battle, embraced an ambiguous opportunity of returning to France and Stephen, count of Chartres, basely deserted the standard which he bore, and the council in which he presided. The soldiers were discouraged by the flight of William, viscount of Melun, surnamed the *Carpenter*, from the weighty strokes of his axe; and the saints were scandalized by the fall of Peter the Hermit, who, after arming Europe against Asia, attempted to escape from the penance of a necessary fast. Of the multitude of recreant warriors, the names (says an historian) are blotted from the book of life; and the opprobrious epithet of the rope-dancers was applied to the deserters who dropped in the night from the walls of Antioch. The emperor Alexius, who seemed to advance to the succor of the Latins, was dismayed by the assurance of their hopeless condition. They expected their fate in silent despair; oaths and punishments were tried without effect; and to rouse the soldiers to the defence of the walls, it was found necessary to set fire to their quarters.

For their salvation and victory, they were indebted to the same fanaticism which had led them to the brink of ruin. In such a cause, and in such an army, visions, prophecies, and miracles, were frequent and familiar. In the distress of Antioch, they were repeated with unusual energy and success: St. Ambrose had assured a pious ecclesiastic, that two years of trial must precede the season of deliverance and grace; the deserters were stopped by the presence and reproaches of Christ himself; the dead had promised to arise and combat with their brethren; the Virgin had obtained the pardon of their sins; and their confidence was revived by a visible sign, the seasonable and splendid discovery of the holy lance. The policy of their chiefs has on this occasion been admired, and might surely be excused; but a pious fraud is seldom produced by the cool conspiracy of many persons; and a voluntary impostor might depend on the support of the wise and the credulity of the people. Of the diocese of Marseilles, there was a priest of low cunning and loose manners, and his name was Peter Bartholemy. He presented himself at the door of the council-chamber, to disclose an apparition of St. Andrew, which had been thrice reiterated in his sleep with a dreadful menace, if he presumed to suppress the commands of Heaven. "At Antioch," said the apostle, "in the church of my brother St. Peter, near the high altar, is concealed the steel head of the lance that pierced the side of our Redeemer. In three days that instrument of eternal, and now of temporal, salvation, will be manifested to his disciples. Search, and ye shall find: bear it aloft in battle; and that mystic weapon shall penetrate the souls of the miscreants." The pope's legate, the bishop of Puy, affected to listen with coldness and distrust; but the revelation was eagerly accepted by Count Raymond, whom his faithful subject, in the name of the apostle, had chosen for the guardian of the holy lance. The experiment was resolved; and on the third day after a due preparation of prayer and fasting, the priest of Marseilles introduced twelve trusty spectators, among whom were the count and his chaplain; and the church doors were barred against the impetuous multitude. The ground was opened in the appointed place; but the workmen, who relieved each other, dug to the depth of twelve feet without discovering the object of their search. In the evening, when Count Raymond had withdrawn to his post, and the weary assistants began to murmur, Bartholemy, in his shirt, and without his shoes, boldly descended into the pit; the darkness of the hour and of the place enabled him to secrete and deposit the head of a Saracen lance; and the first sound, the first gleam, of the steel was saluted with a devout rapture. The holy lance was drawn from its recess, wrapped in a veil of silk and gold, and exposed to the veneration of the crusaders; their anxious suspense burst forth in a general shout of joy and hope, and the desponding troops were again inflamed with the enthusiasm of valor. Whatever had been the arts, and whatever might be the sentiments of the chiefs, they skilfully improved this fortunate revolution by every aid that discipline and devotion could afford. The soldiers were dismissed to their quarters with an injunction to fortify their minds and bodies for the approaching conflict, freely to bestow their last pittance on themselves and their horses, and to expect with the dawn of day the signal of victory. On the festival of St. Peter and St. Paul, the gates of Antioch were thrown open: a martial psalm, "Let the Lord arise, and let his enemies be scattered!" was chanted by a procession of priests and monks; the battle array was marshalled in twelve divisions, in honor of the twelve apostles; and the holy lance, in the absence of Raymond, was intrusted to the hands of his chaplain. The influence of his relic or trophy, was felt by the servants, and perhaps by the enemies, of Christ; and its potent energy was heightened by an accident, a stratagem, or a rumor, of a miraculous complexion. Three knights, in white garments and resplendent arms, either issued, or seemed to issue, from the hills: the voice of Adhemar, the pope's legate, proclaimed them as the martyrs St. George, St. Theodore, and St. Maurice: the tumult of battle allowed no time for doubt or scrutiny; and the welcome apparition dazzled the eyes or the imagination of a fanatic army. In the season of danger and triumph, the revelation of Bartholemy of Marseilles was unanimously asserted; but as soon as the temporary service was accomplished, the personal dignity and liberal arms which the count of Tholouse derived from the custody of the holy lance, provoked the envy, and awakened the reason, of his rivals. A Norman clerk presumed to sift, with a philosophic spirit, the truth of the legend, the circumstances of the discovery, and the character of the prophet; and the pious Bohemond ascribed their deliverance to the merits and intercession of Christ alone. For a while, the

Provincials defended their national palladium with clamors and arms and new visions condemned to death and hell the profane sceptics who presumed to scrutinize the truth and merit of the discovery. The prevalence of incredulity compelled the author to submit his life and veracity to the judgment of God. A pile of dry fagots, four feet high and fourteen long, was erected in the midst of the camp; the flames burnt fiercely to the elevation of thirty cubits; and a narrow path of twelve inches was left for the perilous trial. The unfortunate priest of Marseilles traversed the fire with dexterity and speed; but the thighs and belly were scorched by the intense heat; he expired the next day; and the logic of believing minds will pay some regard to his dying protestations of innocence and truth. Some efforts were made by the Provincials to substitute a cross, a ring, or a tabernacle, in the place of the holy lance, which soon vanished in contempt and oblivion. Yet the revelation of Antioch is gravely asserted by succeeding historians: and such is the progress of credulity, that miracles most doubtful on the spot, and at the moment, will be received with implicit faith at a convenient distance of time and space.

The prudence or fortune of the Franks had delayed their invasion till the decline of the Turkish empire. Under the manly government of the three first sultans, the kingdoms of Asia were united in peace and justice; and the innumerable armies which they led in person were equal in courage, and superior in discipline, to the Barbarians of the West. But at the time of the crusade, the inheritance of Malek Shaw was disputed by his four sons; their private ambition was insensible of the public danger; and, in the vicissitudes of their fortune, the royal vassals were ignorant, or regardless, of the true object of their allegiance. The twenty-eight emirs who marched with the standard or Kerboga were his rivals or enemies: their hasty levies were drawn from the towns and tents of Mesopotamia and Syria; and the Turkish veterans were employed or consumed in the civil wars beyond the Tigris. The caliph of Egypt embraced this opportunity of weakness and discord to recover his ancient possessions; and his sultan Aphdal besieged Jerusalem and Tyre, expelled the children of Ortok, and restored in Palestine the civil and ecclesiastical authority of the Fatimites. They heard with astonishment of the vast armies of Christians that had passed from Europe to Asia, and rejoiced in the sieges and battles which broke the power of the Turks, the adversaries of their sect and monarchy. But the same Christians were the enemies of the prophet; and from the overthrow of Nice and Antioch, the motive of their enterprise, which was gradually understood, would urge them forwards to the banks of the Jordan, or perhaps of the Nile. An intercourse of epistles and embassies, which rose and fell with the events of war, was maintained between the throne of Cairo and the camp of the Latins; and their adverse pride was the result of ignorance and enthusiasm. The ministers of Egypt declared in a haughty, or insinuated in a milder, tone, that their sovereign, the true and lawful commander of the faithful, had rescued Jerusalem from the Turkish yoke; and that the pilgrims, if they would divide their numbers, and lay aside their arms, should find a safe and hospitable reception at the sepulchre of Jesus. In the belief of their lost condition, the caliph Mostali despised their arms and imprisoned their deputies: the conquest and victory of Antioch prompted him to solicit those formidable champions with gifts of horses and silk robes, of vases, and purses of gold and silver; and in his estimate of their merit or power, the first place was assigned to Bohemond, and the second to Godfrey. In either fortune, the answer of the crusaders was firm and uniform: they disdained to inquire into the private claims or possessions of the followers of Mahomet; whatsoever was his name or nation, the usurper of Jerusalem was their enemy; and instead of prescribing the mode and terms of their pilgrimage, it was only by a timely surrender of the city and province, their sacred right, that he could deserve their alliance, or deprecate their impending and irresistible attack.

Yet this attack, when they were within the view and reach of their glorious prize, was suspended above ten months after the defeat of Kerboga. The zeal and courage of the crusaders were chilled in the moment of victory; and instead of marching to improve the consternation, they hastily dispersed to enjoy the luxury, of Syria. The causes of this strange delay may be found in the want of strength and subordination. In the painful and various service of Antioch, the cavalry was annihilated; many thousands of every rank had been lost by famine, sickness, and desertion: the same abuse of plenty had been productive of a third famine; and the alternative of intemperance and distress had generated a pestilence, which swept away above fifty thousand of the pilgrims. Few were able to command, and none were willing to obey; the domestic feuds, which had been stifled by common fear, were again renewed in acts, or at least in sentiments, of hostility; the fortune of Baldwin and Bohemond excited the envy of their companions; the bravest knights were enlisted for the defence of their new principalities; and Count Raymond exhausted his troops and treasures in an idle expedition into the heart of Syria. *

The winter was consumed in discord and disorder; a sense of honor and religion was rekindled in the spring; and the private soldiers, less susceptible of ambition and jealousy, awakened with angry clamors the indolence of their chiefs. In the month of May, the relics of this mighty host proceeded from Antioch to Laodicea: about forty thousand Latins, of whom no more than fifteen hundred horse, and twenty thousand foot, were capable of immediate service. Their easy march was continued between Mount Libanus and the sea-shore: their wants were liberally supplied by the coasting traders of Genoa and Pisa; and they drew large contributions from the emirs of Tripoli, Tyre, Sidon, Acre, and Cæsarea, who granted a free passage, and promised to follow the example of Jerusalem. From Cæsarea they advanced into the midland country; their clerks recognized the sacred geography of Lydda, Ramla, Emmaus, and Bethlem, and as soon as they descried the holy city, the crusaders forgot their toils and claimed their reward.

The First Crusade. – Part Five

JERUSALEM HAS DERIVED SOME reputation from the number and importance of her memorable sieges. It was not till after a long and obstinate contest that Babylon and Rome could prevail against the obstinacy of the people, the craggy ground that might supersede the necessity of fortifications, and the walls and towers that would have fortified the most accessible plain. These obstacles were diminished in the age of the crusades. The bulwarks had been completely destroyed and imperfectly restored: the Jews, their nation, and worship, were forever banished; but nature is less changeable than man, and the site of Jerusalem, though somewhat softened and somewhat removed, was still strong against the assaults of an enemy. By the experience of a recent siege, and a three years' possession, the Saracens of Egypt had been taught to discern, and in some degree to remedy, the defects of a place, which religion as well as honor forbade them to resign. Aladin, or Iftikhar, the caliph's lieutenant, was intrusted with the defence: his policy strove to restrain the native Christians by the dread of their own ruin and that of the holy sepulchre; to animate the Moslems by the assurance of temporal and eternal rewards. His garrison is said to have consisted of forty thousand Turks and Arabians; and if he could muster twenty thousand of the inhabitants, it must be confessed that the besieged were more numerous than the besieging army. Had the diminished strength and numbers of the Latins allowed them to grasp the whole circumference of four thousand yards, (about two English miles and a half,) to what useful purpose should they have descended into the valley of Ben Hinnom and torrent of Cedron, or approach the precipices of the south and east, from whence they had nothing either to hope or fear? Their siege was more reasonably directed against the northern and western sides of the city. Godfrey of Bouillon erected his standard on the first swell of Mount Calvary: to the left, as far as St. Stephen's gate, the line of attack was continued by Tancred and the two Roberts; and Count Raymond established his quarters from the citadel to the foot of Mount Sion, which was no longer included within the precincts of the city. On the fifth day, the crusaders made a general assault, in the fanatic hope of battering down the walls without engines, and of scaling them without ladders. By the dint of brutal force, they burst the first barrier; but they were driven back with shame and slaughter to the camp: the influence of vision and prophecy was deadened by the too frequent abuse of those pious stratagems; and time and labor were found to be the only means of victory. The time of the siege was indeed fulfilled in forty days, but they were forty days of calamity and anguish. A repetition of the old complaint of famine may be imputed in some degree to the voracious or disorderly appetite of the Franks; but the stony soil of Jerusalem is almost destitute of water; the scanty springs and hasty torrents were dry in the summer season; nor was the thirst of the besiegers relieved, as in the city, by the artificial supply of cisterns and aqueducts. The circumjacent country is equally destitute of trees for the uses of shade or building, but some large beams were discovered in a cave by the crusaders: a wood near Sichem, the enchanted grove of Tasso, was cut down: the necessary timber was transported to the camp by the vigor and dexterity of Tancred; and the engines were framed by some Genoese artists, who had fortunately landed in the harbor of Jaffa. Two movable turrets were constructed at the expense, and in the stations, of the duke of Lorraine and the count of Tholouse, and rolled forwards with devout labor, not to the most accessible, but to the most neglected, parts of the fortification. Raymond's Tower was reduced to ashes by the fire of the besieged, but his colleague was more vigilant and successful; the enemies were driven by his archers from the rampart; the draw-bridge was let down; and on a Friday, at three in the afternoon, the day and hour of the passion, Godfrey of Bouillon stood victorious on the walls of Jerusalem. His example was followed on every side by the emulation of valor; and about four hundred and sixty years after the conquest of Omar, the holy city was rescued from the Mahometan yoke. In the pillage of public and private wealth, the adventurers had agreed to respect the exclusive property of the first occupant; and the spoils of the great mosque, seventy lamps and massy vases of gold and silver, rewarded the diligence, and displayed the generosity, of Tancred. A bloody sacrifice was offered by his mistaken votaries to the God of the Christians: resistance might provoke but neither age nor sex could mollify, their implacable rage: they indulged themselves three days in a promiscuous massacre; and the infection of the dead bodies produced an epidemical disease. After seventy thousand Moslems had been put to the sword, and the harmless Jews had been burnt in their synagogue, they could still reserve a multitude of captives, whom interest or lassitude persuaded them to spare. Of these savage heroes of the cross, Tancred alone betrayed some sentiments of compassion; yet we may praise the more selfish lenity of Raymond, who granted a capitulation and safe-conduct to the garrison of the citadel. The holy sepulchre was now free; and the bloody victors prepared to accomplish their vow. Bareheaded and barefoot, with contrite hearts, and in an humble posture, they ascended the hill of Calvary, amidst the loud anthems of the clergy; kissed the stone which had covered the Savior of the world; and bedewed with tears of joy and penitence the monument of their redemption. This union of the fiercest and most tender passions has been variously considered by two philosophers; by the one, as easy and natural; by the other, as absurd and incredible. Perhaps it is too rigorously applied to the same persons and the same hour; the example of the virtuous Godfrey awakened the piety of his companions; while they cleansed their bodies, they purified their minds; nor shall I believe that the most ardent in slaughter and rapine were the foremost in the procession to the holy sepulchre.

Eight days after this memorable event, which Pope Urban did not live to hear, the Latin chiefs proceeded to the election of a king, to guard and govern their conquests in Palestine. Hugh the Great, and Stephen of Chartres, had retired with some loss of reputation, which they strove to regain by a second crusade and an honorable death. Baldwin was established at Edessa, and Bohemond at Antioch; and two Roberts, the duke of Normandy and the count of Flanders, preferred their fair inheritance in the West to a doubtful competition or a barren sceptre. The jealousy and ambition of Raymond were condemned by his own followers, and the free, the just, the unanimous voice of the army proclaimed Godfrey of Bouillon the first and most worthy of the champions of Christendom. His magnanimity accepted a trust as full of danger as of glory; but in a city where his Savior had been crowned with thorns, the devout pilgrim rejected the name and ensigns of royalty; and the founder of the kingdom of Jerusalem contented himself with the modest title of Defender and Baron of the Holy Sepulchre. His government of a single year, too short for the public happiness, was interrupted in the first fortnight by a summons to the field, by the approach of the vizier or sultan of Egypt, who had been too slow to prevent, but who was impatient to avenge, the loss of Jerusalem. His total overthrow in the battle of Ascalon sealed the establishment of the Latins in Syria, and signalized the valor of the French princes who in this action bade a long farewell to the holy wars. Some glory might be derived from the prodigious inequality of numbers, though I shall not count the myriads of horse and foot on the side of the Fatimites; but, except three thousand Ethiopians or Blacks, who were armed with flails or scourges of iron, the Barbarians of the South fled on the first onset, and afforded a pleasing comparison between the active valor of the Turks and the sloth and effeminacy of the natives of Egypt. After suspending before the holy sepulchre the sword and standard of the sultan, the new king (he deserves the title) embraced his departing companions, and could retain only with the gallant Tancred three hundred knights, and two thousand foot-soldiers for the defence of Palestine. His sovereignty was soon attacked by a new enemy, the only one against whom Godfrey was a coward. Adhemar, bishop of Puy, who excelled both in council and action, had been swept away in the last plague at Antioch: the remaining ecclesiastics preserved only the pride and avarice of their character; and their seditious clamors had required that the choice of a bishop should precede that of a king. The revenue and jurisdiction of the lawful patriarch were usurped by the Latin clergy: the exclusion of the Greeks and Syrians was justified by the reproach of heresy or schism; and, under the iron yoke of their deliverers, the Oriental Christians regretted the tolerating government of the Arabian caliphs. Daimbert, archbishop of Pisa, had long been trained in the secret policy of Rome: he brought a fleet at his countrymen to the succor of the Holy Land, and was installed, without a competitor, the spiritual and temporal head of the church. The new patriarch immediately grasped the sceptre which had been acquired by the toil and blood of the victorious pilgrims; and both Godfrey and Bohemond submitted to receive at his hands the investiture of their feudal possessions. Nor was this sufficient; Daimbert claimed the immediate property of Jerusalem and Jaffa; instead of a firm and generous refusal, the hero negotiated with the priest; a quarter of either city was ceded to the church; and the modest bishop was satisfied with an eventual reversion of the rest, on the death of Godfrey without children, or on the future acquisition of a new seat at Cairo or Damascus.

Without this indulgence, the conqueror would have almost been stripped of his infant kingdom, which consisted only of Jerusalem and Jaffa, with about twenty villages and towns of the adjacent country. Within this narrow verge, the Mahometans were still lodged in some impregnable castles: and the husbandman, the trader, and the pilgrim, were exposed to daily and domestic hostility. By the arms of Godfrey himself, and of the two Baldwins, his brother and cousin, who succeeded to the throne, the Latins breathed with more ease and safety; and at length they equalled, in the extent of their dominions, though not in the millions of their subjects, the ancient princes of Judah and Israel. After the reduction of the maritime cities of Laodicea, Tripoli, Tyre, and Ascalon, which were powerfully assisted by the fleets of Venice, Genoa, and Pisa, and even of Flanders and Norway, the range of sea-coast from Scanderoon to the borders of Egypt was possessed by the Christian pilgrims. If the prince of Antioch disclaimed his supremacy, the counts of Edessa and Tripoli owned themselves the vassals of the king of Jerusalem: the Latins reigned beyond the Euphrates; and the four cities of Hems, Hamah, Damascus, and Aleppo, were the only relics of the Mahometan conquests in Syria. The laws and language, the manners and titles, of the French nation and Latin church, were introduced into these transmarine colonies. According to the feudal jurisprudence, the principal states and subordinate baronies descended in the line of male and female succession: but the children of the first conquerors, a motley and degenerate race, were dissolved by the luxury of the climate; the arrival of new crusaders from Europe was a doubtful hope and a casual event. The service of the feudal tenures was performed by six hundred and sixty-six knights, who might expect the aid of two hundred more under the banner of the count of Tripoli; and each knight was attended to the field by four squires or archers on horseback. Five thousand and seventy sergeants, most probably foot-soldiers, were supplied by the churches and cities; and the whole legal militia of the kingdom could not exceed eleven thousand men, a slender defence against the surrounding myriads of Saracens and Turks. But the firmest bulwark of Jerusalem was founded on the knights of the Hospital of St. John, and of the temple of Solomon; on the strange association of a monastic and military life, which fanaticism might suggest, but which policy must approve. The flower of the nobility of Europe aspired to wear the cross, and to profess the vows, of these respectable orders; their spirit and discipline were immortal; and the speedy donation of twenty-eight thousand farms, or manors, enabled them to support a regular force of cavalry and infantry for the defence of Palestine. The austerity of the convent soon evaporated in the exercise of arms; the world was scandalized by the pride, avarice, and corruption of these Christian soldiers; their claims of immunity and jurisdiction disturbed the harmony of the church and state; and the public peace was endangered by their jealous emulation. But in their most dissolute period, the knights of their hospital and temple maintained their fearless and fanatic character: they neglected to live, but they were prepared to die, in the service of Christ; and the spirit of chivalry, the parent and offspring of the crusades, has been transplanted by this institution from the holy sepulchre to the Isle of Malta.

The spirit of freedom, which pervades the feudal institutions, was felt in its strongest energy by the volunteers of the cross, who elected for their chief the most deserving of his peers. Amidst the slaves of Asia, unconscious of the lesson or example, a model of political liberty was introduced; and the laws of the French kingdom are derived from the purest source of equality and justice. Of such laws, the first and indispensable condition is the assent of those whose obedience they require, and for whose benefit they are designed. No sooner had Godfrey of Bouillon accepted the office of supreme magistrate, than he solicited the public and private advice of the Latin pilgrims, who were the best skilled in the statutes and customs of Europe. From these materials, with the counsel and approbation of the patriarch and barons, of the clergy and laity, Godfrey composed the Assise of Jerusalem, a precious monument of feudal jurisprudence. The new code, attested by the seals of the king, the patriarch, and the viscount of Jerusalem, was deposited in the holy sepulchre, enriched with the improvements of succeeding times, and respectfully consulted as often as any doubtful question arose in the tribunals of Palestine. With the kingdom and city all was lost: the fragments of the written law were preserved by jealous tradition and variable practice till the middle of the thirteenth century: the code was restored by the pen of John d'Ibelin, count of Jaffa, one of the principal feudatories; and the final revision was accomplished in the year thirteen hundred and sixty-nine, for the use of the Latin kingdom of Cyprus.

The justice and freedom of the constitution were maintained by two tribunals of unequal dignity, which were instituted by Godfrey of Bouillon after the conquest of Jerusalem. The king, in person, presided in the upper court, the court of the barons. Of these the four most conspicuous were the prince of Galilee, the lord of Sidon and Cæsarea, and the counts of Jaffa and Tripoli, who, perhaps with the constable and marshal, were in a special manner the compeers and judges of each other. But all the nobles, who held their lands immediately of the crown, were entitled and bound to attend the king's court; and each baron exercised a similar jurisdiction on the subordinate assemblies of his own feudatories. The connection of lord and vassal was honorable and voluntary: reverence was due to the benefactor, protection to the dependant; but they mutually pledged their faith to each other; and the obligation on either side might be suspended by neglect or dissolved by injury. The cognizance of marriages and testaments was blended with religion, and usurped by the clergy: but the civil and criminal causes of the nobles, the inheritance and tenure of their fiefs, formed the proper occupation of the supreme court. Each member was the judge and guardian both of public and private rights. It was his duty to assert with his tongue and sword the lawful claims of the lord; but if an unjust superior presumed to violate the freedom or property of a vassal, the confederate peers stood forth to maintain his quarrel by word and deed. They boldly affirmed his innocence and his wrongs; demanded the restitution of his liberty or his lands; suspended, after a fruitless demand, their own service; rescued their brother from prison; and employed every weapon in his defence, without offering direct violence to the person of their lord, which was ever sacred in their eyes. In their pleadings, replies, and rejoinders, the advocates of the court were subtle and copious; but the use of argument and evidence was often superseded by judicial combat; and the Assise of Jerusalem admits in many cases this barbarous institution, which has been slowly abolished by the laws and manners of Europe.

The trial by battle was established in all criminal cases which affected the life, or limb, or honor, of any person; and in all civil transactions, of or above the value of one mark of silver. It appears that in criminal cases the combat was the privilege of the accuser, who, except in a charge of treason, avenged his personal injury, or the death of those persons whom he had a right to represent; but wherever, from the nature of the charge, testimony could be obtained, it was necessary for him to produce witnesses of the fact. In civil cases, the combat was not allowed as the means of establishing the claim of the demandant; but he was obliged to produce witnesses who had, or assumed to have, knowledge of the fact. The combat was then the privilege of the defendant; because he charged the witness with an attempt by perjury to take away his right. He came therefore to be in the same situation as the appellant in criminal cases. It was not then as a mode of proof that the combat was received, nor as making negative evidence, (according to the supposition of Montesquieu;) but in every case the right to offer battle was founded on the right to pursue by arms the redress of an injury; and the judicial combat was fought on the same principle, and with the same spirit, as a private duel. Champions were only allowed to women, and to men maimed or past the age of sixty. The consequence of a defeat was death to the person accused, or to the champion or witness, as well as to the accuser himself: but in civil cases, the demandant was punished with infamy and the loss of his suit, while his witness and champion suffered ignominious death. In many cases it was in the option of the judge to award or to refuse the combat: but two are specified, in which it was the inevitable result of the challenge; if a faithful vassal gave the lie to his compeer, who unjustly claimed any portion of their lord's demesnes; or if an unsuccessful suitor presumed to impeach the judgment and veracity of the court. He might impeach them, but the terms were severe and perilous: in the same day he successively fought *all* the members of the tribunal, even those who had been absent; a single defeat was followed by death and infamy; and where none could hope for victory, it is highly probable that none would adventure the trial. In the Assise of Jerusalem, the legal subtlety of the count of Jaffa is more laudably employed to elude, than to facilitate, the judicial combat, which he derives from a principle of honor rather than of superstition.

Among the causes which enfranchised the plebeians from the yoke of feudal tyranny, the institution of cities and corporations is one of the most powerful; and if those of Palestine are coeval with the first crusade, they may be ranked with the most ancient of the Latin world. Many of the pilgrims had escaped from their lords under the banner of the cross; and it was the policy of the French princes to tempt their stay by the assurance of the rights and privileges of freemen. It is expressly declared in the Assise of Jerusalem, that after instituting, for his knights and barons, the court of peers, in which he presided himself, Godfrey of Bouillon established a second tribunal, in which his person was represented by his viscount. The jurisdiction of this inferior court extended over the burgesses of the kingdom; and it was composed of a select number of the most discreet and worthy citizens, who were sworn to judge, according to the laws of the actions and fortunes of their equals. In the conquest and settlement of new cities, the example of Jerusalem was imitated by the kings and their great vassals; and above thirty similar corporations were founded before the loss of the Holy Land. Another class of subjects, the Syrians, or Oriental Christians, were oppressed by the zeal of the clergy, and protected by the toleration of the state. Godfrey listened to their reasonable prayer, that they might be judged by their own national laws. A third court was instituted for their use, of limited and domestic jurisdiction: the sworn members were Syrians, in blood, language, and religion; but the office of the president (in Arabic, of the *rais*) was sometimes exercised by the viscount of the city. At an immeasurable distance below the *nobles*, the *burgesses*, and the *strangers*, the Assise of Jerusalem condescends to mention the *villains* and *slaves*, the peasants of the land and the captives of war, who were almost equally considered as the objects of property. The relief or protection of these unhappy men was not esteemed worthy of the care of the legislator; but he diligently provides for the recovery, though not indeed for the punishment, of the fugitives. Like hounds, or hawks, who had strayed from the lawful owner, they might be lost and claimed: the slave and falcon were of the same value; but three slaves, or twelve oxen, were accumulated to equal the price of the war-horse; and a sum of three hundred pieces of gold was fixed, in the age of chivalry, as the equivalent of the more noble animal.

END OF VOL. FIVE

CHAPTER FIFTY NINE

The Crusades. – Part One

Preservation of the Greek Empire. – Numbers, Passage, and Event, of the Second and Third Crusades. – St. Bernard. – Reign of Saladin in Egypt and Syria. – His Conquest of Jerusalem. – Naval Crusades. – Richard the First of England. – Pope Innocent the Third; and the Fourth and Fifth Crusades. – The Emperor Frederic the Second. – Louis the Ninth of France; and the Two Last Crusades. – Expulsion of the Latins or Franks by the Mamelukes.

IN A STYLE LESS grave than that of history, I should perhaps compare the emperor Alexius to the jackal, who is said to follow the steps, and to devour the leavings, of the lion. Whatever had been his fears and toils in the passage of the first crusade, they were amply recompensed by the subsequent benefits which he derived from the exploits of the Franks. His dexterity and vigilance secured their first conquest of Nice; and from this threatening station the Turks were compelled to evacuate the neighborhood of Constantinople. While the crusaders, with blind valor, advanced into the midland countries of Asia, the crafty Greek improved the favorable occasion when the emirs of the sea-coast were recalled to the standard of the sultan. The Turks were driven from the Isles of Rhodes and Chios: the cities of Ephesus and Smyrna, of Sardes, Philadelphia, and Laodicea, were restored to the empire, which Alexius enlarged from the Hellespont to the banks of the Mæander, and the rocky shores of Pamphylia. The churches resumed their splendor: the towns were rebuilt and fortified; and the desert country was peopled with colonies of Christians, who were gently removed from the more distant and dangerous frontier. In these paternal cares, we may forgive Alexius, if he forgot the deliverance of the holy sepulchre; but, by the Latins, he was stigmatized with the foul reproach of treason and desertion. They had sworn fidelity and obedience to his throne; but *he* had promised to assist their enterprise in person, or, at least, with his troops and treasures: his base retreat dissolved their obligations; and the sword, which had been the instrument of their victory, was the pledge and title of their just independence. It does not appear that the emperor attempted to revive his obsolete claims over the kingdom of Jerusalem; but the borders of Cilicia and Syria were more recent in his possession, and more accessible to his arms. The great army of the crusaders was annihilated or dispersed; the principality of Antioch was left without a head, by the surprise and captivity of Bohemond; his ransom had oppressed him with a heavy debt; and his Norman followers were insufficient to repel the hostilities of the Greeks and Turks. In this distress, Bohemond embraced a magnanimous resolution, of leaving the defence of Antioch to his kinsman, the faithful Tancred; of arming the West against the Byzantine empire; and of executing the design which he inherited from the lessons and example of his father Guiscard. His embarkation was clandestine: and, if we may credit a tale of the princess Anne, he passed the hostile sea closely secreted in a coffin. But his reception in France was dignified by the public applause, and his marriage with the king's daughter: his return was glorious, since the bravest spirits of the age enlisted under his veteran command; and he repassed the Adriatic at the head of five thousand horse and forty thousand foot, assembled from the most remote climates of Europe. The strength of Durazzo, and prudence of Alexius, the progress of famine and approach of winter, eluded his ambitious hopes; and the venal confederates were seduced from his standard. A treaty of peace suspended the fears of the Greeks; and they were finally delivered by the death of an adversary, whom neither oaths could bind, nor dangers could appal, nor prosperity could satiate. His children succeeded to the principality of Antioch; but the boundaries were strictly defined, the homage was clearly stipulated, and the cities of Tarsus and Malmistra were restored to the Byzantine emperors. Of the coast of Anatolia, they possessed the entire circuit from Trebizond to the Syrian gates. The Seljukian dynasty of Roum was separated on all sides from the sea and their Mussulman brethren; the power of the sultan was shaken by the victories and even the defeats of the Franks; and after the loss of Nice, they removed their throne to Cogni or Iconium, an obscure and in land town above three hundred miles from Constantinople. Instead of trembling for their capital, the Comnenian princes waged an offensive war against the Turks, and the first crusade prevented the fall of the declining empire.

In the twelfth century, three great emigrations marched by land from the West for the relief of Palestine. The soldiers and pilgrims of Lombardy, France, and Germany were excited by the example and success of the first crusade. Forty-eight years after the deliverance of the holy sepulchre, the emperor, and the French king, Conrad the Third and Louis the Seventh, undertook the second crusade to support the falling fortunes of the Latins. A grand division of the third crusade was led by the emperor Frederic Barbarossa, who sympathized with his brothers of France and England in the common loss of Jerusalem. These three expeditions may be compared in their resemblance of the greatness of numbers, their passage through the Greek empire, and the nature and event of their Turkish warfare, and a brief parallel may save the repetition of a tedious narrative. However splendid it may seem, a regular story of the crusades would exhibit the perpetual return of the same causes and effects; and the frequent attempts for the defence or recovery of the Holy Land would appear so many faint and unsuccessful copies of the original.

I. Of the swarms that so closely trod in the footsteps of the first pilgrims, the chiefs were equal in rank, though unequal in fame and merit, to Godfrey of Bouillon and his fellow-adventurers. At their head were displayed the banners of the dukes of Burgundy, Bavaria, and Aquitain; the first a descendant of Hugh Capet, the second, a father of the Brunswick line: the archbishop of Milan, a temporal prince, transported, for the benefit of the Turks, the treasures and ornaments of his church and palace; and the veteran crusaders, Hugh the Great and Stephen of Chartres, returned to consummate their unfinished vow. The huge and disorderly bodies of their followers moved forward in two columns; and if the first consisted of two hundred and sixty thousand persons, the second might possibly amount to sixty thousand horse and one hundred thousand foot. The armies of the second crusade might have claimed the conquest of Asia; the nobles of France and Germany were animated by the presence of their sovereigns; and both the rank and personal character of Conrad and Louis gave a dignity to their cause, and a discipline to their force, which might be vainly expected from the feudatory chiefs. The cavalry of the emperor, and that of the king, was each composed of seventy thousand knights, and their immediate attendants in the field; and if the light-armed troops, the peasant infantry, the women and children, the priests and monks, be rigorously excluded, the full account will scarcely be satisfied with four hundred thousand souls. The West, from Rome to Britain, was called into action; the kings of Poland and Bohemia obeyed the summons of Conrad; and it is affirmed by the Greeks and Latins, that, in the passage of a strait or river, the Byzantine agents, after a tale of nine hundred thousand, desisted from the endless and formidable computation. In the third crusade, as the French and English preferred the navigation of the Mediterranean, the host of Frederic Barbarossa was less numerous. Fifteen thousand knights, and as many squires, were the flower of the German chivalry: sixty thousand horse, and one hundred thousand foot, were mustered by the emperor in the plains of Hungary; and after such repetitions, we shall no longer be startled at the six hundred thousand pilgrims, which credulity has ascribed to this last emigration. Such extravagant reckonings prove only the astonishment of contemporaries; but their astonishment most strongly bears testimony to the existence of an enormous, though indefinite, multitude. The Greeks might applaud their superior knowledge of the arts and stratagems of war, but they confessed the strength and courage of the French cavalry, and the infantry of the Germans; and the strangers are described as an iron race, of gigantic stature, who darted fire from their eyes, and spilt blood like water on the ground. Under the banners of Conrad, a troop of females rode in the attitude and armor of men; and the chief of these Amazons, from her gilt spurs and buskins, obtained the epithet of the Golden-footed Dame.

II. The number and character of the strangers was an object of terror to the effeminate Greeks, and the sentiment of fear is nearly allied to that of hatred. This aversion was suspended or softened by the apprehension of the Turkish power; and the invectives of the Latins will not bias our more candid belief, that the emperor Alexius dissembled their insolence, eluded their hostilities, counselled their rashness, and opened to their ardor the road of pilgrimage and conquest. But when the Turks had been driven from Nice and the sea-coast, when the Byzantine princes no longer dreaded the distant sultans of Cogni, they felt with purer indignation the free and frequent passage of the western Barbarians, who violated the majesty, and endangered the safety, of the empire. The second and third crusades were undertaken under the reign of Manuel Comnenus and Isaac Angelus. Of the former, the passions were always impetuous, and often malevolent; and the natural union of a cowardly and a mischievous temper was exemplified in the latter, who, without merit or mercy, could punish a tyrant, and occupy his throne.

It was secretly, and perhaps tacitly, resolved by the prince and people to destroy, or at least to discourage, the pilgrims, by every species of injury and oppression; and their want of prudence and discipline continually afforded the pretence or the opportunity. The Western monarchs had stipulated a safe passage and fair market in the country of their Christian brethren; the treaty had been ratified by oaths and hostages; and the poorest soldier of Frederic's army was furnished with three marks of silver to defray his expenses on the road. But every engagement was violated by treachery and injustice; and the complaints of the Latins are attested by the honest confession of a Greek historian, who has dared to prefer truth to his country. Instead of a hospitable reception, the gates of the cities, both in Europe and Asia, were closely barred against the crusaders; and the scanty pittance of food was let down in baskets from the walls. Experience or foresight might excuse this timid jealousy; but the common duties of humanity prohibited the mixture of chalk, or other poisonous ingredients, in the bread; and should Manuel be acquitted of any foul connivance, he is guilty of coining base money for the purpose of trading with the pilgrims. In every step of their march they were stopped or misled: the governors had private orders to fortify the passes and break down the bridges against them: the stragglers were pillaged and murdered: the soldiers and horses were pierced in the woods by arrows from an invisible hand; the sick were burnt in their beds; and the dead bodies were hung on gibbets along the highways. These injuries exasperated the champions of the cross, who were not endowed with evangelical patience; and the Byzantine princes, who had provoked the unequal conflict, promoted the embarkation and march of these formidable guests. On the verge of the Turkish frontier Barbarossa spared the guilty Philadelphia, rewarded the hospitable Laodicea, and deplored the hard necessity that had stained his sword with any drops of Christian blood. In their intercourse with the monarchs of Germany and France, the pride of the Greeks was exposed to an anxious trial. They might boast that on the first interview the seat of Louis was a low stool, beside the throne of Manuel; but no sooner had the French king transported his army beyond the Bosphorus, than he refused the offer of a second conference, unless his brother would meet him on equal terms, either on the sea or land. With Conrad and Frederic, the ceremonial was still nicer and more difficult: like the successors of Constantine, they styled themselves emperors of the Romans; and firmly maintained the purity of their title and dignity. The first of these representatives of Charlemagne would only converse with Manuel on horseback in the open field; the second, by passing the Hellespont rather than the Bosphorus, declined the view of Constantinople and its sovereign. An emperor, who had been crowned at Rome, was reduced in the Greek epistles to the humble appellation of *Rex*, or prince, of the Alemanni; and the vain and feeble Angelus affected to be ignorant of the name of one of the greatest men and monarchs of the age. While they viewed with hatred and suspicion the Latin pilgrims the Greek emperors maintained a strict, though secret, alliance with the Turks and Saracens. Isaac Angelus complained, that by his friendship for the great Saladin he had incurred the enmity of the Franks; and a mosque was founded at Constantinople for the public exercise of the religion of Mahomet.

III. The swarms that followed the first crusade were destroyed in Anatolia by famine, pestilence, and the Turkish arrows; and the princes only escaped with some squadrons of horse to accomplish their lamentable pilgrimage. A just opinion may be formed of their knowledge and humanity; of their knowledge, from the design of subduing Persia and Chorasan in their way to Jerusalem; of their humanity, from the massacre of the Christian people, a friendly city, who came out to meet them with palms and crosses in their hands. The arms of Conrad and Louis were less cruel and imprudent; but the event of the second crusade was still more ruinous to Christendom; and the Greek Manuel is accused by his own subjects of giving seasonable intelligence to the sultan, and treacherous guides to the Latin princes. Instead of crushing the common foe, by a double attack at the same time but on different sides, the Germans were urged by emulation, and the French were retarded by jealousy. Louis had scarcely passed the Bosphorus when he was met by the returning emperor, who had lost the greater part of his army in glorious, but unsuccessful, actions on the banks of the Mæander. The contrast of the pomp of his rival hastened the retreat of Conrad: the desertion of his independent vassals reduced him to his hereditary troops; and he borrowed some Greek vessels to execute by sea the pilgrimage of Palestine. Without studying the lessons of experience, or the nature of the war, the king of France advanced through the same country to a similar fate. The vanguard, which bore the royal banner and the oriflamme of St. Denys, had doubled their march with rash and inconsiderate speed; and the rear, which the king commanded in person, no longer found their companions in the evening camp. In darkness and disorder, they were encompassed, assaulted, and overwhelmed, by the innumerable host of Turks, who, in the art of war, were superior to the Christians of the twelfth century. Louis, who climbed a tree in the general discomfiture, was saved by his own valor and the ignorance of his adversaries; and with the dawn of day he escaped alive, but almost alone, to the camp of the vanguard. But instead of pursuing his expedition by land, he was rejoiced to shelter the relics of his army in the friendly seaport of Satalia. From thence he embarked for Antioch; but so penurious was the supply of Greek vessels, that they could only afford room for his knights and nobles; and the plebeian crowd of infantry was left to perish at the foot of the Pamphylian hills. The emperor and the king embraced and wept at Jerusalem; their martial trains, the remnant of mighty armies, were joined to the Christian powers of Syria, and a fruitless siege of Damascus was the final effort of the second crusade. Conrad and Louis embarked for Europe with the personal fame of piety and courage; but the Orientals had braved these potent monarchs of the Franks, with whose names and military forces they had been so often threatened. Perhaps they had still more to fear from the veteran genius of Frederic the First, who in his youth had served in Asia under his uncle Conrad. Forty campaigns in Germany and Italy had taught Barbarossa to command; and his soldiers, even the princes of the empire, were accustomed under his reign to obey. As soon as he lost sight of Philadelphia and Laodicea, the last cities of the Greek frontier, he plunged into the salt and barren desert, a land (says the historian) of horror and tribulation. During twenty days, every step of his fainting and sickly march was besieged by the innumerable hordes of Turkmans, whose numbers and fury seemed after each defeat to multiply and inflame. The emperor continued to struggle and to suffer; and such was the measure of his calamities, that when he reached the gates of Iconium, no more than one thousand knights were able to serve on horseback. By a sudden and resolute assault he defeated the guards, and stormed the capital of the sultan, who humbly sued for pardon and peace. The road was now open, and Frederic advanced in a career of triumph, till he was unfortunately drowned in a petty torrent of Cilicia. The remainder of his Germans was consumed by sickness and desertion: and the emperor's son expired with the greatest part of his Swabian vassals at the siege of Acre. Among the Latin heroes, Godfrey of Bouillon and Frederic Barbarossa could alone achieve the passage of the Lesser Asia; yet even their success was a warning; and in the last and most experienced age of the crusades, every nation preferred the sea to the toils and perils of an inland expedition.

Note: * It is now called the Girama: its course is described in M'Donald Kinneir's Travels. – M.]

The enthusiasm of the first crusade is a natural and simple event, while hope was fresh, danger untried, and enterprise congenial to the spirit of the times. But the obstinate perseverance of Europe may indeed excite our pity and admiration; that no instruction should have been drawn from constant and adverse experience; that the same confidence should have repeatedly grown from the same failures; that six succeeding generations should have rushed headlong down the precipice that was open before them; and that men of every condition should have staked their public and private fortunes on the desperate adventure of possessing or recovering a tombstone two thousand miles from their country. In a period of two centuries after the council of Clermont, each spring and summer produced a new emigration of pilgrim warriors for the defence of the Holy Land; but the seven great armaments or crusades were excited by some impending or recent calamity: the nations were moved by the authority of their pontiffs, and the example of their kings: their zeal was kindled, and their reason was silenced, by the voice of their holy orators; and among these, Bernard, the monk, or the saint, may claim the most honorable place. About eight years before the first conquest of Jerusalem, he was born of a noble family in Burgundy; at the age of three-and-twenty he buried himself in the monastery of Citeaux, then in the primitive fervor of the institution; at the end of two years he led forth her third colony, or daughter, to the valley of Clairvaux in Champagne; and was content, till the hour of his death, with the humble station of abbot of his own community. A philosophic age has abolished, with too liberal and indiscriminate disdain, the honors of these spiritual heroes. The meanest among them are distinguished by some energies of the mind; they were at least superior to their votaries and disciples; and, in the race of superstition, they attained the prize for which such numbers contended. In speech, in writing, in action, Bernard stood high above his rivals and contemporaries; his compositions are not devoid of wit and eloquence; and he seems to have preserved as much reason and humanity as may be reconciled with the character of a saint. In a secular life, he would have shared the seventh part of a private inheritance; by a vow of poverty and penance, by closing his eyes against the visible world, by the refusal of all ecclesiastical dignities, the abbot of Clairvaux became the oracle of Europe, and the founder of one hundred and sixty convents. Princes and pontiffs trembled at the freedom of his apostolical censures: France, England, and Milan, consulted and obeyed his judgment in a schism of the church: the debt was repaid by the gratitude of Innocent the Second; and his successor, Eugenius the Third, was the friend and disciple of the holy Bernard. It was in the proclamation of the second crusade that he shone as the missionary and prophet of God, who called the nations to the defence of his holy sepulchre. At the parliament of Vezelay he spoke before the king; and Louis the Seventh, with his nobles, received their crosses from his hand. The abbot of Clairvaux then marched to the less easy conquest of the emperor Conrad: a phlegmatic people, ignorant of his language, was transported by the pathetic vehemence of his tone and gestures; and his progress, from Constance to Cologne, was the triumph of eloquence and zeal. Bernard applauds his own success in the depopulation of Europe; affirms that cities and castles were emptied of their inhabitants; and computes, that only one man was left behind for the consolation of seven widows. The blind fanatics were desirous of electing him for their general; but the example of the hermit Peter was before his eyes; and while he assured the crusaders of the divine favor, he prudently declined a military command, in which failure and victory would have been almost equally disgraceful to his character. Yet, after the calamitous event, the abbot of Clairvaux was loudly accused as a false prophet, the author of the public and private mourning; his enemies exulted, his friends blushed, and his apology was slow and unsatisfactory. He justifies his obedience to the commands of the pope; expatiates on the mysterious ways of Providence; imputes the misfortunes of the pilgrims to their own sins; and modestly insinuates, that his mission had been approved by signs and wonders. Had the fact been certain, the argument would be decisive; and his faithful disciples, who enumerate twenty or thirty miracles in a day, appeal to the public assemblies of France and Germany, in which they were performed. At the present hour, such prodigies will not obtain credit beyond the precincts of Clairvaux; but in the preternatural cures of the blind, the lame, and the sick, who were presented to the man of God, it is impossible for us to ascertain the separate shares of accident, of fancy, of imposture, and of fiction.

Omnipotence itself cannot escape the murmurs of its discordant votaries; since the same dispensation which was applauded as a deliverance in Europe, was deplored, and perhaps arraigned, as a calamity in Asia. After the loss of Jerusalem, the Syrian fugitives diffused their consternation and sorrow; Bagdad mourned in the dust; the cadhi Zeineddin of Damascus tore his beard in the caliph's presence; and the whole divan shed tears at his melancholy tale. But the commanders of the faithful could only weep; they were themselves captives in the hands of the Turks: some temporal power was restored to the last age of the Abbassides; but their humble ambition was confined to Bagdad and the adjacent province. Their tyrants, the Seljukian sultans, had followed the common law of the Asiatic dynasties, the unceasing round of valor, greatness, discord, degeneracy, and decay; their spirit and power were unequal to the defence of religion; and, in his distant realm of Persia, the Christians were strangers to the name and the arms of Sangiar, the last hero of his race. While the sultans were involved in the silken web of the harem, the pious task was undertaken by their slaves, the Atabeks, a Turkish name, which, like the Byzantine patricians, may be translated by Father of the Prince. Ascansar, a valiant Turk, had been the favorite of Malek Shaw, from whom he received the privilege of standing on the right hand of the throne; but, in the civil wars that ensued on the monarch's death, he lost his head and the government of Aleppo. His domestic emirs persevered in their attachment to his son Zenghi, who proved his first arms against the Franks in the defeat of Antioch: thirty campaigns in the service of the caliph and sultan established his military fame; and he was invested with the command of Mosul, as the only champion that could avenge the cause of the prophet. The public hope was not disappointed: after a siege of twenty-five days, he stormed the city of Edessa, and recovered from the Franks their conquests beyond the Euphrates: the martial tribes of Cúurdistan were subdued by the independent sovereign of Mosul and Aleppo: his soldiers were taught to behold the camp as their only country; they trusted to his liberality for their rewards; and their absent families were protected by the vigilance of Zenghi. At the head of these veterans, his son Noureddin gradually united the Mahometan powers; added the kingdom of Damascus to that of Aleppo, and waged a long and successful war against the Christians of Syria; he spread his ample reign from the Tigris to the Nile, and the Abbassides rewarded their faithful servant with all the titles and prerogatives of royalty. The Latins themselves were compelled to own the wisdom and courage, and even the justice and piety, of this implacable adversary. In his life and government the holy warrior revived the zeal and simplicity of the first caliphs. Gold and silk were banished from his palace; the use of wine from his dominions; the public revenue was scrupulously applied to the public service; and the frugal household of Noureddin was maintained from his legitimate share of the spoil which he vested in the purchase of a private estate. His favorite sultana sighed for some female object of expense. "Alas," replied the king, "I fear God, and am no more than the treasurer of the Moslems. Their property I cannot alienate; but I still possess three shops in the city of Hems: these you may take; and these alone can I bestow." His chamber of justice was the terror of the great and the refuge of the poor. Some years after the sultan's death, an oppressed subject called aloud in the streets of Damascus, "O Noureddin, Noureddin, where art thou now? Arise, arise, to pity and protect us!" A tumult was apprehended, and a living tyrant blushed or trembled at the name of a departed monarch.

CHAPTER FIFTY NINE

The Crusades. – Part Two

By THE ARMS OF the Turks and Franks, the Fatimites had been deprived of Syria. In Egypt the decay of their character and influence was still more essential. Yet they were still revered as the descendants and successors of the prophet; they maintained their invisible state in the palace of Cairo; and their person was seldom violated by the profane eyes of subjects or strangers. The Latin ambassadors have described their own introduction, through a series of gloomy passages, and glittering porticos: the scene was enlivened by the warbling of birds and the murmur of fountains: it was enriched by a display of rich furniture and rare animals; of the Imperial treasures, something was shown, and much was supposed; and the long order of unfolding doors was guarded by black soldiers and domestic eunuchs. The sanctuary of the presence chamber was veiled with a curtain; and the vizier, who conducted the ambassadors, laid aside the cimeter, and prostrated himself three times on the ground; the veil was then removed; and they beheld the commander of the faithful, who signified his pleasure to the first slave of the throne. But this slave was his master: the viziers or sultans had usurped the supreme administration of Egypt; the claims of the rival candidates were decided by arms; and the name of the most worthy, of the strongest, was inserted in the royal patent of command. The factions of Dargham and Shawer alternately expelled each other from the capital and country; and the weaker side implored the dangerous protection of the sultan of Damascus, or the king of Jerusalem, the perpetual enemies of the sect and monarchy of the Fatimites. By his arms and religion the Turk was most formidable; but the Frank, in an easy, direct march, could advance from Gaza to the Nile; while the intermediate situation of his realm compelled the troops of Noureddin to wheel round the skirts of Arabia, a long and painful circuit, which exposed them to thirst, fatigue, and the burning winds of the desert. The secret zeal and ambition of the Turkish prince aspired to reign in Egypt under the name of the Abbassides; but the restoration of the suppliant Shawer was the ostensible motive of the first expedition; and the success was intrusted to the emir Shiracouh, a valiant and veteran commander. Dargham was oppressed and slain; but the ingratitude, the jealousy, the just apprehensions, of his more fortunate rival, soon provoked him to invite the king of Jerusalem to deliver Egypt from his insolent benefactors. To this union the forces of Shiracouh were unequal: he relinquished the premature conquest; and the evacuation of Belbeis or Pelusium was the condition of his safe retreat. As the Turks defiled before the enemy, and their general closed the rear, with a vigilant eye, and a battle axe in his hand, a Frank presumed to ask him if he were not afraid of an attack. "It is doubtless in your power to begin the attack," replied the intrepid emir; "but rest assured, that not one of my soldiers will go to paradise till he has sent an infidel to hell." His report of the riches of the land, the effeminacy of the natives, and the disorders of the government, revived the hopes of Noureddin; the caliph of Bagdad applauded the pious design; and Shiracouh descended into Egypt a second time with twelve thousand Turks and eleven thousand Arabs. Yet his forces were still inferior to the confederate armies of the Franks and Saracens; and I can discern an unusual degree of military art, in his passage of the Nile, his retreat into Thebais, his masterly evolutions in the battle of Babain, the surprise of Alexandria, and his marches and countermarches in the flats and valley of Egypt, from the tropic to the sea. His conduct was seconded by the courage of his troops, and on the eve of action a Mamaluke exclaimed, "If we cannot wrest Egypt from the Christian dogs, why do we not renounce the honors and rewards of the sultan, and retire to labor with the peasants, or to spin with the females of the harem?" Yet, after all his efforts in the field, after the obstinate defence of Alexandria by his nephew Saladin, an honorable capitulation and retreat concluded the second enterprise of Shiracouh; and Noureddin reserved his abilities for a third and more propitious occasion. It was soon offered by the ambition and avarice of Amalric or Amaury, king of Jerusalem, who had imbibed the pernicious maxim, that no faith should be kept with the enemies of God. A religious warrior, the great master of the hospital, encouraged him to proceed; the emperor of Constantinople either gave, or promised, a fleet to act with the armies of Syria; and the perfidious Christian, unsatisfied with spoil and subsidy, aspired to the conquest of Egypt. In this emergency, the Moslems turned their eyes towards the sultan of Damascus; the vizier, whom danger encompassed on all sides, yielded to their unanimous wishes, and Noureddin seemed to be tempted by the fair offer of one third of the revenue of the kingdom. The Franks were already at the gates of Cairo; but the suburbs, the old city, were burnt on their approach; they were deceived by an insidious negotiation, and their vessels were unable to surmount the barriers of the Nile. They prudently declined a contest with the Turks in the midst of a hostile country; and Amaury retired into Palestine with the shame and reproach that always adhere to unsuccessful injustice. After this deliverance, Shiracouh was invested with a robe of honor, which he soon stained with the blood of the unfortunate Shawer. For a while, the Turkish emirs condescended to hold the office of vizier; but this foreign conquest precipitated the fall of the Fatimites themselves; and the bloodless change was accomplished by a message and a word. The caliphs had been degraded by their own weakness and the tyranny of the viziers: their subjects blushed, when the descendant and successor of the prophet presented his naked hand to the rude gripe of a Latin ambassador; they wept when he sent the hair of his women, a sad emblem of their grief and terror, to excite the pity of the sultan of Damascus. By the command of Noureddin, and the sentence of the doctors, the holy names of Abubeker, Omar, and Othman, were solemnly restored: the caliph Mosthadi, of Bagdad, was acknowledged in the public prayers as the true commander of the faithful; and the green livery of the sons of Ali was exchanged for the black color of the Abbassides. The last of his race, the caliph Adhed, who survived only ten days, expired in happy ignorance of his fate; his treasures secured the loyalty of the soldiers, and silenced the murmurs of the sectaries; and in all subsequent revolutions, Egypt has never departed from the orthodox tradition of the Moslems.

The hilly country beyond the Tigris is occupied by the pastoral tribes of the Cúurds; a people hardy, strong, savage impatient of the yoke, addicted to rapine, and tenacious of the government of their national chiefs. The resemblance of name, situation, and manners, seems to identify them with the Carduchians of the Greeks; and they still defend against the Ottoman Porte the antique freedom which they asserted against the successors of Cyrus. Poverty and ambition prompted them to embrace the profession of mercenary soldiers: the service of his father and uncle prepared the reign of the great Saladin; and the son of Job or Ayud, a simple Cúurd, magnanimously smiled at his pedigree, which flattery deduced from the Arabian caliphs. So unconscious was Noureddin of the impending ruin of his house, that he constrained the reluctant youth to follow his uncle Shiracouh into Egypt: his military character was established by the defence of Alexandria; and, if we may believe the Latins, he solicited and obtained from the Christian general the *profane*honors of knighthood. On the death of Shiracouh, the office of grand vizier was bestowed on Saladin, as the youngest and least powerful of the emirs; but with the advice of his father, whom he invited to Cairo, his genius obtained the ascendant over his equals, and attached the army to his person and interest. While Noureddin lived, these ambitious Cúurds were the most humble of his slaves; and the indiscreet murmurs of the divan were silenced by the prudent Ayub, who loudly protested that at the command of the sultan he himself would lead his sons in chains to the foot of the throne. "Such language," he added in private, "was prudent and proper in an assembly of your rivals; but we are now above fear and obedience; and the threats of Noureddin shall not extort the tribute of a sugar-cane." His seasonable death relieved them from the odious and doubtful conflict: his son, a minor of eleven years of age, was left for a while to the emirs of Damascus; and the new lord of Egypt was decorated by the caliph with every title that could sanctify his usurpation in the eyes of the people. Nor was Saladin long content with the possession of Egypt; he despoiled the Christians of Jerusalem, and the Atabeks of Damascus, Aleppo, and Diarbekir: Mecca and Medina acknowledged him for their temporal protector: his brother subdued the distant regions of Yemen, or the happy Arabia; and at the hour of his death, his empire was spread from the African Tripoli to the Tigris, and from the Indian Ocean to the mountains of Armenia. In the judgment of his character, the reproaches of treason and ingratitude strike forcibly on *our* minds, impressed, as they are, with the principle and experience of law and loyalty. But his ambition may in some measure be excused by the revolutions of Asia, which had erased every notion of legitimate succession; by the recent example of the Atabeks themselves; by his reverence to the son of his benefactor; his humane and generous behavior to the collateral branches; by *their* incapacity and *his* merit; by the approbation of the caliph, the sole source of all legitimate power; and, above all, by the wishes and interest of the people, whose happiness is the first object of government. In *his* virtues, and in those of his patron, they admired the singular union of the hero and the saint; for both Noureddin and Saladin are ranked among the Mahometan saints; and the constant meditation of the holy war appears to have shed a serious and sober color over their lives and actions. The youth of the latter was addicted to wine and women: but his aspiring spirit soon renounced the temptations of pleasure for the graver follies of fame and dominion: the garment of Saladin was of coarse woollen; water was his only drink; and, while he emulated the temperance, he surpassed the chastity, of his Arabian prophet. Both in faith and practice he was a rigid Mussulman: he ever deplored that the defence of religion had not allowed him to accomplish the pilgrimage of Mecca; but at the stated hours, five times each day, the sultan devoutly prayed with his brethren: the involuntary omission of fasting was scrupulously repaid; and his perusal of the Koran, on horseback between the approaching armies, may be quoted as a proof, however ostentatious, of piety and courage. The superstitious doctrine of the sect of Shafei was the only study that he deigned to encourage: the poets were safe in his contempt; but all profane science was the object of his aversion; and a philosopher, who had invented some speculative novelties, was seized and strangled by the command of the royal saint. The justice of his divan was accessible to the meanest suppliant against himself and his ministers; and it was only for a kingdom that Saladin would deviate from the rule of equity. While the descendants of Seljuk and Zenghi held his stirrup and smoothed his garments, he was affable and patient with the meanest of his servants. So boundless was his liberality, that he distributed twelve thousand horses at the siege of Acre; and, at the time of his death, no more than forty-seven drams of silver and one piece of gold coin were found in the treasury; yet, in a martial reign, the tributes were diminished, and the wealthy citizens enjoyed, without fear or danger, the fruits of their industry. Egypt, Syria, and Arabia, were adorned by the royal foundations of hospitals, colleges, and mosques; and Cairo was fortified with a wall and citadel; but his works were consecrated to public use: nor did the sultan indulge himself in a garden or palace of private luxury. In a fanatic age, himself a fanatic, the genuine virtues of Saladin commanded the esteem of the Christians; the emperor of Germany gloried in his friendship; the Greek emperor solicited his alliance; and the conquest of Jerusalem diffused, and perhaps magnified, his fame both in the East and West.

During its short existence, the kingdom of Jerusalem was supported by the discord of the Turks and Saracens; and both the Fatimite caliphs and the sultans of Damascus were tempted to sacrifice the cause of their religion to the meaner considerations of private and present advantage. But the powers of Egypt, Syria, and Arabia, were now united by a hero, whom nature and fortune had armed against the Christians. All without now bore the most threatening aspect; and all was feeble and hollow in the internal state of Jerusalem. After the two first Baldwins, the brother and cousin of Godfrey of Bouillon, the sceptre devolved by female succession to Melisenda, daughter of the second Baldwin, and her husband Fulk, count of Anjou, the father, by a former marriage, of our English Plantagenets. Their two sons, Baldwin the Third, and Amaury, waged a strenuous, and not unsuccessful, war against the infidels; but the son of Amaury, Baldwin the Fourth, was deprived, by the leprosy, a gift of the crusades, of the faculties both of mind and body. His sister Sybilla, the mother of Baldwin the Fifth, was his natural heiress: after the suspicious death of her child, she crowned her second husband, Guy of Lusignan, a prince of a handsome person, but of such base renown, that his own brother Jeffrey was heard to exclaim, "Since they have made *him* a king, surely they would have made *me* a god!" The choice was generally blamed; and the most powerful vassal, Raymond count of Tripoli, who had been excluded from the succession and regency, entertained an implacable hatred against the king, and exposed his honor and conscience to the temptations of the sultan. Such were the guardians of the holy city; a leper, a child, a woman, a coward, and a traitor: yet its fate was delayed twelve years by some supplies from Europe, by the valor of the military orders, and by the distant or domestic avocations of their great enemy. At length, on every side, the sinking state was encircled and pressed by a hostile line: and the truce was violated by the Franks, whose existence it protected. A soldier of fortune, Reginald of Chatillon, had seized a fortress on the edge of the desert, from whence he pillaged the caravans, insulted Mahomet, and threatened the cities of Mecca and Medina. Saladin condescended to complain; rejoiced in the denial of justice, and at the head of fourscore thousand horse and foot invaded the Holy Land. The choice of Tiberias for his first siege was suggested by the count of Tripoli, to whom it belonged; and the king of Jerusalem was persuaded to drain his garrison, and to arm his people, for the relief of that important place. By the advice of the perfidious Raymond, the Christians were betrayed into a camp destitute of water: he fled on the first onset, with the curses of both nations: Lusignan was overthrown, with the loss of thirty thousand men; and the wood of the true cross (a dire misfortune!) was left in the power of the infidels. The royal captive was conducted to the tent of Saladin; and as he fainted with thirst and terror, the generous victor presented him with a cup of sherbet, cooled in snow, without suffering his companion, Reginald of Chatillon, to partake of this pledge of hospitality and pardon. "The person and dignity of a king," said the sultan, "are sacred, but this impious robber must instantly acknowledge the prophet, whom he has blasphemed, or meet the death which he has so often deserved." On the proud or conscientious refusal of the Christian warrior, Saladin struck him on the head with his cimeter, and Reginald was despatched by the guards. The trembling Lusignan was sent to Damascus, to an honorable prison and speedy ransom; but the victory was stained by the execution of two hundred and thirty knights of the hospital, the intrepid champions and martyrs of their faith. The kingdom was left without a head; and of the two grand masters of the military orders, the one was slain and the other was a prisoner. From all the cities, both of the sea-coast and the inland country, the garrisons had been drawn away for this fatal field: Tyre and Tripoli alone could escape the rapid inroad of Saladin; and three months after the battle of Tiberias, he appeared in arms before the gates of Jerusalem.

He might expect that the siege of a city so venerable on earth and in heaven, so interesting to Europe and Asia, would rekindle the last sparks of enthusiasm; and that, of sixty thousand Christians, every man would be a soldier, and every soldier a candidate for martyrdom. But Queen Sybilla trembled for herself and her captive husband; and the barons and knights, who had escaped from the sword and chains of the Turks, displayed the same factious and selfish spirit in the public ruin. The most numerous portion of the inhabitants was composed of the Greek and Oriental Christians, whom experience had taught to prefer the Mahometan before the Latin yoke; and the holy sepulchre attracted a base and needy crowd, without arms or courage, who subsisted only on the charity of the pilgrims. Some feeble and hasty efforts were made for the defence of Jerusalem: but in the space of fourteen days, a victorious army drove back the sallies of the besieged, planted their engines, opened the wall to the breadth of fifteen cubits, applied their scaling-ladders, and erected on the breach twelve banners of the prophet and the sultan. It was in vain that a barefoot procession of the queen, the women, and the monks, implored the Son of God to save his tomb and his inheritance from impious violation. Their sole hope was in the mercy of the conqueror, and to their first suppliant deputation that mercy was sternly denied. "He had sworn to avenge the patience and long-suffering of the Moslems; the hour of forgiveness was elapsed, and the moment was now arrived to expiate, in blood, the innocent blood which had been spilt by Godfrey and the first crusaders." But a desperate and successful struggle of the Franks admonished the sultan that his triumph was not yet secure; he listened with reverence to a solemn adjuration in the name of the common Father of mankind; and a sentiment of human sympathy mollified the rigor of fanaticism and conquest. He consented to accept the city, and to spare the inhabitants. The Greek and Oriental Christians were permitted to live under his dominion, but it was stipulated, that in forty days all the Franks and Latins should evacuate Jerusalem, and be safely conducted to the seaports of Syria and Egypt; that ten pieces of gold should be paid for each man, five for each woman, and one for every child; and that those who were unable to purchase their freedom should be detained in perpetual slavery. Of some writers it is a favorite and invidious theme to compare the humanity of Saladin with the massacre of the first crusade. The difference would be merely personal; but we should not forget that the Christians had offered to capitulate, and that the Mahometans of Jerusalem sustained the last extremities of an assault and storm. Justice is indeed due to the fidelity with which the Turkish conqueror fulfilled the conditions of the treaty; and he may be deservedly praised for the glance of pity which he cast on the misery of the vanquished. Instead of a rigorous exaction of his debt, he accepted a sum of thirty thousand byzants, for the ransom of seven thousand poor; two or three thousand more were dismissed by his gratuitous clemency; and the number of slaves was reduced to eleven or fourteen thousand persons. In this interview with the queen, his words, and even his tears suggested the kindest consolations; his liberal alms were distributed among those who had been made orphans or widows by the fortune of war; and while the knights of the hospital were in arms against him, he allowed their more pious brethren to continue, during the term of a year, the care and service of the sick. In these acts of mercy the virtue of Saladin deserves our admiration and love: he was above the necessity of dissimulation, and his stern fanaticism would have prompted him to dissemble, rather than to affect, this profane compassion for the enemies of the Koran. After Jerusalem had been delivered from the presence of the strangers, the sultan made his triumphal entry, his banners waving in the wind, and to the harmony of martial music. The great mosque of Omar, which had been converted into a church, was again consecrated to one God and his prophet Mahomet: the walls and pavement were purified with rose-water; and a pulpit, the labor of Noureddin, was erected in the sanctuary. But when the golden cross that glittered on the dome was cast down, and dragged through the streets, the Christians of every sect uttered a lamentable groan, which was answered by the joyful shouts of the Moslems. In four ivory chests the patriarch had collected the crosses, the images, the vases, and the relics of the holy place; they were seized by the conqueror, who was desirous of presenting the caliph with the trophies of Christian idolatry. He was persuaded, however, to intrust them to the patriarch and prince of Antioch; and the pious pledge was redeemed by Richard of England, at the expense of fifty-two thousand byzants of gold.

The nations might fear and hope the immediate and final expulsion of the Latins from Syria; which was yet delayed above a century after the death of Saladin. In the career of victory, he was first checked by the resistance of Tyre; the troops and garrisons, which had capitulated, were imprudently conducted to the same port: their numbers were adequate to the defence of the place; and the arrival of Conrad of Montferrat inspired the disorderly crowd with confidence and union. His father, a venerable pilgrim, had been made prisoner in the battle of Tiberias; but that disaster was unknown in Italy and Greece, when the son was urged by ambition and piety to visit the inheritance of his royal nephew, the infant Baldwin. The view of the Turkish banners warned him from the hostile coast of Jaffa; and Conrad was unanimously hailed as the prince and champion of Tyre, which was already besieged by the conqueror of Jerusalem. The firmness of his zeal, and perhaps his knowledge of a generous foe, enabled him to brave the threats of the sultan, and to declare, that should his aged parent be exposed before the walls, he himself would discharge the first arrow, and glory in his descent from a Christian martyr. The Egyptian fleet was allowed to enter the harbor of Tyre; but the chain was suddenly drawn, and five galleys were either sunk or taken: a thousand Turks were slain in a sally; and Saladin, after burning his engines, concluded a glorious campaign by a disgraceful retreat to Damascus. He was soon assailed by a more formidable tempest. The pathetic narratives, and even the pictures, that represented in lively colors the servitude and profanation of Jerusalem, awakened the torpid sensibility of Europe: the emperor Frederic Barbarossa, and the kings of France and England, assumed the cross; and the tardy magnitude of their armaments was anticipated by the maritime states of the Mediterranean and the Ocean. The skilful and provident Italians first embarked in the ships of Genoa, Pisa, and Venice. They were speedily followed by the most eager pilgrims of France, Normandy, and the Western Isles. The powerful succor of Flanders, Frise, and Denmark, filled near a hundred vessels: and the Northern warriors were distinguished in the field by a lofty stature and a ponderous battle-axe. Their increasing multitudes could no longer be confined within the walls of Tyre, or remain obedient to the voice of Conrad. They pitied the misfortunes, and revered the dignity, of Lusignan, who was released from prison, perhaps, to divide the army of the Franks. He proposed the recovery of Ptolemais, or Acre, thirty miles to the south of Tyre; and the place was first invested by two thousand horse and thirty thousand foot under his nominal command. I shall not expatiate on the story of this memorable siege; which lasted near two years, and consumed, in a narrow space, the forces of Europe and Asia. Never did the flame of enthusiasm burn with fiercer and more destructive rage; nor could the true believers, a common appellation, who consecrated their own martyrs, refuse some applause to the mistaken zeal and courage of their adversaries. At the sound of the holy trumpet, the Moslems of Egypt, Syria, Arabia, and the Oriental provinces, assembled under the servant of the prophet: his camp was pitched and removed within a few miles of Acre; and he labored, night and day, for the relief of his brethren and the annoyance of the Franks. Nine battles, not unworthy of the name, were fought in the neighborhood of Mount Carmel, with such vicissitude of fortune, that in one attack, the sultan forced his way into the city; that in one sally, the Christians penetrated to the royal tent. By the means of divers and pigeons, a regular correspondence was maintained with the besieged; and, as often as the sea was left open, the exhausted garrison was withdrawn, and a fresh supply was poured into the place. The Latin camp was thinned by famine, the sword and the climate; but the tents of the dead were replenished with new pilgrims, who exaggerated the strength and speed of their approaching countrymen. The vulgar was astonished by the report, that the pope himself, with an innumerable crusade, was advanced as far as Constantinople. The march of the emperor filled the East with more serious alarms: the obstacles which he encountered in Asia, and perhaps in Greece, were raised by the policy of Saladin: his joy on the death of Barbarossa was measured by his esteem; and the Christians were rather dismayed than encouraged at the sight of the duke of Swabia and his way-worn remnant of five thousand Germans. At length, in the spring of the second year, the royal fleets of France and England cast anchor in the Bay of Acre, and the siege was more vigorously prosecuted by the youthful emulation of the two kings, Philip Augustus and Richard Plantagenet. After every resource had been tried, and every hope was exhausted, the defenders of Acre submitted to their fate; a capitulation was granted, but their lives and liberties were taxed at the hard conditions of a ransom of two hundred thousand pieces of gold, the deliverance of one hundred nobles, and fifteen hundred inferior captives, and the restoration of the wood of the holy cross. Some doubts in the agreement, and some delay in the execution, rekindled the fury of the Franks, and three thousand Moslems, almost in the sultan's view, were beheaded by the command of the sanguinary Richard. By the conquest of Acre, the Latin powers acquired a strong town and a convenient harbor; but the advantage was most dearly purchased. The minister and historian of Saladin computes, from the report of the enemy, that their numbers, at different periods, amounted to five or six hundred thousand; that more than one hundred thousand Christians were slain; that a far greater number was lost by disease or shipwreck; and that a small portion of this mighty host could return in safety to their native countries.

The Crusades. – Part Three

PHILIP AUGUSTUS, and Richard the First, are the only kings of France and England who have fought under the same banners; but the holy service in which they were enlisted was incessantly disturbed by their national jealousy; and the two factions, which they protected in Palestine, were more averse to each other than to the common enemy. In the eyes of the Orientals; the French monarch was superior in dignity and power; and, in the emperor's absence, the Latins revered him as their temporal chief. His exploits were not adequate to his fame. Philip was brave, but the statesman predominated in his character; he was soon weary of sacrificing his health and interest on a barren coast: the surrender of Acre became the signal of his departure; nor could he justify this unpopular desertion, by leaving the duke of Burgundy with five hundred knights and ten thousand foot, for the service of the Holy Land. The king of England, though inferior in dignity, surpassed his rival in wealth and military renown; and if heroism be confined to brutal and ferocious valor, Richard Plantagenet will stand high among the heroes of the age. The memory of *Cúur de Lion*, of the lion-hearted prince, was long dear and glorious to his English subjects; and, at the distance of sixty years, it was celebrated in proverbial sayings by the grandsons of the Turks and Saracens, against whom he had fought: his tremendous name was employed by the Syrian mothers to silence their infants; and if a horse suddenly started from the way, his rider was wont to exclaim, "Dost thou think King Richard is in that bush?" His cruelty to the Mahometans was the effect of temper and zeal; but I cannot believe that a soldier, so free and fearless in the use of his lance, would have descended to whet a dagger against his valiant brother Conrad of Montferrat, who was slain at Tyre by some secret assassins. After the surrender of Acre, and the departure of Philip, the king of England led the crusaders to the recovery of the sea-coast; and the cities of Cæsarea and Jaffa were added to the fragments of the kingdom of Lusignan. A march of one hundred miles from Acre to Ascalon was a great and perpetual battle of eleven days. In the disorder of his troops, Saladin remained on the field with seventeen guards, without lowering his standard, or suspending the sound of his brazen kettle-drum: he again rallied and renewed the charge; and his preachers or heralds called aloud on the *unitarians*, manfully to stand up against the Christian idolaters. But the progress of these idolaters was irresistible; and it was only by demolishing the walls and buildings of Ascalon, that the sultan could prevent them from occupying an important fortress on the confines of Egypt. During a severe winter, the armies slept; but in the spring, the Franks advanced within a day's march of Jerusalem, under the leading standard of the English king; and his active spirit intercepted a convoy, or caravan, of seven thousand camels. Saladin had fixed his station in the holy city; but the city was struck with consternation and discord: he fasted; he prayed; he preached; he offered to share the dangers of the siege; but his Mamalukes, who remembered the fate of their companions at Acre, pressed the sultan with loyal or seditious clamors, to reserve *his* person and *their* courage for the future defence of the religion and empire. The Moslems were delivered by the sudden, or, as they deemed, the miraculous, retreat of the Christians; and the laurels of Richard were blasted by the prudence, or envy, of his companions. The hero, ascending a hill, and veiling his face, exclaimed with an indignant voice, "Those who are unwilling to rescue, are unworthy to view, the sepulchre of Christ!" After his return to Acre, on the news that Jaffa was surprised by the sultan, he sailed with some merchant vessels, and leaped foremost on the beach: the castle was relieved by his presence; and sixty thousand Turks and Saracens fled before his arms. The discovery of his weakness, provoked them to return in the morning; and they found him carelessly encamped before the gates with only seventeen knights and three hundred archers. Without counting their numbers, he sustained their charge; and we learn from the evidence of his enemies, that the king of England, grasping his lance, rode furiously along their front, from the right to the left wing, without meeting an adversary who dared to encounter his career. Am I writing the history of Orlando or Amadis?

Note: * Von Hammer (Geschichte der Assassinen, p. 202) sums up against Richard, Wilken (vol. iv. p. 485) as strongly for acquittal. Michaud (vol. ii. p. 420) delivers no decided opinion. This crime was also attributed to Saladin, who is said, by an Oriental authority, (the continuator of Tabari,) to have employed the assassins to murder both Conrad and Richard. It is a melancholy admission, but it must be acknowledged, that such an act would be less inconsistent with the character of the Christian than of the Mahometan king. – M.]

During these hostilities, a languid and tedious negotiation between the Franks and Moslems was started, and continued, and broken, and again resumed, and again broken. Some acts of royal courtesy, the gift of snow and fruit, the exchange of Norway hawks and Arabian horses, softened the asperity of religious war: from the vicissitude of success, the monarchs might learn to suspect that Heaven was neutral in the quarrel; nor, after the trial of each other, could either hope for a decisive victory. The health both of Richard and Saladin appeared to be in a declining state; and they respectively suffered the evils of distant and domestic warfare: Plantagenet was impatient to punish a perfidious rival who had invaded Normandy in his absence; and the indefatigable sultan was subdued by the cries of the people, who was the victim, and of the soldiers, who were the instruments, of his martial zeal. The first demands of the king of England were the restitution of Jerusalem, Palestine, and the true cross; and he firmly declared, that himself and his brother pilgrims would end their lives in the pious labor, rather than return to Europe with ignominy and remorse. But the conscience of Saladin refused, without some weighty compensation, to restore the idols, or promote the idolatry, of the Christians; he asserted, with equal firmness, his religious and civil claim to the sovereignty of Palestine; descanted on the importance and sanctity of Jerusalem; and rejected all terms of the establishment, or partition of the Latins. The marriage which Richard proposed, of his sister with the sultan's brother, was defeated by the difference of faith; the princess abhorred the embraces of a Turk; and Adel, or Saphadin, would not easily renounce a plurality of wives. A personal interview was declined by Saladin, who alleged their mutual ignorance of each other's language; and the negotiation was managed with much art and delay by their interpreters and envoys. The final agreement was equally disapproved by the zealots of both parties, by the Roman pontiff and the caliph of Bagdad. It was stipulated that Jerusalem and the holy sepulchre should be open, without tribute or vexation, to the pilgrimage of the Latin Christians; that, after the demolition of Ascalon, they should inclusively possess the sea-coast from Jaffa to Tyre; that the count of Tripoli and the prince of Antioch should be comprised in the truce; and that, during three years and three months, all hostilities should cease. The principal chiefs of the two armies swore to

the observance of the treaty; but the monarchs were satisfied with giving their word and their right hand; and the royal majesty was excused
from an oath, which always implies some suspicion of falsehood and
dishonor. Richard embarked for Europe, to seek a long captivity and a
premature grave; and the space of a few months concluded the life and
glories of Saladin. The Orientals describe his edifying death, which happened at Damascus; but they seem ignorant of the equal distribution of
his alms among the three religions, or of the display of a shroud, instead
of a standard, to admonish the East of the instability of human greatness. The unity of empire was dissolved by his death; his sons were oppressed by the stronger arm of their uncle Saphadin; the hostile interests
of the sultans of Egypt, Damascus, and Aleppo, were again revived; and
the Franks or Latins stood and breathed, and hoped, in their fortresses
along the Syrian coast.

The noblest monument of a conqueror's fame, and of the terror which
he inspired, is the Saladine tenth, a general tax which was imposed on
the laity, and even the clergy, of the Latin church, for the service of the
holy war. The practice was too lucrative to expire with the occasion:
and this tribute became the foundation of all the tithes and tenths on
ecclesiastical benefices, which have been granted by the Roman pontiffs to Catholic sovereigns, or reserved for the immediate use of the
apostolic see. This pecuniary emolument must have tended to increase
the interest of the popes in the recovery of Palestine: after the death of
Saladin, they preached the crusade, by their epistles, their legates, and
their missionaries; and the accomplishment of the pious work might
have been expected from the zeal and talents of Innocent the Third. Under that young and ambitious priest, the successors of St. Peter attained
the full meridian of their greatness: and in a reign of eighteen years, he
exercised a despotic command over the emperors and kings, whom he
raised and deposed; over the nations, whom an interdict of months or
years deprived, for the offence of their rulers, of the exercise of Christian worship. In the council of the Lateran he acted as the ecclesiastical,
almost as the temporal, sovereign of the East and West. It was at the feet
of his legate that John of England surrendered his crown; and Innocent
may boast of the two most signal triumphs over sense and humanity, the
establishment of transubstantiation, and the origin of the inquisition.
At his voice, two crusades, the fourth and the fifth, were undertaken;
but, except a king of Hungary, the princes of the second order were at
the head of the pilgrims: the forces were inadequate to the design; nor
did the effects correspond with the hopes and wishes of the pope and
the people. The fourth crusade was diverted from Syria to Constanti-

nople; and the conquest of the Greek or Roman empire by the Latins will form the proper and important subject of the next chapter. In the fifth, two hundred thousand Franks were landed at the eastern mouth of the Nile. They reasonably hoped that Palestine must be subdued in Egypt, the seat and storehouse of the sultan; and, after a siege of sixteen months, the Moslems deplored the loss of Damietta. But the Christian army was ruined by the pride and insolence of the legate Pelagius, who, in the pope's name, assumed the character of general: the sickly Franks were encompassed by the waters of the Nile and the Oriental forces; and it was by the evacuation of Damietta that they obtained a safe retreat, some concessions for the pilgrims, and the tardy restitution of the doubtful relic of the true cross. The failure may in some measure be ascribed to the abuse and multiplication of the crusades, which were preached at the same time against the Pagans of Livonia, the Moors of Spain, the Albigeois of France, and the kings of Sicily of the Imperial family. In these meritorious services, the volunteers might acquire at home the same spiritual indulgence, and a larger measure of temporal rewards; and even the popes, in their zeal against a domestic enemy, were sometimes tempted to forget the distress of their Syrian brethren. From the last age of the crusades they derived the occasional command of an army and revenue; and some deep reasoners have suspected that the whole enterprise, from the first synod of Placentia, was contrived and executed by the policy of Rome. The suspicion is not founded, either in nature or in fact. The successors of St. Peter appear to have followed, rather than guided, the impulse of manners and prejudice; without much foresight of the seasons, or cultivation of the soil, they gathered the ripe and spontaneous fruits of the superstition of the times. They gathered these fruits without toil or personal danger: in the council of the Lateran, Innocent the Third declared an ambiguous resolution of animating the crusaders by his example; but the pilot of the sacred vessel could not abandon the helm; nor was Palestine ever blessed with the presence of a Roman pontiff.

The persons, the families, and estates of the pilgrims, were under the immediate protection of the popes; and these spiritual patrons soon claimed the prerogative of directing their operations, and enforcing, by commands and censures, the accomplishment of their vow. Frederic the Second, the grandson of Barbarossa, was successively the pupil, the enemy, and the victim of the church. At the age of twenty-one years, and in obedience to his guardian Innocent the Third, he assumed the cross; the same promise was repeated at his royal and imperial coronations; and his marriage with the heiress of Jerusalem forever bound him to defend the kingdom of his son Conrad. But as Frederic advanced in age and authority, he repented of the rash engagements of his youth: his liberal sense and knowledge taught him to despise the phantoms of superstition and the crowns of Asia: he no longer entertained the same reverence for the successors of Innocent: and his ambition was occupied by the restoration of the Italian monarchy from Sicily to the Alps. But the success of this project would have reduced the popes to their primitive simplicity; and, after the delays and excuses of twelve years, they urged the emperor, with entreaties and threats, to fix the time and place of his departure for Palestine. In the harbors of Sicily and Apulia, he prepared a fleet of one hundred galleys, and of one hundred vessels, that were framed to transport and land two thousand five hundred knights, with their horses and attendants; his vassals of Naples and Germany formed a powerful army; and the number of English crusaders was magnified to sixty thousand by the report of fame. But the inevitable or affected slowness of these mighty preparations consumed the strength and provisions of the more indigent pilgrims: the multitude was thinned by sickness and desertion; and the sultry summer of Calabria anticipated the mischiefs of a Syrian campaign. At length the emperor hoisted sail at Brundusium, with a fleet and army of forty thousand men: but he kept the sea no more than three days; and his hasty retreat, which was ascribed by his friends to a grievous indisposition, was accused by his enemies as a voluntary and obstinate disobedience. For suspending his vow was Frederic excommunicated by Gregory the Ninth; for presuming, the next year, to accomplish his vow, he was again excommunicated by the same pope. While he served under the banner of the cross, a crusade was preached against him in Italy; and after his return he was compelled to ask pardon for the injuries which he had suffered. The clergy and military orders of Palestine were previously instructed to renounce his communion and dispute his commands; and in his own kingdom, the emperor was forced to consent that the orders of the camp should be issued in the name of God and of the Christian republic. Frederic entered Jerusalem in triumph; and with his own hands (for no priest would perform the office) he took the crown from the altar of the holy sepulchre. But the patriarch cast an interdict on the church which his presence had profaned; and the knights of the hospital and temple informed the sultan how easily he might be surprised and slain in his unguarded visit to the River Jordan. In such a state of fanaticism and faction, victory was hopeless, and defence was difficult; but the conclusion of an advantageous peace may be imputed to the discord of the Mahometans, and their personal esteem for the character of Frederic. The enemy of the church is accused of maintaining with the miscreants an intercourse of hospitality and friendship unworthy of a Christian; of despising the barrenness of the land; and of indulging a profane thought, that if Jehovah had seen the kingdom of Naples he never would have selected Palestine for the inheritance of his chosen people. Yet Frederic obtained from the sultan the restitution of Jerusalem, of Bethlem and Nazareth, of Tyre and Sidon; the Latins were allowed to inhabit and fortify the city; an equal code of civil and religious freedom was ratified for the sectaries of Jesus and those of Mahomet; and, while the former worshipped at the holy sepulchre, the latter might pray and preach in the mosque of the temple, from whence the prophet undertook his nocturnal journey to heaven. The clergy deplored this scandalous toleration; and the weaker Moslems were gradually expelled; but every rational object of the crusades was accomplished without bloodshed; the churches were restored, the monasteries were replenished; and, in the space of fifteen years, the Latins of Jerusalem exceeded the number of six thousand. This peace and prosperity, for which they were ungrateful to their benefactor, was terminated by the irruption of the strange and savage hordes of Carizmians. Flying from the arms of the Moguls, those shepherds of the Caspian rolled headlong on Syria; and the union of the Franks with the sultans of Aleppo, Hems, and Damascus, was insufficient to stem the violence of the torrent. Whatever stood against them was cut off by the sword, or dragged into captivity: the military orders were almost exterminated in a single battle; and in the pillage of the city, in the profanation of the holy sepulchre, the Latins confess and regret the modesty and discipline of the Turks and Saracens.

Of the seven crusades, the two last were undertaken by Louis the Ninth, king of France; who lost his liberty in Egypt, and his life on the coast of Africa. Twenty-eight years after his death, he was canonized at Rome; and sixty-five miracles were readily found, and solemnly attested, to justify the claim of the royal saint. The voice of history renders a more honorable testimony, that he united the virtues of a king, a hero, and a man; that his martial spirit was tempered by the love of private and public justice; and that Louis was the father of his people, the friend of his neighbors, and the terror of the infidels. Superstition alone, in all the extent of her baleful influence, corrupted his understanding and his heart: his devotion stooped to admire and imitate the begging friars of Francis and Dominic: he pursued with blind and cruel zeal the enemies of the faith; and the best of kings twice descended from his throne to seek the adventures of a spiritual knight-errant. A monkish historian would have been content to applaud the most despicable part of his character; but the noble and gallant Joinville, who shared the friendship and captivity of Louis, has traced with the pencil of nature the free portrait of his virtues as well as of his failings. From this intimate knowledge we may learn to suspect the political views of depressing their great vassals, which are so often imputed to the royal authors of the crusades. Above all the princes of the middle ages, Louis the Ninth successfully labored to restore the prerogatives of the crown; but it was at home and not in the East, that he acquired for himself and his posterity: his vow was the result of enthusiasm and sickness; and if he were the promoter, he was likewise the victim, of his holy madness. For the invasion of Egypt, France was exhausted of her troops and treasures; he covered the sea of Cyprus with eighteen hundred sails; the most modest enumeration amounts to fifty thousand men; and, if we might trust his own confession, as it is reported by Oriental vanity, he disembarked nine thousand five hundred horse, and one hundred and thirty thousand foot, who performed their pilgrimage under the shadow of his power.

Note: * Compare Wilken, vol. vii. p. 94. – M.]

In complete armor, the oriflamme waving before him, Louis leaped foremost on the beach; and the strong city of Damietta, which had cost his predecessors a siege of sixteen months, was abandoned on the first assault by the trembling Moslems. But Damietta was the first and the last of his conquests; and in the fifth and sixth crusades, the same causes, almost on the same ground, were productive of similar calamities. After a ruinous delay, which introduced into the camp the seeds of an epidemic disease, the Franks advanced from the sea-coast towards the capital of Egypt, and strove to surmount the unseasonable inundation of the Nile, which opposed their progress. Under the eye of their intrepid monarch, the barons and knights of France displayed their invincible contempt of danger and discipline: his brother, the count of Artois, stormed with inconsiderate valor the town of Massoura; and the carrier pigeons announced to the inhabitants of Cairo that all was lost. But a soldier, who afterwards usurped the sceptre, rallied the flying troops: the main body of the Christians was far behind the vanguard; and Artois was overpowered and slain. A shower of Greek fire was incessantly poured on the invaders; the Nile was commanded by the Egyptian galleys, the open country by the Arabs; all provisions were intercepted; each day aggravated the sickness and famine; and about the same time a retreat was found to be necessary and impracticable. The Oriental writers confess, that Louis might have escaped, if he would have deserted his subjects; he was made prisoner, with the greatest part of his nobles; all who could not redeem their lives by service or ransom were inhumanly massacred; and the walls of Cairo were decorated with a circle of Christian heads. The king of France was loaded with chains; but the generous victor, a great-grandson of the brother of Saladin, sent a robe of honor to his royal captive, and his deliverance, with that of his soldiers, was obtained by the restitution of Damietta and the payment of four hundred thousand pieces of gold. In a soft and luxurious climate, the degenerate children of the companions of Noureddin and Saladin were incapable of resisting the flower of European chivalry: they triumphed by the arms of their slaves or Mamalukes, the hardy natives of Tartary, who at a tender age had been purchased of the Syrian merchants, and were educated in the camp and palace of the sultan. But Egypt soon afforded a new example of the danger of prætorian bands; and the rage of these ferocious animals, who had been let loose on the strangers, was provoked to devour their benefactor. In the pride of conquest, Touran Shaw, the last of his race, was murdered by his Mamalukes; and the most daring of the assassins entered the chamber of the captive king, with drawn cimeters, and their hands imbrued in the blood of their sultan. The firmness of Louis commanded their respect; their avarice prevailed over cruelty and zeal; the treaty was accomplished; and the king of France, with the relics of his army, was permitted to embark for Palestine. He wasted four years within the walls of Acre, unable to visit Jerusalem, and unwilling to return without glory to his native country.

Note: * Wilken, vol. vii. p. 257, thinks the proposition could not have been made in earnest. – M.]

The memory of his defeat excited Louis, after sixteen years of wisdom and repose, to undertake the seventh and last of the crusades. His finances were restored, his kingdom was enlarged; a new generation of warriors had arisen, and he advanced with fresh confidence at the head of six thousand horse and thirty thousand foot. The loss of Antioch had provoked the enterprise; a wild hope of baptizing the king of Tunis tempted him to steer for the African coast; and the report of an immense treasure reconciled his troops to the delay of their voyage to the Holy Land. Instead of a proselyte, he found a siege: the French panted and died on the burning sands: St. Louis expired in his tent; and no sooner had he closed his eyes, than his son and successor gave the signal of the retreat. "It is thus," says a lively writer, "that a Christian king died near the ruins of Carthage, waging war against the sectaries of Mahomet, in a land to which Dido had introduced the deities of Syria."

A more unjust and absurd constitution cannot be devised than that which condemns the natives of a country to perpetual servitude, under the arbitrary dominion of strangers and slaves. Yet such has been the state of Egypt above five hundred years. The most illustrious sultans of the Baharite and Borgite dynasties were themselves promoted from the Tartar and Circassian bands; and the four-and-twenty beys, or military chiefs, have ever been succeeded, not by their sons, but by their servants. They produce the great charter of their liberties, the treaty of Selim the First with the republic: and the Othman emperor still accepts from Egypt a slight acknowledgment of tribute and subjection. With some breathing intervals of peace and order, the two dynasties are marked as a period of rapine and bloodshed: but their throne, however shaken, reposed on the two pillars of discipline and valor: their sway extended over Egypt, Nubia, Arabia, and Syria: their Mamalukes were multiplied from eight hundred to twenty-five thousand horse; and their numbers were increased by a provincial militia of one hundred and seven thousand foot, and the occasional aid of sixty-six thousand Arabs. Princes of such power and spirit could not long endure on their coast a hostile and independent nation; and if the ruin of the Franks was postponed about forty years, they were indebted to the cares of an unsettled reign, to the invasion of the Moguls, and to the occasional aid of some warlike pilgrims. Among these, the English reader will observe the name of our first Edward, who assumed the cross in the lifetime of his father Henry. At the head of a thousand soldiers the future conqueror of Wales and Scotland delivered Acre from a siege; marched as far as Nazareth with an army of nine thousand men; emulated the fame of his uncle Richard; extorted, by his valor, a ten years' truce; and escaped, with a dangerous wound, from the dagger of a fanatic *assassin*. Antioch, whose situation had been less exposed to the calamities of the holy war, was finally occupied and ruined by Bondocdar, or Bibars, sultan of Egypt and Syria; the Latin principality was extinguished; and the first seat of the Christian name was dispeopled by the slaughter of seventeen, and the captivity of one hundred, thousand of her inhabitants. The maritime towns of Laodicea, Gabala, Tripoli, Berytus, Sidon, Tyre and Jaffa, and the stronger castles of the Hospitallers and Templars, successively fell; and the whole existence of the Franks was confined to the city and colony of St. John of Acre, which is sometimes described by the more classic title of Ptolemais.

After the loss of Jerusalem, Acre, which is distant about seventy miles, became the metropolis of the Latin Christians, and was adorned with strong and stately buildings, with aqueducts, an artificial port, and a double wall. The population was increased by the incessant streams of pilgrims and fugitives: in the pauses of hostility the trade of the East and West was attracted to this convenient station; and the market could offer the produce of every clime and the interpreters of every tongue. But in this conflux of nations, every vice was propagated and practised: of all the disciples of Jesus and Mahomet, the male and female inhabitants of Acre were esteemed the most corrupt; nor could the abuse of religion be corrected by the discipline of law. The city had many sovereigns, and no government. The kings of Jerusalem and Cyprus, of the house of Lusignan, the princes of Antioch, the counts of Tripoli and Sidon, the great masters of the hospital, the temple, and the Teutonic order, the republics of Venice, Genoa, and Pisa, the pope's legate, the kings of France and England, assumed an independent command: seventeen tribunals exercised the power of life and death; every criminal was protected in the adjacent quarter; and the perpetual jealousy of the nations often burst forth in acts of violence and blood. Some adventurers, who disgraced the ensign of the cross, compensated their want of pay by the plunder of the Mahometan villages: nineteen Syrian merchants, who traded under the public faith, were despoiled and hanged by the Christians; and the denial of satisfaction justified the arms of the sultan Khalil. He marched against Acre, at the head of sixty thousand horse and one hundred and forty thousand foot: his train of artillery (if I may use the word) was numerous and weighty: the separate timbers of a single engine were transported in one hundred wagons; and the royal historian Abulfeda, who served with the troops of Hamah, was himself a spectator of the holy war. Whatever might be the vices of the Franks, their courage was rekindled by enthusiasm and despair; but they were torn by the discord of seventeen chiefs, and overwhelmed on all sides by the powers of the sultan. After a siege of thirty three days, the double wall was forced by the Moslems; the principal tower yielded to their engines; the Mamalukes made a general assault; the city was stormed; and death or slavery was the lot of sixty thousand Christians. The convent, or rather fortress, of the Templars resisted three days longer; but the great master was pierced with an arrow; and, of five hundred knights, only ten were left alive, less happy than the victims of the sword, if they lived to suffer on a scaffold, in the unjust and cruel proscription of the whole order. The king of Jerusalem, the patriarch and the great master of the hospital, effected their retreat to the shore; but the sea was rough, the vessels were insufficient; and great numbers of the fugitives were drowned before they could reach the Isle of Cyprus, which might comfort Lusignan for the loss of Palestine. By the command of the sultan, the churches and fortifications of the Latin cities were demolished: a motive of avarice or fear still opened the holy sepulchre to some devout and defenceless pilgrims; and a mournful and solitary silence prevailed along the coast which had so long resounded with the world's debate.

Note: * After these chapters of Gibbon, the masterly prize composition, "Essai sur 'Influence des Croisades sur l'Europe," par A H. L. Heeren: traduit de l'Allemand par Charles Villars, Paris, 1808,' or the original German, in Heeren's "Vermischte Schriften," may be read with great advantage. – M.]

The Fourth Crusade. – Part One

Schism of the Greeks and Latins. – State of Constantinople. – Revolt of the Bulgarians. – Isaac Angelus Dethroned by his Brother Alexius. – Origin of the Fourth Crusade. – Alliance of the French and Venetians With the Son of Isaac. – Their Naval Expedition to Constantinople. – The Two Sieges and Final Conquest of the City by the Latins.

THE RESTORATION OF THE Western empire by Charlemagne was speedily followed by the separation of the Greek and Latin churches. A religious and national animosity still divides the two largest communions of the Christian world; and the schism of Constantinople, by alienating her most useful allies, and provoking her most dangerous enemies, has precipitated the decline and fall of the Roman empire in the East. In the course of the present History, the aversion of the Greeks for the Latins has been often visible and conspicuous. It was originally derived from the disdain of servitude, inflamed, after the time of Constantine, by the pride of equality or dominion; and finally exasperated by the preference which their rebellious subjects had given to the alliance of the Franks. In every age the Greeks were proud of their superiority in profane and religious knowledge: they had first received the light of Christianity; they had pronounced the decrees of the seven general councils; they alone possessed the language of Scripture and philosophy; nor should the Barbarians, immersed in the darkness of the West, presume to argue on the high and mysterious questions of theological science. Those Barbarians despised in then turn the restless and subtile levity of the Orientals, the authors of every heresy; and blessed their own simplicity, which was content to hold the tradition of the apostolic church. Yet in the seventh century, the synods of Spain, and afterwards of France, improved or corrupted the Nicene creed, on the mysterious subject of the third person of the Trinity. In the long controversies of the East, the nature and generation of the Christ had been scrupulously defined; and the well-known relation of father and son seemed to convey a faint image to the human mind. The idea of birth was less analogous to the Holy Spirit, who, instead of a divine gift or attribute, was considered by the Catholics as a substance, a person, a god; he was not begotten, but in the orthodox style he *proceeded*. Did he proceed from the Father alone, perhaps *by* the Son? or from the Father *and* the Son? The first of these opinions was asserted by the Greeks, the second by the Latins; and the addition to the Nicene creed of the word *filioque*, kindled the flame of discord between the Oriental and the Gallic churches. In the origin of the disputes the Roman pontiffs affected a character of neutrality and moderation: they condemned the innovation, but they acquiesced in the sentiment, of their Transalpine brethren: they seemed desirous of casting a veil of silence and charity over the superfluous research; and in the correspondence of Charlemagne and Leo the Third, the pope assumes the liberality of a statesman, and the prince descends to the passions and prejudices of a priest. But the orthodoxy of Rome spontaneously obeyed the impulse of the temporal policy; and the *filioque*, which Leo wished to erase, was transcribed in the symbol and chanted in the liturgy of the Vatican. The Nicene and Athanasian creeds are held as the Catholic faith, without which none can be saved; and both Papists and Protestants must now sustain and return the anathemas of the Greeks, who deny the procession of the Holy Ghost from the Son, as well as from the Father. Such articles of faith are not susceptible of treaty; but the rules of discipline will vary in remote and independent churches; and the reason, even of divines, might allow, that the difference is inevitable and harmless. The craft or superstition of Rome has imposed on her priests and deacons the rigid obligation of celibacy; among the Greeks it is confined to the bishops; the loss is compensated by dignity or annihilated by age; and the parochial clergy, the papas, enjoy the conjugal society of the wives whom they have married before their entrance into holy orders. A question concerning the *Azyms* was fiercely debated in the eleventh century, and the essence of the Eucharist was supposed in the East and West to depend on the use of leavened or unleavened bread. Shall I mention in a serious history the furious reproaches that were urged against the Latins, who for a long while remained on the defensive? They neglected to abstain, according to the apostolical decree, from things strangled, and from blood: they fasted (a Jewish observance!) on the Saturday of each week: during the first week of Lent they permitted the use of milk and cheese; their infirm monks were indulged in the taste of flesh; and animal grease was substituted for the want of vegetable oil: the holy chrism or unction in baptism was reserved to the episcopal order: the bishops, as the bridegrooms of their churches, were decorated with rings; their priests shaved their faces, and baptized by a single immersion. Such were the crimes which provoked the zeal of the patriarchs of Constantinople; and which were justified with equal zeal by the doctors of the Latin church.

Bigotry and national aversion are powerful magnifiers of every object of dispute; but the immediate cause of the schism of the Greeks may be traced in the emulation of the leading prelates, who maintained the supremacy of the old metropolis superior to all, and of the reigning capital, inferior to none, in the Christian world. About the middle of the ninth century, Photius, an ambitious layman, the captain of the guards and principal secretary, was promoted by merit and favor to the more desirable office of patriarch of Constantinople. In science, even ecclesiastical science, he surpassed the clergy of the age; and the purity of his morals has never been impeached: but his ordination was hasty, his rise was irregular; and Ignatius, his abdicated predecessor, was yet supported by the public compassion and the obstinacy of his adherents. They appealed to the tribunal of Nicholas the First, one of the proudest and most aspiring of the Roman pontiffs, who embraced the welcome opportunity of judging and condemning his rival of the East. Their quarrel was embittered by a conflict of jurisdiction over the king and nation of the Bulgarians; nor was their recent conversion to Christianity of much avail to either prelate, unless he could number the proselytes among the subjects of his power. With the aid of his court the Greek patriarch was victorious; but in the furious contest he deposed in his turn the successor of St. Peter, and involved the Latin church in the reproach of heresy and schism. Photius sacrificed the peace of the world to a short and precarious reign: he fell with his patron, the Cæsar Bardas; and Basil the Macedonian performed an act of justice in the restoration of Ignatius, whose age and dignity had not been sufficiently respected. From his monastery, or prison, Photius solicited the favor of the emperor by pathetic complaints and artful flattery; and the eyes of his rival were scarcely closed, when he was again restored to the throne of Constantinople. After the death of Basil he experienced the vicissitudes of courts and the ingratitude of a royal pupil: the patriarch was again deposed, and in his last solitary hours he might regret the freedom of a secular and studious life. In each revolution, the breath, the nod, of the sovereign had been accepted by a submissive clergy; and a synod of three hundred bishops was always prepared to hail the triumph, or to stigmatize the fall, of the holy, or the execrable, Photius. By a delusive promise of succor or reward, the popes were tempted to countenance these various proceedings; and the synods of Constantinople were ratified by their epistles or legates. But the court and the people, Ignatius and Photius, were equally adverse to their claims; their ministers were insulted or imprisoned; the procession of the Holy Ghost was forgotten; Bulgaria was forever annexed to the Byzantine throne; and the schism was prolonged by their rigid censure of all the multiplied ordinations of an irregular patriarch. The darkness and corruption of the tenth century suspended the intercourse, without reconciling the minds, of the two nations. But when the Norman sword restored the churches of Apulia to the jurisdiction of Rome, the departing flock was warned, by a petulant epistle of the Greek patriarch, to avoid and abhor the errors of the Latins. The rising majesty of Rome could no longer brook the insolence of a rebel; and Michael Cerularius was excommunicated in the heart of Constantinople by the pope's legates. Shaking the dust from their feet, they deposited on the altar of St. Sophia a direful anathema, which enumerates the seven mortal heresies of the Greeks, and devotes the guilty teachers, and their unhappy sectaries, to the eternal society of the devil and his angels. According to the emergencies of the church and state, a friendly correspondence was some times resumed; the language of charity and concord was sometimes affected; but the Greeks have never recanted their errors; the popes have never repealed their sentence; and from this thunderbolt we may date the consummation of the schism. It was enlarged by each ambitious step of the Roman pontiffs: the emperors blushed and trembled at the ignominious fate of their royal brethren of Germany; and the people were scandalized by the temporal power and military life of the Latin clergy.

The aversion of the Greeks and Latins was nourished and manifested in the three first expeditions to the Holy Land. Alexius Comnenus contrived the absence at least of the formidable pilgrims: his successors, Manuel and Isaac Angelus, conspired with the Moslems for the ruin of the greatest princes of the Franks; and their crooked and malignant policy was seconded by the active and voluntary obedience of every order of their subjects. Of this hostile temper, a large portion may doubtless be ascribed to the difference of language, dress, and manners, which severs and alienates the nations of the globe. The pride, as well as the prudence, of the sovereign was deeply wounded by the intrusion of foreign armies, that claimed a right of traversing his dominions, and passing under the walls of his capital: his subjects were insulted and plundered by the rude strangers of the West: and the hatred of the pusillanimous Greeks was sharpened by secret envy of the bold and pious enterprises of the Franks. But these profane causes of national enmity were fortified and inflamed by the venom of religious zeal. Instead of a kind embrace, a hospitable reception from their Christian brethren of the East, every tongue was taught to repeat the names of schismatic and heretic, more odious to an orthodox ear than those of pagan and infidel: instead of being loved for the general conformity of faith and worship, they were abhorred for some rules of discipline, some questions of theology, in which themselves or their teachers might differ from the Oriental church. In the crusade of Louis the Seventh, the Greek clergy washed and purified the altars which had been defiled by the sacrifice of a French priest. The companions of Frederic Barbarossa deplore the injuries which they endured, both in word and deed, from the peculiar rancor of the bishops and monks. Their prayers and sermons excited the people against the impious Barbarians; and the patriarch is accused of declaring, that the faithful might obtain the redemption of all their sins by the extirpation of the schismatics. An enthusiast, named Dorotheus, alarmed the fears, and restored the confidence, of the emperor, by a prophetic assurance, that the German heretic, after assaulting the gate of Blachernes, would be made a signal example of the divine vengeance. The passage of these mighty armies were rare and perilous events; but the crusades introduced a frequent and familiar intercourse between the two nations, which enlarged their knowledge without abating their prejudices. The wealth and luxury of Constantinople demanded the productions of every climate; these imports were balanced by the art and labor of her numerous inhabitants; her situation invites the commerce of the world; and, in every period of her existence, that commerce has been in the hands of foreigners. After the decline of Amalphi, the Venetians, Pisans, and Genoese, introduced their factories and settlements into the capital of the empire: their services were rewarded with honors and immunities; they acquired the possession of lands and houses; their families were multiplied by marriages with the natives; and, after the toleration of a Mahometan mosque, it was impossible to interdict the churches of the Roman rite. The two wives of Manuel Comnenus were of the race of the Franks: the first, a sister-in-law of the emperor Conrad; the second, a daughter of the prince of Antioch: he obtained for his son Alexius a daughter of Philip Augustus, king of France; and he bestowed his own daughter on a marquis of

Montferrat, who was educated and dignified in the palace of Constantinople. The Greek encountered the arms, and aspired to the empire, of the West: he esteemed the valor, and trusted the fidelity, of the Franks; their military talents were unfitly recompensed by the lucrative offices of judges and treasures; the policy of Manuel had solicited the alliance of the pope; and the popular voice accused him of a partial bias to the nation and religion of the Latins. During his reign, and that of his successor Alexius, they were exposed at Constantinople to the reproach of foreigners, heretics, and favorites; and this triple guilt was severely expiated in the tumult, which announced the return and elevation of Andronicus. The people rose in arms: from the Asiatic shore the tyrant despatched his troops and galleys to assist the national revenge; and the hopeless resistance of the strangers served only to justify the rage, and sharpen the daggers, of the assassins. Neither age, nor sex, nor the ties of friendship or kindred, could save the victims of national hatred, and avarice, and religious zeal; the Latins were slaughtered in their houses and in the streets; their quarter was reduced to ashes; the clergy were burnt in their churches, and the sick in their hospitals; and some estimate may be formed of the slain from the clemency which sold above four thousand Christians in perpetual slavery to the Turks. The priests and monks were the loudest and most active in the destruction of the schismatics; and they chanted a thanksgiving to the Lord, when the head of a Roman cardinal, the pope's legate, was severed from his body, fastened to the tail of a dog, and dragged, with savage mockery, through the city. The more diligent of the strangers had retreated, on the first alarm, to their vessels, and escaped through the Hellespont from the scene of blood. In their flight, they burnt and ravaged two hundred miles of the sea-coast; inflicted a severe revenge on the guiltless subjects of the empire; marked the priests and monks as their peculiar enemies; and compensated, by the accumulation of plunder, the loss of their property and friends. On their return, they exposed to Italy and Europe the wealth and weakness, the perfidy and malice, of the Greeks, whose vices were painted as the genuine characters of heresy and schism. The scruples of the first crusaders had neglected the fairest opportunities of securing, by the possession of Constantinople, the way to the Holy Land: domestic revolution invited, and almost compelled, the French and Venetians to achieve the conquest of the Roman empire of the East.

In the series of the Byzantine princes, I have exhibited the hypocrisy and ambition, the tyranny and fall, of Andronicus, the last male of the Comnenian family who reigned at Constantinople. The revolution, which cast him headlong from the throne, saved and exalted Isaac Angelus, who descended by the females from the same Imperial dynasty. The successor of a second Nero might have found it an easy task to deserve the esteem and affection of his subjects; they sometimes had reason to regret the administration of Andronicus. The sound and vigorous mind of the tyrant was capable of discerning the connection between his own and the public interest; and while he was feared by all who could inspire him with fear, the unsuspected people, and the remote provinces, might bless the inexorable justice of their master. But his successor was vain and jealous of the supreme power, which he wanted courage and abilities to exercise: his vices were pernicious, his virtues (if he possessed any virtues) were useless, to mankind; and the Greeks, who imputed their calamities to his negligence, denied him the merit of any transient or accidental benefits of the times. Isaac slept on the throne, and was awakened only by the sound of pleasure: his vacant hours were amused by comedians and buffoons, and even to these buffoons the emperor was an object of contempt: his feasts and buildings exceeded the examples of royal luxury: the number of his eunuchs and domestics amounted to twenty thousand; and a daily sum of four thousand pounds of silver would swell to four millions sterling the annual expense of his household and table. His poverty was relieved by oppression; and the public discontent was inflamed by equal abuses in the collection, and the application, of the revenue. While the Greeks numbered the days of their servitude, a flattering prophet, whom he rewarded with the dignity of patriarch, assured him of a long and victorious reign of thirty-two years; during which he should extend his sway to Mount Libanus, and his conquests beyond the Euphrates. But his only step towards the accomplishment of the prediction was a splendid and scandalous embassy to Saladin, to demand the restitution of the holy sepulchre, and to propose an offensive and defensive league with the enemy of the Christian name. In these unworthy hands, of Isaac and his brother, the remains of the Greek empire crumbled into dust. The Island of Cyprus, whose name excites the ideas of elegance and pleasure, was usurped by his namesake, a Comnenian prince; and by a strange concatenation of events, the sword of our English Richard bestowed that kingdom on the house of Lusignan, a rich compensation for the loss of Jerusalem.

The honor of the monarchy and the safety of the capital were deeply wounded by the revolt of the Bulgarians and Walachians. Since the victory of the second Basil, they had supported, above a hundred and seventy years, the loose dominion of the Byzantine princes; but no effectual measures had been adopted to impose the yoke of laws and manners on these savage tribes. By the command of Isaac, their sole means of subsistence, their flocks and herds, were driven away, to contribute towards the pomp of the royal nuptials; and their fierce warriors were exasperated by the denial of equal rank and pay in the military service. Peter and Asan, two powerful chiefs, of the race of the ancient kings, asserted their own rights and the national freedom; their dæmoniac impostors proclaimed to the crowd, that their glorious patron St. Demetrius had forever deserted the cause of the Greeks; and the conflagration spread from the banks of the Danube to the hills of Macedonia and Thrace. After some faint efforts, Isaac Angelus and his brother acquiesced in their independence; and the Imperial troops were soon discouraged by the bones of their fellow-soldiers, that were scattered along the passes of Mount Hæmus. By the arms and policy of John or Joannices, the second kingdom of Bulgaria was firmly established. The subtle Barbarian sent an embassy to Innocent the Third, to acknowledge himself a genuine son of Rome in descent and religion, and humbly received from the pope the license of coining money, the royal title, and a Latin archbishop or patriarch. The Vatican exulted in the spiritual conquest of Bulgaria, the first object of the schism; and if the Greeks could have preserved the prerogatives of the church, they would gladly have resigned the rights of the monarchy.

The Bulgarians were malicious enough to pray for the long life of Isaac Angelus, the surest pledge of their freedom and prosperity. Yet their chiefs could involve in the same indiscriminate contempt the family and nation of the emperor. "In all the Greeks," said Asan to his troops, "the same climate, and character, and education, will be productive of the same fruits. Behold my lance," continued the warrior, "and the long streamers that float in the wind. They differ only in color; they are formed of the same silk, and fashioned by the same workman; nor has the stripe that is stained in purple any superior price or value above its fellows." Several of these candidates for the purple successively rose and fell under the empire of Isaac; a general, who had repelled the fleets of Sicily, was driven to revolt and ruin by the ingratitude of the prince; and his luxurious repose was disturbed by secret conspiracies and popular insurrections. The emperor was saved by accident, or the merit of his servants: he was at length oppressed by an ambitious brother, who, for the hope of a precarious diadem, forgot the obligations of nature, of loyalty, and of friendship. While Isaac in the Thracian valleys pursued the idle and solitary pleasures of the chase, his brother, Alexius Angelus, was invested with the purple, by the unanimous suffrage of the camp; the capital and the clergy subscribed to their choice; and the vanity of the new sovereign rejected the name of his fathers for the lofty and royal appellation of the Comnenian race. On the despicable character of Isaac I have exhausted the language of contempt, and can only add, that, in a reign of eight years, the baser Alexius was supported by the masculine vices of his wife Euphrosyne. The first intelligence of his fall was conveyed to the late emperor by the hostile aspect and pursuit of the guards, no longer his own: he fled before them above fifty miles, as far as Stagyra, in Macedonia; but the fugitive, without an object or a follower, was arrested, brought back to Constantinople, deprived of his eyes, and confined in a lonesome tower, on a scanty allowance of bread and water. At the moment of the revolution, his son Alexius, whom he educated in the hope of empire, was twelve years of age. He was spared by the usurper, and reduced to attend his triumph both in peace and war; but as the army was encamped on the sea-shore, an Italian vessel facilitated the escape of the royal youth; and, in the disguise of a common sailor, he eluded the search of his enemies, passed the Hellespont, and found a secure refuge in the Isle of Sicily. After saluting the threshold of the apostles, and imploring the protection of Pope Innocent the Third, Alexius accepted the kind invitation of his sister Irene, the wife of Philip of Swabia, king of the Romans. But in his passage through Italy, he heard that the flower of Western chivalry was assembled at Venice for the deliverance of the Holy Land; and a ray of hope was kindled in his bosom, that their invincible swords might be employed in his father's restoration.

About ten or twelve years after the loss of Jerusalem, the nobles of France were again summoned to the holy war by the voice of a third prophet, less extravagant, perhaps, than Peter the hermit, but far below St. Bernard in the merit of an orator and a statesman. An illiterate priest of the neighborhood of Paris, Fulk of Neuilly, forsook his parochial duty, to assume the more flattering character of a popular and itinerant missionary. The fame of his sanctity and miracles was spread over the land; he declaimed, with severity and vehemence, against the vices of the age; and his sermons, which he preached in the streets of Paris, converted the robbers, the usurers, the prostitutes, and even the doctors and scholars of the university. No sooner did Innocent the Third ascend the chair of St. Peter, than he proclaimed in Italy, Germany, and France, the obligation of a new crusade. The eloquent pontiff described the ruin of Jerusalem, the triumph of the Pagans, and the shame of Christendom; his liberality proposed the redemption of sins, a plenary indulgence to all who should serve in Palestine, either a year in person, or two years by a substitute; and among his legates and orators who blew the sacred trumpet, Fulk of Neuilly was the loudest and most successful. The situation of the principal monarchs was averse to the pious summons. The emperor Frederic the Second was a child; and his kingdom of Germany was disputed by the rival houses of Brunswick and Swabia, the memorable factions of the Guelphs and Ghibelines. Philip Augustus of France had performed, and could not be persuaded to renew, the perilous vow; but as he was not less ambitious of praise than of power, he cheerfully instituted a perpetual fund for the defence of the Holy Land. Richard of England was satiated with the glory and misfortunes of his first adventure; and he presumed to deride the exhortations of Fulk of Neuilly, who was not abashed in the presence of kings. "You advise me," said Plantagenet, "to dismiss my three daughters, pride, avarice, and incontinence: I bequeath them to the most deserving; my pride to the knights templars, my avarice to the monks of Cisteaux, and my incontinence to the prelates." But the preacher was heard and obeyed by the great vassals, the princes of the second order; and Theobald, or Thibaut, count of Champagne, was the foremost in the holy race. The valiant youth, at the age of twenty-two years, was encouraged by the domestic examples of his father, who marched in the second crusade, and of his elder brother, who had ended his days in Palestine with the title of King of Jerusalem; two thousand two hundred knights owed service and homage to his peerage; the nobles of Champagne excelled in all the exercises of war; and, by his marriage with the heiress of Navarre, Thibaut could draw a band of hardy Gascons from either side of the Pyrenæan mountains. His companion in arms was Louis, count of Blois and Chartres; like himself of regal lineage, for both the princes were nephews, at the same time, of the kings of France and England. In a crowd of prelates and barons, who imitated their zeal, I distinguish the birth and merit of Matthew of Montmorency; the famous Simon of Montfort, the scourge of the Albigeois; and a valiant noble, Jeffrey of Villehardouin, marshal of Champagne, who has condescended, in the rude idiom of his age and country, to write or dictate an original narrative of the councils and actions in which he bore a memorable part. At the same time, Baldwin, count of Flanders, who had married the sister of Thibaut, assumed the cross at Bruges, with his brother Henry, and the principal knights and citizens of that rich and industrious province. The vow which the chiefs had pronounced in churches, they ratified in tournaments; the operations of the war were debated in full and frequent assemblies; and it was resolved to seek the deliverance of Palestine in Egypt, a country, since Saladin's death, which was almost ruined by famine and civil war. But the fate of so many royal armies displayed the toils and perils of a land expedition; and if the Flemings dwelt along the ocean, the French barons were destitute of ships and ignorant of navigation. They embraced the wise resolution of choosing six deputies or representatives, of whom Villehardouin was one, with a discretionary trust to direct the motions, and to pledge the faith, of the whole confederacy. The maritime states of Italy were alone possessed of the means of transporting the holy warriors with their arms and horses; and the six deputies proceeded to Venice, to solicit, on motives of piety or interest, the aid of that powerful republic.

In the invasion of Italy by Attila, I have mentioned the flight of the Venetians from the fallen cities of the continent, and their obscure shelter in the chain of islands that line the extremity of the Adriatic Gulf. In the midst of the waters, free, indigent, laborious, and inaccessible, they gradually coalesced into a republic: the first foundations of Venice were laid in the Island of Rialto; and the annual election of the twelve tribunes was superseded by the permanent office of a duke or doge. On the verge of the two empires, the Venetians exult in the belief of primitive and perpetual independence. Against the Latins, their antique freedom has been asserted by the sword, and may be justified by the pen. Charlemagne himself resigned all claims of sovereignty to the islands of the Adriatic Gulf: his son Pepin was repulsed in the attacks of the *lagunas* or canals, too deep for the cavalry, and too shallow for the vessels; and in every age, under the German Cæsars, the lands of the republic have been clearly distinguished from the kingdom of Italy. But the inhabitants of Venice were considered by themselves, by strangers, and by their sovereigns, as an inalienable portion of the Greek empire: in the ninth and tenth centuries, the proofs of their subjection are numerous and unquestionable; and the vain titles, the servile honors, of the Byzantine court, so ambitiously solicited by their dukes, would have degraded the magistrates of a free people. But the bands of this dependence, which was never absolute or rigid, were imperceptibly relaxed by the ambition of Venice and the weakness of Constantinople. Obedience was softened into respect, privilege ripened into prerogative, and the freedom of domestic government was fortified by the independence of foreign dominion. The maritime cities of Istria and Dalmatia bowed to the sovereigns of the Adriatic; and when they armed against the Normans in the cause of Alexius, the emperor applied, not to the duty of his subjects, but to the gratitude and generosity of his faithful allies. The sea was their patrimony: the western parts of the

Mediterranean, from Tuscany to Gibraltar, were indeed abandoned to their rivals of Pisa and Genoa; but the Venetians acquired an early and lucrative share of the commerce of Greece and Egypt. Their riches increased with the increasing demand of Europe; their manufactures of silk and glass, perhaps the institution of their bank, are of high antiquity; and they enjoyed the fruits of their industry in the magnificence of public and private life. To assert her flag, to avenge her injuries, to protect the freedom of navigation, the republic could launch and man a fleet of a hundred galleys; and the Greeks, the Saracens, and the Normans, were encountered by her naval arms. The Franks of Syria were assisted by the Venetians in the reduction of the sea coast; but their zeal was neither blind nor disinterested; and in the conquest of Tyre, they shared the sovereignty of a city, the first seat of the commerce of the world. The policy of Venice was marked by the avarice of a trading, and the insolence of a maritime, power; yet her ambition was prudent: nor did she often forget that if armed galleys were the effect and safeguard, merchant vessels were the cause and supply, of her greatness. In her religion, she avoided the schisms of the Greeks, without yielding a servile obedience to the Roman pontiff; and a free intercourse with the infidels of every clime appears to have allayed betimes the fever of superstition. Her primitive government was a loose mixture of democracy and monarchy; the doge was elected by the votes of the general assembly; as long as he was popular and successful, he reigned with the pomp and authority of a prince; but in the frequent revolutions of the state, he was deposed, or banished, or slain, by the justice or injustice of the multitude. The twelfth century produced the first rudiments of the wise and jealous aristocracy, which has reduced the doge to a pageant, and the people to a cipher.

The Fourth Crusade. – Part Two

WHEN THE SIX AMBASSADORS of the French pilgrims arrived at Venice, they were hospitably entertained in the palace of St. Mark, by the reigning duke; his name was Henry Dandolo; and he shone in the last period of human life as one of the most illustrious characters of the times. Under the weight of years, and after the loss of his eyes, Dandolo retained a sound understanding and a manly courage: the spirit of a hero, ambitious to signalize his reign by some memorable exploits; and the wisdom of a patriot, anxious to build his fame on the glory and advantage of his country. He praised the bold enthusiasm and liberal confidence of the barons and their deputies: in such a cause, and with such associates, he should aspire, were he a private man, to terminate his life; but he was the servant of the republic, and some delay was requisite to consult, on this arduous business, the judgment of his colleagues. The proposal of the French was first debated by the six *sages* who had been recently appointed to control the administration of the doge: it was next disclosed to the forty members of the council of state; and finally communicated to the legislative assembly of four hundred and fifty representatives, who were annually chosen in the six quarters of the city. In peace and war, the doge was still the chief of the republic; his legal authority was supported by the personal reputation of Dandolo: his arguments of public interest were balanced and approved; and he was authorized to inform the ambassadors of the following conditions of the treaty. It was proposed that the crusaders should assemble at Venice, on the feast of St. John of the ensuing year; that flat-bottomed vessels should be prepared for four thousand five hundred horses, and nine thousand squires, with a number of ships sufficient for the embarkation of four thousand five hundred knights, and twenty thousand foot; that during a term of nine months they should be supplied with provisions, and transported to whatsoever coast the service of God and Christendom should require; and that the republic should join the armament with a squadron of fifty galleys. It was required, that the pilgrims should pay, before their departure, a sum of eighty-five thousand marks of silver; and that all conquests, by sea and land, should be equally divided between the confederates. The terms were hard; but the emergency was pressing, and the French barons were not less profuse of money than of blood. A general assembly was convened to ratify the treaty: the stately chapel and place of St. Mark were filled with ten thousand citizens; and the noble deputies were taught a new lesson of humbling themselves before the majesty of the people. "Illustrious Venetians," said the marshal of Champagne, "we are sent by the greatest and most powerful barons of France to implore the aid of the masters of the sea for the deliverance of Jerusalem. They have enjoined us to fall prostrate at your feet; nor will we rise from the ground till you have promised to avenge with us the injuries of Christ." The eloquence of their words and tears, their martial aspect, and suppliant attitude, were applauded by a universal shout; as it were, says Jeffrey, by the sound of an earthquake. The venerable doge ascended the pulpit to urge their request by those motives of honor and virtue, which alone can be offered to a popular assembly: the treaty was transcribed on parchment, attested with oaths and seals, mutually accepted by the weeping and joyful representatives of France and Venice; and despatched to Rome for the approbation of Pope Innocent the Third. Two thousand marks were borrowed of the merchants for the first expenses of the armament. Of the six deputies, two repassed the Alps to announce their success, while their four companions made a fruitless trial of the zeal and emulation of the republics of Genoa and Pisa.

The execution of the treaty was still opposed by unforeseen difficulties and delays. The marshal, on his return to Troyes, was embraced and approved by Thibaut count of Champagne, who had been unanimously chosen general of the confederates. But the health of that valiant youth already declined, and soon became hopeless; and he deplored the untimely fate, which condemned him to expire, not in a field of battle, but on a bed of sickness. To his brave and numerous vassals, the dying prince distributed his treasures: they swore in his presence to accomplish his vow and their own; but some there were, says the marshal, who accepted his gifts and forfeited their words. The more resolute champions of the cross held a parliament at Soissons for the election of a new general; but such was the incapacity, or jealousy, or reluctance, of the princes of France, that none could be found both able and willing to assume the conduct of the enterprise. They acquiesced in the choice of a stranger, of Boniface marquis of Montferrat, descended of a race of heroes, and himself of conspicuous fame in the wars and negotiations of the times; nor could the piety or ambition of the Italian chief decline this honorable invitation. After visiting the French court, where he was received as a friend and kinsman, the marquis, in the church of Soissons, was invested with the cross of a pilgrim and the staff of a general; and immediately repassed the Alps, to prepare for the distant expedition of the East. About the festival of the Pentecost he displayed his banner, and marched towards Venice at the head of the Italians: he was preceded or followed by the counts of Flanders and Blois, and the most respectable barons of France; and their numbers were swelled by the pilgrims of Germany, whose object and motives were similar to their own. The Venetians had fulfilled, and even surpassed, their engagements: stables were constructed for the horses, and barracks for the troops: the magazines were abundantly replenished with forage and provisions; and the fleet of transports, ships, and galleys, was ready to hoist sail as soon as the republic had received the price of the freight and armament. But that price far exceeded the wealth of the crusaders who were assembled at Venice. The Flemings, whose obedience to their count was voluntary and precarious, had embarked in their vessels for the long navigation of the ocean and Mediterranean; and many of the French and Italians had preferred a cheaper and more convenient passage from Marseilles and Apulia to the Holy Land. Each pilgrim might complain, that after he had furnished his own contribution, he was made responsible for the deficiency of his absent brethren: the gold and silver plate of the chiefs, which they freely delivered to the treasury of St. Marks, was a generous but inadequate sacrifice; and after all their efforts, thirty-four thousand marks were still wanting to complete the stipulated sum. The obstacle was removed by the policy and patriotism of the doge, who proposed to the barons, that if they would join their arms in reducing some revolted cities of Dalmatia, he would expose his person in the holy war, and obtain from the republic a long indulgence, till some wealthy conquest should afford the means of satisfying the debt. After much scruple and hesitation, they chose rather to accept the offer than to relinquish the enterprise; and the first hostilities of the fleet and army were directed against Zara, a strong city of the Sclavonian coast, which had renounced its allegiance to Venice, and implored the protection of the king of Hungary. The crusaders burst the chain or boom of the harbor; landed their horses, troops, and military engines; and compelled the inhabitants, after a defence of five days, to surrender at discretion: their lives were spared, but the revolt was punished by the pillage of their houses and the demolition of their walls. The season was far advanced; the French and Venetians resolved to pass the winter in a secure harbor and plentiful country; but their repose was disturbed by national and tumultuous quarrels of the soldiers and mariners. The conquest of Zara had scattered the seeds of discord and scandal: the arms of the allies had been stained in their outset with the blood, not of infidels, but of Christians: the king of Hungary and his new subjects were themselves enlisted under the banner of the cross; and the scruples of the devout were magnified by the fear of lassitude of the reluctant pilgrims. The pope had excommunicated the false crusaders who had pillaged and massacred their brethren, and only the marquis Boniface and Simon of Montfort escaped these spiritual thunders; the one by his absence from the siege, the other by his final departure from the camp. Innocent might absolve the simple and submissive penitents of France; but he was provoked by the stubborn reason of the Venetians, who refused to confess their guilt, to accept their pardon, or to allow, in their temporal concerns, the interposition of a priest.

The assembly of such formidable powers by sea and land had revived the hopes of young Alexius; and both at Venice and Zara, he solicited the arms of the crusaders, for his own restoration and his father's deliverance. The royal youth was recommended by Philip king of Germany: his prayers and presence excited the compassion of the camp; and his cause was embraced and pleaded by the marquis of Montferrat and the doge of Venice. A double alliance, and the dignity of Cæsar, had connected with the Imperial family the two elder brothers of Boniface: he expected to derive a kingdom from the important service; and the more generous ambition of Dandolo was eager to secure the inestimable benefits of trade and dominion that might accrue to his country. Their influence procured a favorable audience for the ambassadors of Alexius; and if the magnitude of his offers excited some suspicion, the motives and rewards which he displayed might justify the delay and diversion of those forces which had been consecrated to the deliverance of Jerusalem. He promised in his own and his father's name, that as soon as they should be seated on the throne of Constantinople, they would terminate the long schism of the Greeks, and submit themselves and their people to the lawful supremacy of the Roman church. He engaged to recompense the labors and merits of the crusaders, by the immediate payment of two hundred thousand marks of silver; to accompany them in person to Egypt; or, if it should be judged more advantageous, to maintain, during a year, ten thousand men, and, during his life, five hundred knights, for the service of the Holy Land. These tempting conditions were accepted by the republic of Venice; and the eloquence of the doge and marquis persuaded the counts of Flanders, Blois, and St. Pol, with eight barons of France, to join in the glorious enterprise. A treaty of offensive and defensive alliance was confirmed by their oaths and seals; and each individual, according to his situation and character, was swayed by the hope of public or private advantage; by the honor of restoring an exiled monarch; or by the sincere and probable opinion, that their efforts in Palestine would be fruitless and unavailing, and that the acquisition of Constantinople must precede and prepare the recovery of Jerusalem. But they were the chiefs or equals of a valiant band of freemen and volunteers, who thought and acted for themselves: the soldiers and clergy were divided; and, if a large majority subscribed to the alliance, the numbers and arguments of the dissidents were strong and respectable. The boldest hearts were appalled by the report of the naval power and impregnable strength of Constantinople; and their apprehensions were disguised to the world, and perhaps to themselves, by the more decent objections of religion and duty. They alleged the sanctity of a vow, which had drawn them from their families and homes to the rescue of the holy sepulchre; nor should the dark and crooked counsels of human policy divert them from a pursuit, the event of which was in the hands of the Almighty. Their first offence, the attack of Zara, had been severely punished by the reproach of their conscience and the censures of the pope; nor would they again imbrue their hands in the blood of their fellow-Christians. The apostle of Rome had pronounced; nor would they usurp the right of avenging with the sword the schism of the Greeks and the doubtful usurpation of the Byzantine monarch. On these principles or pretences, many pilgrims, the most distinguished for their valor and piety, withdrew from the camp; and their retreat was less pernicious than the open or secret opposition of a discontented party, that labored, on every occasion, to separate the army and disappoint the enterprise.

Notwithstanding this defection, the departure of the fleet and army was vigorously pressed by the Venetians, whose zeal for the service of the royal youth concealed a just resentment to his nation and family. They were mortified by the recent preference which had been given to Pisa, the rival of their trade; they had a long arrear of debt and injury to liquidate with the Byzantine court; and Dandolo might not discourage the popular tale, that he had been deprived of his eyes by the emperor Manuel, who perfidiously violated the sanctity of an ambassador. A similar armament, for ages, had not rode the Adriatic: it was composed of one hundred and twenty flat-bottomed vessels or *palanders* for the horses; two hundred and forty transports filled with men and arms; seventy store-ships laden with provisions; and fifty stout galleys, well prepared for the encounter of an enemy. While the wind was favorable, the sky serene, and the water smooth, every eye was fixed with wonder and delight on the scene of military and naval pomp which overspread the sea. The shields of the knights and squires, at once an ornament and a defence, were arranged on either side of the ships; the banners of the nations and families were displayed from the stern; our modern artillery was supplied by three hundred engines for casting stones and darts: the fatigues of the way were cheered with the sound of music; and the spirits of the adventurers were raised by the mutual assurance, that forty thousand Christian heroes were equal to the conquest of the world. In the navigation from Venice and Zara, the fleet was successfully steered by the skill and experience of the Venetian pilots: at Durazzo, the confederates first landed on the territories of the Greek empire: the Isle of Corfu afforded a station and repose; they doubled, without accident, the perilous cape of Malea, the southern point of Peloponnesus or the Morea; made a descent in the islands of Negropont and Andros; and cast anchor at Abydus on the Asiatic side of the Hellespont. These preludes of conquest were easy and bloodless: the Greeks of the provinces, without patriotism or courage, were crushed by an irresistible force: the presence of the lawful heir might justify their obedience; and it was rewarded by the modesty and discipline of the Latins. As they penetrated through the Hellespont, the magnitude of their navy was compressed in a narrow channel, and the face of the waters was darkened with innumerable sails. They again expanded in the basin of the Propontis, and traversed that placid sea, till they approached the European shore, at the abbey of St. Stephen, three leagues to the west of Constantinople. The prudent doge dissuaded them from dispersing themselves in a populous and hostile land; and, as their stock of provisions was reduced, it was resolved, in the season of harvest, to replenish their store-ships in the fertile islands of the Propontis. With this resolution, they directed their course: but a strong gale, and their own impatience, drove them to the eastward; and so near did they run to the shore and the city, that some volleys of stones and darts were exchanged between the ships and the rampart. As they passed along, they gazed with admiration on the capital of the East, or, as it should seem, of the earth; rising from her seven hills, and towering over the continents of Europe and Asia. The swelling domes and lofty spires of five hundred palaces and churches were gilded by the sun and reflected in the waters: the walls were crowded with soldiers and spectators, whose numbers they beheld, of whose temper they were ignorant; and each heart was chilled by the reflection, that, since the beginning of the world, such an enterprise had never been undertaken by such a handful of warriors. But the momentary apprehension was dispelled by hope and valor; and every man, says the marshal of Champagne, glanced his eye on the sword or lance which he must speedily use in the glorious conflict. The Latins cast anchor before Chalcedon; the mariners only were left in the vessels: the soldiers, horses, and arms, were safely landed; and, in the luxury of an Imperial palace, the barons tasted the first fruits of their success. On the third day, the fleet and army moved towards Scutari, the Asiatic suburb of Constantinople: a detachment of five hundred Greek horse was surprised and defeated by fourscore French knights; and in a halt of nine days, the camp was plentifully supplied with forage and provisions.

In relating the invasion of a great empire, it may seem strange that I have not described the obstacles which should have checked the progress of the strangers. The Greeks, in truth, were an unwarlike people; but they were rich, industrious, and subject to the will of a single man: had that man been capable of fear, when his enemies were at a distance, or of courage, when they approached his person. The first rumor of his nephew's alliance with the French and Venetians was despised by the usurper Alexius: his flatterers persuaded him, that in this contempt he was bold and sincere; and each evening, in the close of the banquet, he thrice discomfited the Barbarians of the West. These Barbarians had been justly terrified by the report of his naval power; and the sixteen hundred fishing boats of Constantinople could have manned a fleet, to sink them in the Adriatic, or stop their entrance in the mouth of the Hellespont. But all force may be annihilated by the negligence of the prince and the venality of his ministers. The great duke, or admiral, made a scandalous, almost a public, auction of the sails, the masts, and the rigging: the royal forests were reserved for the more important purpose of the chase; and the trees, says Nicetas, were guarded by the eunuchs, like the groves of religious worship. From his dream of pride, Alexius was awakened by the siege of Zara, and the rapid advances of the Latins; as soon as he saw the danger was real, he thought it inevitable, and his vain presumption was lost in abject despondency and despair. He suffered these contemptible Barbarians to pitch their camp in the sight of the palace; and his apprehensions were thinly disguised by the pomp and menace of a suppliant embassy. The sovereign of the Romans was astonished (his ambassadors were instructed to say) at the hostile appearance of the strangers. If these pilgrims were sincere in their vow for the deliverance of Jerusalem, his voice must applaud, and his treasures should assist, their pious design but should they dare to invade the sanctuary of empire, their numbers, were they ten times more considerable, should not protect them from his just resentment. The answer of the doge and barons was simple and magnanimous. "In the cause of honor and justice," they said, "we despise the usurper of Greece, his threats, and his offers. *Our* friendship and *his* allegiance are due to the lawful heir, to the young prince, who is seated among us, and to his father, the emperor Isaac, who has been deprived of his sceptre, his freedom, and his eyes, by the crime of an ungrateful brother. Let that brother confess his guilt, and implore forgiveness, and we ourselves will intercede, that he may be permitted to live in affluence and security. But let him not insult us by a second message; our reply will be made in arms, in the palace of Constantinople."

On the tenth day of their encampment at Scutari, the crusaders prepared themselves, as soldiers and as Catholics, for the passage of the Bosphorus. Perilous indeed was the adventure; the stream was broad and rapid: in a calm the current of the Euxine might drive down the liquid and unextinguishable fires of the Greeks; and the opposite shores of Europe were defended by seventy thousand horse and foot in formidable array. On this memorable day, which happened to be bright and pleasant, the Latins were distributed in six battles or divisions; the first, or vanguard, was led by the count of Flanders, one of the most powerful of the Christian princes in the skill and number of his crossbows. The four successive battles of the French were commanded by his brother Henry, the counts of St. Pol and Blois, and Matthew of Montmorency; the last of whom was honored by the voluntary service of the marshal and nobles of Champagne. The sixth division, the rear-guard and reserve of the army, was conducted by the marquis of Montferrat, at the head of the Germans and Lombards. The chargers, saddled, with their long caparisons dragging on the ground, were embarked in the flat *palanders*; and the knights stood by the side of their horses, in complete armor, their helmets laced, and their lances in their hands. The numerous train of sergeants and archers occupied the transports; and each transport was towed by the strength and swiftness of a galley. The six divisions traversed the Bosphorus, without encountering an enemy or an obstacle: to land the foremost was the wish, to conquer or die was the resolution, of every division and of every soldier. Jealous of the preeminence of danger, the knights in their heavy armor leaped into the sea, when it rose as high as their girdle; the sergeants and archers were animated by their valor; and the squires, letting down the draw-bridges of the palanders, led the horses to the shore. Before their squadrons could mount, and form, and couch their Lances, the seventy thousand Greeks had vanished from their sight: the timid Alexius gave the example to his troops; and it was only by the plunder of his rich pavilions that the Latins were informed that they had fought against an emperor. In the first consternation of the flying enemy, they resolved, by a double attack, to open the entrance of the harbor. The tower of Galata, in the suburb of Pera, was attacked and stormed by the French, while the Venetians assumed the more difficult task of forcing the boom or chain that was stretched from that tower to the Byzantine shore. After some fruitless attempts, their intrepid perseverance prevailed: twenty ships of war, the relics of the Grecian navy, were either sunk or taken: the enormous and massy links of iron were cut asunder by the shears, or broken by the weight, of the galleys; and the Venetian fleet, safe and triumphant, rode at anchor in the port of Constantinople. By these daring achievements, a remnant of twenty thousand Latins solicited the license of besieging a capital which contained above four hundred thousand inhabitants, able, though not willing, to bear arms in defence of their country. Such an account would indeed suppose a population of near two millions; but whatever abatement may be required in the numbers of the Greeks, the *belief* of those numbers will equally exalt the fearless spirit of their assailants.

In the choice of the attack, the French and Venetians were divided by their habits of life and warfare. The former affirmed with truth, that Constantinople was most accessible on the side of the sea and the harbor. The latter might assert with honor, that they had long enough trusted their lives and fortunes to a frail bark and a precarious element, and loudly demanded a trial of knighthood, a firm ground, and a close onset, either on foot or on horseback. After a prudent compromise, of employing the two nations by sea and land, in the service best suited to their character, the fleet covering the army, they both proceeded from the entrance to the extremity of the harbor: the stone bridge of the river was hastily repaired; and the six battles of the French formed their encampment against the front of the capital, the basis of the triangle which runs about four miles from the port to the Propontis. On the edge of a broad ditch, at the foot of a lofty rampart, they had leisure to contemplate the difficulties of their enterprise. The gates to the right and left of their narrow camp poured forth frequent sallies of cavalry and light-infantry, which cut off their stragglers, swept the country of provisions,

sounded the alarm five or six times in the course of each day, and compelled them to plant a palisade, and sink an intrenchment, for their immediate safety. In the supplies and convoys the Venetians had been too
sparing, or the Franks too voracious: the usual complaints of hunger
and scarcity were heard, and perhaps felt their stock of flour would be
exhausted in three weeks; and their disgust of salt meat tempted them
to taste the flesh of their horses. The trembling usurper was supported
by Theodore Lascaris, his son-in-law, a valiant youth, who aspired to
save and to rule his country; the Greeks, regardless of that country,
were awakened to the defence of their religion; but their firmest hope
was in the strength and spirit of the Varangian guards, of the Danes and
English, as they are named in the writers of the times. After ten days'
incessant labor, the ground was levelled, the ditch filled, the approaches
of the besiegers were regularly made, and two hundred and fifty engines of assault exercised their various powers to clear the rampart, to
batter the walls, and to sap the foundations. On the first appearance of
a breach, the scaling-ladders were applied: the numbers that defended
the vantage ground repulsed and oppressed the adventurous Latins;
but they admired the resolution of fifteen knights and sergeants, who
had gained the ascent, and maintained their perilous station till they
were precipitated or made prisoners by the Imperial guards. On the
side of the harbor the naval attack was more successfully conducted by
the Venetians; and that industrious people employed every resource
that was known and practiced before the invention of gunpowder. A
double line, three bow-shots in front, was formed by the galleys and
ships; and the swift motion of the former was supported by the weight
and loftiness of the latter, whose decks, and poops, and turret, were
the platforms of military engines, that discharged their shot over the
heads of the first line. The soldiers, who leaped from the galleys on
shore, immediately planted and ascended their scaling-ladders, while
the large ships, advancing more slowly into the intervals, and lowering
a draw-bridge, opened a way through the air from their masts to the
rampart. In the midst of the conflict, the doge, a venerable and conspicuous form, stood aloft in complete armor on the prow of his galley.
The great standard of St. Mark was displayed before him; his threats,
promises, and exhortations, urged the diligence of the rowers; his vessel
was the first that struck; and Dandolo was the first warrior on the shore.
The nations admired the magnanimity of the blind old man, without
reflecting that his age and infirmities diminished the price of life, and
enhanced the value of immortal glory. On a sudden, by an invisible
hand, (for the standard-bearer was probably slain,) the banner of the

republic was fixed on the rampart: twenty-five towers were rapidly occupied; and, by the cruel expedient of fire, the Greeks were driven from the adjacent quarter. The doge had despatched the intelligence of his success, when he was checked by the danger of his confederates. Nobly declaring that he would rather die with the pilgrims than gain a victory by their destruction, Dandolo relinquished his advantage, recalled his troops, and hastened to the scene of action. He found the six weary diminutive *battles* of the French encompassed by sixty squadrons of the Greek cavalry, the least of which was more numerous than the largest of their divisions. Shame and despair had provoked Alexius to the last effort of a general sally; but he was awed by the firm order and manly aspect of the Latins; and, after skirmishing at a distance, withdrew his troops in the close of the evening. The silence or tumult of the night exasperated his fears; and the timid usurper, collecting a treasure of ten thousand pounds of gold, basely deserted his wife, his people, and his fortune; threw himself into a bark; stole through the Bosphorus; and landed in shameful safety in an obscure harbor of Thrace. As soon as they were apprised of his flight, the Greek nobles sought pardon and peace in the dungeon where the blind Isaac expected each hour the visit of the executioner. Again saved and exalted by the vicissitudes of fortune, the captive in his Imperial robes was replaced on the throne, and surrounded with prostrate slaves, whose real terror and affected joy he was incapable of discerning. At the dawn of day, hostilities were suspended, and the Latin chiefs were surprised by a message from the lawful and reigning emperor, who was impatient to embrace his son, and to reward his generous deliverers.

The Fourth Crusade. – Part Three

BUT THESE GENEROUS DELIVERERS were unwilling to release their hostage, till they had obtained from his father the payment, or at least the promise, of their recompense. They chose four ambassadors, Matthew of Montmorency, our historian the marshal of Champagne, and two Venetians, to congratulate the emperor. The gates were thrown open on their approach, the streets on both sides were lined with the battle axes of the Danish and English guard: the presence-chamber glittered with gold and jewels, the false substitute of virtue and power: by the side of the blind Isaac his wife was seated, the sister of the king of Hungary: and by her appearance, the noble matrons of Greece were drawn from their domestic retirement, and mingled with the circle of senators and soldiers. The Latins, by the mouth of the marshal, spoke like men conscious of their merits, but who respected the work of their own hands; and the emperor clearly understood, that his son's engagements with Venice and the pilgrims must be ratified without hesitation or delay. Withdrawing into a private chamber with the empress, a chamberlain, an interpreter, and the four ambassadors, the father of young Alexius inquired with some anxiety into the nature of his stipulations. The submission of the Eastern empire to the pope, the succor of the Holy Land, and a present contribution of two hundred thousand marks of silver. – "These conditions are weighty," was his prudent reply: "they are hard to accept, and difficult to perform. But no conditions can exceed the measure of your services and deserts." After this satisfactory assurance, the barons mounted on horseback, and introduced the heir of Constantinople to the city and palace: his youth and marvellous adventures engaged every heart in his favor, and Alexius was solemnly crowned with his father in the dome of St. Sophia. In the first days of his reign, the people, already blessed with the restoration of plenty and peace, was delighted by the joyful catastrophe of the tragedy; and the discontent of the nobles, their regret, and their fears, were covered by the polished surface of pleasure and loyalty The mixture of two discordant nations in the same capital might have been pregnant with mischief and danger; and the suburb of Galata, or Pera, was assigned for the quarters of the French and Venetians. But the liberty of trade and familiar intercourse was allowed between the friendly nations: and each day the pilgrims were tempted by devotion or curiosity to visit the churches and palaces of Constantinople. Their rude minds, insensible perhaps of the finer arts, were astonished by the magnificent scenery: and the poverty of their native towns enhanced the populousness and riches of the first metropolis of Christendom. Descending from his state, young Alexius was prompted by interest and gratitude to repeat his frequent and familiar visits to his Latin allies; and in the freedom of the table, the gay petulance of the French sometimes forgot the emperor of the East. In their most serious conferences, it was agreed, that the reunion of the two churches must be the result of patience and time; but avarice was less tractable than zeal; and a larger sum was instantly disbursed to appease the wants, and silence the importunity, of the crusaders. Alexius was alarmed by the approaching hour of their departure: their absence might have relieved him from the engagement which he was yet incapable of performing; but his friends would have left him, naked and alone, to the caprice and prejudice of a perfidious nation. He wished to bribe their stay, the delay of a year, by undertaking to defray their expense, and to satisfy, in their name, the freight of the Venetian vessels. The offer was agitated in the council of the barons; and, after a repetition of their debates and scruples, a majority of votes again acquiesced in the advice of the doge and the prayer of the young emperor. At the price of sixteen hundred pounds of gold, he prevailed on the marquis of Montferrat to lead him with an army round the provinces of Europe; to establish his authority, and pursue his uncle, while Constantinople was awed by the presence of Baldwin and his confederates of France and Flanders. The expedition was successful: the blind emperor exulted in the success of his arms, and listened to the predictions of his flatterers, that the same Providence which had raised him from the dungeon to the throne, would heal his gout, restore his sight, and watch over the long prosperity of his reign. Yet the mind of the suspicious old man was tormented by the rising glories of his son; nor could his pride conceal from his envy, that, while his own name was pronounced in faint and reluctant acclamations, the royal youth was the theme of spontaneous and universal praise.

By the recent invasion, the Greeks were awakened from a dream of nine centuries; from the vain presumption that the capital of the Roman empire was impregnable to foreign arms. The strangers of the West had violated the city, and bestowed the sceptre, of Constantine: their Imperial clients soon became as unpopular as themselves: the well-known vices of Isaac were rendered still more contemptible by his infirmities, and the young Alexius was hated as an apostate, who had renounced the manners and religion of his country. His secret covenant with the Latins was divulged or suspected; the people, and especially the clergy, were devoutly attached to their faith and superstition; and every convent, and every shop, resounded with the danger of the church and the tyranny of the pope. An empty treasury could ill supply the demands of regal luxury and foreign extortion: the Greeks refused to avert, by a general tax, the impending evils of servitude and pillage; the oppression of the rich excited a more dangerous and personal resentment; and if the emperor melted the plate, and despoiled the images, of the sanctuary, he seemed to justify the complaints of heresy and sacrilege. During the absence of Marquis Boniface and his Imperial pupil, Constantinople was visited with a calamity which might be justly imputed to the zeal and indiscretion of the Flemish pilgrims. In one of their visits to the city, they were scandalized by the aspect of a mosque or synagogue, in which one God was worshipped, without a partner or a son. Their effectual mode of controversy was to attack the infidels with the sword, and their habitation with fire: but the infidels, and some Christian neighbors, presumed to defend their lives and properties; and the flames which bigotry had kindled, consumed the most orthodox and innocent structures. During eight days and nights, the conflagration spread above a league in front, from the harbor to the Propontis, over the thickest and most populous regions of the city. It is not easy to count the stately churches and palaces that were reduced to a smoking ruin, to value the merchandise that perished in the trading streets, or to number the families that were involved in the common destruction. By this outrage, which the doge and the barons in vain affected to disclaim, the name of the Latins became still more unpopular; and the colony of that nation, above fifteen thousand persons, consulted their safety in a hasty retreat from the city to the protection of their standard in the suburb of Pera. The emperor returned in triumph; but the firmest and most dexterous policy would have been insufficient to steer him through the tempest, which overwhelmed the person and government of that unhappy youth. His own inclination, and his father's advice, attached him to his benefactors; but Alexius hesitated between gratitude and patriotism, between the fear of his subjects and of his allies. By his feeble and fluctuating conduct he lost the esteem and confidence of both; and, while he invited the marquis of Monferrat to occupy the palace, he suffered the nobles to conspire, and the people to arm, for the deliverance of their country. Regardless of his painful situation, the Latin chiefs repeated their demands, resented his delays, suspected his intentions, and exacted a decisive answer of peace or war. The haughty summons was delivered by three French knights and three Venetian deputies, who girded their swords, mounted their horses, pierced through the angry multitude, and entered, with a fearful countenance, the palace and presence of the Greek emperor. In a peremptory tone, they recapitulated their services and his engagements; and boldly declared, that unless their just claims were fully and immediately satisfied, they should no longer hold him either as a sovereign or a friend. After this defiance, the first that had ever wounded an Imperial ear, they departed without betraying any symptoms of fear; but their escape from a servile palace and a furious city astonished the ambassadors themselves; and their return to the camp was the signal of mutual hostility.

Among the Greeks, all authority and wisdom were overborne by the impetuous multitude, who mistook their rage for valor, their numbers for strength, and their fanaticism for the support and inspiration of Heaven. In the eyes of both nations Alexius was false and contemptible; the base and spurious race of the Angeli was rejected with clamorous disdain; and the people of Constantinople encompassed the senate, to demand at their hands a more worthy emperor. To every senator, conspicuous by his birth or dignity, they successively presented the purple: by each senator the deadly garment was repulsed: the contest lasted three days; and we may learn from the historian Nicetas, one of the members of the assembly, that fear and weaknesses were the guardians of their loyalty. A phantom, who vanished in oblivion, was forcibly proclaimed by the crowd: but the author of the tumult, and the leader of the war, was a prince of the house of Ducas; and his common appellation of Alexius must be discriminated by the epithet of Mourzoufle, which in the vulgar idiom expressed the close junction of his black and shaggy eyebrows. At once a patriot and a courtier, the perfidious Mourzoufle, who was not destitute of cunning and courage, opposed the Latins both in speech and action, inflamed the passions and prejudices of the Greeks, and insinuated himself into the favor and confidence of Alexius, who trusted him with the office of great chamberlain, and tinged his buskins with the colors of royalty. At the dead of night, he rushed into the bed-chamber with an affrighted aspect, exclaiming, that the palace was attacked by the people and betrayed by the guards. Starting from his couch, the unsuspecting prince threw himself into the arms of his enemy, who had contrived his escape by a private staircase. But that staircase terminated in a prison: Alexius was seized, stripped, and loaded with chains; and, after tasting some days the bitterness of death, he was poisoned, or strangled, or beaten with clubs, at the command, or in the presence, of the tyrant. The emperor Isaac Angelus soon followed his son to the grave; and Mourzoufle, perhaps, might spare the superfluous crime of hastening the extinction of impotence and blindness.

The death of the emperors, and the usurpation of Mourzoufle, had changed the nature of the quarrel. It was no longer the disagreement of allies who overvalued their services, or neglected their obligations: the French and Venetians forgot their complaints against Alexius, dropped a tear on the untimely fate of their companion, and swore revenge against the perfidious nation who had crowned his assassin. Yet the prudent doge was still inclined to negotiate: he asked as a debt, a subsidy, or a fine, fifty thousand pounds of gold, about two millions sterling; nor would the conference have been abruptly broken, if the zeal, or policy, of Mourzoufle had not refused to sacrifice the Greek church to the safety of the state. Amidst the invectives of his foreign and domestic enemies, we may discern, that he was not unworthy of the character which he had assumed, of the public champion: the second siege of Constantinople was far more laborious than the first; the treasury was replenished, and discipline was restored, by a severe inquisition into the abuses of the former reign; and Mourzoufle, an iron mace in his hand, visiting the posts, and affecting the port and aspect of a warrior, was an object of terror to his soldiers, at least, and to his kinsmen. Before and after the death of Alexius, the Greeks made two vigorous and well-conducted attempts to burn the navy in the harbor; but the skill and courage of the Venetians repulsed the fire-ships; and the vagrant flames wasted themselves without injury in the sea. In a nocturnal sally the Greek emperor was vanquished by Henry, brother of the count of Flanders: the advantages of number and surprise aggravated the shame of his defeat: his buckler was found on the field of battle; and the Imperial standard, a divine image of the Virgin, was presented, as a trophy and a relic to the Cistercian monks, the disciples of St. Bernard. Near three months, without excepting the holy season of Lent, were consumed in skirmishes and preparations, before the Latins were ready or resolved for a general assault. The land fortifications had been found impregnable; and the Venetian pilots represented, that, on the shore of the Propontis, the anchorage was unsafe, and the ships must be driven by the current far away to the straits of the Hellespont; a prospect not unpleasing to the reluctant pilgrims, who sought every opportunity of breaking the army. From the harbor, therefore, the assault was determined by the assailants, and expected by the besieged; and the emperor had placed his scarlet pavilions on a neighboring height, to direct and animate the efforts of his troops. A fearless spectator, whose mind could entertain the ideas of pomp and pleasure, might have admired the long array of two embattled armies, which extended above half a league, the one on the ships and galleys, the other on the walls and towers raised above the ordinary level by several stages of wooden turrets. Their first fury was spent in the discharge of darts, stones, and fire, from the engines; but the water was deep; the French were bold; the Venetians were skilful; they approached the walls; and a desperate conflict of swords, spears, and battle-axes, was fought on the trembling bridges that grappled the floating, to the stable, batteries. In more than a hundred places, the assault was urged, and the defence was sustained; till the superiority of ground and numbers finally prevailed, and the Latin trumpets sounded a retreat. On the ensuing days, the attack was renewed with equal vigor, and a similar event; and, in the night, the doge and the barons held a council, apprehensive only for the public danger: not a voice pronounced the words of escape or treaty; and each warrior, according to his temper, embraced the hope of victory, or the assurance of a glorious death. By the experience of the former siege, the Greeks were instructed, but the Latins were animated; and the knowledge that Constantinople might be taken, was of more avail than the local precautions which that knowledge had inspired for its defence. In the third assault, two ships were linked together to double their strength; a strong north wind drove them on the shore; the bishops of Troyes and Soissons led the van; and the auspicious names of the *pilgrim* and the *paradise* resounded along the line. The episcopal banners were displayed on the walls; a hundred marks of silver had been promised to the first adventurers; and if their reward was intercepted by death, their names have been immortalized by fame. Four towers were scaled; three gates were burst open; and the French knights, who might tremble on the waves, felt themselves invincible on horseback on the solid ground. Shall I relate that the thousands who guarded the emperor's person fled on the approach, and before the lance, of a single warrior? Their ignominious flight is attested by their countryman Nicetas: an army of phantoms marched with the French hero, and he was magnified to a giant in the eyes of the Greeks. While the fugitives deserted their posts and cast away their arms, the Latins entered the city under the banners of their leaders: the streets and gates opened for their passage; and either design or accident kindled a third conflagration, which consumed in a few hours the measure of three of the largest cities of France. In the close of evening, the barons checked their troops, and fortified their stations: They were awed by the extent and populousness of the capital, which might yet require the labor of a month, if the churches and palaces were conscious of their internal strength. But in the morning, a suppliant procession, with crosses and images, announced the submission of the Greeks, and deprecated the wrath of the conquerors: the usurper escaped through the golden gate: the palaces of Blachernæ and Boucoleon were occupied by the count of Flanders and the marquis of Montferrat; and the empire, which still bore the name of Constantine, and the title of Roman, was subverted by the arms of the Latin pilgrims.

Constantinople had been taken by storm; and no restraints, except those of religion and humanity, were imposed on the conquerors by the laws of war. Boniface, marquis of Montferrat, still acted as their general; and the Greeks, who revered his name as that of their future sovereign, were heard to exclaim in a lamentable tone, "Holy marquis-king, have mercy upon us!" His prudence or compassion opened the gates of the city to the fugitives; and he exhorted the soldiers of the cross to spare the lives of their fellow-Christians. The streams of blood that flowed down the pages of Nicetas may be reduced to the slaughter of two thousand of his unresisting countrymen; and the greater part was massacred, not by the strangers, but by the Latins, who had been driven from the city, and who exercised the revenge of a triumphant faction. Yet of these exiles, some were less mindful of injuries than of benefits; and Nicetas himself was indebted for his safety to the generosity of a Venetian merchant. Pope Innocent the Third accuses the pilgrims for respecting, in their lust, neither age nor sex, nor religious profession; and bitterly laments that the deeds of darkness, fornication, adultery, and incest, were perpetrated in open day; and that noble matrons and holy nuns were polluted by the grooms and peasants of the Catholic camp. It is indeed probable that the license of victory prompted and covered a multitude of sins: but it is certain, that the capital of the East contained a stock of venal or willing beauty, sufficient to satiate the desires of twenty thousand pilgrims; and female prisoners were no longer subject to the right or abuse of domestic slavery. The marquis of Montferrat was the patron of discipline and decency; the count of Flanders was the mirror of chastity: they had forbidden, under pain of death, the rape of married women, or virgins, or nuns; and the proclamation was sometimes invoked by the vanquished and respected by the victors. Their cruelty and lust were moderated by the authority of the chiefs, and feelings of the soldiers; for we are no longer describing an irruption of the northern savages; and however ferocious they might still appear, time, policy, and religion had civilized the manners of the French, and still more of the Italians. But a free scope was allowed to their avarice, which was glutted, even in the holy week, by the pillage of Constantinople. The right of victory, unshackled by any promise or treaty, had confiscated the public and private wealth of the Greeks; and every hand, according to its size and strength, might lawfully execute the sentence and seize the forfeiture. A portable and universal standard of exchange was found in the coined and uncoined metals of gold and silver, which each captor, at home or abroad, might convert into the possessions most suitable to his temper and situation. Of the treasures, which trade and luxury had accumulated, the silks, velvets, furs, the gems, spices, and rich movables, were the most precious, as they could not be procured for money in the ruder countries of Europe. An order of rapine was instituted; nor was the share of each individual abandoned to industry or chance. Under the tremendous penalties of perjury, excommunication, and death, the Latins were bound to deliver their plunder into the common stock: three churches were selected for the deposit and distribution of the spoil: a single share was allotted to a foot-soldier; two for a sergeant on horseback; four to a knight; and larger proportions according to the rank and merit of the barons and princes. For violating this sacred engagement, a knight belonging to the count of St. Paul was hanged with his shield and coat of arms round his neck; his example might render similar offenders more artful and discreet; but avarice was more powerful than fear; and it is generally believed that the secret far exceeded the acknowledged plunder. Yet the magnitude of the prize surpassed the largest scale of experience or expectation. After the whole had been equally divided between the French and Venetians, fifty thousand marks were deducted to satisfy the debts of the former and the demands of the latter. The residue of the French amounted to four hundred thousand marks of silver, about eight hundred thousand pounds sterling; nor can I better appreciate the value of that sum in the public and private transactions of the age, than by defining it as seven times the annual revenue of the kingdom of England.

In this great revolution we enjoy the singular felicity of comparing the narratives of Villehardouin and Nicetas, the opposite feelings of the marshal of Champagne and the Byzantine senator. At the first view it should seem that the wealth of Constantinople was only transferred from one nation to another; and that the loss and sorrow of the Greeks is exactly balanced by the joy and advantage of the Latins. But in the miserable account of war, the gain is never equivalent to the loss, the pleasure to the pain; the smiles of the Latins were transient and fallacious; the Greeks forever wept over the ruins of their country; and their real calamities were aggravated by sacrilege and mockery. What benefits accrued to the conquerors from the three fires which annihilated so vast a portion of the buildings and riches of the city? What a stock of such things, as could neither be used nor transported, was maliciously or wantonly destroyed! How much treasure was idly wasted in gaming, debauchery, and riot! And what precious objects were bartered for a vile price by the impatience or ignorance of the soldiers, whose reward was stolen by the base industry of the last of the Greeks! These alone, who had nothing to lose, might derive some profit from the revolution; but the misery of the upper ranks of society is strongly painted in the personal adventures of Nicetas himself. His stately palace had been reduced to ashes in the second conflagration; and the senator, with his family and friends, found an obscure shelter in another house which he possessed near the church of St. Sophia. It was the door of this mean habitation that his friend, the Venetian merchant, guarded in the disguise of a soldier, till Nicetas could save, by a precipitate flight, the relics of his fortune and the chastity of his daughter. In a cold, wintry season, these fugitives, nursed in the lap of prosperity, departed on foot; his wife was with child; the desertion of their slaves compelled them to carry their baggage on their own shoulders; and their women, whom they placed in the centre, were exhorted to conceal their beauty with dirt, instead of adorning it with paint and jewels Every step was exposed to insult and danger: the threats of the strangers were less painful than the taunts of the plebeians, with whom they were now levelled; nor did the exiles breathe in safety till their mournful pilgrimage was concluded at Selymbria, above forty miles from the capital. On the way they overtook the patriarch, without attendance and almost without apparel, riding on an ass, and reduced to a state of apostolical poverty, which, had it been voluntary, might perhaps have been meritorious. In the mean while, his desolate churches were profaned by the licentiousness and party zeal of the Latins. After stripping the gems and pearls, they converted the chalices into drinking-cups; their tables, on which they gamed and feasted, were covered with the pictures of Christ and the saints; and they trampled under foot the most venerable objects of the Christian worship. In the cathedral of St. Sophia, the ample veil of the sanctuary was rent asunder for the sake of the golden fringe; and the altar, a monument of art and riches, was broken in pieces and shared among the captors. Their mules and horses were laden with the wrought silver and gilt carvings, which they tore down from the doors and pulpit; and if the beasts stumbled under the burden, they were stabbed by their impatient drivers, and the holy pavement streamed with their impure blood. A prostitute was seated on the throne of the patriarch; and that daughter of Belial, as she is styled, sung and danced in the church, to ridicule the hymns and processions of the Orientals. Nor were the repositories of the royal dead secure from violation: in the church of the Apostles, the tombs of the emperors were rifled; and it is said, that after six centuries the corpse of Justinian was found without any signs of decay or putrefaction. In the streets, the French and Flemings clothed themselves and their horses in painted robes and flowing head-dresses of linen; and the coarse intemperance of their feasts insulted the splendid sobriety of the East. To expose the arms of a people of scribes and scholars, they affected to display a pen, an inkhorn, and a sheet of paper, without discerning that the instruments of science and valor were *alike* feeble and useless in the hands of the modern Greeks.

Their reputation and their language encouraged them, however, to despise the ignorance and to overlook the progress of the Latins. In the love of the arts, the national difference was still more obvious and real; the Greeks preserved with reverence the works of their ancestors, which they could not imitate; and, in the destruction of the statues of Constantinople, we are provoked to join in the complaints and invectives of the Byzantine historian. We have seen how the rising city was adorned by the vanity and despotism of the Imperial founder: in the ruins of paganism, some gods and heroes were saved from the axe of superstition; and the forum and hippodrome were dignified with the relics of a better age. Several of these are described by Nicetas, in a florid and affected style; and from his descriptions I shall select some interesting particulars. . The victorious charioteers were cast in bronze, at their own or the public charge, and fitly placed in the hippodrome: they stood aloft in their chariots, wheeling round the goal: the spectators could admire their attitude, and judge of the resemblance; and of these figures, the most perfect might have been transported from the Olympic stadium. . The sphinx, river-horse, and crocodile, denote the climate and manufacture of Egypt and the spoils of that ancient province. . The she-wolf suckling Romulus and Remus, a subject alike pleasing to the *old* and the *new* Romans, but which could really be treated before the decline of the Greek sculpture. . An eagle holding and tearing a serpent in his talons, a domestic monument of the Byzantines, which they ascribed, not to a human artist, but to the magic power of the philosopher Apollonius, who, by this talisman, delivered the city from such venomous reptiles. . An ass and his driver, which were erected by Augustus in his colony of Nicopolis, to commemorate a verbal omen of the victory of Actium. . An equestrian statue which passed, in the vulgar opinion, for Joshua, the Jewish conqueror, stretching out his hand to stop the course of the descending sun. A more classical tradition recognized the figures of Bellerophon and Pegasus; and the free attitude of the steed seemed to mark that he trod on air, rather than on the earth. . A square and lofty obelisk of brass; the sides were embossed with a variety of picturesque and rural scenes, birds singing; rustics laboring, or playing on their pipes; sheep bleating; lambs skipping; the sea, and a scene of fish and fishing; little naked cupids laughing, playing, and pelting each other with apples; and, on the summit, a female figure, turning with the slightest breath, and thence denominated *the wind's attendant.* . The Phrygian shepherd presenting to Venus the prize of beauty, the apple of discord. . The incomparable statue of Helen, which is delineated by Nicetas in the words of admiration and love: her well-turned feet, snowy arms, rosy lips, bewitching smiles, swimming eyes, arched eyebrows, the harmony of her shape, the lightness of her drapery, and her flowing locks that waved in the wind; a beauty that might have moved her Barbarian destroyers to pity and remorse. . The manly or divine form of Hercules, as he was restored to life by the masterhand of Lysippus; of such magnitude, that his thumb was equal to his waist, his leg to the stature, of a common man: his chest ample, his shoulders broad, his limbs strong and muscular, his hair curled, his aspect commanding. Without his bow, or quiver, or club, his lion's skin carelessly thrown over him, he was seated on an osier basket, his right leg and arm stretched to the utmost, his left knee bent, and supporting his elbow, his head reclining on his left hand, his countenance indignant and pensive. . A colossal statue of Juno, which had once adorned her temple of Samos, the enormous head by four yoke of oxen was laboriously drawn to the palace. . Another colossus, of Pallas or Minerva, thirty feet in height, and representing with admirable spirit the attributes and character of the martial maid. Before we accuse the Latins, it is just to remark, that this Pallas was destroyed after the first siege, by the fear and superstition of the Greeks themselves. The other statues of brass which I have enumerated were broken and melted by the unfeeling avarice of the crusaders: the cost and labor were consumed in a moment; the soul of genius evaporated in smoke; and the remnant of base metal was coined into money for the payment of the troops. Bronze is not the most durable of monuments: from the marble forms of Phidias and Praxiteles, the Latins might turn aside with stupid contempt; but unless they were crushed by some accidental injury, those useless stones stood secure on their pedestals. The most enlightened of the strangers, above the gross and sensual pursuits of their countrymen, more piously exercised the right of conquest in the search and seizure of the relics of the saints. Immense was the supply of heads and bones, crosses and images, that were scattered by this revolution over the churches of Europe; and such was the increase of pilgrimage and oblation, that no branch, perhaps, of more lucrative plunder was imported from the East. Of the writings of antiquity, many that still existed in the twelfth century, are now lost. But the pilgrims were not solicitous to save or transport the volumes of an unknown tongue: the perishable substance of paper or parchment can only be preserved by the multiplicity of copies; the literature of the Greeks had almost centred in the metropolis; and, without computing the extent of our loss, we may drop a tear over the libraries that have perished in the triple fire of Constantinople.

Partition of the Empire by the French and Venetians. – Part One

Partition of the Empire by the French and
Venetians, – Five Latin Emperors of the
Houses of Flanders and Courtenay. – Their
Wars against the Bulgarians and Greeks. –
Weakness and Poverty of the Latin Empire.
– Recovery of Constantinople by the Greeks.
– General Consequences of the Crusades.

AFTER THE DEATH OF the lawful princes, the French and Venetians, confident of justice and victory, agreed to divide and regulate their future possessions. It was stipulated by treaty, that twelve electors, six of either nation, should be nominated; that a majority should choose the emperor of the East; and that, if the votes were equal, the decision of chance should ascertain the successful candidate. To him, with all the titles and prerogatives of the Byzantine throne, they assigned the two palaces of Boucoleon and Blachernæ, with a fourth part of the Greek monarchy. It was defined that the three remaining portions should be equally shared between the republic of Venice and the barons of France; that each feudatory, with an honorable exception for the doge, should acknowledge and perform the duties of homage and military service to the supreme head of the empire; that the nation which gave an emperor, should resign to their brethren the choice of a patriarch; and that the pilgrims, whatever might be their impatience to visit the Holy Land, should devote another year to the conquest and defence of the Greek provinces. After the conquest of Constantinople by the Latins, the treaty was confirmed and executed; and the first and most important step was the creation of an emperor. The six electors of the French nation were all ecclesiastics, the abbot of Loces, the archbishop elect of Acre in Palestine, and the bishops of Troyes, Soissons, Halberstadt, and Bethlehem, the last of whom exercised in the camp the office of pope's legate: their profession and knowledge were respectable; and as *they* could not be the objects, they were best qualified to be the authors of the choice. The six Venetians were the principal servants of the state, and in this list the noble families of Querini and Contarini are still proud to discover their ancestors. The twelve assembled in the chapel of the palace; and after the solemn invocation of the Holy Ghost, they proceeded to deliberate and vote. A just impulse of respect and gratitude prompted them to crown the virtues of the doge; his wisdom had inspired their enterprise; and the most youthful knights might envy and applaud the exploits of blindness and age. But the patriot Dandolo was devoid of all personal ambition, and fully satisfied that he had been judged worthy to reign. His nomination was overruled by the Venetians themselves: his countrymen, and perhaps his friends, represented, with the eloquence of truth, the mischiefs that might arise to national freedom and the common cause, from the union of two incompatible characters, of the first magistrate of a republic and the emperor of the East. The exclusion of the doge left room for the more equal merits of Boniface and Baldwin; and at their names all meaner candidates respectfully withdrew. The marquis of Montferrat was recommended by his mature age and fair reputation, by the choice of the adventurers, and the wishes of the Greeks; nor can I believe that Venice, the mistress of the sea, could be seriously apprehensive of a petty lord at the foot of the Alps. But the count of Flanders was the chief of a wealthy and warlike people: he was valiant, pious, and chaste; in the prime of life, since he was only thirty-two years of age; a descendant of Charlemagne, a cousin of the king of France, and a compeer of the prelates and barons who had yielded with reluctance to the command of a foreigner. Without the chapel, these barons, with the doge and marquis at their head, expected the decision of the twelve electors. It was announced by the bishop of Soissons, in the name of his colleagues: "Ye have sworn to obey the prince whom we should choose: by our unanimous suffrage, Baldwin count of Flanders and Hainault is now your sovereign, and the emperor of the East." He was saluted with loud applause, and the proclamation was reechoed through the city by the joy of the Latins, and the trembling adulation of the Greeks. Boniface was the first to kiss the hand of his rival, and to raise him on the buckler: and Baldwin was transported to the cathedral, and solemnly invested with the purple buskins. At the end of three weeks he was crowned by the legate, in the vacancy of the patriarch; but the Venetian clergy soon filled the chapter of St. Sophia, seated Thomas Morosini on the ecclesiastical throne, and employed every art to perpetuate in their own nation the honors and benefices of the Greek church. Without delay the successor of Constantine instructed Palestine, France, and Rome, of this memorable revolution. To Palestine he sent, as a trophy, the gates of Constantinople, and the chain of the harbor; and adopted, from the Assise of Jerusalem, the laws or customs best adapted to a French colony and conquest in the East. In his epistles, the natives of France are encouraged to swell that colony, and to secure that conquest, to people a magnificent city and a fertile land, which will reward the labors both of the priest and the soldier. He congratulates the Roman pontiff on the restoration of his authority in the East; invites him to extinguish the Greek schism by his presence in a general council; and implores his blessing and forgiveness for the disobedient pilgrims. Prudence and dignity are blended in the answer of Innocent. In the subversion of the Byzantine empire, he arraigns the vices of man, and adores the providence of God; the conquerors will be absolved or condemned by their future conduct; the validity of their treaty depends on the judgment of St. Peter; but he inculcates their most sacred duty of establishing a just subordination of obedience and tribute, from the Greeks to the Latins, from the magistrate to the clergy, and from the clergy to the pope.

In the division of the Greek provinces, the share of the Venetians was more ample than that of the Latin emperor. No more than one fourth was appropriated to his domain; a clear moiety of the remainder was reserved for Venice; and the other moiety was distributed among the adventurers of France and Lombardy. The venerable Dandolo was proclaimed despot of Romania, and invested after the Greek fashion with the purple buskins. He ended at Constantinople his long and glorious life; and if the prerogative was personal, the title was used by his successors till the middle of the fourteenth century, with the singular, though true, addition of lords of one fourth and a half of the Roman empire. The doge, a slave of state, was seldom permitted to depart from the helm of the republic; but his place was supplied by the *bail*, or regent, who exercised a supreme jurisdiction over the colony of Venetians: they possessed three of the eight quarters of the city; and his independent tribunal was composed of six judges, four counsellors, two chamberlains two fiscal advocates, and a constable. Their long experience of the Eastern trade enabled them to select their portion with discernment: they had rashly accepted the dominion and defence of Adrianople; but it was the more reasonable aim of their policy to form a chain of factories, and cities, and islands, along the maritime coast, from the neighborhood of Ragusa to the Hellespont and the Bosphorus. The labor and cost of such extensive conquests exhausted their treasury: they abandoned their maxims of government, adopted a feudal system, and contented themselves with the homage of their nobles, for the possessions which these private vassals undertook to reduce and maintain. And thus it was that the family of Sanut acquired the duchy of Naxos, which involved the greatest part of the archipelago. For the price of ten thousand marks, the republic purchased of the marquis of Montferrat the fertile Island of Crete or Candia, with the ruins of a hundred cities; but its improvement was stinted by the proud and narrow spirit of an aristocracy; and the wisest senators would confess that the sea, not the land, was the treasury of St. Mark. In the moiety of the adventurers the marquis Boniface might claim the most liberal reward; and, besides the Isle of Crete, his exclusion from the throne was compensated by the royal title and the provinces beyond the Hellespont. But he prudently exchanged that distant and difficult conquest for the kingdom of Thessalonica Macedonia, twelve days' journey from the capital, where he might be supported by the neighboring powers of his brother-in-law the king of Hungary. His progress was hailed by the voluntary or reluctant acclamations of the natives; and Greece, the proper and ancient Greece, again received a Latin conqueror, who trod with indifference that classic ground. He viewed with a careless eye the beauties of the valley of Tempe; traversed with a cautious step the straits of Thermopylæ; occupied the unknown cities of Thebes, Athens, and Argos; and assaulted the fortifications of Corinth and Napoli, which resisted his arms. The lots of the Latin pilgrims were regulated by chance, or choice, or subsequent exchange; and they abused, with intemperate joy, their triumph over the lives and fortunes of a great people. After a minute survey of the provinces, they weighed in the scales of avarice the revenue of each district, the advantage of the situation, and the ample or scanty supplies for the maintenance of soldiers and horses. Their presumption claimed and divided the long-lost dependencies of the Roman sceptre: the Nile and Euphrates rolled through their imaginary realms; and happy was the warrior who drew for his prize the palace of the Turkish sultan of Iconium. I shall not descend to the pedigree of families and the rent-roll of estates, but I wish to specify that the counts of Blois and St. Pol were invested with the duchy of Nice and the lordship of Demotica: the principal fiefs were held by the service of constable, chamberlain, cup-bearer, butler, and chief cook; and our historian, Jeffrey of Ville-hardouin, obtained a fair establishment on the banks of the Hebrus, and united the double office of marshal of Champagne and Romania. At the head of his knights and archers, each baron mounted on horse-back to secure the possession of his share, and their first efforts were generally successful. But the public force was weakened by their dispersion; and a thousand quarrels must arise under a law, and among men, whose sole umpire was the sword. Within three months after the conquest of Constantinople, the emperor and the king of Thessalonica drew their hostile followers into the field; they were reconciled by the authority of the doge, the advice of the marshal, and the firm freedom of their peers.

Two fugitives, who had reigned at Constantinople, still asserted the title of emperor; and the subjects of their fallen throne might be moved to pity by the misfortunes of the elder Alexius, or excited to revenge by the spirit of Mourzoufle. A domestic alliance, a common interest, a similar guilt, and the merit of extinguishing his enemies, a brother and a nephew, induced the more recent usurper to unite with the former the relics of his power. Mourzoufle was received with smiles and honors in the camp of his father Alexius; but the wicked can never love, and should rarely trust, their fellow-criminals; he was seized in the bath, deprived of his eyes, stripped of his troops and treasures, and turned out to wander an object of horror and contempt to those who with more propriety could hate, and with more justice could punish, the assassin of the emperor Isaac and his son. As the tyrant, pursued by fear or remorse, was stealing over to Asia, he was seized by the Latins of Constantinople, and condemned, after an open trial, to an ignominious death. His judges debated the mode of his execution, the axe, the wheel, or the stake; and it was resolved that Mourzoufle should ascend the Theodosian column, a pillar of white marble of one hundred and forty-seven feet in height. From the summit he was cast down headlong, and dashed in pieces on the pavement, in the presence of innumerable spectators, who filled the forum of Taurus, and admired the accomplishment of an old prediction, which was explained by this singular event. The fate of Alexius is less tragical: he was sent by the marquis a captive to Italy, and a gift to the king of the Romans; but he had not much to applaud his fortune, if the sentence of imprisonment and exile were changed from a fortress in the Alps to a monastery in Asia. But his daughter, before the national calamity, had been given in marriage to a young hero who continued the succession, and restored the throne, of the Greek princes. The valor of Theodore Lascaris was signalized in the two sieges of Constantinople. After the flight of Mourzoufle, when the Latins were already in the city, he offered himself as their emperor to the soldiers and people; and his ambition, which might be virtuous, was undoubtedly brave. Could he have infused a soul into the multitude, they might have crushed the strangers under their feet: their abject despair refused his aid; and Theodore retired to breathe the air of freedom in Anatolia, beyond the immediate view and pursuit of the conquerors. Under the title, at first of despot, and afterwards of emperor, he drew to his standard the bolder spirits, who were fortified against slavery by the contempt of life; and as every means was lawful for the public safety implored without scruple the alliance of the Turkish sultan Nice, where Theodore established his residence, Prusa and Philadelphia, Smyrna and Ephesus, opened their gates to their deliverer: he derived strength and reputation from his victories, and even from his defeats; and the successor of Constantine preserved a fragment of the empire from the banks of the Mæander to the suburbs of Nicomedia, and at length of Constantinople. Another portion, distant and obscure, was possessed by the lineal heir of the Comneni, a son of the virtuous Manuel, a grandson of the tyrant Andronicus. His name was Alexius; and the epithet of great was applied perhaps to his stature, rather than to his exploits. By the indulgence of the Angeli, he was appointed governor or duke of Trebizond: his birth gave him ambition, the revolution independence; and, without changing his title, he reigned in peace from Sinope to the Phasis, along the coast of the Black Sea. His nameless son and successor is described as the vassal of the sultan, whom he served with two hundred lances: that Comnenian prince was no more than duke of Trebizond, and the title of emperor was first assumed by the pride and envy of the grandson of Alexius. In the West, a third fragment was saved from the common shipwreck by Michael, a bastard of the house of Angeli, who, before the revolution, had been known as a hostage, a soldier, and a rebel. His flight from the camp of the marquis Boniface secured his freedom; by his marriage with the governor's daughter, he commanded the important place of Durazzo, assumed the title of despot, and founded a strong and conspicuous principality in Epirus, Ætolia, and Thessaly, which have ever been peopled by a warlike race. The Greeks, who had offered their service to their new sovereigns, were excluded by the haughty Latins from all civil and military honors, as a nation born to tremble and obey. Their resentment prompted them to show that they might have been useful friends, since they could be dangerous enemies: their nerves were braced by adversity: whatever was learned or holy, whatever was noble or valiant, rolled away into the independent states of Trebizond, Epirus, and Nice; and a single patrician is marked by the ambiguous praise of attachment and loyalty to the Franks. The vulgar herd of the cities and the country would have gladly submitted to a mild and regular servitude; and the transient disorders of war would have been obliterated by some years of industry and peace. But peace was banished, and industry was crushed, in the disorders of the feudal system. The *Roman* emperors of Constantinople, if they were endowed with abilities, were armed with power for the protection of their subjects: their laws were wise, and their administration was simple. The Latin throne was filled by a titular prince, the chief, and often the servant, of his licentious confederates; the fiefs of the empire, from a kingdom to a castle, were held and ruled by the sword of the barons; and their discord, poverty, and ignorance, extended the ramifications of tyranny to the most sequestered villages. The Greeks were oppressed by the double weight of the priests, who were invested with temporal power, and of the soldier, who was inflamed by fanatic hatred; and the insuperable bar of religion and language forever separated the stranger and the native. As long as the crusaders were united at Constantinople, the memory of their conquest, and the terror of their arms, imposed silence on the captive land: their dispersion betrayed the smallness of their numbers and the defects of their discipline; and some failures and mischances revealed the secret, that they were not invincible. As the fears of the Greeks abated, their hatred increased. They murdered; they conspired; and before a year of slavery had elapsed, they implored, or accepted, the succor of a Barbarian, whose power they had felt, and whose gratitude they trusted.

The Latin conquerors had been saluted with a solemn and early embassy from John, or Joannice, or Calo-John, the revolted chief of the Bulgarians and Walachians. He deemed himself their brother, as the votary of the Roman pontiff, from whom he had received the regal title and a holy banner; and in the subversion of the Greek monarchy, he might aspire to the name of their friend and accomplice. But Calo-John was astonished to find, that the Count of Flanders had assumed the pomp and pride of the successors of Constantine; and his ambassadors were dismissed with a haughty message, that the rebel must deserve a pardon, by touching with his forehead the footstool of the

Imperial throne. His resentment would have exhaled in acts of violence and blood: his cooler policy watched the rising discontent of the Greeks; affected a tender concern for their sufferings; and promised, that their first struggles for freedom should be supported by his person and kingdom. The conspiracy was propagated by national hatred, the firmest band of association and secrecy: the Greeks were impatient to sheathe their daggers in the breasts of the victorious strangers; but the execution was prudently delayed, till Henry, the emperor's brother, had transported the flower of his troops beyond the Hellespont. Most of the towns and villages of Thrace were true to the moment and the signal; and the Latins, without arms or suspicion, were slaughtered by the vile and merciless revenge of their slaves. From Demotica, the first scene of the massacre, the surviving vassals of the count of St. Pol escaped to Adrianople; but the French and Venetians, who occupied that city, were slain or expelled by the furious multitude: the garrisons that could effect their retreat fell back on each other towards the metropolis; and the fortresses, that separately stood against the rebels, were ignorant of each other's and of their sovereign's fate. The voice of fame and fear announced the revolt of the Greeks and the rapid approach of their Bulgarian ally; and Calo-John, not depending on the forces of his own kingdom, had drawn from the Scythian wilderness a body of fourteen thousand Comans, who drank, as it was said, the blood of their captives, and sacrificed the Christians on the altars of their gods.

Alarmed by this sudden and growing danger, the emperor despatched a swift messenger to recall Count Henry and his troops; and had Baldwin expected the return of his gallant brother, with a supply of twenty thousand Armenians, he might have encountered the invader with equal numbers and a decisive superiority of arms and discipline. But the spirit of chivalry could seldom discriminate caution from cowardice; and the emperor took the field with a hundred and forty knights, and their train of archers and sergeants. The marshal, who dissuaded and obeyed, led the vanguard in their march to Adrianople; the main body was commanded by the count of Blois; the aged doge of Venice followed with the rear; and their scanty numbers were increased from all sides by the fugitive Latins. They undertook to besiege the rebels of Adrianople; and such was the pious tendency of the crusades that they employed the holy week in pillaging the country for their subsistence, and in framing engines for the destruction of their fellow-Christians. But the Latins were soon interrupted and alarmed by the light cavalry of the Comans, who boldly skirmished to the edge of their imperfect lines: and a proclamation was issued by the marshal of Romania, that, on the trumpet's sound, the cavalry should mount and form; but that none, under pain of death, should abandon themselves to a desultory and dangerous pursuit. This wise injunction was first disobeyed by the count of Blois, who involved the emperor in his rashness and ruin. The Comans, of the Parthian or Tartar school, fled before their first charge; but after a career of two leagues, when the knights and their horses were almost breathless, they suddenly turned, rallied, and encompassed the heavy squadrons of the Franks. The count was slain on the field; the emperor was made prisoner; and if the one disdained to fly, if the other refused to yield, their personal bravery made a poor atonement for their ignorance, or neglect, of the duties of a general.

Partition of the Empire by the French and Venetians. – Part Two

PROUD OF HIS VICTORY and his royal prize, the Bulgarian advanced to relieve Adrianople and achieve the destruction of the Latins. They must inevitably have been destroyed, if the marshal of Romania had not displayed a cool courage and consummate skill; uncommon in all ages, but most uncommon in those times, when war was a passion, rather than a science. His grief and fears were poured into the firm and faithful bosom of the doge; but in the camp he diffused an assurance of safety, which could only be realized by the general belief. All day he maintained his perilous station between the city and the Barbarians: Villehardouin decamped in silence at the dead of night; and his masterly retreat of three days would have deserved the praise of Xenophon and the ten thousand. In the rear, the marshal supported the weight of the pursuit; in the front, he moderated the impatience of the fugitives; and wherever the Comans approached, they were repelled by a line of impenetrable spears. On the third day, the weary troops beheld the sea, the solitary town of Rodosta, and their friends, who had landed from the Asiatic shore. They embraced, they wept; but they united their arms and counsels; and in his brother's absence, Count Henry assumed the regency of the empire, at once in a state of childhood and caducity. If the Comans withdrew from the summer heats, seven thousand Latins, in the hour of danger, deserted Constantinople, their brethren, and their vows. Some partial success was overbalanced by the loss of one hundred and twenty knights in the field of Rusium; and of the Imperial domain, no more was left than the capital, with two or three adjacent fortresses on the shores of Europe and Asia. The king of Bulgaria was resistless and inexorable; and Calo-John respectfully eluded the demands of the pope, who conjured his new proselyte to restore peace and the emperor to the afflicted Latins. The deliverance of Baldwin was no longer, he said, in the power of man: that prince had died in prison; and the manner of his death is variously related by ignorance and credulity. The lovers of a tragic legend will be pleased to hear, that the royal captive was tempted by the amorous queen of the Bulgarians; that his chaste refusal exposed him to the falsehood of a woman and the jealousy of a savage; that his hands and feet were severed from his body; that his bleeding trunk was cast among the carcasses of dogs and horses; and that he breathed three days, before he was devoured by the birds of prey. About twenty years afterwards, in a wood of the Netherlands, a hermit announced himself as the true Baldwin, the emperor of Constantinople, and lawful sovereign of Flanders. He related the wonders of his escape, his adventures, and his penance, among a people prone to believe and to rebel; and, in the first transport, Flanders acknowledged her long-lost sovereign. A short examination before the French court detected the impostor, who was punished with an ignominious death; but the Flemings still adhered to the pleasing error; and the countess Jane is accused by the gravest historians of sacrificing to her ambition the life of an unfortunate father.

In all civilized hostility, a treaty is established for the exchange or ransom of prisoners; and if their captivity be prolonged, their condition is known, and they are treated according to their rank with humanity or honor. But the savage Bulgarian was a stranger to the laws of war: his prisons were involved in darkness and silence; and above a year elapsed before the Latins could be assured of the death of Baldwin, before his brother, the regent Henry, would consent to assume the title of emperor. His moderation was applauded by the Greeks as an act of rare and inimitable virtue. Their light and perfidious ambition was eager to seize or anticipate the moment of a vacancy, while a law of succession, the guardian both of the prince and people, was gradually defined and confirmed in the hereditary monarchies of Europe. In the support of the Eastern empire, Henry was gradually left without an associate, as the heroes of the crusade retired from the world or from the war. The doge of Venice, the venerable Dandolo, in the fulness of years and glory, sunk into the grave. The marquis of Montferrat was slowly recalled from the Peloponnesian war to the revenge of Baldwin and the defence of Thessalonica. Some nice disputes of feudal homage and service were reconciled in a personal interview between the emperor and the king; they were firmly united by mutual esteem and the common danger; and their alliance was sealed by the nuptials of Henry with the daughter of the Italian prince. He soon deplored the loss of his friend and father. At the persuasion of some faithful Greeks, Boniface made a bold and successful inroad among the hills of Rhodope: the Bulgarians fled on his approach; they assembled to harass his retreat. On the intelligence that his rear was attacked, without waiting for any defensive armor, he leaped on horseback, couched his lance, and drove the enemies before him; but in the rash pursuit he was pierced with a mortal wound; and the head of the king of Thessalonica was presented to Calo-John, who enjoyed the honors, without the merit, of victory. It is here, at this melancholy event, that the pen or the voice of Jeffrey of Villehardouin seems to drop or to expire; and if he still exercised his military office of marshal of Romania, his subsequent exploits are buried in oblivion. The character of Henry was not unequal to his arduous situation: in the siege of Constantinople, and beyond the Hellespont, he had deserved the fame of a valiant knight and a skilful commander; and his courage was tempered with a degree of prudence and mildness unknown to his impetuous brother. In the double war against the Greeks of Asia and the Bulgarians of Europe, he was ever the foremost on shipboard or on horseback; and though he cautiously provided for the success of his arms, the drooping Latins were often roused by his example to save and to second their fearless emperor. But such efforts, and some supplies of men and money from France, were of less avail than the errors, the cruelty, and death, of their most formidable adversary. When the despair of the Greek subjects invited Calo-John as their deliverer, they hoped that he would protect their liberty and adopt their laws: they were soon taught to compare the degrees of national ferocity, and to execrate the savage conqueror, who no longer dissembled his intention of dispeopling Thrace, of demolishing the cities, and of transplanting the inhabitants beyond the Danube. Many towns and villages of Thrace were already evacuated: a heap of ruins marked the place of Philippopolis, and a similar calamity was expected at Demotica and Adrianople, by the first authors of the revolt. They raised a cry of grief and repentance to the throne of Henry; the emperor alone had the magnanimity to forgive and trust them. No more than four hundred knights, with their sergeants and archers, could be assembled under his banner; and with this slender force he fought and repulsed the Bulgarian, who, besides his infantry, was at the head of forty thousand horse. In this expedition, Henry felt the difference between a hostile and a friendly country: the remaining cities were preserved by his arms; and the savage, with shame and loss, was compelled to relinquish his prey. The siege of Thessalonica was the last of the evils which Calo-John inflicted or suffered: he was stabbed in the night in his tent; and the general, perhaps the assassin, who found him weltering in his blood, ascribed the blow, with general applause, to the lance of St. Demetrius. After several victories, the prudence of Henry concluded an honorable peace with the successor of the tyrant, and with the Greek princes of Nice and Epirus. If he ceded some doubtful limits, an ample kingdom was reserved for himself and his feudatories; and his reign, which lasted only ten years, afforded a short interval of prosperity and peace. Far above the narrow policy of Baldwin and Boniface, he freely intrusted to the Greeks the most important offices of the state and army; and this liberality of sentiment and practice was the more seasonable, as the princes of Nice and Epirus had already learned to seduce and employ the mercenary valor of the Latins. It was the aim of Henry to unite and reward his deserving subjects, of every nation and language; but he appeared less solicitous to accomplish the impracticable union of the two churches. Pelagius, the pope's legate, who acted as the sovereign of Constantinople, had interdicted the worship of the Greeks, and sternly imposed the payment of tithes, the double procession of the Holy Ghost, and a blind obedience to the Roman pontiff. As the weaker party, they pleaded the duties of conscience, and implored the rights of toleration: "Our bodies," they said, "are Cæsar's, but our souls belong only to God." The persecution was checked by the firmness of the emperor: and if we can believe that the same prince was poisoned by the Greeks themselves, we must entertain a contemptible idea of the sense and gratitude of mankind. His valor was a vulgar attribute, which he shared with ten thousand knights; but Henry possessed the superior courage to oppose, in a superstitious age, the pride and avarice of the clergy. In the cathedral of St. Sophia he presumed to place his throne on the right hand of the patriarch; and this presumption excited the sharpest censure of Pope Innocent the Third. By a salutary edict, one of the first examples of the laws of mortmain, he prohibited the alienation of fiefs: many of the Latins, desirous of returning to Europe, resigned their estates to the church for a spiritual or temporal reward; these holy lands were immediately discharged from military service, and a colony of soldiers would have been gradually transformed into a college of priests.

The virtuous Henry died at Thessalonica, in the defence of that kingdom, and of an infant, the son of his friend Boniface. In the two first emperors of Constantinople the male line of the counts of Flanders was extinct. But their sister Yolande was the wife of a French prince, the mother of a numerous progeny; and one of her daughters had married Andrew king of Hungary, a brave and pious champion of the cross. By seating him on the Byzantine throne, the barons of Romania would have acquired the forces of a neighboring and warlike kingdom; but the prudent Andrew revered the laws of succession; and the princess Yolande, with her husband Peter of Courtenay, count of Auxerre, was invited by the Latins to assume the empire of the East. The royal birth of his father, the noble origin of his mother, recommended to the barons of France the first cousin of their king. His reputation was fair, his possessions were ample, and in the bloody crusade against the Albigeois, the soldiers and the priests had been abundantly satisfied of his zeal and valor. Vanity might applaud the elevation of a French emperor of Constantinople; but prudence must pity, rather than envy, his treacherous and imaginary greatness. To assert and adorn his title, he was reduced to sell or mortgage the best of his patrimony. By these expedients, the liberality of his royal kinsman Philip Augustus, and the national spirit of chivalry, he was enabled to pass the Alps at the head of one hundred and forty knights, and five thousand five hundred sergeants and archers. After some hesitation, Pope Honorius the Third was persuaded to crown the successor of Constantine: but he performed the ceremony in a church without the walls, lest he should seem to imply or to bestow any right of sovereignty over the ancient capital of the empire. The Venetians had engaged to transport Peter and his forces beyond the Adriatic, and the empress, with her four children, to the Byzantine palace; but they required, as the price of their service, that he should recover Durazzo from the despot of Epirus. Michael Angelus, or Comnenus, the first of his dynasty, had bequeathed the succession of his power and ambition to Theodore, his legitimate brother, who already threatened and invaded the establishments of the Latins. After discharging his debt by a fruitless assault, the emperor raised the siege to prosecute a long and perilous journey over land from Durazzo to Thessalonica. He was soon lost in the mountains of Epirus: the passes were fortified; his provisions exhausted; he was delayed and deceived by a treacherous negotiation; and, after Peter of Courtenay and the Roman legate had been arrested in a banquet, the French troops, without leaders or hopes, were eager to exchange their arms for the delusive promise of mercy and bread. The Vatican thundered; and the impious Theodore was threatened with the vengeance of earth and heaven; but the captive emperor and his soldiers were forgotten, and the reproaches of the pope are confined to the imprisonment of his legate. No sooner was he satisfied by the deliverance of the priests and a promise of spiritual obedience, than he pardoned and protected the despot of Epirus. His peremptory commands suspended the ardor of the Venetians and the king of Hungary; and it was only by a natural or untimely death that Peter of Courtenay was released from his hopeless captivity.

The long ignorance of his fate, and the presence of the lawful sovereign, of Yolande, his wife or widow, delayed the proclamation of a new emperor. Before her death, and in the midst of her grief, she was delivered of a son, who was named Baldwin, the last and most unfortunate of the Latin princes of Constantinople. His birth endeared him to the barons of Romania; but his childhood would have prolonged the troubles of a minority, and his claims were superseded by the elder claims of his brethren. The first of these, Philip of Courtenay, who derived from his mother the inheritance of Namur, had the wisdom to prefer the substance of a marquisate to the shadow of an empire; and on his refusal, Robert, the second of the sons of Peter and Yolande, was called to the throne of Constantinople. Warned by his father's mischance, he pursued his slow and secure journey through Germany and along the Danube: a passage was opened by his sister's marriage with the king of Hungary; and the emperor Robert was crowned by the patriarch in the cathedral of St. Sophia. But his reign was an æra of calamity and disgrace; and the colony, as it was styled, of New France yielded on all sides to the Greeks of Nice and Epirus. After a victory, which he owed to his perfidy rather than his courage, Theodore Angelus entered the kingdom of Thessalonica, expelled the feeble Demetrius, the son of the marquis Boniface, erected his standard on the walls of Adrianople; and added, by his vanity, a third or a fourth name to the list of rival emperors. The relics of the Asiatic province were swept away by John Vataces, the son-in-law and successor of Theodore Lascaris, and who, in a triumphant reign of thirty-three years, displayed the virtues both of peace and war. Under his discipline, the swords of the French mercenaries were the most effectual instruments of his conquests, and their desertion from the service of their country was at once a symptom and a cause of the rising ascendant of the Greeks. By the construction of a fleet, he obtained the command of the Hellespont, reduced the islands of Lesbos and Rhodes, attacked the Venetians of Candia, and intercepted the rare and parsimonious succors of the West. Once, and once only, the Latin emperor sent an army against Vataces; and in the defeat of that army, the veteran knights, the last of the original conquerors, were left on the field of battle. But the success of a foreign enemy was less painful to the pusillanimous Robert than the insolence of his Latin subjects, who confounded the weakness of the emperor and of the empire. His personal misfortunes will prove the anarchy of the government and the ferociousness of the times. The amorous youth had neglected his Greek bride, the daughter of Vataces, to introduce into the palace a beautiful maid, of a private, though noble family of Artois; and her mother had been tempted by the lustre of the purple to forfeit her engagements with a gentleman of Burgundy. His love was converted into rage; he assembled his friends, forced the palace gates, threw the mother into the sea, and inhumanly cut off the nose and lips of the wife or concubine of the emperor. Instead of punishing the offender, the barons avowed and applauded the savage deed, which, as a prince and as a man, it was impossible that Robert should forgive. He escaped from the guilty city to implore the justice or compassion of the pope: the emperor was coolly exhorted to return to his station; before he could obey, he sunk under the weight of grief, shame, and impotent resentment.

It was only in the age of chivalry, that valor could ascend from a private station to the thrones of Jerusalem and Constantinople. The titular kingdom of Jerusalem had devolved to Mary, the daughter of Isabella and Conrad of Montferrat, and the granddaughter of Almeric or Amaury. She was given to John of Brienne, of a noble family in Champagne, by the public voice, and the judgment of Philip Augustus, who named him as the most worthy champion of the Holy Land. In the fifth crusade, he led a hundred thousand Latins to the conquest of Egypt: by him the siege of Damietta was achieved; and the subsequent failure was justly ascribed to the pride and avarice of the legate. After the marriage of his daughter with Frederic the Second, he was provoked by the emperor's ingratitude to accept the command of the army of the church; and though advanced in life, and despoiled of royalty, the sword and spirit of John of Brienne were still ready for the service of Christendom. In the seven years of his brother's reign, Baldwin of Courtenay had not emerged from a state of childhood, and the barons of Romania felt the strong necessity of placing the sceptre in the hands of a man and a hero. The veteran king of Jerusalem might have disdained the name and office of regent; they agreed to invest him for his life with the title and prerogatives of emperor, on the sole condition that Baldwin should marry his second daughter, and succeed at a mature age to the throne of Constantinople. The expectation, both of the Greeks and Latins, was kindled by the renown, the choice, and the presence of John of Brienne; and they admired his martial aspect, his green and vigorous age of more than fourscore years, and his size and stature, which surpassed the common measure of mankind. But avarice, and the love of ease, appear to have chilled the ardor of enterprise: his troops were disbanded, and two years rolled away without action or honor, till he was awakened by the dangerous alliance of Vataces emperor of Nice, and of Azan king of Bulgaria. They besieged Constantinople by sea and land, with an army of one hundred thousand men, and a fleet of three hundred ships of war; while the entire force of the Latin emperor was reduced to one hundred and sixty knights, and a small addition of sergeants and archers. I tremble to relate, that instead of defending the city, the hero made a sally at the head of his cavalry; and that of forty-eight squadrons of the enemy, no more than three escaped from the edge of his invincible sword. Fired by his example, the infantry and the citizens boarded the vessels that anchored close to the walls; and twenty-five were dragged in triumph into the harbor of Constantinople. At the summons of the emperor, the vassals and allies armed in her defence; broke through every obstacle that opposed their passage; and, in the succeeding year, obtained a second victory over the same enemies. By the rude poets of the age, John of Brienne is compared to Hector, Roland, and Judas Machabæus: but their credit, and his glory, receive some abatement from the silence of the Greeks. The empire was soon deprived of the last of her champions; and the dying monarch was ambitious to enter paradise in the habit of a Franciscan friar.

> *N'Aie, Ector, Roll' ne Ogiers*
> *Ne Judas Machabeus li fiers*
> *Tant ne fit d'armes en estors*
> *Com fist li Rois Jehans cel jors*
> *Et il defors et il dedans*
> *La paru sa force et ses sens*
> *Et li hardiment qu'il avoit.]*

In the double victory of John of Brienne, I cannot discover the name or exploits of his pupil Baldwin, who had attained the age of military service, and who succeeded to the imperial dignity on the decease of his adoptive father. The royal youth was employed on a commission more suitable to his temper; he was sent to visit the Western courts, of the pope more especially, and of the king of France; to excite their pity by the view of his innocence and distress; and to obtain some supplies of men or money for the relief of the sinking empire. He thrice repeated these mendicant visits, in which he seemed to prolong his stay and postpone his return; of the five-and-twenty years of his reign, a greater number were spent abroad than at home; and in no place did the emperor deem himself less free and secure than in his native country and his capital.

On some public occasions, his vanity might be soothed by the title of Augustus, and by the honors of the purple; and at the general council of Lyons, when Frederic the Second was excommunicated and deposed, his Oriental colleague was enthroned on the right hand of the pope. But how often was the exile, the vagrant, the Imperial beggar, humbled with scorn, insulted with pity, and degraded in his own eyes and those of the nations! In his first visit to England, he was stopped at Dover by a severe reprimand, that he should presume, without leave, to enter an independent kingdom. After some delay, Baldwin, however, was permitted to pursue his journey, was entertained with cold civility, and thankfully departed with a present of seven hundred marks. From the avarice of Rome he could only obtain the proclamation of a crusade, and a treasure of indulgences; a coin whose currency was depreciated by too frequent and indiscriminate abuse. His birth and misfortunes recommended him to the generosity of his cousin Louis the Ninth; but the martial zeal of the saint was diverted from Constantinople to Egypt and Palestine; and the public and private poverty of Baldwin was alleviated, for a moment, by the alienation of the marquisate of Namur and the lordship of Courtenay, the last remains of his inheritance. By such shameful or ruinous expedients, he once more returned to Romania, with an army of thirty thousand soldiers, whose numbers were doubled in the apprehension of the Greeks. His first despatches to France and England announced his victories and his hopes: he had reduced the country round the capital to the distance of three days' journey; and if he succeeded against an important, though nameless, city, (most probably Chiorli,) the frontier would be safe and the passage accessible. But these expectations (if Baldwin was sincere) quickly vanished like a dream: the troops and treasures of France melted away in his unskilful hands; and the throne of the Latin emperor was protected by a dishonorable alliance with the Turks and Comans. To secure the former, he consented to bestow his niece on the unbelieving sultan of Cogni; to please the latter, he complied with their Pagan rites; a dog was sacrificed between the two armies; and the contracting parties tasted each other's blood, as a pledge of their fidelity. In the palace, or prison, of Constantinople, the successor of Augustus demolished the vacant houses for winter fuel, and stripped the lead from the churches for the daily expense of his family. Some usurious loans were dealt with a scanty hand by the merchants of Italy; and Philip, his son and heir, was pawned at Venice as the security for a debt. Thirst, hunger, and nakedness, are positive evils: but wealth is relative; and a prince who would be rich in a private station, may be exposed by the increase of his wants to all the anxiety and bitterness of poverty.

Partition of the Empire by the French and Venetians. – Part Three

BUT IN THIS ABJECT distress, the emperor and empire were still possessed of an ideal treasure, which drew its fantastic value from the superstition of the Christian world. The merit of the true cross was somewhat impaired by its frequent division; and a long captivity among the infidels might shed some suspicion on the fragments that were produced in the East and West. But another relic of the Passion was preserved in the Imperial chapel of Constantinople; and the crown of thorns which had been placed on the head of Christ was equally precious and authentic. It had formerly been the practice of the Egyptian debtors to deposit, as a security, the mummies of their parents; and both their honor and religion were bound for the redemption of the pledge. In the same manner, and in the absence of the emperor, the barons of Romania borrowed the sum of thirteen thousand one hundred and thirty-four pieces of gold on the credit of the holy crown: they failed in the performance of their contract; and a rich Venetian, Nicholas Querini, undertook to satisfy their impatient creditors, on condition that the relic should be lodged at Venice, to become his absolute property, if it were not redeemed within a short and definite term. The barons apprised their sovereign of the hard treaty and impending loss and as the empire could not afford a ransom of seven thousand pounds sterling, Baldwin was anxious to snatch the prize from the Venetians, and to vest it with more honor and emolument in the hands of the most Christian king. Yet the negotiation was attended with some delicacy. In the purchase of relics, the saint would have started at the guilt of simony; but if the mode of expression were changed, he might lawfully repay the debt, accept the gift, and acknowledge the obligation. His ambassadors, two Dominicans, were despatched to Venice to redeem and receive the holy crown which had escaped the dangers of the sea and the galleys of Vataces. On opening a wooden box, they recognized the seals of the doge and barons, which were applied on a shrine of silver; and within this shrine the monument of the Passion was enclosed in a golden vase. The reluctant Venetians yielded to justice and power: the emperor Frederic granted a free and honorable passage; the court of France advanced as far as Troyes in Champagne, to meet with devotion this inestimable relic: it was borne in triumph through Paris by the king himself, barefoot, and in his shirt; and a free gift of ten thousand marks of silver reconciled Baldwin to his loss. The success of this transaction tempted the Latin emperor to offer with the same generosity the remaining furniture of his chapel; a large and authentic portion of the true cross; the baby-linen of the Son of God, the lance, the sponge, and the chain, of his Passion; the rod of Moses, and part of the skull of St. John the Baptist. For the reception of these spiritual treasures, twenty thousand marks were expended by St. Louis on a stately foundation, the holy chapel of Paris, on which the muse of Boileau has bestowed a comic immortality. The truth of such remote and ancient relics, which cannot be proved by any human testimony, must be admitted by those who believe in the miracles which they have performed. About the middle of the last age, an inveterate ulcer was touched and cured by a holy prickle of the holy crown: the prodigy is attested by the most pious and enlightened Christians of France; nor will the fact be easily disproved, except by those who are armed with a general antidote against religious credulity.

The Latins of Constantinople were on all sides encompassed and pressed; their sole hope, the last delay of their ruin, was in the division of their Greek and Bulgarian enemies; and of this hope they were deprived by the superior arms and policy of Vataces, emperor of Nice. From the Propontis to the rocky coast of Pamphylia, Asia was peaceful and prosperous under his reign; and the events of every campaign extended his influence in Europe. The strong cities of the hills of Macedonia and Thrace were rescued from the Bulgarians; and their kingdom was circumscribed by its present and proper limits, along the southern banks of the Danube. The sole emperor of the Romans could no longer brook that a lord of Epirus, a Comnenian prince of the West, should presume to dispute or share the honors of the purple; and the humble Demetrius changed the color of his buskins, and accepted with gratitude the appellation of despot. His own subjects were exasperated by his baseness and incapacity; they implored the protection of their supreme lord. After some resistance, the kingdom of Thessalonica was united to the empire of Nice; and Vataces reigned without a competitor from the Turkish borders to the Adriatic Gulf. The princes of Europe revered his merit and power; and had he subscribed an orthodox creed, it should seem that the pope would have abandoned without reluctance the Latin throne of Constantinople. But the death of Vataces, the short and busy reign of Theodore his son, and the helpless infancy of his grandson John, suspended the restoration of the Greeks. In the next chapter, I shall explain their domestic revolutions; in this place, it will be sufficient to observe, that the young prince was oppressed by the ambition of his guardian and colleague, Michael Palæologus, who displayed the virtues and vices that belong to the founder of a new dynasty. The emperor Baldwin had flattered himself, that he might recover some provinces or cities by an impotent negotiation. His ambassadors were dismissed from Nice with mockery and contempt. At every place which they named, Palæologus alleged some special reason, which rendered it dear and valuable in his eyes: in the one he was born; in another he had been first promoted to military command; and in a third he had enjoyed, and hoped long to enjoy, the pleasures of the chase. "And what then do you propose to give us?" said the astonished deputies. "Nothing," replied the Greek, "not a foot of land. If your master be desirous of peace, let him pay me, as an annual tribute, the sum which he receives from the trade and customs of Constantinople. On these terms, I may allow him to reign. If he refuses, it is war. I am not ignorant of the art of war, and I trust the event to God and my sword." An expedition against the despot of Epirus was the first prelude of his arms. If a victory was followed by a defeat; if the race of the Comneni or Angeli survived in those mountains his efforts and his reign; the captivity of Villehardouin, prince of Achaia, deprived the Latins of the most active and powerful vassal of their expiring monarchy. The republics of Venice and Genoa disputed, in the first of their naval wars, the command of the sea and the commerce of the East. Pride and interest attached the Venetians to the defence of Constantinople; their rivals were tempted to promote the designs of her enemies, and the alliance of the Genoese with the schismatic conqueror provoked the indignation of the Latin church.

Intent on his great object, the emperor Michael visited in person and strengthened the troops and fortifications of Thrace. The remains of the Latins were driven from their last possessions: he assaulted without success the suburb of Galata; and corresponded with a perfidious baron, who proved unwilling, or unable, to open the gates of the metropolis. The next spring, his favorite general, Alexius Strategopulus, whom he had decorated with the title of Cæsar, passed the Hellespont with eight hundred horse and some infantry, on a secret expedition. His instructions enjoined him to approach, to listen, to watch, but not to risk any doubtful or dangerous enterprise against the city. The adjacent territory between the Propontis and the Black Sea was cultivated by a hardy race of peasants and outlaws, exercised in arms, uncertain in their allegiance, but inclined by language, religion, and present advantage, to the party of the Greeks. They were styled the *volunteers*; and by their free service the army of Alexius, with the regulars of Thrace and the Coman auxiliaries, was augmented to the number of five-and-twenty thousand men. By the ardor of the volunteers, and by his own ambition, the Cæsar was stimulated to disobey the precise orders of his master, in the just confidence that success would plead his pardon and reward. The weakness of Constantinople, and the distress and terror of the Latins, were familiar to the observation of the volunteers; and they represented the present moment as the most propitious to surprise and conquest. A rash youth, the new governor of the Venetian colony, had sailed away with thirty galleys, and the best of the French knights, on a wild expedition to Daphnusia, a town on the Black Sea, at the distance of forty leagues; and the remaining Latins were without strength or suspicion. They were informed that Alexius had passed the Hellespont; but their apprehensions were lulled by the smallness of his original numbers; and their imprudence had not watched the subsequent increase of his army. If he left his main body to second and support his operations, he might advance unperceived in the night with a chosen detachment. While some applied scaling-ladders to the lowest part of the walls, they were secure of an old Greek, who would introduce their companions through a subterraneous passage into his house; they could soon on the inside break an entrance through the golden gate, which had been long obstructed; and the conqueror would be in the heart of the city before the Latins were conscious of their danger. After some debate, the Cæsar resigned himself to the faith of the volunteers; they were trusty, bold, and successful; and in describing the plan, I have already related the execution and success. But no sooner had Alexius passed the threshold of the golden gate, than he trembled at his own rashness; he paused, he deliberated; till the desperate volunteers urged him forwards, by the assurance that in retreat lay the greatest and most inevitable danger. Whilst the Cæsar kept his regulars in firm array, the Comans dispersed themselves on all sides; an alarm was sounded, and the threats of fire and pillage compelled the citizens to a decisive resolution. The Greeks of Constantinople remembered their native sovereigns; the Genoese merchants their recent alliance and Venetian foes; every quarter was in arms; and the air resounded with a general acclamation of "Long life and victory to Michael and John, the august emperors of the Romans!" Their rival, Baldwin, was awakened by the sound; but the most pressing danger could not prompt him to draw his sword in the defence of a city which he deserted, perhaps, with more pleasure than regret: he fled from the palace to the seashore, where he descried the welcome sails of the fleet returning from the vain and fruitless attempt on Daphnusia. Constantinople was irrecoverably lost; but the Latin emperor and the principal families embarked on board the Venetian galleys, and steered for the Isle of Euba, and afterwards for Italy, where the royal fugitive was entertained by the pope and Sicilian king with a mixture of contempt and pity. From the loss of Constantinople to his death, he consumed thirteen years, soliciting the Catholic powers to join in his restoration: the lesson had been familiar to his youth; nor was his last exile more indigent or shameful than his three former pilgrimages to the courts of Europe. His son Philip was the heir of an ideal empire; and the pretensions of his daughter Catherine were transported by her marriage to Charles of Valois, the brother of Philip the Fair, king of France. The house of Courtenay was represented in the female line by successive alliances, till the title of emperor of Constantinople, too bulky and sonorous for a private name, modestly expired in silence and oblivion.

After this narrative of the expeditions of the Latins to Palestine and Constantinople, I cannot dismiss the subject without resolving the general consequences on the countries that were the scene, and on the nations that were the actors, of these memorable crusades. As soon as the arms of the Franks were withdrawn, the impression, though not the memory, was erased in the Mahometan realms of Egypt and Syria. The faithful disciples of the prophet were never tempted by a profane desire to study the laws or language of the idolaters; nor did the simplicity of their primitive manners receive the slightest alteration from their intercourse in peace and war with the unknown strangers of the West. The Greeks, who thought themselves proud, but who were only vain, showed a disposition somewhat less inflexible. In the efforts for the recovery of their empire, they emulated the valor, discipline, and tactics of their antagonists. The modern literature of the West they might justly despise; but its free spirit would instruct them in the rights of man; and some institutions of public and private life were adopted from the French. The correspondence of Constantinople and Italy diffused the knowledge of the Latin tongue; and several of the fathers and classics were at length honored with a Greek version. But the national and religious prejudices of the Orientals were inflamed by persecution, and the reign of the Latins confirmed the separation of the two churches.

If we compare the æra of the crusades, the Latins of Europe with the Greeks and Arabians, their respective degrees of knowledge, industry, and art, our rude ancestors must be content with the third rank in the scale of nations. Their successive improvement and present superiority may be ascribed to a peculiar energy of character, to an active and imitative spirit, unknown to their more polished rivals, who at that time were in a stationary or retrograde state. With such a disposition, the Latins should have derived the most early and essential benefits from a series of events which opened to their eyes the prospect of the world, and introduced them to a long and frequent intercourse with the more cultivated regions of the East. The first and most obvious progress was in trade and manufactures, in the arts which are strongly prompted by the thirst of wealth, the calls of necessity, and the gratification of the sense or vanity. Among the crowd of unthinking fanatics, a captive or a pilgrim might sometimes observe the superior refinements of Cairo and Constantinople: the first importer of windmills was the benefactor of nations; and if such blessings are enjoyed without any grateful remembrance, history has condescended to notice the more apparent luxuries of silk and sugar, which were transported into Italy from Greece and Egypt. But the intellectual wants of the Latins were more slowly felt and supplied; the ardor of studious curiosity was awakened in Europe by different causes and more recent events; and, in the age of the crusades, they viewed with careless indifference the literature of the Greeks and Arabians. Some rudiments of mathematical and medicinal knowledge might be imparted in practice and in figures; necessity might produce some interpreters for the grosser business of merchants and soldiers; but the commerce of the Orientals had not diffused the study and knowledge of their languages in the schools of Europe. If a similar principle of religion repulsed the idiom of the Koran, it should have excited their patience and curiosity to understand the original text of the gospel; and the same grammar would have unfolded the sense of Plato and the beauties of Homer. Yet in a reign of sixty years, the Latins of Constantinople disdained the speech and learning of their subjects; and the manuscripts were the only treasures which the natives might enjoy without rapine or envy. Aristotle was indeed the oracle of the Western universities, but it was a barbarous Aristotle; and, instead of ascending to the fountain head, his Latin votaries humbly accepted a corrupt and remote version, from the Jews and Moors of Andalusia. The principle of the crusades was a savage fanaticism; and the most important effects were analogous to the cause. Each pilgrim was ambitious to return with his sacred spoils, the relics of Greece and Palestine; and each relic was preceded and followed by a train of miracles and visions. The belief of the Catholics was corrupted by new legends, their practice by new superstitions; and the establishment of the inquisition, the mendicant orders of monks and friars, the last abuse of indulgences, and the final progress of idolatry, flowed from the baleful fountain of the holy war. The active spirit of the Latins preyed on the vitals of their reason and religion; and if the ninth and tenth centuries were the times of darkness, the thirteenth and fourteenth were the age of absurdity and fable.

Partition of the Empire by the French and Venetians. – Part Four

IN THE PROFESSION OF Christianity, in the cultivation of a fertile land, the northern conquerors of the Roman empire insensibly mingled with the provincials, and rekindled the embers of the arts of antiquity. Their settlements about the age of Charlemagne had acquired some degree of order and stability, when they were overwhelmed by new swarms of invaders, the Normans, Saracens, and Hungarians, who replunged the western countries of Europe into their former state of anarchy and barbarism. About the eleventh century, the second tempest had subsided by the expulsion or conversion of the enemies of Christendom: the tide of civilization, which had so long ebbed, began to flow with a steady and accelerated course; and a fairer prospect was opened to the hopes and efforts of the rising generations. Great was the increase, and rapid the progress, during the two hundred years of the crusades; and some philosophers have applauded the propitious influence of these holy wars, which appear to me to have checked rather than forwarded the maturity of Europe. The lives and labors of millions, which were buried in the East, would have been more profitably employed in the improvement of their native country: the accumulated stock of industry and wealth would have overflowed in navigation and trade; and the Latins would have been enriched and enlightened by a pure and friendly correspondence with the climates of the East. In one respect I can indeed perceive the accidental operation of the crusades, not so much in producing a benefit as in removing an evil. The larger portion of the inhabitants of Europe was chained to the soil, without freedom, or property, or knowledge; and the two orders of ecclesiastics and nobles, whose numbers were comparatively small, alone deserved the name of citizens and men. This oppressive system was supported by the arts of the clergy and the swords of the barons. The authority of the priests operated in the darker ages as a salutary antidote: they prevented the total extinction of letters, mitigated the fierceness of the times, sheltered the poor and defenceless, and preserved or revived the peace and order of civil society. But the independence, rapine, and discord of the feudal lords were unmixed with any semblance of good; and every hope of industry and improvement was crushed by the iron weight of the martial aristocracy. Among the causes that undermined that Gothic edifice, a conspicuous place must be allowed to the crusades. The estates of the barons were dissipated, and their race was often extinguished, in these costly and perilous expeditions. Their poverty extorted from their pride those charters of freedom which unlocked the fetters of the slave, secured the farm of the peasant and the shop of the artificer, and gradually restored a substance and a soul to the most numerous and useful part of the community. The conflagration which destroyed the tall and barren trees of the forest gave air and scope to the vegetation of the smaller and nutritive plants of the soil.

Digression On The Family Of Courtenay.

The purple of three emperors, who have reigned at Constantinople, will authorize or excuse a digression on the origin and singular fortunes of the house of Courtenay, in the three principal branches: I. Of Edessa; II. Of France; and III. Of England; of which the last only has survived the revolutions of eight hundred years.

I. Before the introduction of trade, which scatters riches, and of knowledge, which dispels prejudice, the prerogative of birth is most strongly felt and most humbly acknowledged. In every age, the laws and manners of the Germans have discriminated the ranks of society; the dukes and counts, who shared the empire of Charlemagne, converted their office to an inheritance; and to his children, each feudal lord bequeathed his honor and his sword. The proudest families are content to lose, in the darkness of the middle ages, the tree of their pedigree, which, however deep and lofty, must ultimately rise from a plebeian root; and their historians must descend ten centuries below the Christian æra, before they can ascertain any lineal succession by the evidence of surnames, of arms, and of authentic records. With the first rays of light, we discern the nobility and opulence of Atho, a French knight; his nobility, in the rank and title of a nameless father; his opulence, in the foundation of the castle of Courtenay in the district of Gatinois, about fifty-six miles to the south of Paris. From the reign of Robert, the son of Hugh Capet, the barons of Courtenay are conspicuous among the immediate vassals of the crown; and Joscelin, the grandson of Atho and a noble dame, is enrolled among the heroes of the first crusade. A domestic alliance (their mothers were sisters) attached him to the standard of Baldwin of Bruges, the second count of Edessa; a princely fief, which he was worthy to receive, and able to maintain, announces the number of his martial followers; and after the departure of his cousin, Joscelin himself was invested with the county of Edessa on both sides of the Euphrates. By economy in peace, his territories were replenished with Latin and Syrian subjects; his magazines with corn, wine, and oil; his castles with gold and silver, with arms and horses. In a holy warfare of thirty years, he was alternately a conqueror and a captive: but he died like a soldier, in a horse litter at the head of his troops; and his last glance beheld the flight of the Turkish invaders who had presumed on his age and infirmities. His son and successor, of the same name, was less deficient in valor than in vigilance; but he sometimes forgot that dominion is acquired and maintained by the same arms. He challenged the hostility of the Turks, without securing the friendship of the prince of Antioch; and, amidst the peaceful luxury of Turbessel, in Syria, Joscelin neglected the defence of the Christian frontier beyond the Euphrates. In his absence, Zenghi, the first of the Atabeks, besieged and stormed his capital, Edessa, which was feebly defended by a timorous and disloyal crowd of Orientals: the Franks were oppressed in a bold attempt for its recovery, and Courtenay ended his days in the prison of Aleppo. He still left a fair and ample patrimony But the victorious Turks oppressed on all sides the weakness of a widow and orphan; and, for the equivalent of an annual pension, they resigned to the Greek emperor the charge of defending, and the shame of losing, the last relics of the Latin conquest. The countess-dowager of Edessa retired to Jerusalem with her two children; the daughter, Agnes, became the wife and mother of a king; the son, Joscelin the Third, accepted the office of seneschal, the first of the kingdom, and held his new estates in Palestine by the service of fifty knights. His name appears with honor in the transactions of peace and war; but he finally vanishes in the fall of Jerusalem; and the name of Courtenay, in this branch of Edessa, was lost by the marriage of his two daughters with a French and German baron.

II. While Joscelin reigned beyond the Euphrates, his elder brother Milo, the son of Joscelin, the son of Atho, continued, near the Seine, to possess the castle of their fathers, which was at length inherited by Rainaud, or Reginald, the youngest of his three sons. Examples of genius or virtue must be rare in the annals of the oldest families; and, in a remote age their pride will embrace a deed of rapine and violence; such, however, as could not be perpetrated without some superiority of courage, or, at least, of power. A descendant of Reginald of Courtenay may blush for the public robber, who stripped and imprisoned several merchants, after they had satisfied the king's duties at Sens and Orleans. He will glory in the offence, since the bold offender could not be compelled to obedience and restitution, till the regent and the count of Champagne prepared to march against him at the head of an army. Reginald bestowed his estates on his eldest daughter, and his daughter on the seventh son of King Louis the Fat; and their marriage was crowned with a numerous offspring. We might expect that a private should have merged in a royal name; and that the descendants of Peter of France and Elizabeth of Courtenay would have enjoyed the titles and honors of princes of the blood. But this legitimate claim was long neglected, and finally denied; and the causes of their disgrace will represent the story of this second branch. . Of all the families now extant, the most ancient, doubtless, and the most illustrious, is the house of France, which has occupied the same throne above eight hundred years, and descends, in a clear and lineal series of males, from the middle of the ninth century. In the age of the crusades, it was already revered both in the East and West. But from Hugh Capet to the marriage of Peter, no more than five reigns or generations had elapsed; and so precarious was their title, that the eldest sons, as a necessary precaution, were previously crowned during the lifetime of their fathers. The peers of France have long maintained their precedency before the younger branches of the royal line, nor had the princes of the blood, in the twelfth century, acquired that hereditary lustre which is now diffused over the most remote candidates for the succession. . The barons of Courtenay must have stood high in their own estimation, and in that of the world, since they could impose on the son of a king the obligation of adopting for himself and all his descendants the name and arms of their daughter and his wife. In the marriage of an heiress with her inferior or her equal, such exchange was often required and allowed: but as they continued to diverge from the regal stem, the sons of Louis the Fat were insensibly confounded with their maternal ancestors; and the new Courtenays might deserve to forfeit the honors of their birth, which a motive of interest had tempted them to renounce. . The shame was far more permanent than the reward, and a momentary blaze was followed by a long darkness. The eldest son of these nuptials, Peter of Courtenay, had married, as I have already mentioned, the sister of the counts of Flanders, the two first emperors of Constantinople: he rashly accepted the invitation of the barons of Romania; his two sons, Robert and Baldwin, successively held and lost the remains of the Latin empire in the East, and the granddaughter of Baldwin the Second again mingled her blood with the blood of France and of Valois. To support the expenses of a troubled and transitory reign, their patrimonial estates were mortgaged or sold: and the last emperors of Constantinople depended on the annual charity of Rome and Naples.

While the elder brothers dissipated their wealth in romantic adventures, and the castle of Courtenay was profaned by a plebeian owner, the younger branches of that adopted name were propagated and multiplied. But their splendor was clouded by poverty and time: after the decease of Robert, great butler of France, they descended from princes to barons; the next generations were confounded with the simple gentry; the descendants of Hugh Capet could no longer be visible in the rural lords of Tanlay and of Champignelles. The more adventurous embraced without dishonor the profession of a soldier: the least active and opulent might sink, like their cousins of the branch of Dreux, into the condition of peasants. Their royal descent, in a dark period of four hundred years, became each day more obsolete and ambiguous; and their pedigree, instead of being enrolled in the annals of the kingdom, must be painfully searched by the minute diligence of heralds and genealogists. It was not till the end of the sixteenth century, on the accession of a family almost as remote as their own, that the princely spirit of the Courtenays again revived; and the question of the nobility provoked them to ascertain the royalty of their blood. They appealed to the justice and compassion of Henry the Fourth; obtained a favorable opinion from twenty lawyers of Italy and Germany, and modestly compared themselves to the descendants of King David, whose prerogatives were not impaired by the lapse of ages or the trade of a carpenter. But every ear was deaf, and every circumstance was adverse, to their lawful claims. The Bourbon kings were justified by the neglect of the Valois; the princes of the blood, more recent and lofty, disdained the alliance of his humble kindred: the parliament, without denying their proofs, eluded a dangerous precedent by an arbitrary distinction, and established St. Louis as the first father of the royal line. A repetition of complaints and protests was repeatedly disregarded; and the hopeless pursuit was terminated in the present century by the death of the last male of the family. Their painful and anxious situation was alleviated by the pride of conscious virtue: they sternly rejected the temptations of fortune and favor; and a dying

Courtenay would have sacrificed his son, if the youth could have renounced, for any temporal interest, the right and title of a legitimate
prince of the blood of France.

III. According to the old register of Ford Abbey, the Courtenays of
Devonshire are descended from Prince *Florus*, the second son of Peter,
and the grandson of Louis the Fat. This fable of the grateful or venal
monks was too respectfully entertained by our antiquaries, Cambden
and Dugdale: but it is so clearly repugnant to truth and time, that
the rational pride of the family now refuses to accept this imaginary
founder. Their most faithful historians believe, that, after giving his
daughter to the king's son, Reginald of Courtenay abandoned his possessions in France, and obtained from the English monarch a second
wife and a new inheritance. It is certain, at least, that Henry the Second distinguished in his camps and councils a Reginald, of the name
and arms, and, as it may be fairly presumed, of the genuine race, of
the Courtenays of France. The right of wardship enabled a feudal lord
to reward his vassal with the marriage and estate of a noble heiress;
and Reginald of Courtenay acquired a fair establishment in Devonshire, where his posterity has been seated above six hundred years.
From a Norman baron, Baldwin de Brioniis, who had been invested
by the Conqueror, Hawise, the wife of Reginald, derived the honor of
Okehampton, which was held by the service of ninety-three knights;
and a female might claim the manly offices of hereditary viscount or
sheriff, and of captain of the royal castle of Exeter. Their son Robert
married the sister of the earl of Devon: at the end of a century, on the
failure of the family of Rivers, his great-grandson, Hugh the Second,
succeeded to a title which was still considered as a territorial dignity; and twelve earls of Devonshire, of the name of Courtenay, have
flourished in a period of two hundred and twenty years. They were
ranked among the chief of the barons of the realm; nor was it till after
a strenuous dispute, that they yielded to the fief of Arundel the first
place in the parliament of England: their alliances were contracted
with the noblest families, the Veres, Despensers, St. Johns, Talbots,
Bohuns, and even the Plantagenets themselves; and in a contest with
John of Lancaster, a Courtenay, bishop of London, and afterwards
archbishop of Canterbury, might be accused of profane confidence in
the strength and number of his kindred. In peace, the earls of Devon resided in their numerous castles and manors of the west; their
ample revenue was appropriated to devotion and hospitality; and the
epitaph of Edward, surnamed from his misfortune, the *blind*, from
his virtues, the *good*, earl, inculcates with much ingenuity a moral

sentence, which may, however, be abused by thoughtless generosity. After a grateful commemoration of the fifty-five years of union and happiness which he enjoyed with Mabe his wife, the good earl thus speaks from the tomb: –

"What we gave, we have;
What we spent, we had;
What we left, we lost."

But their *losses*, in this sense, were far superior to their gifts and expenses; and their heirs, not less than the poor, were the objects of their paternal care. The sums which they paid for livery and seizin attest the greatness of their possessions; and several estates have remained in their family since the thirteenth and fourteenth centuries. In war, the Courtenays of England fulfilled the duties, and deserved the honors, of chivalry. They were often intrusted to levy and command the militia of Devonshire and Cornwall; they often attended their supreme lord to the borders of Scotland; and in foreign service, for a stipulated price, they sometimes maintained fourscore men-at-arms and as many archers. By sea and land they fought under the standard of the Edwards and Henries: their names are conspicuous in battles, in tournaments, and in the original list of the Order of the Garter; three brothers shared the Spanish victory of the Black Prince; and in the lapse of six generations, the English Courtenays had learned to despise the nation and country from which they derived their origin. In the quarrel of the two roses, the earls of Devon adhered to the house of Lancaster; and three brothers successively died either in the field or on the scaffold. Their honors and estates were restored by Henry the Seventh; a daughter of Edward the Fourth was not disgraced by the nuptials of a Courtenay; their son, who was created Marquis of Exeter, enjoyed the favor of his cousin Henry the Eighth; and in the camp of Cloth of Gold, he broke a lance against the French monarch. But the favor of Henry was the prelude of disgrace; his disgrace was the signal of death; and of the victims of the jealous tyrant, the marquis of Exeter is one of the most noble and guiltless. His son Edward lived a prisoner in the Tower, and died in exile at Padua; and the secret love of Queen Mary, whom he slighted, perhaps for the princess Elizabeth, has shed a romantic color on the story of this beautiful youth. The relics of his patrimony were conveyed into strange families by the marriages of his four aunts; and his personal honors, as if they had been legally extinct, were revived by the patents of succeeding princes. But there still survived a lineal descendant of Hugh, the first earl of Devon, a younger branch of the Courtenays, who have been seated at Powderham Castle above four hundred years, from the reign of Edward the Third to the present hour. Their estates have been increased by the grant and improvement of lands in Ireland, and they have been recently restored to the honors of the peerage. Yet the Courtenays still retain the plaintive motto, which asserts the innocence, and deplores the fall, of their ancient house. While they sigh for past greatness, they are doubtless sensible of present blessings: in the long series of the Courtenay annals, the most splendid æra is likewise the most unfortunate; nor can an opulent peer of Britain be inclined to envy the emperors of Constantinople, who wandered over Europe to solicit alms for the support of their dignity and the defence of their capital.

CHAPTER SIXTY TWO

Greek Emperors of Nice and Constantinople. – Part One

The Greek Emperors of Nice and Constantinople. – Elevation and Reign of Michael Palæologus. – His False Union with the Pope and the Latin Church. – Hostile Designs of Charles of Anjou. – Revolt of Sicily. – War of the Catalans in Asia and Greece. – Revolutions and Present State of Athens.

THE LOSS OF CONSTANTINOPLE restored a momentary vigor to the Greeks. From their palaces, the princes and nobles were driven into the field; and the fragments of the falling monarchy were grasped by the hands of the most vigorous or the most skilful candidates. In the long and barren pages of the Byzantine annals, it would not be an easy task to equal the two characters of Theodore Lascaris and John Ducas Vataces, who replanted and upheld the Roman standard at Nice in Bithynia. The difference of their virtues was happily suited to the diversity of their situation. In his first efforts, the fugitive Lascaris commanded only three cities and two thousand soldiers: his reign was the season of generous and active despair: in every military operation he staked his life and crown; and his enemies of the Hellespont and the Mæander, were surprised by his celerity and subdued by his boldness. A victorious reign of eighteen years expanded the principality of Nice to the magnitude of an empire. The throne of his successor and son-in-law Vataces was founded on a more solid basis, a larger scope, and more plentiful resources; and it was the temper, as well as the interest, of Vataces to calculate the risk, to expect the moment, and to insure the success, of his ambitious designs. In the decline of the Latins, I have briefly exposed the progress of the Greeks; the prudent and gradual advances of a conqueror, who, in a reign of thirty-three years, rescued the provinces from national and foreign usurpers, till he pressed on all sides the Imperial city, a leafless and sapless trunk, which must full at the first stroke of the axe. But his interior and peaceful administration is still more deserving of notice and praise. The calamities of the times had wasted the numbers and the substance of the Greeks; the motives and the means of agriculture were extirpated; and the most fertile lands were left without cultivation or inhabitants. A portion of this vacant property was occupied and improved by the command, and for the benefit, of the emperor: a powerful hand and a vigilant eye supplied and surpassed, by a skilful management, the minute diligence of a private farmer: the royal domain became the garden and granary of Asia; and without impoverishing the people, the sovereign acquired a fund of innocent and productive wealth. According to the nature of the soil, his lands were sown with corn or planted with vines; the pastures were filled with horses and oxen, with sheep and hogs; and when Vataces presented to the empress a crown of diamonds and pearls, he informed her, with a smile, that this precious ornament arose from the sale of the eggs of his innumerable poultry. The produce of his domain was applied to the maintenance of his palace and hospitals, the calls of dignity and benevolence: the lesson was still more useful than the revenue: the plough was restored to its ancient security and honor; and the nobles were taught to seek a sure and independent revenue from their estates, instead of adorning their splendid beggary by the oppression of the people, or (what is almost the same) by the favors of the court. The superfluous stock of corn and cattle was eagerly purchased by the Turks, with whom Vataces preserved a strict and sincere alliance; but he discouraged the importation of foreign manufactures, the costly silks of the East, and the curious labors of the Italian looms. "The demands of nature and necessity," was he accustomed to say, "are indispensable; but the influence of fashion may rise and sink at the breath of a monarch;" and both his precept and example recommended simplicity of manners and the use of domestic industry. The education of youth and the revival of learning were the most serious objects of his care; and, without deciding the precedency, he pronounced with truth, that a prince and a philosopher are the two most eminent characters of human society. His first wife was Irene, the daughter of Theodore Lascaris, a woman more illustrious by her personal merit, the milder virtues of her sex, than by the blood of the Angeli and Comneni that flowed in her veins, and transmitted the inheritance of the empire. After her death he was contracted to Anne, or Constance, a natural daughter of the emperor Frederic the Second; but as the bride had not attained the years of puberty, Vataces placed in his solitary bed an Italian damsel of her train; and his amorous weakness bestowed on the concubine the honors, though not the title, of a lawful empress. His frailty was censured as a flagitious and damnable sin by the monks; and their rude invectives exercised and displayed the patience of the royal lover. A philosophic age may excuse a single vice, which was redeemed by a crowd of virtues; and in the review of his faults, and the more intemperate passions of Lascaris, the judgment of their contemporaries was softened by gratitude to the second founders of the empire. The slaves of the Latins, without law or peace, applauded the happiness of their brethren who had resumed their national freedom; and Vataces employed the laudable policy of convincing the Greeks of every dominion that it was their interest to be enrolled in the number of his subjects.

A strong shade of degeneracy is visible between John Vataces and his son Theodore; between the founder who sustained the weight, and the heir who enjoyed the splendor, of the Imperial crown. Yet the character of Theodore was not devoid of energy; he had been educated in the school of his father, in the exercise of war and hunting; Constantinople was yet spared; but in the three years of a short reign, he thrice led his armies into the heart of Bulgaria. His virtues were sullied by a choleric and suspicious temper: the first of these may be ascribed to the ignorance of control; and the second might naturally arise from a dark and imperfect view of the corruption of mankind. On a march in Bulgaria, he consulted on a question of policy his principal ministers; and the Greek logothete, George Acropolita, presumed to offend him by the declaration of a free and honest opinion. The emperor half unsheathed his cimeter; but his more deliberate rage reserved Acropolita for a baser punishment. One of the first officers of the empire was ordered to dismount, stripped of his robes, and extended on the ground in the presence of the prince and army. In this posture he was chastised with so many and such heavy blows from the clubs of two guards or executioners, that when Theodore commanded them to cease, the great logothete was scarcely able to rise and crawl away to his tent. After a seclusion of some days, he was recalled by a peremptory mandate to his seat in council; and so dead were the Greeks to the sense of honor and shame, that it is from the narrative of the sufferer himself that we acquire the knowledge of his disgrace. The cruelty of the emperor was exasperated by the pangs of sickness, the approach of a premature end, and the suspicion of poison and magic. The lives and fortunes, the eyes and limbs, of his kinsmen and nobles, were sacrificed to each sally of passion; and before he died, the son of Vataces might deserve from the people, or at least from the court, the appellation of tyrant. A matron of the family of the Palæologi had provoked his anger by refusing to bestow her beauteous daughter on the vile plebeian who was recommended by his caprice. Without regard to her birth or age, her body, as high as the neck, was enclosed in a sack with several cats, who were pricked with pins to irritate their fury against their unfortunate fellow-captive. In his last hours the emperor testified a wish to forgive and be forgiven, a just anxiety for the fate of John his son and successor, who, at the age of eight years, was condemned to the dangers of a long minority. His last choice intrusted the office of guardian to the sanctity of the patriarch Arsenius, and to the courage of George Muzalon, the great domestic, who was equally distinguished by the royal favor and the public hatred. Since their connection with the Latins, the names and privileges of hereditary rank had insinuated themselves into the Greek monarchy; and the noble families were provoked by the elevation of a worthless favorite, to whose influence they imputed the errors and calamities of the late reign. In the first council, after the emperor's death, Muzalon, from a lofty throne, pronounced a labored apology of his conduct and intentions: his modesty was subdued by a unanimous assurance of esteem and fidelity; and his most inveterate enemies were the loudest to salute him as the guardian and savior of the Romans. Eight days were sufficient to prepare the execution of the conspiracy. On the ninth, the obsequies of the deceased monarch were solemnized in the cathedral of Magnesia, an Asiatic city, where he expired, on the banks of the Hermus, and at the foot of Mount Sipylus. The holy rites were interrupted by a sedition of the guards; Muzalon, his brothers, and his adherents, were massacred at the foot of the altar; and the absent patriarch was associated with a new colleague, with Michael Palæologus, the most illustrious, in birth and merit, of the Greek nobles.

Of those who are proud of their ancestors, the far greater part must be content with local or domestic renown; and few there are who dare trust the memorials of their family to the public annals of their country. As early as the middle of the eleventh century, the noble race of the Palæologi stands high and conspicuous in the Byzantine history: it was the valiant George Palæologus who placed the father of the Comneni on the throne; and his kinsmen or descendants continue, in each generation, to lead the armies and councils of the state. The purple was not dishonored by their alliance, and had the law of succession, and female succession, been strictly observed, the wife of Theodore Lascaris must have yielded to her elder sister, the mother of Michael Palæologus, who afterwards raised his family to the throne. In his person, the splendor of birth was dignified by the merit of the soldier and statesman: in his early youth he was promoted to the office of *constable* or commander of the French mercenaries; the private expense of a day never exceeded three pieces of gold; but his ambition was rapacious and profuse; and his gifts were doubled by the graces of his conversation and manners. The love of the soldiers and people excited the jealousy of the court, and Michael thrice escaped from the dangers in which he was involved by his own imprudence or that of his friends. I. Under the reign of Justice and Vataces, a dispute arose between two officers, one of whom accused the other of maintaining the hereditary right of the Palæologi The cause was decided, according to the new jurisprudence of the Latins, by single combat; the defendant was overthrown; but he persisted in declaring that himself alone was guilty; and that he had uttered these rash or treasonable speeches without the approbation or knowledge of his patron. Yet a cloud of suspicion hung over the innocence of the constable; he was still pursued by the whispers of malevolence; and a subtle courtier, the archbishop of Philadelphia, urged him to accept the judgment of God in the fiery proof of the ordeal. Three days before the trial, the patient's arm was enclosed in a bag, and secured by the royal signet; and it was incumbent on him to bear a red-hot ball of iron three times from the altar to the rails of the sanctuary, without artifice and without injury. Palæologus eluded the dangerous experiment with sense and pleasantry. "I am a soldier," said he, "and will boldly enter the lists with my accusers; but a layman, a sinner like myself, is not endowed with the gift of miracles. *Your* piety, most holy prelate, may deserve the interposition of Heaven, and from your hands I will receive the fiery globe, the pledge of my innocence." The archbishop started; the emperor smiled; and the absolution or pardon of Michael was approved by new rewards and new services. II. In the succeeding reign, as he held the government of Nice, he was secretly informed, that the mind of the absent prince was poisoned with jealousy; and that death, or blindness, would be his final reward. Instead of awaiting the return and sentence of Theodore, the constable, with some followers, escaped from the city and the empire; and though he was plundered by the Turkmans of the desert, he found a hospitable refuge in the court of the sultan. In the ambiguous state of an exile, Michael reconciled the duties of gratitude and loyalty: drawing his sword against the Tartars; admonishing the garrisons of the Roman limit; and promoting, by his influence, the restoration of peace, in which his pardon and recall were honorably included. III. While he guarded the West against the despot of Epirus, Michael was again suspected and condemned in the palace; and such was his loyalty or weakness, that he submitted to be led in chains above six hundred miles from Durazzo to Nice. The civility of the messenger alleviated his disgrace; the emperor's sickness dispelled his danger; and the last breath of Theodore, which recommended his infant son, at once acknowledged the innocence and the power of Palæologus.

But his innocence had been too unworthily treated, and his power was too strongly felt, to curb an aspiring subject in the fair field that was opened to his ambition. In the council, after the death of Theodore, he was the first to pronounce, and the first to violate, the oath of allegiance to Muzalon; and so dexterous was his conduct, that he reaped the benefit, without incurring the guilt, or at least the reproach, of the subsequent massacre. In the choice of a regent, he balanced the interests and passions of the candidates; turned their envy and hatred from himself against each other, and forced every competitor to own, that after his own claims, those of Palæologus were best entitled to the preference. Under the title of great duke, he accepted or assumed, during a long minority, the active powers of government; the patriarch was a venerable name; and the factious nobles were seduced, or oppressed, by the ascendant of his genius. The fruits of the economy of Vataces were deposited in a strong castle on the banks of the Hermus, in the custody of the faithful Varangians: the constable retained his command or influence over the foreign troops; he employed the guards to possess the treasure, and the treasure to corrupt the guards; and whatsoever might be the abuse of the public money, his character was above the suspicion of private avarice. By himself, or by his emissaries, he strove to persuade every rank of subjects, that their own prosperity would rise in just proportion to the establishment of his authority. The weight of taxes was suspended, the perpetual theme of popular complaint; and he prohibited the trials by the ordeal and judicial combat. These Barbaric institutions were already abolished or undermined in France and England; and the appeal to the sword offended the sense of a civilized, and the temper of an unwarlike, people. For the future maintenance of their wives and children, the veterans were grateful: the priests and the philosophers applauded his ardent zeal for the advancement of religion and learning; and his vague promise of rewarding merit was applied by every candidate to his own hopes. Conscious of the influence of the clergy, Michael successfully labored to secure the suffrage of that powerful order. Their expensive journey from Nice to Magnesia, afforded a decent and ample pretence:

the leading prelates were tempted by the liberality of his nocturnal visits; and the incorruptible patriarch was flattered by the homage of his new colleague, who led his mule by the bridle into the town, and removed to a respectful distance the importunity of the crowd. Without renouncing his title by royal descent, Palæologus encouraged a free discussion into the advantages of elective monarchy; and his adherents asked, with the insolence of triumph, what patient would trust his health, or what merchant would abandon his vessel, to the *hereditary* skill of a physician or a pilot? The youth of the emperor, and the impending dangers of a minority, required the support of a mature and experienced guardian; of an associate raised above the envy of his equals, and invested with the name and prerogatives of royalty. For the interest of the prince and people, without any selfish views for himself or his family, the great duke consented to guard and instruct the son of Theodore; but he sighed for the happy moment when he might restore to his firmer hands the administration of his patrimony, and enjoy the blessings of a private station. He was first invested with the title and prerogatives of *despot*, which bestowed the purple ornaments and the second place in the Roman monarchy. It was afterwards agreed that John and Michael should be proclaimed as joint emperors, and raised on the buckler, but that the preeminence should be reserved for the birthright of the former. A mutual league of amity was pledged between the royal partners; and in case of a rupture, the subjects were bound, by their oath of allegiance, to declare themselves against the aggressor; an ambiguous name, the seed of discord and civil war. Palæologus was content; but, on the day of the coronation, and in the cathedral of Nice, his zealous adherents most vehemently urged the just priority of his age and merit. The unseasonable dispute was eluded by postponing to a more convenient opportunity the coronation of John Lascaris; and he walked with a slight diadem in the train of his guardian, who alone received the Imperial crown from the hands of the patriarch. It was not without extreme reluctance that Arsenius abandoned the cause of his pupil; out the Varangians brandished their battle-axes; a sign of assent was extorted from the trembling youth; and some voices were heard, that the life of a child should no longer impede the settlement of the nation. A full harvest of honors and employments was distributed among his friends by the grateful Palæologus. In his own family he created a despot and two sebastocrators; Alexius Strategopulus was decorated with the title of Cæsar; and that veteran commander soon repaid the obligation, by restoring Constantinople to the Greek emperor.

It was in the second year of his reign, while he resided in the palace and gardens of Nymphæum, near Smyrna, that the first messenger arrived at the dead of night; and the stupendous intelligence was imparted to Michael, after he had been gently waked by the tender precaution of his sister Eulogia. The man was unknown or obscure; he produced no letters from the victorious Cæsar; nor could it easily be credited, after the defeat of Vataces and the recent failure of Palæologus himself, that the capital had been surprised by a detachment of eight hundred soldiers. As a hostage, the doubtful author was confined, with the assurance of death or an ample recompense; and the court was left some hours in the anxiety of hope and fear, till the messengers of Alexius arrived with the authentic intelligence, and displayed the trophies of the conquest, the sword and sceptre, the buskins and bonnet, of the usurper Baldwin, which he had dropped in his precipitate flight. A general assembly of the bishops, senators, and nobles, was immediately convened, and never perhaps was an event received with more heartfelt and universal joy. In a studied oration, the new sovereign of Constantinople congratulated his own and the public fortune. "There was a time," said he, "a far distant time, when the Roman empire extended to the Adriatic, the Tigris, and the confines of Æthiopia. After the loss of the provinces, our capital itself, in these last and calamitous days, has been wrested from our hands by the Barbarians of the West. From the lowest ebb, the tide of prosperity has again returned in our favor; but our prosperity was that of fugitives and exiles: and when we were asked, which was the country of the Romans, we indicated with a blush the climate of the globe, and the quarter of the heavens. The divine Providence has now restored to our arms the city of Constantine, the sacred seat of religion and empire; and it will depend on our valor and conduct to render this important acquisition the pledge and omen of future victories." So eager was the impatience of the prince and people, that Michael made his triumphal entry into Constantinople only twenty days after the expulsion of the Latins. The golden gate was thrown open at his approach; the devout conqueror dismounted from his horse; and a miraculous image of Mary the Conductress was borne before him, that the divine Virgin in person might appear to conduct him to the temple of her Son, the cathedral of St. Sophia. But after the first transport of devotion and pride, he sighed at the dreary prospect of solitude and ruin. The palace was defiled with smoke and dirt, and the gross intemperance of the Franks; whole streets had been consumed by fire, or were decayed by the injuries of time; the sacred and profane edifices were stripped of their ornaments: and, as if they were conscious of their approaching exile, the industry of the Latins had been confined to the work of pillage and destruction. Trade had expired under the pressure of anarchy and distress, and the numbers of inhabitants had decreased with the opulence of the city. It was the first care of the Greek monarch to reinstate the nobles in the palaces of their fathers; and the houses or the ground which they occupied were restored to the families that could exhibit a legal right of inheritance. But the far greater part was extinct or lost; the vacant property had devolved to the lord; he repeopled Constantinople by a liberal invitation to the provinces; and the brave *volunteers* were seated in the capital which had been recovered by their arms. The French barons and the principal families had retired with their emperor; but the patient and humble crowd of Latins was attached to the country, and indifferent to the change of masters. Instead of banishing the factories of the Pisans, Venetians, and Genoese, the prudent conqueror accepted their oaths of allegiance, encouraged their industry, confirmed their privileges, and allowed them to live under the jurisdiction of their proper magistrates. Of these nations, the Pisans and Venetians preserved their respective quarters in the city; but the services and power of the Genoese deserved at the same time the gratitude and the jealousy of the Greeks. Their independent colony was first planted at the seaport town of Heraclea in Thrace. They were speedily recalled, and settled in the exclusive possession of the suburb of Galata, an advantageous post, in which they revived the commerce, and insulted the majesty, of the Byzantine empire.

The recovery of Constantinople was celebrated as the æra of a new empire: the conqueror, alone, and by the right of the sword, renewed his coronation in the church of St. Sophia; and the name and honors of John Lascaris, his pupil and lawful sovereign, were insensibly abolished. But his claims still lived in the minds of the people; and the royal youth must speedily attain the years of manhood and ambition. By fear or conscience, Palæologus was restrained from dipping his hands in innocent and royal blood; but the anxiety of a usurper and a parent urged him to secure his throne by one of those imperfect crimes so familiar to the modern Greeks. The loss of sight incapacitated the young prince for the active business of the world; instead of the brutal violence of tearing out his eyes, the visual nerve was destroyed by the intense glare of a red-hot basin, and John Lascaris was removed to a distant castle, where he spent many years in privacy and oblivion. Such cool and deliberate guilt may seem incompatible with remorse; but if Michael could trust the mercy of Heaven, he was not inaccessible to the reproaches and vengeance of mankind, which he had provoked by cruelty and treason. His cruelty imposed on a servile court the duties of applause or silence; but the clergy had a right to speak in the name of their invisible Master; and their holy legions were led by a prelate, whose character was above the temptations of hope or fear. After a short abdication of his dignity, Arsenius had consented to ascend the ecclesiastical throne of Constantinople, and to preside in the restoration of the church. His pious simplicity was long deceived by the arts of Palæologus; and his patience and submission might soothe the usurper, and protect the safety of the young prince. On the news of his inhuman treatment, the patriarch unsheathed the spiritual sword; and superstition, on this occasion, was enlisted in the cause of humanity and justice. In a synod of bishops, who were stimulated by the example of his zeal, the patriarch pronounced a sentence of excommunication; though his prudence still repeated the name of Michael in the public prayers. The Eastern prelates had not adopted the dangerous maxims of ancient Rome; nor did they presume to enforce their censures, by deposing princes, or absolving nations from their oaths of allegiance. But the Christian, who had been separated from God and the church, became an object of horror; and, in a turbulent and fanatic capital, that horror might arm the hand of an assassin, or inflame a sedition of the people. Palæologus felt his danger, confessed his guilt, and deprecated his judge: the act was irretrievable; the prize was obtained; and the most rigorous penance, which he solicited, would have raised the sinner to the reputation of a saint. The unrelenting patriarch refused to announce any means of atonement or any hopes of mercy; and condescended only to pronounce, that for so great a crime, great indeed must be the satisfaction. "Do you require," said Michael, "that I should abdicate the empire?" and at these words, he offered, or seemed to offer, the sword of state. Arsenius eagerly grasped this pledge of sovereignty; but when he perceived that the emperor was unwilling to purchase absolution at so dear a rate, he indignantly escaped to his cell, and left the royal sinner kneeling and weeping before the door.

CHAPTER SIXTY TWO

Greek Emperors of Nice and Constantinople. – Part Two

THE DANGER AND SCANDAL of this excommunication subsisted above three years, till the popular clamor was assuaged by time and repentance; till the brethren of Arsenius condemned his inflexible spirit, so repugnant to the unbounded forgiveness of the gospel. The emperor had artfully insinuated, that, if he were still rejected at home, he might seek, in the Roman pontiff, a more indulgent judge; but it was far more easy and effectual to find or to place that judge at the head of the Byzantine church. Arsenius was involved in a vague rumor of conspiracy and disaffection; some irregular steps in his ordination and government were liable to censure; a synod deposed him from the episcopal office; and he was transported under a guard of soldiers to a small island of the Propontis. Before his exile, he sullenly requested that a strict account might be taken of the treasures of the church; boasted, that his sole riches, three pieces of gold, had been earned by transcribing the psalms; continued to assert the freedom of his mind; and denied, with his last breath, the pardon which was implored by the royal sinner. After some delay, Gregory, bishop of Adrianople, was translated to the Byzantine throne; but his authority was found insufficient to support the absolution of the emperor; and Joseph, a reverend monk, was substituted to that important function. This edifying scene was represented in the presence of the senate and the people; at the end of six years the humble penitent was restored to the communion of the faithful; and humanity will rejoice, that a milder treatment of the captive Lascaris was stipulated as a proof of his remorse. But the spirit of Arsenius still survived in a powerful faction of the monks and clergy, who persevered about forty-eight years in an obstinate schism. Their scruples were treated with tenderness and respect by Michael and his son; and the reconciliation of the Arsenites was the serious labor of the church and state. In the confidence of fanaticism, they had proposed to try their cause by a miracle; and when the two papers, that contained their own and the adverse cause, were cast into a fiery brazier, they expected that the Catholic verity would be respected by the flames. Alas! the two papers were indiscriminately consumed, and this unforeseen accident produced the union of a day, and renewed the quarrel of an age. The final treaty displayed the victory of the Arsenites: the clergy abstained during forty days from all ecclesiastical functions; a slight penance was imposed on the laity; the body of Arsenius was deposited in the sanctuary; and, in the name of the departed saint, the prince and people were released from the sins of their fathers.

The establishment of his family was the motive, or at least the pretence, of the crime of Palæologus; and he was impatient to confirm the succession, by sharing with his eldest son the honors of the purple. Andronicus, afterwards surnamed the Elder, was proclaimed and crowned emperor of the Romans, in the fifteenth year of his age; and, from the first æra of a prolix and inglorious reign, he held that august title nine years as the colleague, and fifty as the successor, of his father. Michael himself, had he died in a private station, would have been thought more worthy of the empire; and the assaults of his temporal and spiritual enemies left him few moments to labor for his own fame or the happiness of his subjects. He wrested from the Franks several of the noblest islands of the Archipelago, Lesbos, Chios, and Rhodes: his brother Constantine was sent to command in Malvasia and Sparta; and the eastern side of the Morea, from Argos and Napoli to Cape Thinners, was repossessed by the Greeks. This effusion of Christian blood was loudly condemned by the patriarch; and the insolent priest presumed to interpose his fears and scruples between the arms of princes. But in the prosecution of these western conquests, the countries beyond the Hellespont were left naked to the Turks; and their depredations verified the prophecy of a dying senator, that the recovery of Constantinople would be the ruin of Asia. The victories of Michael were achieved by his lieutenants; his sword rusted in the palace; and, in the transactions of the emperor with the popes and the king of Naples, his political acts were stained with cruelty and fraud.

I. The Vatican was the most natural refuge of a Latin emperor, who had been driven from his throne; and Pope Urban the Fourth appeared to pity the misfortunes, and vindicate the cause, of the fugitive Baldwin. A crusade, with plenary indulgence, was preached by his command against the schismatic Greeks: he excommunicated their allies and adherents; solicited Louis the Ninth in favor of his kinsman; and demanded a tenth of the ecclesiastical revenues of France and England for the service of the holy war. The subtle Greek, who watched the rising tempest of the West, attempted to suspend or soothe the hostility of the pope, by suppliant embassies and respectful letters; but he insinuated that the establishment of peace must prepare the reconciliation and obedience of the Eastern church. The Roman court could not be deceived by so gross an artifice; and Michael was admonished, that the repentance of the son should precede the forgiveness of the father; and that *faith* (an ambiguous word) was the only basis of friendship and alliance. After a long and affected delay, the approach of danger, and the importunity of Gregory the Tenth, compelled him to enter on a more serious negotiation: he alleged the example of the great Vataces; and the Greek clergy, who understood the intentions of their prince, were not alarmed by the first steps of reconciliation and respect. But when he pressed the conclusion of the treaty, they strenuously declared, that the Latins, though not in name, were heretics in fact, and that they despised those strangers as the vilest and most despicable portion of the human race. It was the task of the emperor to persuade, to corrupt, to intimidate the most popular ecclesiastics, to gain the vote of each individual, and alternately to urge the arguments of Christian charity and the public welfare. The texts of the fathers and the arms of the Franks were balanced in the theological and political scale; and without approving the addition to the Nicene creed, the most moderate were taught to confess, that the two hostile propositions of proceeding from the Father by the Son, and of proceeding from the Father and the Son, might be reduced to a safe and Catholic sense. The supremacy of the pope was a doctrine more easy to conceive, but more painful to acknowledge: yet Michael represented to his monks and prelates, that they might submit to name the Roman bishop as the first of the patriarchs; and that their distance and discretion would guard the liberties of the Eastern church from the mischievous consequences of the right of appeal. He protested that he would sacrifice his life and empire rather than yield the smallest point of orthodox faith or national independence; and this declaration was sealed and ratified by a golden bull. The patriarch Joseph withdrew to a monastery, to resign or resume his throne, according to the event of the treaty: the letters of union and obedience were subscribed by the emperor, his son Andronicus, and thirty-five archbishops and metropolitans, with their respective synods; and the episcopal list was multiplied by many dioceses which were annihilated under the yoke of the infidels. An embassy was composed of some trusty ministers and prelates: they embarked for Italy, with rich ornaments and rare perfumes for the altar of St. Peter; and their secret orders authorized and recommended a boundless compliance. They were received in the general council of Lyons, by Pope Gregory the Tenth, at the head of five hundred bishops. He embraced with tears his long-lost and repentant children; accepted the oath of the ambassadors, who abjured the schism in the name of the two emperors; adorned the prelates with the ring and mitre; chanted in Greek and Latin the Nicene creed with the addition of *filioque*; and rejoiced in the union of the East and West, which had been reserved for his reign. To consummate this pious work, the Byzantine deputies were speedily followed by the pope's nuncios; and their instruction discloses the policy of the Vatican, which could not be satisfied with the vain title of supremacy. After viewing the temper of the prince and people, they were enjoined to absolve the schismatic clergy, who should subscribe and swear their abjuration and obedience; to establish in all the churches the use of the perfect creed; to prepare the entrance of a cardinal legate, with the full powers and dignity of his office; and to instruct the emperor in the advantages which he might derive from the temporal protection of the Roman pontiff.

But they found a country without a friend, a nation in which the names of Rome and Union were pronounced with abhorrence. The patriarch Joseph was indeed removed: his place was filled by Veccus, an ecclesiastic of learning and moderation; and the emperor was still urged by the same motives, to persevere in the same professions. But in his private language Palæologus affected to deplore the pride, and to blame the innovations, of the Latins; and while he debased his character by this double hypocrisy, he justified and punished the opposition of his subjects. By the joint suffrage of the new and the ancient Rome, a sentence of excommunication was pronounced against the obstinate schismatics; the censures of the church were executed by the sword of Michael; on the failure of persuasion, he tried the arguments of prison and exile, of whipping and mutilation; those touchstones, says an historian, of cowards and the brave. Two Greeks still reigned in Ætolia, Epirus, and Thessaly, with the appellation of despots: they had yielded to the sovereign of Constantinople, but they rejected the chains of the Roman pontiff, and supported their refusal by successful arms. Under their protection, the fugitive monks and bishops assembled in hostile synods; and retorted the name of heretic with the galling addition of apostate: the prince of Trebizond was tempted to assume the forfeit title of emperor; and even the Latins of Negropont, Thebes, Athens, and the Morea, forgot the merits of the convert, to join, with open or clandestine aid, the enemies of Palæologus. His favorite generals, of his own blood, and family, successively deserted, or betrayed, the sacrilegious trust. His sister Eulogia, a niece, and two female cousins, conspired against him; another niece, Mary queen of Bulgaria, negotiated his ruin with the sultan of Egypt; and, in the public eye, their treason was consecrated as the most sublime virtue. To the pope's nuncios, who urged the consummation of the work, Palæologus exposed a naked recital of all that he had done and suffered for their sake. They were assured that the guilty sectaries, of both sexes and every rank, had been deprived of their honors, their fortunes, and their liberty; a spreading list of confiscation and punishment, which involved many persons, the dearest to the emperor, or the best deserving of his favor. They were conducted to the prison, to behold four princes of the royal blood chained in the four corners, and shaking their fetters in an agony of grief and rage. Two of these captives were afterwards released; the one by submission, the other by death: but the obstinacy of their two companions was chastised by the loss of their eyes; and the Greeks, the least adverse to the union, deplored that cruel and inauspicious tragedy. Persecutors must expect the hatred of those whom they oppress; but they commonly find some consolation in the testimony of their conscience, the applause of their party, and, perhaps, the success of their undertaking. But the hypocrisy of Michael, which was prompted only by political motives, must have forced him to hate himself, to despise his followers, and to esteem and envy the rebel champions by whom he was detested and despised. While his violence was abhorred at Constantinople, at Rome his slowness was arraigned, and his sincerity suspected; till at length Pope Martin the Fourth excluded the Greek emperor from the pale of a church, into which he was striving to reduce a schismatic people. No sooner had the tyrant expired, than the union was dissolved, and abjured by unanimous consent; the churches were purified; the penitents were reconciled; and his son Andronicus, after weeping the sins and errors of his youth most piously denied his father the burial of a prince and a Christian.

II. In the distress of the Latins, the walls and towers of Constantinople had fallen to decay: they were restored and fortified by the policy of Michael, who deposited a plenteous store of corn and salt provisions, to sustain the siege which he might hourly expect from the resentment of the Western powers. Of these, the sovereign of the Two Sicilies was the most formidable neighbor: but as long as they were possessed by Mainfroy, the bastard of Frederic the Second, his monarchy was the bulwark, rather than the annoyance, of the Eastern empire. The usurper, though a brave and active prince, was sufficiently employed in the defence of his throne: his proscription by successive popes had separated Mainfroy from the common cause of the Latins; and the forces that might have besieged Constantinople were detained in a crusade against the domestic enemy of Rome. The prize of her avenger, the crown of the Two Sicilies, was won and worn by the brother of St Louis, by Charles count of Anjou and Provence, who led the chivalry of France on this holy expedition. The disaffection of his Christian subjects compelled Mainfroy to enlist a colony of Saracens whom his father had planted in Apulia; and this odious succor will explain the defiance of the Catholic hero, who rejected all terms of accommodation. "Bear this message," said Charles, "to the sultan of Nocera, that God and the sword are umpire between us; and that he shall either send me to paradise, or I will send him to the pit of hell." The armies met: and though I am ignorant of Mainfroy's doom in the other world, in this he lost his friends, his kingdom, and his life, in the bloody battle of Benevento. Naples and Sicily were immediately peopled with a warlike race of French nobles; and their aspiring leader embraced the future conquest of Africa, Greece, and Palestine. The most specious reasons might point his first arms against the Byzantine empire; and Palæologus, diffident of his own strength, repeatedly appealed from the ambition of Charles to the humanity of St. Louis, who still preserved a just ascendant over the mind of his ferocious brother. For a while the attention of that brother was confined at home by the invasion of Conradin, the last heir to the imperial house of Swabia; but the hapless boy sunk in the unequal conflict; and his execution on a public scaffold taught the rivals of Charles to tremble for their heads as well as their dominions. A second respite was obtained by the last crusade of St. Louis to the African coast; and the double motive of interest and duty urged the king of Naples to assist, with his powers and his presence, the holy enterprise. The death of St. Louis released him from the importunity of a virtuous censor: the king of Tunis confessed himself the tributary and vassal of the crown of Sicily; and the boldest of the French knights were free to enlist under his banner against the Greek empire. A treaty and a marriage united his interest with the house of Courtenay; his daughter Beatrice was promised to Philip, son and heir of the emperor Baldwin; a pension of six hundred ounces of gold was allowed for his maintenance; and his generous father distributed among his aliens the kingdoms and provinces of the East, reserving only Constantinople, and one day's journey round the city for the imperial domain. In this perilous moment, Palæologus was the most eager to subscribe the creed, and implore the protection, of the Roman pontiff, who assumed, with propriety and weight, the character of an angel of peace, the common father of the Christians. By his voice, the sword of Charles was chained in the scabbard; and the Greek ambassadors beheld him, in the pope's antechamber, biting his ivory sceptre in a transport of fury, and deeply resenting the refusal to enfranchise and consecrate his arms. He appears to have respected the disinterested mediation of Gregory the Tenth; but Charles was insensibly disgusted by the pride and partiality of Nicholas the Third; and his attachment to his kindred, the Ursini family, alienated the most strenuous champion from the service of the church. The hostile league against the Greeks, of Philip the Latin emperor, the king of the Two Sicilies, and the republic of Venice, was ripened into execution; and the election of Martin the Fourth, a French pope, gave a sanction to the cause. Of the allies, Philip supplied his name; Martin, a bull of excommunication; the Venetians, a squadron of forty galleys; and the formidable powers of Charles consisted of forty counts, ten thousand men at arms, a numerous body of infantry, and a fleet of more than three hundred ships and transports. A distant day was appointed for assembling this mighty force in the harbor of Brindisi; and a previous attempt was risked with a detachment of three hundred knights, who invaded Albania, and besieged the fortress of Belgrade. Their defeat might amuse with a triumph the vanity of Constantinople; but the more sagacious Michael, despairing of his arms, depended on the effects of a conspiracy; on the secret workings of a rat, who gnawed the bowstring of the Sicilian tyrant.

Among the proscribed adherents of the house of Swabia, John of Procida forfeited a small island of that name in the Bay of Naples. His birth was noble, but his education was learned; and in the poverty of exile, he was relieved by the practice of physic, which he had studied in the school of Salerno. Fortune had left him nothing to lose, except life; and to despise life is the first qualification of a rebel. Procida was endowed with the art of negotiation, to enforce his reasons and disguise his motives; and in his various transactions with nations and men, he could persuade each party that he labored solely for *their* interest. The new kingdoms of Charles were afflicted by every species of fiscal and military oppression; and the lives and fortunes of his Italian subjects were sacrificed to the greatness of their master and the licentiousness of his followers. The hatred of Naples was repressed by his presence; but the looser government of his vicegerents excited the contempt, as well as the aversion, of the Sicilians: the island was roused to a sense of freedom by the eloquence of Procida; and he displayed to every baron his private interest in the common cause. In the confidence of foreign aid, he successively visited the courts of the Greek emperor, and of Peter king of Arragon, who possessed the maritime countries of Valentia and Catalonia. To the ambitious Peter a crown was presented, which he might justly claim by his marriage with the sister of Mainfroy, and by the dying voice of Conradin, who from the scaffold had cast a ring to his heir and avenger. Palæologus was easily persuaded to divert his enemy from a foreign war by a rebellion at home; and a Greek subsidy of twenty-five thousand ounces of gold was most profitably applied to arm a Catalan fleet, which sailed under a holy banner to the specious attack of the Saracens of Africa. In the disguise of a monk or beggar, the indefatigable missionary of revolt flew from Constantinople to Rome, and from Sicily to Saragossa: the treaty was sealed with the signet of Pope Nicholas himself, the enemy of Charles; and his deed of gift transferred the fiefs of St. Peter from the house of Anjou to that of Arragon. So widely diffused and so freely circulated, the secret was preserved above two years with impenetrable discretion; and each of the conspirators imbibed the maxim of Peter, who declared that he would cut off his left hand if it were conscious of the intentions of his right. The mine was prepared with deep and dangerous artifice; but it may be questioned, whether the instant explosion of Palermo were the effect of accident or design.

On the vigil of Easter, a procession of the disarmed citizens visited a church without the walls; and a noble damsel was rudely insulted by a French soldier. The ravisher was instantly punished with death; and if the people was at first scattered by a military force, their numbers and fury prevailed: the conspirators seized the opportunity; the flame spread over the island; and eight thousand French were exterminated in a promiscuous massacre, which has obtained the name of the Sicilian Vespers. From every city the banners of freedom and the church were displayed: the revolt was inspired by the presence or the soul of Procida and Peter of Arragon, who sailed from the African coast to Palermo, was saluted as the king and savior of the isle. By the rebellion of a people on whom he had so long trampled with impunity, Charles was astonished and confounded; and in the first agony of grief and devotion, he was heard to exclaim, "O God! if thou hast decreed to humble me, grant me at least a gentle and gradual descent from the pinnacle of greatness!" His fleet and army, which already filled the seaports of Italy, were hastily recalled from the service of the Grecian war; and the situation of Messina exposed that town to the first storm of his revenge.

Feeble in themselves, and yet hopeless of foreign succor, the citizens would have repented, and submitted on the assurance of full pardon and their ancient privileges. But the pride of the monarch was already rekindled; and the most fervent entreaties of the legate could extort no more than a promise, that he would forgive the remainder, after a chosen list of eight hundred rebels had been yielded to his discretion. The despair of the Messinese renewed their courage: Peter of Arragon approached to their relief; and his rival was driven back by the failure of provision and the terrors of the equinox to the Calabrian shore. At the same moment, the Catalan admiral, the famous Roger de Loria, swept the channel with an invincible squadron: the French fleet, more numerous in transports than in galleys, was either burnt or destroyed; and the same blow assured the independence of Sicily and the safety of the Greek empire. A few days before his death, the emperor Michael rejoiced in the fall of an enemy whom he hated and esteemed; and perhaps he might be content with the popular judgment, that had they not been matched with each other, Constantinople and Italy must speedily have obeyed the same master. From this disastrous moment, the life of Charles was a series of misfortunes: his capital was insulted, his son was made prisoner, and he sunk into the grave without recovering the Isle of Sicily, which, after a war of twenty years, was finally severed from the throne of Naples, and transferred, as an independent kingdom, to a younger branch of the house of Arragon.

Greek Emperors of Nice and Constantinople. – Part Three

I SHALL NOT, I trust, be accused of superstition; but I must remark that, even in this world, the natural order of events will sometimes afford the strong appearances of moral retribution. The first Palæologus had saved his empire by involving the kingdoms of the West in rebellion and blood; and from these scenes of discord uprose a generation of iron men, who assaulted and endangered the empire of his son. In modern times our debts and taxes are the secret poison which still corrodes the bosom of peace: but in the weak and disorderly government of the middle ages, it was agitated by the present evil of the disbanded armies. Too idle to work, too proud to beg, the mercenaries were accustomed to a life of rapine: they could rob with more dignity and effect under a banner and a chief; and the sovereign, to whom their service was useless, and their presence importunate, endeavored to discharge the torrent on some neighboring countries. After the peace of Sicily, many thousands of Genoese, *Catalans*, &c., who had fought, by sea and land, under the standard of Anjou or Arragon, were blended into one nation by the resemblance of their manners and interest. They heard that the Greek provinces of Asia were invaded by the Turks: they resolved to share the harvest of pay and plunder: and Frederic king of Sicily most liberally contributed the means of their departure. In a warfare of twenty years, a ship, or a camp, was become their country; arms were their sole profession and property; valor was the only virtue which they knew; their women had imbibed the fearless temper of their lovers and husbands: it was reported, that, with a stroke of their broadsword, the Catalans could cleave a horseman and a horse; and the report itself was a powerful weapon. Roger de Flor was the most popular of their chiefs; and his personal merit overshadowed the dignity of his prouder rivals of Arragon. The offspring of a marriage between a German gentleman of the court of Frederic the Second and a damsel of Brindisi, Roger was successively a templar, an apostate, a pirate, and at length the richest and most powerful admiral of the Mediterranean. He sailed from Messina to Constantinople, with eighteen galleys, four great ships, and eight thousand adventurers; and his previous treaty was faithfully accomplished by Andronicus the elder, who accepted with joy and terror this formidable succor. A palace was allotted for his reception, and a niece of the emperor was given in marriage to the valiant stranger, who was immediately created great duke or admiral of Romania. After a decent repose, he transported his troops over the Propontis, and boldly led them against the Turks: in two bloody battles thirty thousand of the Moslems were slain: he raised the siege of Philadelphia, and deserved the name of the deliverer of Asia. But after a short season of prosperity, the cloud of slavery and ruin again burst on that unhappy province. The inhabitants escaped (says a Greek historian) from the smoke into the flames; and the hostility of the Turks was less pernicious than the friendship of the Catalans. The lives and fortunes which they had rescued they considered as their own: the willing or reluctant maid was saved from the race of circumcision for the embraces of a Christian soldier: the exaction of fines and supplies was enforced by licentious rapine and arbitrary executions; and, on the resistance of Magnesia, the great duke besieged a city of the Roman empire. These disorders he excused by the wrongs and passions of a victorious army; nor would his own authority or person have been safe, had he dared to punish his faithful followers, who were defrauded of the just and covenanted price of their services. The threats and complaints of Andronicus disclosed the nakedness of the empire. His golden bull had invited no more than five hundred horse and a thousand foot soldiers; yet the crowds of volunteers, who migrated to the East, had been enlisted and fed by his spontaneous bounty. While his bravest allies were content with three byzants or pieces of gold, for their monthly pay, an ounce, or even two ounces, of gold were assigned to the Catalans, whose annual pension would thus amount to near a hundred pounds sterling: one of their chiefs had modestly rated at three hundred thousand crowns the value of his *future* merits; and above a million had been issued from the treasury for the maintenance of these costly mercenaries. A cruel tax had been imposed on the corn of the husbandman: one third was retrenched from the salaries of the public officers; and the standard of the coin was so shamefully debased, that of the four-and-twenty parts only five were of pure gold. At the summons of the emperor, Roger evacuated a province which no longer supplied the materials of rapine; but he refused to disperse his troops; and while his style was respectful, his conduct was independent and hostile. He protested, that if the emperor should march against him, he would advance forty paces to kiss the ground before him; but in rising from this prostrate attitude Roger had a life and sword at the service of his friends. The great duke of Romania condescended to accept the title and ornaments of Cæsar; but he rejected the new proposal of the government of Asia with a subsidy of corn and money, on condition that he should reduce his troops to the harmless number of three thousand men. Assassination is the last resource of cowards. The Cæsar was tempted to visit the royal residence of Adrianople; in the apartment, and before the eyes, of the empress he was stabbed by the Alani guards; and though the deed was imputed to their private revenge, his countrymen, who dwelt at Constantinople in the security of peace, were involved in the same proscription by the prince or people. The loss of their leader intimidated the crowd of adventurers, who hoisted the sails of flight, and were soon scattered round the coasts of the Mediterranean. But a veteran band of fifteen hundred Catalans, or French, stood firm in the strong fortress of Gallipoli on the Hellespont, displayed the banners of Arragon, and offered to revenge and justify their chief, by an equal combat of ten or a hundred warriors. Instead of accepting this bold defiance, the emperor Michael, the son and colleague of Andronicus, resolved to oppress them with the weight of multitudes: every nerve was strained to form an army of thirteen thousand horse and thirty thousand foot; and the Propontis was covered with the ships of the Greeks and Genoese. In two battles by sea and land, these mighty forces were encountered and overthrown by the despair and discipline of the Catalans: the young emperor fled to the palace; and an insufficient guard of light-horse was left for the protection of the open country. Victory renewed the hopes and numbers of the adventures: every nation was blended under the name and standard of the *great company*; and three thousand Turkish proselytes deserted from the Imperial service to join this military association. In the possession of Gallipoli, the Catalans intercepted the trade of Constantinople and the Black Sea, while they spread their devastation on either side of the Hellespont over the confines of Europe and Asia. To prevent their approach, the greatest part of the Byzantine territory was laid waste by the Greeks themselves: the peasants and their cattle retired into the city; and myriads of sheep and oxen, for which neither place nor food could be procured, were unprofitably slaughtered on the same day. Four times the emperor Andronicus sued for peace, and four times he was inflexibly repulsed, till the want of provisions, and the discord of the chiefs, compelled the Catalans to evacuate the banks of the Hellespont and the neighborhood of the capital. After their separation from the Turks, the remains of the great company pursued their march through Macedonia and Thessaly, to seek a new establishment in the heart of Greece.

After some ages of oblivion, Greece was awakened to new misfortunes by the arms of the Latins. In the two hundred and fifty years between the first and the last conquest of Constantinople, that venerable land was disputed by a multitude of petty tyrants; without the comforts of freedom and genius, her ancient cities were again plunged in foreign and intestine war; and, if servitude be preferable to anarchy, they might repose with joy under the Turkish yoke. I shall not pursue the obscure and various dynasties, that rose and fell on the continent or in the isles; but our silence on the fate of Athens would argue a strange ingratitude to the first and purest school of liberal science and amusement. In the partition of the empire, the principality of Athens and Thebes was assigned to Otho de la Roche, a noble warrior of Burgundy, with the title of great duke, which the Latins understood in their own sense, and the Greeks more foolishly derived from the age of Constantine. Otho followed the standard of the marquis of Montferrat: the ample state which he acquired by a miracle of conduct or fortune, was peaceably inherited by his son and two grandsons, till the family, though not the nation, was changed, by the marriage of an heiress into the elder branch of the house of Brienne. The son of that marriage, Walter de Brienne, succeeded to the duchy of Athens; and, with the aid of some Catalan mercenaries, whom he invested with fiefs, reduced above thirty castles of the vassal or neighboring lords. But when he was informed of the approach and ambition of the great company, he collected a force of seven hundred knights, six thousand four hundred horse, and eight thousand foot, and boldly met them on the banks of the River Cephisus in Búotia. The Catalans amounted to no more than three thousand five hundred horse, and four thousand foot; but the deficiency of numbers was compensated by stratagem and order. They formed round their camp an artificial inundation; the duke and his knights advanced without fear or precaution on the verdant meadow; their horses plunged into the bog; and he was cut in pieces, with the greatest part of the French cavalry. His family and nation were expelled; and his son Walter de Brienne, the titular duke of Athens, the tyrant of Florence, and the constable of France, lost his life in the field of Poitiers Attica and Búotia were the rewards of the victorious Catalans; they married the widows and daughters of the slain; and during fourteen years, the great company was the terror of the Grecian states. Their factions drove them to acknowledge the sovereignty of the house of Arragon; and during the remainder of the fourteenth century, Athens, as a government or an appanage, was successively bestowed by the kings of Sicily. After the French and Catalans, the third dynasty was that of the Accaioli, a family, plebeian at Florence, potent at Naples, and sovereign in Greece. Athens, which they embellished with new buildings, became the capital of a state, that extended over Thebes, Argos, Corinth, Delphi, and a part of Thessaly; and their reign was finally determined by Mahomet the Second, who strangled the last duke, and educated his sons in the discipline and religion of the seraglio.

Athens, though no more than the shadow of her former self, still contains about eight or ten thousand inhabitants; of these, three fourths are Greeks in religion and language; and the Turks, who compose the remainder, have relaxed, in their intercourse with the citizens, somewhat of the pride and gravity of their national character. The olive-tree, the gift of Minerva, flourishes in Attica; nor has the honey of Mount Hymettus lost any part of its exquisite flavor: but the languid trade is monopolized by strangers, and the agriculture of a barren land is abandoned to the vagrant Walachians. The Athenians are still distinguished by the subtlety and acuteness of their understandings; but these qualities, unless ennobled by freedom, and enlightened by study, will degenerate into a low and selfish cunning: and it is a proverbial saying of the country, "From the Jews of Thessalonica, the Turks of Negropont, and the Greeks of Athens, good Lord deliver us!" This artful people has eluded the tyranny of the Turkish bashaws, by an expedient which alleviates their servitude and aggravates their shame. About the middle of the last century, the Athenians chose for their protector the Kislar Aga, or chief black eunuch of the seraglio. This Æthiopian slave, who possesses the sultan's ear, condescends to accept the tribute of thirty thousand crowns: his lieutenant, the Waywode, whom he annually confirms, may reserve for his own about five or six thousand more; and such is the policy of the citizens, that they seldom fail to remove and punish an oppressive governor. Their private differences are decided by the archbishop, one of the richest prelates of the Greek church, since he possesses a revenue of one thousand pounds sterling; and by a tribunal of the eight *geronti* or elders, chosen in the eight quarters of the city: the noble families cannot trace their pedigree above three hundred years; but their principal members are distinguished by a grave demeanor, a fur cap, and the lofty appellation of *archon*. By some, who delight in the contrast, the modern language of Athens is represented as the most corrupt and barbarous of the seventy dialects of the vulgar Greek: this picture is too darkly colored: but it would not be easy, in the country of Plato and Demosthenes, to find a reader or a copy of their works. The Athenians walk with supine indifference among the glorious ruins of antiquity; and such is the debasement of their character, that they are incapable of admiring the genius of their predecessors.

CHAPTER SIXTY THREE

Civil Wars and the Ruin of the Greek Empire. – Part One

Civil Wars, and Ruin of the Greek Empire. – Reigns of Andronicus, the Elder and Younger, and John Palæologus. – Regency, Revolt, Reign, and Abdication of John Cantacuzene. – Establishment of a Genoese Colony at Pera or Galata. – Their Wars with The Empire and City of Constantinople.

THE LONG REIGN OF Andronicus the elder is chiefly memorable by the disputes of the Greek church, the invasion of the Catalans, and the rise of the Ottoman power. He is celebrated as the most learned and virtuous prince of the age; but such virtue, and such learning, contributed neither to the perfection of the individual, nor to the happiness of society. A slave of the most abject superstition, he was surrounded on all sides by visible and invisible enemies; nor were the flames of hell less dreadful to his fancy, than those of a Catalan or Turkish war. Under the reign of the Palæologi, the choice of the patriarch was the most important business of the state; the heads of the Greek church were ambitious and fanatic monks; and their vices or virtues, their learning or ignorance, were equally mischievous or contemptible. By his intemperate discipline, the patriarch Athanasius excited the hatred of the clergy and people: he was heard to declare, that the sinner should swallow the last dregs of the cup of penance; and the foolish tale was propagated of his punishing a sacrilegious ass that had tasted the lettuce of a convent garden. Driven from the throne by the universal clamor, Athanasius composed before his retreat two papers of a very opposite cast. His public testament was in the tone of charity and resignation; the private codicil breathed the direst anathemas against the authors of his disgrace, whom he excluded forever from the communion of the holy trinity, the angels, and the saints. This last paper he enclosed in an earthen pot, which was placed, by his order, on the top of one of the pillars, in the dome of St. Sophia, in the distant hope of discovery and revenge. At the end of four years, some youths, climbing by a ladder in search of pigeons' nests, detected the fatal secret; and, as Andronicus felt himself touched and bound by the excommunication, he trembled on the brink of the abyss which had been so treacherously dug under his feet. A synod of bishops was instantly convened to debate this important question: the rashness of these clandestine anathemas was generally condemned; but as the knot could be untied only by the same hand, as that hand was now deprived of the crosier, it appeared that this posthumous decree was irrevocable by any earthly power. Some faint testimonies of repentance and pardon were extorted from the author of the mischief; but the conscience of the emperor was still wounded, and he desired, with no less ardor than Athanasius himself, the restoration of a patriarch, by whom alone he could be healed. At the dead of night, a monk rudely knocked at the door of the royal bed-chamber, announcing a revelation of plague and famine, of inundations and earthquakes. Andronicus started from his bed, and spent the night in prayer, till he felt, or thought that he felt, a slight motion of the earth. The emperor on foot led the bishops and monks to the cell of Athanasius; and, after a proper resistance, the saint, from whom this message had been sent, consented to absolve the prince, and govern the church of Constantinople. Untamed by disgrace, and hardened by solitude, the shepherd was again odious to the flock, and his enemies contrived a singular, and as it proved, a successful, mode of revenge. In the night, they stole away the footstool or foot-cloth of his throne, which they secretly replaced with the decoration of a satirical picture. The emperor was painted with a bridle in his mouth, and Athanasius leading the tractable beast to the feet of Christ. The authors of the libel were detected and punished; but as their lives had been spared, the Christian priest in sullen indignation retired to his cell; and the eyes of Andronicus, which had been opened for a moment, were again closed by his successor.

If this transaction be one of the most curious and important of a reign of fifty years, I cannot at least accuse the brevity of my materials, since I reduce into some few pages the enormous folios of Pachymer, Cantacuzene, and Nicephorus Gregoras, who have composed the prolix and languid story of the times. The name and situation of the emperor John Cantacuzene might inspire the most lively curiosity.

His memorials of forty years extend from the revolt of the younger Andronicus to his own abdication of the empire; and it is observed, that, like Moses and Cæsar, he was the principal actor in the scenes which he describes. But in this eloquent work we should vainly seek the sincerity of a hero or a penitent. Retired in a cloister from the vices and passions of the world, he presents not a confession, but an apology, of the life of an ambitious statesman. Instead of unfolding the true counsels and characters of men, he displays the smooth and specious surface of events, highly varnished with his own praises and those of his friends. Their motives are always pure; their ends always legitimate: they conspire and rebel without any views of interest; and the violence which they inflict or suffer is celebrated as the spontaneous effect of reason and virtue.

After the example of the first of the Palæologi, the elder Andronicus associated his son Michael to the honors of the purple; and from the age of eighteen to his premature death, that prince was acknowledged, above twenty-five years, as the second emperor of the Greeks. At the head of an army, he excited neither the fears of the enemy, nor the jealousy of the court; his modesty and patience were never tempted to compute the years of his father; nor was that father compelled to repent of his liberality either by the virtues or vices of his son. The son of Michael was named Andronicus from his grandfather, to whose early favor he was introduced by that nominal resemblance. The blossoms of wit and beauty increased the fondness of the elder Andronicus; and, with the common vanity of age, he expected to realize in the second, the hope which had been disappointed in the first, generation. The boy was educated in the palace as an heir and a favorite; and in the oaths and acclamations of the people, the *august triad* was formed by the names of the father, the son, and the grandson. But the younger Andronicus was speedily corrupted by his infant greatness, while he beheld with puerile impatience the double obstacle that hung, and might long hang, over his rising ambition. It was not to acquire fame, or to diffuse happiness, that he so eagerly aspired: wealth and impunity were in his eyes the most precious attributes of a monarch; and his first indiscreet demand was the sovereignty of some rich and fertile island, where he might lead a life of independence and pleasure. The emperor was offended by the loud and frequent intemperance which disturbed his capital; the sums which his parsimony denied were supplied by the Genoese usurers of Pera; and the oppressive debt, which consolidated the interest of a faction, could be discharged only by a revolution. A beautiful female, a matron in rank, a prostitute in manners, had instructed the younger

Andronicus in the rudiments of love; but he had reason to suspect the nocturnal visits of a rival; and a stranger passing through the street was pierced by the arrows of his guards, who were placed in ambush at her door. That stranger was his brother, Prince Manuel, who languished and died of his wound; and the emperor Michael, their common father, whose health was in a declining state, expired on the eighth day, lamenting the loss of both his children. However guiltless in his intention, the younger Andronicus might impute a brother's and a father's death to the consequence of his own vices; and deep was the sigh of thinking and feeling men, when they perceived, instead of sorrow and repentance, his ill-dissembled joy on the removal of two odious competitors. By these melancholy events, and the increase of his disorders, the mind of the elder emperor was gradually alienated; and, after many fruitless reproofs, he transferred on another grandson his hopes and affection. The change was announced by the new oath of allegiance to the reigning sovereign, and the *person* whom he should appoint for his successor; and the acknowledged heir, after a repetition of insults and complaints, was exposed to the indignity of a public trial. Before the sentence, which would probably have condemned him to a dungeon or a cell, the emperor was informed that the palace courts were filled with the armed followers of his grandson; the judgment was softened to a treaty of reconciliation; and the triumphant escape of the prince encouraged the ardor of the younger faction.

Yet the capital, the clergy, and the senate, adhered to the person, or at least to the government, of the old emperor; and it was only in the provinces, by flight, and revolt, and foreign succor, that the malecontents could hope to vindicate their cause and subvert his throne. The soul of the enterprise was the great domestic John Cantacuzene; the sally from Constantinople is the first date of his actions and memorials; and if his own pen be most descriptive of his patriotism, an unfriendly historian has not refused to celebrate the zeal and ability which he displayed in the service of the young emperor. That prince escaped from the capital under the pretence of hunting; erected his standard at Adrianople; and, in a few days, assembled fifty thousand horse and foot, whom neither honor nor duty could have armed against the Barbarians. Such a force might have saved or commanded the empire; but their counsels were discordant, their motions were slow and doubtful, and their progress was checked by intrigue and negotiation. The quarrel of the two Andronici was protracted, and suspended, and renewed, during a ruinous period of seven years. In the first treaty, the relics of the Greek empire were divided: Constantinople, Thessalonica, and the islands, were left to the elder, while the younger acquired the sovereignty of the greatest part of Thrace, from Philippi to the Byzantine limit. By the second treaty, he stipulated the payment of his troops, his immediate coronation, and an adequate share of the power and revenue of the state. The third civil war was terminated by the surprise of Constantinople, the final retreat of the old emperor, and the sole reign of his victorious grandson. The reasons of this delay may be found in the characters of the men and of the times. When the heir of the monarchy first pleaded his wrongs and his apprehensions, he was heard with pity and applause: and his adherents repeated on all sides the inconsistent promise, that he would increase the pay of the soldiers and alleviate the burdens of the people. The grievances of forty years were mingled in his revolt; and the rising generation was fatigued by the endless prospect of a reign, whose favorites and maxims were of other times. The youth of Andronicus had been without spirit, his age was without reverence: his taxes produced an unusual revenue of five hundred thousand pounds; yet the richest of the sovereigns of Christendom was incapable of maintaining three thousand horse and twenty galleys, to resist the destructive progress of the Turks. "How different," said the younger Andronicus, "is my situation from that of the son of Philip! Alexander might complain, that his father would leave him nothing to conquer: alas! my grandsire will leave me nothing to lose." But the Greeks were soon admonished, that the public disorders could not be healed by a civil war; and that their young favorite was not destined to be the savior of a falling empire. On the first repulse, his party was broken by his own levity, their intestine discord, and the intrigues of the ancient court, which tempted each malecontent to desert or betray the cause of the rebellion. Andronicus the younger was touched with remorse, or fatigued with business, or deceived by negotiation: pleasure rather than power was his aim; and the license of maintaining a thousand hounds, a thousand hawks, and a thousand huntsmen, was sufficient to sully his fame and disarm his ambition.

Let us now survey the catastrophe of this busy plot, and the final situation of the principal actors. The age of Andronicus was consumed in civil discord; and, amidst the events of war and treaty, his power and reputation continually decayed, till the fatal night in which the gates of the city and palace were opened without resistance to his grandson. His principal commander scorned the repeated warnings of danger; and retiring to rest in the vain security of ignorance, abandoned the feeble monarch, with some priests and pages, to the terrors of a sleepless night.

These terrors were quickly realized by the hostile shouts, which proclaimed the titles and victory of Andronicus the younger; and the aged emperor, falling prostrate before an image of the Virgin, despatched a suppliant message to resign the sceptre, and to obtain his life at the hands of the conqueror. The answer of his grandson was decent and pious; at the prayer of his friends, the younger Andronicus assumed the sole administration; but the elder still enjoyed the name and preeminence of the first emperor, the use of the great palace, and a pension of twenty-four thousand pieces of gold, one half of which was assigned on the royal treasury, and the other on the fishery of Constantinople. But his impotence was soon exposed to contempt and oblivion; the vast silence of the palace was disturbed only by the cattle and poultry of the neighborhood, which roved with impunity through the solitary courts; and a reduced allowance of ten thousand pieces of gold was all that he could ask, and more than he could hope. His calamities were imbittered by the gradual extinction of sight; his confinement was rendered each day more rigorous; and during the absence and sickness of his grandson, his inhuman keepers, by the threats of instant death, compelled him to exchange the purple for the monastic habit and profession. The monk *Antony* had renounced the pomp of the world; yet he had occasion for a coarse fur in the winter season, and as wine was forbidden by his confessor, and water by his physician, the sherbet of Egypt was his common drink. It was not without difficulty that the late emperor could procure three or four pieces to satisfy these simple wants; and if he bestowed the gold to relieve the more painful distress of a friend, the sacrifice is of some weight in the scale of humanity and religion. Four years after his abdication, Andronicus or Antony expired in a cell, in the seventy-fourth year of his age: and the last strain of adulation could only promise a more splendid crown of glory in heaven than he had enjoyed upon earth.

Nor was the reign of the younger, more glorious or fortunate than that of the elder, Andronicus. He gathered the fruits of ambition; but the taste was transient and bitter: in the supreme station he lost the remains of his early popularity; and the defects of his character became still more conspicuous to the world. The public reproach urged him to march in person against the Turks; nor did his courage fail in the hour of trial; but a defeat and a wound were the only trophies of his expedition in Asia, which confirmed the establishment of the Ottoman monarchy. The abuses of the civil government attained their full maturity and perfection: his neglect of forms, and the confusion of national dresses, are deplored by the Greeks as the fatal symptoms of the decay of the empire. Andronicus was old before his time; the intemperance of youth had accelerated the infirmities of age; and after being rescued from a dangerous malady by nature, or physic, or the Virgin, he was snatched away before he had accomplished his forty-fifth year. He was twice married; and, as the progress of the Latins in arms and arts had softened the prejudices of the Byzantine court, his two wives were chosen in the princely houses of Germany and Italy. The first, Agnes at home, Irene in Greece, was daughter of the duke of Brunswick. Her father was a petty lord in the poor and savage regions of the north of Germany: yet he derived some revenue from his silver mines; and his family is celebrated by the Greeks as the most ancient and noble of the Teutonic name. After the death of this childish princess, Andronicus sought in marriage Jane, the sister of the count of Savoy; and his suit was preferred to that of the French king. The count respected in his sister the superior majesty of a Roman empress: her retinue was composed of knights and ladies; she was regenerated and crowned in St. Sophia, under the more orthodox appellation of Anne; and, at the nuptial feast, the Greeks and Italians vied with each other in the martial exercises of tilts and tournaments.

The empress Anne of Savoy survived her husband: their son, John Palæologus, was left an orphan and an emperor in the ninth year of his age; and his weakness was protected by the first and most deserving of the Greeks. The long and cordial friendship of his father for John Cantacuzene is alike honorable to the prince and the subject. It had been formed amidst the pleasures of their youth: their families were almost equally noble; and the recent lustre of the purple was amply compensated by the energy of a private education. We have seen that the young emperor was saved by Cantacuzene from the power of his grandfather; and, after six years of civil war, the same favorite brought him back in triumph to the palace of Constantinople. Under the reign of Andronicus the younger, the great domestic ruled the emperor and the empire; and it was by his valor and conduct that the Isle of Lesbos and the principality of Ætolia were restored to their ancient allegiance. His enemies confess, that, among the public robbers, Cantacuzene alone was moderate and abstemious; and the free and voluntary account which he produces of his own wealth may sustain the presumption that he was devolved by inheritance, and not accumulated by rapine. He does not indeed specify the value of his money, plate, and jewels; yet, after a voluntary gift of two hundred vases of silver, after much had been secreted by his friends and plundered by his foes, his forfeit treasures were sufficient for the equipment of a fleet of seventy galleys. He does not measure the size and number of his estates; but his granaries were heaped with an incredible store of wheat and barley; and the labor of a thousand yoke of oxen might cultivate, according to the practice of antiquity, about sixty-two thousand five hundred acres of arable land. His pastures were stocked with two thousand five hundred brood mares, two hundred camels, three hundred mules, five hundred asses, five thousand horned cattle, fifty thousand hogs, and seventy thousand sheep: a precious record of rural opulence, in the last period of the empire, and in a land, most probably in Thrace, so repeatedly wasted by foreign and domestic hostility. The favor of Cantacuzene was above his fortune. In the moments of familiarity, in the hour of sickness, the emperor was desirous to level the distance between them and pressed his friend to accept the diadem and purple. The virtue of the great domestic, which is attested by his own pen, resisted the dangerous proposal; but the last testament of Andronicus the younger named him the guardian of his son, and the regent of the empire.

Had the regent found a suitable return of obedience and gratitude, perhaps he would have acted with pure and zealous fidelity in the service of his pupil. A guard of five hundred soldiers watched over his person and the palace; the funeral of the late emperor was decently performed; the capital was silent and submissive; and five hundred letters, which Cantacuzene despatched in the first month, informed the provinces of their loss and their duty. The prospect of a tranquil minority was blasted by the great duke or admiral Apocaucus, and to exaggerate *his* perfidy, the Imperial historian is pleased to magnify his own imprudence, in raising him to that office against the advice of his more sagacious sovereign. Bold and subtle, rapacious and profuse, the avarice and ambition of Apocaucus were by turns subservient to each other; and his talents were applied to the ruin of his country. His arrogance was heightened by the command of a naval force and an impregnable castle, and under the mask of oaths and flattery he secretly conspired against his benefactor. The female court of the empress was bribed and directed; he encouraged Anne of Savoy to assert, by the law of nature, the tutelage of her son; the love of power was disguised by the anxiety of maternal tenderness: and the founder of the Palæologi had instructed his posterity to dread the example of a perfidious guardian. The patriarch John of Apri was a proud and feeble old man, encompassed by a numerous and hungry kindred. He produced an obsolete epistle of Andronicus, which bequeathed the prince and people to his pious care: the fate of his predecessor Arsenius prompted him to prevent, rather than punish, the crimes of a usurper; and Apocaucus smiled at the success of his own flattery, when he beheld the Byzantine priest assuming the state and temporal claims of the Roman pontiff. Between three persons so different in their situation and character, a private league was concluded: a shadow of authority was restored to the senate; and the people was tempted by the name of freedom. By this powerful confederacy, the great domestic was assaulted at first with clandestine, at length with open, arms. His prerogatives were disputed; his opinions slighted; his friends persecuted; and his safety was threatened both in the camp and city. In his absence on the public service, he was accused of treason; proscribed as an enemy of the church and state; and delivered with all his adherents to the sword of justice, the vengeance of the people, and the power of the devil; his fortunes were confiscated; his aged mother was cast into prison; all his past services were buried in oblivion; and he was driven by injustice to perpetrate the crime of which he was accused. From the review of his preceding conduct, Cantacuzene appears to have been guiltless of any treasonable designs; and the only suspicion of his innocence must arise from the vehemence of his protestations, and the sublime purity which he ascribes to his own virtue. While the empress and the patriarch still affected the appearances of harmony, he repeatedly solicited the permission of retiring to a private, and even a monastic, life. After he had been declared a public enemy, it was his fervent wish to throw himself at the feet of the young emperor, and to receive without a murmur the stroke of the executioner: it was not without reluctance that he listened to the voice of reason, which inculcated the sacred duty of saving his family and friends, and proved that he could only save them by drawing the sword and assuming the Imperial title.

Civil Wars and the Ruin of the Greek Empire. – Part Two

IN THE STRONG CITY of Demotica, his peculiar domain, the emperor John Cantacuzenus was invested with the purple buskins: his right leg was clothed by his noble kinsmen, the left by the Latin chiefs, on whom he conferred the order of knighthood. But even in this act of revolt, he was still studious of loyalty; and the titles of John Palæologus and Anne of Savoy were proclaimed before his own name and that of his wife Irene. Such vain ceremony is a thin disguise of rebellion, nor are there perhaps any personal wrongs that can authorize a subject to take arms against his sovereign: but the want of preparation and success may confirm the assurance of the usurper, that this decisive step was the effect of necessity rather than of choice. Constantinople adhered to the young emperor; the king of Bulgaria was invited to the relief of Adrianople: the principal cities of Thrace and Macedonia, after some hesitation, renounced their obedience to the great domestic; and the leaders of the troops and provinces were induced, by their private interest, to prefer the loose dominion of a woman and a priest. The army of Cantacuzene, in sixteen divisions, was stationed on the banks of the Melas to tempt or to intimidate the capital: it was dispersed by treachery or fear; and the officers, more especially the mercenary Latins, accepted the bribes, and embraced the service, of the Byzantine court. After this loss, the rebel emperor (he fluctuated between the two characters) took the road of Thessalonica with a chosen remnant; but he failed in his enterprise on that important place; and he was closely pursued by the great duke, his enemy Apocaucus, at the head of a superior power by sea and land. Driven from the coast, in his march, or rather flight, into the mountains of

Servia, Cantacuzene assembled his troops to scrutinize those who were worthy and willing to accompany his broken fortunes. A base majority bowed and retired; and his trusty band was diminished to two thousand, and at last to five hundred, volunteers. The *cral*, or despot of the Servians received him with general hospitality; but the ally was insensibly degraded to a suppliant, a hostage, a captive; and in this miserable dependence, he waited at the door of the Barbarian, who could dispose of the life and liberty of a Roman emperor. The most tempting offers could not persuade the cral to violate his trust; but he soon inclined to the stronger side; and his friend was dismissed without injury to a new vicissitude of hopes and perils. Near six years the flame of discord burnt with various success and unabated rage: the cities were distracted by the faction of the nobles and the plebeians; the Cantacuzeni and Palæologi: and the Bulgarians, the Servians, and the Turks, were invoked on both sides as the instruments of private ambition and the common ruin. The regent deplored the calamities, of which he was the author and victim: and his own experience might dictate a just and lively remark on the different nature of foreign and civil war. "The former," said he, "is the external warmth of summer, always tolerable, and often beneficial; the latter is the deadly heat of a fever, which consumes without a remedy the vitals of the constitution."

The introduction of barbarians and savages into the contests of civilized nations, is a measure pregnant with shame and mischief; which the interest of the moment may compel, but which is reprobated by the best principles of humanity and reason. It is the practice of both sides to accuse their enemies of the guilt of the first alliances; and those who fail in their negotiations are loudest in their censure of the example which they envy and would gladly imitate. The Turks of Asia were less barbarous perhaps than the shepherds of Bulgaria and Servia; but their religion rendered them implacable foes of Rome and Christianity. To acquire the friendship of their emirs, the two factions vied with each other in baseness and profusion: the dexterity of Cantacuzene obtained the preference: but the succor and victory were dearly purchased by the marriage of his daughter with an infidel, the captivity of many thousand Christians, and the passage of the Ottomans into Europe, the last and fatal stroke in the fall of the Roman empire. The inclining scale was decided in his favor by the death of Apocaucus, the just though singular retribution of his crimes. A crowd of nobles or plebeians, whom he feared or hated, had been seized by his orders in the capital and the provinces; and the old palace of Constantine was assigned as the place of their confinement. Some alterations in raising the walls, and narrowing the cells, had been ingeniously contrived to prevent their escape, and aggravate their misery; and the work was incessantly pressed by the daily visits of the tyrant. His guards watched at the gate, and as he stood in the inner court to overlook the architects, without fear or suspicion, he was assaulted and laid breathless on the ground, by two resolute prisoners of the Palæologian race, who were armed with sticks, and animated by despair. On the rumor of revenge and liberty, the captive multitude broke their fetters, fortified their prison, and exposed from the battlements the tyrant's head, presuming on the favor of the people and the clemency of the empress. Anne of Savoy might rejoice in the fall of a haughty and ambitious minister, but while she delayed to resolve or to act, the populace, more especially the mariners, were excited by the widow of the great duke to a sedition, an assault, and a massacre. The prisoners (of whom the far greater part were guiltless or inglorious of the deed) escaped to a neighboring church: they were slaughtered at the foot of the altar; and in his death the monster was not less bloody and venomous than in his life. Yet his talents alone upheld the cause of the young emperor; and his surviving associates, suspicious of each other, abandoned the conduct of the war, and rejected the fairest terms of accommodation. In the beginning of the dispute, the empress felt, and complained, that she was deceived by the enemies of Cantacuzene: the patriarch was employed to preach against the forgiveness of injuries; and her promise of immortal hatred was sealed by an oath, under the penalty of excommunication. But Anne soon learned to hate without a teacher: she beheld the misfortunes of the empire with the indifference of a stranger: her jealousy was exasperated by the competition of a rival empress; and on the first symptoms of a more yielding temper, she threatened the patriarch to convene a synod, and degrade him from his office. Their incapacity and discord would have afforded the most decisive advantage; but the civil war was protracted by the weakness of both parties; and the moderation of Cantacuzene has not escaped the reproach of timidity and indolence. He successively recovered the provinces and cities; and the realm of his pupil was measured by the walls of Constantinople; but the metropolis alone counterbalanced the rest of the empire; nor could he attempt that important conquest till he had secured in his favor the public voice and a private correspondence. An Italian, of the name of Facciolati, had succeeded to the office of great duke: the ships, the guards, and the golden gate, were subject to his command; but his humble ambition was bribed to become the instrument of treachery; and the revolution was accomplished without danger or bloodshed. Destitute of the powers of resistance, or the hope of relief, the inflexible Anne would have still defended the palace, and have smiled to behold the capital in flames, rather than in the possession of a rival. She yielded to the prayers of her friends and enemies; and the treaty was dictated by the conqueror, who professed a loyal and zealous attachment to the son of his benefactor. The marriage of his daughter with John Palæologus was at length consummated: the hereditary right of the pupil was acknowledged; but the sole administration during ten years was vested in the guardian. Two emperors and three empresses were seated on the Byzantine throne; and a general amnesty quieted the apprehensions, and confirmed the property, of the most guilty subjects. The festival of the coronation and nuptials was celebrated with the appearances of concord and magnificence, and both were equally fallacious. During the late troubles, the treasures of the state, and even the furniture of the palace, had been alienated or embezzled; the royal banquet was served in pewter or earthenware; and such was the proud poverty of the times, that the absence of gold and jewels was supplied by the paltry artifices of glass and gilt-leather.

I hasten to conclude the personal history of John Cantacuzene. He triumphed and reigned; but his reign and triumph were clouded by the discontent of his own and the adverse faction. His followers might style the general amnesty an act of pardon for his enemies, and of oblivion for his friends: in his cause their estates had been forfeited or plundered; and as they wandered naked and hungry through the streets, they cursed the selfish generosity of a leader, who, on the throne of the empire, might relinquish without merit his private inheritance. The adherents of the empress blushed to hold their lives and fortunes by the precarious favor of a usurper; and the thirst of revenge was concealed by a tender concern for the succession, and even the safety, of her son. They were justly alarmed by a petition of the friends of Cantacuzene, that they might be released from their oath of allegiance to the Palæologi, and intrusted with the defence of some cautionary towns; a measure supported with argument and eloquence; and which was rejected (says the Imperial historian) "by *my* sublime, and almost incredible virtue." His repose was disturbed by the sound of plots and seditions; and he trembled lest the lawful prince should be stolen away by some foreign or domestic enemy, who would inscribe his name and his wrongs in the banners of rebellion. As the son of Andronicus advanced in the years of manhood, he began to feel and to act for himself; and his rising ambition was rather stimulated than checked by the imitation of his father's vices. If we may trust his own professions,

Cantacuzene labored with honest industry to correct these sordid and sensual appetites, and to raise the mind of the young prince to a level with his fortune. In the Servian expedition, the two emperors showed themselves in cordial harmony to the troops and provinces; and the younger colleague was initiated by the elder in the mysteries of war and government. After the conclusion of the peace, Palæologus was left at Thessalonica, a royal residence, and a frontier station, to secure by his absence the peace of Constantinople, and to withdraw his youth from the temptations of a luxurious capital. But the distance weakened the powers of control, and the son of Andronicus was surrounded with artful or unthinking companions, who taught him to hate his guardian, to deplore his exile, and to vindicate his rights. A private treaty with the cral or despot of Servia was soon followed by an open revolt; and Cantacuzene, on the throne of the elder Andronicus, defended the cause of age and prerogative, which in his youth he had so vigorously attacked. At his request the empress-mother undertook the voyage of Thessalonica, and the office of mediation: she returned without success; and unless Anne of Savoy was instructed by adversity, we may doubt the sincerity, or at least the fervor, of her zeal. While the regent grasped the sceptre with a firm and vigorous hand, she had been instructed to declare, that the ten years of his legal administration would soon elapse; and that, after a full trial of the vanity of the world, the emperor Cantacuzene sighed for the repose of a cloister, and was ambitious only of a heavenly crown. Had these sentiments been genuine, his voluntary abdication would have restored the peace of the empire, and his conscience would have been relieved by an act of justice. Palæologus alone was responsible for his future government; and whatever might be his vices, they were surely less formidable than the calamities of a civil war, in which the Barbarians and infidels were again invited to assist the Greeks in their mutual destruction. By the arms of the Turks, who now struck a deep and everlasting root in Europe, Cantacuzene prevailed in the third contest in which he had been involved; and the young emperor, driven from the sea and land, was compelled to take shelter among the Latins of the Isle of Tenedos. His insolence and obstinacy provoked the victor to a step which must render the quarrel irreconcilable; and the association of his son Matthew, whom he invested with the purple, established the succession in the family of the Cantacuzeni. But Constantinople was still attached to the blood of her ancient princes; and this last injury accelerated the restoration of the rightful heir. A noble Genoese espoused the cause of Palæologus, obtained a promise of his sister, and achieved the revolution with two galleys and two thousand five hundred auxiliaries. Under the pretence of distress, they were admitted into the lesser port; a gate was opened, and the Latin shout of, "Long life and victory to the emperor, John Palæologus!" was answered by a general rising in his favor. A numerous and loyal party yet adhered to the standard of Cantacuzene: but he asserts in his history (does he hope for belief?) that his tender conscience rejected the assurance of conquest; that, in free obedience to the voice of religion and philosophy, he descended from the throne and embraced with pleasure the monastic habit and profession. So soon as he ceased to be a prince, his successor was not unwilling that he should be a saint: the remainder of his life was devoted to piety and learning; in the cells of Constantinople and Mount Athos, the monk Joasaph was respected as the temporal and spiritual father of the emperor; and if he issued from his retreat, it was as the minister of peace, to subdue the obstinacy, and solicit the pardon, of his rebellious son.

Yet in the cloister, the mind of Cantacuzene was still exercised by theological war. He sharpened a controversial pen against the Jews and Mahometans; and in every state he defended with equal zeal the divine light of Mount Thabor, a memorable question which consummates the religious follies of the Greeks. The fakirs of India, and the monks of the Oriental church, were alike persuaded, that in the total abstraction of the faculties of the mind and body, the purer spirit may ascend to the enjoyment and vision of the Deity. The opinion and practice of the monasteries of Mount Athos will be best represented in the words of an abbot, who flourished in the eleventh century. "When thou art alone in thy cell," says the ascetic teacher, "shut thy door, and seat thyself in a corner: raise thy mind above all things vain and transitory; recline thy beard and chin on thy breast; turn thy eyes and thy thoughts toward the middle of thy belly, the region of the navel; and search the place of the heart, the seat of the soul. At first, all will be dark and comfortless; but if you persevere day and night, you will feel an ineffable joy; and no sooner has the soul discovered the place of the heart, than it is involved in a mystic and ethereal light." This light, the production of a distempered fancy, the creature of an empty stomach and an empty brain, was adored by the Quietists as the pure and perfect essence of God himself; and as long as the folly was confined to Mount Athos, the simple solitaries were not inquisitive how the divine essence could be a *material* substance, or how an *immaterial* substance could be perceived by the eyes of the body. But in the reign of the younger Andronicus, these monasteries were visited by Barlaam, a Calabrian monk, who was equally skilled in philosophy and theology; who possessed the language of the Greeks and Latins; and whose versatile genius could maintain their opposite creeds, according to the interest of the moment. The indiscretion of an ascetic revealed to the curious traveller the secrets of mental prayer and Barlaam embraced the opportunity of ridiculing the Quietists, who placed the soul in the navel; of accusing the monks of Mount Athos of heresy and blasphemy. His attack compelled the more learned to renounce or dissemble the simple devotion of their brethren; and Gregory Palamas introduced a scholastic distinction between the essence and operation of God. His inaccessible essence dwells in the midst of an uncreated and eternal light; and this beatific vision of the saints had been manifested to the disciples on Mount Thabor, in the transfiguration of Christ. Yet this distinction could not escape the reproach of polytheism; the eternity of the light of Thabor was fiercely denied; and Barlaam still charged the Palamites with holding two eternal substances, a visible and an invisible God. From the rage of the monks of Mount Athos, who threatened his life, the Calabrian retired to Constantinople, where his smooth and specious manners introduced him to the favor of the great domestic and the emperor. The court and the city were involved in this theological dispute, which flamed amidst the civil war; but the doctrine of Barlaam was disgraced by his flight and apostasy: the Palamites triumphed; and their adversary, the patriarch John of Apri, was deposed by the consent of the adverse factions of the state. In the character of emperor and theologian, Cantacuzene presided in the synod of the Greek church, which established, as an article of faith, the uncreated light of Mount Thabor; and, after so many insults, the reason of mankind was slightly wounded by the addition of a single absurdity. Many rolls of paper or parchment have been blotted; and the impenitent sectaries, who refused to subscribe the orthodox creed, were deprived of the honors of Christian burial; but in the next age the question was forgotten; nor can I learn that the axe or the fagot were employed for the extirpation of the Barlaamite heresy.

For the conclusion of this chapter, I have reserved the Genoese war, which shook the throne of Cantacuzene, and betrayed the debility of the Greek empire. The Genoese, who, after the recovery of Constantinople, were seated in the suburb of Pera or Galata, received that honorable fief from the bounty of the emperor. They were indulged in the use of their laws and magistrates; but they submitted to the duties of vassals and subjects; the forcible word of *liegemen*43 was borrowed from the Latin jurisprudence; and their *podesta*, or chief, before he entered on his office, saluted the emperor with loyal acclamations and vows of fidelity. Genoa sealed a firm alliance with the Greeks; and, in case of a defensive war, a supply of fifty empty galleys and a succor of fifty galleys, completely armed and manned, was promised by the republic to the empire. In the revival of a naval force, it was the aim of Michael Palæologus to deliver himself from a foreign aid; and his vigorous government contained the Genoese of Galata within those limits which the insolence of wealth and freedom provoked them to exceed. A sailor threatened that they should soon be masters of Constantinople, and slew the Greek who resented this national affront; and an armed vessel, after refusing to salute the palace, was guilty of some acts of piracy in the Black Sea. Their countrymen threatened to support their cause; but the long and open village of Galata was instantly surrounded by the Imperial troops; till, in the moment of the assault, the prostrate Genoese implored the clemency of their sovereign. The defenceless situation which secured their obedience exposed them to the attack of their Venetian rivals, who, in the reign of the elder Andronicus, presumed to violate the majesty of the throne. On the approach of their fleets, the Genoese, with their families and effects, retired into the city: their empty habitations were reduced to ashes; and the feeble prince, who had viewed the destruction of his suburb, expressed his resentment, not by arms, but by ambassadors. This misfortune, however, was advantageous to the Genoese, who obtained, and imperceptibly abused, the dangerous license of surrounding Galata with a strong wall; of introducing into the ditch the waters of the sea; of erecting lofty turrets; and of mounting a train of military engines on the rampart. The narrow bounds in which they had been circumscribed were insufficient for the growing colony; each day they acquired some addition of landed property; and the adjacent hills were covered with their villas and castles, which they joined and protected by new fortifications. The navigation and trade of the Euxine was the patrimony of the Greek emperors, who commanded the narrow entrance, the gates, as it were, of that inland sea. In the reign of Michael Palæologus, their prerogative was acknowledged by the sultan of Egypt, who solicited and obtained the liberty of sending an annual ship for the purchase of slaves in Circassia and the Lesser Tartary: a liberty pregnant with mischief to the Christian cause; since these youths were transformed by education and discipline into the formidable Mamalukes. From the colony of Pera, the Genoese engaged with superior advantage in the lucrative trade of the Black Sea; and their industry supplied the Greeks with fish and corn; two articles of food almost equally important to a superstitious people. The spontaneous bounty of nature appears to have bestowed the harvests of Ukraine, the produce of a rude and savage husbandry; and the endless exportation of salt fish and caviare is annually renewed by the enormous sturgeons that are caught at the mouth of the Don or Tanais, in their last station of the rich mud and shallow water of the Mæotis. The waters of the Oxus, the Caspian, the Volga, and the Don, opened a rare and laborious passage for the gems and spices of India; and after three months' march the caravans of Carizme met the Italian vessels in the harbors of Crimæa. These various branches of trade were monopolized by the diligence and power of the Genoese. Their rivals of Venice and Pisa were forcibly expelled; the natives were awed by the castles and cities, which arose on the foundations of their humble factories; and their principal establishment of Caffa was besieged without effect by the Tartar powers. Destitute of a navy, the Greeks were oppressed by these haughty merchants, who fed, or famished, Constantinople, according to their interest. They proceeded to usurp the customs, the fishery, and even the toll, of the Bosphorus; and while they derived from these objects a revenue of two hundred thousand pieces of gold, a remnant of thirty thousand was reluctantly allowed to the emperor. The colony of Pera or Galata acted, in peace and war, as an independent state; and, as it will happen in distant settlements, the Genoese podesta too often forgot that he was the servant of his own masters.

These usurpations were encouraged by the weakness of the elder Andronicus, and by the civil wars that afflicted his age and the minority of his grandson. The talents of Cantacuzene were employed to the ruin, rather than the restoration, of the empire; and after his domestic victory, he was condemned to an ignominious trial, whether the Greeks or the Genoese should reign in Constantinople. The merchants of Pera were offended by his refusal of some contiguous land, some commanding heights, which they proposed to cover with new fortifications; and in the absence of the emperor, who was detained at Demotica by sickness, they ventured to brave the debility of a female reign. A Byzantine vessel, which had presumed to fish at the mouth of the harbor, was sunk by these audacious strangers; the fishermen were murdered. Instead of suing for pardon, the Genoese demanded satisfaction; required, in a haughty strain, that the Greeks should renounce the exercise of navigation; and encountered with regular arms the first sallies of the popular indignation. They instantly occupied the debatable land; and by the labor of a whole people, of either sex and of every age, the wall was raised, and the ditch was sunk, with incredible speed. At the same time, they attacked and burnt two Byzantine galleys; while the three others, the remainder of the Imperial navy, escaped from their hands: the habitations without the gates, or along the shore, were pillaged and destroyed; and the care of the regent, of the empress Irene, was confined to the preservation of the city. The return of Cantacuzene dispelled the public consternation: the emperor inclined to peaceful counsels; but he yielded to the obstinacy of his enemies, who rejected all reasonable terms, and to the ardor of his subjects, who threatened, in the style of Scripture, to break them in pieces like a potter's vessel. Yet they reluctantly paid the taxes, that he imposed for the construction of ships, and the expenses of the war; and as the two nations were masters, the one of the land, the other of the sea, Constantinople and Pera were pressed by the evils of a mutual siege. The merchants of the colony, who had believed that a few days would terminate the war, already murmured at their losses: the succors from their mother-country were delayed by the factions of Genoa; and the most cautious embraced the opportunity of a Rhodian vessel to remove their families and effects from the scene of hostility. In the spring, the Byzantine fleet, seven galleys and a train of smaller vessels, issued from the mouth of the harbor, and steered in a single line along the shore of Pera; unskilfully presenting their sides to the beaks of the adverse squadron. The crews were composed of peasants and mechanics; nor was their ignorance compensated by the native courage of Barbarians: the wind was strong, the waves were rough; and no sooner did the Greeks perceive a distant and inactive enemy, than they leaped headlong into the sea, from a doubtful, to an inevitable peril. The troops that marched to the attack of the lines of Pera were struck at the same moment with a similar panic; and the Genoese were astonished, and almost ashamed, at their double victory. Their triumphant vessels, crowned with flowers, and dragging after them the captive galleys, repeatedly passed and repassed before the palace: the only virtue of the emperor was patience; and the hope of revenge his sole consolation. Yet the distress of both parties interposed a temporary agreement; and the shame of the empire was disguised by a thin veil of dignity and power. Summoning the chiefs of the colony, Cantacuzene affected to despise the trivial object of the debate; and, after a mild reproof, most liberally granted the lands, which had been previously resigned to the seeming custody of his officers.

But the emperor was soon solicited to violate the treaty, and to join his arms with the Venetians, the perpetual enemies of Genoa and her colonies. While he compared the reasons of peace and war, his moderation was provoked by a wanton insult of the inhabitants of Pera, who discharged from their rampart a large stone that fell in the midst of Constantinople. On his just complaint, they coldly blamed the imprudence of their engineer; but the next day the insult was repeated; and they exulted in a second proof that the royal city was not beyond the reach of their artillery. Cantacuzene instantly signed his treaty with the Venetians; but the weight of the Roman empire was scarcely felt in the balance of these opulent and powerful republics. From the Straits of Gibraltar to the mouth of the Tanais, their fleets encountered each other with various success; and a memorable battle was fought in the narrow sea, under the walls of Constantinople. It would not be an easy task to reconcile the accounts of the Greeks, the Venetians, and the Genoese; and while I depend on the narrative of an impartial historian, I shall borrow from each nation the facts that redound to their own disgrace, and the honor of their foes. The Venetians, with their allies the Catalans, had the advantage of number; and their fleet, with the poor addition of eight Byzantine galleys, amounted to seventy-five sail: the Genoese did not exceed sixty-four; but in those times their ships of war were distinguished by the superiority of their size and strength. The names and families of their naval commanders, Pisani and Doria, are illustrious in the annals of their country; but the personal merit of the former was eclipsed by the fame and abilities of his rival. They engaged in tempestuous weather; and the tumultuary conflict was continued from the dawn to the extinction of light. The enemies of the Genoese applaud their prowess; the friends of the Venetians are dissatisfied with their behavior; but all parties agree in praising the skill and boldness of the Catalans, who, with many wounds, sustained the brunt of the action. On the separation of the fleets, the event might appear doubtful; but the thirteen Genoese galleys, that had been sunk or taken, were compensated by a double loss of the allies; of fourteen Venetians, ten Catalans, and two Greeks; and even the grief of the conquerors expressed the assurance and habit of more decisive victories. Pisani confessed his defeat, by retiring into a fortified harbor, from whence, under the pretext of the orders of the senate, he steered with a broken and flying squadron for the Isle of Candia, and abandoned to his rivals the sovereignty of the sea. In a public epistle, addressed to the doge and senate, Petrarch employs his eloquence to reconcile the maritime powers, the two luminaries of Italy. The orator celebrates the valor and victory of the Genoese, the first of men in the exercise of naval war: he drops a tear on the misfortunes of their Venetian brethren; but he exhorts them to pursue with fire and sword the base and perfidious Greeks; to purge the metropolis of the East from the heresy with which it was infected.

Deserted by their friends, the Greeks were incapable of resistance; and three months after the battle, the emperor Cantacuzene solicited and subscribed a treaty, which forever banished the Venetians and Catalans, and granted to the Genoese a monopoly of trade, and almost a right of dominion. The Roman empire (I smile in transcribing the name) might soon have sunk into a province of Genoa, if the ambition of the republic had not been checked by the ruin of her freedom and naval power. A long contest of one hundred and thirty years was determined by the triumph of Venice; and the factions of the Genoese compelled them to seek for domestic peace under the protection of a foreign lord, the duke of Milan, or the French king. Yet the spirit of commerce survived that of conquest; and the colony of Pera still awed the capital and navigated the Euxine, till it was involved by the Turks in the final servitude of Constantinople itself.

Moguls, Ottoman Turks. – Part One

Conquests of Zingis Khan and the Moguls from China to Poland. – Escape of Constantinople and the Greeks. – Origin of the Ottoman Turks in Bithynia. – Reigns and Victories of Othman, Orchan, Amurath the First, and Bajazet the First. – Foundation and Progress of the Turkish Monarchy in Asia and Europe. – Danger of Constantinople and the Greek Empire.

FROM THE PETTY QUARRELS of a city and her suburbs, from the cowardice and discord of the falling Greeks, I shall now ascend to the victorious Turks; whose domestic slavery was ennobled by martial discipline, religious enthusiasm, and the energy of the national character. The rise and progress of the Ottomans, the present sovereigns of Constantinople, are connected with the most important scenes of modern history; but they are founded on a previous knowledge of the great eruption of the Moguls and Tartars; whose rapid conquests may be compared with the primitive convulsions of nature, which have agitated and altered the surface of the globe. I have long since asserted my claim to introduce the nations, the immediate or remote authors of the fall of the Roman empire; nor can I refuse myself to those events, which, from their uncommon magnitude, will interest a philosophic mind in the history of blood.

From the spacious highlands between China, Siberia, and the Caspian Sea, the tide of emigration and war has repeatedly been poured. These ancient seats of the Huns and Turks were occupied in the twelfth century by many pastoral tribes, of the same descent and similar manners, which were united and led to conquest by the formidable Zingis.

In his ascent to greatness, that Barbarian (whose private appellation was Temugin) had trampled on the necks of his equals. His birth was noble; but it was the pride of victory, that the prince or people deduced his seventh ancestor from the immaculate conception of a virgin. His father had reigned over thirteen hordes, which composed about thirty or forty thousand families: above two thirds refused to pay tithes or obedience to his infant son; and at the age of thirteen, Temugin fought a battle against his rebellious subjects. The future conqueror of Asia was reduced to fly and to obey; but he rose superior to his fortune, and in his fortieth year he had established his fame and dominion over the circumjacent tribes. In a state of society, in which policy is rude and valor is universal, the ascendant of one man must be founded on his power and resolution to punish his enemies and recompense his friends. His first military league was ratified by the simple rites of sacrificing a horse and tasting of a running stream: Temugin pledged himself to divide with his followers the sweets and the bitters of life; and when he had shared among them his horses and apparel, he was rich in their gratitude and his own hopes. After his first victory, he placed seventy caldrons on the fire, and seventy of the most guilty rebels were cast headlong into the boiling water. The sphere of his attraction was continually enlarged by the ruin of the proud and the submission of the prudent; and the boldest chieftains might tremble, when they beheld, enchased in silver, the skull of the khan of Keraites; who, under the name of Prester John, had corresponded with the Roman pontiff and the princes of Europe. The ambition of Temugin condescended to employ the arts of superstition; and it was from a naked prophet, who could ascend to heaven on a white horse, that he accepted the title of Zingis, the *most great*; and a divine right to the conquest and dominion of the earth. In a general *couroultai*, or diet, he was seated on a felt, which was long afterwards revered as a relic, and solemnly proclaimed great khan, or emperor of the Moguls and Tartars. Of these kindred, though rival, names, the former had given birth to the imperial race; and the latter has been extended by accident or error over the spacious wilderness of the north.

The code of laws which Zingis dictated to his subjects was adapted to the preservation of a domestic peace, and the exercise of foreign hostility. The punishment of death was inflicted on the crimes of adultery, murder, perjury, and the capital thefts of a horse or ox; and the fiercest of men were mild and just in their intercourse with each other. The future election of the great khan was vested in the princes of his family and the heads of the tribes; and the regulations of the chase were essential to the pleasures and plenty of a Tartar camp. The victorious nation was held sacred from all servile labors, which were abandoned to slaves and strangers; and every labor was servile except the profession of arms. The service and discipline of the troops, who were armed with bows, cimeters, and iron maces, and divided by hundreds, thousands, and ten thousands, were the institutions of a veteran commander. Each officer and soldier was made responsible, under pain of death, for the safety and honor of his companions; and the spirit of conquest breathed in the law, that peace should never be granted unless to a vanquished and suppliant enemy. But it is the religion of Zingis that best deserves our wonder and applause. The Catholic inquisitors of Europe, who defended nonsense by cruelty, might have been confounded by the example of a Barbarian, who anticipated the lessons of philosophy, and established by his laws a system of pure theism and perfect toleration. His first and only article of faith was the existence of one God, the Author of all good; who fills by his presence the heavens and earth, which he has created by his power. The Tartars and Moguls were addicted to the idols of their peculiar tribes; and many of them had been converted by the foreign missionaries to the religions of Moses, of Mahomet, and of Christ. These various systems in freedom and concord were taught and practised within the precincts of the same camp; and the Bonze, the Imam, the Rabbi, the Nestorian, and the Latin priest, enjoyed the same honorable exemption from service and tribute: in the mosque of Bochara, the insolent victor might trample the Koran under his horse's feet, but the calm legislator respected the prophets and pontiffs of the most hostile sects. The reason of Zingis was not informed by books: the khan could neither read nor write; and, except the tribe of the Igours, the greatest part of the Moguls and Tartars were as illiterate as their sovereign. The memory of their exploits was preserved by tradition: sixty-eight years after the death of Zingis, these traditions were collected and transcribed; the brevity of their domestic annals may be supplied by the Chinese, Persians, Armenians, Syrians, Arabians, Greeks, Russians, Poles, Hungarians, and Latins; and each nation will deserve credit in the relation of their own disasters and defeats.

Moguls, Ottoman Turks. – Part Two

THE ARMS OF ZINGIS and his lieutenants successively reduced the hordes of the desert, who pitched their tents between the wall of China and the Volga; and the Mogul emperor became the monarch of the pastoral world, the lord of many millions of shepherds and soldiers, who felt their united strength, and were impatient to rush on the mild and wealthy climates of the south. His ancestors had been the tributaries of the Chinese emperors; and Temugin himself had been disgraced by a title of honor and servitude. The court of Pekin was astonished by an embassy from its former vassal, who, in the tone of the king of nations, exacted the tribute and obedience which he had paid, and who affected to treat the *son of heaven* as the most contemptible of mankind. A haughty answer disguised their secret apprehensions; and their fears were soon justified by the march of innumerable squadrons, who pierced on all sides the feeble rampart of the great wall. Ninety cities were stormed, or starved, by the Moguls; ten only escaped; and Zingis, from a knowledge of the filial piety of the Chinese, covered his vanguard with their captive parents; an unworthy, and by degrees a fruitless, abuse of the virtue of his enemies. His invasion was supported by the revolt of a hundred thousand Khitans, who guarded the frontier: yet he listened to a treaty; and a princess of China, three thousand horses, five hundred youths, and as many virgins, and a tribute of gold and silk, were the price of his retreat. In his second expedition, he compelled the Chinese emperor to retire beyond the yellow river to a more southern residence. The siege of Pekin was long and laborious: the inhabitants were reduced by famine to decimate and devour their fellow-citizens; when their ammunition was spent, they discharged ingots of gold and silver from their engines; but the Moguls introduced a mine to the centre of the capital; and the conflagration of the palace burnt above thirty days. China was desolated by Tartar war and domestic faction; and the five northern provinces were added to the empire of Zingis.

In the West, he touched the dominions of Mohammed, sultan of Carizme, who reigned from the Persian Gulf to the borders of India and Turkestan; and who, in the proud imitation of Alexander the Great, forgot the servitude and ingratitude of his fathers to the house of Seljuk. It was the wish of Zingis to establish a friendly and commercial intercourse with the most powerful of the Moslem princes: nor could he be tempted by the secret solicitations of the caliph of Bagdad, who sacrificed to his personal wrongs the safety of the church and state. A rash and inhuman deed provoked and justified the Tartar arms in the invasion of the southern Asia. A caravan of three ambassadors and one hundred and fifty merchants were arrested and murdered at Otrar, by the command of Mohammed; nor was it till after a demand and denial of justice, till he had prayed and fasted three nights on a mountain, that the Mogul emperor appealed to the judgment of God and his sword. Our European battles, says a philosophic writer, are petty skirmishes, if compared to the numbers that have fought and fallen in the fields of Asia. Seven hundred thousand Moguls and Tartars are said to have marched under the standard of Zingis and his four sons. In the vast plains that extend to the north of the Sihon or Jaxartes, they were encountered by four hundred thousand soldiers of the sultan; and in the first battle, which was suspended by the night, one hundred and sixty thousand Carizmians were slain. Mohammed was astonished by the multitude and valor of his enemies: he withdrew from the scene of danger, and distributed his troops in the frontier towns; trusting that the Barbarians, invincible in the field, would be repulsed by the length and difficulty of so many regular sieges. But the prudence of Zingis had formed a body of Chinese engineers, skilled in the mechanic arts; informed perhaps of the secret of gunpowder, and capable, under his discipline, of attacking a foreign country with more vigor and success than they had defended their own. The Persian historians will relate the sieges and reduction of Otrar, Cogende, Bochara, Samarcand, Carizme, Herat, Merou, Nisabour, Balch, and Candahar; and the conquest of the rich and populous countries of Transoxiana, Carizme, and Chorazan. The destructive hostilities of Attila and the Huns have long since been elucidated by the example of Zingis and the Moguls; and in this more proper place I shall be content to observe, that, from the Caspian to the Indus, they ruined a tract of many hundred miles, which was adorned with the habitations and labors of mankind, and that five centuries have not been sufficient to repair the ravages of four years. The Mogul emperor encouraged or indulged the fury of his troops: the hope of future possession was lost in the ardor of rapine and slaughter; and the cause of the war exasperated their native fierceness by the pretence of justice and revenge. The downfall and death of the sultan Mohammed, who expired, unpitied and alone, in a desert island of the Caspian Sea, is a poor atonement for the calamities of which he was the author. Could the Carizmian empire have been saved by a single hero, it would have been saved by his son Gelaleddin, whose active valor repeatedly checked the Moguls in the career of victory. Retreating, as he fought, to the banks of the Indus, he was oppressed by their innumerable host, till, in the last moment of despair, Gelaleddin spurred his horse into the waves, swam one of the broadest and most rapid rivers of Asia, and extorted the admiration and applause of Zingis himself. It was in this camp that the Mogul conqueror yielded with reluctance to the murmurs of his weary and wealthy troops, who sighed for the enjoyment of their native land. Eucumbered with the spoils of Asia, he slowly measured back his footsteps, betrayed some pity for the misery of the vanquished, and declared his intention of rebuilding the cities which had been swept away by the tempest of his arms. After he had repassed the Oxus and Jaxartes, he was joined by two generals, whom he had detached with thirty thousand horse, to subdue the western provinces of Persia. They had trampled on the nations which opposed their passage, penetrated through the gates of Derbent, traversed the Volga and the desert, and accomplished the circuit of the Caspian Sea, by an expedition which had never been attempted, and has never been repeated. The return of Zingis was signalized by the overthrow of the rebellious or independent kingdoms of Tartary; and he died in the fulness of years and glory, with his last breath exhorting and instructing his sons to achieve the conquest of the Chinese empire.

The harem of Zingis was composed of five hundred wives and concubines; and of his numerous progeny, four sons, illustrious by their birth and merit, exercised under their father the principal offices of peace and war. Toushi was his great huntsman, Zagatai his judge, Octai his minister, and Tuli his general; and their names and actions are often conspicuous in the history of his conquests. Firmly united for their own and the public interest, the three brothers and their families were content with dependent sceptres; and Octai, by general consent, was proclaimed great khan, or emperor of the Moguls and Tartars. He was succeeded by his son Gayuk, after whose death the empire devolved to his cousins Mangou and Cublai, the sons of Tuli, and the grandsons of Zingis. In the sixty-eight years of his four first successors, the Mogul subdued almost all Asia, and a large portion of Europe. Without confining myself to the order of time, without expatiating on the detail of events, I shall present a general picture of the progress of their arms; I. In the East; II. In the South; III. In the West; and IV. In the North.

I. Before the invasion of Zingis, China was divided into two empires or dynasties of the North and South; and the difference of origin and interest was smoothed by a general conformity of laws, language, and national manners. The Northern empire, which had been dismembered by Zingis, was finally subdued seven years after his death. After the loss of Pekin, the emperor had fixed his residence at Kaifong, a city many leagues in circumference, and which contained, according to the Chinese annals, fourteen hundred thousand families of inhabitants and fugitives. He escaped from thence with only seven horsemen, and made his last stand in a third capital, till at length the hopeless monarch, protesting his innocence and accusing his fortune, ascended a funeral pile, and gave orders, that, as soon as he had stabbed himself, the fire should be kindled by his attendants. The dynasty of the *Song*, the native and ancient sovereigns of the whole empire, survived about forty-five years the fall of the Northern usurpers; and the perfect conquest was reserved for the arms of Cublai. During this interval, the Moguls were often diverted by foreign wars; and, if the Chinese seldom dared to meet their victors in the field, their passive courage presented and endless succession of cities to storm and of millions to slaughter. In the attack and defence of places, the engines of antiquity and the Greek fire were alternately employed: the use of gunpowder in cannon and bombs appears as a familiar practice; and the sieges were conducted by the Mahometans and Franks, who had been liberally invited into the service of Cublai. After passing the great river, the troops and artillery were conveyed along a series of canals, till they invested the royal residence of Hamcheu, or Quinsay, in the country of silk, the most delicious climate of China. The emperor, a defenceless youth, surrendered his person and sceptre; and before he was sent in exile into Tartary, he struck nine times the ground with his forehead, to adore in prayer or thanksgiving the mercy of the great khan. Yet the war (it was now styled a rebellion) was still maintained in the southern provinces from Hamcheu to Canton; and the obstinate remnant of independence and hostility was transported from the land to the sea. But when the fleet of the *Song* was surrounded and oppressed by a superior armament, their last champion leaped into the waves with his infant emperor in his arms. "It is more glorious," he cried, "to die a prince, than to live a slave." A hundred thousand Chinese imitated his example; and the whole empire, from Tonkin to the great wall, submitted to the dominion of Cublai. His boundless ambition aspired to the conquest of Japan: his fleet was twice shipwrecked; and the lives of a hundred thousand Moguls and Chinese were sacrificed in the fruitless expedition. But the circumjacent kingdoms, Corea, Tonkin, Cochinchina, Pegu, Bengal, and Thibet, were reduced in different degrees of tribute and obedience by the effort or terror of his arms. He explored the Indian Ocean with a fleet of a thousand ships: they sailed in sixty-eight days, most probably to the Isle of Borneo, under the equinoctial line; and though they returned not without spoil or glory, the emperor was dissatisfied that the savage king had escaped from their hands.

II. The conquest of Hindostan by the Moguls was reserved in a later period for the house of Timour; but that of Iran, or Persia, was achieved by Holagou Khan, the grandson of Zingis, the brother and lieutenant of the two successive emperors, Mangou and Cublai. I shall not enumerate the crowd of sultans, emirs, and atabeks, whom he trampled into dust; but the extirpation of the *Assassins*, or Ismaelians of Persia, may be considered as a service to mankind. Among the hills to the south of the Caspian, these odious sectaries had reigned with impunity above a hundred and sixty years; and their prince, or Imam, established his lieutenant to lead and govern the colony of Mount Libanus, so famous and formidable in the history of the crusades. With the fanaticism of the Koran the Ismaelians had blended the Indian transmigration, and the visions of their own prophets; and it was their first duty to devote their souls and bodies in blind obedience to the vicar of God. The daggers of his missionaries were felt both in the East and West: the Christians and the Moslems enumerate, and persons multiply, the illustrious victims that were sacrificed to the zeal, avarice, or resentment of *the old man* (as he was corruptly styled) *of the mountain*. But these daggers, his only arms, were broken by the sword of Holagou, and not a vestige is left of the enemies of mankind, except the word *assassin*, which, in the most odious sense, has been adopted in the languages of Europe. The extinction of the Abbassides cannot be indifferent to the spectators of their greatness and decline. Since the fall of their Seljukian tyrants the caliphs had recovered their lawful dominion of Bagdad and the Arabian Irak; but the city was distracted by theological factions, and the commander of the faithful was lost in a harem of seven hundred concubines. The invasion of the Moguls he encountered with feeble arms and haughty embassies. "On the divine decree," said the caliph Mostasem, "is founded the throne of the sons of Abbas: and their foes shall surely be destroyed in this world and in the next. Who is this Holagou that dares to rise against them? If he be desirous of peace, let him instantly depart from the sacred territory; and perhaps he may obtain from our clemency the pardon of his fault." This presumption was cherished by a perfidious vizier, who assured his master, that, even if the Barbarians had entered the city, the women and children, from the terraces, would be sufficient to overwhelm them with stones. But when Holagou touched the phantom, it instantly vanished into smoke. After a siege of two months, Bagdad was stormed and sacked by the Moguls; and their savage commander pronounced the death of the caliph Mostasem, the last of the temporal successors of Mahomet; whose noble kinsmen, of the race of Abbas, had reigned in Asia above five hundred years. Whatever might be the designs of the conqueror, the holy cities of Mecca and Medina were protected by the Arabian desert; but the Moguls spread beyond the Tigris and Euphrates, pillaged Aleppo and Damascus, and threatened to join the Franks in the deliverance of Jerusalem. Egypt was lost, had she been defended only by her feeble offspring; but the Mamalukes had breathed in their infancy the keenness of a Scythian air: equal in valor, superior in discipline, they met the Moguls in many a well-fought field; and drove back the stream of hostility to the eastward of the Euphrates. But it overflowed with resistless violence the kingdoms of Armenia and Anatolia, of which the former was possessed by the Christians, and the latter by the Turks. The sultans of Iconium opposed some resistance to the Mogul arms, till Azzadin sought a refuge among the Greeks of Constantinople, and his feeble successors, the last of the Seljukian dynasty, were finally extirpated by the khans of Persia.

III. No sooner had Octai subverted the northern empire of China, than he resolved to visit with his arms the most remote countries of the West. Fifteen hundred thousand Moguls and Tartars were inscribed on the military roll: of these the great khan selected a third, which he intrusted to the command of his nephew Batou, the son of Tuli; who reigned over his father's conquests to the north of the Caspian Sea. After a festival of forty days, Batou set forwards on this great expedition; and such was the speed and ardor of his innumerable squadrons, than in less than six years they had measured a line of ninety degrees of longitude, a fourth part of the circumference of the globe. The great rivers of Asia and Europe, the Volga and Kama, the Don and Borysthenes, the Vistula and Danube, they either swam with their horses or passed on the ice, or traversed in leathern boats, which followed the camp, and transported their wagons and artillery. By the first victories of Batou, the remains of national freedom were eradicated in the immense plains of Turkestan and Kipzak. In his rapid progress, he overran the kingdoms, as they are now styled, of Astracan and Cazan; and the troops which he detached towards Mount Caucasus explored the most secret recesses of Georgia and Circassia. The civil discord of the great dukes, or princes, of Russia, betrayed their country to the Tartars. They spread from Livonia to the Black Sea, and both Moscow and Kiow, the modern and the ancient capitals, were reduced to ashes; a temporary ruin, less fatal than the deep, and perhaps indelible, mark, which a servitude of two hundred years has imprinted on the character of the Russians. The Tartars ravaged with equal fury the countries which they hoped to possess, and those which they were hastening to leave. From the permanent conquest of Russia they made a deadly, though transient, inroad into the heart of Poland, and as far as the borders of Germany. The cities of Lublin and Cracow were obliterated: they approached the shores of the Baltic; and in the battle of Lignitz they defeated the dukes of Silesia, the Polish palatines, and the great master of the Teutonic order, and filled nine sacks with the right ears of the slain. From Lignitz, the extreme point of their western march, they turned aside to the invasion of Hungary; and the presence or spirit of Batou inspired the host of five hundred thousand men: the Carpathian hills could not be long impervious to their divided columns; and their approach had been fondly disbelieved till it was irresistibly felt. The king, Bela the Fourth, assembled the military force of his counts and bishops; but he had alienated the nation by adopting a vagrant horde of forty thousand families of Comans, and these savage guests were provoked to revolt by the suspicion of treachery and the murder of their prince. The whole country north of the Danube was lost in a day, and depopulated in a summer; and the ruins of cities and churches were overspread with the bones of the natives, who expiated the sins of their Turkish ancestors. An ecclesiastic, who fled from the sack of Waradin, describes the calamities which he had seen, or suffered; and the sanguinary rage of sieges and battles is far less atrocious than the treatment of the fugitives, who had been allured from the woods under a promise of peace and pardon and who were coolly slaughtered as soon as they had performed the labors of the harvest and vintage. In the winter the Tartars passed the Danube on the ice, and advanced to Gran or Strigonium, a German colony, and the metropolis of the kingdom. Thirty engines were planted against the walls; the ditches were filled with sacks of earth and dead bodies; and after a promiscuous massacre, three hundred noble matrons were slain in the presence of the khan. Of all the cities and fortresses of Hungary, three alone survived the Tartar invasion, and the unfortunate Bata hid his head among the islands of the Adriatic.

The Latin world was darkened by this cloud of savage hostility: a Russian fugitive carried the alarm to Sweden; and the remote nations of the Baltic and the ocean trembled at the approach of the Tartars, whom their fear and ignorance were inclined to separate from the human species. Since the invasion of the Arabs in the eighth century, Europe had never been exposed to a similar calamity: and if the disciples of Mahomet would have oppressed her religion and liberty, it might be apprehended that the shepherds of Scythia would extinguish her cities, her arts, and all the institutions of civil society. The Roman pontiff attempted to appease and convert these invincible Pagans by a mission of Franciscan and Dominican friars; but he was astonished by the reply of the khan, that the sons of God and of Zingis were invested with a divine power to subdue or extirpate the nations; and that the pope would be involved in the universal destruction, unless he visited in person, and as a suppliant, the royal horde. The emperor Frederic the Second embraced a more generous mode of defence; and his letters to the kings of France and England, and the princes of Germany, represented the common danger, and urged them to arm their vassals in this just and rational crusade. The Tartars themselves were awed by the fame and valor of the Franks; the town of Newstadt in Austria was bravely defended against them by fifty knights and twenty crossbows; and they raised the siege on the appearance of a German army. After wasting the adjacent kingdoms of Servia, Bosnia, and Bulgaria, Batou slowly retreated from the Danube to the Volga to enjoyed the rewards of victory in the city and palace of Serai, which started at his command from the midst of the desert.

IV. Even the poor and frozen regions of the north attracted the arms of the Moguls: Sheibani khan, the brother of the great Batou, led a horde of fifteen thousand families into the wilds of Siberia; and his descendants reigned at Tobolskoi above three centuries, till the Russian conquest. The spirit of enterprise which pursued the course of the Oby and Yenisei must have led to the discovery of the icy sea. After brushing away the monstrous fables, of men with dogs' heads and cloven feet, we shall find, that, fifteen years after the death of Zingis, the Moguls were informed of the name and manners of the Samoyedes in the neighborhood of the polar circle, who dwelt in subterraneous huts, and derived their furs and their food from the sole occupation of hunting.

While China, Syria, and Poland, were invaded at the same time by the Moguls and Tartars, the authors of the mighty mischief were content with the knowledge and declaration, that their word was the sword of death. Like the first caliphs, the first successors of Zingis seldom appeared in person at the head of their victorious armies. On the banks of the Onon and Selinga, the royal or *golden horde* exhibited the contrast of simplicity and greatness; of the roasted sheep and mare's milk which composed their banquets; and of a distribution in one day of five hundred wagons of gold and silver. The ambassadors and princes of Europe and Asia were compelled to undertake this distant and laborious pilgrimage; and the life and reign of the great dukes of Russia, the kings of Georgia and Armenia, the sultans of Iconium, and the emirs of Persia, were decided by the frown or smile of the great khan. The sons and grandsons of Zingis had been accustomed to the pastoral life; but the village of Caracorum was gradually ennobled by their election and residence. A change of manners is implied in the removal of Octai and Mangou from a tent to a house; and their example was imitated by the princes of their family and the great officers of the empire. Instead of the boundless forest, the enclosure of a park afforded the more indolent pleasures of the chase; their new habitations were decorated with painting and sculpture; their superfluous treasures were cast in fountains, and basins, and statues of massy silver; and the artists of China and Paris vied with each other in the service of the great khan. Caracorum contained two streets, the one of Chinese mechanics, the other of Mahometan traders; and the places of religious worship, one Nestorian church, two mosques, and twelve temples of various idols, may represent in some degree the number and division of inhabitants. Yet a French missionary declares, that the town of St. Denys, near Paris, was more considerable than the Tartar capital; and that the whole palace of Mangou was scarcely equal to a tenth part of that Benedictine abbey. The conquests of Russia and Syria might amuse the vanity of the great khans; but they were seated on the borders of China; the acquisition of that empire was the nearest and most interesting object; and they might learn from their pastoral economy, that it is for the advantage of the shepherd to protect and propagate his flock. I have already celebrated the wisdom and virtue of a Mandarin who prevented the desolation of five populous and cultivated provinces. In a spotless administration of thirty years, this friend of his country and of mankind continually labored to mitigate, or suspend, the havoc of war; to save the monuments, and to rekindle the flame, of science; to restrain the military commander by the restoration of civil magistrates; and to instil the love of peace and justice into the minds of the Moguls. He struggled with the barbarism of the first conquerors; but his salutary lessons produced a rich harvest in the second generation. The northern, and by degrees the southern, empire acquiesced in the government of Cublai, the lieutenant, and afterwards the successor, of Mangou; and the nation was loyal to a prince who had been educated in the manners of China. He restored the forms of her venerable constitution; and the victors submitted to the laws, the fashions, and even the prejudices, of the vanquished people. This peaceful triumph, which has been more than once repeated, may be ascribed, in a great measure, to the numbers and servitude of the Chinese. The Mogul army was dissolved in a vast and populous country; and their emperors adopted with pleasure a political system, which gives to the prince the solid substance of despotism, and leaves to the subject the empty names of philosophy, freedom, and filial obedience. Under the reign of Cublai, letters and commerce, peace and justice, were restored; the great canal, of five hundred miles, was opened from Nankin to the capital: he fixed his residence at Pekin; and displayed in his court the magnificence of the greatest monarch of Asia. Yet this learned prince declined from the pure and simple religion of his great ancestor: he sacrificed to the idol Fo; and his blind attachment to the lamas of Thibet and the bonzes of China provoked the censure of the disciples of Confucius. His successors polluted the palace with a crowd of eunuchs, physicians, and astrologers, while thirteen millions of their subjects were consumed in the provinces by famine. One hundred and forty years after the death of Zingis, his degenerate race, the dynasty of the Yuen, was expelled by a revolt of the native Chinese; and the Mogul emperors were lost in the oblivion of the desert. Before this revolution, they had forfeited their supremacy over the dependent branches of their house, the khans of Kipzak and Russia, the khans of Zagatai, or Transoxiana, and the khans of Iran or Persia. By their distance and power, these royal lieutenants had soon been released from the duties of obedience; and after the death of Cublai, they scorned to accept a sceptre or a title from his unworthy successors. According to their respective situations, they maintained the simplicity of the pastoral life, or assumed the luxury of the cities of Asia; but the princes and their hordes were alike disposed for the reception of a foreign worship. After some hesitation between the Gospel and the Koran, they conformed to the religion of Mahomet; and while they adopted for their brethren the Arabs and Persians, they renounced all intercourse with the ancient Moguls, the idolaters of China.

Moguls, Ottoman Turks. – Part Three

IN THIS SHIPWRECK OF nations, some surprise may be excited by the escape of the Roman empire, whose relics, at the time of the Mogul invasion, were dismembered by the Greeks and Latins. Less potent than Alexander, they were pressed, like the Macedonian, both in Europe and Asia, by the shepherds of Scythia; and had the Tartars undertaken the siege, Constantinople must have yielded to the fate of Pekin, Samarcand, and Bagdad. The glorious and voluntary retreat of Batou from the Danube was insulted by the vain triumph of the Franks and Greeks; and in a second expedition death surprised him in full march to attack the capital of the Cæsars. His brother Borga carried the Tartar arms into Bulgaria and Thrace; but he was diverted from the Byzantine war by a visit to Novogorod, in the fifty-seventh degree of latitude, where he numbered the inhabitants and regulated the tributes of Russia. The Mogul khan formed an alliance with the Mamalukes against his brethren of Persia: three hundred thousand horse penetrated through the gates of Derbend; and the Greeks might rejoice in the first example of domestic war. After the recovery of Constantinople, Michael Palæologus, at a distance from his court and army, was surprised and surrounded in a Thracian castle, by twenty thousand Tartars. But the object of their march was a private interest: they came to the deliverance of Azzadin, the Turkish sultan; and were content with his person and the treasure of the emperor. Their general Noga, whose name is perpetuated in the hordes of Astracan, raised a formidable rebellion against Mengo Timour, the third of the khans of Kipzak; obtained in marriage Maria, the natural daughter of Palæologus; and guarded the dominions of his friend and father. The subsequent invasions of a Scythian cast were those of outlaws and fugitives: and some thousands of Alani and Comans, who had been driven from their native seats, were reclaimed from a vagrant life, and enlisted in the service of the empire. Such was the influence in Europe of the invasion of the Moguls. The first terror of their arms secured, rather than disturbed, the peace of the Roman Asia. The sultan of Iconium solicited a personal interview with John Vataces; and his artful policy encouraged the Turks to defend their barrier against the common enemy. That barrier indeed was soon overthrown; and the servitude and ruin of the Seljukians exposed the nakedness of the Greeks. The formidable Holagou threatened to march to Constantinople at the head of four hundred thousand men; and the groundless panic of the citizens of Nice will present an image of the terror which he had inspired. The accident of a procession, and the sound of a doleful litany, "From the fury of the Tartars, good Lord, deliver us," had scattered the hasty report of an assault and massacre. In the blind credulity of fear, the streets of Nice were crowded with thousands of both sexes, who knew not from what or to whom they fled; and some hours elapsed before the firmness of the military officers could relieve the city from this imaginary foe. But the ambition of Holagou and his successors was fortunately diverted by the conquest of Bagdad, and a long vicissitude of Syrian wars; their hostility to the Moslems inclined them to unite with the Greeks and Franks; and their generosity or contempt had offered the kingdom of Anatolia as the reward of an Armenian vassal. The fragments of the Seljukian monarchy were disputed by the emirs who had occupied the cities or the mountains; but they all confessed the supremacy of the khans of Persia; and he often interposed his authority, and sometimes his arms, to check their depredations, and to preserve the peace and balance of his Turkish frontier. The death of Cazan, one of the greatest and most accomplished princes of the house of Zingis, removed this salutary control; and the decline of the Moguls gave a free scope to the rise and progress of the Ottoman Empire.

After the retreat of Zingis, the sultan Gelaleddin of Carizme had returned from India to the possession and defence of his Persian kingdoms. In the space of eleven years, that hero fought in person fourteen battles; and such was his activity, that he led his cavalry in seventeen days from Teflis to Kerman, a march of a thousand miles. Yet he was oppressed by the jealousy of the Moslem princes, and the innumerable armies of the Moguls; and after his last defeat, Gelaleddin perished ignobly in the mountains of Cúurdistan. His death dissolved a veteran and adventurous army, which included under the name of Carizmians or Corasmins many Turkman hordes, that had attached themselves to the sultan's fortune. The bolder and more powerful chiefs invaded

Syria, and violated the holy sepulchre of Jerusalem: the more humble engaged in the service of Aladin, sultan of Iconium; and among these were the obscure fathers of the Ottoman line. They had formerly pitched their tents near the southern banks of the Oxus, in the plains of Mahan and Nesa; and it is somewhat remarkable, that the same spot should have produced the first authors of the Parthian and Turkish empires. At the head, or in the rear, of a Carizmian army, Soliman Shah was drowned in the passage of the Euphrates: his son Orthogrul became the soldier and subject of Aladin, and established at Surgut, on the banks of the Sangar, a camp of four hundred families or tents, whom he governed fifty-two years both in peace and war. He was the father of Thaman, or Athman, whose Turkish name has been melted into the appellation of the caliph Othman; and if we describe that pastoral chief as a shepherd and a robber, we must separate from those characters all idea of ignominy and baseness. Othman possessed, and perhaps surpassed, the ordinary virtues of a soldier; and the circumstances of time and place were propitious to his independence and success. The Seljukian dynasty was no more; and the distance and decline of the Mogul khans soon enfranchised him from the control of a superior. He was situate on the verge of the Greek empire: the Koran sanctified his *gazi*, or holy war, against the infidels; and their political errors unlocked the passes of Mount Olympus, and invited him to descend into the plains of Bithynia. Till the reign of Palæologus, these passes had been vigilantly guarded by the militia of the country, who were repaid by their own safety and an exemption from taxes. The emperor abolished their privilege and assumed their office; but the tribute was rigorously collected, the custody of the passes was neglected, and the hardy mountaineers degenerated into a trembling crowd of peasants without spirit or discipline. It was on the twenty-seventh of July, in the year twelve hundred and ninety-nine of the Christian æra, that Othman first invaded the territory of Nicomedia; and the singular accuracy of the date seems to disclose some foresight of the rapid and destructive growth of the monster. The annals of the twenty-seven years of his reign would exhibit a repetition of the same inroads; and his hereditary troops were multiplied in each campaign by the accession of captives and volunteers. Instead of retreating to the hills, he maintained the most useful and defensive posts; fortified the towns and castles which he had first pillaged; and renounced the pastoral life for the baths and palaces of his infant capitals. But it was not till Othman was oppressed by age and infirmities, that he received the welcome news of the conquest of Prusa, which had been surrendered by famine or treachery to the arms of his son Orchan. The glory of Othman is chiefly founded on that of his descendants; but the Turks have transcribed or composed a royal testament of his last counsels of justice and moderation.

From the conquest of Prusa, we may date the true æra of the Ottoman empire. The lives and possessions of the Christian subjects were redeemed by a tribute or ransom of thirty thousand crowns of gold; and the city, by the labors of Orchan, assumed the aspect of a Mahometan capital; Prusa was decorated with a mosque, a college, and a hospital, of royal foundation; the Seljukian coin was changed for the name and impression of the new dynasty: and the most skilful professors, of human and divine knowledge, attracted the Persian and Arabian students from the ancient schools of Oriental learning. The office of vizier was instituted for Aladin, the brother of Orchan; and a different habit distinguished the citizens from the peasants, the Moslems from the infidels. All the troops of Othman had consisted of loose squadrons of Turkman cavalry; who served without pay and fought without discipline: but a regular body of infantry was first established and trained by the prudence of his son. A great number of volunteers was enrolled with a small stipend, but with the permission of living at home, unless they were summoned to the field: their rude manners, and seditious temper, disposed Orchan to educate his young captives as his soldiers and those of the prophet; but the Turkish peasants were still allowed to mount on horseback, and follow his standard, with the appellation and the hopes of *freebooters*. By these arts he formed an army of twenty-five thousand Moslems: a train of battering engines was framed for the use of sieges; and the first successful experiment was made on the cities of Nice and Nicomedia. Orchan granted a safe-conduct to all who were desirous of departing with their families and effects; but the widows of the slain were given in marriage to the conquerors; and the sacrilegious plunder, the books, the vases, and the images, were sold or ransomed at Constantinople. The emperor Andronicus the Younger was vanquished and wounded by the son of Othman: he subdued the whole province or kingdom of Bithynia, as far as the shores of the Bosphorus and Hellespont; and the Christians confessed the justice and clemency of a reign which claimed the voluntary attachment of the Turks of Asia. Yet Orchan was content with the modest title of emir; and in the list of his compeers, the princes of Roum or Anatolia, his military forces were surpassed by the emirs of Ghermian and Caramania, each of whom could bring into the field an army of forty thousand men. Their domains were situate in the heart of the Seljukian kingdom; but the holy warriors, though of inferior note, who formed new principalities on the Greek empire, are more conspicuous in the light of history. The maritime country from the Propontis to the Mæander and the Isle of Rhodes, so long threatened and so often pillaged, was finally lost about the thirteenth year of Andronicus the Elder. Two Turkish chieftains, Sarukhan and Aidin, left their names to their conquests, and their conquests to their posterity. The captivity or ruin of the *seven* churches of Asia was consummated; and the barbarous lords of Ionia and Lydia still trample on the monuments of classic and Christian antiquity. In the loss of Ephesus, the Christians deplored the fall of the first angel, the extinction of the first candlestick, of the Revelations; the desolation is complete; and the temple of Diana, or the church of Mary, will equally elude the search of the curious traveller. The circus and three stately theatres of Laodicea are now peopled with wolves and foxes; Sardes is reduced to a miserable village; the God of Mahomet, without a rival or a son, is invoked in the mosques of Thyatira and Pergamus; and the populousness of Smyrna is supported by the foreign trade of the Franks and Armenians. Philadelphia alone has been saved by prophecy, or courage. At a distance from the sea, forgotten by the emperors, encompassed on all sides by the Turks, her valiant citizens defended their religion and freedom above fourscore years; and at length capitulated with the proudest of the Ottomans. Among the Greek colonies and churches of Asia, Philadelphia is still erect; a column in a scene of ruins; a pleasing example, that the paths of honor and safety may sometimes be the same. The servitude of Rhodes was delayed about two centuries by the establishment of the knights of St. John of Jerusalem: under the discipline of the order, that island emerged into fame and opulence; the noble and warlike monks were renowned by land and sea: and the bulwark of Christendom provoked, and repelled, the arms of the Turks and Saracens.

The Greeks, by their intestine divisions, were the authors of their final ruin. During the civil wars of the elder and younger Andronicus, the son of Othman achieved, almost without resistance, the conquest of Bithynia; and the same disorders encouraged the Turkish emirs of Lydia and Ionia to build a fleet, and to pillage the adjacent islands and the sea-coast of Europe. In the defence of his life and honor, Cantacuzene was tempted to prevent, or imitate, his adversaries, by calling to his aid the public enemies of his religion and country. Amir, the son of Aidin, concealed under a Turkish garb the humanity and politeness of a Greek; he was united with the great domestic by mutual esteem and reciprocal services; and their friendship is compared, in the vain rhetoric of the times, to the perfect union of Orestes and Pylades. On the report of the danger of his friend, who was persecuted by an ungrateful court, the prince of Ionia assembled at Smyrna a fleet of three hundred vessels, with an army of twenty-nine thousand men; sailed in the depth of winter, and cast anchor at the mouth of the Hebrus. From thence, with a chosen band of two thousand Turks, he marched along the banks of the river, and rescued the empress, who was besieged in Demotica by the wild Bulgarians. At that disastrous moment, the life or death of his beloved Cantacuzene was concealed by his flight into Servia: but the grateful Irene, impatient to behold her deliverer, invited him to enter the city, and accompanied her message with a present of rich apparel and a hundred horses. By a peculiar strain of delicacy, the Gentle Barbarian refused, in the absence of an unfortunate friend, to visit his wife, or to taste the luxuries of the palace; sustained in his tent the rigor of the winter; and rejected the hospitable gift, that he might share the hardships of two thousand companions, all as deserving as himself of that honor and distinction. Necessity and revenge might justify his predatory excursions by sea and land: he left nine thousand five hundred men for the guard of his fleet; and persevered in the fruitless search of Cantacuzene, till his embarkation was hastened by a fictitious letter, the severity of the season, the clamors of his independent troops, and the weight of his spoil and captives. In the prosecution of the civil war, the prince of Ionia twice returned to Europe; joined his arms with those of the emperor; besieged Thessalonica, and threatened Constantinople. Calumny might affix some reproach on his imperfect aid, his hasty departure, and a bribe of ten thousand crowns, which he accepted from the Byzantine court; but his friend was satisfied; and the conduct of Amir is excused by the more sacred duty of defending against the Latins his hereditary dominions. The maritime power of the Turks had united the pope, the king of Cyprus, the republic of Venice, and the order of St. John, in a laudable crusade; their galleys invaded the coast of Ionia; and Amir was slain with an arrow, in the attempt to wrest from the Rhodian knights the citadel of Smyrna. Before his death, he generously recommended another ally of his own nation; not more sincere or zealous than himself, but more able to afford a prompt and powerful succor, by his situation along the Propontis and in the front of Constantinople. By the prospect of a more advantageous treaty, the Turkish prince of Bithynia was detached from his engagements with Anne of Savoy; and the pride of Orchan dictated the most solemn protestations, that if he could obtain the daughter of Cantacuzene, he would invariably fulfil the duties of a subject and a son. Parental tenderness was silenced by the voice of ambition: the Greek clergy connived at the marriage of a Christian princess with a sectary of Mahomet; and the father of Theodora describes, with shameful satisfaction, the dishonor of the purple. A body of Turkish cavalry attended the ambassadors, who disembarked from thirty vessels, before his camp of Selybria. A stately pavilion was erected, in which the empress Irene passed the night with her daughters. In the morning, Theodora ascended a throne, which was surrounded with curtains of silk and gold: the troops were under arms; but the emperor alone was on horseback. At a signal the curtains were suddenly withdrawn to disclose the bride, or the victim, encircled by kneeling eunuchs and hymeneal torches: the sound of flutes and trumpets proclaimed the joyful event; and her pretended happiness was the theme of the nuptial song, which was chanted by such poets as the age could produce. Without the rites of the church, Theodora was delivered to her barbarous lord: but it had been stipulated, that she should preserve her religion in the harem of Bursa; and her father celebrates her charity and devotion in this ambiguous situation. After his peaceful establishment on the throne of Constantinople, the Greek emperor visited his Turkish ally, who with four sons, by various wives, expected him at Scutari, on the Asiatic shore. The two princes partook, with seeming cordiality, of the pleasures of the banquet and the chase; and Theodora was permitted to repass the Bosphorus, and to enjoy some days in the society of her mother. But the friendship of Orchan was subservient to his religion and interest; and in the Genoese war he joined without a blush the enemies of Cantacuzene.

In the treaty with the empress Anne, the Ottoman prince had inserted a singular condition, that it should be lawful for him to sell his prisoners at Constantinople, or transport them into Asia. A naked crowd of Christians of both sexes and every age, of priests and monks, of matrons and virgins, was exposed in the public market; the whip was frequently used to quicken the charity of redemption; and the indigent Greeks deplored the fate of their brethren, who were led away to the worst evils of temporal and spiritual bondage Cantacuzene was reduced to subscribe the same terms; and their execution must have been still more pernicious to the empire: a body of ten thousand Turks had been detached to the assistance of the empress Anne; but the entire forces of Orchan were exerted in the service of his father. Yet these calamities were of a transient nature; as soon as the storm had passed away, the fugitives might return to their habitations; and at the conclusion of the civil and foreign wars, Europe was completely evacuated by the Moslems of Asia. It was in his last quarrel with his pupil that Cantacuzene inflicted the deep and deadly wound, which could never be healed by his successors, and which is poorly expiated by his theological dialogues against the prophet Mahomet. Ignorant of their own history, the modern Turks confound their first and their final passage of the Hellespont, and describe the son of Orchan as a nocturnal robber, who, with eighty companions, explores by stratagem a hostile and unknown shore. Soliman, at the head of ten thousand horse, was transported in the vessels, and entertained as the friend, of the Greek emperor. In the civil wars of Romania, he performed some service and perpetrated more mischief; but the Chersonesus was insensibly filled with a Turkish colony; and the Byzantine court solicited in vain the restitution of the fortresses of Thrace. After some artful delays between the Ottoman prince and his son, their ransom was valued at sixty thousand crowns, and the first payment had been made when an earthquake shook the walls and cities of the provinces; the dismantled places were occupied by the Turks; and Gallipoli, the key of the Hellespont, was rebuilt and repeopled by the policy of Soliman. The abdication of Cantacuzene dissolved the feeble bands of domestic alliance; and his last advice admonished his countrymen to decline a rash contest, and to compare their own weakness with the numbers and valor, the discipline and enthusiasm, of the Moslems. His prudent counsels were despised by the headstrong vanity of youth, and soon justified by the victories of the Ottomans. But as he practised in the field the exercise of the *jerid*, Soliman was killed by a fall from his horse; and the aged Orchan wept and expired on the tomb of his valiant son.

Moguls, Ottoman Turks. – Part Four

BUT THE GREEKS HAD not time to rejoice in the death of their enemies; and the Turkish cimeter was wielded with the same spirit by Amurath the First, the son of Orchan, and the brother of Soliman. By the pale and fainting light of the Byzantine annals, we can discern, that he subdued without resistance the whole province of Romania or Thrace, from the Hellespont to Mount Hæmus, and the verge of the capital; and that Adrianople was chosen for the royal seat of his government and religion in Europe. Constantinople, whose decline is almost coeval with her foundation, had often, in the lapse of a thousand years, been assaulted by the Barbarians of the East and West; but never till this fatal hour had the Greeks been surrounded, both in Asia and Europe, by the arms of the same hostile monarchy. Yet the prudence or generosity of Amurath postponed for a while this easy conquest; and his pride was satisfied with the frequent and humble attendance of the emperor John Palæologus and his four sons, who followed at his summons the court and camp of the Ottoman prince. He marched against the Sclavonian nations between the Danube and the Adriatic, the Bulgarians, Servians, Bosnians, and Albanians; and these warlike tribes, who had so often insulted the majesty of the empire, were repeatedly broken by his destructive inroads. Their countries did not abound either in gold or silver; nor were their rustic hamlets and townships enriched by commerce or decorated by the arts of luxury. But the natives of the soil have been distinguished in every age by their hardiness of mind and body; and they were converted by a prudent institution into the firmest and most faithful supporters of the Ottoman greatness. The vizier of Amurath reminded his sovereign that, according to the Mahometan law, he was entitled to a fifth part of the spoil and captives; and that the duty might easily be levied, if vigilant officers were stationed in Gallipoli, to watch the passage, and to select for his use the stoutest and most beautiful of the Christian youth. The advice was followed: the edict was proclaimed; many thousands of the European captives were educated in religion and arms; and the new militia was consecrated and named by a celebrated dervis. Standing in the front of their ranks, he stretched the sleeve of his gown over the head of the foremost soldier, and his blessing was delivered in these words: "Let them be called Janizaries, (*Yengi cheri*, or new soldiers;) may their countenance be ever bright! their hand victorious! their sword keen! may their spear always hang over the heads of their enemies! and wheresoever they go, may they return with a *white face!*" Such was the origin of these haughty troops, the terror of the nations, and sometimes of the sultans themselves. Their valor has declined, their discipline is relaxed, and their tumultuary array is incapable of contending with the order and weapons of modern tactics; but at the time of their institution, they possessed a decisive superiority in war; since a regular body of infantry, in constant exercise and pay, was not maintained by any of the princes of Christendom. The Janizaries fought with the zeal of proselytes against their *idolatrous* countrymen; and in the battle of Cossova, the league and independence of the Sclavonian tribes was finally crushed. As the conqueror walked over the field, he observed that the greatest part of the slain consisted of beardless youths; and listened to the flattering reply of his vizier, that age and wisdom would have taught them not to oppose his irresistible arms. But the sword of his Janizaries could not defend him from the dagger of despair; a Servian soldier started from the crowd of dead bodies, and Amurath was pierced in the belly with a mortal wound. The grandson of Othman was mild in his temper, modest in his apparel, and a lover of learning and virtue; but the Moslems were scandalized at his absence from public worship; and he was corrected by the firmness of the mufti, who dared to reject his testimony in a civil cause: a mixture of servitude and freedom not unfrequent in Oriental history.

The character of Bajazet, the son and successor of Amurath, is strongly expressed in his surname of *Ilderim*, or the lightning; and he might glory in an epithet, which was drawn from the fiery energy of his soul and the rapidity of his destructive march. In the fourteen years of his reign, he incessantly moved at the head of his armies, from Boursa to Adrianople, from the Danube to the Euphrates; and, though he strenuously labored for the propagation of the law, he invaded, with impartial ambition, the Christian and Mahometan princes of Europe

and Asia. From Angora to Amasia and Erzeroum, the northern regions of Anatolia were reduced to his obedience: he stripped of their
hereditary possessions his brother emirs of Ghermian and Caramania,
of Aidin and Sarukhan; and after the conquest of Iconium the ancient
kingdom of the Seljukians again revived in the Ottoman dynasty. Nor
were the conquests of Bajazet less rapid or important in Europe. No
sooner had he imposed a regular form of servitude on the Servians
and Bulgarians, than he passed the Danube to seek new enemies and
new subjects in the heart of Moldavia. Whatever yet adhered to the
Greek empire in Thrace, Macedonia, and Thessaly, acknowledged a
Turkish master: an obsequious bishop led him through the gates of
Thermopylæ into Greece; and we may observe, as a singular fact, that
the widow of a Spanish chief, who possessed the ancient seat of the
oracle of Delphi, deserved his favor by the sacrifice of a beauteous
daughter. The Turkish communication between Europe and Asia had
been dangerous and doubtful, till he stationed at Gallipoli a fleet of
galleys, to command the Hellespont and intercept the Latin succors of
Constantinople. While the monarch indulged his passions in a boundless range of injustice and cruelty, he imposed on his soldiers the most
rigid laws of modesty and abstinence; and the harvest was peaceably
reaped and sold within the precincts of his camp. Provoked by the
loose and corrupt administration of justice, he collected in a house the
judges and lawyers of his dominions, who expected that in a few moments the fire would be kindled to reduce them to ashes. His ministers
trembled in silence: but an Æthiopian buffoon presumed to insinuate
the true cause of the evil; and future venality was left without excuse,
by annexing an adequate salary to the office of cadhi. The humble title
of emir was no longer suitable to the Ottoman greatness; and Bajazet
condescended to accept a patent of sultan from the caliphs who served
in Egypt under the yoke of the Mamalukes: a last and frivolous homage that was yielded by force to opinion; by the Turkish conquerors
to the house of Abbas and the successors of the Arabian prophet. The
ambition of the sultan was inflamed by the obligation of deserving this
august title; and he turned his arms against the kingdom of Hungary,
the perpetual theatre of the Turkish victories and defeats. Sigismond,
the Hungarian king, was the son and brother of the emperors of the
West: his cause was that of Europe and the church; and, on the report
of his danger, the bravest knights of France and Germany were eager to
march under his standard and that of the cross. In the battle of Nicopolis, Bajazet defeated a confederate army of a hundred thousand Christians, who had proudly boasted, that if the sky should fall, they could

uphold it on their lances. The far greater part were slain or driven into the Danube; and Sigismond, escaping to Constantinople by the river and the Black Sea, returned after a long circuit to his exhausted kingdom. In the pride of victory, Bajazet threatened that he would besiege Buda; that he would subdue the adjacent countries of Germany and Italy, and that he would feed his horse with a bushel of oats on the altar of St. Peter at Rome. His progress was checked, not by the miraculous interposition of the apostle, not by a crusade of the Christian powers, but by a long and painful fit of the gout. The disorders of the moral, are sometimes corrected by those of the physical, world; and an acrimonious humor falling on a single fibre of one man, may prevent or suspend the misery of nations.

Such is the general idea of the Hungarian war; but the disastrous adventure of the French has procured us some memorials which illustrate the victory and character of Bajazet. The duke of Burgundy, sovereign of Flanders, and uncle of Charles the Sixth, yielded to the ardor of his son, John count of Nevers; and the fearless youth was accompanied by four princes, his *cousins*, and those of the French monarch. Their inexperience was guided by the Sire de Coucy, one of the best and oldest captain of Christendom; but the constable, admiral, and marshal of France commanded an army which did not exceed the number of a thousand knights and squires. These splendid names were the source of presumption and the bane of discipline. So many might aspire to command, that none were willing to obey; their national spirit despised both their enemies and their allies; and in the persuasion that Bajazet *would* fly, or *must* fall, they began to compute how soon they should visit Constantinople and deliver the holy sepulchre. When their scouts announced the approach of the Turks, the gay and thoughtless youths were at table, already heated with wine; they instantly clasped their armor, mounted their horses, rode full speed to the vanguard, and resented as an affront the advice of Sigismond, which would have deprived them of the right and honor of the foremost attack. The battle of Nicopolis would not have been lost, if the French would have obeyed the prudence of the Hungarians; but it might have been gloriously won, had the Hungarians imitated the valor of the French. They dispersed the first line, consisting of the troops of Asia; forced a rampart of stakes, which had been planted against the cavalry; broke, after a bloody conflict, the Janizaries themselves; and were at length overwhelmed by the numerous squadrons that issued from the woods, and charged on all sides this handful of intrepid warriors. In the speed and secrecy of his march, in the order and evolutions of the battle, his enemies felt and admired the military talents of Bajazet. They accuse his cruelty in the use of victory. After reserving the count of Nevers, and four-and-twenty lords, whose birth and riches were attested by his Latin interpreters, the remainder of the French captives, who had survived the slaughter of the day, were led before his throne; and, as they refused to abjure their faith, were successively beheaded in his presence. The sultan was exasperated by the loss of his bravest Janizaries; and if it be true, that, on the eve of the engagement, the French had massacred their Turkish prisoners, they might impute to themselves the consequences of a just retaliation. A knight, whose life had been spared, was permitted to return to Paris, that he might relate the deplorable tale, and solicit the ransom of the noble captives. In the mean while, the count of Nevers, with the princes and barons of France, were dragged along in the marches of the Turkish camp, exposed as a grateful trophy to the Moslems of Europe and Asia, and strictly confined at Boursa, as often as Bajazet resided in his capital. The sultan was pressed each day to expiate with their blood the blood of his martyrs; but he had pronounced that they should live, and either for mercy or destruction his word was irrevocable. He was assured of their value and importance by the return of the messenger, and the gifts and intercessions of the kings of France and of Cyprus. Lusignan presented him with a gold saltcellar of curious workmanship, and of the price of ten thousand ducats; and Charles the Sixth despatched by the way of Hungary a cast of Norwegian hawks, and six horse-loads of scarlet cloth, of fine linen of Rheims, and of Arras tapestry, representing the battles of the great Alexander. After much delay, the effect of distance rather than of art, Bajazet agreed to accept a ransom of two hundred thousand ducats for the count of Nevers and the surviving princes and barons: the marshal Boucicault, a famous warrior, was of the number of the fortunate; but the admiral of France had been slain in battle; and the constable, with the Sire de Coucy, died in the prison of Boursa. This heavy demand, which was doubled by incidental costs, fell chiefly on the duke of Burgundy, or rather on his Flemish subjects, who were bound by the feudal laws to contribute for the knighthood and captivity of the eldest son of their lord. For the faithful discharge of the debt, some merchants of Genoa gave security to the amount of five times the sum; a lesson to those warlike times, that commerce and credit are the links of the society of nations. It had been stipulated in the treaty, that the French captives should swear never to bear arms against the person of their conqueror; but the ungenerous restraint was abolished by Bajazet himself. "I despise," said he to the heir of Burgundy, "thy oaths and thy arms. Thou art young, and mayest be ambitious of effacing the disgrace or misfortune of thy first chivalry. Assemble thy powers, proclaim thy design, and be assured that Bajazet will rejoice to meet thee a second time in a field of battle." Before their departure, they were indulged in the freedom and hospitality of the court of Boursa. The French princes admired the magnificence of the Ottoman, whose hunting and hawking equipage was composed of seven thousand huntsmen and seven thousand falconers. In their presence, and at his command, the belly of one of his chamberlains was cut open, on a complaint against him for drinking the goat's milk of a poor woman. The strangers were astonished by this act of justice; but it was the justice of a sultan who disdains to balance the weight of evidence, or to measure the degrees of guilt.

After his enfranchisement from an oppressive guardian, John Palæologus remained thirty-six years, the helpless, and, as it should seem, the careless spectator of the public ruin. Love, or rather lust, was his only vigorous passion; and in the embraces of the wives and virgins of the city, the Turkish slave forgot the dishonor of the emperor of the *Romans* Andronicus, his eldest son, had formed, at Adrianople, an intimate and guilty friendship with Sauzes, the son of Amurath; and the two youths conspired against the authority and lives of their parents. The presence of Amurath in Europe soon discovered and dissipated their rash counsels; and, after depriving Sauzes of his sight, the Ottoman threatened his vassal with the treatment of an accomplice and an enemy, unless he inflicted a similar punishment on his own son. Palæologus trembled and obeyed; and a cruel precaution involved in the same sentence the childhood and innocence of John, the son of the criminal. But the operation was so mildly, or so unskilfully, performed, that the one retained the sight of an eye, and the other was afflicted only with the infirmity of squinting. Thus excluded from the succession, the two princes were confined in the tower of Anema; and the piety of Manuel, the second son of the reigning monarch, was rewarded with the gift of the Imperial crown. But at the end of two years, the turbulence of the Latins and the levity of the Greeks, produced a revolution; and the two emperors were buried in the tower from whence the two prisoners were exalted to the throne. Another period of two years afforded Palæologus and Manuel the means of escape: it was contrived by the magic or subtlety of a monk, who was alternately named the angel or the devil: they fled to Scutari; their adherents armed in their cause; and the two Byzantine factions displayed the ambition and animosity with which Cæsar and Pompey had disputed the empire of the world. The Roman world was now contracted to a corner of Thrace, between the Propontis and the Black Sea, about fifty miles in length and thirty in breadth; a space of ground not more extensive than the lesser principalities of Germany or Italy, if the remains of Constantinople had not still represented the wealth and populousness of a kingdom. To restore the public peace, it was found necessary to divide this fragment of the empire; and while Palæologus and Manuel were left in possession of the capital, almost all that lay without the walls was ceded to the blind princes, who fixed their residence at Rhodosto and Selybria. In the tranquil slumber of royalty, the passions of John Palæologus survived his reason and his strength: he deprived his favorite and heir of a blooming princess of Trebizond; and while the feeble emperor labored to consummate his nuptials, Manuel, with a hundred of the noblest Greeks, was sent on a peremptory summons to the Ottoman *porte*. They served with honor in the wars of Bajazet; but a plan of fortifying Constantinople excited his jealousy: he threatened their lives; the new works were instantly demolished; and we shall bestow a praise, perhaps above the merit of Palæologus, if we impute this last humiliation as the cause of his death.

The earliest intelligence of that event was communicated to Manuel, who escaped with speed and secrecy from the palace of Boursa to the Byzantine throne. Bajazet affected a proud indifference at the loss of this valuable pledge; and while he pursued his conquests in Europe and Asia, he left the emperor to struggle with his blind cousin John of Selybria, who, in eight years of civil war, asserted his right of primogeniture. At length, the ambition of the victorious sultan pointed to the conquest of Constantinople; but he listened to the advice of his vizier, who represented that such an enterprise might unite the powers of Christendom in a second and more formidable crusade. His epistle to the emperor was conceived in these words: "By the divine clemency, our invincible cimeter has reduced to our obedience almost all Asia, with many and large countries in Europe, excepting only the city of Constantinople; for beyond the walls thou hast nothing left. Resign that city; stipulate thy reward; or tremble, for thyself and thy unhappy people, at the consequences of a rash refusal." But his ambassadors were instructed to soften their tone, and to propose a treaty, which was subscribed with submission and gratitude. A truce of ten years was purchased by an annual tribute of thirty thousand crowns of gold; the Greeks deplored the public toleration of the law of Mahomet, and Bajazet enjoyed the glory of establishing a Turkish cadhi, and founding a royal mosque in the metropolis of the Eastern church. Yet this truce was soon violated by the restless sultan: in the cause of the prince of Selybria, the lawful emperor, an army of Ottomans again threatened Constantinople; and the distress of Manuel implored the protection of the king of France. His plaintive embassy obtained much pity and some relief; and the conduct of the succor was intrusted to the marshal Boucicault, whose religious chivalry was inflamed by the desire of revenging his captivity on the infidels. He sailed with four ships of war, from Aiguesmortes to the Hellespont; forced the passage, which was guarded by seventeen Turkish galleys; landed at Constantinople a supply of six hundred men-at-arms and sixteen hundred archers; and reviewed them in the adjacent plain, without condescending to number or array the multitude of Greeks. By his presence, the blockade was raised both by sea and land; the flying squadrons of Bajazet were driven to a more respectful distance; and several castles in Europe and Asia were stormed by the emperor and the marshal, who fought with equal valor by each other's side. But the Ottomans soon returned with an increase of numbers; and the intrepid Boucicault, after a year's struggle, resolved to evacuate a country which could no longer afford either pay or provisions for his soldiers. The marshal offered to conduct Manuel to the French court, where he might solicit in person a supply of men and money; and advised, in the mean while, that, to extinguish all domestic discord, he should leave his blind competitor on the throne. The proposal was embraced: the prince of Selybria was introduced to the capital; and such was the public misery, that the lot of the exile seemed more fortunate than that of the sovereign. Instead of applauding the success of his vassal, the Turkish sultan claimed the city as his own; and on the refusal of the emperor John, Constantinople was more closely pressed by the calamities of war and famine. Against such an enemy prayers and resistance were alike unavailing; and the savage would have devoured his prey, if, in the fatal moment, he had not been overthrown by another savage stronger than himself. By the victory of Timour or Tamerlane, the fall of Constantinople was delayed about fifty years; and this important, though accidental, service may justly introduce the life and character of the Mogul conqueror.

CHAPTER SIXTY FIVE

Elevation of Timour or Tamerlane, and his Death. – Part One

Elevation of Timour or Tamerlane to the Throne of Samarcand. – His Conquests in Persia, Georgia, Tartary Russia, India, Syria, and Anatolia. – His Turkish War. – Defeat and Captivity of Bajazet. – Death of Timour. – Civil War of the Sons of Bajazet. – Restoration of the Turkish Monarchy by Mahomet the First. – Siege of Constantinople by Amurath the Second.

THE CONQUEST AND MONARCHY of the world was the first object of the ambition of Timour. To live in the memory and esteem of future ages was the second wish of his magnanimous spirit. All the civil and military transactions of his reign were diligently recorded in the journals of his secretaries: the authentic narrative was revised by the persons best informed of each particular transaction; and it is believed in the empire and family of Timour, that the monarch himself composed the *commentaries* of his life, and the *institutions* of his government. But these cares were ineffectual for the preservation of his fame, and these precious memorials in the Mogul or Persian language were concealed from the world, or, at least, from the knowledge of Europe. The nations which he vanquished exercised a base and impotent revenge; and ignorance has long repeated the tale of calumny, which had disfigured the birth and character, the person, and even the name, of *Tamerlane*. Yet his real merit would be enhanced, rather than debased, by the elevation of a peasant to the throne of Asia; nor can his lameness be a theme of reproach, unless he had the weakness to blush at a natural, or perhaps an honorable, infirmity.

In the eyes of the Moguls, who held the indefeasible succession of the house of Zingis, he was doubtless a rebel subject; yet he sprang from the noble tribe of Berlass: his fifth ancestor, Carashar Nevian, had been the vizier of Zagatai, in his new realm of Transoxiana; and in the ascent of some generations, the branch of Timour is confounded, at least by the females, with the Imperial stem. He was born forty miles to the south of Samarcand in the village of Sebzar, in the fruitful territory of Cash, of which his fathers were the hereditary chiefs, as well as of a toman of ten thousand horse. His birth was cast on one of those periods of anarchy, which announce the fall of the Asiatic dynasties, and open a new field to adventurous ambition. The khans of Zagatai were extinct; the emirs aspired to independence; and their domestic feuds could only be suspended by the conquest and tyranny of the khans of Kashgar, who, with an army of Getes or Calmucks, invaded the Transoxian kingdom. From the twelfth year of his age, Timour had entered the field of action; in the twenty-fifth he stood forth as the deliverer of his country; and the eyes and wishes of the people were turned towards a hero who suffered in their cause. The chiefs of the law and of the army had pledged their salvation to support him with their lives and fortunes; but in the hour of danger they were silent and afraid; and, after waiting seven days on the hills of Samarcand, he retreated to the desert with only sixty horsemen. The fugitives were overtaken by a thousand Getes, whom he repulsed with incredible slaughter, and his enemies were forced to exclaim, "Timour is a wonderful man: fortune and the divine favor are with him." But in this bloody action his own followers were reduced to ten, a number which was soon diminished by the desertion of three Carizmians. He wandered in the desert with his wife, seven companions, and four horses; and sixty-two days was he plunged in a loathsome dungeon, from whence he escaped by his own courage and the remorse of the oppressor. After swimming the broad and rapid steam of the Jihoon, or Oxus, he led, during some months, the life of a vagrant and outlaw, on the borders of the adjacent states. But his fame shone brighter in adversity; he learned to distinguish the friends of his person, the associates of his fortune, and to apply the various characters of men for their advantage, and, above all, for his own. On his return to his native country, Timour was successively joined by the parties of his confederates, who anxiously sought him in the desert; nor can I refuse to describe, in his pathetic simplicity, one of their fortunate encounters. He presented himself as a guide to three chiefs, who were at the head of seventy horse. "When their eyes fell upon me," says Timour, "they were overwhelmed with joy; and they alighted from their horses; and they came and kneeled; and they kissed my stirrup. I also came down from my horse, and took each of them in my arms. And I put my turban on the head of the first chief; and my girdle, rich in jewels and wrought with gold, I bound on the loins of the second; and the third I clothed in my own coat. And they wept, and I wept also; and the hour of prayer was arrived, and we prayed. And we mounted our horses, and came to my dwelling; and I collected my people, and made a feast." His trusty bands were soon increased by the bravest of the tribes; he led them against a superior foe; and, after some vicissitudes of war the Getes were finally driven from the kingdom of Transoxiana. He had done much for his own glory; but much remained to be done, much art to be exerted, and some blood to be spilt, before he could teach his equals to obey him as their master. The birth and power of emir Houssein compelled him to accept a vicious and unworthy colleague, whose sister was the best beloved of his wives. Their union was short and jealous; but the policy of Timour, in their frequent quarrels, exposed his rival to the reproach of injustice and perfidy; and, after a final defeat, Houssein was slain by some sagacious friends, who presumed, for the last time, to disobey the commands of their lord. At the age of thirty-four, and in a general diet or *couroultai*, he was invested with *Imperial* command, but he affected to revere the house of Zingis; and while the emir Timour reigned over Zagatai and the East, a nominal khan served as a private officer in the armies of his servant. A fertile kingdom, five hundred miles in length and in breadth, might have satisfied the ambition of a subject; but Timour aspired to the dominion of the world; and before his death, the crown of Zagatai was one of the twenty-seven crowns which he had placed on his head. Without expatiating on the victories of thirty-five campaigns; without describing the lines of march, which he repeatedly traced over the continent of Asia; I shall briefly represent his conquests in, I. Persia, II. Tartary, and, III. India, and from thence proceed to the more interesting narrative of his Ottoman war.

I. For every war, a motive of safety or revenge, of honor or zeal, of right or convenience, may be readily found in the jurisprudence of conquerors. No sooner had Timour reunited to the patrimony of Zagatai the dependent countries of Carizme and Candahar, than he turned his eyes towards the kingdoms of Iran or Persia. From the Oxus to the Tigris, that extensive country was left without a lawful sovereign since the death of Abousaid, the last of the descendants of the great Holacou. Peace and justice had been banished from the land above forty years; and the Mogul invader might seem to listen to the cries of an oppressed people. Their petty tyrants might have opposed him with confederate arms: they separately stood, and successively fell; and the difference of their fate was only marked by the promptitude of submission or the obstinacy of resistance. Ibrahim, prince of Shirwan, or Albania, kissed the footstool of the Imperial throne. His peace-offerings of silks, horses, and jewels, were composed, according to the Tartar fashion, each article of nine pieces; but a critical spectator observed, that there were only eight slaves. "I myself am the ninth," replied Ibrahim, who was prepared for the remark; and his flattery was rewarded by the smile of Timour. Shah Mansour, prince of Fars, or the proper Persia, was one of the least powerful, but most dangerous, of his enemies. In a battle under the walls of Shiraz, he broke, with three or four thousand soldiers, the *coul* or main body of thirty thousand horse, where the emperor fought in person. No more than fourteen or fifteen guards remained near the standard of Timour: he stood firm as a rock, and received on his helmet two weighty strokes of a cimeter: the Moguls rallied; the head of Mansour was thrown at his feet; and he declared his esteem of the valor of a foe, by extirpating all the males of so intrepid a race. From Shiraz, his troops advanced to the Persian Gulf; and the richness and weakness of Ormuz were displayed in an annual tribute of six hundred thousand dinars of gold. Bagdad was no longer the city of peace, the seat of the caliphs; but the noblest conquest of Holacou could not be overlooked by his ambitious successor. The whole course of the Tigris and Euphrates, from the mouth to the sources of those rivers, was reduced to his obedience: he entered Edessa; and the Turkmans of the black sheep were chastised for the sacrilegious pillage of a caravan of Mecca. In the mountains of Georgia, the native Christians still braved the law and the sword of Mahomet, by three expeditions he obtained the merit of the *gazie*, or holy war; and the prince of Teflis became his proselyte and friend.

II. A just retaliation might be urged for the invasion of Turkestan, or the Eastern Tartary. The dignity of Timour could not endure the impunity of the Getes: he passed the Sihoon, subdued the kingdom of Kashgar, and marched seven times into the heart of their country. His most distant camp was two months' journey, or four hundred and eighty leagues to the north-east of Samarcand; and his emirs, who traversed the River Irtish, engraved in the forests of Siberia a rude memorial of their exploits. The conquest of Kipzak, or the Western Tartary, was founded on the double motive of aiding the distressed, and chastising the ungrateful. Toctamish, a fugitive prince, was entertained and protected in his court: the ambassadors of Auruss Khan were dismissed with a haughty denial, and followed on the same day by the armies of

Zagatai; and their success established Toctamish in the Mogul empire of the North. But, after a reign of ten years, the new khan forgot the merits and the strength of his benefactor; the base usurper, as he deemed him, of the sacred rights of the house of Zingis. Through the gates of Derbend, he entered Persia at the head of ninety thousand horse: with the innumerable forces of Kipzak, Bulgaria, Circassia, and Russia, he passed the Sihoon, burnt the palaces of Timour, and compelled him, amidst the winter snows, to contend for Samarcand and his life. After a mild expostulation, and a glorious victory, the emperor resolved on revenge; and by the east, and the west, of the Caspian, and the Volga, he twice invaded Kipzak with such mighty powers, that thirteen miles were measured from his right to his left wing. In a march of five months, they rarely beheld the footsteps of man; and their daily subsistence was often trusted to the fortune of the chase. At length the armies encountered each other; but the treachery of the standard-bearer, who, in the heat of action, reversed the Imperial standard of Kipzak, determined the victory of the Zagatais; and Toctamish (I speak the language of the Institutions) gave the tribe of Toushi to the wind of desolation. He fled to the Christian duke of Lithuania; again returned to the banks of the Volga; and, after fifteen battles with a domestic rival, at last perished in the wilds of Siberia. The pursuit of a flying enemy carried Timour into the tributary provinces of Russia: a duke of the reigning family was made prisoner amidst the ruins of his capital; and Yeletz, by the pride and ignorance of the Orientals, might easily be confounded with the genuine metropolis of the nation. Moscow trembled at the approach of the Tartar, and the resistance would have been feeble, since the hopes of the Russians were placed in a miraculous image of the Virgin, to whose protection they ascribed the casual and voluntary retreat of the conqueror. Ambition and prudence recalled him to the South, the desolate country was exhausted, and the Mogul soldiers were enriched with an immense spoil of precious furs, of linen of Antioch, and of ingots of gold and silver. On the banks of the Don, or Tanais, he received an humble deputation from the consuls and merchants of Egypt, Venice, Genoa, Catalonia, and Biscay, who occupied the commerce and city of Tana, or Azoph, at the mouth of the river. They offered their gifts, admired his magnificence, and trusted his royal word. But the peaceful visit of an emir, who explored the state of the magazines and harbor, was speedily followed by the destructive presence of the Tartars. The city was reduced to ashes; the Moslems were pillaged and dismissed; but all the Christians, who had not fled to their ships, were condemned either to death or slavery. Revenge prompted him to burn the cities of Serai and Astrachan, the monuments of rising civilization; and his vanity proclaimed, that he had penetrated to the region of perpetual daylight, a strange phenomenon, which authorized his Mahometan doctors to dispense with the obligation of evening prayer.

III. When Timour first proposed to his princes and emirs the invasion of India or Hindostan, he was answered by a murmur of discontent: "The rivers! and the mountains and deserts! and the soldiers clad in armor! and the elephants, destroyers of men!" But the displeasure of the emperor was more dreadful than all these terrors; and his superior reason was convinced, that an enterprise of such tremendous aspect was safe and easy in the execution. He was informed by his spies of the weakness and anarchy of Hindostan: the soubahs of the provinces had erected the standard of rebellion; and the perpetual infancy of Sultan Mahmoud was despised even in the harem of Delhi. The Mogul army moved in three great divisions; and Timour observes with pleasure, that the ninety-two squadrons of a thousand horse most fortunately corresponded with the ninety-two names or epithets of the prophet Mahomet. Between the Jihoon and the Indus they crossed one of the ridges of mountains, which are styled by the Arabian geographers The Stony Girdles of the Earth. The highland robbers were subdued or extirpated; but great numbers of men and horses perished in the snow; the emperor himself was let down a precipice on a portable scaffold – the ropes were one hundred and fifty cubits in length; and before he could reach the bottom, this dangerous operation was five times repeated. Timour crossed the Indus at the ordinary passage of Attok; and successively traversed, in the footsteps of Alexander, the *Punjab*, or five rivers, that fall into the master stream. From Attok to Delhi, the high road measures no more than six hundred miles; but the two conquerors deviated to the south-east; and the motive of Timour was to join his grandson, who had achieved by his command the conquest of Moultan. On the eastern bank of the Hyphasis, on the edge of the desert, the Macedonian hero halted and wept: the Mogul entered the desert, reduced the fortress of Batmir, and stood in arms before the gates of Delhi, a great and flourishing city, which had subsisted three centuries under the dominion of the Mahometan kings. The siege, more especially of the castle, might have been a work of time; but he tempted, by the appearance of weakness, the sultan Mahmoud and his vizier to descend into the plain, with ten thousand cuirassiers, forty thousand of his foot-guards, and one hundred and twenty elephants, whose tusks are said to have been armed with sharp and poisoned daggers. Against these monsters, or rather against the imagination of his troops, he condescended to use some extraordinary precautions of fire and a ditch, of iron spikes and a rampart of bucklers; but the event taught the Moguls to smile at their own fears; and as soon as these unwieldy animals were routed, the inferior species (the men of India) disappeared from the field. Timour made his triumphal entry into the capital of Hindostan; and admired, with a view to imitate, the architecture of the stately mosque; but the order or license of a general pillage and massacre polluted the festival of his victory. He resolved to purify his soldiers in the blood of the idolaters, or Gentoos, who still surpass, in the proportion of ten to one, the numbers of the Moslems. In this pious design, he advanced one hundred miles to the north-east of Delhi, passed the Ganges, fought several battles by land and water, and penetrated to the famous rock of Coupele, the statue of the cow, that *seems* to discharge the mighty river, whose source is far distant among the mountains of Thibet. His return was along the skirts of the northern hills; nor could this rapid campaign of one year justify the strange foresight of his emirs, that their children in a warm climate would degenerate into a race of Hindoos.

It was on the banks of the Ganges that Timour was informed, by his speedy messengers, of the disturbances which had arisen on the confines of Georgia and Anatolia, of the revolt of the Christians, and the ambitious designs of the sultan Bajazet. His vigor of mind and body was not impaired by sixty-three years, and innumerable fatigues; and, after enjoying some tranquil months in the palace of Samarcand, he proclaimed a new expedition of seven years into the western countries of Asia. To the soldiers who had served in the Indian war he granted the choice of remaining at home, or following their prince; but the troops of all the provinces and kingdoms of Persia were commanded to assemble at Ispahan, and wait the arrival of the Imperial standard. It was first directed against the Christians of Georgia, who were strong only in their rocks, their castles, and the winter season; but these obstacles were overcome by the zeal and perseverance of Timour: the rebels submitted to the tribute or the Koran; and if both religions boasted of their martyrs, that name is more justly due to the Christian prisoners, who were offered the choice of abjuration or death. On his descent from the hills, the emperor gave audience to the first ambassadors of Bajazet, and opened the hostile correspondence of complaints and menaces, which fermented two years before the final explosion. Between two jealous and haughty neighbors, the motives of quarrel will seldom be wanting. The Mogul and Ottoman conquests now touched each other in the neighborhood of Erzeroum, and the Euphrates; nor had the doubtful limit been ascertained by time and treaty. Each of these ambitious monarchs might accuse his rival of violating his territory, of threatening his vassals, and protecting his rebels; and, by the name of rebels, each understood the fugitive princes, whose kingdoms he had usurped, and whose life or liberty he implacably pursued. The resemblance of character was still more dangerous than the opposition of interest; and in their victorious career, Timour was impatient of an equal, and Bajazet was ignorant of a superior. The first epistle of the Mogul emperor must have provoked, instead of reconciling, the Turkish sultan, whose family and nation he affected to despise. "Dost thou not know, that the greatest part of Asia is subject to our arms and our laws? that our invincible forces extend from one sea to the other? that the potentates of the earth form a line before our gate? and that we have compelled Fortune herself to watch over the prosperity of our empire. What is the foundation of thy insolence and folly? Thou hast fought some battles in the woods of Anatolia; contemptible trophies! Thou hast obtained some victories over the Christians of Europe; thy sword was blessed by the apostle of God; and thy obedience to the precept of the Koran, in waging war against the infidels, is the sole consideration that prevents us from destroying thy country, the frontier and bulwark of the Moslem world. Be wise in time; reflect; repent; and avert the thunder of our vengeance, which is yet suspended over thy head. Thou art no more than a pismire; why wilt thou seek to provoke the elephants? Alas! they will trample thee under their feet." In his replies, Bajazet poured forth the indignation of a soul which was deeply stung by such unusual contempt. After retorting the basest reproaches on the thief and rebel of the desert, the Ottoman recapitulates his boasted victories in Iran, Touran, and the Indies; and labors to prove, that Timour had never triumphed unless by his own perfidy and the vices of his foes. "Thy armies are innumerable: be they so; but what are the arrows of the flying Tartar against the cimeters and battle-axes of my firm and invincible Janizaries? I will guard the princes who have implored my protection: seek them in my tents. The cities of Arzingan and Erzeroum are mine; and unless the tribute be duly paid, I will demand the arrears under the walls of Tauris and Sultania." The ungovernable rage of the sultan at length betrayed him to an insult of a more domestic kind. "If I fly from thy arms," said he, "may *my* wives be thrice divorced from my bed: but if thou hast not courage to meet me in the field, mayest thou again receive *thy* wives after they have thrice endured the embraces of a stranger." Any violation by word or deed of the secrecy of the harem is an unpardonable offence among the Turkish nations; and the political quarrel of the two monarchs was imbittered by private and personal resentment. Yet in his first expedition, Timour was satisfied with the siege and destruction of Siwas or Sebaste, a strong city on the borders of Anatolia; and he revenged the indiscretion of the Ottoman, on a garrison of four thousand Armenians, who were buried alive for the brave and faithful discharge of their duty. As a Mussulman, he seemed to respect the pious occupation of Bajazet, who was still engaged in the blockade of Constantinople; and after this salutary lesson, the Mogul conqueror checked his pursuit, and turned aside to the invasion of Syria and Egypt. In these transactions, the Ottoman prince, by the Orientals, and even by Timour, is styled the *Kaissar of Roum*, the Cæsar of the Romans; a title which, by a small anticipation, might be given to a monarch who possessed the provinces, and threatened the city, of the successors of Constantine.

Elevation of Timour or Tamerlane, and his Death. – Part Two

THE MILITARY REPUBLIC OF the Mamalukes still reigned in Egypt and Syria: but the dynasty of the Turks was overthrown by that of the Circassians; and their favorite Barkok, from a slave and a prisoner, was raised and restored to the throne. In the midst of rebellion and discord, he braved the menaces, corresponded with the enemies, and detained the ambassadors, of the Mogul, who patiently expected his decease, to revenge the crimes of the father on the feeble reign of his son Farage. The Syrian emirs were assembled at Aleppo to repel the invasion: they confided in the fame and discipline of the Mamalukes, in the temper of their swords and lances of the purest steel of Damascus, in the strength of their walled cities, and in the populousness of sixty thousand villages; and instead of sustaining a siege, they threw open their gates, and arrayed their forces in the plain. But these forces were not cemented by virtue and union; and some powerful emirs had been seduced to desert or betray their more loyal companions. Timour's front was covered with a line of Indian elephants, whose turrets were filled with archers and Greek fire: the rapid evolutions of his cavalry completed the dismay and disorder; the Syrian crowds fell back on each other: many thousands were stifled or slaughtered in the entrance of the great street; the Moguls entered with the fugitives; and after a short defence, the citadel, the impregnable citadel of Aleppo, was surrendered by cowardice or treachery. Among the suppliants and captives, Timour distinguished the doctors of the law, whom he invited to the dangerous honor of a personal conference. The Mogul prince was a zealous Mussulman; but his Persian schools had taught him to revere the memory of Ali and

Hosein; and he had imbibed a deep prejudice against the Syrians, as the enemies of the son of the daughter of the apostle of God. To these doctors he proposed a captious question, which the casuists of Bochara, Samarcand, and Herat, were incapable of resolving. "Who are the true martyrs, of those who are slain on my side, or on that of my enemies?" But he was silenced, or satisfied, by the dexterity of one of the cadhis of Aleppo, who replied in the words of Mahomet himself, that the motive, not the ensign, constitutes the martyr; and that the Moslems of either party, who fight only for the glory of God, may deserve that sacred appellation. The true succession of the caliphs was a controversy of a still more delicate nature; and the frankness of a doctor, too honest for his situation, provoked the emperor to exclaim, "Ye are as false as those of Damascus: Moawiyah was a usurper, Yezid a tyrant, and Ali alone is the lawful successor of the prophet." A prudent explanation restored his tranquillity; and he passed to a more familiar topic of conversation. "What is your age?" said he to the cadhi. "Fifty years." – "It would be the age of my eldest son: you see me here (continued Timour) a poor lame, decrepit mortal. Yet by my arm has the Almighty been pleased to subdue the kingdoms of Iran, Touran, and the Indies. I am not a man of blood; and God is my witness, that in all my wars I have never been the aggressor, and that my enemies have always been the authors of their own calamity." During this peaceful conversation the streets of Aleppo streamed with blood, and reechoed with the cries of mothers and children, with the shrieks of violated virgins. The rich plunder that was abandoned to his soldiers might stimulate their avarice; but their cruelty was enforced by the peremptory command of producing an adequate number of heads, which, according to his custom, were curiously piled in columns and pyramids: the Moguls celebrated the feast of victory, while the surviving Moslems passed the night in tears and in chains. I shall not dwell on the march of the destroyer from Aleppo to Damascus, where he was rudely encountered, and almost overthrown, by the armies of Egypt. A retrograde motion was imputed to his distress and despair: one of his nephews deserted to the enemy; and Syria rejoiced in the tale of his defeat, when the sultan was driven by the revolt of the Mamalukes to escape with precipitation and shame to his palace of Cairo. Abandoned by their prince, the inhabitants of Damascus still defended their walls; and Timour consented to raise the siege, if they would adorn his retreat with a gift or ransom; each article of nine pieces. But no sooner had he introduced himself into the city, under color of a truce, than he perfidiously violated the treaty; imposed a contribution of ten millions of gold; and animated his troops to chastise the posterity of those Syrians who had executed, or approved, the murder of the grandson of Mahomet. A family which had given honorable burial to the head of Hosein, and a colony of artificers, whom he sent to labor at Samarcand, were alone reserved in the general massacre, and after a period of seven centuries, Damascus was reduced to ashes, because a Tartar was moved by religious zeal to avenge the blood of an Arab. The losses and fatigues of the campaign obliged Timour to renounce the conquest of Palestine and Egypt; but in his return to the Euphrates he delivered Aleppo to the flames; and justified his pious motive by the pardon and reward of two thousand sectaries of Ali, who were desirous to visit the tomb of his son. I have expatiated on the personal anecdotes which mark the character of the Mogul hero; but I shall briefly mention, that he erected on the ruins of Bagdad a pyramid of ninety thousand heads; again visited Georgia; encamped on the banks of Araxes; and proclaimed his resolution of marching against the Ottoman emperor. Conscious of the importance of the war, he collected his forces from every province: eight hundred thousand men were enrolled on his military list; but the splendid commands of five, and ten, thousand horse, may be rather expressive of the rank and pension of the chiefs, than of the genuine number of effective soldiers. In the pillage of Syria, the Moguls had acquired immense riches: but the delivery of their pay and arrears for seven years more firmly attached them to the Imperial standard.

During this diversion of the Mogul arms, Bajazet had two years to collect his forces for a more serious encounter. They consisted of four hundred thousand horse and foot, whose merit and fidelity were of an unequal complexion. We may discriminate the Janizaries, who have been gradually raised to an establishment of forty thousand men; a national cavalry, the Spahis of modern times; twenty thousand cuirassiers of Europe, clad in black and impenetrable armor; the troops of Anatolia, whose princes had taken refuge in the camp of Timour, and a colony of Tartars, whom he had driven from Kipzak, and to whom Bajazet had assigned a settlement in the plains of Adrianople. The fearless confidence of the sultan urged him to meet his antagonist; and, as if he had chosen that spot for revenge, he displayed his banner near the ruins of the unfortunate Suvas. In the mean while, Timour moved from the Araxes through the countries of Armenia and Anatolia: his boldness was secured by the wisest precautions; his speed was guided by order and discipline; and the woods, the mountains, and the rivers, were diligently explored by the flying squadrons, who marked his road and preceded his standard. Firm in his plan of fighting in the heart of the Ottoman kingdom, he avoided their camp; dexterously inclined to the left; occupied Cæsarea; traversed the salt desert and the River Halys; and invested Angora: while the sultan, immovable and ignorant in his post, compared the Tartar swiftness to the crawling of a snail; he returned on the wings of indignation to the relief of Angora: and as both generals were alike impatient for action, the plains round that city were the scene of a memorable battle, which has immortalized the glory of Timour and the shame of Bajazet. For this signal victory the Mogul emperor was indebted to himself, to the genius of the moment, and the discipline of thirty years. He had improved the tactics, without violating the manners, of his nation, whose force still consisted in the missile weapons, and rapid evolutions, of a numerous cavalry. From a single troop to a great army, the mode of attack was the same: a foremost line first advanced to the charge, and was supported in a just order by the squadrons of the great vanguard. The general's eye watched over the field, and at his command the front and rear of the right and left wings successively moved forwards in their several divisions, and in a direct or oblique line: the enemy was pressed by eighteen or twenty attacks; and each attack afforded a chance of victory. If they all proved fruitless or unsuccessful, the occasion was worthy of the emperor himself, who gave the signal of advancing to the standard and main body, which he led in person. But in the battle of Angora, the main body itself was supported, on the flanks and in the rear, by the bravest squadrons of the reserve, commanded by the sons and grandsons of Timour. The conqueror of Hindostan ostentatiously showed a line of elephants, the trophies, rather than the instruments, of victory; the use of the Greek fire was familiar to the Moguls and Ottomans; but had they borrowed from Europe the recent invention of gunpowder and cannon, the artificial thunder, in the hands of either nation, must have turned the fortune of the day. In that day Bajazet displayed the qualities of a soldier and a chief: but his genius sunk under a stronger ascendant; and, from various motives, the greatest part of his troops failed him in the decisive moment. His rigor and avarice had provoked a mutiny among the Turks; and even his son Soliman too hastily withdrew from the field. The forces of Anatolia, loyal in their revolt, were drawn away to the banners of their lawful princes. His Tartar allies had been tempted by the letters and emissaries of Timour; who reproached their ignoble servitude under the slaves of their fathers; and offered to their hopes the dominion of their new, or the liberty of their ancient, country. In the right wing of Bajazet the cuirassiers of Europe charged, with faithful hearts and irresistible arms: but these men of iron were soon broken by an artful flight and headlong pursuit; and the Janizaries, alone, without cavalry or missile weapons, were encompassed by the circle of the Mogul hunters. Their valor was at length oppressed by heat, thirst, and the weight of numbers; and the unfortunate sultan, afflicted with the gout in his hands and feet, was transported from the field on the fleetest of his horses. He was pursued and taken by the titular khan of Zagatai; and, after his capture, and the defeat of the Ottoman powers, the kingdom of Anatolia submitted to the conqueror, who planted his standard at Kiotahia, and dispersed on all sides the ministers of rapine and destruction. Mirza Mehemmed Sultan, the eldest and best beloved of his grandsons, was despatched to Boursa, with thirty thousand horse; and such was his youthful ardor, that he arrived with only four thousand at the gates of the capital, after performing in five days a march of two hundred and thirty miles. Yet fear is still more rapid in its course; and Soliman, the son of Bajazet, had already passed over to Europe with the royal treasure. The spoil, however, of the palace and city was immense: the inhabitants had escaped; but the buildings, for the most part of wood, were reduced to ashes. From Boursa, the grandson of Timour advanced to Nice, ever yet a fair and flourishing city; and the Mogul squadrons were only stopped by the waves of the Propontis. The same success attended the other mirzas and emirs in their excursions; and Smyrna, defended by the zeal and courage of the Rhodian knights, alone deserved the presence of the emperor himself. After an obstinate defence, the place was taken by storm: all that breathed was put to the sword; and the heads of the Christian heroes were launched from the engines, on board of two carracks, or great ships of Europe, that rode at anchor in the harbor. The Moslems of Asia rejoiced in their deliverance from a dangerous and domestic foe; and a parallel was drawn between the two rivals, by observing that Timour, in fourteen days, had reduced a fortress which had sustained seven years the siege, or at least the blockade, of Bajazet.

The *iron cage* in which Bajazet was imprisoned by Tamerlane, so long and so often repeated as a moral lesson, is now rejected as a fable by the modern writers, who smile at the vulgar credulity. They appeal with confidence to the Persian history of Sherefeddin Ali, which has been given to our curiosity in a French version, and from which I shall collect and abridge a more specious narrative of this memorable transaction. No sooner was Timour informed that the captive Ottoman was at the door of his tent, than he graciously stepped forwards to receive him, seated him by his side, and mingled with just reproaches a soothing pity for his rank and misfortune. "Alas!" said the emperor, "the decree of fate is now accomplished by your own fault; it is the web which you have woven, the thorns of the tree which yourself have planted. I wished to spare, and even to assist, the champion of the Moslems; you braved our threats; you despised our friendship; you forced us to enter your kingdom with our invincible armies. Behold the event. Had you vanquished, I am not ignorant of the fate which you reserved for myself and my troops. But I disdain to retaliate: your life and honor are secure; and I shall express my gratitude to God by my clemency to man." The royal captive showed some signs of repentance, accepted the humiliation of a robe of honor, and embraced with tears his son Mousa, who, at his request, was sought and found among the captives of the field. The Ottoman princes were lodged in a splendid pavilion; and the respect of the guards could be surpassed only by their vigilance. On the arrival of the harem from Boursa, Timour restored the queen Despina and her daughter to their father and husband; but he piously required, that the Servian princess, who had hitherto been indulged in the profession of Christianity, should embrace without delay the religion of the prophet. In the feast of victory, to which Bajazet was invited, the Mogul emperor placed a crown on his head and a sceptre in his hand, with a solemn assurance of restoring him with an increase of glory to the throne of his ancestors. But the effect of his promise was disappointed by the sultan's untimely death: amidst the care of the most skilful physicians, he expired of an apoplexy at Akshehr, the Antioch of Pisidia, about nine months after his defeat. The victor dropped a tear over his grave: his body, with royal pomp, was conveyed to the mausoleum which he had erected at Boursa; and his son Mousa, after receiving a rich present of gold and jewels, of horses and arms, was invested by a patent in red ink with the kingdom of Anatolia.

Such is the portrait of a generous conqueror, which has been extracted from his own memorials, and dedicated to his son and grandson, nineteen years after his decease; and, at a time when the truth was remembered by thousands, a manifest falsehood would have implied a satire on his real conduct. Weighty indeed is this evidence, adopted by all the Persian histories; yet flattery, more especially in the East, is base and audacious; and the harsh and ignominious treatment of Bajazet is attested by a chain of witnesses, some of whom shall be produced in the order of their time and country. . The reader has not forgot the garrison of French, whom the marshal Boucicault left behind him for the defence of Constantinople. They were on the spot to receive the earliest and most faithful intelligence of the overthrow of their great adversary; and it is more than probable, that some of them accompanied the Greek embassy to the camp of Tamerlane. From their account, the *hardships* of the prison and death of Bajazet are affirmed by the marshal's servant and historian, within the distance of seven years. . The name of Poggius the Italian is deservedly famous among the revivers of learning in the fifteenth century. His elegant dialogue on the vicissitudes of fortune was composed in his fiftieth year, twenty-eight years after the Turkish victory of Tamerlane; whom he celebrates as not inferior to the illustrious Barbarians of antiquity. Of his exploits and discipline Poggius was informed by several ocular witnesses; nor does he forget an example so apposite to his theme as the Ottoman monarch, whom the Scythian confined like a wild beast in an iron cage, and exhibited a spectacle to Asia. I might add the authority of two Italian chronicles, perhaps of an earlier date, which would prove at least that the same story, whether false or true, was imported into Europe with the first tidings of the revolution. . At the time when Poggius flourished at Rome, Ahmed Ebn Arabshah composed at Damascus the florid and malevolent history of Timour, for which he had collected materials in his journeys over Turkey and Tartary. Without any possible correspondence between the Latin and the Arabian writer, they agree in the fact of the iron cage; and their agreement is a striking proof of their common veracity. Ahmed Arabshah likewise relates another outrage, which Bajazet endured, of a more domestic and tender nature. His indiscreet mention of women and divorces was deeply resented by the jealous Tartar: in the feast of victory the wine was served by female cupbearers, and the sultan beheld his own concubines and wives confounded among the slaves, and exposed without a veil to the eyes of intemperance. To escape a similar indignity, it is said that his successors, except in a single instance, have abstained from legitimate nuptials; and the Ottoman practice and belief, at least in the sixteenth century, is asserted by the observing Busbequius, ambassador from the court of Vienna to the great Soliman. . Such is the separation of language, that the testimony of a Greek is not less independent than that of a Latin or an Arab. I suppress the names of Chalcondyles and Ducas, who flourished in the latter period, and who speak in a less positive tone; but more attention is due to George Phranza, protovestiare of the last emperors, and who was born a year before the battle of Angora. Twenty-two years after that event, he was sent ambassador to Amurath the Second; and the historian might converse with some veteran Janizaries, who had been made prisoners with the sultan, and had themselves seen him in his iron cage. 5. The last evidence, in every sense, is that of the Turkish annals, which have been consulted or transcribed by Leunclavius, Pocock, and Cantemir. They unanimously deplore the captivity of the iron cage; and some credit may be allowed to national historians, who cannot stigmatize the Tartar without uncovering the shame of their king and country.

From these opposite premises, a fair and moderate conclusion may be deduced. I am satisfied that Sherefeddin Ali has faithfully described the first ostentatious interview, in which the conqueror, whose spirits were harmonized by success, affected the character of generosity. But his mind was insensibly alienated by the unseasonable arrogance of Bajazet; the complaints of his enemies, the Anatolian princes, were just and vehement; and Timour betrayed a design of leading his royal captive in triumph to Samarcand. An attempt to facilitate his escape, by digging a mine under the tent, provoked the Mogul emperor to impose a harsher restraint; and in his perpetual marches, an iron cage on a wagon might be invented, not as a wanton insult, but as a rigorous precaution. Timour had read in some fabulous history a similar treatment of one of his predecessors, a king of Persia; and Bajazet was condemned to represent the person, and expiate the guilt, of the Roman Cæsar But the strength of his mind and body fainted under the trial, and his premature death might, without injustice, be ascribed to the severity of Timour. He warred not with the dead: a tear and a sepulchre were all that he could bestow on a captive who was delivered from his power; and if Mousa, the son of Bajazet, was permitted to reign over the ruins of Boursa, the greatest part of the province of Anatolia had been restored by the conqueror to their lawful sovereigns.

From the Irtish and Volga to the Persian Gulf, and from the Ganges to Damascus and the Archipelago, Asia was in the hand of Timour: his armies were invincible, his ambition was boundless, and his zeal might aspire to conquer and convert the Christian kingdoms of the West, which already trembled at his name. He touched the utmost verge of the land; but an insuperable, though narrow, sea rolled between the two continents of Europe and Asia; and the lord of so many *tomans*, or myriads, of horse, was not master of a single galley. The two passages of the Bosphorus and Hellespont, of Constantinople and Gallipoli, were possessed, the one by the Christians, the other by the Turks. On this great occasion, they forgot the difference of religion, to act with union and firmness in the common cause: the double straits were guarded with ships and fortifications; and they separately withheld the transports which Timour demanded of either nation, under the pretence of attacking their enemy. At the same time, they soothed his pride with tributary gifts and suppliant embassies, and prudently tempted him to retreat with the honors of victory. Soliman, the son of Bajazet, implored his clemency for his father and himself; accepted, by a red patent, the investiture of the kingdom of Romania, which he already held by the sword; and reiterated his ardent wish, of casting himself in person at the feet of the king of the world. The Greek emperor (either John or Manuel) submitted to pay the same tribute which he had stipulated with the Turkish sultan, and ratified the treaty by an oath of allegiance, from which he could absolve his conscience so soon as the Mogul arms had retired from Anatolia. But the fears and fancy of nations ascribed to the ambitious Tamerlane a new design of vast and romantic compass; a design of subduing Egypt and Africa, marching from the Nile to the Atlantic Ocean, entering Europe by the Straits of Gibraltar, and, after imposing his yoke on the kingdoms of Christendom, of returning home by the deserts of Russia and Tartary. This remote, and perhaps imaginary, danger was averted by the submission of the sultan of Egypt: the honors of the prayer and the coin attested at Cairo the supremacy of Timour; and a rare gift of a *giraffe*, or camelopard, and nine ostriches, represented at Samarcand the tribute of the African world. Our imagination is not less astonished by the portrait of a Mogul, who, in his camp before Smyrna, meditates, and almost accomplishes, the invasion of the Chinese empire. Timour was urged to this enterprise by national honor and religious zeal. The torrents which he had shed of Mussulman blood could be expiated only by an equal destruction of the infidels; and as he now stood at the gates of paradise, he might best secure his glorious entrance by demolishing the idols of China, founding mosques in every city, and establishing the profession of faith in one God, and his prophet Mahomet. The recent expulsion of the house of Zingis was an insult on the Mogul name; and the disorders of the empire afforded the fairest opportunity for revenge. The illustrious Hongvou, founder of the dynasty of *Ming*, died four years before the battle of Angora; and his grandson, a weak and unfortunate youth, was burnt in his palace, after a million of Chinese had perished in the civil war. Before he evacuated Anatolia, Timour despatched beyond the Sihoon a numerous army, or rather colony, of his old and new subjects, to open the road, to subdue the Pagan Calmucks and Mungals, and to found cities and magazines in the desert; and, by the diligence of his lieutenant, he soon received a perfect map and description of the unknown regions, from the source of the Irtish to the wall of China. During these preparations, the emperor achieved the final conquest of Georgia; passed the winter on the banks of the Araxes; appeased the troubles of Persia; and slowly returned to his capital, after a campaign of four years and nine months.

Elevation of Timour or Tamerlane, and his Death. – Part Three

ON THE THRONE OF Samarcand, he displayed, in a short repose, his magnificence and power; listened to the complaints of the people; distributed a just measure of rewards and punishments; employed his riches in the architecture of palaces and temples; and gave audience to the ambassadors of Egypt, Arabia, India, Tartary, Russia, and Spain, the last of whom presented a suit of tapestry which eclipsed the pencil of the Oriental artists. The marriage of six of the emperor's grandsons was esteemed an act of religion as well as of paternal tenderness; and the pomp of the ancient caliphs was revived in their nuptials. They were celebrated in the gardens of Canighul, decorated with innumerable tents and pavilions, which displayed the luxury of a great city and the spoils of a victorious camp. Whole forests were cut down to supply fuel for the kitchens; the plain was spread with pyramids of meat, and vases of every liquor, to which thousands of guests were courteously invited: the orders of the state, and the nations of the earth, were marshalled at the royal banquet; nor were the ambassadors of Europe (says the haughty Persian) excluded from the feast; since even the *casses*, the smallest of fish, find their place in the ocean. The public joy was testified by illuminations and masquerades; the trades of Samarcand passed in review; and every trade was emulous to execute some quaint device, some marvellous pageant, with the materials of their peculiar art. After the marriage contracts had been ratified by the cadhis, the bride-grooms and their brides retired to the nuptial chambers: nine times, according to the Asiatic fashion, they were dressed and undressed; and at each change of apparel, pearls and rubies were showered on their heads, and contemptuously abandoned to their attendants. A general indulgence was proclaimed: every law was relaxed, every pleasure was allowed; the people was free, the sovereign was idle; and the historian of Timour may remark, that, after devoting fifty years to the attainment of empire, the only happy period of his life were the two months in which he ceased to exercise his power. But he was soon awakened to the cares of government and war. The standard was unfurled for the invasion of China: the emirs made their report of two hundred thousand, the select and veteran soldiers of Iran and Touran: their baggage and provisions were transported by five hundred great wagons, and an immense train of horses and camels; and the troops might prepare for a long absence, since more than six months were employed in the tranquil journey of a caravan from Samarcand to Pekin. Neither age, nor the severity of the winter, could retard the impatience of Timour; he mounted on horseback, passed the Sihoon on the ice, marched seventy-six parasangs, three hundred miles, from his capital, and pitched his last camp in the neighborhood of Otrar, where he was expected by the angel of death. Fatigue, and the indiscreet use of iced water, accelerated the progress of his fever; and the conqueror of Asia expired in the seventieth year of his age, thirty-five years after he had ascended the throne of Zagatai. His designs were lost; his armies were disbanded; China was saved; and fourteen years after his decease, the most powerful of his children sent an embassy of friendship and commerce to the court of Pekin.

The fame of Timour has pervaded the East and West: his posterity is still invested with the Imperial *title*; and the admiration of his subjects, who revered him almost as a deity, may be justified in some degree by the praise or confession of his bitterest enemies. Although he was lame of a hand and foot, his form and stature were not unworthy of his rank; and his vigorous health, so essential to himself and to the world, was corroborated by temperance and exercise. In his familiar discourse he was grave and modest, and if he was ignorant of the Arabic language, he spoke with fluency and elegance the Persian and Turkish idioms. It was his delight to converse with the learned on topics of history and science; and the amusement of his leisure hours was the game of chess, which he improved or corrupted with new refinements. In his religion he was a zealous, though not perhaps an orthodox, Mussulman; but his sound understanding may tempt us to believe, that a superstitious reverence for omens and prophecies, for saints and astrologers, was only affected as an instrument of policy. In the government of a vast empire, he stood alone and absolute, without a rebel to oppose his power, a favorite to seduce his affections, or a minister to mislead his judgment. It was his

firmest maxim, that whatever might be the consequence, the word of
the prince should never be disputed or recalled; but his foes have maliciously observed, that the commands of anger and destruction were
more strictly executed than those of beneficence and favor. His sons
and grandsons, of whom Timour left six-and-thirty at his decease, were
his first and most submissive subjects; and whenever they deviated
from their duty, they were corrected, according to the laws of Zingis,
with the bastinade, and afterwards restored to honor and command.
Perhaps his heart was not devoid of the social virtues; perhaps he was
not incapable of loving his friends and pardoning his enemies; but the
rules of morality are founded on the public interest; and it may be sufficient to applaud the *wisdom* of a monarch, for the liberality by which
he is not impoverished, and for the justice by which he is strengthened
and enriched. To maintain the harmony of authority and obedience,
to chastise the proud, to protect the weak, to reward the deserving, to
banish vice and idleness from his dominions, to secure the traveller
and merchant, to restrain the depredations of the soldier, to cherish the
labors of the husbandman, to encourage industry and learning, and,
by an equal and moderate assessment, to increase the revenue, without
increasing the taxes, are indeed the duties of a prince; but, in the discharge of these duties, he finds an ample and immediate recompense.
Timour might boast, that, at his accession to the throne, Asia was the
prey of anarchy and rapine, whilst under his prosperous monarchy a
child, fearless and unhurt, might carry a purse of gold from the East to
the West. Such was his confidence of merit, that from this reformation
he derived an excuse for his victories, and a title to universal dominion.
The four following observations will serve to appreciate his claim to the
public gratitude; and perhaps we shall conclude, that the Mogul emperor was rather the scourge than the benefactor of mankind. . If some
partial disorders, some local oppressions, were healed by the sword of
Timour, the remedy was far more pernicious than the disease. By their
rapine, cruelty, and discord, the petty tyrants of Persia might afflict their
subjects; but whole nations were crushed under the footsteps of the reformer. The ground which had been occupied by flourishing cities was
often marked by his abominable trophies, by columns, or pyramids, of
human heads. Astracan, Carizme, Delhi, Ispahan, Bagdad, Aleppo, Damascus, Boursa, Smyrna, and a thousand others, were sacked, or burnt,
or utterly destroyed, in his presence, and by his troops: and perhaps
his conscience would have been startled, if a priest or philosopher had
dared to number the millions of victims whom he had sacrificed to
the establishment of peace and order. . His most destructive wars were

rather inroads than conquests. He invaded Turkestan, Kipzak, Russia, Hindostan, Syria, Anatolia, Armenia, and Georgia, without a hope or a desire of preserving those distant provinces. From thence he departed laden with spoil; but he left behind him neither troops to awe the contumacious, nor magistrates to protect the obedient, natives. When he had broken the fabric of their ancient government, he abandoned them to the evils which his invasion had aggravated or caused; nor were these evils compensated by any present or possible benefits. . The kingdoms of Transoxiana and Persia were the proper field which he labored to cultivate and adorn, as the perpetual inheritance of his family. But his peaceful labors were often interrupted, and sometimes blasted, by the absence of the conqueror. While he triumphed on the Volga or the Ganges, his servants, and even his sons, forgot their master and their duty. The public and private injuries were poorly redressed by the tardy rigor of inquiry and punishment; and we must be content to praise the *Institutions* of Timour, as the specious idea of a perfect monarchy. . Whatsoever might be the blessings of his administration, they evaporated with his life. To reign, rather than to govern, was the ambition of his children and grandchildren; the enemies of each other and of the people. A fragment of the empire was upheld with some glory by Sharokh, his youngest son; but after *his* decease, the scene was again involved in darkness and blood; and before the end of a century, Transoxiana and Persia were trampled by the Uzbeks from the north, and the Turkmans of the black and white sheep. The race of Timour would have been extinct, if a hero, his descendant in the fifth degree, had not fled before the Uzbek arms to the conquest of Hindostan. His successors (the great Moguls) extended their sway from the mountains of Cashmir to Cape Comorin, and from Candahar to the Gulf of Bengal. Since the reign of Aurungzebe, their empire had been dissolved; their treasures of Delhi have been rifled by a Persian robber; and the richest of their kingdoms is now possessed by a company of Christian merchants, of a remote island in the Northern Ocean.

Far different was the fate of the Ottoman monarchy. The massy trunk was bent to the ground, but no sooner did the hurricane pass away, than it again rose with fresh vigor and more lively vegetation. When Timour, in every sense, had evacuated Anatolia, he left the cities without a palace, a treasure, or a king. The open country was overspread with hordes of shepherds and robbers of Tartar or Turkman origin; the recent conquests of Bajazet were restored to the emirs, one of whom, in base revenge, demolished his sepulchre; and his five sons were eager, by civil discord, to consume the remnant of their patrimony. I shall enumerate their names in the order of their age and actions. . It is doubtful, whether I relate the story of the true *Mustapha*, or of an impostor who personated that lost prince. He fought by his father's side in the battle of Angora: but when the captive sultan was permitted to inquire for his children, Mousa alone could be found; and the Turkish historians, the slaves of the triumphant faction, are persuaded that his brother was confounded among the slain. If Mustapha escaped from that disastrous field, he was concealed twelve years from his friends and enemies; till he emerged in Thessaly, and was hailed by a numerous party, as the son and successor of Bajazet. His first defeat would have been his last, had not the true, or false, Mustapha been saved by the Greeks, and restored, after the decease of his brother Mahomet, to liberty and empire. A degenerate mind seemed to argue his spurious birth; and if, on the throne of Adrianople, he was adored as the Ottoman sultan, his flight, his fetters, and an ignominious gibbet, delivered the impostor to popular contempt. A similar character and claim was asserted by several rival pretenders: thirty persons are said to have suffered under the name of Mustapha; and these frequent executions may perhaps insinuate, that the Turkish court was not perfectly secure of the death of the lawful prince. . After his father's captivity, Isa reigned for some time in the neighborhood of Angora, Sinope, and the Black Sea; and his ambassadors were dismissed from the presence of Timour with fair promises and honorable gifts. But their master was soon deprived of his province and life, by a jealous brother, the sovereign of Amasia; and the final event suggested a pious allusion, that the law of Moses and Jesus, of *Isa* and *Mousa*, had been abrogated by the greater Mahomet. . *Soliman* is not numbered in the list of the Turkish emperors: yet he checked the victorious progress of the Moguls; and after their departure, united for a while the thrones of Adrianople and Boursa. In war he was brave, active, and fortunate; his courage was softened by clemency; but it was likewise inflamed by presumption, and corrupted by intemperance and idleness. He relaxed the nerves of discipline, in a government where either the subject or the sovereign must continually tremble: his vices alienated the chiefs of the army and the law; and his daily drunkenness, so contemptible in a prince and a man, was doubly odious in a disciple of the prophet. In the slumber of intoxication he was surprised by his brother Mousa; and as he fled from Adrianople towards the Byzantine capital, Soliman was overtaken and slain in a bath, after a reign of seven years and ten months. . The investiture of Mousa degraded him as the slave of the Moguls: his tributary kingdom of Anatolia was confined within a narrow limit, nor could his broken militia and empty treasury contend with the hardy and veteran bands of the sovereign of Romania. Mousa fled in disguise from the palace of Boursa; traversed the Propontis in an open boat; wandered over the Walachian and Servian hills; and after some vain attempts, ascended the throne of Adrianople, so recently stained with the blood of Soliman. In a reign of three years and a half, his troops were victorious against the Christians of Hungary and the Morea; but Mousa was ruined by his timorous disposition and unseasonable clemency. After resigning the sovereignty of Anatolia, he fell a victim to the perfidy of his ministers, and the superior ascendant of his brother Mahomet. .The final victory of Mahomet was the just recompense of his prudence and moderation. Before his father's captivity, the royal youth had been intrusted with the government of Amasia, thirty days' journey from Constantinople, and the Turkish frontier against the Christians of Trebizond and Georgia. The castle, in Asiatic warfare, was esteemed impregnable; and the city of Amasia, which is equally divided by the River Iris, rises on either side in the form of an amphitheatre, and represents on a smaller scale the image of Bagdad. In his rapid career, Timour appears to have overlooked this obscure and contumacious angle of Anatolia; and Mahomet, without provoking the conqueror, maintained his silent independence, and chased from the province the last stragglers of the Tartar host. He relieved himself from the dangerous neighborhood of Isa; but in the contests of their more powerful brethren his firm neutrality was respected; till, after the triumph of Mousa, he stood forth the heir and avenger of the unfortunate Soliman. Mahomet obtained Anatolia by treaty, and Romania by arms; and the soldier who presented him with the head of Mousa was rewarded as the benefactor of his king and country. The eight years of his sole and peaceful reign were usefully employed in banishing the vices of civil discord, and restoring on a firmer basis the fabric of the Ottoman monarchy. His last care was the choice of two viziers, Bajazet and Ibrahim, who might guide the youth of his son Amurath; and such was their union and prudence, that they concealed above forty days the emperor's death, till the arrival of his successor in the palace of Boursa. A new war was kindled in Europe by the prince, or impostor, Mustapha; the first vizier lost his army and his head; but the more fortunate Ibrahim, whose name and family are still revered, extinguished the last pretender to the throne of Bajazet, and closed the scene of domestic hostility.

In these conflicts, the wisest Turks, and indeed the body of the nation, were strongly attached to the unity of the empire; and Romania and Anatolia, so often torn asunder by private ambition, were animated by a strong and invincible tendency of cohesion. Their efforts might have instructed the Christian powers; and had they occupied, with a confederate fleet, the Straits of Gallipoli, the Ottomans, at least in Europe, must have been speedily annihilated. But the schism of the West, and the factions and wars of France and England, diverted the Latins from this generous enterprise: they enjoyed the present respite, without a thought of futurity; and were often tempted by a momentary interest to serve the common enemy of their religion. A colony of Genoese, which had been planted at Phocæa on the Ionian coast, was enriched by the lucrative monopoly of alum; and their tranquillity, under the Turkish empire, was secured by the annual payment of tribute. In the last civil war of the Ottomans, the Genoese governor, Adorno, a bold and ambitious youth, embraced the party of Amurath; and undertook, with seven stout galleys, to transport him from Asia to Europe. The sultan and five hundred guards embarked on board the admiral's ship; which was manned by eight hundred of the bravest Franks. His life and liberty were in their hands; nor can we, without reluctance, applaud the fidelity of Adorno, who, in the midst of the passage, knelt before him, and gratefully accepted a discharge of his arrears of tribute. They landed in sight of Mustapha and Gallipoli; two thousand Italians, armed with lances and battle-axes, attended Amurath to the conquest of Adrianople; and this venal service was soon repaid by the ruin of the commerce and colony of Phocæa.

If Timour had generously marched at the request, and to the relief, of the Greek emperor, he might be entitled to the praise and gratitude of the Christians. But a Mussulman, who carried into Georgia the sword of persecution, and respected the holy warfare of Bajazet, was not disposed to pity or succor the *idolaters* of Europe. The Tartar followed the impulse of ambition; and the deliverance of Constantinople was the accidental consequence. When Manuel abdicated the government, it was his prayer, rather than his hope, that the ruin of the church and state might be delayed beyond his unhappy days; and after his return from a western pilgrimage, he expected every hour the news of the sad catastrophe. On a sudden, he was astonished and rejoiced by the intelligence of the retreat, the overthrow, and the captivity of the Ottoman. Manuel immediately sailed from Modon in the Morea; ascended the throne of Constantinople, and dismissed his blind competitor to an easy exile in the Isle of Lesbos. The ambassadors of the son of Bajazet were soon introduced to his presence; but their pride was fallen, their tone was modest: they were awed by the just apprehension, lest the Greeks should open to the Moguls the gates of Europe. Soliman saluted the emperor by the name of father; solicited at his hands the government or gift of Romania; and promised to deserve his favor by inviolable friendship, and the restitution of Thessalonica, with the most important places along the Strymon, the Propontis, and the Black Sea. The alliance of Soliman exposed the emperor to the enmity and revenge of Mousa: the Turks appeared in arms before the gates of Constantinople; but they were repulsed by sea and land; and unless the city was guarded by some foreign mercenaries, the Greeks must have wondered at their own triumph. But, instead of prolonging the division of the Ottoman powers, the policy or passion of Manuel was tempted to assist the most formidable of the sons of Bajazet. He concluded a treaty with Mahomet, whose progress was checked by the insuperable barrier of Gallipoli: the sultan and his troops were transported over the Bosphorus; he was hospitably entertained in the capital; and his successful sally was the first step to the conquest of Romania. The ruin was suspended by the prudence and moderation of the conqueror: he faithfully discharged his own obligations and those of Soliman, respected the laws of gratitude and peace; and left the emperor guardian of his two younger sons, in the vain hope of saving them from the jealous cruelty of their brother Amurath. But the execution of his last testament would have offended the national honor and religion; and the divan unanimously pronounced, that the royal youths should never be abandoned to the custody and education of a Christian dog. On this refusal, the Byzantine councils were divided; but the age and caution of Manuel yielded to the presumption of his son John; and they unsheathed a dangerous weapon of revenge, by dismissing the true or false Mustapha, who had long been detained as a captive and hostage, and for whose maintenance they received an annual pension of three hundred thousand aspers. At the door of his prison, Mustapha subscribed to every proposal; and the keys of Gallipoli, or rather of Europe, were stipulated as the price of his deliverance. But no sooner was he seated on the throne of Romania, than he dismissed the Greek ambassadors with a smile of contempt, declaring, in a pious tone, that, at the day of judgment, he would rather answer for the violation of an oath, than for the surrender of a Mussulman city into the hands of the infidels. The emperor was at once the enemy of the two rivals; from whom he had sustained, and to whom he had offered, an injury; and the victory of Amurath was followed, in the ensuing spring, by the siege of Constantinople.

The religious merit of subduing the city of the Cæsars attracted from Asia a crowd of volunteers, who aspired to the crown of martyrdom: their military ardor was inflamed by the promise of rich spoils and beautiful females; and the sultan's ambition was consecrated by the presence and prediction of Seid Bechar, a descendant of the prophet, who arrived in the camp, on a mule, with a venerable train of five hundred disciples. But he might blush, if a fanatic could blush, at the failure of his assurances. The strength of the walls resisted an army of two hundred thousand Turks; their assaults were repelled by the sallies of the Greeks and their foreign mercenaries; the old resources of defence were opposed to the new engines of attack; and the enthusiasm of the dervis, who was snatched to heaven in visionary converse with Mahomet, was answered by the credulity of the Christians, who *beheld* the Virgin Mary, in a violet garment, walking on the rampart and animating their courage. After a siege of two months, Amurath was recalled to Boursa by a domestic revolt, which had been kindled by Greek treachery, and was soon extinguished by the death of a guiltless brother. While he led his Janizaries to new conquests in Europe and Asia, the Byzantine empire was indulged in a servile and precarious respite of thirty years. Manuel sank into the grave; and John Palæologus was permitted to reign, for an annual tribute of three hundred thousand aspers, and the dereliction of almost all that he held beyond the suburbs of Constantinople.

In the establishment and restoration of the Turkish empire, the first merit must doubtless be assigned to the personal qualities of the sultans; since, in human life, the most important scenes will depend on the character of a single actor. By some shades of wisdom and virtue, they may be discriminated from each other; but, except in a single instance, a period of nine reigns, and two hundred and sixty-five years, is occupied, from the elevation of Othman to the death of Soliman, by a rare series of warlike and active princes, who impressed their subjects with obedience and their enemies with terror. Instead of the slothful luxury of the seraglio, the heirs of royalty were educated in the council and the field: from early youth they were intrusted by their fathers with the command of provinces and armies; and this manly institution, which was often productive of civil war, must have essentially contributed to the discipline and vigor of the monarchy. The Ottomans cannot style themselves, like the Arabian caliphs, the descendants or successors of the apostle of God; and the kindred which they claim with the Tartar khans of the house of Zingis appears to be founded in flattery rather than in truth. Their origin is obscure; but their sacred and indefeasible right, which no time can erase, and no violence can infringe, was soon and unalterably implanted in the minds of their subjects. A weak or vicious sultan may be deposed and strangled; but his inheritance devolves to an infant or an idiot: nor has the most daring rebel presumed to ascend the throne of his lawful sovereign.

While the transient dynasties of Asia have been continually subverted by a crafty vizier in the palace, or a victorious general in the camp, the Ottoman succession has been confirmed by the practice of five centuries, and is now incorporated with the vital principle of the Turkish nation.

To the spirit and constitution of that nation, a strong and singular influence may, however, be ascribed. The primitive subjects of Othman were the four hundred families of wandering Turkmans, who had followed his ancestors from the Oxus to the Sangar; and the plains of Anatolia are still covered with the white and black tents of their rustic brethren. But this original drop was dissolved in the mass of voluntary and vanquished subjects, who, under the name of Turks, are united by the common ties of religion, language, and manners. In the cities, from Erzeroum to Belgrade, that national appellation is common to all the Moslems, the first and most honorable inhabitants; but they have abandoned, at least in Romania, the villages, and the cultivation of the land, to the Christian peasants. In the vigorous age of the Ottoman government, the Turks were themselves excluded from all civil and military honors; and a servile class, an artificial people, was raised by the discipline of education to obey, to conquer, and to command. From the time of Orchan and the first Amurath, the sultans were persuaded that a government of the sword must be renewed in each generation with new soldiers; and that such soldiers must be sought, not in effeminate Asia, but among the hardy and warlike natives of Europe. The provinces of Thrace, Macedonia, Albania, Bulgaria, and Servia, became the perpetual seminary of the Turkish army; and when the royal fifth of the captives was diminished by conquest, an inhuman tax of the fifth child, or of every fifth year, was rigorously levied on the Christian families. At the age of twelve or fourteen years, the most robust youths were torn from their parents; their names were enrolled in a book; and from that moment they were clothed, taught, and maintained, for the public service. According to the promise of their appearance, they were selected for the royal schools of Boursa, Pera, and Adrianople, intrusted to the care of the bashaws, or dispersed in the houses of the Anatolian peasantry. It was the first care of their masters to instruct them in the Turkish language: their bodies were exercised by every labor that could fortify their strength; they learned to wrestle, to leap, to run, to shoot with the bow, and afterwards with the musket; till they were drafted into the chambers and companies of the Janizaries, and severely trained in the military or monastic discipline of the order. The youths most conspicuous for birth, talents, and beauty, were admitted into the inferior class of *Agiamoglans*, or the more liberal rank of *Ichoglans*, of whom the former were attached to the palace, and the latter to the person, of the prince. In four successive schools, under the rod of the white eunuchs, the arts of horsemanship and of darting the javelin were their daily exercise, while those of a more studious cast applied themselves to the study of the Koran, and the knowledge of the Arabic and Persian tongues. As they advanced in seniority and merit, they were gradually dismissed to military, civil, and even ecclesiastical employments: the longer their stay, the higher was their expectation; till, at a mature period, they were admitted into the number of the forty agas, who stood before the sultan, and were promoted by his choice to the government of provinces and the first honors of the empire. Such a mode of institution was admirably adapted to the form and spirit of a despotic monarchy. The ministers and generals were, in the strictest sense, the slaves of the emperor, to whose bounty they were indebted for their instruction and support. When they left the seraglio, and suffered their beards to grow as the symbol of enfranchisement, they found themselves in an important office, without faction or friendship, without parents and without heirs, dependent on the hand which had raised them from the dust, and which, on the slightest displeasure, could break in pieces these statues of glass, as they were aptly termed by the Turkish proverb. In the slow and painful steps of education, their characters and talents were unfolded to a discerning eye: the *man*, naked and alone, was reduced to the standard of his personal merit; and, if the sovereign had wisdom to choose, he possessed a pure and boundless liberty of choice. The Ottoman candidates were trained by the virtues of abstinence to those of action; by the habits of submission to those of command. A similar spirit was diffused among the troops; and their silence and sobriety, their patience and modesty, have extorted the reluctant praise of their Christian enemies. Nor can the victory appear doubtful, if we compare the discipline and exercise of the Janizaries with the pride of birth, the independence of chivalry, the ignorance of the new levies, the mutinous temper of the veterans, and the vices of intemperance and disorder, which so long contaminated the armies of Europe.

The only hope of salvation for the Greek empire, and the adjacent kingdoms, would have been some more powerful weapon, some discovery in the art of war, that would give them a decisive superiority over their Turkish foes. Such a weapon was in their hands; such a discovery had been made in the critical moment of their fate. The chemists of China or Europe had found, by casual or elaborate experiments, that a mixture of saltpetre, sulphur, and charcoal, produces, with a spark of fire, a tremendous explosion. It was soon observed, that if the expansive force were compressed in a strong tube, a ball of stone or iron might be expelled with irresistible and destructive velocity. The precise æra of the invention and application of gunpowder is involved in doubtful traditions and equivocal language; yet we may clearly discern, that it was known before the middle of the fourteenth century; and that before the end of the same, the use of artillery in battles and sieges, by sea and land, was familiar to the states of Germany, Italy, Spain, France, and England. The priority of nations is of small account; none could derive any exclusive benefit from their previous or superior knowledge; and in the common improvement, they stood on the same level of relative power and military science. Nor was it possible to circumscribe the secret within the pale of the church; it was disclosed to the Turks by the treachery of apostates and the selfish policy of rivals; and the sultans had sense to adopt, and wealth to reward, the talents of a Christian engineer. The Genoese, who transported Amurath into Europe, must be accused as his preceptors; and it was probably by their hands that his cannon was cast and directed at the siege of Constantinople. The first attempt was indeed unsuccessful; but in the general warfare of the age, the advantage was on *their* side, who were most commonly the assailants: for a while the proportion of the attack and defence was suspended; and this thundering artillery was pointed against the walls and towers which had been erected only to resist the less potent engines of antiquity. By the Venetians, the use of gunpowder was communicated without reproach to the sultans of Egypt and Persia, their allies against the Ottoman power; the secret was soon propagated to the extremities of Asia; and the advantage of the European was confined to his easy victories over the savages of the new world. If we contrast the rapid progress of this mischievous discovery with the slow and laborious advances of reason, science, and the arts of peace, a philosopher, according to his temper, will laugh or weep at the folly of mankind.

Union of the Greek and Latin Churches. – Part One

Applications of the Eastern Emperors to the Popes. – Visits to the West, of John the First, Manuel, and John the Second, Palæologus. – Union of the Greek and Latin Churches, Promoted by the Council of Basil, and Concluded at Ferrara and Florence. – State of Literature at Constantinople. – Its Revival in Italy by the Greek Fugitives. – Curiosity and Emulation of the Latins.

IN THE FOUR LAST centuries of the Greek emperors, their friendly or hostile aspect towards the pope and the Latins may be observed as the thermometer of their prosperity or distress; as the scale of the rise and fall of the Barbarian dynasties. When the Turks of the house of Seljuk pervaded Asia, and threatened Constantinople, we have seen, at the council of Placentia, the suppliant ambassadors of Alexius imploring the protection of the common father of the Christians. No sooner had the arms of the French pilgrims removed the sultan from Nice to Iconium, than the Greek princes resumed, or avowed, their genuine hatred and contempt for the schismatics of the West, which precipitated the first downfall of their empire. The date of the Mogul invasion is marked in the soft and charitable language of John Vataces. After the recovery of Constantinople, the throne of the first Palæologus was encompassed by foreign and domestic enemies; as long as the sword of Charles was suspended over his head, he basely courted the favor of the Roman pontiff; and sacrificed to the present danger his faith, his virtue, and the affection of his subjects. On the decease of Michael, the prince and people asserted the independence of their church, and the purity of their creed: the elder Andronicus neither feared nor loved the Latins; in his last distress, pride was the safeguard of superstition; nor could he decently retract in his age the firm and orthodox declarations of his youth. His grandson, the younger Andronicus, was less a slave in his temper and situation; and the conquest of Bithynia by the Turks admonished him to seek a temporal and spiritual alliance with the Western princes. After a separation and silence of fifty years, a secret agent, the monk Barlaam, was despatched to Pope Benedict the Twelfth; and his artful instructions appear to have been drawn by the master-hand of the great domestic. "Most holy father," was he commissioned to say, "the emperor is not less desirous than yourself of a union between the two churches: but in this delicate transaction, he is obliged to respect his own dignity and the prejudices of his subjects. The ways of union are twofold; force and persuasion. Of force, the inefficacy has been already tried; since the Latins have subdued the empire, without subduing the minds, of the Greeks. The method of persuasion, though slow, is sure and permanent. A deputation of thirty or forty of our doctors would probably agree with those of the Vatican, in the love of truth and the unity of belief; but on their return, what would be the use, the recompense, of such an agreement? the scorn of their brethren, and the reproaches of a blind and obstinate nation. Yet that nation is accustomed to reverence the general councils, which have fixed the articles of our faith; and if they reprobate the decrees of Lyons, it is because the Eastern churches were neither heard nor represented in that arbitrary meeting. For this salutary end, it will be expedient, and even necessary, that a well-chosen legate should be sent into Greece, to convene the patriarchs of Constantinople, Alexandria, Antioch, and Jerusalem; and, with their aid, to prepare a free and universal synod. But at this moment," continued the subtle agent, "the empire is assaulted and endangered by the Turks, who have occupied four of the greatest cities of Anatolia. The Christian inhabitants have expressed a wish of returning to their allegiance and religion; but the forces and revenues of the emperor are insufficient for their deliverance: and the Roman legate must be accompanied, or preceded, by an army of Franks, to expel the infidels, and open a way to the holy sepulchre." If the suspicious Latins should require some pledge, some previous effect of the sincerity of the Greeks, the answers of Barlaam were perspicuous and rational. "1. A general synod can alone consummate the union of the churches; nor can such a synod be held till the three Oriental patriarchs, and a great number of bishops, are enfranchised from the Mahometan yoke. . The Greeks are alienated by a long series of oppression and injury: they must be reconciled by some act of brotherly love, some effectual succor, which may fortify the authority and arguments of the emperor, and the friends of the union. . If some difference of faith or ceremonies should be found incurable, the Greeks, however, are the disciples of Christ; and the Turks are the common enemies of the Christian name. The Armenians, Cyprians, and Rhodians, are equally attacked; and it will become the piety of the French princes to draw their swords in the general defence of religion. . Should the subjects of Andronicus be treated as the worst of schismatics, of heretics, of pagans, a judicious policy may yet instruct the powers of the West to embrace a useful ally, to uphold a sinking empire, to guard the confines of Europe; and rather to join the Greeks against the Turks, than to expect the union of the Turkish arms with the troops and treasures of captive Greece." The reasons, the offers, and the demands, of Andronicus were eluded with cold and stately indifference. The kings of France and Naples declined the dangers and glory of a crusade; the pope refused to call a new synod to determine old articles of faith; and his regard for the obsolete claims of the Latin emperor and clergy engaged him to use an offensive superscription, – "To the *moderator* of the Greeks, and the persons who style themselves the patriarchs of the Eastern churches." For such an embassy, a time and character less propitious could not easily have been found. Benedict the Twelfth was a dull peasant, perplexed with scruples, and immersed in sloth and wine: his pride might enrich with a third crown the papal tiara, but he was alike unfit for the regal and the pastoral office.

After the decease of Andronicus, while the Greeks were distracted by intestine war, they could not presume to agitate a general union of the Christians. But as soon as Cantacuzene had subdued and pardoned his enemies, he was anxious to justify, or at least to extenuate, the introduction of the Turks into Europe, and the nuptials of his daughter with a Mussulman prince. Two officers of state, with a Latin interpreter, were sent in his name to the Roman court, which was transplanted to Avignon, on the banks of the Rhône, during a period of seventy years: they represented the hard necessity which had urged him to embrace the alliance of the miscreants, and pronounced by his command the specious and edifying sounds of union and crusade. Pope Clement the Sixth, the successor of Benedict, received them with hospitality and honor, acknowledged the innocence of their sovereign, excused his distress, applauded his magnanimity, and displayed a clear knowledge of the state and revolutions of the Greek empire, which he had imbibed from the honest accounts of a Savoyard lady, an attendant of the empress Anne.

If Clement was ill endowed with the virtues of a priest, he possessed, however, the spirit and magnificence of a prince, whose liberal hand distributed benefices and kingdoms with equal facility. Under his reign Avignon was the seat of pomp and pleasure: in his youth he had surpassed the licentiousness of a baron; and the palace, nay, the bed-chamber of the pope, was adorned, or polluted, by the visits of his female favorites. The wars of France and England were adverse to the holy enterprise; but his vanity was amused by the splendid idea; and the Greek ambassadors returned with two Latin bishops, the ministers of the pontiff. On their arrival at Constantinople, the emperor and the nuncios admired each other's piety and eloquence; and their frequent conferences were filled with mutual praises and promises, by which both parties were amused, and neither could be deceived. "I am delighted," said the devout Cantacuzene, "with the project of our holy war, which must redound to my personal glory, as well as to the public benefit of Christendom. My dominions will give a free passage to the armies of France: my troops, my galleys, my treasures, shall be consecrated to the common cause; and happy would be my fate, could I deserve and obtain the crown of martyrdom. Words are insufficient to express the ardor with which I sigh for the reunion of the scattered members of Christ. If my death could avail, I would gladly present my sword and my neck: if the spiritual phúnix could arise from my ashes, I would erect the pile, and kindle the flame with my own hands." Yet the Greek emperor presumed to observe, that the articles of faith which divided the two churches had been introduced by the pride and precipitation of the Latins: he disclaimed the servile and arbitrary steps of the first Palæologus; and firmly declared, that he would never submit his conscience unless to the decrees of a free and universal synod. "The situation of the times," continued he, "will not allow the pope and myself to meet either at Rome or Constantinople; but some maritime city may be chosen on the verge of the two empires, to unite the bishops, and to instruct the faithful, of the East and West." The nuncios seemed content with the proposition; and Cantacuzene affects to deplore the failure of his hopes, which were soon overthrown by the death of Clement, and the different temper of his successor. His own life was prolonged, but it was prolonged in a cloister; and, except by his prayers, the humble monk was incapable of directing the counsels of his pupil or the state.

Yet of all the Byzantine princes, that pupil, John Palæologus, was the best disposed to embrace, to believe, and to obey, the shepherd of the West. His mother, Anne of Savoy, was baptized in the bosom of the Latin church: her marriage with Andronicus imposed a change of name, of apparel, and of worship, but her heart was still faithful to her country and religion: she had formed the infancy of her son, and she governed the emperor, after his mind, or at least his stature, was enlarged to the size of man. In the first year of his deliverance and restoration, the Turks were still masters of the Hellespont; the son of Cantacuzene was in arms at Adrianople; and Palæologus could depend neither on himself nor on his people. By his mother's advice, and in the hope of foreign aid, he abjured the rights both of the church and state; and the act of slavery, subscribed in purple ink, and sealed with the *golden* bull, was privately intrusted to an Italian agent. The first article of the treaty is an oath of fidelity and obedience to Innocent the Sixth and his successors, the supreme pontiffs of the Roman and Catholic church. The emperor promises to entertain with due reverence their legates and nuncios; to assign a palace for their residence, and a temple for their worship; and to deliver his second son Manuel as the hostage of his faith. For these condescensions he requires a prompt succor of fifteen galleys, with five hundred men at arms, and a thousand archers, to serve against his Christian and Mussulman enemies. Palæologus engages to impose on his clergy and people the same spiritual yoke; but as the resistance of the Greeks might be justly foreseen, he adopts the two effectual methods of corruption and education. The legate was empowered to distribute the vacant benefices among the ecclesiastics who should subscribe the creed of the Vatican: three schools were instituted to instruct the youth of Constantinople in the language and doctrine of the Latins; and the name of Andronicus, the heir of the empire, was enrolled as the first student. Should he fail in the measures of persuasion or force, Palæologus declares himself unworthy to reign; transferred to the pope all regal and paternal authority; and invests Innocent with full power to regulate the family, the government, and the marriage, of his son and successor. But this treaty was neither executed nor published: the Roman galleys were as vain and imaginary as the submission of the Greeks; and it was only by the secrecy that their sovereign escaped the dishonor of this fruitless humiliation.

The tempest of the Turkish arms soon burst on his head; and after the loss of Adrianople and Romania, he was enclosed in his capital, the vassal of the haughty Amurath, with the miserable hope of being the last devoured by the savage. In this abject state, Palæologus embraced the resolution of embarking for Venice, and casting himself at the feet of the pope: he was the first of the Byzantine princes who had ever visited the unknown regions of the West, yet in them alone he could seek consolation or relief; and with less violation of his dignity he might appear in the sacred college than at the Ottoman *Porte*. After a long absence, the Roman pontiffs were returning from Avignon to the banks of the Tyber: Urban the Fifth, of a mild and virtuous character, encouraged or allowed the pilgrimage of the Greek prince; and, within the same year, enjoyed the glory of receiving in the Vatican the two Imperial shadows who represented the majesty of Constantine and Charlemagne. In this suppliant visit, the emperor of Constantinople, whose vanity was lost in his distress, gave more than could be expected of empty sounds and formal submissions. A previous trial was imposed; and, in the presence of four cardinals, he acknowledged, as a true Catholic, the supremacy of the pope, and the double procession of the Holy Ghost. After this purification, he was introduced to a public audience in the church of St. Peter: Urban, in the midst of the cardinals, was seated on his throne; the Greek monarch, after three genuflections, devoutly kissed the feet, the hands, and at length the mouth, of the holy father, who celebrated high mass in his presence, allowed him to lead the bridle of his mule, and treated him with a sumptuous banquet in the Vatican. The entertainment of Palæologus was friendly and honorable; yet some difference was observed between the emperors of the East and West; nor could the former be entitled to the rare privilege of chanting the gospel in the rank of a deacon. In favor of his proselyte, Urban strove to rekindle the zeal of the French king and the other powers of the West; but he found them cold in the general cause, and active only in their domestic quarrels. The last hope of the emperor was in an English mercenary, John Hawkwood, or Acuto, who, with a band of adventurers, the white brotherhood, had ravaged Italy from the Alps to Calabria; sold his services to the hostile states; and incurred a just excommunication by shooting his arrows against the papal residence. A special license was granted to negotiate with the outlaw, but the forces, or the spirit, of Hawkwood, were unequal to the enterprise: and it was for the advantage, perhaps, of Palæologus to be disappointed of succor, that must have been costly, that could not be effectual, and which might have been dangerous. The disconsolate Greek prepared for his return, but even his return was impeded by a most ignominious obstacle. On his arrival at Venice, he had borrowed large sums at exorbitant usury; but his coffers were empty, his creditors were impatient, and his person was detained as the best security for the payment. His eldest son, Andronicus, the regent of Constantinople, was repeatedly urged to exhaust every resource; and even by stripping the churches, to extricate his father from captivity and disgrace. But the unnatural youth was insensible of the disgrace, and secretly pleased with the captivity of the emperor: the state was poor, the clergy were obstinate; nor could some religious scruple be wanting to excuse the guilt of his indifference and delay. Such undutiful neglect was severely reproved by the piety of his brother Manuel, who instantly sold or mortgaged all that he possessed, embarked for Venice, relieved his father, and pledged his own freedom to be responsible for the debt. On his return to Constantinople, the parent and king distinguished his two sons with suitable rewards; but the faith and manners of the slothful Palæologus had not been improved by his Roman pilgrimage; and his apostasy or conversion, devoid of any spiritual or temporal effects, was speedily forgotten by the Greeks and Latins.

Thirty years after the return of Palæologus, his son and successor, Manuel, from a similar motive, but on a larger scale, again visited the countries of the West. In a preceding chapter I have related his treaty with Bajazet, the violation of that treaty, the siege or blockade of Constantinople, and the French succor under the command of the gallant Boucicault. By his ambassadors, Manuel had solicited the Latin powers; but it was thought that the presence of a distressed monarch would draw tears and supplies from the hardest Barbarians; and the marshal who advised the journey prepared the reception of the Byzantine prince. The land was occupied by the Turks; but the navigation of Venice was safe and open: Italy received him as the first, or, at least, as the second, of the Christian princes; Manuel was pitied as the champion and confessor of the faith; and the dignity of his behavior prevented that pity from sinking into contempt. From Venice he proceeded to Padua and Pavia; and even the duke of Milan, a secret ally of Bajazet, gave him safe and honorable conduct to the verge of his dominions. On the confines of France the royal officers undertook the care of his person, journey, and expenses; and two thousand of the richest citizens, in arms and on horseback, came forth to meet him as far as Charenton, in the neighborhood of the capital. At the gates of Paris, he was saluted by the chancellor and the parliament; and Charles the Sixth, attended by his princes and nobles, welcomed his brother with a cordial embrace. The successor of Constantine was clothed in a robe of white silk, and mounted on a milk-white steed, a circumstance, in the French ceremonial, of singular importance: the white color is considered as the symbol of sovereignty; and, in a late visit, the German emperor, after a haughty demand and a peevish refusal, had been reduced to content himself with a black courser. Manuel was lodged in the Louvre; a succession of feasts and balls, the pleasures of the banquet and the chase, were ingeniously varied by the politeness of the French, to display their magnificence, and amuse his grief: he was indulged in the liberty of his chapel; and the doctors of the Sorbonne were astonished, and possibly scandalized, by the language, the rites, and the vestments, of his Greek clergy. But the slightest glance on the state of the kingdom must teach him to despair of any effectual assistance. The unfortunate Charles, though he enjoyed some lucid intervals, continually relapsed into furious or stupid insanity: the reins of government were alternately seized by his brother and uncle, the dukes of Orleans and Burgundy, whose factious competition prepared the miseries of civil war. The former was a gay youth, dissolved in luxury and love: the latter was the father of John count of Nevers, who had so lately been ransomed from Turkish captivity; and, if the fearless son was ardent to revenge his defeat, the more prudent Burgundy was content with the cost and peril of the first experiment. When Manuel had satiated the curiosity, and perhaps fatigued the patience, of the French, he resolved on a visit to the adjacent island. In his progress from Dover, he was entertained at Canterbury with due reverence by the prior and monks of St. Austin; and, on Blackheath, King Henry the Fourth, with the English court, saluted the Greek hero, (I copy our old historian,) who, during many days, was lodged and treated in London as emperor of the East. But the state of England was still more adverse to the design of the holy war. In the same year, the hereditary sovereign had been deposed and murdered: the reigning prince was a successful usurper, whose ambition was punished by jealousy and remorse: nor could Henry of Lancaster withdraw his person or forces from the defence of a throne incessantly shaken by conspiracy and rebellion. He pitied, he praised, he feasted, the emperor of Constantinople; but if the English monarch assumed the cross, it was only to appease his people, and perhaps his conscience, by the merit or semblance of his pious intention. Satisfied, however, with gifts and honors, Manuel returned to Paris; and, after a residence of two years in the West, shaped his course through Germany and Italy, embarked at Venice, and patiently expected, in the Morea, the moment of his ruin or deliverance. Yet he had escaped the ignominious necessity of offering his religion to public or private sale. The Latin church was distracted by the great schism; the kings, the nations, the universities, of Europe were divided in their obedience between the popes of Rome and Avignon; and the emperor, anxious to conciliate the friendship of both parties, abstained from any correspondence with the indigent and unpopular rivals. His journey coincided with the year of the jubilee; but he passed through Italy without desiring, or deserving, the plenary indulgence which abolished the guilt or penance of the sins of the faithful. The Roman pope was offended by this neglect; accused him of irreverence to an image of Christ; and exhorted the princes of Italy to reject and abandon the obstinate schismatic.

Union of the Greek and Latin Churches. – Part Two

DURING THE PERIOD OF the crusades, the Greeks beheld with astonishment and terror the perpetual stream of emigration that flowed, and continued to flow, from the unknown climates of their West. The visits of their last emperors removed the veil of separation, and they disclosed to their eyes the powerful nations of Europe, whom they no longer presumed to brand with the name of Barbarians. The observations of Manuel, and his more inquisitive followers, have been preserved by a Byzantine historian of the times: his scattered ideas I shall collect and abridge; and it may be amusing enough, perhaps instructive, to contemplate the rude pictures of Germany, France, and England, whose ancient and modern state are so familiar to *our* minds. I. Germany (says the Greek Chalcondyles) is of ample latitude from Vienna to the ocean; and it stretches (a strange geography) from Prague in Bohemia to the River Tartessus, and the Pyrenæan Mountains. The soil, except in figs and olives, is sufficiently fruitful; the air is salubrious; the bodies of the natives are robust and healthy; and these cold regions are seldom visited with the calamities of pestilence, or earthquakes. After the Scythians or Tartars, the Germans are the most numerous of nations: they are brave and patient; and were they united under a single head, their force would be irresistible. By the gift of the pope, they have acquired the privilege of choosing the Roman emperor; nor is any people more devoutly attached to the faith and obedience of the Latin patriarch. The greatest part of the country is divided among the princes and prelates; but Strasburg, Cologne, Hamburgh, and more than two hundred free cities, are governed by sage and equal laws, according to the will, and for the advantage, of the whole community. The use of duels, or single combats on foot, prevails among them in peace and war: their industry excels in all the mechanic arts; and the Germans may boast of the invention of gunpowder and cannon, which is now diffused over the greatest part of the world. II. The kingdom of France is spread above fifteen or twenty days' journey from Germany to Spain, and from the Alps to the British Ocean; containing many flourishing cities, and among these Paris, the seat of the king, which surpasses the rest in riches and luxury. Many princes and lords alternately wait in his palace, and acknowledge him as their sovereign: the most powerful are the dukes of Bretagne and Burgundy; of whom the latter possesses the wealthy province of Flanders, whose harbors are frequented by the ships and merchants of our own, and the more remote, seas. The French are an ancient and opulent people; and their language and manners, though somewhat different, are not dissimilar from those of the Italians. Vain of the Imperial dignity of Charlemagne, of their victories over the Saracens, and of the exploits of their heroes, Oliver and Rowland, they esteem themselves the first of the western nations; but this foolish arrogance has been recently humbled by the unfortunate events of their wars against the English, the inhabitants of the British island. III. Britain, in the ocean, and opposite to the shores of Flanders, may be considered either as one, or as three islands; but the whole is united by a common interest, by the same manners, and by a similar government. The measure of its circumference is five thousand stadia: the land is overspread with towns and villages: though destitute of wine, and not abounding in fruit-trees, it is fertile in wheat and barley; in honey and wool; and much cloth is manufactured by the inhabitants. In populousness and power, in richness and luxury, London, the metropolis of the isle, may claim a preeminence over all the cities of the West. It is situate on the Thames, a broad and rapid river, which at the distance of thirty miles falls into the Gallic Sea; and the daily flow and ebb of the tide affords a safe entrance and departure to the vessels of commerce. The king is head of a powerful and turbulent aristocracy: his principal vassals hold their estates by a free and unalterable tenure; and the laws define the limits of his authority and their obedience. The kingdom has been often afflicted by foreign conquest and domestic sedition: but the natives are bold and hardy, renowned in arms and victorious in war. The form of their shields or targets is derived from the Italians, that of their swords from the Greeks; the use of the long bow is the peculiar and decisive advantage of the English. Their language bears no affinity to the idioms of the Continent: in the habits of domestic life, they are not easily distinguished from their neighbors of France: but the most singular circumstance of their manners is their disregard of conjugal honor and of female chastity. In their mutual visits, as the first act of hospitality, the guest is welcomed in the embraces of their wives and daughters: among friends they are lent and borrowed without shame; nor are the islanders offended at this strange commerce, and its inevitable consequences. Informed as we are of the customs of Old England and assured of the virtue of our mothers, we may smile at the credulity, or resent the injustice, of the Greek, who must have confounded a modest salute with a criminal embrace. But his credulity and injustice may teach an important lesson; to distrust the accounts of foreign and remote nations, and to suspend our belief of every tale that deviates from the laws of nature and the character of man.

After his return, and the victory of Timour, Manuel reigned many years in prosperity and peace. As long as the sons of Bajazet solicited his friendship and spared his dominions, he was satisfied with the national religion; and his leisure was employed in composing twenty theological dialogues for its defence. The appearance of the Byzantine ambassadors at the council of Constance, announces the restoration of the Turkish power, as well as of the Latin church: the conquest of the sultans, Mahomet and Amurath, reconciled the emperor to the Vatican; and the siege of Constantinople almost tempted him to acquiesce in the double procession of the Holy Ghost. When Martin the Fifth ascended without a rival the chair of St. Peter, a friendly intercourse of letters and embassies was revived between the East and West. Ambition on one side, and distress on the other, dictated the same decent language of charity and peace: the artful Greek expressed a desire of marrying his six sons to Italian princesses; and the Roman, not less artful, despatched the daughter of the marquis of Montferrat, with a company of noble virgins, to soften, by their charms, the obstinacy of the schismatics. Yet under this mask of zeal, a discerning eye will perceive that all was hollow and insincere in the court and church of Constantinople. According to the vicissitudes of danger and repose, the emperor advanced or retreated; alternately instructed and disavowed his ministers; and escaped from the importunate pressure by urging the duty of inquiry, the obligation of collecting the sense of his patriarchs and bishops, and the impossibility of convening them at a time when the Turkish arms were at the gates of his capital. From a review of the public transactions it will appear that the Greeks insisted on three successive measures, a succor, a council, and a final reunion, while the Latins eluded the second, and only promised the first, as a consequential and voluntary reward of the third. But we have an opportunity of unfolding the most secret intentions of Manuel, as he explained them in a private conversation without artifice or disguise. In his declining age, the emperor had associated John Palæologus, the second of the name, and the eldest of his sons, on whom he devolved the greatest part of the authority and weight of government. One day, in the presence only of the historian Phranza, his favorite chamberlain, he opened to his colleague and successor the true principle of his negotiations with the pope. "Our last resource," said Manuel, against the Turks, "is their fear of our union with the Latins, of the warlike nations of the West, who may arm for our relief and for their destruction. As often as you are threatened by the miscreants, present this danger before their eyes. Propose a council; consult on the means; but ever delay and avoid the convocation of an assembly, which cannot tend either to our spiritual or temporal emolument. The Latins are proud; the Greeks are obstinate; neither party will recede or retract; and the attempt of a perfect union will confirm the schism, alienate the churches, and leave us, without hope or defence, at the mercy of the Barbarians." Impatient of this salutary lesson, the royal youth arose from his seat, and departed in silence; and the wise monarch (continued Phranza) casting his eyes on me, thus resumed his discourse: "My son deems himself a great and heroic prince; but, alas! our miserable age does not afford scope for heroism or greatness. His daring spirit might have suited the happier times of our ancestors; but the present state requires not an emperor, but a cautious steward of the last relics of our fortunes. Well do I remember the lofty expectations which he built on our alliance with Mustapha; and much do I fear, that this rash courage will urge the ruin of our house, and that even religion may precipitate our downfall." Yet the experience and authority of Manuel preserved the peace, and eluded the council; till, in the seventy-eighth year of his age, and in the habit of a monk, he terminated his career, dividing his precious movables among his children and the poor, his physicians and his favorite servants. Of his six sons, Andronicus the Second was invested with the principality of Thessalonica, and died of a leprosy soon after the sale of that city to the Venetians and its final conquest by the Turks. Some fortunate incidents had restored Peloponnesus, or the Morea, to the empire; and in his more prosperous days, Manuel had fortified the narrow isthmus of six miles with a stone wall and one hundred and fifty-three towers. The wall was overthrown by the first blast of the Ottomans; the fertile peninsula might have been sufficient for the four younger brothers, Theodore and Constantine, Demetrius and Thomas; but they wasted in domestic contests the remains of their strength; and the least successful of the rivals were reduced to a life of dependence in the Byzantine palace.

The eldest of the sons of Manuel, John Palæologus the Second, was acknowledged, after his father's death, as the sole emperor of the Greeks. He immediately proceeded to repudiate his wife, and to contract a new marriage with the princess of Trebizond: beauty was in his eyes the first qualification of an empress; and the clergy had yielded to his firm assurance, that unless he might be indulged in a divorce, he would retire to a cloister, and leave the throne to his brother Constantine. The first, and in truth the only, victory of Palæologus, was over a Jew, whom, after a long and learned dispute, he converted to the Christian faith; and this momentous conquest is carefully recorded in the history of the times. But he soon resumed the design of uniting the East and West; and, regardless of his father's advice, listened, as it should seem with sincerity, to the proposal of meeting the pope in a general council beyond the Adriatic. This dangerous project was encouraged by Martin the Fifth, and coldly entertained by his successor Eugenius, till, after a tedious negotiation, the emperor received a summons from the Latin assembly of a new character, the independent prelates of Basil, who styled themselves the representatives and judges of the Catholic church.

The Roman pontiff had fought and conquered in the cause of ecclesiastical freedom; but the victorious clergy were soon exposed to the tyranny of their deliverer; and his sacred character was invulnerable to those arms which they found so keen and effectual against the civil magistrate. Their great charter, the right of election, was annihilated by appeals, evaded by trusts or commendams, disappointed by reversionary grants, and superseded by previous and arbitrary reservations. A public auction was instituted in the court of Rome: the cardinals and favorites were enriched with the spoils of nations; and every country might complain that the most important and valuable benefices were accumulated on the heads of aliens and absentees. During their residence at Avignon, the ambition of the popes subsided in the meaner passions of avarice and luxury: they rigorously imposed on the clergy the tributes of first-fruits and tenths; but they freely tolerated the impunity of vice, disorder, and corruption. These manifold scandals were aggravated by the great schism of the West, which continued above fifty years. In the furious conflicts of Rome and Avignon, the vices of the rivals were mutually exposed; and their precarious situation degraded their authority, relaxed their discipline, and multiplied their wants and exactions. To heal the wounds, and restore the monarchy, of the church, the synods of Pisa and Constance were successively convened; but these great assemblies, conscious of their strength, resolved to vindicate the privileges of the Christian aristocracy. From a personal sentence against two pontiffs, whom they rejected, and a third, their acknowledged sovereign, whom they deposed, the fathers of Constance proceeded to examine the nature and limits of the Roman supremacy; nor did they separate till they had established the authority, above the pope, of a general council. It was enacted, that, for the government and reformation of the church, such assemblies should be held at regular intervals; and that each synod, before its dissolution, should appoint the time and place of the subsequent meeting. By the influence of the court of Rome, the next convocation at Sienna was easily eluded; but the bold and vigorous proceedings of the council of Basil had almost been fatal to the reigning pontiff, Eugenius the Fourth. A just suspicion of his design prompted the fathers to hasten the promulgation of their first decree, that the representatives of the church-militant on earth were invested with a divine and spiritual jurisdiction over all Christians, without excepting the pope; and that a general council could not be dissolved, prorogued, or transferred, unless by their free deliberation and consent. On the notice that Eugenius had fulminated a bull for that purpose, they ventured to summon, to admonish, to threaten, to censure the contumacious successor of St. Peter. After many delays, to allow time for repentance, they finally declared, that, unless he submitted within the term of sixty days, he was suspended from the exercise of all temporal and ecclesiastical authority. And to mark their jurisdiction over the prince as well as the priest, they assumed the government of Avignon, annulled the alienation of the sacred patrimony, and protected Rome from the imposition of new taxes. Their boldness was justified, not only by the general opinion of the clergy, but by the support and power of the first monarchs of Christendom: the emperor Sigismond declared himself the servant and protector of the synod; Germany and France adhered to their cause; the duke of Milan was the enemy of Eugenius; and he was driven from the Vatican by an insurrection of the Roman people. Rejected at the same time by temporal and spiritual subjects, submission was his only choice: by a most humiliating bull, the pope repealed his own acts, and ratified those of the council; incorporated his legates and cardinals with that venerable body; and *seemed* to resign himself to the decrees of the supreme legislature. Their fame pervaded the countries of the East: and it was in their presence that Sigismond received the ambassadors of the Turkish sultan, who laid at his feet twelve large vases, filled with robes of silk and pieces of gold. The fathers of Basil aspired to the glory of reducing the Greeks, as well as the Bohemians, within the pale of the church; and their deputies invited the emperor and patriarch of Constantinople to unite with an assembly which possessed the confidence of the Western nations. Palæologus was not averse to the proposal; and his ambassadors were introduced with due honors into the Catholic senate. But the choice of the place appeared to be an insuperable obstacle, since he refused to pass the Alps, or the sea of Sicily, and positively required that the synod should be adjourned to some convenient city in Italy, or at least on the Danube. The other articles of this treaty were more readily stipulated: it was agreed to defray the travelling expenses of the emperor, with a train of seven hundred persons, to remit an immediate sum of eight thousand ducats for the accommodation of the Greek clergy; and in his absence to grant a supply of ten thousand ducats, with three hundred archers and some galleys, for the protection of Constantinople. The city of Avignon advanced the funds for the preliminary expenses; and the embarkation was prepared at Marseilles with some difficulty and delay.

In his distress, the friendship of Palæologus was disputed by the ecclesiastical powers of the West; but the dexterous activity of a monarch prevailed over the slow debates and inflexible temper of a republic. The decrees of Basil continually tended to circumscribe the despotism of the pope, and to erect a supreme and perpetual tribunal in the church. Eugenius was impatient of the yoke; and the union of the Greeks might afford a decent pretence for translating a rebellious synod from the Rhine to the Po. The independence of the fathers was lost if they passed the Alps: Savoy or Avignon, to which they acceded with reluctance, were described at Constantinople as situate far beyond the pillars of Hercules; the emperor and his clergy were apprehensive of the dangers of a long navigation; they were offended by a haughty declaration, that after suppressing the *new* heresy of the Bohemians, the council would soon eradicate the *old* heresy of the Greeks. On the side of Eugenius, all was smooth, and yielding, and respectful; and he invited the Byzantine monarch to heal by his presence the schism of the Latin, as well as of the Eastern, church. Ferrara, near the coast of the Adriatic, was proposed for their amicable interview; and with some indulgence of forgery and theft, a surreptitious decree was procured, which transferred the synod, with its own consent, to that Italian city. Nine galleys were equipped for the service at Venice, and in the Isle of Candia; their diligence anticipated the slower vessels of Basil: the Roman admiral was commissioned to burn, sink, and destroy; and these priestly squadrons might have encountered each other in the same seas where Athens and Sparta had formerly contended for the preeminence of glory. Assaulted by the importunity of the factions, who were ready to fight for the possession of his person, Palæologus hesitated before he left his palace and country on a perilous experiment. His father's advice still dwelt on his memory; and reason must suggest, that since the Latins were divided among themselves, they could never unite in a foreign cause. Sigismond dissuaded the unreasonable adventure; his advice was impartial, since he adhered to the council; and it was enforced by the strange belief, that the German Cæsar would nominate a Greek his heir and successor in the empire of the West. Even the Turkish sultan was a counsellor whom it might be unsafe to trust, but whom it was dangerous to offend. Amurath was unskilled in the disputes, but he was apprehensive of the union, of the Christians. From his own treasures, he offered to relieve the wants of the Byzantine court; yet he declared with seeming magnanimity, that Constantinople should be secure and inviolate, in the absence of her sovereign. The resolution of Palæologus was decided by the most splendid gifts and the most specious promises: he wished to escape for a while from a scene of danger and distress and after dismissing with an ambiguous answer the messengers of the council, he declared his intention of embarking in the Roman galleys. The age of the patriarch Joseph was more susceptible of fear than of hope; he trembled at the perils of the sea, and expressed his apprehension, that his feeble voice, with thirty perhaps of his orthodox brethren, would be oppressed in a foreign land by the power and numbers of a Latin synod. He yielded to the royal mandate, to the flattering assurance, that he would be heard as the oracle of nations, and to the secret wish of learning from his brother of the West, to deliver the church from the yoke of kings. The five *cross-bearers*, or dignitaries, of St. Sophia, were bound to attend his person; and one of these, the great ecclesiarch or preacher, Sylvester Syropulus, has composed a free and curious history of the *false* union. Of the clergy that reluctantly obeyed the summons of the emperor and the patriarch, submission was the first duty, and patience the most useful virtue. In a chosen list of twenty bishops, we discover the metropolitan titles of Heracleæ and Cyzicus, Nice and Nicomedia, Ephesus and Trebizond, and the personal merit of Mark and Bessarion who, in the confidence of their learning and eloquence, were promoted to the episcopal rank. Some monks and philosophers were named to display the science and sanctity of the

Greek church; and the service of the choir was performed by a select band of singers and musicians. The patriarchs of Alexandria, Antioch, and Jerusalem, appeared by their genuine or fictitious deputies; the primate of Russia represented a national church, and the Greeks might contend with the Latins in the extent of their spiritual empire. The precious vases of St. Sophia were exposed to the winds and waves, that the patriarch might officiate with becoming splendor: whatever gold the emperor could procure, was expended in the massy ornaments of his bed and chariot; and while they affected to maintain the prosperity of their ancient fortune, they quarrelled for the division of fifteen thousand ducats, the first alms of the Roman pontiff. After the necessary preparations, John Palæologus, with a numerous train, accompanied by his brother Demetrius, and the most respectable persons of the church and state, embarked in eight vessels with sails and oars which steered through the Turkish Straits of Gallipoli to the Archipelago, the Morea, and the Adriatic Gulf.

Union of the Greek and Latin Churches. – Part Three

AFTER A TEDIOUS AND troublesome navigation of seventy-seven days, this religious squadron cast anchor before Venice; and their reception proclaimed the joy and magnificence of that powerful republic. In the command of the world, the modest Augustus had never claimed such honors from his subjects as were paid to his feeble successor by an independent state. Seated on the poop on a lofty throne, he received the visit, or, in the Greek style, the *adoration* of the doge and senators. They sailed in the Bucentaur, which was accompanied by twelve stately galleys: the sea was overspread with innumerable gondolas of pomp and pleasure; the air resounded with music and acclamations; the mariners, and even the vessels, were dressed in silk and gold; and in all the emblems and pageants, the Roman eagles were blended with the lions of St. Mark. The triumphal procession, ascending the great canal, passed under the bridge of the Rialto; and the Eastern strangers gazed with admiration on the palaces, the churches, and the populousness of a city, that seems to float on the bosom of the waves. They sighed to behold the spoils and trophies with which it had been decorated after the sack of Constantinople. After a hospitable entertainment of fifteen days, Palæologus pursued his journey by land and water from Venice to Ferrara; and on this occasion the pride of the Vatican was tempered by policy to indulge the ancient dignity of the emperor of the East. He made his entry on a *black* horse; but a milk-white steed, whose trappings were embroidered with golden eagles, was led before him; and the canopy was borne over his head by the princes of Este, the sons or kinsmen of Nicholas, marquis of the city, and a sovereign more powerful than himself. Palæologus did not alight till he reached the bottom of the staircase: the pope advanced to the door of the apartment; refused his proffered genuflection; and, after a paternal embrace, conducted the emperor to a seat on his left hand. Nor would the patriarch descend from his galley, till a ceremony almost equal, had been stipulated between the bishops of Rome and Constantinople. The latter was saluted by his brother with a kiss of union and charity; nor would any of the Greek ecclesiastics submit to kiss the feet of the Western primate. On the opening of the synod, the place of honor in the centre was claimed by the temporal and ecclesiastical chiefs; and it was only by alleging that his predecessors had not assisted in person at Nice or Chalcedon, that Eugenius could evade the ancient precedents of Constantine and Marcian. After much debate, it was agreed that the right and left sides of the church should be occupied by the two nations; that the solitary chair of St. Peter should be raised the first of the Latin line; and that the throne of the Greek emperor, at the head of his clergy, should be equal and opposite to the second place, the vacant seat of the emperor of the West.

But as soon as festivity and form had given place to a more serious treaty, the Greeks were dissatisfied with their journey, with themselves, and with the pope. The artful pencil of his emissaries had painted him in a prosperous state; at the head of the princes and prelates of Europe, obedient at his voice, to believe and to arm. The thin appearance of the universal synod of Ferrara betrayed his weakness: and the Latins opened the first session with only five archbishops, eighteen bishops, and ten abbots, the greatest part of whom were the subjects or countrymen of the Italian pontiff. Except the duke of Burgundy, none of the potentates of the West condescended to appear in person, or by their ambassadors; nor was it possible to suppress the judicial acts of Basil against the dignity and person of Eugenius, which were finally concluded by a new election. Under these circumstances, a truce or delay was asked and granted, till Palæologus could expect from the consent of the Latins some temporal reward for an unpopular union; and after the first session, the public proceedings were adjourned above six months. The emperor, with a chosen band of his favorites and *Janizaries*, fixed his summer residence at a pleasant, spacious monastery, six miles from Ferrara; forgot, in the pleasures of the chase, the distress of the church and state; and persisted in destroying the game, without listening to the just complaints of the marquis or the husbandman. In the mean while, his unfortunate Greeks were exposed to all the miseries of exile and poverty; for the support of each stranger, a monthly allowance was assigned of three or four gold florins; and although the entire sum did not amount to seven hundred florins, a long arrear was repeatedly incurred by the indigence or policy of the Roman court. They sighed for a speedy deliverance, but their escape was prevented by a triple chain: a passport from their superiors was required at the gates of Ferrara; the government of Venice had engaged to arrest and send back the fugitives; and inevitable punishment awaited them at Constantinople; excommunication, fines, and a sentence, which did not respect the sacerdotal dignity, that they should be stripped naked and publicly whipped. It was only by the alternative of hunger or dispute that the Greeks could be persuaded to open the first conference; and they yielded with extreme reluctance to attend from Ferrara to Florence the rear of a flying synod. This new translation was urged by inevitable necessity: the city was visited by the plague; the fidelity of the marquis might be suspected; the mercenary troops of the duke of Milan were at the gates; and as they occupied Romagna, it was not without difficulty and danger that the pope, the emperor, and the bishops, explored their way through the unfrequented paths of the Apennine.

Yet all these obstacles were surmounted by time and policy. The violence of the fathers of Basil rather promoted than injured the cause of Eugenius; the nations of Europe abhorred the schism, and disowned the election, of Felix the Fifth, who was successively a duke of Savoy, a hermit, and a pope; and the great princes were gradually reclaimed by his competitor to a favorable neutrality and a firm attachment. The legates, with some respectable members, deserted to the Roman army, which insensibly rose in numbers and reputation; the council of Basil was reduced to thirty-nine bishops, and three hundred of the inferior clergy; while the Latins of Florence could produce the subscriptions of the pope himself, eight cardinals, two patriarchs, eight archbishops, fifty two bishops, and forty-five abbots, or chiefs of religious orders. After the labor of nine months, and the debates of twenty-five sessions, they attained the advantage and glory of the reunion of the Greeks. Four principal questions had been agitated between the two churches; . The use of unleavened bread in the communion of Christ's body. . The nature of purgatory. . The supremacy of the pope. And, . The single or double procession of the Holy Ghost. The cause of either nation was managed by ten theological champions: the Latins were supported by the inexhaustible eloquence of Cardinal Julian; and Mark of Ephesus and Bessarion of Nice were the bold and able leaders of the Greek forces. We may bestow some praise on the progress of human reason, by observing that the first of these questions was now treated as an immaterial rite, which might innocently vary with the fashion of the age and country. With regard to the second, both parties were agreed in the belief of an intermediate state of purgation for the venial sins of the faithful; and whether their souls were purified by elemental fire was a doubtful point, which in a few years might be conveniently settled on the spot by the disputants. The claims of supremacy appeared of a more weighty and substantial kind; yet by the Orientals the Roman bishop had ever been respected as the first of the five patriarchs; nor did they scruple to admit, that his jurisdiction should be exercised agreeably to the holy canons; a vague allowance, which might be defined or eluded by occasional convenience. The procession of the Holy Ghost from the Father alone, or from the Father and the Son, was an article of faith which had sunk much deeper into the minds of men; and in the sessions of Ferrara and Florence, the Latin addition of *filioque* was subdivided into two questions, whether it were legal, and whether it were orthodox. Perhaps it may not be necessary to boast on this subject of my own impartial indifference; but I must think that the Greeks were strongly supported by the prohibition of the council of Chalcedon, against adding any article whatsoever to the creed of Nice, or rather of Constantinople. In earthly affairs, it is not easy to conceive how an assembly equal of legislators can bind their successors invested with powers equal to their own. But the dictates of inspiration must be true and unchangeable; nor should a private bishop, or a provincial synod, have presumed to innovate against the judgment of the Catholic church. On the substance of the doctrine, the controversy was equal and endless: reason is confounded by the procession of a deity: the gospel, which lay on the altar, was silent; the various texts of the fathers might be corrupted by fraud or entangled by sophistry; and the Greeks were ignorant of the characters and writings of the Latin saints. Of this at least we may be sure, that neither side could be convinced by the arguments of their opponents. Prejudice may be enlightened by reason, and a superficial glance may be rectified by a clear and more perfect view of an object adapted to our faculties. But the bishops and monks had been taught from their infancy to repeat a form of mysterious words: their national and personal honor depended on the repetition of the same sounds; and their narrow minds were hardened and inflamed by the acrimony of a public dispute.

While they were most in a cloud of dust and darkness, the Pope and emperor were desirous of a seeming union, which could alone accomplish the purposes of their interview; and the obstinacy of public dispute was softened by the arts of private and personal negotiation. The patriarch Joseph had sunk under the weight of age and infirmities; his dying voice breathed the counsels of charity and concord, and his vacant benefice might tempt the hopes of the ambitious clergy. The ready and active obedience of the archbishops of Russia and Nice, of Isidore and Bessarion, was prompted and recompensed by their speedy promotion to the dignity of cardinals. Bessarion, in the first debates, had stood forth the most strenuous and eloquent champion of the Greek church; and if the apostate, the bastard, was reprobated by his country, he appears in ecclesiastical story a rare example of a patriot who was recommended to court favor by loud opposition and well-timed compliance. With the aid of his two spiritual coadjutors, the emperor applied his arguments to the general situation and personal characters of the bishops, and each was successively moved by authority and example. Their revenues were in the hands of the Turks, their persons in those of the Latins: an episcopal treasure, three robes and forty ducats, was soon exhausted: the hopes of their return still depended on the ships of Venice and the alms of Rome; and such was their indigence, that their arrears, the payment of a debt, would be accepted as a favor, and might operate as a bribe. The danger and relief of Constantinople might excuse some prudent and pious dissimulation; and it was insinuated, that the obstinate heretics who should resist the consent of the East and West would be abandoned in a hostile land to the revenge or justice of the Roman pontiff. In the first private assembly of the Greeks, the formulary of union was approved by twenty-four, and rejected by twelve, members; but the five *cross-bearers* of St. Sophia, who aspired to represent the patriarch, were disqualified by ancient discipline; and their right of voting was transferred to the obsequious train of monks, grammarians, and profane laymen. The will of the monarch produced a false and servile unanimity, and no more than two patriots had courage to speak their own sentiments and those of their country. Demetrius, the emperor's brother, retired to Venice, that he might not be witness of the union; and Mark of Ephesus, mistaking perhaps his pride for his conscience, disclaimed all communion with the Latin heretics, and avowed himself the champion and confessor of the orthodox creed. In the treaty between the two nations, several forms of consent were proposed, such as might satisfy the Latins, without dishonoring the Greeks; and they weighed the scruples of words and syllables, till the theological balance trembled with a slight preponderance in favor of the Vatican. It was agreed (I must entreat the attention of the reader) that the Holy Ghost proceeds from the Father *and* the Son, as from one principle and one substance; that he proceeds *by* the Son, being of the same nature and substance, and that he proceeds from the Father *and* the Son, by one *spiration* and production. It is less difficult to understand the articles of the preliminary treaty; that the pope should defray all the expenses of the Greeks in their return home; that he should annually maintain two galleys and three hundred soldiers for the defence of Constantinople: that all the ships which transported pilgrims to Jerusalem should be obliged to touch at that port; that as often as they were required, the pope should furnish ten galleys for a year, or twenty for six months; and that he should powerfully solicit the princes of Europe, if the emperor had occasion for land forces.

The same year, and almost the same day, were marked by the deposition of Eugenius at Basil; and, at Florence, by his reunion of the Greeks and Latins. In the former synod, (which he styled indeed an assembly of dæmons,) the pope was branded with the guilt of simony, perjury, tyranny, heresy, and schism; and declared to be incorrigible in his vices, unworthy of any title, and incapable of holding any ecclesiastical office. In the latter, he was revered as the true and holy vicar of Christ, who, after a separation of six hundred years, had reconciled the Catholics of the East and West in one fold, and under one shepherd. The act of union was subscribed by the pope, the emperor, and the principal members of both churches; even by those who, like Syropulus, had been deprived of the right of voting. Two copies might have sufficed for the East and West; but Eugenius was not satisfied, unless four authentic and similar transcripts were signed and attested as the monuments of his victory. On a memorable day, the sixth of July, the successors of St. Peter and Constantine ascended their thrones the two nations assembled in the cathedral of Florence; their representatives, Cardinal Julian and Bessarion archbishop of Nice, appeared in the pulpit, and, after reading in their respective tongues the act of union, they mutually embraced, in the name and the presence of their applauding brethren. The pope and his ministers then officiated according to the Roman liturgy; the creed was chanted with the addition of *filioque*; the acquiescence of the Greeks was poorly excused by their ignorance of the harmonious, but inarticulate sounds; and the more scrupulous Latins refused any public celebration of the Byzantine rite. Yet the emperor and his clergy were not totally unmindful of national honor. The treaty was ratified by their consent: it was tacitly agreed that no innovation should be attempted in their creed or ceremonies: they spared, and secretly respected, the generous firmness of Mark of Ephesus; and, on the decease of the patriarch, they refused to elect his successor, except in the cathedral of St. Sophia. In the distribution of public and private rewards, the liberal pontiff exceeded their hopes and his promises: the Greeks, with less pomp and pride, returned by the same road of Ferrara and Venice; and their reception at Constantinople was such as will be described in the following chapter. The success of the first trial encouraged Eugenius to repeat the same edifying scenes; and the deputies of the Armenians, the Maronites, the Jacobites of Syria and Egypt, the Nestorians and the Æthiopians, were successively introduced, to kiss the feet of the Roman pontiff, and to announce the obedience and the orthodoxy of the East. These Oriental embassies, unknown in the countries which they presumed to represent, diffused over the West the fame of Eugenius; and a clamor was artfully propagated against the remnant of a schism in Switzerland and Savoy, which alone impeded the harmony of the Christian world. The vigor of opposition was succeeded by the lassitude of despair: the council of Basil was silently dissolved; and Felix, renouncing the tiara, again withdrew to the devout or delicious hermitage of Ripaille. A general peace was secured by mutual acts of oblivion and indemnity: all ideas of reformation subsided; the popes continued to exercise and abuse their ecclesiastical despotism; nor has Rome been since disturbed by the mischiefs of a contested election.

The journeys of three emperors were unavailing for their temporal, or perhaps their spiritual, salvation; but they were productive of a beneficial consequence – the revival of the Greek learning in Italy, from whence it was propagated to the last nations of the West and North. In their lowest servitude and depression, the subjects of the Byzantine throne were still possessed of a golden key that could unlock the treasures of antiquity; of a musical and prolific language, that gives a soul to the objects of sense, and a body to the abstractions of philosophy. Since the barriers of the monarchy, and even of the capital, had been trampled under foot, the various Barbarians had doubtless corrupted the form and substance of the national dialect; and ample glossaries have been composed, to interpret a multitude of words, of Arabic, Turkish, Sclavonian, Latin, or French origin. But a purer idiom was spoken in the court and taught in the college; and the flourishing state of the language is described, and perhaps embellished, by a learned Italian, who, by a long residence and noble marriage, was naturalized at Constantinople about thirty years before the Turkish conquest. "The vulgar speech," says Philelphus, "has been depraved by the people, and infected by the multitude of strangers and merchants, who every day flock to the city and mingle with the inhabitants. It is from the disciples of such a school that the Latin language received the versions of Aristotle and Plato; so obscure in sense, and in spirit so poor. But the Greeks who have escaped the contagion, are those whom *we* follow; and they alone are worthy of our imitation. In familiar discourse, they still speak the tongue of Aristophanes and Euripides, of the historians and philosophers of Athens; and the style of their writings is still more elaborate and correct. The persons who, by their birth and offices, are attached to the Byzantine court, are those who maintain, with the least alloy, the ancient standard of elegance and purity; and the native graces of language most conspicuously shine among the noble matrons, who are excluded from all intercourse with foreigners. With foreigners do I say? They live retired and sequestered from the eyes of their fellow-citizens. Seldom are they seen in the streets; and when they leave their houses, it is in the dusk of evening, on visits to the churches and their nearest kindred. On these occasions, they are on horseback, covered with a veil, and encompassed by their parents, their husbands, or their servants."

Among the Greeks a numerous and opulent clergy was dedicated to the service of religion: their monks and bishops have ever been distinguished by the gravity and austerity of their manners; nor were they diverted, like the Latin priests, by the pursuits and pleasures of a secular, and even military, life. After a large deduction for the time and talent that were lost in the devotion, the laziness, and the discord, of the church and cloister, the more inquisitive and ambitious minds would explore the sacred and profane erudition of their native language. The ecclesiastics presided over the education of youth; the schools of philosophy and eloquence were perpetuated till the fall of the empire; and it may be affirmed, that more books and more knowledge were included within the walls of Constantinople, than could be dispersed over the extensive countries of the West. But an important distinction has been already noticed: the Greeks were stationary or retrograde, while the Latins were advancing with a rapid and progressive motion. The nations were excited by the spirit of independence and emulation; and even the little world of the Italian states contained more people and industry than the decreasing circle of the Byzantine empire. In Europe, the lower ranks of society were relieved from the yoke of feudal servitude; and freedom is the first step to curiosity and knowledge. The use, however rude and corrupt, of the Latin tongue had been preserved by superstition; the universities, from Bologna to Oxford, were peopled with thousands of scholars; and their misguided ardor might be directed to more liberal and manly studies. In the resurrection of science, Italy was the first that cast away her shroud; and the eloquent Petrarch, by his lessons and his example, may justly be applauded as the first harbinger of day. A purer style of composition, a more generous and rational strain of sentiment, flowed from the study and imitation of the writers of ancient Rome; and the disciples of Cicero and Virgil approached, with reverence and love, the sanctuary of their Grecian masters. In the sack of Constantinople, the French, and even the Venetians, had despised and destroyed the works of Lysippus and Homer: the monuments of art may be annihilated by a single blow; but the immortal mind is renewed and multiplied by the copies of the pen; and such copies it was the ambition of Petrarch and his friends to possess and understand. The arms of the Turks undoubtedly pressed the flight of the Muses; yet we may tremble at the thought, that Greece might have been overwhelmed, with her schools and libraries, before Europe had emerged from the deluge of barbarism; that the seeds of science might have been scattered by the winds, before the Italian soil was prepared for their cultivation.

Union of the Greek and Latin Churches. – Part Four

The most learned Italians of the fifteenth century have confessed and applauded the restoration of Greek literature, after a long oblivion of many hundred years. Yet in that country, and beyond the Alps, some names are quoted; some profound scholars, who in the darker ages were honorably distinguished by their knowledge of the Greek tongue; and national vanity has been loud in the praise of such rare examples of erudition. Without scrutinizing the merit of individuals, truth must observe, that their science is without a cause, and without an effect; that it was easy for them to satisfy themselves and their more ignorant contemporaries; and that the idiom, which they had so marvellously acquired was transcribed in few manuscripts, and was not taught in any university of the West. In a corner of Italy, it faintly existed as the popular, or at least as the ecclesiastical dialect. The first impression of the Doric and Ionic colonies has never been completely erased: the Calabrian churches were long attached to the throne of Constantinople: and the monks of St. Basil pursued their studies in Mount Athos and the schools of the East. Calabria was the native country of Barlaam, who has already appeared as a sectary and an ambassador; and Barlaam was the first who revived, beyond the Alps, the memory, or at least the writings, of Homer. He is described, by Petrarch and Boccace, as a man of diminutive stature, though truly great in the measure of learning and genius; of a piercing discernment, though of a slow and painful elocution. For many ages (as they affirm) Greece had not produced his equal in the knowledge of history, grammar, and philosophy; and his merit was celebrated in the attestations of the princes and doctors of Constantinople. One of these attestations is still extant; and the emperor Cantacuzene, the protector of his adversaries, is forced to allow, that Euclid, Aristotle, and Plato, were familiar to that profound and subtle logician. In the court of Avignon, he formed an intimate connection with Petrarch, the first of the Latin scholars; and the desire of mutual instruction was the principle of their literary commerce. The Tuscan applied himself with eager curiosity and assiduous diligence to the study of the Greek language; and in a laborious struggle with the dryness and difficulty of the first rudiments, he began to reach the sense, and to feel the spirit, of poets and philosophers, whose minds were congenial to his own. But he was soon deprived of the society and lessons of this useful assistant: Barlaam relinquished his fruitless embassy; and, on his return to Greece, he rashly provoked the swarms of fanatic monks, by attempting to substitute the light of reason to that of their navel. After a separation of three years, the two friends again met in the court of Naples: but the generous pupil renounced the fairest occasion of improvement; and by his recommendation Barlaam was finally settled in a small bishopric of his native Calabria. The manifold avocations of Petrarch, love and friendship, his various correspondence and frequent journeys, the Roman laurel, and his elaborate compositions in prose and verse, in Latin and Italian, diverted him from a foreign idiom; and as he advanced in life, the attainment of the Greek language was the object of his wishes rather than of his hopes. When he was about fifty years of age, a Byzantine ambassador, his friend, and a master of both tongues, presented him with a copy of Homer; and the answer of Petrarch is at one expressive of his eloquence, gratitude, and regret. After celebrating the generosity of the donor, and the value of a gift more precious in his estimation than gold or rubies, he thus proceeds: "Your present of the genuine and original text of the divine poet, the fountain of all inventions, is worthy of yourself and of me: you have fulfilled your promise, and satisfied my desires. Yet your liberality is still imperfect: with Homer you should have given me yourself; a guide, who could lead me into the fields of light, and disclose to my wondering eyes the spacious miracles of the Iliad and Odyssey. But, alas! Homer is dumb, or I am deaf; nor is it in my power to enjoy the beauty which I possess. I have seated him by the side of Plato, the prince of poets near the prince of philosophers; and I glory in the sight of my illustrious guests. Of their immortal writings, whatever had been translated into the Latin idiom, I had already acquired; but, if there be no profit, there is some pleasure, in beholding these venerable Greeks in their proper and national habit. I am delighted with the aspect of Homer; and as often as I embrace the silent volume, I exclaim with a sigh, Illustrious bard! with what pleasure should I listen to thy song, if my sense of hearing were not obstructed and lost by the death of one friend, and in the much-lamented absence of another. Nor do I yet despair; and the example of Cato suggests some comfort and hope, since it was in the last period of age that he attained the knowledge of the Greek letters."

The prize which eluded the efforts of Petrarch, was obtained by the fortune and industry of his friend Boccace, the father of the Tuscan prose. That popular writer, who derives his reputation from the Decameron, a hundred novels of pleasantry and love, may aspire to the more serious praise of restoring in Italy the study of the Greek language. In the year one thousand three hundred and sixty, a disciple of Barlaam, whose name was Leo, or Leontius Pilatus, was detained in his way to Avignon by the advice and hospitality of Boccace, who lodged the stranger in his house, prevailed on the republic of Florence to allow him an annual stipend, and devoted his leisure to the first Greek professor, who taught that language in the Western countries of Europe. The appearance of Leo might disgust the most eager disciple, he was clothed in the mantle of a philosopher, or a mendicant; his countenance was hideous; his face was overshadowed with black hair; his beard long and uncombed; his deportment rustic; his temper gloomy and inconstant; nor could he grace his discourse with the ornaments, or even the perspicuity, of Latin elocution. But his mind was stored with a treasure of Greek learning: history and fable, philosophy and grammar, were alike at his command; and he read the poems of Homer in the schools of Florence. It was from his explanation that Boccace composed and transcribed a literal prose version of the Iliad and Odyssey, which satisfied the thirst of his friend Petrarch, and which, perhaps, in the succeeding century, was clandestinely used by Laurentius Valla, the Latin interpreter. It was from his narratives that the same Boccace collected the materials for his treatise on the genealogy of the heathen gods, a work, in that age, of stupendous erudition, and which he ostentatiously sprinkled with Greek characters and passages, to excite the wonder and applause of his more ignorant readers. The first steps of learning are slow and laborious; no more than ten votaries of Homer could be enumerated in all Italy; and neither Rome, nor Venice, nor Naples, could add a single name to this studious catalogue. But their numbers would have multiplied, their progress would have been accelerated, if the inconstant Leo, at the end of three years, had not relinquished an honorable and beneficial station. In his passage, Petrarch entertained him at Padua a short time: he enjoyed the scholar, but was justly offended with the gloomy and unsocial temper of the man. Discontented with the world and with himself, Leo depreciated his present enjoyments, while absent persons and objects were dear to his imagination. In Italy he was a Thessalian, in Greece a native of Calabria: in the company of the Latins he disdained their language, religion, and manners: no sooner was he landed at Constantinople, than he again sighed for the wealth of Venice and the elegance of Florence. His Italian friends were deaf to his importunity: he depended on their curiosity and indulgence, and embarked on a second voyage; but on his entrance into the Adriatic, the ship was assailed by a tempest, and the unfortunate teacher, who like Ulysses had fastened himself to the mast, was struck dead by a flash of lightning. The humane Petrarch dropped a tear on his disaster; but he was most anxious to learn whether some copy of Euripides or Sophocles might not be saved from the hands of the mariners.

But the faint rudiments of Greek learning, which Petrarch had encouraged and Boccace had planted, soon withered and expired. The succeeding generation was content for a while with the improvement of Latin eloquence; nor was it before the end of the fourteenth century that a new and perpetual flame was rekindled in Italy. Previous to his own journey the emperor Manuel despatched his envoys and orators to implore the compassion of the Western princes. Of these envoys, the most conspicuous, or the most learned, was Manuel Chrysoloras, of noble birth, and whose Roman ancestors are supposed to have migrated with the great Constantine. After visiting the courts of France and England, where he obtained some contributions and more promises, the envoy was invited to assume the office of a professor; and Florence had again the honor of this second invitation. By his knowledge, not only of the Greek, but of the Latin tongue, Chrysoloras deserved the stipend, and surpassed the expectation, of the republic. His school was frequented by a crowd of disciples of every rank and age; and one of these, in a general history, has described his motives and his success. "At that time," says Leonard Aretin, "I was a student of the civil law; but my soul was inflamed with the love of letters; and I bestowed some application on the sciences of logic and rhetoric. On the arrival of Manuel, I hesitated whether I should desert my legal studies, or relinquish this golden opportunity; and thus, in the ardor of youth, I communed with my own mind – Wilt thou be wanting to thyself and thy fortune? Wilt thou refuse to be introduced to a familiar converse with Homer, Plato, and Demosthenes; with those poets, philosophers, and orators, of whom such wonders are related, and who are celebrated by every age as the great masters of human science? Of professors and scholars in civil law, a sufficient supply will always be found in our universities; but a teacher, and such a teacher, of the Greek language, if he once be suffered to escape, may never afterwards be retrieved. Convinced by these reasons, I gave myself to Chrysoloras; and so strong was my passion, that the lessons which I had imbibed in the day were the constant object of my nightly dreams." At the same time and place, the Latin classics were explained by John of Ravenna, the domestic pupil of Petrarch; the Italians, who illustrated their age and country, were formed in this double school; and Florence became the fruitful seminary of Greek and Roman erudition. The presence of the emperor recalled Chrysoloras from the college to the court; but he afterwards taught at Pavia and Rome with equal industry and applause. The remainder of his life, about fifteen years, was divided between Italy and Constantinople, between embassies and lessons. In the noble office of enlightening a foreign nation, the grammarian was not unmindful of a more sacred duty to his prince and country; and Emanuel Chrysoloras died at Constance on a public mission from the emperor to the council.

After his example, the restoration of the Greek letters in Italy was prosecuted by a series of emigrants, who were destitute of fortune, and endowed with learning, or at least with language. From the terror or oppression of the Turkish arms, the natives of Thessalonica and Constantinople escaped to a land of freedom, curiosity, and wealth. The synod introduced into Florence the lights of the Greek church, and the oracles of the Platonic philosophy; and the fugitives who adhered to the union, had the double merit of renouncing their country, not only for the Christian, but for the catholic cause. A patriot, who sacrifices his party and conscience to the allurements of favor, may be possessed, however, of the private and social virtues: he no longer hears the reproachful epithets of slave and apostate; and the consideration which he acquires among his new associates will restore in his own eyes the dignity of his character. The prudent conformity of Bessarion was rewarded with the Roman purple: he fixed his residence in Italy; and the Greek cardinal, the titular patriarch of Constantinople, was respected as the chief and protector of his nation: his abilities were exercised in the legations of Bologna, Venice, Germany, and France; and his election to the chair of St. Peter floated for a moment on the uncertain breath of a conclave. His ecclesiastical honors diffused a splendor and preeminence over his literary merit and service: his palace was a school; as often as the cardinal visited the Vatican, he was attended by a learned train of both nations; of men applauded by themselves and the public; and whose writings, now overspread with dust, were popular and useful in their own times. I shall not attempt to enumerate the restorers of Grecian literature in the fifteenth century; and it may be sufficient to mention with gratitude the names of Theodore Gaza, of George of Trebizond, of John Argyropulus, and Demetrius Chalcocondyles, who taught their native language in the schools of Florence and Rome. Their labors were not inferior to those of Bessarion, whose purple they revered, and whose fortune was the secret object of their envy. But the lives of these grammarians were humble and obscure: they had declined the lucrative paths of the church; their dress and manners secluded them from the commerce of the world; and since they were confined to the merit, they might be content with the rewards, of learning. From this character, Janus Lascaris will deserve an exception. His eloquence, politeness, and Imperial descent, recommended him to the French monarch; and in the same cities he was alternately employed to teach and to negotiate. Duty and interest prompted them to cultivate the study of the Latin language; and the most successful attained the faculty of writing and speaking with fluency and elegance in a foreign idiom. But they ever retained the inveterate vanity of their country: their praise, or at least their esteem, was reserved for the national writers, to whom they owed their fame and subsistence; and they sometimes betrayed their contempt in licentious criticism or satire on Virgil's poetry, and the oratory of Tully. The superiority of these masters arose from the familiar use of a living language; and their first disciples were incapable of discerning how far they had degenerated from the knowledge, and even the practice of their ancestors. A vicious pronunciation, which they introduced, was banished from the schools by the reason of the succeeding age. Of the power of the Greek accents they were ignorant; and those musical notes, which, from an Attic tongue, and to an Attic ear, must have been the secret soul of harmony, were to their eyes, as to our own, no more than minute and unmeaning marks, in prose superfluous and troublesome in verse. The art of grammar they truly possessed; the valuable fragments of Apollonius and Herodian were transfused into their lessons; and their treatises of syntax and etymology, though devoid of philosophic spirit, are still useful to the Greek student. In the shipwreck of the Byzantine libraries, each fugitive seized a fragment of treasure, a copy of some author, who without his industry might have perished: the transcripts were multiplied by an assiduous, and sometimes an elegant pen; and the text was corrected and explained by their own comments, or those of the elder scholiasts. The sense, though not the spirit, of the Greek classics, was interpreted to the Latin world: the beauties of style evaporate in a version; but the judgment of Theodore Gaza selected the more solid works of Aristotle and Theophrastus, and their natural histories of animals and plants opened a rich fund of genuine and experimental science.

Yet the fleeting shadows of metaphysics were pursued with more curiosity and ardor. After a long oblivion, Plato was revived in Italy by a venerable Greek, who taught in the house of Cosmo of Medicis. While the synod of Florence was involved in theological debate, some beneficial consequences might flow from the study of his elegant philosophy: his style is the purest standard of the Attic dialect, and his sublime thoughts are sometimes adapted to familiar conversation, and sometimes adorned with the richest colors of poetry and eloquence. The dialogues of Plato are a dramatic picture of the life and death of a sage; and, as often as he descends from the clouds, his moral system inculcates the love of truth, of our country, and of mankind. The precept and example of Socrates recommended a modest doubt and liberal inquiry; and if the Platonists, with blind devotion, adored the visions and errors of their divine master, their enthusiasm might correct the dry, dogmatic method of the Peripatetic school. So equal, yet so opposite, are the merits of Plato and Aristotle, that they may be balanced in endless controversy; but some spark of freedom may be produced by the collision of adverse servitude. The modern Greeks were divided between the two sects: with more fury than skill they fought under the banner of their leaders; and the field of battle was removed in their flight from Constantinople to Rome. But this philosophical debate soon degenerated into an angry and personal quarrel of grammarians; and Bessarion, though an advocate for Plato, protected the national honor, by interposing the advice and authority of a mediator. In the gardens of the Medici, the academical doctrine was enjoyed by the polite and learned: but their philosophic society was quickly dissolved; and if the writings of the Attic sage were perused in the closet, the more powerful Stagyrite continued to reign, the oracle of the church and school.

I have fairly represented the literary merits of the Greeks; yet it must be confessed, that they were seconded and surpassed by the ardor of the Latins. Italy was divided into many independent states; and at that time it was the ambition of princes and republics to vie with each other in the encouragement and reward of literature. The fame of Nicholas the Fifth has not been adequate to his merits. From a plebeian origin he raised himself by his virtue and learning: the character of the man prevailed over the interest of the pope; and he sharpened those weapons which were soon pointed against the Roman church. He had been the friend of the most eminent scholars of the age: he became their patron; and such was the humility of his manners, that the change was scarcely discernible either to them or to himself. If he pressed the acceptance of a liberal gift, it was not as the measure of desert, but as the proof of benevolence; and when modest merit declined his bounty, "Accept it," would he say, with a consciousness of his own worth: "ye will not always have a Nicholas among you." The influence of the holy see pervaded Christendom; and he exerted that influence in the search, not of benefices, but of books. From the ruins of the Byzantine libraries, from the darkest monasteries of Germany and Britain, he collected the dusty manuscripts of the writers of antiquity; and wherever the original could not be removed, a faithful copy was transcribed and transmitted for his use. The Vatican, the old repository for bulls and legends, for superstition and forgery, was daily replenished with more precious furniture; and such was the industry of Nicholas, that in a reign of eight years he formed a library of five thousand volumes. To his munificence the Latin world was indebted for the versions of Xenophon, Diodorus, Polybius, Thucydides, Herodotus, and Appian; of Strabo's Geography, of the Iliad, of the most valuable works of Plato and Aristotle, of Ptolemy and Theophrastus, and of the fathers of the Greek church. The example of the Roman pontiff was preceded or imitated by a Florentine merchant, who governed the republic without arms and without a title. Cosmo of Medicis was the father of a line of princes, whose name and age are almost synonymous with the restoration of learning: his credit was ennobled into fame; his riches were dedicated to the service of mankind; he corresponded at once with Cairo and London: and a cargo of Indian spices and Greek books was often imported in the same vessel. The genius and education of his grandson Lorenzo rendered him not only a patron, but a judge and candidate, in the literary race. In his palace, distress was entitled to relief, and merit to reward: his leisure hours were delightfully spent in the Platonic academy; he encouraged the emulation of Demetrius Chalcocondyles and Angelo Politian; and his active missionary Janus Lascaris returned from the East with a treasure of two hundred manuscripts, fourscore of which were as yet unknown in the libraries of Europe. The rest of Italy was animated by a similar spirit, and the progress of the nation repaid the liberality of their princes. The Latins held the exclusive property of their own literature; and these disciples of Greece were soon capable of transmitting and improving the lessons which they had imbibed. After a short succession of foreign teachers, the tide of emigration subsided; but the language of Constantinople was spread beyond the Alps and the natives of France, Germany, and England, imparted to their country the sacred fire which they had kindled in the schools of Florence and Rome. In the productions of the mind, as in those of the soil, the gifts of nature are excelled by industry and skill: the Greek authors, forgotten on the banks of the Ilissus, have been illustrated on those of the Elbe and the Thames: and Bessarion or Gaza might have envied the superior science of the Barbarians; the accuracy of Budæus, the taste of Erasmus, the copiousness of Stephens, the erudition of Scaliger, the discernment of Reiske, or of Bentley. On the side of the Latins, the discovery of printing was a casual advantage: but this useful art has been applied by Aldus, and his innumerable successors, to perpetuate and multiply the works of antiquity. A single manuscript imported from Greece is revived in ten thousand copies; and each copy is fairer than the original. In this form, Homer and Plato would peruse with more satisfaction their own writings; and their scholiasts must resign the prize to the labors of our Western editors.

Before the revival of classic literature, the Barbarians in Europe were immersed in ignorance; and their vulgar tongues were marked with the rudeness and poverty of their manners. The students of the more perfect idioms of Rome and Greece were introduced to a new world of light and science; to the society of the free and polished nations of antiquity; and to a familiar converse with those immortal men who spoke the sublime language of eloquence and reason. Such an intercourse must tend to refine the taste, and to elevate the genius, of the moderns; and yet, from the first experiments, it might appear that the study of the ancients had given fetters, rather than wings, to the human mind. However laudable, the spirit of imitation is of a servile cast; and the first disciples of the Greeks and Romans were a colony of strangers in the midst of their age and country. The minute and laborious diligence which explored the antiquities of remote times might have improved or adorned the present state of society, the critic and metaphysician were the slaves of Aristotle; the poets, historians, and orators, were proud to repeat the thoughts and words of the Augustan age: the works of nature were observed with the eyes of Pliny and Theophrastus; and some Pagan votaries professed a secret devotion to the gods of Homer and Plato. The Italians were oppressed by the strength and number of their ancient auxiliaries: the century after the deaths of Petrarch and Boccace was filled with a crowd of Latin imitators, who decently repose on our shelves; but in that æra of learning it will not be easy to discern a real discovery of science, a work of invention or eloquence, in the popular language of the country. But as soon as it had been deeply saturated with the celestial dew, the soil was quickened into vegetation and life; the modern idioms were refined; the classics of Athens and Rome inspired a pure taste and a generous emulation; and in Italy, as afterwards in France and England, the pleasing reign of poetry and fiction was succeeded by the light of speculative and experimental philosophy. Genius may anticipate the season of maturity; but in the education of a people, as in that of an individual, memory must be exercised, before the powers of reason and fancy can be expanded: nor may the artist hope to equal or surpass, till he has learned to imitate, the works of his predecessors.

CHAPTER SIXTY SEVEN

Schism of the Greeks and Latins.
– Part One

Schism of the Greeks and Latins. – Reign and Character of Amurath the Second. – Crusade of Ladislaus, King of Hungary. – His Defeat and Death. – John Huniades. – Scanderbeg. – Constantine Palæologus, Last Emperor of the East.

THE RESPECTIVE MERITS OF Rome and Constantinople are compared and celebrated by an eloquent Greek, the father of the Italian schools. The view of the ancient capital, the seat of his ancestors, surpassed the most sanguine expectations of Emanuel Chrysoloras; and he no longer blamed the exclamation of an old sophist, that Rome was the habitation, not of men, but of gods. Those gods, and those men, had long since vanished; but to the eye of liberal enthusiasm, the majesty of ruin restored the image of her ancient prosperity. The monuments of the consuls and Cæsars, of the martyrs and apostles, engaged on all sides the curiosity of the philosopher and the Christian; and he confessed that in every age the arms and the religion of Rome were destined to reign over the earth. While Chrysoloras admired the venerable beauties of the mother, he was not forgetful of his native country, her fairest daughter, her Imperial colony; and the Byzantine patriot expatiates with zeal and truth on the eternal advantages of nature, and the more transitory glories of art and dominion, which adorned, or had adorned, the city of Constantine. Yet the perfection of the copy still redounds (as he modestly observes) to the honor of the original, and parents are delighted to be renewed, and even excelled, by the superior merit of their children. "Constantinople," says the orator, "is situate on a commanding point, between Europe and Asia, between the Archipelago and the

Euxine. By her interposition, the two seas, and the two continents, are united for the common benefit of nations; and the gates of commerce may be shut or opened at her command. The harbor, encompassed on all sides by the sea, and the continent, is the most secure and capacious in the world. The walls and gates of Constantinople may be compared with those of Babylon: the towers many; each tower is a solid and lofty structure; and the second wall, the outer fortification, would be sufficient for the defence and dignity of an ordinary capital. A broad and rapid stream may be introduced into the ditches and the artificial island may be encompassed, like Athens, by land or water." Two strong and natural causes are alleged for the perfection of the model of new Rome. The royal founder reigned over the most illustrious nations of the globe; and in the accomplishment of his designs, the power of the Romans was combined with the art and science of the Greeks. Other cities have been reared to maturity by accident and time: their beauties are mingled with disorder and deformity; and the inhabitants, unwilling to remove from their natal spot, are incapable of correcting the errors of their ancestors, and the original vices of situation or climate. But the free idea of Constantinople was formed and executed by a single mind; and the primitive model was improved by the obedient zeal of the subjects and successors of the first monarch. The adjacent isles were stored with an inexhaustible supply of marble; but the various materials were transported from the most remote shores of Europe and Asia; and the public and private buildings, the palaces, churches, aqueducts, cisterns, porticos, columns, baths, and hippodromes, were adapted to the greatness of the capital of the East. The superfluity of wealth was spread along the shores of Europe and Asia; and the Byzantine territory, as far as the Euxine, the Hellespont, and the long wall, might be considered as a populous suburb and a perpetual garden. In this flattering picture, the past and the present, the times of prosperity and decay, are artfully confounded; but a sigh and a confession escape, from the orator, that his wretched country was the shadow and sepulchre of its former self. The works of ancient sculpture had been defaced by Christian zeal or Barbaric violence; the fairest structures were demolished; and the marbles of Paros or Numidia were burnt for lime, or applied to the meanest uses. Of many a statue, the place was marked by an empty pedestal; of many a column, the size was determined by a broken capital; the tombs of the emperors were scattered on the ground; the stroke of time was accelerated by storms and earthquakes; and the vacant space was adorned, by vulgar tradition, with fabulous monuments of gold and silver. From these wonders, which lived only in memory or belief, he distinguishes, however, the porphyry pillar, the column and colossus of Justinian, and the church, more especially the dome, of St. Sophia; the best conclusion, since it could not be described according to its merits, and after it no other object could deserve to be mentioned. But he forgets that, a century before, the trembling fabrics of the colossus and the church had been saved and supported by the timely care of Andronicus the Elder. Thirty years after the emperor had fortified St. Sophia with two new buttresses or pyramids, the eastern hemisphere suddenly gave way: and the images, the altars, and the sanctuary, were crushed by the falling ruin. The mischief indeed was speedily repaired; the rubbish was cleared by the incessant labor of every rank and age; and the poor remains of riches and industry were consecrated by the Greeks to the most stately and venerable temple of the East.

The last hope of the falling city and empire was placed in the harmony of the mother and daughter, in the maternal tenderness of Rome, and the filial obedience of Constantinople. In the synod of Florence, the Greeks and Latins had embraced, and subscribed, and promised; but these signs of friendship were perfidious or fruitless; and the baseless fabric of the union vanished like a dream. The emperor and his prelates returned home in the Venetian galleys; but as they touched at the Morea and the Isles of Corfu and Lesbos, the subjects of the Latins complained that the pretended union would be an instrument of oppression. No sooner did they land on the Byzantine shore, than they were saluted, or rather assailed, with a general murmur of zeal and discontent. During their absence, above two years, the capital had been deprived of its civil and ecclesiastical rulers; fanaticism fermented in anarchy; the most furious monks reigned over the conscience of women and bigots; and the hatred of the Latin name was the first principle of nature and religion. Before his departure for Italy, the emperor had flattered the city with the assurance of a prompt relief and a powerful succor; and the clergy, confident in their orthodoxy and science, had promised themselves and their flocks an easy victory over the blind shepherds of the West. The double disappointment exasperated the Greeks; the conscience of the subscribing prelates was awakened; the hour of temptation was past; and they had more to dread from the public resentment, than they could hope from the favor of the emperor or the pope. Instead of justifying their conduct, they deplored their weakness, professed their contrition, and cast themselves on the mercy of God and of their brethren. To the reproachful question, what had been the event or the use of their Italian synod? they answered with sighs and tears, "Alas! we have made a new faith; we have exchanged piety for impiety; we have betrayed the immaculate sacrifice; and we are become *Azymites.*" (The Azymites were those who celebrated the communion with unleavened bread; and I must retract or qualify the praise which I have bestowed on the growing philosophy of the times.) "Alas! we have been seduced by distress, by fraud, and by the hopes and fears of a transitory life. The hand that has signed the union should be cut off; and the tongue that has pronounced the Latin creed deserves to be torn from the root." The best proof of their repentance was an increase of zeal for the most trivial rites and the most incomprehensible doctrines; and an absolute separation from all, without excepting their prince, who preserved some regard for honor and consistency. After the decease of the patriarch Joseph, the archbishops of Heraclea and Trebizond had courage to refuse the vacant office; and Cardinal Bessarion preferred the warm and comfortable shelter of the Vatican. The choice of the emperor and his clergy was confined to Metrophanes of Cyzicus: he was consecrated in St. Sophia, but the temple was vacant. The cross-bearers abdicated their service; the infection spread from the city to the villages; and Metrophanes discharged, without effect, some ecclesiastical thunders against a nation of schismatics. The eyes of the Greeks were directed to Mark of Ephesus, the champion of his country; and the sufferings of the holy confessor were repaid with a tribute of admiration and applause. His example and writings propagated the flame of religious discord; age and infirmity soon removed him from the world; but the gospel of Mark was not a law of forgiveness; and he requested with his dying breath, that none of the adherents of Rome might attend his obsequies or pray for his soul.

The schism was not confined to the narrow limits of the Byzantine empire. Secure under the Mamaluke sceptre, the three patriarchs of Alexandria, Antioch, and Jerusalem, assembled a numerous synod; disowned their representatives at Ferrara and Florence; condemned the creed and council of the Latins; and threatened the emperor of Constantinople with the censures of the Eastern church. Of the sectaries of the Greek communion, the Russians were the most powerful, ignorant, and superstitious. Their primate, the cardinal Isidore, hastened from Florence to Moscow, to reduce the independent nation under the Roman yoke. But the Russian bishops had been educated at Mount Athos; and the prince and people embraced the theology of their priests. They were scandalized by the title, the pomp, the Latin cross of the legate, the friend of those impious men who shaved their beards, and performed the divine office with gloves on their hands and rings on their fingers: Isidore was condemned by a synod; his person was imprisoned in a monastery; and it was with extreme difficulty that the cardinal could escape from the hands of a fierce and fanatic people. The Russians refused a passage to the missionaries of Rome who aspired to convert the Pagans beyond the Tanais; and their refusal was justified by the maxim, that the guilt of idolatry is less damnable than that of schism. The errors of the Bohemians were excused by their abhorrence for the pope; and a deputation of the Greek clergy solicited the friendship of those sanguinary enthusiasts. While Eugenius triumphed in the union and orthodoxy of the Greeks, his party was contracted to the walls, or rather to the palace of Constantinople. The zeal of Palæologus had been excited by interest; it was soon cooled by opposition: an attempt to violate the national belief might endanger his life and crown; not could the pious rebels be destitute of foreign and domestic aid. The sword of his brother Demetrius, who in Italy had maintained a prudent and popular silence, was half unsheathed in the cause of religion; and Amurath, the Turkish sultan, was displeased and alarmed by the seeming friendship of the Greeks and Latins.

"Sultan Murad, or Amurath, lived forty-nine, and reigned thirty years, six months, and eight days. He was a just and valiant prince, of a great soul, patient of labors, learned, merciful, religious, charitable; a lover and encourager of the studious, and of all who excelled in any art or science; a good emperor and a great general. No man obtained more or greater victories than Amurath; Belgrade alone withstood his attacks. Under his reign, the soldier was ever victorious, the citizen rich and secure. If he subdued any country, his first care was to build mosques and caravansaras, hospitals, and colleges. Every year he gave a thousand pieces of gold to the sons of the Prophet; and sent two thousand five hundred to the religious persons of Mecca, Medina, and Jerusalem." This portrait is transcribed from the historian of the Othman empire: but the applause of a servile and superstitious people has been lavished on the worst of tyrants; and the virtues of a sultan are often the vices most useful to himself, or most agreeable to his subjects. A nation ignorant of the equal benefits of liberty and law, must be awed by the flashes of arbitrary power: the cruelty of a despot will assume the character of justice; his profusion, of liberality; his obstinacy, of firmness. If the most reasonable excuse be rejected, few acts of obedience will be found impossible; and guilt must tremble, where innocence cannot always be secure. The tranquillity of the people, and the discipline of the troops, were best maintained by perpetual action in the field; war was the trade of the Janizaries; and those who survived the peril, and divided the spoil, applauded the generous ambition of their sovereign. To propagate the true religion, was the duty of a faithful Mussulman: the unbelievers were *his* enemies, and those of the Prophet; and, in the hands of the Turks, the cimeter was the only instrument of conversion. Under these circumstances, however, the justice and moderation of Amurath are attested by his conduct, and acknowledged by the Christians themselves; who consider a prosperous reign and a peaceful death as the reward of his singular merits. In the vigor of his age and military power, he seldom engaged in war till he was justified by a previous and adequate provocation: the victorious sultan was disarmed by submission; and in the observance of treaties, his word was inviolate and sacred. The Hungarians were commonly the aggressors; he was provoked by the revolt of Scanderbeg; and the perfidious Caramanian was twice vanquished, and twice pardoned, by the Ottoman monarch. Before he invaded the Morea, Thebes had been surprised by the despot: in the conquest of Thessalonica, the grandson of Bajazet might dispute the recent purchase of the Venetians; and after the first siege of Constantinople, the sultan was never tempted, by the distress, the absence, or the injuries of Palæologus, to extinguish the dying light of the Byzantine empire.

But the most striking feature in the life and character of Amurath is the double abdication of the Turkish throne; and, were not his motives debased by an alloy of superstition, we must praise the royal philosopher, who at the age of forty could discern the vanity of human greatness. Resigning the sceptre to his son, he retired to the pleasant residence of Magnesia; but he retired to the society of saints and hermits. It was not till the fourth century of the Hegira, that the religion of Mahomet had been corrupted by an institution so adverse to his genius; but in the age of the crusades, the various orders of Dervises were multiplied by the example of the Christian, and even the Latin, monks. The lord of nations submitted to fast, and pray, and turn round in endless rotation with the fanatics, who mistook the giddiness of the head for the illumination of the spirit. But he was soon awakened from his dreams of enthusiasm by the Hungarian invasion; and his obedient son was the foremost to urge the public danger and the wishes of the people. Under the banner of their veteran leader, the Janizaries fought and conquered but he withdrew from the field of Varna, again to pray, to fast, and to turn round with his Magnesian brethren. These pious occupations were again interrupted by the danger of the state. A victorious army disdained the inexperience of their youthful ruler: the city of Adrianople was abandoned to rapine and slaughter; and the unanimous divan implored his presence to appease the tumult, and prevent the rebellion, of the Janizaries. At the well-known voice of their master, they trembled and obeyed; and the reluctant sultan was compelled to support his splendid servitude, till at the end of four years, he was relieved by the angel of death. Age or disease, misfortune or caprice, have tempted several princes to descend from the throne; and they have had leisure to repent of their irretrievable step. But Amurath alone, in the full liberty of choice, after the trial of empire and solitude, has *repeated* his preference of a private life.

After the departure of his Greek brethren, Eugenius had not been unmindful of their temporal interest; and his tender regard for the Byzantine empire was animated by a just apprehension of the Turks, who approached, and might soon invade, the borders of Italy. But the spirit of the crusades had expired; and the coldness of the Franks was not less unreasonable than their headlong passion. In the eleventh century, a fanatic monk could precipitate Europe on Asia for the recovery of the holy sepulchre; but in the fifteenth, the most pressing motives of religion and policy were insufficient to unite the Latins in the defence of Christendom. Germany was an inexhaustible storehouse of men and arms: but that complex and languid body required the impulse of a vigorous hand; and Frederic the Third was alike impotent in his personal character and his Imperial dignity. A long war had impaired the strength, without satiating the animosity, of France and England: but Philip duke of Burgundy was a vain and magnificent prince; and he enjoyed, without danger or expense, the adventurous piety of his subjects, who sailed, in a gallant fleet, from the coast of Flanders to the Hellespont. The maritime republics of Venice and Genoa were less remote from the scene of action; and their hostile fleets were associated under the standard of St. Peter. The kingdoms of Hungary and Poland, which covered as it were the interior pale of the Latin church, were the most nearly concerned to oppose the progress of the Turks. Arms were the patrimony of the Scythians and Sarmatians; and these nations might appear equal to the contest, could they point, against the common foe, those swords that were so wantonly drawn in bloody and domestic quarrels. But the same spirit was adverse to concord and obedience: a poor country and a limited monarch are incapable of maintaining a standing force; and the loose bodies of Polish and Hungarian horse were not armed with the sentiments and weapons which, on some occasions, have given irresistible weight to the French chivalry. Yet, on this side, the designs of the Roman pontiff, and the eloquence of Cardinal Julian, his legate, were promoted by the circumstances of the times: by the union of the two crowns on the head of Ladislaus, a young and ambitious soldier;

by the valor of a hero, whose name, the name of John Huniades, was already popular among the Christians, and formidable to the Turks. An endless treasure of pardons and indulgences was scattered by the legate; many private warriors of France and Germany enlisted under the holy banner; and the crusade derived some strength, or at least some reputation, from the new allies both of Europe and Asia. A fugitive despot of Servia exaggerated the distress and ardor of the Christians beyond the Danube, who would unanimously rise to vindicate their religion and liberty. The Greek emperor, with a spirit unknown to his fathers, engaged to guard the Bosphorus, and to sally from Constantinople at the head of his national and mercenary troops. The sultan of Caramania announced the retreat of Amurath, and a powerful diversion in the heart of Anatolia; and if the fleets of the West could occupy at the same moment the Straits of the Hellespont, the Ottoman monarchy would be dissevered and destroyed. Heaven and earth must rejoice in the perdition of the miscreants; and the legate, with prudent ambiguity, instilled the opinion of the invisible, perhaps the visible, aid of the Son of God, and his divine mother.

Of the Polish and Hungarian diets, a religious war was the unanimous cry; and Ladislaus, after passing the Danube, led an army of his confederate subjects as far as Sophia, the capital of the Bulgarian kingdom. In this expedition they obtained two signal victories, which were justly ascribed to the valor and conduct of Huniades. In the first, with a vanguard of ten thousand men, he surprised the Turkish camp; in the second, he vanquished and made prisoner the most renowned of their generals, who possessed the double advantage of ground and numbers. The approach of winter, and the natural and artificial obstacles of Mount Hæmus, arrested the progress of the hero, who measured a narrow interval of six days' march from the foot of the mountains to the hostile towers of Adrianople, and the friendly capital of the Greek empire. The retreat was undisturbed; and the entrance into Buda was at once a military and religious triumph. An ecclesiastical procession was followed by the king and his warriors on foot: he nicely balanced the merits and rewards of the two nations; and the pride of conquest was blended with the humble temper of Christianity. Thirteen bashaws, nine standards, and four thousand captives, were unquestionable trophies; and as all were willing to believe, and none were present to contradict, the crusaders multiplied, with unblushing confidence, the myriads of Turks whom they had left on the field of battle. The most solid proof, and the most salutary consequence, of victory, was a deputation from the divan to solicit peace, to restore Servia, to ransom the prisoners, and to evacuate the Hungarian frontier. By this treaty, the rational objects of the war were obtained: the king, the despot, and Huniades himself, in the diet of Segedin, were satisfied with public and private emolument; a truce of ten years was concluded; and the followers of Jesus and Mahomet, who swore on the Gospel and the Koran, attested the word of God as the guardian of truth and the avenger of perfidy. In the place of the Gospel, the Turkish ministers had proposed to substitute the Eucharist, the real presence of the Catholic deity; but the Christians refused to profane their holy mysteries; and a superstitious conscience is less forcibly bound by the spiritual energy, than by the outward and visible symbols of an oath.

During the whole transaction, the cardinal legate had observed a sullen silence, unwilling to approve, and unable to oppose, the consent of the king and people. But the diet was not dissolved before Julian was fortified by the welcome intelligence, that Anatolia was invaded by the Caramanian, and Thrace by the Greek emperor; that the fleets of Genoa, Venice, and Burgundy, were masters of the Hellespont; and that the allies, informed of the victory, and ignorant of the treaty, of Ladislaus, impatiently waited for the return of his victorious army. "And is it thus," exclaimed the cardinal, "that you will desert their expectations and your own fortune? It is to them, to your God, and your fellow-Christians, that you have pledged your faith; and that prior obligation annihilates a rash and sacrilegious oath to the enemies of Christ. His vicar on earth is the Roman pontiff; without whose sanction you can neither promise nor perform. In his name I absolve your perjury and sanctify your arms: follow my footsteps in the paths of glory and salvation; and if still ye have scruples, devolve on my head the punishment and the sin." This mischievous casuistry was seconded by his respectable character, and the levity of popular assemblies: war was resolved, on the same spot where peace had so lately been sworn; and, in the execution of the treaty, the Turks were assaulted by the Christians; to whom, with some reason, they might apply the epithet of Infidels. The falsehood of Ladislaus to his word and oath was palliated by the religion of the times: the most perfect, or at least the most popular, excuse would have been the success of his arms and the deliverance of the Eastern church. But the same treaty which should have bound his conscience had diminished his strength. On the proclamation of the peace, the French and German volunteers departed with indignant murmurs: the Poles were exhausted by distant warfare, and perhaps disgusted with foreign command; and their palatines accepted the first license, and hastily retired to their provinces and castles. Even Hungary was divided by faction, or restrained by a laudable scruple; and the relics of the crusade that marched in the second expedition were reduced to an inadequate force of twenty thousand men. A Walachian chief, who joined the royal standard with his vassals, presumed to remark that their numbers did not exceed the hunting retinue that sometimes attended the sultan; and the gift of two horses of matchless speed might admonish Ladislaus of his secret foresight of the event. But the despot of Servia, after the restoration of his country and children, was tempted by the promise of new realms; and the inexperience of the king, the enthusiasm of the legate, and the martial presumption of Huniades himself, were persuaded that every obstacle must yield to the invincible virtue of the sword and the cross. After the passage of the Danube, two roads might lead to Constantinople and the Hellespont: the one direct, abrupt, and difficult through the mountains of Hæmus; the other more tedious and secure, over a level country, and along the shores of the Euxine; in which their flanks, according to the Scythian discipline, might always be covered by a movable fortification of wagons. The latter was judiciously preferred: the Catholics marched through the plains of Bulgaria, burning, with wanton cruelty, the churches and villages of the Christian natives; and their last station was at Warna, near the sea-shore; on which the defeat and death of Ladislaus have bestowed a memorable name.

Schism of the Greeks and Latins. – Part Two

It was on this fatal spot, that, instead of finding a confederate fleet to second their operations, they were alarmed by the approach of Amurath himself, who had issued from his Magnesian solitude, and transported the forces of Asia to the defence of Europe. According to some writers, the Greek emperor had been awed, or seduced, to grant the passage of the Bosphorus; and an indelible stain of corruption is fixed on the Genoese, or the pope's nephew, the Catholic admiral, whose mercenary connivance betrayed the guard of the Hellespont. From Adrianople, the sultan advanced by hasty marches, at the head of sixty thousand men; and when the cardinal, and Huniades, had taken a nearer survey of the numbers and order of the Turks, these ardent warriors proposed the tardy and impracticable measure of a retreat. The king alone was resolved to conquer or die; and his resolution had almost been crowned with a glorious and salutary victory. The princes were opposite to each other in the centre; and the Beglerbegs, or generals of Anatolia and Romania, commanded on the right and left, against the adverse divisions of the despot and Huniades. The Turkish wings were broken on the first onset: but the advantage was fatal; and the rash victors, in the heat of the pursuit, were carried away far from the annoyance of the enemy, or the support of their friends. When Amurath beheld the flight of his squadrons, he despaired of his fortune and that of the empire: a veteran Janizary seized his horse's bridle; and he had magnanimity to pardon and reward the soldier who dared to perceive the terror, and arrest the flight, of his sovereign. A copy of the treaty, the monument of Christian perfidy, had been displayed in the front of battle; and it is said, that the sultan in his distress, lifting his eyes and his hands to heaven, implored the protection of the God of truth; and called on the prophet Jesus himself to avenge the impious mockery of his name and religion. With inferior numbers and disordered ranks, the king of Hungary rushed forward in the confidence of victory, till his career was stopped by the impenetrable phalanx of the Janizaries. If we may credit the Ottoman annals, his horse was pierced by the javelin of Amurath; he fell among the spears of the infantry; and a Turkish soldier proclaimed with a loud voice, "Hungarians, behold the head of your king!" The death of Ladislaus was the signal of their defeat. On his return from an intemperate pursuit, Huniades deplored his error, and the public loss; he strove to rescue the royal body, till he was overwhelmed by the tumultuous crowd of the victors and vanquished; and the last efforts of his courage and conduct were exerted to save the remnant of his Walachian cavalry. Ten thousand Christians were slain in the disastrous battle of Warna: the loss of the Turks, more considerable in numbers, bore a smaller proportion to their total strength; yet the philosophic sultan was not ashamed to confess, that his ruin must be the consequence of a second and similar victory. At his command a column was erected on the spot where Ladislaus had fallen; but the modest inscription, instead of accusing the rashness, recorded the valor, and bewailed the misfortune, of the Hungarian youth.

Before I lose sight of the field of Warna, I am tempted to pause on the character and story of two principal actors, the cardinal Julian and John Huniades. Julian Cæsarini was born of a noble family of Rome: his studies had embraced both the Latin and Greek learning, both the sciences of divinity and law; and his versatile genius was equally adapted to the schools, the camp, and the court. No sooner had he been invested with the Roman purple, than he was sent into Germany to arm the empire against the rebels and heretics of Bohemia. The spirit of persecution is unworthy of a Christian; the military profession ill becomes a priest; but the former is excused by the times; and the latter was ennobled by the courage of Julian, who stood dauntless and alone in the disgraceful flight of the German host. As the pope's legate, he opened the council of Basil; but the president soon appeared the most strenuous champion of ecclesiastical freedom; and an opposition of seven years was conducted by his ability and zeal. After promoting the strongest measures against the authority and person of Eugenius, some secret motive of interest or conscience engaged him to desert on a sudden the popular party. The cardinal withdrew himself from Basil to Ferrara; and, in the debates of the Greeks and Latins, the two nations admired the dexterity of his arguments and the depth of his theological erudition. In his Hungarian embassy, we have already seen the mischievous effects of his sophistry and eloquence, of which Julian himself was the first victim. The cardinal, who performed the duties of a priest and a soldier, was lost in the defeat of Warna. The circumstances of his death are variously related; but it is believed, that a weighty encumbrance of gold impeded his flight, and tempted the cruel avarice of some Christian fugitives.

From an humble, or at least a doubtful origin, the merit of John Huniades promoted him to the command of the Hungarian armies. His father was a Walachian, his mother a Greek: her unknown race might possibly ascend to the emperors of Constantinople; and the claims of the Walachians, with the surname of Corvinus, from the place of his nativity, might suggest a thin pretence for mingling his blood with the patricians of ancient Rome. In his youth he served in the wars of Italy, and was retained, with twelve horsemen, by the bishop of Zagrab: the valor of the *white knight* was soon conspicuous; he increased his fortunes by a noble and wealthy marriage; and in the defence of the Hungarian borders he won in the same year three battles against the Turks. By his influence, Ladislaus of Poland obtained the crown of Hungary; and the important service was rewarded by the title and office of Waivod of Transylvania. The first of Julian's crusades added two Turkish laurels on his brow; and in the public distress the fatal errors of Warna were forgotten. During the absence and minority of Ladislaus of Austria, the titular king, Huniades was elected supreme captain and governor of Hungary; and if envy at first was silenced by terror, a reign of twelve years supposes the arts of policy as well as of war. Yet the idea of a consummate general is not delineated in his campaigns; the white knight fought with the hand rather than the head, as the chief of desultory Barbarians, who attack without fear and fly without shame; and his military life is composed of a romantic alternative of victories and escapes. By the Turks, who employed his name to frighten their perverse children, he was corruptly denominated *Jancus Lain*, or the Wicked: their hatred is the proof of their esteem; the kingdom which he guarded was inaccessible to their arms; and they felt him most daring and formidable, when they fondly believed the captain and his country irrecoverably lost. Instead of confining himself to a defensive war, four years after the defeat of Warna he again penetrated into the heart of Bulgaria, and in the plain of Cossova, sustained, till the third day, the shock of the Ottoman army, four times more numerous than his own. As he fled alone through the woods of Walachia, the hero was surprised by two robbers; but while they disputed a gold chain that hung at his neck, he recovered his sword, slew the one, terrified the other, and, after new perils of captivity or death, consoled by his presence an afflicted kingdom. But the last and most glorious action of his life was the defence of Belgrade against the powers of Mahomet the Second in person. After a siege of forty days, the Turks, who had already entered the town, were compelled to retreat; and the joyful nations celebrated Huniades and Belgrade as the bulwarks of Christendom. About a month after this great deliverance, the champion expired; and his most splendid epitaph is the regret of the Ottoman prince, who sighed that he could no longer hope for revenge against the single antagonist who had triumphed over his arms. On the first vacancy of the throne, Matthias Corvinus, a youth of eighteen years of age, was elected and crowned by the grateful Hungarians. His reign was prosperous and long: Matthias aspired to the glory of a conqueror and a saint: but his purest merit is the encouragement of learning; and the Latin orators and historians, who were invited from Italy by the son, have shed the lustre of their eloquence on the father's character.

In the list of heroes, John Huniades and Scanderbeg are commonly associated; and they are both entitled to our notice, since their occupation of the Ottoman arms delayed the ruin of the Greek empire. John Castriot, the father of Scanderbeg, was the hereditary prince of a small district of Epirus or Albania, between the mountains and the Adriatic Sea. Unable to contend with the sultan's power, Castriot submitted to the hard conditions of peace and tribute: he delivered his four sons as the pledges of his fidelity; and the Christian youths, after receiving the mark of circumcision, were instructed in the Mahometan religion, and trained in the arms and arts of Turkish policy. The three elder brothers were confounded in the crowd of slaves; and the poison to which their deaths are ascribed cannot be verified or disproved by any positive evidence. Yet the suspicion is in a great measure removed by the kind and paternal treatment of George Castriot, the fourth brother, who, from his tender youth, displayed the strength and spirit of a soldier. The successive overthrow of a Tartar and two Persians, who carried a proud defiance to the Turkish court, recommended him to the favor of Amurath, and his Turkish appellation of Scanderbeg, (*Iskender beg,*) or the lord Alexander, is an indelible memorial of his glory and servitude. His father's principality was reduced into a province; but the loss was compensated by the rank and title of Sanjiak, a command of five thousand horse, and the prospect of the first dignities of the empire. He served with honor in the wars of Europe and Asia; and we may smile at the art or credulity of the historian, who supposes, that in every encounter he spared the Christians, while he fell with a thundering arm on his Mussulman foes. The glory of Huniades is without reproach: he fought in the defence of his religion and country; but the enemies who applaud the patriot, have branded his rival with the name of traitor and apostate. In the eyes of the Christian, the rebellion of Scanderbeg is justified by his father's wrongs, the ambiguous death of his three brothers, his own degradation, and the slavery of his country; and they adore the generous, though tardy, zeal, with which he asserted the faith and independence of his ancestors. But he had imbibed from his ninth year the doctrines of the Koran; he was ignorant of the Gospel; the religion of a soldier is determined by authority and habit; nor is it easy to conceive what new illumination at the age of forty could be poured into his soul. His motives would be less exposed to the suspicion of interest or revenge, had he broken his chain from the moment that he was sensible of its weight: but a long oblivion had surely impaired his original right; and every year of obedience and reward had cemented the mutual bond of the sultan and his subject. If Scanderbeg had long harbored the belief of Christianity and the intention of revolt, a worthy mind must condemn the base dissimulation, that could serve only to betray, that could promise only to be forsworn, that could actively join in the temporal and spiritual perdition of so many thousands of his unhappy brethren. Shall we praise a secret correspondence with Huniades, while he commanded the vanguard of the Turkish army? shall we excuse the desertion of his standard, a treacherous desertion which abandoned the victory to the enemies of his benefactor? In the confusion of a defeat, the eye of Scanderbeg was fixed on the Reis Effendi or principal secretary: with the dagger at his breast, he extorted a firman or patent for the government of Albania; and the murder of the guiltless scribe and his train prevented the consequences of an immediate discovery. With some bold companions, to whom he had revealed his design he escaped in the night, by rapid marches, from the field or battle to his paternal mountains. The gates of Croya were opened to the royal mandate; and no sooner did he command the fortress, than George Castriot dropped the mask of dissimulation; abjured the prophet and the sultan, and proclaimed himself the avenger of his family and country. The names of religion and liberty provoked a general revolt: the Albanians, a martial race, were unanimous to live and die with their hereditary prince; and the Ottoman garrisons were indulged in the choice of martyrdom or baptism. In the assembly of the states of Epirus, Scanderbeg was elected general of the Turkish war; and each of the allies engaged to furnish his respective proportion of men and money. From these contributions, from his patrimonial estate, and from the valuable salt-pits of Selina, he drew an annual revenue of two hundred thousand ducats; and the entire sum, exempt from the demands of luxury, was strictly appropriated to the public use. His manners were popular; but his discipline was severe; and every superfluous vice was banished from his camp: his example strengthened his command; and under his conduct, the Albanians were invincible in their own opinion and that of their enemies. The bravest adventurers of France and Germany were allured by his fame and retained in his service: his standing militia consisted of eight thousand horse and seven thousand foot; the horses were small, the men were active; but he viewed with a discerning eye the difficulties and resources of the mountains; and, at the blaze of the beacons, the whole nation was distributed in the strongest posts. With such unequal arms Scanderbeg resisted twenty-three years the powers of the Ottoman empire; and two conquerors, Amurath the Second, and his greater son, were repeatedly baffled by a rebel, whom they pursued with seeming contempt and implacable resentment. At the head of sixty thousand horse and forty thousand Janizaries, Amurath entered Albania: he might ravage the open country, occupy the defenceless towns, convert the churches into mosques, circumcise the Christian youths, and punish with death his adult and obstinate captives: but the conquests of the sultan were confined to the petty fortress of Sfetigrade; and the garrison, invincible to his arms, was oppressed by a paltry artifice and a superstitious scruple. Amurath retired with shame and loss from the walls of Croya, the castle and residence of the Castriots; the march, the siege, the retreat, were harassed by a vexatious, and almost invisible, adversary; and the disappointment might tend to imbitter, perhaps to shorten, the last days of the sultan. In the fulness of conquest, Mahomet the Second still felt at his bosom this domestic thorn: his lieutenants were permitted to negotiate a truce; and the Albanian prince may justly be praised as a firm and able champion of his national independence. The enthusiasm of chivalry and religion has ranked him with the names of Alexander and Pyrrhus; nor would they blush to acknowledge their intrepid countryman: but his narrow dominion, and slender powers, must leave him at an humble distance below the heroes of antiquity, who triumphed over the East and the Roman legions. His splendid achievements, the bashaws whom he encountered, the armies that he discomfited, and the three thousand Turks who were slain by his single hand, must be weighed in the scales of suspicious criticism. Against an illiterate enemy, and in the dark solitude of Epirus, his partial biographers may safely indulge the latitude of romance: but their fictions are exposed by the light of Italian history; and they afford a strong presumption against their own truth, by a fabulous tale of his exploits, when he passed the Adriatic with eight hundred horse to the succor of the king of Naples. Without disparagement to his fame, they might have owned, that he was finally oppressed by the Ottoman powers: in his extreme danger he applied to Pope Pius the Second for a refuge in the ecclesiastical state; and his resources were almost exhausted, since Scanderbeg died a fugitive at Lissus, on the Venetian territory. His sepulchre was soon violated by the Turkish conquerors; but the Janizaries, who wore his bones enchased in a bracelet, declared by this superstitious amulet their involuntary reverence for his valor. The instant ruin of his country may redound to the hero's glory; yet, had he balanced the consequences of submission and resistance, a patriot perhaps would have declined the unequal contest which must depend on the life and genius of one man. Scanderbeg might indeed be supported by the rational, though fallacious, hope, that the pope, the king of Naples, and the Venetian republic, would join in the defence of a free and Christian people, who guarded the sea-coast of the Adriatic, and the narrow passage from Greece to Italy. His infant son was saved from the national shipwreck; the Castriots were invested with a Neapolitan dukedom, and their blood continues to flow in the noblest families of the realm. A colony of Albanian fugitives obtained a settlement in Calabria, and they preserve at this day the language and manners of their ancestors.

In the long career of the decline and fall of the Roman empire, I have reached at length the last reign of the princes of Constantinople, who so feebly sustained the name and majesty of the Cæsars. On the decease of John Palæologus, who survived about four years the Hungarian crusade, the royal family, by the death of Andronicus and the monastic profession of Isidore, was reduced to three princes, Constantine, Demetrius, and Thomas, the surviving sons of the emperor Manuel. Of these the first and the last were far distant in the Morea; but Demetrius, who possessed the domain of Selybria, was in the suburbs, at the head of a party: his ambition was not chilled by the public distress; and his conspiracy with the Turks and the schismatics had already disturbed the peace of his country. The funeral of the late emperor was accelerated with singular and even suspicious haste: the claim of Demetrius to the vacant throne was justified by a trite and flimsy sophism, that he was born in the purple, the eldest son of his father's reign. But the empress-mother, the senate and soldiers, the clergy and people, were unanimous in the cause of the lawful successor: and the despot Thomas, who, ignorant of the change, accidentally returned to the capital, asserted with becoming zeal the interest of his absent brother. An ambassador, the historian Phranza, was immediately despatched to the court of Adrianople. Amurath received him with honor and dismissed him with gifts; but the gracious approbation of the Turkish sultan announced his supremacy, and the approaching downfall of the Eastern empire. By the hands of two illustrious deputies, the Imperial crown was placed at Sparta on the head of Constantine. In the spring he sailed from the Morea, escaped the encounter of a Turkish squadron, enjoyed the acclamations of his subjects, celebrated the festival of a new reign, and exhausted by his donatives the treasure, or rather the indigence, of the state. The emperor immediately resigned to his brothers the possession of the Morea; and the brittle friendship of the two princes, Demetrius and Thomas, was confirmed in their mother's presence by the frail security of oaths and embraces. His next occupation was the choice of a consort. A daughter of the doge of Venice had been proposed; but the Byzantine nobles objected the distance between an hereditary monarch and an elective magistrate; and in their subsequent distress, the chief of that powerful republic was not unmindful of the affront. Constantine afterwards hesitated between the royal families of Trebizond and Georgia; and the embassy of Phranza represents in his public and private life the last days of the Byzantine empire.

The *protovestiare*, or great chamberlain, Phranza sailed from Constantinople as the minister of a bridegroom; and the relics of wealth and luxury were applied to his pompous appearance. His numerous retinue consisted of nobles and guards, of physicians and monks: he was attended by a band of music; and the term of his costly embassy was protracted above two years. On his arrival in Georgia or Iberia, the natives from the towns and villages flocked around the strangers; and such was their simplicity, that they were delighted with the effects, without understanding the cause, of musical harmony. Among the crowd was an old man, above a hundred years of age, who had formerly been carried away a captive by the Barbarians, and who amused his hearers with a tale of the wonders of India, from whence he had returned to Portugal by an unknown sea. From this hospitable land, Phranza proceeded to the court of Trebizond, where he was informed by the Greek prince of the recent decease of Amurath. Instead of rejoicing in the deliverance, the experienced statesman expressed his apprehension, that an ambitious youth would not long adhere to the sage and pacific system of his father. After the sultan's decease, his Christian wife, Maria, the daughter of the Servian despot, had been honorably restored to her parents; on the fame of her beauty and merit, she was recommended by the ambassador as the most worthy object of the royal choice; and Phranza recapitulates and refutes the specious objections that might be raised against the proposal. The majesty of the purple would ennoble an unequal alliance; the bar of affinity might be removed by liberal alms and the dispensation of the church; the disgrace of Turkish nuptials had been repeatedly over-looked; and, though the fair Maria was nearly fifty years of age, she might yet hope to give an heir to the empire. Constantine listened to the advice, which was transmitted in the first ship that sailed from Trebizond; but the factions of the court opposed his marriage; and it was finally prevented by the pious vow of the sultana, who ended her days in the monastic profession. Reduced to the first alternative, the choice of Phranza was decided in favor of a Georgian princess; and the vanity of her father was dazzled by the glorious alliance. Instead of demanding, according to the primitive and national custom, a price for his daughter, he offered a portion of fifty-six thousand, with an an-nual pension of five thousand, ducats; and the services of the ambas-sador were repaid by an assurance, that, as his son had been adopted in baptism by the emperor, the establishment of his daughter should be the peculiar care of the empress of Constantinople. On the return of Phranza, the treaty was ratified by the Greek monarch, who with his own hand impressed three vermilion crosses on the golden bull, and assured the Georgian envoy that in the spring his galleys should conduct the bride to her Imperial palace. But Constantine embraced his faithful servant, not with the cold approbation of a sovereign, but with the warm confidence of a friend, who, after a long absence, is impatient to pour his secrets into the bosom of his friend. "Since the death of my mother and of Cantacuzene, who alone advised me with-out interest or passion, I am surrounded," said the emperor, "by men whom I can neither love nor trust, nor esteem. You are not a stranger to Lucas Notaras, the great admiral; obstinately attached to his own sentiments, he declares, both in private and public, that his sentiments are the absolute measure of my thoughts and actions. The rest of the courtiers are swayed by their personal or factious views; and how can I consult the monks on questions of policy and marriage? I have yet much employment for your diligence and fidelity. In the spring you shall engage one of my brothers to solicit the succor of the Western powers; from the Morea you shall sail to Cyprus on a particular com-mission; and from thence proceed to Georgia to receive and conduct the future empress." – "Your commands," replied Phranza, "are irre-sistible; but deign, great sir," he added, with a serious smile, "to consider, that if I am thus perpetually absent from my family, my wife may be tempted either to seek another husband, or to throw herself into a monastery." After laughing at his apprehensions, the emperor more gravely consoled him by the pleasing assurance that *this* should be his last service abroad, and that he destined for his son a wealthy and noble heiress; for himself, the important office of great logothete, or principal minister of state. The marriage was immediately stipulated: but the office, however incompatible with his own, had been usurped by the ambition of the admiral. Some delay was requisite to negotiate a consent and an equivalent; and the nomination of Phranza was half declared, and half suppressed, lest it might be displeasing to an insolent and powerful favorite. The winter was spent in the preparations of his embassy; and Phranza had resolved, that the youth his son should embrace this opportunity of foreign travel, and be left, on the appearance of danger, with his maternal kindred of the Morea. Such were the private and public designs, which were interrupted by a Turkish war, and finally buried in the ruins of the empire.

Reign of Mahomet the Second, Extinction of Eastern Empire. – Part One

Reign and Character of Mahomet the Second. – Siege, Assault, and Final Conquest, of Constantinople by the Turks. – Death of Constantine Palæologus. – Servitude of the Greeks. – Extinction of the Roman Empire in the East. – Consternation of Europe. – Conquests and Death of Mahomet the Second.

THE SIEGE OF CONSTANTINOPLE by the Turks attracts our first attention to the person and character of the great destroyer. Mahomet the Second was the son of the second Amurath; and though his mother has been decorated with the titles of Christian and princess, she is more probably confounded with the numerous concubines who peopled from every climate the harem of the sultan. His first education and sentiments were those of a devout Mussulman; and as often as he conversed with an infidel, he purified his hands and face by the legal rites of ablution. Age and empire appear to have relaxed this narrow bigotry: his aspiring genius disdained to acknowledge a power above his own; and in his looser hours he presumed (it is said) to brand the prophet of Mecca as a robber and impostor. Yet the sultan persevered in a decent reverence for the doctrine and discipline of the Koran: his private indiscretion must have been sacred from the vulgar ear; and we should suspect the credulity of strangers and sectaries, so prone to believe that a mind which is hardened against truth must be armed with superior contempt for absurdity and error. Under the tuition of the most skilful masters, Mahomet advanced with an early and rapid progress in the paths of knowledge; and besides his native tongue it is affirmed that he spoke or understood five languages, the Arabic, the Persian, the Chaldæan or Hebrew, the Latin, and the Greek. The Persian might indeed contribute to his amusement, and the Arabic to his edification; and such studies are familiar to the Oriental youth. In the intercourse of the Greeks and Turks, a conqueror might wish to converse with the people over which he was ambitious to reign: his own praises in Latin poetry or prose might find a passage to the royal ear; but what use or merit could recommend to the statesman or the scholar the uncouth dialect of his Hebrew slaves? The history and geography of the world were familiar to his memory: the lives of the heroes of the East, perhaps of the West, excited his emulation: his skill in astrology is excused by the folly of the times, and supposes some rudiments of mathematical science; and a profane taste for the arts is betrayed in his liberal invitation and reward of the painters of Italy. But the influence of religion and learning were employed without effect on his savage and licentious nature. I will not transcribe, nor do I firmly believe, the stories of his fourteen pages, whose bellies were ripped open in search of a stolen melon; or of the beauteous slave, whose head he severed from her body, to convince the Janizaries that their master was not the votary of love. His sobriety is attested by the silence of the Turkish annals, which accuse three, and three only, of the Ottoman line of the vice of drunkenness. But it cannot be denied that his passions were at once furious and inexorable; that in the palace, as in the field, a torrent of blood was spilt on the slightest provocation; and that the noblest of the captive youth were often dishonored by his unnatural lust. In the Albanian war he studied the lessons, and soon surpassed the example, of his father; and the conquest of two empires, twelve kingdoms, and two hundred cities, a vain and flattering account, is ascribed to his invincible sword. He was doubtless a soldier, and possibly a general; Constantinople has sealed his glory; but if we compare the means, the obstacles, and the achievements, Mahomet the Second must blush to sustain a parallel with Alexander or Timour. Under his command, the Ottoman forces were always more numerous than their enemies; yet their progress was bounded by the Euphrates and the Adriatic; and his arms were checked by Huniades and Scanderbeg, by the Rhodian knights and by the Persian king.

In the reign of Amurath, he twice tasted of royalty, and twice descended from the throne: his tender age was incapable of opposing his father's restoration, but never could he forgive the viziers who had recommended that salutary measure. His nuptials were celebrated with the daughter of a Turkman emir; and, after a festival of two months, he departed from Adrianople with his bride, to reside in the government of Magnesia. Before the end of six weeks, he was recalled by a sudden message from the divan, which announced the decease of Amurath, and the mutinous spirit of the Janizaries. His speed and vigor commanded their obedience: he passed the Hellespont with a chosen guard: and at the distance of a mile from Adrianople, the viziers and emirs, the imams and cadhis, the soldiers and the people, fell prostrate before the new sultan. They affected to weep, they affected to rejoice: he ascended the throne at the age of twenty-one years, and removed the cause of sedition by the death, the inevitable death, of his infant brothers. The ambassadors of Europe and Asia soon appeared to congratulate his accession and solicit his friendship; and to all he spoke the language of moderation and peace. The confidence of the Greek emperor was revived by the solemn oaths and fair assurances with which he sealed the ratification of the treaty: and a rich domain on the banks of the Strymon was assigned for the annual payment of three hundred thousand aspers, the pension of an Ottoman prince, who was detained at his request in the Byzantine court. Yet the neighbors of Mahomet might tremble at the severity with which a youthful monarch reformed the pomp of his father's household: the expenses of luxury were applied to those of ambition, and a useless train of seven thousand falconers was either dismissed from his service, or enlisted in his troops. In the first summer of his reign, he visited with an army the Asiatic provinces; but after humbling the pride, Mahomet accepted the submission, of the Caramanian, that he might not be diverted by the smallest obstacle from the execution of his great design.

The Mahometan, and more especially the Turkish casuists, have pronounced that no promise can bind the faithful against the interest and duty of their religion; and that the sultan may abrogate his own treaties and those of his predecessors. The justice and magnanimity of Amurath had scorned this immoral privilege; but his son, though the proudest of men, could stoop from ambition to the basest arts of dissimulation and deceit. Peace was on his lips, while war was in his heart: he incessantly sighed for the possession of Constantinople; and the Greeks, by their own indiscretion, afforded the first pretence of the fatal rupture. Instead of laboring to be forgotten, their ambassadors pursued his camp, to demand the payment, and even the increase, of their annual stipend: the divan was importuned by their complaints, and the vizier, a secret friend of the Christians, was constrained to deliver the sense of his brethren. "Ye foolish and miserable Romans," said Calil, "we know your devices, and ye are ignorant of your own danger! The scrupulous Amurath is no more; his throne is occupied by a young conqueror, whom no laws can bind, and no obstacles can resist: and if you escape from his hands, give praise to the divine clemency, which yet delays the chastisement of your sins. Why do ye seek to affright us by vain and indirect menaces? Release the fugitive Orchan, crown him sultan of Romania; call the Hungarians from beyond the Danube; arm against us the nations of the West; and be assured, that you will only provoke and precipitate your ruin." But if the fears of the ambassadors were alarmed by the stern language of the vizier, they were soothed by the courteous audience and friendly speeches of the Ottoman prince; and Mahomet assured them that on his return to Adrianople he would redress the grievances, and consult the true interests, of the Greeks. No sooner had he repassed the Hellespont, than he issued a mandate to suppress their pension, and to expel their officers from the banks of the Strymon: in this measure he betrayed a hostile mind; and the second order announced, and in some degree commenced, the siege of Constantinople. In the narrow pass of the Bosphorus, an Asiatic fortress had formerly been raised by his grandfather; in the opposite situation, on the European side, he resolved to erect a more formidable castle; and a thousand masons were commanded to assemble in the spring on a spot named Asomaton, about five miles from the Greek metropolis. Persuasion is the resource of the feeble; and the feeble can seldom persuade: the ambassadors of the emperor attempted, without success, to divert Mahomet from the execution of his design. They represented, that his grandfather had solicited the permission of Manuel to build a castle on his own territories; but that this double fortification, which would command the strait, could only tend to violate the alliance of the nations; to intercept the Latins who traded in the Black Sea, and perhaps to annihilate the subsistence of the city. "I form no enterprise," replied the perfidious sultan, "against the city; but the empire of Constantinople is measured by her walls. Have you forgot the distress to which my father was reduced when you formed a league with the Hungarians; when they invaded our country by land, and the Hellespont was occupied by the French galleys? Amurath was compelled to force the passage of the Bosphorus; and your strength was not equal to your malevolence. I was then a child at Adrianople; the Moslems trembled; and, for a while, the *Gabours* insulted our disgrace. But when my father had triumphed in the field of Warna, he vowed to erect a fort on the western shore, and that vow it is my duty to accomplish. Have ye the right, have ye the power, to control my actions on my own ground? For that ground is my own: as far as the shores of the Bosphorus, Asia is inhabited by the Turks, and

Europe is deserted by the Romans. Return, and inform your king, that the present Ottoman is far different from his predecessors; that *his* resolutions surpass *their* wishes; and that *he* performs more *than* they could resolve. Return in safety – but the next who delivers a similar message may expect to be flayed alive." After this declaration, Constantine, the first of the Greeks in spirit as in rank, had determined to unsheathe the sword, and to resist the approach and establishment of the Turks on the Bosphorus. He was disarmed by the advice of his civil and ecclesiastical ministers, who recommended a system less generous, and even less prudent, than his own, to approve their patience and long-suffering, to brand the Ottoman with the name and guilt of an aggressor, and to depend on chance and time for their own safety, and the destruction of a fort which could not long be maintained in the neighborhood of a great and populous city. Amidst hope and fear, the fears of the wise, and the hopes of the credulous, the winter rolled away; the proper business of each man, and each hour, was postponed; and the Greeks shut their eyes against the impending danger, till the arrival of the spring and the sultan decide the assurance of their ruin.

Of a master who never forgives, the orders are seldom disobeyed. On the twenty-sixth of March, the appointed spot of Asomaton was covered with an active swarm of Turkish artificers; and the materials by sea and land were diligently transported from Europe and Asia. The lime had been burnt in Cataphrygia; the timber was cut down in the woods of Heraclea and Nicomedia; and the stones were dug from the Anatolian quarries. Each of the thousand masons was assisted by two workmen; and a measure of two cubits was marked for their daily task. The fortress was built in a triangular form; each angle was flanked by a strong and massy tower; one on the declivity of the hill, two along the sea-shore: a thickness of twenty-two feet was assigned for the walls, thirty for the towers; and the whole building was covered with a solid platform of lead. Mahomet himself pressed and directed the work with indefatigable ardor: his three viziers claimed the honor of finishing their respective towers; the zeal of the cadhis emulated that of the Janizaries; the meanest labor was ennobled by the service of God and the sultan; and the diligence of the multitude was quickened by the eye of a despot, whose smile was the hope of fortune, and whose frown was the messenger of death. The Greek emperor beheld with terror the irresistible progress of the work; and vainly strove, by flattery and gifts, to assuage an implacable foe, who sought, and secretly fomented, the slightest occasion of a quarrel. Such occasions must soon and inevitably be found. The ruins of stately churches, and even the marble columns which had been consecrated to Saint Michael the archangel, were employed without scruple by the profane and rapacious Moslems; and some Christians, who presumed to oppose the removal, received from their hands the crown of martyrdom. Constantine had solicited a Turkish guard to protect the fields and harvests of his subjects: the guard was fixed; but their first order was to allow free pasture to the mules and horses of the camp, and to defend their brethren if they should be molested by the natives. The retinue of an Ottoman chief had left their horses to pass the night among the ripe corn; the damage was felt; the insult was resented; and several of both nations were slain in a tumultuous conflict. Mahomet listened with joy to the complaint; and a detachment was commanded to exterminate the guilty village: the guilty had fled; but forty innocent and unsuspecting reapers were massacred by the soldiers. Till this provocation, Constantinople had been opened to the visits of commerce and curiosity: on the first alarm, the gates were shut; but the emperor, still anxious for peace, released on the third day his Turkish captives; and expressed, in a last message, the firm resignation of a Christian and a soldier. "Since neither oaths, nor treaty, nor submission, can secure peace, pursue," said he to Mahomet, "your impious warfare. My trust is in God alone; if it should please him to mollify your heart, I shall rejoice in the happy change; if he delivers the city into your hands, I submit without a murmur to his holy will. But until the Judge of the earth shall pronounce between us, it is my duty to live and die in the defence of my people." The sultan's answer was hostile and decisive: his fortifications were completed; and before his departure for Adrianople, he stationed a vigilant Aga and four hundred Janizaries, to levy a tribute on the ships of every nation that should pass within the reach of their cannon. A Venetian vessel, refusing obedience to the new lords of the Bosphorus, was sunk with a single bullet. The master and thirty sailors escaped in the boat; but they were dragged in chains to the *Porte*: the chief was impaled; his companions were beheaded; and the historian Ducas beheld, at Demotica, their bodies exposed to the wild beasts. The siege of Constantinople was deferred till the ensuing spring; but an Ottoman army marched into the Morea to divert the force of the brothers of Constantine. At this æra of calamity, one of these princes, the despot Thomas, was blessed or afflicted with the birth of a son; "the last heir," says the plaintive Phranza, "of the last spark of the Roman empire."

The Greeks and the Turks passed an anxious and sleepless winter: the former were kept awake by their fears, the latter by their hopes; both by the preparations of defence and attack; and the two emperors, who had the most to lose or to gain, were the most deeply affected by the national sentiment. In Mahomet, that sentiment was inflamed by the ardor of his youth and temper: he amused his leisure with building at Adrianople the lofty palace of Jehan Numa, (the watchtower of the world;) but his serious thoughts were irrevocably bent on the conquest of the city of Cæsar. At the dead of night, about the second watch, he started from his bed, and commanded the instant attendance of his prime vizier. The message, the hour, the prince, and his own situation, alarmed the guilty conscience of Calil Basha; who had possessed the confidence, and advised the restoration, of Amurath. On the accession of the son, the vizier was confirmed in his office and the appearances of favor; but the veteran statesman was not insensible that he trod on a thin and slippery ice, which might break under his footsteps, and plunge him in the abyss. His friendship for the Christians, which might be innocent under the late reign, had stigmatized him with the name of Gabour Ortachi, or foster-brother of the infidels; and his avarice entertained a venal and treasonable correspondence, which was detected and punished after the conclusion of the war. On receiving the royal mandate, he embraced, perhaps for the last time, his wife and children; filled a cup with pieces of gold, hastened to the palace, adored the sultan, and offered, according to the Oriental custom, the slight tribute of his duty and gratitude. "It is not my wish," said Mahomet, "to resume my gifts, but rather to heap and multiply them on thy head. In my turn, I ask a present far more valuable and important; – Constantinople." As soon as the vizier had recovered from his surprise, "The same God," said he, "who has already given thee so large a portion of the Roman empire, will not deny the remnant, and the capital. His providence, and thy power, assure thy success; and myself, with the rest of thy faithful slaves, will sacrifice our lives and fortunes." – "Lala," (or preceptor,) continued the sultan, "do you see this pillow? All the night, in my agitation, I have pulled it on one side and the other; I have risen from my bed, again have I lain down; yet sleep has not visited these weary eyes. Beware of the gold and silver of the Romans: in arms we are superior; and with the aid of God, and the prayers of the prophet, we shall speedily become masters of Constantinople." To sound the disposition of his soldiers, he often wandered through the streets alone, and in disguise; and it was fatal to discover the sultan, when he wished to escape from the vulgar eye. His hours were spent in delineating the plan of the hostile city; in debating with his generals and engineers, on what spot he should erect his batteries; on which side he should assault the walls; where he should spring his mines; to what place he should apply his scaling-ladders: and the exercises of the day repeated and proved the lucubrations of the night.

Reign of Mahomet the Second, Extinction of Eastern Empire. – Part Two

AMONG THE IMPLEMENTS OF destruction, he studied with peculiar care the recent and tremendous discovery of the Latins; and his artillery surpassed whatever had yet appeared in the world. A founder of cannon, a Dane or Hungarian, who had been almost starved in the Greek service, deserted to the Moslems, and was liberally entertained by the Turkish sultan. Mahomet was satisfied with the answer to his first question, which he eagerly pressed on the artist. "Am I able to cast a cannon capable of throwing a ball or stone of sufficient size to batter the walls of Constantinople? I am not ignorant of their strength; but were they more solid than those of Babylon, I could oppose an engine of superior power: the position and management of that engine must be left to your engineers." On this assurance, a foundry was established at Adrianople: the metal was prepared; and at the end of three months, Urban produced a piece of brass ordnance of stupendous, and almost incredible magnitude; a measure of twelve palms is assigned to the bore; and the stone bullet weighed above six hundred pounds. A vacant place before the new palace was chosen for the first experiment; but to prevent the sudden and mischievous effects of astonishment and fear, a proclamation was issued, that the cannon would be discharged the ensuing day. The explosion was felt or heard in a circuit of a hundred furlongs: the ball, by the force of gunpowder, was driven above a mile; and on the spot where it fell, it buried itself a fathom deep in the ground. For the conveyance of this destructive engine, a frame or carriage of thirty wagons was linked together and drawn along by a team of sixty oxen: two hundred men on both sides were stationed, to poise and support the rolling weight; two hundred and fifty workmen marched before to smooth the way and repair the bridges; and near two months were employed in a laborious journey of one hundred and fifty miles. A lively philosopher derides on this occasion the credulity of the Greeks, and observes, with much reason, that we should always distrust the exaggerations of a vanquished people. He calculates, that a ball, even of two hundred pounds, would require a charge of one hundred and fifty pounds of powder; and that the stroke would be feeble and impotent, since not a fifteenth part of the mass could be inflamed at the same moment. A stranger as I am to the art of destruction, I can discern that the modern improvements of artillery prefer the number of pieces to the weight of metal; the quickness of the fire to the sound, or even the consequence, of a single explosion. Yet I dare not reject the positive and unanimous evidence of contemporary writers; nor can it seem improbable, that the first artists, in their rude and ambitious efforts, should have transgressed the standard of moderation. A Turkish cannon, more enormous than that of Mahomet, still guards the entrance of the Dardanelles; and if the use be inconvenient, it has been found on a late trial that the effect was far from contemptible. A stone bullet of *eleven* hundred pounds' weight was once discharged with three hundred and thirty pounds of powder: at the distance of six hundred yards it shivered into three rocky fragments; traversed the strait; and leaving the waters in a foam, again rose and bounded against the opposite hill.

While Mahomet threatened the capital of the East, the Greek emperor implored with fervent prayers the assistance of earth and heaven. But the invisible powers were deaf to his supplications; and Christendom beheld with indifference the fall of Constantinople, while she derived at least some promise of supply from the jealous and temporal policy of the sultan of Egypt. Some states were too weak, and others too remote; by some the danger was considered as imaginary by others as inevitable: the Western princes were involved in their endless and domestic quarrels; and the Roman pontiff was exasperated by the falsehood or obstinacy of the Greeks. Instead of employing in their favor the arms and treasures of Italy, Nicholas the Fifth had foretold their approaching ruin; and his honor was engaged in the accomplishment of his prophecy. Perhaps he was softened by the last extremity of their distress; but his compassion was tardy; his efforts were faint and unavailing; and Constantinople had fallen, before the squadrons of Genoa and Venice could sail from their harbors. Even the princes of the Morea and of the Greek islands affected a cold neutrality: the Genoese colony of Galata negotiated a private treaty; and the sultan indulged them in the delusive hope, that by his clemency they might survive the ruin of the empire. A plebeian crowd, and some Byzantine nobles basely withdrew from the danger of their country; and the avarice of the rich denied the emperor, and reserved for the Turks, the secret treasures which might have raised in their defence whole armies of mercenaries. The indigent and solitary prince prepared, however, to sustain his formidable adversary; but if his courage were equal to the peril, his strength was inadequate to the contest. In the beginning of the spring, the Turkish vanguard swept the towns and villages as far as the gates of Constantinople: submission was spared and protected; whatever presumed to resist was exterminated with fire and sword. The Greek places on the Black Sea, Mesembria, Acheloum, and Bizon, surrendered on the first summons; Selybria alone deserved the honors of a siege or blockade; and the bold inhabitants, while they were invested by land, launched their boats, pillaged the opposite coast of Cyzicus, and sold their captives in the public market. But on the approach of Mahomet himself all was silent and prostrate: he first halted at the distance of five miles; and from thence advancing in battle array, planted before the gates of St. Romanus the Imperial standard; and on the sixth day of April formed the memorable siege of Constantinople.

> *The groaning Greeks dig up the golden caverns.*
> *The accumulated wealth of hoarding ages;*
> *That wealth which, granted to their weeping prince,*
> *Had ranged embattled nations at their gates.*

The troops of Asia and Europe extended on the right and left from the Propontis to the harbor; the Janizaries in the front were stationed before the sultan's tent; the Ottoman line was covered by a deep intrenchment; and a subordinate army enclosed the suburb of Galata, and watched the doubtful faith of the Genoese. The inquisitive Philelphus, who resided in Greece about thirty years before the siege, is confident, that all the Turkish forces of any name or value could not exceed the number of sixty thousand horse and twenty thousand foot; and he upbraids the pusillanimity of the nations, who had tamely yielded to a handful of Barbarians. Such indeed might be the regular establishment of the *Capiculi*, the troops of the Porte who marched with the prince, and were paid from his royal treasury. But the bashaws, in their respective governments, maintained or levied a provincial militia; many lands were held by a military tenure; many volunteers were attracted by the hope of spoil and the sound of the holy trumpet invited a swarm of hungry and fearless fanatics, who might contribute at least to multiply the terrors, and in a first attack to blunt the swords, of the Christians. The whole mass of the Turkish powers is magnified by Ducas, Chalcondyles, and Leonard of Chios, to the amount of three or four hundred thousand men; but Phranza was a less remote and more accurate judge; and his precise definition of two hundred and fifty-eight thousand does not exceed the measure of experience and probability. The navy of the besiegers was less formidable: the Propontis was overspread with three hundred and twenty sail; but of these no more than eighteen could be rated as galleys of war; and the far greater part must be degraded to the condition of store-ships and transports, which poured into the camp fresh supplies of men, ammunition, and provisions. In her last decay, Constantinople was still peopled with more than a hundred thousand inhabitants; but these numbers are found in the accounts, not of war, but of captivity; and they mostly consisted of mechanics, of priests, of women, and of men devoid of that spirit which even women have sometimes exerted for the common safety. I can suppose, I could almost excuse, the reluctance of subjects to serve on a distant frontier, at the will of a tyrant; but the man who dares not expose his life in the defence of his children and his property, has lost in society the first and most active energies of nature. By the emperor's command, a particular inquiry had been made through the streets and houses, how many of the citizens, or even of the monks, were able and willing to bear arms for their country. The lists were intrusted to Phranza; and, after a diligent addition, he informed his master, with grief and surprise, that the national defence was reduced to four thousand nine hundred and seventy *Romans*. Between Constantine and his faithful minister this comfortless secret was preserved; and a sufficient proportion of shields, cross-bows, and muskets, were distributed from the arsenal to the city bands. They derived some accession from a body of two thousand strangers, under the command of John Justiniani, a noble Genoese; a liberal donative was advanced to these auxiliaries; and a princely recompense, the Isle of Lemnos, was promised to the valor and victory of their chief. A strong chain was drawn across the mouth of the harbor: it was supported by some Greek and Italian vessels of war and merchandise; and the ships of every Christian nation, that successively arrived from Candia and the Black Sea, were detained for the public service. Against the powers of the Ottoman empire, a city of the extent of thirteen, perhaps of sixteen, miles was defended by a scanty garrison of seven or eight thousand soldiers. Europe and

Asia were open to the besiegers; but the strength and provisions of the Greeks must sustain a daily decrease; nor could they indulge the expectation of any foreign succor or supply.

The primitive Romans would have drawn their swords in the resolution of death or conquest. The primitive Christians might have embraced each other, and awaited in patience and charity the stroke of martyrdom. But the Greeks of Constantinople were animated only by the spirit of religion, and that spirit was productive only of animosity and discord. Before his death, the emperor John Palæologus had renounced the unpopular measure of a union with the Latins; nor was the idea revived, till the distress of his brother Constantine imposed a last trial of flattery and dissimulation. With the demand of temporal aid, his ambassadors were instructed to mingle the assurance of spiritual obedience: his neglect of the church was excused by the urgent cares of the state; and his orthodox wishes solicited the presence of a Roman legate. The Vatican had been too often deluded; yet the signs of repentance could not decently be overlooked; a legate was more easily granted than an army; and about six months before the final destruction, the cardinal Isidore of Russia appeared in that character with a retinue of priests and soldiers. The emperor saluted him as a friend and father; respectfully listened to his public and private sermons; and with the most obsequious of the clergy and laymen subscribed the act of union, as it had been ratified in the council of Florence. On the twelfth of December, the two nations, in the church of St. Sophia, joined in the communion of sacrifice and prayer; and the names of the two pontiffs were solemnly commemorated; the names of Nicholas the Fifth, the vicar of Christ, and of the patriarch Gregory, who had been driven into exile by a rebellious people.

But the dress and language of the Latin priest who officiated at the altar were an object of scandal; and it was observed with horror, that he consecrated a cake or wafer of *unleavened* bread, and poured cold water into the cup of the sacrament. A national historian acknowledges with a blush, that none of his countrymen, not the emperor himself, were sincere in this occasional conformity. Their hasty and unconditional submission was palliated by a promise of future revisal; but the best, or the worst, of their excuses was the confession of their own perjury. When they were pressed by the reproaches of their honest brethren, "Have patience," they whispered, "have patience till God shall have delivered the city from the great dragon who seeks to devour us. You shall then perceive whether we are truly reconciled with the Azymites." But patience is not the attribute of zeal; nor can the arts of a court be adapted to the freedom and violence of popular enthusiasm. From the dome of St. Sophia the inhabitants of either sex, and of every degree, rushed in crowds to the cell of the monk Gennadius, to consult the oracle of the church. The holy man was invisible; entranced, as it should seem, in deep meditation, or divine rapture: but he had exposed on the door of his cell a speaking tablet; and they successively withdrew, after reading those tremendous words: "O miserable Romans, why will ye abandon the truth? and why, instead of confiding in God, will ye put your trust in the Italians? In losing your faith you will lose your city. Have mercy on me, O Lord! I protest in thy presence that I am innocent of the crime. O miserable Romans, consider, pause, and repent. At the same moment that you renounce the religion of your fathers, by embracing impiety, you submit to a foreign servitude." According to the advice of Gennadius, the religious virgins, as pure as angels, and as proud as dæmons, rejected the act of union, and abjured all communion with the present and future associates of the Latins; and their example was applauded and imitated by the greatest part of the clergy and people. From the monastery, the devout Greeks dispersed themselves in the taverns; drank confusion to the slaves of the pope; emptied their glasses in honor of the image of the holy Virgin; and besought her to defend against Mahomet the city which she had formerly saved from Chosroes and the Chagan. In the double intoxication of zeal and wine, they valiantly exclaimed, "What occasion have we for succor, or union, or Latins? Far from us be the worship of the Azymites!" During the winter that preceded the Turkish conquest, the nation was distracted by this epidemical frenzy; and the season of Lent, the approach of Easter, instead of breathing charity and love, served only to fortify the obstinacy and influence of the zealots. The confessors scrutinized and alarmed the conscience of their votaries, and a rigorous penance was imposed on those who had received the communion from a priest who had given an express or tacit consent to the union. His service at the altar propagated the infection to the mute and simple spectators of the ceremony: they forfeited, by the impure spectacle, the virtue of the sacerdotal character; nor was it lawful, even in danger of sudden death, to invoke the assistance of their prayers or absolution. No sooner had the church of St. Sophia been polluted by the Latin sacrifice, than it was deserted as a Jewish synagogue, or a heathen temple, by the clergy and people; and a vast and gloomy silence prevailed in that venerable dome, which had so often smoked with a cloud of incense, blazed with innumerable lights, and resounded with the voice of prayer and thanksgiving. The Latins were the most odious of heretics and infidels; and the first minister of the empire, the great duke, was heard to declare, that he had rather behold in Constantinople the turban of Mahomet, than the pope's tiara or a cardinal's hat. A sentiment so unworthy of Christians and patriots was familiar and fatal to the Greeks: the emperor was deprived of the affection and support of his subjects; and their native cowardice was sanctified by resignation to the divine decree, or the visionary hope of a miraculous deliverance.

Of the triangle which composes the figure of Constantinople, the two sides along the sea were made inaccessible to an enemy; the Propontis by nature, and the harbor by art. Between the two waters, the basis of the triangle, the land side was protected by a double wall, and a deep ditch of the depth of one hundred feet. Against this line of fortification, which Phranza, an eye-witness, prolongs to the measure of six miles, the Ottomans directed their principal attack; and the emperor, after distributing the service and command of the most perilous stations, undertook the defence of the external wall. In the first days of the siege the Greek soldiers descended into the ditch, or sallied into the field; but they soon discovered, that, in the proportion of their numbers, one Christian was of more value than twenty Turks: and, after these bold preludes, they were prudently content to maintain the rampart with their missile weapons. Nor should this prudence be accused of pusillanimity. The nation was indeed pusillanimous and base; but the last Constantine deserves the name of a hero: his noble band of volunteers was inspired with Roman virtue; and the foreign auxiliaries supported the honor of the Western chivalry. The incessant volleys of lances and arrows were accompanied with the smoke, the sound, and the fire, of their musketry and cannon. Their small arms discharged at the same time either five, or even ten, balls of lead, of the size of a walnut; and, according to the closeness of the ranks and the force of the powder, several breastplates and bodies were transpierced by the same shot. But the Turkish approaches were soon sunk in trenches, or covered with ruins. Each day added to the science of the Christians; but their inadequate stock of gunpowder was wasted in the operations of each day. Their ordnance was not powerful, either in size or number; and if they possessed some heavy cannon, they feared to plant them on the walls, lest the aged structure should be shaken and overthrown by the explosion. The same destructive secret had been revealed to the Moslems; by whom it was employed with the superior energy of zeal, riches, and despotism. The great cannon of Mahomet has been separately noticed; an important and visible object in the history of the times: but that enormous engine was flanked by two fellows almost of equal magnitude: the long order of the Turkish artillery was pointed against the walls; fourteen batteries thundered at once on the most accessible places; and of one of these it is ambiguously expressed, that it was mounted with one hundred and thirty guns, or that it discharged one hundred and thirty bullets. Yet in the power and activity of the sultan, we may discern the infancy of the new science. Under a master who counted the moments, the great cannon could be loaded and fired no more than seven times in one day. The heated metal unfortunately burst; several workmen were destroyed; and the skill of an artist was admired who bethought himself of preventing the danger and the accident, by pouring oil, after each explosion, into the mouth of the cannon.

The first random shots were productive of more sound than effect; and it was by the advice of a Christian, that the engineers were taught to level their aim against the two opposite sides of the salient angles of a bastion. However imperfect, the weight and repetition of the fire made some impression on the walls; and the Turks, pushing their approaches to the edge of the ditch, attempted to fill the enormous chasm, and to build a road to the assault. Innumerable fascines, and hogsheads, and trunks of trees, were heaped on each other; and such was the impetuosity of the throng, that the foremost and the weakest were pushed headlong down the precipice, and instantly buried under the accumulated mass. To fill the ditch was the toil of the besiegers; to clear away the rubbish was the safety of the besieged; and after a long and bloody conflict, the web that had been woven in the day was still unravelled in the night. The next resource of Mahomet was the practice of mines; but the soil was rocky; in every attempt he was stopped and undermined by the Christian engineers; nor had the art been yet invented of replenishing those subterraneous passages with gunpowder, and blowing whole towers and cities into the air. A circumstance that distinguishes the siege of Constantinople is the reunion of the ancient and modern artillery. The cannon were intermingled with the mechanical engines for casting stones and darts; the bullet and the battering-ram were directed against the same walls: nor had the discovery of gunpowder superseded the use of the liquid and unextinguishable fire. A wooden turret of the largest size was advanced on rollers; this portable magazine of ammunition and fascines was protected by a threefold covering of bulls' hides: incessant volleys were securely discharged from the loop-holes; in the front, three doors were contrived for the alternate sally and retreat of the soldiers and workmen. They ascended by a staircase to the upper platform, and, as high as the level of that platform, a scaling-ladder could be raised by pulleys to form a bridge, and grapple with the adverse rampart. By these various arts of annoyance, some as new as they were pernicious to the Greeks, the tower of St. Romanus was at length overturned: after a severe struggle, the Turks were repulsed from the breach, and interrupted by darkness; but they trusted that with the return of light they should renew the attack with fresh vigor and decisive success. Of this pause of action, this interval of hope, each moment was improved, by the activity of the emperor and Justiniani, who passed the night on the spot, and urged the labors which involved the safety of the church and city. At the dawn of day, the impatient sultan perceived, with astonishment and grief, that his wooden turret had been reduced to ashes: the ditch was cleared and restored; and the tower of St. Romanus was again strong and entire. He deplored the failure of his design; and uttered a profane exclamation, that the word of the thirty-seven thousand prophets should not have compelled him to believe that such a work, in so short a time, could have been accomplished by the infidels.

Reign of Mahomet the Second, Extinction of Eastern Empire. – Part Three

THE GENEROSITY OF THE Christian princes was cold and tardy; but in the first apprehension of a siege, Constantine had negotiated, in the isles of the Archipelago, the Morea, and Sicily, the most indispensable supplies. As early as the beginning of April, five great ships, equipped for merchandise and war, would have sailed from the harbor of Chios, had not the wind blown obstinately from the north. One of these ships bore the Imperial flag; the remaining four belonged to the Genoese; and they were laden with wheat and barley, with wine, oil, and vegetables, and, above all, with soldiers and mariners for the service of the capital. After a tedious delay, a gentle breeze, and, on the second day, a strong gale from the south, carried them through the Hellespont and the Propontis: but the city was already invested by sea and land; and the Turkish fleet, at the entrance of the Bosphorus, was stretched from shore to shore, in the form of a crescent, to intercept, or at least to repel, these bold auxiliaries. The reader who has present to his mind the geographical picture of Constantinople, will conceive and admire the greatness of the spectacle. The five Christian ships continued to advance with joyful shouts, and a full press both of sails and oars, against a hostile fleet of three hundred vessels; and the rampart, the camp, the coasts of Europe and Asia, were lined with innumerable spectators, who anxiously awaited the event of this momentous succor. At the first view that event could not appear doubtful; the superiority of the Moslems was beyond all measure or account: and, in a calm, their numbers and valor must inevitably have prevailed. But their hasty and imperfect navy had been created, not by the genius of the people, but by the will of the sultan: in the height of their prosperity, the Turks have acknowledged, that if God had given them the earth, he had left the sea to the infidels; and a series of defeats, a rapid progress of decay, has established the truth of their modest confession. Except eighteen galleys of some force, the rest of their fleet consisted of open boats, rudely constructed and awkwardly managed, crowded with troops, and destitute of cannon; and since courage arises in a great measure from the consciousness of strength, the bravest of the Janizaries might tremble on a new element. In the Christian squadron, five stout and lofty ships were guided by skilful pilots, and manned with the veterans of Italy and Greece, long practised in the arts and perils of the sea. Their weight was directed to sink or scatter the weak obstacles that impeded their passage: their artillery swept the waters: their liquid fire was poured on the heads of the adversaries, who, with the design of boarding, presumed to approach them; and the winds and waves are always on the side of the ablest navigators. In this conflict, the Imperial vessel, which had been almost overpowered, was rescued by the Genoese; but the Turks, in a distant and closer attack, were twice repulsed with considerable loss. Mahomet himself sat on horseback on the beach to encourage their valor by his voice and presence, by the promise of reward, and by fear more potent than the fear of the enemy. The passions of his soul, and even the gestures of his body, seemed to imitate the actions of the combatants; and, as if he had been the lord of nature, he spurred his horse with a fearless and impotent effort into the sea. His loud reproaches, and the clamors of the camp, urged the Ottomans to a third attack, more fatal and bloody than the two former; and I must repeat, though I cannot credit, the evidence of Phranza, who affirms, from their own mouth, that they lost above twelve thousand men in the slaughter of the day. They fled in disorder to the shores of Europe and Asia, while the Christian squadron, triumphant and unhurt, steered along the Bosphorus, and securely anchored within the chain of the harbor. In the confidence of victory, they boasted that the whole Turkish power must have yielded to their arms; but the admiral, or captain bashaw, found some consolation for a painful wound in his eye, by representing that accident as the cause of his defeat. Balthi Ogli was a renegade of the race of the Bulgarian princes: his military character was tainted with the unpopular vice of avarice; and under the despotism of the prince or people, misfortune is a sufficient evidence of guilt. His rank and services were annihilated by the displeasure of Mahomet. In the royal presence, the captain bashaw was extended on the ground by four slaves, and received one hundred strokes with a golden rod: his death had been pronounced; and he adored the clemency of the sultan, who was satisfied with the milder punishment of confiscation and exile. The introduction of this supply revived the hopes of the Greeks, and accused the supineness of their Western allies. Amidst the deserts of Anatolia and the rocks of Palestine, the millions of the crusades had buried themselves in a voluntary and inevitable grave; but the situation of the Imperial city was strong against her enemies, and accessible to her friends; and a rational and moderate armament of the marine states might have saved the relics of the Roman name, and maintained a Christian fortress in the heart of the Ottoman empire. Yet this was the sole and feeble attempt for the deliverance of Constantinople: the more distant powers were insensible of its danger; and the ambassador of Hungary, or at least of Huniades, resided in the Turkish camp, to remove the fears, and to direct the operations, of the sultan.

It was difficult for the Greeks to penetrate the secret of the divan; yet the Greeks are persuaded, that a resistance so obstinate and surprising, had fatigued the perseverance of Mahomet. He began to meditate a retreat; and the siege would have been speedily raised, if the ambition and jealousy of the second vizier had not opposed the perfidious advice of Calil Bashaw, who still maintained a secret correspondence with the Byzantine court. The reduction of the city appeared to be hopeless, unless a double attack could be made from the harbor as well as from the land; but the harbor was inaccessible: an impenetrable chain was now defended by eight large ships, more than twenty of a smaller size, with several galleys and sloops; and, instead of forcing this barrier, the Turks might apprehend a naval sally, and a second encounter in the open sea. In this perplexity, the genius of Mahomet conceived and executed a plan of a bold and marvellous cast, of transporting by land his lighter vessels and military stores from the Bosphorus into the higher part of the harbor. The distance is about ten miles; the ground is uneven, and was overspread with thickets; and, as the road must be opened behind the suburb of Galata, their free passage or total destruction must depend on the option of the Genoese. But these selfish merchants were ambitious of the favor of being the last devoured; and the deficiency of art was supplied by the strength of obedient myriads. A level way was covered with a broad platform of strong and solid planks; and to render them more slippery and smooth, they were anointed with the fat of sheep and oxen. Fourscore light galleys and brigantines, of fifty and thirty oars, were disembarked on the Bosphorus shore; arranged successively on rollers; and drawn forwards by the power of men and pulleys. Two guides or pilots were stationed at the helm, and the prow, of each vessel: the sails were unfurled to the winds; and the labor was cheered by song and acclamation. In the course of a single night, this Turkish fleet painfully climbed the hill, steered over the plain, and was launched from the declivity into the shallow waters of the harbor, far above the molestation of the deeper vessels of the Greeks. The real importance of this operation was magnified by the consternation and confidence which it inspired: but the notorious, unquestionable fact was displayed before the eyes, and is recorded by the pens, of the two nations. A similar stratagem had been repeatedly practised by the ancients; the Ottoman galleys (I must again repeat) should be considered as large boats; and, if we compare the magnitude and the distance, the obstacles and the means, the boasted miracle has perhaps been equalled by the industry of our own times. As soon as Mahomet had occupied the upper harbor with a fleet and army, he constructed, in the narrowest part, a bridge, or rather mole, of fifty cubits in breadth, and one hundred in length: it was formed of casks and hogsheads; joined with rafters, linked with iron, and covered with a solid floor. On this floating battery he planted one of his largest cannon, while the fourscore galleys, with troops and scaling ladders, approached the most accessible side, which had formerly been stormed by the Latin conquerors. The indolence of the Christians has been accused for not destroying these unfinished works; but their fire, by a superior fire, was controlled and silenced; nor were they wanting in a nocturnal attempt to burn the vessels as well as the bridge of the sultan. His vigilance prevented their approach; their foremost galiots were sunk or taken; forty youths, the bravest of Italy and Greece, were inhumanly massacred at his command; nor could the emperor's grief be assuaged by the just though cruel retaliation, of exposing from the walls the heads of two hundred and sixty Mussulman captives. After a siege of forty days, the fate of Constantinople could no longer be averted. The diminutive garrison was exhausted by a double attack: the fortifications, which had stood for ages against hostile violence, were dismantled on all sides by the Ottoman cannon: many breaches were opened; and near the gate of St. Romanus, four towers had been levelled with the ground. For the payment of his feeble and mutinous troops, Constantine was compelled to despoil the churches with the promise of a fourfold restitution; and his sacrilege offered a new reproach to the enemies of the union. A spirit of discord impaired the remnant of the Christian strength; the

Genoese and Venetian auxiliaries asserted the preeminence of their respective service; and Justiniani and the great duke, whose ambition was not extinguished by the common danger, accused each other of treachery and cowardice.

During the siege of Constantinople, the words of peace and capitulation had been sometimes pronounced; and several embassies had passed between the camp and the city. The Greek emperor was humbled by adversity; and would have yielded to any terms compatible with religion and royalty. The Turkish sultan was desirous of sparing the blood of his soldiers; still more desirous of securing for his own use the Byzantine treasures: and he accomplished a sacred duty in presenting to the *Gabours* the choice of circumcision, of tribute, or of death. The avarice of Mahomet might have been satisfied with an annual sum of one hundred thousand ducats; but his ambition grasped the capital of the East: to the prince he offered a rich equivalent, to the people a free toleration, or a safe departure: but after some fruitless treaty, he declared his resolution of finding either a throne, or a grave, under the walls of Constantinople. A sense of honor, and the fear of universal reproach, forbade Palæologus to resign the city into the hands of the Ottomans; and he determined to abide the last extremities of war. Several days were employed by the sultan in the preparations of the assault; and a respite was granted by his favorite science of astrology, which had fixed on the twenty-ninth of May, as the fortunate and fatal hour. On the evening of the twenty-seventh, he issued his final orders; assembled in his presence the military chiefs, and dispersed his heralds through the camp to proclaim the duty, and the motives, of the perilous enterprise. Fear is the first principle of a despotic government; and his menaces were expressed in the Oriental style, that the fugitives and deserters, had they the wings of a bird, should not escape from his inexorable justice. The greatest part of his bashaws and Janizaries were the offspring of Christian parents: but the glories of the Turkish name were perpetuated by successive adoption; and in the gradual change of individuals, the spirit of a legion, a regiment, or an *oda*, is kept alive by imitation and discipline. In this holy warfare, the Moslems were exhorted to purify their minds with prayer, their bodies with seven ablutions; and to abstain from food till the close of the ensuing day. A crowd of dervises visited the tents, to instil the desire of martyrdom, and the assurance of spending an immortal youth amidst the rivers and gardens of paradise, and in the embraces of the black-eyed virgins. Yet Mahomet principally trusted to the efficacy of temporal and visible rewards. A double pay was promised to the victorious troops: "The city and the buildings," said Mahomet, "are mine; but

I resign to your valor the captives and the spoil, the treasures of gold and beauty; be rich and be happy. Many are the provinces of my empire: the intrepid soldier who first ascends the walls of Constantinople shall be rewarded with the government of the fairest and most wealthy; and my gratitude shall accumulate his honors and fortunes above the measure of his own hopes." Such various and potent motives diffused among the Turks a general ardor, regardless of life and impatient for action: the camp reechoed with the Moslem shouts of "God is God: there is but one God, and Mahomet is the apostle of God;" and the sea and land, from Galata to the seven towers, were illuminated by the blaze of their nocturnal fires.

> *Should the fierce North, upon his frozen wings.*
> *Bear him aloft above the wondering clouds,*
> *And seat him in the Pleiads' golden chariot –*
> *Then should my fury drag him down to tortures.*
> *'Ark-on q' hn kai amaxan epiklhsin kaleouein. Il. S. 487.]*

Far different was the state of the Christians; who, with loud and impotent complaints, deplored the guilt, or the punishment, of their sins. The celestial image of the Virgin had been exposed in solemn procession; but their divine patroness was deaf to their entreaties: they accused the obstinacy of the emperor for refusing a timely surrender; anticipated the horrors of their fate; and sighed for the repose and security of Turkish servitude. The noblest of the Greeks, and the bravest of the allies, were summoned to the palace, to prepare them, on the evening of the twenty-eighth, for the duties and dangers of the general assault. The last speech of Palæologus was the funeral oration of the Roman empire: he promised, he conjured, and he vainly attempted to infuse the hope which was extinguished in his own mind. In this world all was comfortless and gloomy; and neither the gospel nor the church have proposed any conspicuous recompense to the heroes who fall in the service of their country. But the example of their prince, and the confinement of a siege, had armed these warriors with the courage of despair, and the pathetic scene is described by the feelings of the historian Phranza, who was himself present at this mournful assembly. They wept, they embraced; regardless of their families and fortunes, they devoted their lives; and each commander, departing to his station, maintained all night a vigilant and anxious watch on the rampart. The emperor, and some faithful companions, entered the dome of St. Sophia, which in a few hours was to be converted into a mosque; and devoutly received, with tears and prayers, the sacrament of the holy communion. He reposed some moments in the palace, which resounded with cries and lamentations; solicited the pardon of all whom he might have injured; and mounted on horseback to visit the guards, and explore the motions of the enemy. The distress and fall of the last Constantine are more glorious than the long prosperity of the Byzantine Cæsars.

In the confusion of darkness, an assailant may sometimes succeed; but in this great and general attack, the military judgment and astrological knowledge of Mahomet advised him to expect the morning, the memorable twenty-ninth of May, in the fourteen hundred and fifty-third year of the Christian æra. The preceding night had been strenuously employed: the troops, the cannons, and the fascines, were advanced to the edge of the ditch, which in many parts presented a smooth and level passage to the breach; and his fourscore galleys almost touched, with the prows and their scaling-ladders, the less defensible walls of the harbor. Under pain of death, silence was enjoined: but the physical laws of motion and sound are not obedient to discipline or fear; each individual might suppress his voice and measure his footsteps; but the march and labor of thousands must inevitably produce a strange confusion of dissonant clamors, which reached the ears of the watchmen of the towers. At daybreak, without the customary signal of the morning gun, the Turks assaulted the city by sea and land; and the similitude of a twined or twisted thread has been applied to the closeness and continuity of their line of attack. The foremost ranks consisted of the refuse of the host, a voluntary crowd who fought without order or command; of the feebleness of age or childhood, of peasants and vagrants, and of all who had joined the camp in the blind hope of plunder and martyrdom. The common impulse drove them onwards to the wall; the most audacious to climb were instantly precipitated; and not a dart, not a bullet, of the Christians, was idly wasted on the accumulated throng. But their strength and ammunition were exhausted in this laborious defence: the ditch was filled with the bodies of the slain; they supported the footsteps of their companions; and of this devoted vanguard the death was more serviceable than the life. Under their respective bashaws and sanjaks, the troops of Anatolia and Romania were successively led to the charge: their progress was various and doubtful; but, after a conflict of two hours, the Greeks still maintained, and improved their advantage; and the voice of the emperor was heard, encouraging his soldiers to achieve, by a last effort, the deliverance of their country. In that fatal moment, the Janizaries arose, fresh, vigorous, and invincible. The sultan himself on horseback, with an iron mace in his hand, was the spectator and judge of their valor: he was surrounded by ten thousand of his domestic troops, whom he reserved for the decisive occasion; and the tide of battle was directed and impelled by his voice and eye. His numerous ministers of justice were posted behind the line, to urge, to restrain, and to punish; and if danger was in the front, shame and inevitable death were in the rear, of the fugitives. The cries of fear and of pain were drowned in the martial music of drums, trumpets, and attaballs; and experience has proved, that the mechanical operation of sounds, by quickening the circulation of the blood and spirits, will act on the human machine more forcibly than the eloquence of reason and honor. From the lines, the galleys, and the bridge, the Ottoman artillery thundered on all sides; and the camp and city, the Greeks and the Turks, were involved in a cloud of smoke which could only be dispelled by the final deliverance or destruction of the Roman empire. The single combats of the heroes of history or fable amuse our fancy and engage our affections: the skilful evolutions of war may inform the mind, and improve a necessary, though pernicious, science. But in the uniform and odious pictures of a general assault, all is blood, and horror, and confusion; nor shall I strive, at the distance of three centuries, and a thousand miles, to delineate a scene of which there could be no spectators, and of which the actors themselves were incapable of forming any just or adequate idea.

The immediate loss of Constantinople may be ascribed to the bullet, or arrow, which pierced the gauntlet of John Justiniani. The sight of his blood, and the exquisite pain, appalled the courage of the chief, whose arms and counsels were the firmest rampart of the city. As he withdrew from his station in quest of a surgeon, his flight was perceived and stopped by the indefatigable emperor. "Your wound," exclaimed Palæologus, "is slight; the danger is pressing: your presence is necessary; and whither will you retire?" – "I will retire," said the trembling Genoese, "by the same road which God has opened to the Turks;" and at these words he hastily passed through one of the breaches of the inner wall. By this pusillanimous act he stained the honors of a military life; and the few days which he survived in Galata, or the Isle of Chios, were embittered by his own and the public reproach. His example was imitated by the greatest part of the Latin auxiliaries, and the defence began to slacken when the attack was pressed with redoubled vigor. The number of the Ottomans was fifty, perhaps a hundred, times superior to that of the Christians; the double walls were reduced by the cannon to a heap of ruins: in a circuit of several miles, some places must be found more easy of access, or more feebly guarded; and if the besiegers could penetrate in a single point, the whole city was irrecoverably lost. The first who deserved the sultan's reward was Hassan the Janizary, of gigantic stature and strength. With his cimeter in one hand and his buckler in the other, he ascended the outward fortification: of the thirty Janizaries, who were emulous of his valor, eighteen perished in the bold adventure. Hassan and his twelve companions had reached the summit: the giant was precipitated from the rampart: he rose on one knee, and was again oppressed by a shower of darts and stones. But his success had proved that the achievement was possible: the walls and towers were instantly covered with a swarm of Turks; and the Greeks, now driven from the vantage ground, were overwhelmed by increasing multitudes. Amidst these multitudes, the emperor, who accomplished all the duties of a general and a soldier, was long seen and finally lost. The nobles, who fought round his person, sustained, till their last breath, the honorable names of Palæologus and Cantacuzene: his mournful exclamation was heard, "Cannot there be found a Christian to cut off my head?" and his last fear was that of falling alive into the hands of the infidels. The prudent despair of Constantine cast away the purple: amidst the tumult he fell by an unknown hand, and his body was buried under a mountain of the slain. After his death, resistance and order were no more: the Greeks fled towards the city; and many were pressed and stifled in the narrow pass of the gate of St. Romanus. The victorious Turks rushed through the breaches of the inner wall; and as they advanced into the streets, they were soon joined by their brethren, who had forced the gate Phenar on the side of the harbor. In the first heat of the pursuit, about two thousand Christians were put to the sword; but avarice soon prevailed over cruelty; and the victors acknowledged, that they should immediately have given quarter if the valor of the emperor and his chosen bands had not prepared them for a similar opposition in every part of the capital. It was thus, after a siege of fifty-three days, that Constantinople, which had defied the power of Chosroes, the Chagan, and the caliphs, was irretrievably subdued by the arms of Mahomet the Second. Her empire only had been subverted by the Latins: her religion was trampled in the dust by the Moslem conquerors.

> *As to Sebastian, let them search the field;*
> *And where they find a mountain of the slain,*
> *Send one to climb, and looking down beneath,*
> *There they will find him at his manly length,*
> *With his face up to heaven, in that red monument*
> *Which his good sword had digged.]*

The tidings of misfortune fly with a rapid wing; yet such was the extent of Constantinople, that the more distant quarters might prolong, some moments, the happy ignorance of their ruin. But in the general consternation, in the feelings of selfish or social anxiety, in the tumult and thunder of the assault, a *sleepless* night and morning must have elapsed; nor can I believe that many Grecian ladies were awakened by the Janizaries from a sound and tranquil slumber. On the assurance of the public calamity, the houses and convents were instantly deserted; and the trembling inhabitants flocked together in the streets, like a herd of timid animals, as if accumulated weakness could be productive of strength, or in the vain hope, that amid the crowd each individual might be safe and invisible. From every part of the capital, they flowed into the church of St. Sophia: in the space of an hour, the sanctuary, the choir, the nave, the upper and lower galleries, were filled with the multitudes of fathers and husbands, of women and children, of priests, monks, and religious virgins: the doors were barred on the inside, and they sought protection from the sacred dome, which they had so lately abhorred as a profane and polluted edifice. Their confidence was founded on the prophecy of an enthusiast or impostor; that one day the Turks would enter Constantinople, and pursue the Romans as far as the column of Constantine in the square before St. Sophia: but that this would be the term of their calamities: that an angel would descend from heaven, with a sword in his hand, and would deliver the empire, with that celestial weapon, to a poor man seated at the foot of the column. "Take this sword," would he say, "and avenge the people of the Lord." At these animating words, the Turks would instantly fly, and the victorious Romans would drive them from the West, and from all Anatolia as far as the frontiers of Persia. It is on this occasion that Ducas, with some fancy and much truth, upbraids the discord and obstinacy of the Greeks. "Had that angel appeared," exclaims the historian, "had he offered to exterminate your foes if you would consent to the union of the church, even event then, in that fatal moment, you would have rejected your safety, or have deceived your God."

Reign of Mahomet the Second, Extinction of Eastern Empire. – Part Four

WHILE THEY EXPECTED THE descent of the tardy angel, the doors were broken with axes; and as the Turks encountered no resistance, their bloodless hands were employed in selecting and securing the multitude of their prisoners. Youth, beauty, and the appearance of wealth, attracted their choice; and the right of property was decided among themselves by a prior seizure, by personal strength, and by the authority of command. In the space of an hour, the male captives were bound with cords, the females with their veils and girdles. The senators were linked with their slaves; the prelates, with the porters of the church; and young men of the plebeian class, with noble maids, whose faces had been invisible to the sun and their nearest kindred. In this common captivity, the ranks of society were confounded; the ties of nature were cut asunder; and the inexorable soldier was careless of the father's groans, the tears of the mother, and the lamentations of the children. The loudest in their wailings were the nuns, who were torn from the altar with naked bosoms, outstretched hands, and dishevelled hair; and we should piously believe that few could be tempted to prefer the vigils of the harem to those of the monastery. Of these unfortunate Greeks, of these domestic animals, whole strings were rudely driven through the streets; and as the conquerors were eager to return for more prey, their trembling pace was quickened with menaces and blows. At the same hour, a similar rapine was exercised in all the churches and monasteries, in all the palaces and habitations, of the capital; nor could any place, however sacred or sequestered, protect the persons or the property of the Greeks. Above sixty thousand of this devoted people were transported from the city to the camp and fleet; exchanged or sold according to the caprice or interest of their masters, and dispersed in remote servitude through the provinces of the Ottoman empire. Among these we may notice some remarkable characters. The historian Phranza, first chamberlain and principal secretary, was involved with his family in the common lot. After suffering four months the hardships of slavery, he recovered his freedom: in the ensuing winter he ventured to Adrianople, and ransomed his wife from the *mir bashi*, or master of the horse; but his two children, in the flower of youth and beauty, had been seized for the use of Mahomet himself. The daughter of Phranza died in the seraglio, perhaps a virgin: his son, in the fifteenth year of his age, preferred death to infamy, and was stabbed by the hand of the royal lover. A deed thus inhuman cannot surely be expiated by the taste and liberality with which he released a Grecian matron and her two daughters, on receiving a Latin doe From ode from Philelphus, who had chosen a wife in that noble family. The pride or cruelty of Mahomet would have been most sensibly gratified by the capture of a Roman legate; but the dexterity of Cardinal Isidore eluded the search, and he escaped from Galata in a plebeian habit. The chain and entrance of the outward harbor was still occupied by the Italian ships of merchandise and war. They had signalized their valor in the siege: they embraced the moment of retreat, while the Turkish mariners were dissipated in the pillage of the city. When they hoisted sail, the beach was covered with a suppliant and lamentable crowd; but the means of transportation were scanty: the Venetians and Genoese selected their countrymen; and, notwithstanding the fairest promises of the sultan, the inhabitants of Galata evacuated their houses, and embarked with their most precious effects.

In the fall and the sack of great cities, an historian is condemned to repeat the tale of uniform calamity: the same effects must be produced by the same passions; and when those passions may be indulged without control, small, alas! is the difference between civilized and savage man. Amidst the vague exclamations of bigotry and hatred, the Turks are not accused of a wanton or immoderate effusion of Christian blood: but according to their maxims, (the maxims of antiquity,) the lives of the vanquished were forfeited; and the legitimate reward of the conqueror was derived from the service, the sale, or the ransom, of his captives of both sexes. The wealth of Constantinople had been granted by the sultan to his victorious troops; and the rapine of an hour is more productive than the industry of years. But as no regular division was attempted of the spoil, the respective shares were not determined by merit; and the rewards of valor were stolen away by the followers of the camp, who had declined the toil and danger of the battle. The narrative of their depredations could not afford either amusement or instruction: the total amount, in the last poverty of the empire, has been valued at four millions of ducats; and of this sum a small part was the property of the Venetians, the Genoese, the Florentines, and the merchants of Ancona. Of these foreigners, the stock was improved in quick and perpetual circulation: but the riches of the Greeks were displayed in the idle ostentation of palaces and wardrobes, or deeply buried in treasures of ingots and old coin, lest it should be demanded at their hands for the defence of their country. The profanation and plunder of the monasteries and churches excited the most tragic complaints. The dome of St. Sophia itself, the earthly heaven, the second firmament, the vehicle of the cherubim, the throne of the glory of God, was despoiled of the oblation of ages; and the gold and silver, the pearls and jewels, the vases and sacerdotal ornaments, were most wickedly converted to the service of mankind. After the divine images had been stripped of all that could be valuable to a profane eye, the canvas, or the wood, was torn, or broken, or burnt, or trod under foot, or applied, in the stables or the kitchen, to the vilest uses. The example of sacrilege was imitated, however, from the Latin conquerors of Constantinople; and the treatment which Christ, the Virgin, and the saints, had sustained from the guilty Catholic, might be inflicted by the zealous Mussulman on the monuments of idolatry. Perhaps, instead of joining the public clamor, a philosopher will observe, that in the decline of the arts the workmanship could not be more valuable than the work, and that a fresh supply of visions and miracles would speedily be renewed by the craft of the priests and the credulity of the people. He will more seriously deplore the loss of the Byzantine libraries, which were destroyed or scattered in the general confusion: one hundred and twenty thousand manuscripts are said to have disappeared; ten volumes might be purchased for a single ducat; and the same ignominious price, too high perhaps for a shelf of theology, included the whole works of Aristotle and Homer, the noblest productions of the science and literature of ancient Greece. We may reflect with pleasure that an inestimable portion of our classic treasures was safely deposited in Italy; and that the mechanics of a German town had invented an art which derides the havoc of time and barbarism.

From the first hour of the memorable twenty-ninth of May, disorder and rapine prevailed in Constantinople, till the eighth hour of the same day; when the sultan himself passed in triumph through the gate of St. Romanus. He was attended by his viziers, bashaws, and guards, each of whom (says a Byzantine historian) was robust as Hercules, dexterous as Apollo, and equal in battle to any ten of the race of ordinary mortals. The conqueror gazed with satisfaction and wonder on the strange, though splendid, appearance of the domes and palaces, so dissimilar from the style of Oriental architecture. In the hippodrome, or *atmeidan*, his eye was attracted by the twisted column of the three serpents; and, as a trial of his strength, he shattered with his iron mace or battle-axe the under jaw of one of these monsters, which in the eyes of the Turks were the idols or talismans of the city. At the principal door of St. Sophia, he alighted from his horse, and entered the dome; and such was his jealous regard for that monument of his glory, that on observing a zealous Mussulman in the act of breaking the marble pavement, he admonished him with his cimeter, that, if the spoil and captives were granted to the soldiers, the public and private buildings had been reserved for the prince. By his command the metropolis of the Eastern church was transformed into a mosque: the rich and portable instruments of superstition had been removed; the crosses were thrown down; and the walls, which were covered with images and mosaics, were washed and purified, and restored to a state of naked simplicity. On the same day, or on the ensuing Friday, the *muezin*, or crier, ascended the most lofty turret, and proclaimed the *ezan*, or public invitation in the name of God and his prophet; the imam preached; and Mahomet and Second performed the *namaz* of prayer and thanksgiving on the great altar, where the Christian mysteries had so lately been celebrated before the last of the Cæsars. From St. Sophia he proceeded to the august, but desolate mansion of a hundred successors of the great Constantine, but which in a few hours had been stripped of the pomp of royalty. A melancholy reflection on the vicissitudes of human greatness forced itself on his mind; and he repeated an elegant distich of Persian poetry: "The spider has wove his web in the Imperial palace; and the owl hath sung her watch-song on the towers of Afrasiab."

Yet his mind was not satisfied, nor did the victory seem complete, till he was informed of the fate of Constantine; whether he had escaped, or been made prisoner, or had fallen in the battle. Two Janizaries claimed the honor and reward of his death: the body, under a heap of slain, was discovered by the golden eagles embroidered on his shoes; the Greeks acknowledged, with tears, the head of their late emperor; and, after exposing the bloody trophy, Mahomet bestowed on his rival the honors of a decent funeral. After his decease, Lucas Notaras, great duke, and first minister of the empire, was the most important prisoner. When he offered his person and his treasures at the foot of the throne, "And why," said the indignant sultan, "did you not employ these treasures in the defence of your prince and country?" – "They were yours," answered the slave; "God had reserved them for your hands." – "If he reserved them for me," replied the despot, "how have you presumed to withhold them so long by a fruitless and fatal resistance?" The great duke alleged the obstinacy of the strangers, and some secret encouragement from the Turkish vizier; and from this perilous interview he was at length dismissed with the assurance of pardon and protection. Mahomet condescended to visit his wife, a venerable princess oppressed with sickness and grief; and his consolation for her misfortunes was in the most tender strain of humanity and filial reverence. A similar clemency was extended to the principal officers of state, of whom several were ransomed at his expense; and during some days he declared himself the friend and father of the vanquished people. But the scene was soon changed; and before his departure, the hippodrome streamed with the blood of his noblest captives. His perfidious cruelty is execrated by the Christians: they adorn with the colors of heroic martyrdom the execution of the great duke and his two sons; and his death is ascribed to the generous refusal of delivering his children to the tyrant's lust. Yet a Byzantine historian has dropped an unguarded word of conspiracy, deliverance, and Italian succor: such treason may be glorious; but the rebel who bravely ventures, has justly forfeited his life; nor should we blame a conqueror for destroying the enemies whom he can no longer trust. On the eighteenth of June the victorious sultan returned to Adrianople; and smiled at the base and hollow embassies of the Christian princes, who viewed their approaching ruin in the fall of the Eastern empire.

Constantinople had been left naked and desolate, without a prince or a people. But she could not be despoiled of the incomparable situation which marks her for the metropolis of a great empire; and the genius of the place will ever triumph over the accidents of time and fortune. Boursa and Adrianople, the ancient seats of the Ottomans, sunk into provincial towns; and Mahomet the Second established his own residence, and that of his successors, on the same commanding spot which had been chosen by Constantine. The fortifications of Galata, which might afford a shelter to the Latins, were prudently destroyed; but the damage of the Turkish cannon was soon repaired; and before the month of August, great quantities of lime had been burnt for the restoration of the walls of the capital. As the entire property of the soil and buildings, whether public or private, or profane or sacred, was now transferred to the conqueror, he first separated a space of eight furlongs from the point of the triangle for the establishment of his seraglio or palace. It is here, in the bosom of luxury, that the *Grand Signor* (as he has been emphatically named by the Italians) appears to reign over Europe and Asia; but his person on the shores of the Bosphorus may not always be secure from the insults of a hostile navy. In the new character of a mosque, the cathedral of St. Sophia was endowed with an ample revenue, crowned with lofty minarets, and surrounded with groves and fountains, for the devotion and refreshment of the Moslems. The same model was imitated in the *jami*, or royal mosques; and the first of these was built, by Mahomet himself, on the ruins of the church of the holy apostles, and the tombs of the Greek emperors. On the third day after the conquest, the grave of Abu Ayub, or Job, who had fallen in the first siege of the Arabs, was revealed in a vision; and it is before the sepulchre of the martyr that the new sultans are girded with the sword of empire. Constantinople no longer appertains to the Roman historian; nor shall I enumerate the civil and religious edifices that were profaned or erected by its Turkish masters: the population was speedily renewed; and before the end of September, five thousand families of Anatolia and Romania had obeyed the royal mandate, which enjoined them, under pain of death, to occupy their new habitations in the capital. The throne of Mahomet was guarded by the numbers and fidelity of his Moslem subjects: but his rational policy aspired to collect the remnant of the Greeks; and they returned in crowds, as soon as they were assured of their lives, their liberties, and the free exercise of their religion. In the election and investiture of a patriarch, the ceremonial of the Byzantine court was revived and imitated. With a mixture of satisfaction and horror, they beheld the sultan on his throne; who delivered into the hands of Gennadius the crosier or pastoral staff, the symbol of his ecclesiastical office; who conducted the patriarch to the gate of the seraglio, presented him with a horse richly caparisoned, and directed the viziers and bashaws to lead him to the palace which had been allotted for his residence. The churches of Constantinople were shared between the two religions: their limits were marked; and, till it was infringed by Selim, the grandson of Mahomet, the Greeks enjoyed above sixty years the benefit of this equal partition. Encouraged by the ministers of the divan, who wished to elude the fanaticism of the sultan, the Christian advocates presumed to allege that this division had been an act, not of generosity, but of justice; not a concession, but a compact; and that if one half of the city had been taken by storm, the other moiety had surrendered on the faith of a sacred capitulation. The original grant had indeed been consumed by fire: but the loss was supplied by the testimony of three aged Janizaries who remembered the transaction; and their venal oaths are of more weight in the opinion of Cantemir, than the positive and unanimous consent of the history of the times.

The remaining fragments of the Greek kingdom in Europe and Asia I shall abandon to the Turkish arms; but the final extinction of the two last dynasties which have reigned in Constantinople should terminate the decline and fall of the Roman empire in the East. The despots of the Morea, Demetrius and Thomas, the two surviving brothers of the name of Palæologus, were astonished by the death of the emperor Constantine, and the ruin of the monarchy. Hopeless of defence, they prepared, with the noble Greeks who adhered to their fortune, to seek a refuge in Italy, beyond the reach of the Ottoman thunder. Their first apprehensions were dispelled by the victorious sultan, who contented himself with a tribute of twelve thousand ducats; and while his ambition explored the continent and the islands, in search of prey, he indulged the Morea in a respite of seven years. But this respite was a period of grief, discord, and misery. The *hexamilion*, the rampart of the Isthmus, so often raised and so often subverted, could not long be defended by three hundred Italian archers: the keys of Corinth were seized by the Turks: they returned from their summer excursions with a train of captives and spoil; and the complaints of the injured Greeks were heard with indifference and disdain. The Albanians, a vagrant tribe of shepherds and robbers, filled the peninsula with rapine and murder: the two despots implored the dangerous and humiliating aid of a neighboring bashaw; and when he had quelled the revolt, his lessons inculcated the rule of their future conduct. Neither the ties of blood, nor the oaths which they repeatedly pledged in the communion and before the altar, nor the stronger pressure of necessity, could reconcile or suspend their domestic quarrels. They ravaged each other's patrimony with fire and sword: the alms and succors of the West were consumed in civil hostility; and their power was only exerted in savage and arbitrary executions. The distress and revenge of the weaker rival invoked their supreme lord; and, in the season of maturity and revenge, Mahomet declared himself the friend of Demetrius, and marched into the Morea with an irresistible force. When he had taken possession of Sparta, "You are too weak," said the sultan, "to control this turbulent province: I will take your daughter to my bed; and you shall pass the remainder of your life in security and honor." Demetrius sighed and obeyed; surrendered his daughter and his castles; followed to Adrianople his sovereign and his son; and received for his own maintenance, and that of his followers, a city in Thrace and the adjacent isles of Imbros, Lemnos, and Samothrace. He was joined the next year by a companion of misfortune, the last of the Comnenian race, who, after the taking of Constantinople by the Latins, had founded a new empire on the coast of the Black Sea. In the progress of his Anatolian conquest, Mahomet invested with a fleet and army the capital of David, who presumed to style himself emperor of Trebizond; and the negotiation was comprised in a short and peremptory question, "Will you secure your life and treasures by resigning your kingdom? or had you rather forfeit your kingdom, your treasures, and your life?" The feeble Comnenus was subdued by his own fears, and the example of a Mussulman neighbor, the prince of Sinope, who, on a similar summons, had yielded a fortified city, with four hundred cannon and ten or twelve thousand soldiers. The capitulation of Trebizond was faithfully performed: and the emperor, with his family, was transported to a castle in Romania; but on a slight suspicion of corresponding with the Persian king, David, and the whole Comnenian race, were sacrificed to the jealousy or avarice of the conqueror. Nor could the name of father long protect the unfortunate Demetrius from exile and confiscation; his abject submission moved the pity and contempt of the sultan; his followers were transplanted to Constantinople; and his poverty was alleviated by a pension of fifty thousand aspers, till a monastic habit and a tardy death released Palæologus from an earthly master. It is not easy to pronounce whether the servitude of Demetrius, or the exile of his brother Thomas, be the most inglorious. On the conquest of the Morea, the despot escaped to Corfu, and from thence to Italy, with some naked adherents: his name, his sufferings, and the head of the apostle St. Andrew, entitled him to the hospitality of the Vatican; and his misery was prolonged by a pension of six thousand ducats from the pope and cardinals. His two sons, Andrew and Manuel, were educated in Italy; but the eldest, contemptible to his enemies and burdensome to his friends, was degraded by the baseness of his life and marriage. A title was his sole inheritance; and that inheritance he successively sold to the kings of France and Arragon. During his transient prosperity, Charles the Eighth was ambitious of joining the empire of the East with the kingdom of Naples: in a public festival, he assumed the appellation and the purple of *Augustus*: the Greeks rejoiced and the Ottoman already trembled, at the approach of the French chivalry. Manuel Palæologus, the second son, was tempted to revisit his native country: his return might be grateful, and could not be dangerous, to the Porte: he was maintained at Constantinople in safety and ease; and an honorable train of Christians and Moslems attended him to the grave. If there be some animals of so generous a nature that they refuse to propagate in a domestic state, the last of the Imperial race must be ascribed to an inferior kind: he accepted from the sultan's liberality two beautiful females; and his surviving son was lost in the habit and religion of a Turkish slave.

The importance of Constantinople was felt and magnified in its loss: the pontificate of Nicholas the Fifth, however peaceful and prosperous, was dishonored by the fall of the Eastern empire; and the grief and terror of the Latins revived, or seemed to revive, the old enthusiasm of the crusades. In one of the most distant countries of the West, Philip duke of Burgundy entertained, at Lisle in Flanders, an assembly of his nobles; and the pompous pageants of the feast were skilfully adapted to their fancy and feelings. In the midst of the banquet a gigantic Saracen entered the hall, leading a fictitious elephant with a castle on his back: a matron in a mourning robe, the symbol of religion, was seen to issue from the castle: she deplored her oppression, and accused the slowness of her champions: the principal herald of the golden fleece advanced, bearing on his fist a live pheasant, which, according to the rites of chivalry, he presented to the duke. At this extraordinary summons, Philip, a wise and aged prince, engaged his person and powers in the holy war against the Turks: his example was imitated by the barons and knights of the assembly: they swore to God, the Virgin, the ladies and the *pheasant*; and their particular vows were not less extravagant than the general sanction of their oath. But the performance was made to depend on some future and foreign contingency; and during twelve years, till the last hour of his life, the duke of Burgundy might be scrupulously, and perhaps sincerely, on the eve of his departure. Had every breast glowed with the same ardor; had the union of the Christians corresponded with their bravery; had every country, from Sweden to Naples, supplied a just proportion of cavalry and infantry, of men and money, it is indeed probable that Constantinople would have been delivered, and that the Turks might have been chased beyond the Hellespont or the Euphrates. But the secretary of the emperor, who composed every epistle, and attended every meeting, Æneas Sylvius, a statesman and orator, describes from his own experience the repugnant state and spirit of Christendom. "It is a body," says he, "without a head; a republic without laws or magistrates. The pope and the emperor may shine as lofty titles, as splendid images; but *they* are unable to command, and none are willing to obey: every state has a separate prince, and every prince has a separate interest. What eloquence could unite so many discordant and hostile powers under the same standard? Could they be assembled in arms, who would dare to assume the office of general? What order could be maintained? – what military discipline? Who would undertake to feed such an enormous multitude? Who would understand their various languages, or direct their stranger and incompatible manners? What mortal could reconcile the Germans with the French, Genoa with Arragon, the Germans with the natives of Hungary and Bohemia? If a small number enlisted in the holy war, they must be overthrown by the infidels; if many, by their own weight and confusion." Yet the same Æneas, when he was raised to the papal throne, under the name of Pius the Second, devoted his life to the prosecution of the Turkish war. In the council of Mantua he excited some sparks of a false or feeble enthusiasm; but when the pontiff appeared at Ancona, to embark in person with the troops, engagements vanished in excuses; a precise day was adjourned to an indefinite term; and his effective army consisted of some German pilgrims, whom he was obliged to disband with indulgences and arms. Regardless of futurity, his successors and the powers of Italy were involved in the schemes of present and domestic ambition; and the distance or proximity of each object determined in their eyes its apparent magnitude. A more enlarged view of their interest would have taught them to maintain a defensive and naval war against the common enemy; and the support of Scanderbeg and his brave Albanians might have prevented the subsequent invasion of the kingdom of Naples. The siege and sack of Otranto by the Turks diffused a general consternation; and Pope Sixtus was preparing to fly beyond the Alps, when the storm was instantly dispelled by the death of Mahomet the Second, in the fifty-first year of his age. His lofty genius aspired to the conquest of Italy: he was possessed of a strong city and a capacious harbor; and the same reign might have been decorated with the trophies of the New and the Ancient Rome.

State of Rome from the Twelfth Century. – Part One

State of Rome from the Twelfth Century.
– Temporal Dominion of the Popes. – Sedi-
tions of the City. – Political Heresy of Arnold
of Brescia. – Restoration of the Republic. –
The Senators. – Pride of the Romans. – Their
Wars. – They are Deprived of the Election and
Presence of the Popes, who Retire to Avignon.
– The Jubilee. – Noble Families of Rome. –
Feud of the Colonna and Ursini.

IN THE FIRST AGES of the decline and fall of the Roman empire, our
eye is invariably fixed on the royal city, which had given laws to the
fairest portion of the globe. We contemplate her fortunes, at first with
admiration, at length with pity, always with attention, and when that
attention is diverted from the capital to the provinces, they are considered as so many branches which have been successively severed from
the Imperial trunk. The foundation of a second Rome, on the shores
of the Bosphorus, has compelled the historian to follow the successors
of Constantine; and our curiosity has been tempted to visit the most
remote countries of Europe and Asia, to explore the causes and the authors of the long decay of the Byzantine monarchy. By the conquest of
Justinian, we have been recalled to the banks of the Tyber, to the deliverance of the ancient metropolis; but that deliverance was a change, or
perhaps an aggravation, of servitude. Rome had been already stripped
of her trophies, her gods, and her Cæsars; nor was the Gothic dominion more inglorious and oppressive than the tyranny of the Greeks. In
the eighth century of the Christian æra, a religious quarrel, the wor-

ship of images, provoked the Romans to assert their independence: their bishop became the temporal, as well as the spiritual, father of a free people; and of the Western empire, which was restored by Charlemagne, the title and image still decorate the singular constitution of modern Germany. The name of Rome must yet command our involuntary respect: the climate (whatsoever may be its influence) was no longer the same: the purity of blood had been contaminated through a thousand channels; but the venerable aspect of her ruins, and the memory of past greatness, rekindled a spark of the national character. The darkness of the middle ages exhibits some scenes not unworthy of our notice. Nor shall I dismiss the present work till I have reviewed the state and revolutions of the Roman City, which acquiesced under the absolute dominion of the popes, about the same time that Constantinople was enslaved by the Turkish arms.

In the beginning of the twelfth century, the æra of the first crusade, Rome was revered by the Latins, as the metropolis of the world, as the throne of the pope and the emperor, who, from the eternal city, derived their title, their honors, and the right or exercise of temporal dominion. After so long an interruption, it may not be useless to repeat that the successors of Charlemagne and the Othos were chosen beyond the Rhine in a national diet; but that these princes were content with the humble names of kings of Germany and Italy, till they had passed the Alps and the Apennine, to seek their Imperial crown on the banks of the Tyber. At some distance from the city, their approach was saluted by a long procession of the clergy and people with palms and crosses; and the terrific emblems of wolves and lions, of dragons and eagles, that floated in the military banners, represented the departed legions and cohorts of the republic. The royal path to maintain the liberties of Rome was thrice reiterated, at the bridge, the gate, and on the stairs of the Vatican; and the distribution of a customary donative feebly imitated the magnificence of the first Cæsars. In the church of St. Peter, the coronation was performed by his successor: the voice of God was confounded with that of the people; and the public consent was declared in the acclamations of "Long life and victory to our lord the pope! long life and victory to our lord the emperor! long life and victory to the Roman and Teutonic armies!" The names of Cæsar and Augustus, the laws of Constantine and Justinian, the example of Charlemagne and Otho, established the supreme dominion of the emperors: their title and image was engraved on the papal coins; and their jurisdiction was marked by the sword of justice, which they delivered to the præfect of the city. But every Roman prejudice was awakened by the name, the language, and the manners, of a Barbarian lord. The Cæsars of Saxony or Franconia were the chiefs of a feudal aristocracy; nor could they exercise the discipline of civil and military power, which alone secures the obedience of a distant people, impatient of servitude, though perhaps incapable of freedom. Once, and once only, in his life, each emperor, with an army of Teutonic vassals, descended from the Alps. I have described the peaceful order of his entry and coronation; but that order was commonly disturbed by the clamor and sedition of the Romans, who encountered their sovereign as a foreign invader: his departure was always speedy, and often shameful; and, in the absence of a long reign, his authority was insulted, and his name was forgotten. The progress of independence in Germany and Italy undermined the foundations of the Imperial sovereignty, and the triumph of the popes was the deliverance of Rome.

Of her two sovereigns, the emperor had precariously reigned by the right of conquest; but the authority of the pope was founded on the soft, though more solid, basis of opinion and habit. The removal of a foreign influence restored and endeared the shepherd to his flock. Instead of the arbitrary or venal nomination of a German court, the vicar of Christ was freely chosen by the college of cardinals, most of whom were either natives or inhabitants of the city. The applause of the magistrates and people confirmed his election, and the ecclesiastical power that was obeyed in Sweden and Britain had been ultimately derived from the suffrage of the Romans. The same suffrage gave a prince, as well as a pontiff, to the capital. It was universally believed, that Constantine had invested the popes with the temporal dominion of Rome; and the boldest civilians, the most profane skeptics, were satisfied with disputing the right of the emperor and the validity of his gift. The truth of the fact, the authenticity of his donation, was deeply rooted in the ignorance and tradition of four centuries; and the fabulous origin was lost in the real and permanent effects. The name of *Dominus* or Lord was inscribed on the coin of the bishops: their title was acknowledged by acclamations and oaths of allegiance, and with the free, or reluctant, consent of the German Cæsars, they had long exercised a supreme or subordinate jurisdiction over the city and patrimony of St. Peter. The reign of the popes, which gratified the prejudices, was not incompatible with the liberties, of Rome; and a more critical inquiry would have revealed a still nobler source of their power; the gratitude of a nation, whom they had rescued from the heresy and oppression of the Greek tyrant. In an age of superstition, it should seem that the union of the royal and sacerdotal characters would mutually fortify each other; and that the keys of Paradise would be the surest pledge of earthly obedience. The sanctity of the office might indeed be degraded by the personal vices of the man. But the scandals of the tenth century were obliterated by the austere and more dangerous virtues of Gregory the Seventh and his successors; and in the ambitious contests which they maintained for the rights of the church, their sufferings or their success must equally tend to increase the popular veneration. They sometimes wandered in poverty and exile, the victims of persecution; and the apostolic zeal with which they offered themselves to martyrdom must engage the favor and sympathy of every Catholic breast. And sometimes, thundering from the Vatican, they created, judged, and deposed the kings of the world; nor could the proudest Roman be disgraced by submitting to a priest, whose feet were kissed, and whose stirrup was held, by the successors of Charlemagne. Even the temporal interest of the city should have protected in peace and honor the residence of the popes; from whence a vain and lazy people derived the greatest part of their subsistence and riches. The fixed revenue of the popes was probably impaired; many of the old patrimonial estates, both in Italy and the provinces, had been invaded by sacrilegious hands; nor could the loss be compensated by the claim, rather than the possession, of the more ample gifts of Pepin and his descendants. But the Vatican and Capitol were nourished by the incessant and increasing swarms of pilgrims and suppliants: the pale of Christianity was enlarged, and the pope and cardinals were overwhelmed by the judgment of ecclesiastical and secular causes. A new jurisprudence had established in the Latin church the right and practice of appeals; and from the North and West the bishops and abbots were invited or summoned to solicit, to complain, to accuse, or to justify, before the threshold of the apostles. A rare prodigy is once recorded, that two horses, belonging to the archbishops of Mentz and Cologne, repassed the Alps, yet laden with gold and silver: but it was soon understood, that the success, both of the pilgrims and clients, depended much less on the justice of their cause than on the value of their offering. The wealth and piety of these strangers were ostentatiously displayed; and their expenses, sacred or profane, circulated in various channels for the emolument of the Romans.

Such powerful motives should have firmly attached the voluntary and pious obedience of the Roman people to their spiritual and temporal father. But the operation of prejudice and interest is often disturbed by the sallies of ungovernable passion. The Indian who fells the tree, that he may gather the fruit, and the Arab who plunders the caravans of commerce, are actuated by the same impulse of savage nature, which overlooks the future in the present, and relinquishes for momentary rapine the long and secure possession of the most important blessings. And it was thus, that the shrine of St. Peter was profaned by the thoughtless Romans; who pillaged the offerings, and wounded the pilgrims, without computing the number and value of similar visits, which they prevented by their inhospitable sacrilege. Even the influence of superstition is fluctuating and precarious; and the slave, whose reason is subdued, will often be delivered by his avarice or pride. A credulous devotion for the fables and oracles of the priesthood most powerfully acts on the mind of a Barbarian; yet such a mind is the least capable of preferring imagination to sense, of sacrificing to a distant motive, to an invisible, perhaps an ideal, object, the appetites and interests of the present world. In the vigor of health and youth, his practice will perpetually contradict his belief; till the pressure of age, or sickness, or calamity, awakens his terrors, and compels him to satisfy the double debt of piety and remorse. I have already observed, that the modern times of religious indifference are the most favorable to the peace and security of the clergy. Under the reign of superstition, they had much to hope from the ignorance, and much to fear from the violence, of mankind. The wealth, whose constant increase must have rendered them the sole proprietors of the earth, was alternately bestowed by the repentant father and plundered by the rapacious son: their persons were adored or violated; and the same idol, by the hands of the same votaries, was placed on the altar, or trampled in the dust. In the feudal system of Europe, arms were the title of distinction and the measure of allegiance; and amidst their tumult, the still voice of law and reason was seldom heard or obeyed. The turbulent Romans disdained the yoke, and insulted the impotence, of their bishop: nor would his education or character allow him to exercise, with decency or effect, the power of the sword. The motives of his election and the frailties of his life were exposed to their familiar observation; and proximity must diminish the reverence which his name and his decrees impressed on a barbarous world. This difference has not escaped the notice of our philosophic historian: "Though the name and authority of the court of Rome were so terrible in the remote countries of Europe, which were sunk in profound ignorance, and were entirely unacquainted with its character and conduct, the pope was so little revered at home, that his inveterate enemies surrounded the gates of Rome itself, and even controlled his government in that city; and the ambassadors, who, from a distant extremity of Europe, carried to him the humble, or rather abject, submissions of the greatest potentate of the age, found the utmost difficulty to make their way to him, and to throw themselves at his feet."

Since the primitive times, the wealth of the popes was exposed to envy, their powers to opposition, and their persons to violence. But the long hostility of the mitre and the crown increased the numbers, and inflamed the passions, of their enemies. The deadly factions of the Guelphs and Ghibelines, so fatal to Italy, could never be embraced with truth or constancy by the Romans, the subjects and adversaries both of the bishop and emperor; but their support was solicited by both parties, and they alternately displayed in their banners the keys of St. Peter and the German eagle. Gregory the Seventh, who may be adored or detested as the founder of the papal monarchy, was driven from Rome, and died in exile at Salerno. Six-and-thirty of his successors, till their retreat to Avignon, maintained an unequal contest with the Romans: their age and dignity were often violated; and the churches, in the solemn rites of religion, were polluted with sedition and murder. A repetition of such capricious brutality, without connection or design, would be tedious and disgusting; and I shall content myself with some events of the twelfth century, which represent the state of the popes and the city. On Holy Thursday, while Paschal officiated before the altar, he was interrupted by the clamors of the multitude, who imperiously demanded the confirmation of a favorite magistrate. His silence exasperated their fury; his pious refusal to mingle the affairs of earth and heaven was encountered with menaces, and oaths, that he should be the cause and the witness of the public ruin. During the festival of Easter, while the bishop and the clergy, barefooted and in procession, visited the tombs of the martyrs, they were twice assaulted, at the bridge of St. Angelo, and before the Capitol, with volleys of stones and darts. The houses of his adherents were levelled with the ground: Paschal escaped with difficulty and danger; he levied an army in the patrimony of St. Peter; and his last days were embittered by suffering and inflicting the calamities of civil war. The scenes that followed the election of his successor Gelasius the Second were still more scandalous to the church and city. Cencio Frangipani, a potent and factious baron, burst into the assembly furious and in arms: the cardinals were stripped, beaten, and trampled under foot; and he seized, without pity or respect, the vicar of Christ by the throat. Gelasius was dragged by the hair along the ground, buffeted with blows, wounded with spurs, and bound with an iron chain in the house of his brutal tyrant. An insurrection of the people delivered their bishop: the rival families opposed the violence of the Frangipani; and Cencio, who sued for pardon, repented of the failure, rather than of the guilt, of his enterprise. Not many days had elapsed, when the pope was again assaulted at the altar. While his friends and enemies were engaged in a bloody contest, he escaped in his sacerdotal garments. In this unworthy flight, which excited the compassion of the Roman matrons, his attendants were scattered or unhorsed; and, in the fields behind the church of St. Peter, his successor was found alone and half dead with fear and fatigue. Shaking the dust from his feet, the *apostle* withdrew from a city in which his dignity was insulted and his person was endangered; and the vanity of sacerdotal ambition is revealed in the involuntary confession, that one emperor was more tolerable than twenty. These examples might suffice; but I cannot forget the sufferings of two pontiffs of the same age, the second and third of the name of Lucius. The former, as he ascended in battle array to assault the Capitol, was struck on the temple by a stone, and expired in a few days. The latter was severely wounded in the person of his servants. In a civil commotion, several of his priests had been made prisoners; and the inhuman Romans, reserving one as a guide for his brethren, put out their eyes, crowned them with ludicrous mitres, mounted them on asses with their faces towards the tail, and extorted an oath, that, in this wretched condition, they should offer themselves as a lesson to the head of the church. Hope or fear, lassitude or remorse, the characters of the men, and the circumstances of the times, might sometimes obtain an interval of peace and obedience; and the pope was restored with joyful acclamations to the Lateran or Vatican, from whence he had been driven with threats and violence. But the root of mischief was deep and perennial; and a momentary calm was preceded and followed by such tempests as had almost sunk the bark of St. Peter. Rome continually presented the aspect of war and discord: the churches and palaces were fortified and assaulted by the factions and families; and, after giving peace to Europe, Calistus the Second alone had resolution and power to prohibit the use of private arms in the metropolis. Among the nations who revered the apostolic throne, the tumults of Rome provoked a general indignation; and in a letter to his disciple Eugenius the Third, St. Bernard, with the sharpness of his wit and zeal, has stigmatized the vices of the rebellious people. "Who is ignorant," says the monk of Clairvaux, "of the vanity and arrogance of the Romans? a nation nursed in sedition, untractable, and scorning to obey, unless they are too feeble to resist. When they promise to serve, they aspire to reign; if they swear allegiance, they watch the opportunity of revolt; yet they vent their discontent in loud clamors, if your doors, or your counsels, are shut against them. Dexterous in mischief, they have never learned the science of doing good. Odious to earth and heaven, impious to God, seditious among themselves, jealous of their neighbors, inhuman to strangers, they love no one, by no one are they beloved; and while they wish to inspire fear, they live in base and continual apprehension. They will not submit; they know not how to govern faithless to their superiors, intolerable to their equals, ungrateful to their benefactors, and alike impudent in their demands and their refusals. Lofty in promise, poor in execution; adulation and calumny, perfidy and treason, are the familiar arts of their policy." Surely this dark portrait is not colored by the pencil of Christian charity; yet the features, however harsh or ugly, express a lively resemblance of the Roman of the twelfth century.

The Jews had rejected the Christ when he appeared among them in a plebeian character; and the Romans might plead their ignorance of his vicar when he assumed the pomp and pride of a temporal sovereign. In the busy age of the crusades, some sparks of curiosity and reason were rekindled in the Western world: the heresy of Bulgaria, the Paulician sect, was successfully transplanted into the soil of Italy and France; the Gnostic visions were mingled with the simplicity of the gospel; and the enemies of the clergy reconciled their passions with their conscience, the desire of freedom with the profession of piety. The trumpet of Roman liberty was first sounded by Arnold of Brescia, whose promotion in the church was confined to the lowest rank, and who wore the monastic habit rather as a garb of poverty than as a uniform of obedience. His adversaries could not deny the wit and eloquence which they severely felt; they confess with reluctance the specious purity of his morals; and his errors were recommended to the public by a mixture of important and beneficial truths. In his theological studies, he had been the disciple of the famous and unfortunate Abelard, who was likewise involved in the suspicion of heresy: but the lover of Eloisa was of a soft and flexible nature; and his ecclesiastic judges were edified and disarmed by the humility of his repentance. From this master, Arnold most probably imbibed some metaphysical definitions of the Trinity, repugnant to the taste of the times: his ideas of baptism and the eucharist are loosely censured; but a political heresy was the source of his fame and misfortunes. He presumed to quote the declaration of Christ, that his kingdom is not of this world: he boldly maintained, that the sword and the sceptre were intrusted to the civil magistrate; that temporal honors and possessions were lawfully vested in secular persons; that the abbots, the bishops, and the pope himself, must renounce either their state or their salvation; and that after the loss of their revenues, the voluntary tithes and oblations of the faithful would suffice, not indeed for luxury and avarice, but for a frugal life in the exercise of spiritual labors. During a short time, the preacher was revered as a patriot; and the discontent, or revolt, of Brescia against her bishop, was the first fruits of his dangerous lessons. But the favor of the people is less permanent than the resentment of the priest; and after the heresy of Arnold had been condemned by Innocent the Second, in the general council of the Lateran, the magistrates themselves were urged by prejudice and fear to execute the sentence of the church. Italy could no longer afford a refuge; and the disciple of Abelard escaped beyond the Alps, till he found a safe and hospitable shelter in Zurich, now the first of the Swiss cantons. From a Roman station, a royal villa, a chapter of noble virgins, Zurich had gradually increased to a free and flourishing city; where the appeals of the Milanese were sometimes tried by the Imperial commissaries. In an age less ripe for reformation, the precursor of Zuinglius was heard with applause: a brave and simple people imbibed, and long retained, the color of his opinions; and his art, or merit, seduced the bishop of Constance, and even the pope's legate, who forgot, for his sake, the interest of their master and their order. Their tardy zeal was quickened by the fierce exhortations of St. Bernard; and the enemy of the church was driven by persecution to the desperate measures of erecting his standard in Rome itself, in the face of the successor of St. Peter.

> – – *Damnatus ab illo*
> *Præsule, qui numeros vetitum contingere nostros*
> *Nomen ad innocuâ ducit laudabile vitâ.*

State of Rome from the Twelfth Century. – Part Two

YET THE COURAGE OF Arnold was not devoid of discretion: he was protected, and had perhaps been invited, by the nobles and people; and in the service of freedom, his eloquence thundered over the seven hills. Blending in the same discourse the texts of Livy and St. Paul, uniting the motives of gospel, and of classic, enthusiasm, he admonished the Romans, how strangely their patience and the vices of the clergy had degenerated from the primitive times of the church and the city. He exhorted them to assert the inalienable rights of men and Christians; to restore the laws and magistrates of the republic; to respect the *name* of the emperor; but to confine their shepherd to the spiritual government of his flock. Nor could his spiritual government escape the censure and control of the reformer; and the inferior clergy were taught by his lessons to resist the cardinals, who had usurped a despotic command over the twenty-eight regions or parishes of Rome. The revolution was not accomplished without rapine and violence, the diffusion of blood and the demolition of houses: the victorious faction was enriched with the spoils of the clergy and the adverse nobles. Arnold of Brescia enjoyed, or deplored, the effects of his mission: his reign continued above ten years, while two popes, Innocent the Second and Anastasius the Fourth, either trembled in the Vatican, or wandered as exiles in the adjacent cities. They were succeeded by a more vigorous and fortunate pontiff. Adrian the Fourth, the only Englishman who has ascended the throne of St. Peter; and whose merit emerged from the mean condition of a monk, and almost a beggar, in the monastery of St. Albans. On the first provocation, of a cardinal killed or wounded in the streets, he cast an interdict on the guilty people; and from Christmas to Easter, Rome was deprived of the real or imaginary comforts of religious worship. The Romans had despised their temporal prince: they submitted with grief and terror to the censures of their spiritual father: their guilt was expiated by penance, and the banishment of the seditious preacher was the price of their absolution. But the revenge of Adrian was yet unsatisfied, and the approaching coronation of Frederic Barbarossa was fatal to the bold reformer, who had offended, though not in an equal degree, the heads of the church and state. In their interview at Viterbo, the pope represented to the emperor the furious, ungovernable spirit of the Romans; the insults, the injuries, the fears, to which his person and his clergy were continually exposed; and the pernicious tendency of the heresy of Arnold, which must subvert the principles of civil, as well as ecclesiastical, subordination. Frederic was convinced by these arguments, or tempted by the desire of the Imperial crown: in the balance of ambition, the innocence or life of an individual is of small account; and their common enemy was sacrificed to a moment of political concord. After his retreat from Rome, Arnold had been protected by the viscounts of Campania, from whom he was extorted by the power of Cæsar: the præfect of the city pronounced his sentence: the martyr of freedom was burned alive in the presence of a careless and ungrateful people; and his ashes were cast into the Tyber, lest the heretics should collect and worship the relics of their master. The clergy triumphed in his death: with his ashes, his sect was dispersed; his memory still lived in the minds of the Romans. From his school they had probably derived a new article of faith, that the metropolis of the Catholic church is exempt from the penalties of excommunication and interdict. Their bishops might argue, that the supreme jurisdiction, which they exercised over kings and nations, more especially embraced the city and diocese of the prince of the apostles. But they preached to the winds, and the same principle that weakened the effect, must temper the abuse, of the thunders of the Vatican.

> *Consiliis armisque sua moderamina summa*
> *Arbitrio tractare suo: nil juris in hâc re*
> *Pontifici summo, modicum concedere regi*
> *Suadebat populo. Sic læsâ stultus utrâque*
> *Majestate, reum geminæ se fecerat aulæ.*

The love of ancient freedom has encouraged a belief that as early as the tenth century, in their first struggles against the Saxon Othos, the commonwealth was vindicated and restored by the senate and people of Rome; that two consuls were annually elected among the nobles, and that ten or twelve plebeian magistrates revived the name and office of the tribunes of the commons. But this venerable structure disappears before the light of criticism. In the darkness of the middle ages, the appellations of senators, of consuls, of the sons of consuls, may sometimes be discovered. They were bestowed by the emperors, or assumed by the most powerful citizens, to denote their rank, their honors, and perhaps the claim of a pure and patrician descent: but they float on the surface, without a series or a substance, the titles of men, not the orders of government; and it is only from the year of Christ one thousand one hundred and forty-four that the establishment of the senate is dated, as a glorious æra, in the acts of the city. A new constitution was hastily framed by private ambition or popular enthusiasm; nor could Rome, in the twelfth century, produce an antiquary to explain, or a legislator to restore, the harmony and proportions of the ancient model. The assembly of a free, of an armed, people, will ever speak in loud and weighty acclamations. But the regular distribution of the thirty-five tribes, the nice balance of the wealth and numbers of the centuries, the debates of the adverse orators, and the slow operations of votes and ballots, could not easily be adapted by a blind multitude, ignorant of the arts, and insensible of the benefits, of legal government. It was proposed by Arnold to revive and discriminate the equestrian order; but what could be the motive or measure of such distinction? The pecuniary qualification of the knights must have been reduced to the poverty of the times: those times no longer required their civil functions of judges and farmers of the revenue; and their primitive duty, their military service on horseback, was more nobly supplied by feudal tenures and the spirit of chivalry. The jurisprudence of the republic was useless and unknown: the nations and families of Italy who lived under the Roman and Barbaric laws were insensibly mingled in a common mass; and some faint tradition, some imperfect fragments, preserved the memory of the Code and Pandects of Justinian. With their liberty the Romans might doubtless have restored the appellation and office of consuls; had they not disdained a title so promiscuously adopted in the Italian cities, that it has finally settled on the humble station of the agents of commerce in a foreign land. But the rights of the tribunes, the formidable word that arrested the public counsels, suppose or must produce a legitimate democracy. The old patricians were the subjects, the modern barons the tyrants, of the state; nor would the enemies of peace and order, who insulted the vicar of Christ, have long respected the unarmed sanctity of a plebeian magistrate.

Quin etiam titulos urbis renovare vetustos;
Nomine plebeio secernere nomen equestre,
Jura tribunorum, sanctum reparare senatum,
Et senio fessas mutasque reponere leges.
Lapsa ruinosis, et adhuc pendentia muris
Reddere primævo Capitolia prisca nitori.

In the revolution of the twelfth century, which gave a new existence and æra to Rome, we may observe the real and important events that marked or confirmed her political independence. I. The Capitoline hill, one of her seven eminences, is about four hundred yards in length, and two hundred in breadth. A flight of a hundred steps led to the summit of the Tarpeian rock; and far steeper was the ascent before the declivities had been smoothed and the precipices filled by the ruins of fallen edifices. From the earliest ages, the Capitol had been used as a temple in peace, a fortress in war: after the loss of the city, it maintained a siege against the victorious Gauls, and the sanctuary of the empire was occupied, assaulted, and burnt, in the civil wars of Vitellius and Vespasian. The temples of Jupiter and his kindred deities had crumbled into dust; their place was supplied by monasteries and houses; and the solid walls, the long and shelving porticos, were decayed or ruined by the lapse of time. It was the first act of the Romans, an act of freedom, to restore the strength, though not the beauty, of the Capitol; to fortify the seat of their arms and counsels; and as often as they ascended the hill, the coldest minds must have glowed with the remembrance of their ancestors. II. The first Cæsars had been invested with the exclusive coinage of the gold and silver; to the senate they abandoned the baser metal of bronze or copper: the emblems and legends were inscribed on a more ample field by the genius of flattery; and the prince was relieved from the care of celebrating his own virtues. The successors of Diocletian despised even the flattery of the senate: their royal officers at Rome, and in the provinces, assumed the sole direction of the mint; and the same prerogative was inherited by the Gothic kings of Italy, and the long series of the Greek, the French, and the German dynasties. After an abdication of eight hundred years, the Roman senate asserted this honorable and lucrative privilege; which was tacitly renounced by the popes, from Paschal the Second to the establishment of their residence beyond the Alps. Some of these republican coins of the twelfth and thirteenth centuries are shown in the cabinets of the curious. On one of these, a gold medal, Christ is depictured holding in his left hand a book with this inscription: "The vow of the Roman senate and people: Rome the capital of the world;" on the reverse, St. Peter delivering a banner to a kneeling senator in his cap and gown, with the name and arms of his family impressed on a shield. III. With the empire, the præfect of the city had declined to a municipal officer; yet he still exercised in the last appeal the civil and criminal jurisdiction; and a drawn sword, which he received from the successors of Otho, was the mode of his investiture and the emblem of his functions. The dignity was confined to the noble families of Rome: the choice of the people was ratified by the pope; but a triple oath of fidelity must have often embarrassed the præfect in the conflict of adverse duties. A servant, in whom they possessed but a third share, was dismissed by the independent Romans: in his place they elected a patrician; but this title, which Charlemagne had not disdained, was too lofty for a citizen or a subject; and, after the first fervor of rebellion, they consented without reluctance to the restoration of the præfect. About fifty years after this event, Innocent the Third, the most ambitious, or at least the most fortunate, of the Pontiffs, delivered the Romans and himself from this badge of foreign dominion: he invested the præfect with a banner instead of a sword, and absolved him from all dependence of oaths or service to the German emperors. In his place an ecclesiastic, a present or future cardinal, was named by the pope to the civil government of Rome; but his jurisdiction has been reduced to a narrow compass; and in the days of freedom, the right or exercise was derived from the senate and people. IV. After the revival of the senate, the conscript fathers (if I may use the expression) were invested with the legislative and executive power; but their views seldom reached beyond the present day; and that day was most frequently disturbed by violence and tumult. In its utmost plenitude, the order or assembly consisted of fifty-six senators, the most eminent of whom were distinguished by the title of counsellors: they were nominated, perhaps annually, by the people; and a previous choice of their electors, ten persons in each region, or parish, might afford a basis for a free and permanent constitution. The popes, who in this tempest submitted rather to bend than to break, confirmed by treaty the establishment and privileges of the senate, and expected from time, peace, and religion, the restoration of their government. The motives of public and private interest might sometimes draw from the Romans an occasional and temporary sacrifice of their claims; and they renewed their oath of allegiance to the successor of St. Peter and Constantine, the lawful head of the church and the republic.

The union and vigor of a public council was dissolved in a lawless city; and the Romans soon adopted a more strong and simple mode of administration. They condensed the name and authority of the senate in a single magistrate, or two colleagues; and as they were changed at the end of a year, or of six months, the greatness of the trust was compensated by the shortness of the term. But in this transient reign, the senators of Rome indulged their avarice and ambition: their justice was perverted by the interest of their family and faction; and as they punished only their enemies, they were obeyed only by their adherents. Anarchy, no longer tempered by the pastoral care of their bishop, admonished the Romans that they were incapable of governing themselves; and they sought abroad those blessings which they were hopeless of finding at home. In the same age, and from the same motives, most of the Italian republics were prompted to embrace a measure, which, however strange it may seem, was adapted to their situation, and productive of the most salutary effects. They chose, in some foreign but friendly city, an impartial magistrate of noble birth and unblemished character, a soldier and a statesman, recommended by the voice of fame and his country, to whom they delegated for a time the supreme administration of peace and war. The compact between the governor and the governed was sealed with oaths and subscriptions; and the duration of his power, the measure of his stipend, the nature of their mutual obligations, were defined with scrupulous precision. They swore to obey him as their lawful superior: he pledged his faith to unite the indifference of a stranger with the zeal of a patriot. At his choice, four or six knights and civilians, his assessors in arms and justice, attended the *Podesta*, who maintained at his own expense a decent retinue of servants and horses: his wife, his son, his brother, who might bias the affections of the judge, were left behind: during the exercise of his office he was not permitted to purchase land, to contract an alliance, or even to accept an invitation in the house of a citizen; nor could he honorably depart till he had satisfied the complaints that might be urged against his government.

> *Hujus qui trahitur prætextam sumere mavis;*
> *An Fidenarum Gabiorumque esse Potestas.*
> Juvenal. Satir. x. 99.11]

State of Rome from the Twelfth Century. – Part Three

IT WAS THUS, about the middle of the thirteenth century, that the Romans called from Bologna the senator Brancaleone, whose fame and merit have been rescued from oblivion by the pen of an English historian. A just anxiety for his reputation, a clear foresight of the difficulties of the task, had engaged him to refuse the honor of their choice: the statutes of Rome were suspended, and his office prolonged to the term of three years. By the guilty and licentious he was accused as cruel; by the clergy he was suspected as partial; but the friends of peace and order applauded the firm and upright magistrate by whom those blessings were restored. No criminals were so powerful as to brave, so obscure as to elude, the justice of the senator. By his sentence two nobles of the Annibaldi family were executed on a gibbet; and he inexorably demolished, in the city and neighborhood, one hundred and forty towers, the strong shelters of rapine and mischief. The bishop, as a simple bishop, was compelled to reside in his diocese; and the standard of Brancaleone was displayed in the field with terror and effect. His services were repaid by the ingratitude of a people unworthy of the happiness which they enjoyed. By the public robbers, whom he had provoked for their sake, the Romans were excited to depose and imprison their benefactor; nor would his life have been spared, if Bologna had not possessed a pledge for his safety. Before his departure, the prudent senator had required the exchange of thirty hostages of the noblest families of Rome: on the news of his danger, and at the prayer of his wife, they were more strictly guarded; and Bologna, in the cause of honor, sustained the thunders of a papal interdict. This generous resistance allowed the Romans to compare the present with the past; and Brancaleone was conducted from the prison to the Capitol amidst the acclamations of a repentant people. The remainder of his government was firm and fortunate; and as soon as envy was appeased by death, his head, enclosed in a precious vase, was deposited on a lofty column of marble.

The impotence of reason and virtue recommended in Italy a more effectual choice: instead of a private citizen, to whom they yielded a voluntary and precarious obedience, the Romans elected for their senator some prince of independent power, who could defend them from their enemies and themselves. Charles of Anjou and Provence, the most ambitious and warlike monarch of the age, accepted at the same time the kingdom of Naples from the pope, and the office of senator from the Roman people. As he passed through the city, in his road to victory, he received their oath of allegiance, lodged in the Lateran palace, and smoothed in a short visit the harsh features of his despotic character. Yet even Charles was exposed to the inconstancy of the people, who saluted with the same acclamations the passage of his rival, the unfortunate Conradin; and a powerful avenger, who reigned in the Capitol, alarmed the fears and jealousy of the popes. The absolute term of his life was superseded by a renewal every third year; and the enmity of Nicholas the Third obliged the Sicilian king to abdicate the government of Rome. In his bull, a perpetual law, the imperious pontiff asserts the truth, validity, and use of the donation of Constantine, not less essential to the peace of the city than to the independence of the church; establishes the annual election of the senator; and formally disqualifies all emperors, kings, princes, and persons of an eminent and conspicuous rank. This prohibitory clause was repealed in his own behalf by Martin the Fourth, who humbly solicited the suffrage of the Romans. In the presence, and by the authority, of the people, two electors conferred, not on the pope, but on the noble and faithful Martin, the dignity of senator, and the supreme administration of the republic, to hold during his natural life, and to exercise at pleasure by himself or his deputies. About fifty years afterwards, the same title was granted to the emperor Lewis of Bavaria; and the liberty of Rome was acknowledged by her two sovereigns, who accepted a municipal office in the government of their own metropolis.

In the first moments of rebellion, when Arnold of Brescia had inflamed their minds against the church, the Romans artfully labored to conciliate the favor of the empire, and to recommend their merit and services in the cause of Cæsar. The style of their ambassadors to Conrad the Third and Frederic the First is a mixture of flattery and pride, the tradition and the ignorance of their own history. After some complaint of his silence and neglect, they exhort the former of these princes to pass the Alps, and assume from their hands the Imperial crown. "We beseech your majesty not to disdain the humility of your sons and vassals, not to listen to the accusations of our common enemies; who calumniate the senate as hostile to your throne, who sow the seeds of discord, that they may reap the harvest of destruction. The pope and the *Sicilian* are united in an impious league to oppose *our* liberty and *your* coronation. With the blessing of God, our zeal and courage has hitherto defeated their attempts. Of their powerful and factious adherents, more especially the Frangipani, we have taken by assault the houses and turrets: some of these are occupied by our troops, and some are levelled with the ground. The Milvian bridge, which they had broken, is restored and fortified for your safe passage; and your army may enter the city without being annoyed from the castle of St. Angelo. All that we have done, and all that we design, is for your honor and service, in the loyal hope, that you will speedily appear in person, to vindicate those rights which have been invaded by the clergy, to revive the dignity of the empire, and to surpass the fame and glory of your predecessors. May you fix your residence in Rome, the capital of the world; give laws to Italy, and the Teutonic kingdom; and imitate the example of Constantine and Justinian, who, by the vigor of the senate and people, obtained the sceptre of the earth." But these splendid and fallacious wishes were not cherished by Conrad the Franconian, whose eyes were fixed on the Holy Land, and who died without visiting Rome soon after his return from the Holy Land.

His nephew and successor, Frederic Barbarossa, was more ambitious of the Imperial crown; nor had any of the successors of Otho acquired such absolute sway over the kingdom of Italy. Surrounded by his ecclesiastical and secular princes, he gave audience in his camp at Sutri to the ambassadors of Rome, who thus addressed him in a free and florid oration: "Incline your ear to the queen of cities; approach with a peaceful and friendly mind the precincts of Rome, which has cast away the yoke of the clergy, and is impatient to crown her legitimate emperor. Under your auspicious influence, may the primitive times be restored. Assert the prerogatives of the eternal city, and reduce under her monarchy the insolence of the world. You are not ignorant, that, in former ages, by the wisdom of the senate, by the valor and discipline of the equestrian order, she extended her victorious arms to the East and West, beyond the Alps, and over the islands of the ocean. By our sins, in the absence of our princes, the noble institution of the senate has sunk in oblivion;

and with our prudence, our strength has likewise decreased. We have revived the senate, and the equestrian order: the counsels of the one, the arms of the other, will be devoted to your person and the service of the empire. Do you not hear the language of the Roman matron? You were a guest, I have adopted you as a citizen; a Transalpine stranger, I have elected you for my sovereign; and given you myself, and all that is mine. Your first and most sacred duty is to swear and subscribe, that you will shed your blood for the republic; that you will maintain in peace and justice the laws of the city and the charters of your predecessors; and that you will reward with five thousand pounds of silver the faithful senators who shall proclaim your titles in the Capitol. With the name, assume the character, of Augustus." The flowers of Latin rhetoric were not yet exhausted; but Frederic, impatient of their vanity, interrupted the orators in the high tone of royalty and conquest. "Famous indeed have been the fortitude and wisdom of the ancient Romans; but your speech is not seasoned with wisdom, and I could wish that fortitude were conspicuous in your actions. Like all sublunary things, Rome has felt the vicissitudes of time and fortune. Your noblest families were translated to the East, to the royal city of Constantine; and the remains of your strength and freedom have long since been exhausted by the Greeks and Franks. Are you desirous of beholding the ancient glory of Rome, the gravity of the senate, the spirit of the knights, the discipline of the camp, the valor of the legions? you will find them in the German republic. It is not empire, naked and alone, the ornaments and virtues of empire have likewise migrated beyond the Alps to a more deserving people: they will be employed in your defence, but they claim your obedience. You pretend that myself or my predecessors have been invited by the Romans: you mistake the word; they were not invited, they were implored. From its foreign and domestic tyrants, the city was rescued by Charlemagne and Otho, whose ashes repose in our country; and their dominion was the price of your deliverance. Under that dominion your ancestors lived and died. I claim by the right of inheritance and possession, and who shall dare to extort you from my hands? Is the hand of the Franks and Germans enfeebled by age? Am I vanquished? Am I a captive? Am I not encompassed with the banners of a potent and invincible army? You impose conditions on your master; you require oaths: if the conditions are just, an oath is superfluous; if unjust, it is criminal. Can you doubt my equity? It is extended to the meanest of my subjects. Will not my sword be unsheathed in the defence of the Capitol? By that sword the northern kingdom of Denmark has been restored to the Roman empire. You prescribe the measure and the objects of my bounty, which flows in a copious but a voluntary stream. All will be given to patient merit; all will be denied to rude importunity." Neither the emperor nor the senate could maintain these lofty pretensions of dominion and liberty. United with the pope, and suspicious of the Romans, Frederic continued his march to the Vatican; his coronation was disturbed by a sally from the Capitol; and if the numbers and valor of the Germans prevailed in the bloody conflict, he could not safely encamp in the presence of a city of which he styled himself the sovereign. About twelve years afterwards, he besieged Rome, to seat an antipope in the chair of St. Peter; and twelve Pisan galleys were introduced into the Tyber: but the senate and people were saved by the arts of negotiation and the progress of disease; nor did Frederic or his successors reiterate the hostile attempt. Their laborious reigns were exercised by the popes, the crusades, and the independence of Lombardy and Germany: they courted the alliance of the Romans; and Frederic the Second offered in the Capitol the great standard, the *Caroccio* of Milan. After the extinction of the house of Swabia, they were banished beyond the Alps: and their last coronations betrayed the impotence and poverty of the Teutonic Cæsars.

> *Ave decus orbis, ave! victus tibi destinor, ave!*
> *Cúurrus ab Augusto Frederico Cæsare justo.*
> *Væ Mediolanum! jam sentis spernere vanum*
> *Imperii vires, proprias tibi tollere vires.*
> *Ergo triumphorum urbs potes memor esse priorum*
> *Quos tibi mittebant reges qui bella gerebant.*

Under the reign of Adrian, when the empire extended from the Euphrates to the ocean, from Mount Atlas to the Grampian hills, a fanciful historian amused the Romans with the picture of their ancient wars. "There was a time," says Florus, "when Tibur and Præneste, our summer retreats, were the objects of hostile vows in the Capitol, when we dreaded the shades of the Arician groves, when we could triumph without a blush over the nameless villages of the Sabines and Latins, and even Corioli could afford a title not unworthy of a victorious general." The pride of his contemporaries was gratified by the contrast of the past and the present: they would have been humbled by the prospect of futurity; by the prediction, that after a thousand years, Rome, despoiled of empire, and contracted to her primæval limits, would renew the same hostilities, on the same ground which was then decorated with her villas and gardens. The adjacent territory on either side of the Tyber was always claimed, and sometimes possessed, as the patrimony of St. Peter; but the barons assumed a lawless independence, and the cities too faithfully copied the revolt and discord of the metropolis. In the twelfth and thirteenth centuries the Romans incessantly labored to reduce or destroy the contumacious vassals of the church and senate; and if their headstrong and selfish ambition was moderated by the pope, he often encouraged their zeal by the alliance of his spiritual arms. Their warfare was that of the first consuls and dictators, who were taken from the plough. The assembled in arms at the foot of the Capitol; sallied from the gates, plundered or burnt the harvests of their neighbors, engaged in tumultuary conflict, and returned home after an expedition of fifteen or twenty days. Their sieges were tedious and unskilful: in the use of victory, they indulged the meaner passions of jealousy and revenge; and instead of adopting the valor, they trampled on the misfortunes, of their adversaries. The captives, in their shirts, with a rope round their necks, solicited their pardon: the fortifications, and even the buildings, of the rival cities, were demolished, and the inhabitants were scattered in the adjacent villages. It was thus that the seats of the cardinal bishops, Porto, Ostia, Albanum, Tusculum, Præneste, and Tibur or Tivoli, were successively overthrown by the ferocious hostility of the Romans. Of these, Porto and Ostia, the two keys of the Tyber, are still vacant and desolate: the marshy and unwholesome banks are peopled with herds of buffaloes, and the river is lost to every purpose of navigation and trade. The hills, which afford a shady retirement from the autumnal heats, have again smiled with the blessings of peace; Frescati has arisen near the ruins of Tusculum; Tibur or Tivoli has resumed the honors of a city, and the meaner towns of Albano and Palestrina are decorated with the villas of the cardinals and princes of Rome. In the work of destruction, the ambition of the Romans was often checked and repulsed by the neighboring cities and their allies: in the first siege of Tibur, they were driven from their camp; and the battles of Tusculum and Viterbo might be compared in their relative state to the memorable fields of Thrasymene and Cannæ. In the first of these petty wars, thirty thousand Romans were overthrown by a thousand German horse, whom Frederic Barbarossa had detached to the relief of Tusculum: and if we number the slain at three, the prisoners at two, thousand, we shall embrace the most authentic and moderate account. Sixty-eight years afterwards they marched against Viterbo in the ecclesiastical state with the whole force of the city; by a rare coalition the Teutonic eagle was blended, in the adverse banners, with the keys of St. Peter; and the pope's auxiliaries were commanded by a count of

Thoulouse and a bishop of Winchester. The Romans were discomfited with shame and slaughter: but the English prelate must have indulged the vanity of a pilgrim, if he multiplied their numbers to one hundred, and their loss in the field to thirty, thousand men. Had the policy of the senate and the discipline of the legions been restored with the Capitol, the divided condition of Italy would have offered the fairest opportunity of a second conquest. But in arms, the modern Romans were not *above*, and in arts, they were far *below*, the common level of the neighboring republics. Nor was their warlike spirit of any long continuance; after some irregular sallies, they subsided in the national apathy, in the neglect of military institutions, and in the disgraceful and dangerous use of foreign mercenaries.

Ambition is a weed of quick and early vegetation in the vineyard of Christ. Under the first Christian princes, the chair of St. Peter was disputed by the votes, the venality, the violence, of a popular election: the sanctuaries of Rome were polluted with blood; and, from the third to the twelfth century, the church was distracted by the mischief of frequent schisms. As long as the final appeal was determined by the civil magistrate, these mischiefs were transient and local: the merits were tried by equity or favor; nor could the unsuccessful competitor long disturb the triumph of his rival. But after the emperors had been divested of their prerogatives, after a maxim had been established that the vicar of Christ is amenable to no earthly tribunal, each vacancy of the holy see might involve Christendom in controversy and war. The claims of the cardinals and inferior clergy, of the nobles and people, were vague and litigious: the freedom of choice was overruled by the tumults of a city that no longer owned or obeyed a superior. On the decease of a pope, two factions proceeded in different churches to a double election: the number and weight of votes, the priority of time, the merit of the candidates, might balance each other: the most respectable of the clergy were divided; and the distant princes, who bowed before the spiritual throne, could not distinguish the spurious, from the legitimate, idol. The emperors were often the authors of the schism, from the political motive of opposing a friendly to a hostile pontiff; and each of the competitors was reduced to suffer the insults of his enemies, who were not awed by conscience, and to purchase the support of his adherents, who were instigated by avarice or ambition a peaceful and perpetual succession was ascertained by Alexander the Third, who finally abolished the tumultuary votes of the clergy and people, and defined the right of election in the sole college of cardinals. The three orders of bishops, priests, and deacons, were assimilated to each other by this important privilege; the parochial clergy of Rome obtained the first rank in the hierarchy: they were indifferently chosen among the nations of Christendom; and the possession of the richest benefices, of the most important bishoprics, was not incompatible with their title and office. The senators of the Catholic church, the coadjutors and legates of the supreme pontiff, were robed in purple, the symbol of martyrdom or royalty; they claimed a proud equality with kings; and their dignity was enhanced by the smallness of their number, which, till the reign of Leo the Tenth, seldom exceeded twenty or twenty-five persons. By this wise regulation, all doubt and scandal were removed, and the root of schism was so effectually destroyed, that in a period of six hundred years a double choice has only once divided the unity of the sacred college. But as the concurrence of two thirds of the votes had been made necessary, the election was often delayed by the private interest and passions of the cardinals; and while they prolonged their independent reign, the Christian world was left destitute of a head. A vacancy of almost three years had preceded the elevation of George the Tenth, who resolved to prevent the future abuse; and his bull, after some opposition, has been consecrated in the code of the canon law. Nine days are allowed for the obsequies of the deceased pope, and the arrival of the absent cardinals; on the tenth, they are imprisoned, each with one domestic, in a common apartment or *conclave*, without any separation of walls or curtains: a small window is reserved for the introduction of necessaries; but the door is locked on both sides and guarded by the magistrates of the city, to seclude them from all correspondence with the world. If the election be not consummated in three days, the luxury of their table is contracted to a single dish at dinner and supper; and after the eighth day, they are reduced to a scanty allowance of bread, water, and wine. During the vacancy of the holy see, the cardinals are prohibited from touching the revenues, or assuming, unless in some rare emergency, the government of the church: all agreements and promises among the electors are formally annulled; and their integrity is fortified by their solemn oath and the prayers of the Catholics. Some articles of inconvenient or superfluous rigor have been gradually relaxed, but the principle of confinement is vigorous and entire: they are still urged, by the personal motives of health and freedom, to accelerate the moment of their deliverance; and the improvement of ballot or secret votes has wrapped the struggles of the conclave in the silky veil of charity and politeness. By these institutions the Romans were excluded from the election of their prince and bishop; and in the fever of wild and precarious liberty, they seemed insensible of the loss of this inestimable privilege. The emperor Lewis of Bavaria revived the example of the great Otho. After some negotiation with the magistrates, the Roman people were assembled in the square before St. Peter's: the pope of Avignon, John the Twenty-second, was deposed: the choice of his successor was ratified by their consent and applause. They freely voted for a new law, that their bishop should never be absent more than three months in the year, and two days' journey from the city; and that if he neglected to return on the third summons, the public servant should be degraded and dismissed. But Lewis forgot his own debility and the prejudices of the times: beyond the precincts of a German camp, his useless phantom was rejected; the Romans despised their own workmanship; the antipope implored the mercy of his lawful sovereign; and the exclusive right of the cardinals was more firmly established by this unseasonable attack.

Had the election been always held in the Vatican, the rights of the senate and people would not have been violated with impunity. But the Romans forgot, and were forgotten. in the absence of the successors of Gregory the Seventh, who did not keep as a divine precept their ordinary residence in the city and diocese. The care of that diocese was less important than the government of the universal church; nor could the popes delight in a city in which their authority was always opposed, and their person was often endangered. From the persecution of the emperors, and the wars of Italy, they escaped beyond the Alps into the hospitable bosom of France; from the tumults of Rome they prudently withdrew to live and die in the more tranquil stations of Anagni, Perugia, Viterbo, and the adjacent cities. When the flock was offended or impoverished by the absence of the shepherd, they were recalled by a stern admonition, that St. Peter had fixed his chair, not in an obscure village, but in the capital of the world; by a ferocious menace, that the Romans would march in arms to destroy the place and people that should dare to afford them a retreat. They returned with timorous obedience; and were saluted with the account of a heavy debt, of all the losses which their desertion had occasioned, the hire of lodgings, the sale of provisions, and the various expenses of servants and strangers who attended the court. After a short interval of peace, and perhaps of authority, they were again banished by new tumults, and again summoned by the imperious or respectful invitation of the senate. In these occasional retreats, the exiles and fugitives of the Vatican were seldom long, or far, distant from the metropolis; but in the beginning of the fourteenth century, the apostolic throne was transported, as it might seem forever, from the Tyber to the Rhône; and the cause of the transmigration may be deduced from the furious contest between Boniface the Eighth and the king of France. The spiritual arms of excommunication and interdict were repulsed by the union of the three estates, and the privileges of the Gallican church; but the pope was not prepared against the carnal weapons which Philip the Fair had courage to employ. As the pope resided at Anagni, without the suspicion of danger, his palace and person were assaulted by three hundred horse, who had been secretly levied by William of Nogaret, a French minister, and Sciarra Colonna, of a noble but hostile family of Rome. The cardinals fled; the inhabitants of Anagni were seduced from their allegiance and gratitude; but the dauntless Boniface, unarmed and alone, seated himself in his chair, and awaited, like the conscript fathers of old, the swords of the Gauls. Nogaret, a foreign adversary, was content to execute the orders of his master: by the domestic enmity of Colonna, he was insulted with words and blows; and during a confinement of three days his life was threatened by the hardships which they inflicted on the obstinacy which they provoked. Their strange delay gave time and courage to the adherents of the church, who rescued him from sacrilegious violence; but his imperious soul was wounded in the vital part; and Boniface expired at Rome in a frenzy of rage and revenge. His memory is stained with the glaring vices of avarice and pride; nor has the courage of a martyr promoted this ecclesiastical champion to the honors of a saint; a magnanimous sinner, (say the chronicles of the times,) who entered like a fox, reigned like a lion, and died like a dog. He was succeeded by Benedict the Eleventh, the mildest of mankind. Yet he excommunicated the impious emissaries of Philip, and devoted the city and people of Anagni by a tremendous curse, whose effects are still visible to the eyes of superstition.

State of Rome from the
Twelfth Century. – Part Four

AFTER HIS DECEASE, the tedious and equal suspense of the conclave was fixed by the dexterity of the French faction. A specious offer was made and accepted, that, in the term of forty days, they would elect one of the three candidates who should be named by their opponents. The archbishop of Bourdeaux, a furious enemy of his king and country, was the first on the list; but his ambition was known; and his conscience obeyed the calls of fortune and the commands of a benefactor, who had been informed by a swift messenger that the choice of a pope was now in his hands. The terms were regulated in a private interview; and with such speed and secrecy was the business transacted, that the unanimous conclave applauded the elevation of Clement the Fifth. The cardinals of both parties were soon astonished by a summons to attend him beyond the Alps; from whence, as they soon discovered, they must never hope to return. He was engaged, by promise and affection, to prefer the residence of France; and, after dragging his court through Poitou and Gascony, and devouring, by his expense, the cities and convents on the road, he finally reposed at Avignon, which flourished above seventy years the seat of the Roman pontiff and the metropolis of Christendom. By land, by sea, by the Rhône, the position of Avignon was on all sides accessible; the southern provinces of France do not yield to Italy itself; new palaces arose for the accommodation of the pope and cardinals; and the arts of luxury were soon attracted by the treasures of the church. They were already possessed of the adjacent territory, the Venaissin county, a populous and fertile spot; and the sovereignty of Avignon was afterwards purchased from the youth and distress of Jane, the first queen of Naples and countess of Provence, for the inadequate price of fourscore thousand florins. Under the shadow of a French monarchy, amidst an obedient people, the popes enjoyed an honorable and tranquil state, to which they long had been strangers: but Italy deplored their absence; and Rome, in solitude and poverty, might repent of the ungovernable freedom which had driven from the Vatican the successor of St. Peter. Her repentance was tardy and fruitless: after the death of the old members, the sacred college was filled with French cardinals, who beheld Rome and Italy with abhorrence and contempt, and perpetuated a series of national, and even provincial, popes, attached by the most indissoluble ties to their native country.

The progress of industry had produced and enriched the Italian republics: the æra of their liberty is the most flourishing period of population and agriculture, of manufactures and commerce; and their mechanic labors were gradually refined into the arts of elegance and genius. But the position of Rome was less favorable, the territory less fruitful: the character of the inhabitants was debased by indolence and elated by pride; and they fondly conceived that the tribute of subjects must forever nourish the metropolis of the church and empire. This prejudice was encouraged in some degree by the resort of pilgrims to the shrines of the apostles; and the last legacy of the popes, the institution of the holy year, was not less beneficial to the people than to the clergy. Since the loss of Palestine, the gift of plenary indulgences, which had been applied to the crusades, remained without an object; and the most valuable treasure of the church was sequestered above eight years from public circulation. A new channel was opened by the diligence of Boniface the Eighth, who reconciled the vices of ambition and avarice; and the pope had sufficient learning to recollect and revive the secular games which were celebrated in Rome at the conclusion of every century. To sound without danger the depth of popular credulity, a sermon was seasonably pronounced, a report was artfully scattered, some aged witnesses were produced; and on the first of January of the year thirteen hundred, the church of St. Peter was crowded with the faithful, who demanded the customary indulgence of the holy time. The pontiff, who watched and irritated their devout impatience, was soon persuaded by ancient testimony of the justice of their claim; and he proclaimed a plenary absolution to all Catholics who, in the course of that year, and at every similar period, should respectfully visit the apostolic churches of St. Peter and St. Paul. The welcome sound was propagated through Christendom; and at first from the nearest provinces of Italy, and at length from the remote kingdoms of Hungary and Britain, the highways were thronged with a swarm of pilgrims who sought to expiate their sins in a journey, however costly or laborious, which was exempt from the perils of military service. All exceptions of rank or sex, of age or infirmity, were forgotten in the common transport; and in the streets and churches many persons were trampled to death by the eagerness of devotion. The calculation of their numbers could not be easy nor accurate; and they have probably been magnified by a dexterous clergy, well apprised of the contagion of example: yet we are assured by a judicious historian, who assisted at the ceremony, that Rome was never replenished with less than two hundred thousand strangers; and another spectator has fixed at two millions the total concourse of the year. A trifling oblation from each individual would accumulate a royal treasure; and two priests stood night and day, with rakes in their hands, to collect, without counting, the heaps of gold and silver that were poured on the altar of St. Paul. It was fortunately a season of peace and plenty; and if forage was scarce, if inns and lodgings were extravagantly dear, an inexhaustible supply of bread and wine, of meat and fish, was provided by the policy of Boniface and the venal hospitality of the Romans. From a city without trade or industry, all casual riches will speedily evaporate: but the avarice and envy of the next generation solicited Clement the Sixth to anticipate the distant period of the century. The gracious pontiff complied with their wishes; afforded Rome this poor consolation for his loss; and justified the change by the name and practice of the Mosaic Jubilee. His summons was obeyed; and the number, zeal, and liberality of the pilgrims did not yield to the primitive festival. But they encountered the triple scourge of war, pestilence, and famine: many wives and virgins were violated in the castles of Italy; and many strangers were pillaged or murdered by the savage Romans, no longer moderated by the presence of their bishops. To the impatience of the popes we may ascribe the successive reduction to fifty, thirty-three, and twenty-five years; although the second of these terms is commensurate with the life of Christ. The profusion of indulgences, the revolt of the Protestants, and the decline of superstition, have much diminished the value of the jubilee; yet even the nineteenth and last festival was a year of pleasure and profit to the Romans; and a philosophic smile will not disturb the triumph of the priest or the happiness of the people.

In the beginning of the eleventh century, Italy was exposed to the feudal tyranny, alike oppressive to the sovereign and the people. The rights of human nature were vindicated by her numerous republics, who soon extended their liberty and dominion from the city to the adjacent country. The sword of the nobles was broken; their slaves were enfranchised; their castles were demolished; they assumed the habits of society and obedience; their ambition was confined to municipal honors, and in the proudest aristocracy of Venice on Genoa, each patrician was subject to the laws. But the feeble and disorderly government of Rome was unequal to the task of curbing her rebellious sons, who scorned the authority of the magistrate within and without the walls. It was no longer a civil contention between the nobles and plebeians for the government of the state: the barons asserted in arms their personal independence; their palaces and castles were fortified against a siege; and their private quarrels were maintained by the numbers of their vassals and retainers. In origin and affection, they were aliens to their country: and a genuine Roman, could such have been produced, might have renounced these haughty strangers, who disdained the appellation of citizens, and proudly styled themselves the princes, of Rome. After a dark series of revolutions, all records of pedigree were lost; the distinction of surnames was abolished; the blood of the nations was mingled in a thousand channels; and the Goths and Lombards, the Greeks and Franks, the Germans and Normans, had obtained the fairest possessions by royal bounty, or the prerogative of valor. These examples might be readily presumed; but the elevation of a Hebrew race to the rank of senators and consuls is an event without a parallel in the long captivity of these miserable exiles. In the time of Leo the Ninth, a wealthy and learned Jew was converted to Christianity, and honored at his baptism with the name of his godfather, the reigning Pope. The zeal and courage of Peter the son of Leo were signalized in the cause of Gregory the Seventh, who intrusted his faithful adherent with the government of Adrian's mole, the tower of Crescentius, or, as it is now called, the castle of St. Angelo. Both the father and the son were the parents of a numerous progeny: their riches, the fruits of usury, were shared with the noblest families of the city; and so extensive was their alliance, that the grandson of the proselyte was exalted by the weight of his kindred to the throne of St. Peter. A majority of the clergy and people supported his cause: he reigned several years in the Vatican; and it is only the eloquence of St. Bernard, and the final triumph of Innocence the Second, that has branded Anacletus with the epithet of antipope. After his defeat and death, the posterity of Leo is no longer conspicuous; and none will be found of the modern nobles ambitious of descending from a Jewish stock. It is not my design to enumerate the Roman families which have failed at different periods, or those which are continued in different degrees of splendor to the present time. The old consular line of the *Frangipani* discover their name in the generous act of *breaking* or dividing bread in a time of famine; and such benevolence is more truly glorious than to have enclosed, with their allies the *Corsi*, a spacious quarter of the city in the chains of their fortifications; the *Savelli*, as it should seem a Sabine race, have maintained their original dignity; the obsolete surname of the *Capizucchi* is inscribed on the coins of the first senators; the *Conti* preserve the honor, without the estate, of the counts of Signia; and the *Annibaldi* must have been very ignorant, or very modest, if they had not descended from the Carthaginian hero.

> *Interea titulis redimiti sanguine et armis*
> *Illustresque viri Romanâ a stirpe trahentes*
> *Nomen in emeritos tantæ virtutis honores*
> *Insulerant sese medios festumque colebant*
> *Aurata fulgente togâ, sociante catervâ.*
> *Ex ipsis devota domus præstantis ab Ursâ*
> *Ecclesiæ, vultumque gerens demissius altum*
> *Festa Columna jocis, necnon Sabellia mitis;*
> *Stephanides senior, Comites, Annibalica proles,*
> *Præfectusque urbis magnum sine viribus nomen.*
> *(l. ii. c. 5, 100, p. 647, 648.)*

But among, perhaps above, the peers and princes of the city, I distinguish the rival houses of Colonna and Ursini, whose private story is an essential part of the annals of modern Rome. I. The name and arms of Colonna have been the theme of much doubtful etymology; nor have the orators and antiquarians overlooked either Trajan's pillar, or the columns of Hercules, or the pillar of Christ's flagellation, or the luminous column that guided the Israelites in the desert. Their first historical appearance in the year eleven hundred and four attests the power and antiquity, while it explains the simple meaning, of the name. By the usurpation of Cavæ, the Colonna provoked the arms of Paschal the Second; but they lawfully held in the Campagna of Rome the hereditary fiefs of Zagarola and *Colonna*; and the latter of these towns was probably adorned with some lofty pillar, the relic of a villa or temple. They likewise possessed one moiety of the neighboring city of Tusculum, a strong presumption of their descent from the counts of Tusculum, who in the tenth century were the tyrants of the apostolic see. According to their own and the public opinion, the primitive and remote source was derived from the banks of the Rhine; and the sovereigns of Germany were not ashamed of a real or fabulous affinity with a noble race, which in the revolutions of seven hundred years has been often illustrated by merit and always by fortune. About the end of the thirteenth century, the most powerful branch was composed of an uncle and six bothers, all conspicuous in arms, or in the honors of the church. Of these, Peter was elected senator of Rome, introduced to the Capitol in a triumphal car, and hailed in some vain acclamations with the title of Cæsar; while John and Stephen were declared marquis of Ancona and count of Romagna, by Nicholas the Fourth, a patron so partial to their family, that he has been delineated in satirical portraits, imprisoned as it were in a hollow pillar. After his decease their haughty behavior provoked the displeasure of the most implacable of mankind. The two cardinals, the uncle and the nephew, denied the election of Boniface the Eighth; and the Colonna were oppressed for a moment by his temporal and spiritual arms. He proclaimed a crusade against his personal enemies; their estates were confiscated; their fortresses on either side of the Tyber were besieged by the troops of St. Peter and those of the rival nobles; and after the ruin of Palestrina or Præneste, their principal seat, the ground was marked with a ploughshare, the emblem of perpetual desolation. Degraded, banished, proscribed, the six brothers, in disguise and danger, wandered over Europe without renouncing the hope of deliverance and revenge. In this double hope, the French court was their surest asylum; they prompted and directed the enterprise of Philip; and I should praise their magnanimity, had they respected the misfortune and courage of the captive tyrant. His civil acts were annulled by the Roman people, who restored the honors and possessions of the Colonna; and some estimate may be formed of their wealth by their losses, of their losses by the damages of one hundred thousand gold florins which were granted them against the accomplices and heirs of the deceased pope. All the spiritual censures and disqualifications were abolished by his prudent successors; and the fortune of the house was more firmly established by this transient hurricane. The boldness of Sciarra Colonna was signalized in the captivity of Boniface, and long afterwards in the coronation of Lewis of Bavaria; and by the gratitude of the emperor, the pillar in their arms was encircled with a royal crown. But the first of the family in fame and merit was the elder Stephen, whom Petrarch loved and esteemed as a hero superior to his own times, and not unworthy of ancient Rome. Persecution and exile displayed to the nations his abilities in peace and war; in his distress he was an object, not of pity, but of reverence; the aspect of danger provoked him to avow his name and country; and when he was asked, "Where is now your fortress?" he laid his hand on his heart, and answered, "Here." He supported with the same virtue the return of prosperity; and, till the ruin of his declining age, the ancestors, the character, and the children of Stephen Colonna, exalted his dignity in the Roman republic, and at the court of Avignon. II. The Ursini migrated from Spoleto; the sons of Ursus, as they are styled in the twelfth century, from some eminent person, who is only known as the father of their race. But they were soon distinguished among the nobles of Rome, by the number and bravery of their kinsmen, the strength of their towers, the honors of the senate and sacred college, and the elevation of two popes, Celestin the Third and Nicholas the Third, of their name and lineage. Their riches may be accused as an early abuse of nepotism: the estates of St. Peter were alienated in their favor by the liberal Celestin; and Nicholas was ambitious for their sake to solicit the alliance of monarchs; to found new kingdoms in Lombardy and Tuscany; and to invest them with the perpetual office of senators of Rome. All that has been observed of the greatness of the Colonna will likewise redound to the glory of the Ursini, their constant and equal antagonists in the long hereditary feud, which distracted above two hundred and fifty years the ecclesiastical state. The jealously of preeminence and power was the true ground of their quarrel; but as a specious badge of distinction, the Colonna embraced the name of Ghibelines and the party of the empire; the Ursini espoused the title of Guelphs and the cause of the church. The eagle and the keys were displayed in their adverse banners; and the two factions of Italy most furiously raged when the origin and nature of the dispute were long since forgotten. After the retreat of the popes to Avignon they disputed in arms the vacant republic; and the mischiefs of discord were perpetuated by the wretched compromise of electing each year two rival senators. By their private hostilities the city and country were desolated, and the fluctuating balance inclined with their alternate success. But none of either family had fallen by the sword, till the most renowned champion of the Ursini was surprised and slain by the younger Stephen Colonna. His triumph is stained with the reproach of violating the truce; their defeat was basely avenged by the assassination, before the church door, of an innocent boy and his two servants. Yet the victorious Colonna, with an annual colleague, was declared senator of Rome during the term of five years. And the muse of Petrarch inspired a wish, a hope, a prediction, that the generous youth, the son of his venerable hero, would restore Rome and Italy to their pristine glory; that his justice would extirpate the wolves and lions, the serpents and *bears*, who labored to subvert the eternal basis of the marble column.

– – – – Vallis te proxima misit,
Appenninigenæ qua prata virentia sylvæ
Spoletana metunt armenta gregesque protervi.
– – – – genuit quem nobilis Ursæ (Ursi?)
Progenies, Romana domus, veterataque magnis
Fascibus in clero, pompasque experta senatûs,
Bellorumque manû grandi stipata parentum
Cardineos apices necnon fastigia dudum
Papatûs iterata tenens.
Orsi, lupi, leoni, aquile e serpi
Al una gran marmorea colexna
Fanno noja sovente e à se danno.]

Final Settlement of the Ecclesiastical State. – Part One

Character and Coronation of Petrarch. – Restoration of the Freedom and Government of Rome by the Tribune Rienzi. – His Virtues and Vices, his Expulsion and Death. – Return of the Popes from Avignon. – Great Schism of the West. – Reunion of the Latin Church. – Last Struggles of Roman Liberty. – Statutes of Rome. – Final Settlement of the Ecclesiastical State.

IN THE APPREHENSION OF modern times, Petrarch is the Italian songster of Laura and love. In the harmony of his Tuscan rhymes, Italy applauds, or rather adores, the father of her lyric poetry; and his verse, or at least his name, is repeated by the enthusiasm, or affectation, of amorous sensibility. Whatever may be the private taste of a stranger, his slight and superficial knowledge should humbly acquiesce in the judgment of a learned nation; yet I may hope or presume, that the Italians do not compare the tedious uniformity of sonnets and elegies with the sublime compositions of their epic muse, the original wildness of Dante, the regular beauties of Tasso, and the boundless variety of the incomparable Ariosto. The merits of the lover I am still less qualified to appreciate: nor am I deeply interested in a metaphysical passion for a nymph so shadowy, that her existence has been questioned; for a matron so prolific, that she was delivered of eleven legitimate children, while her amorous swain sighed and sung at the fountain of Vaucluse. But in the eyes of Petrarch, and those of his graver contemporaries, his love was a sin, and Italian verse a frivolous amusement. His Latin works of philosophy, poetry, and eloquence, established his serious reputation, which was soon diffused from Avignon over France and Italy: his friends and disciples were multiplied in every city; and if the ponderous volume of his writings be now abandoned to a long repose, our gratitude must applaud the man, who by precept and example revived the spirit and study of the Augustan age. From his earliest youth, Petrarch aspired to the poetic crown. The academical honors of the three faculties had introduced a royal degree of master or doctor in the art of poetry; and the title of poet-laureate, which custom, rather than vanity, perpetuates in the English court, was first invented by the Cæsars of Germany. In the musical games of antiquity, a prize was bestowed on the victor: the belief that Virgil and Horace had been crowned in the Capitol inflamed the emulation of a Latin bard; and the laurel was endeared to the lover by a verbal resemblance with the name of his mistress. The value of either object was enhanced by the difficulties of the pursuit; and if the virtue or prudence of Laura was inexorable, he enjoyed, and might boast of enjoying, the nymph of poetry. His vanity was not of the most delicate kind, since he applauds the success of his own *labors*; his name was popular; his friends were active; the open or secret opposition of envy and prejudice was surmounted by the dexterity of patient merit. In the thirty-sixth year of his age, he was solicited to accept the object of his wishes; and on the same day, in the solitude of Vaucluse, he received a similar and solemn invitation from the senate of Rome and the university of Paris. The learning of a theological school, and the ignorance of a lawless city, were alike unqualified to bestow the ideal though immortal wreath which genius may obtain from the free applause of the public and of posterity: but the candidate dismissed this troublesome reflection; and after some moments of complacency and suspense, preferred the summons of the metropolis of the world.

The ceremony of his coronation was performed in the Capitol, by his friend and patron the supreme magistrate of the republic. Twelve patrician youths were arrayed in scarlet; six representatives of the most illustrious families, in green robes, with garlands of flowers, accompanied the procession; in the midst of the princes and nobles, the senator, count of Anguillara, a kinsman of the Colonna, assumed his throne; and at the voice of a herald Petrarch arose. After discoursing on a text of Virgil, and thrice repeating his vows for the prosperity of Rome, he knelt before the throne, and received from the senator a laurel crown, with a more precious declaration, "This is the reward of merit." The people shouted, "Long life to the Capitol and the poet!" A sonnet in praise of Rome was accepted as the effusion of genius and gratitude; and after the whole procession had visited the Vatican, the profane wreath was suspended before the shrine of St. Peter. In the act or diploma which was presented to Petrarch, the title and prerogatives of poet-laureate are revived in the Capitol, after the lapse of thirteen hundred years; and he receives the perpetual privilege of wearing, at his choice, a crown of laurel, ivy, or myrtle, of assuming the poetic habit, and of teaching, disputing, interpreting, and composing, in all places whatsoever, and on all subjects of literature. The grant was ratified by the authority of the senate and people; and the character of citizen was the recompense of his affection for the Roman name. They did him honor, but they did him justice. In the familiar society of Cicero and Livy, he had imbibed the ideas of an ancient patriot; and his ardent fancy kindled every idea to a sentiment, and every sentiment to a passion. The aspect of the seven hills and their majestic ruins confirmed these lively impressions; and he loved a country by whose liberal spirit he had been crowned and adopted. The poverty and debasement of Rome excited the indignation and pity of her grateful son; he dissembled the faults of his fellow-citizens; applauded with partial fondness the last of their heroes and matrons; and in the remembrance of the past, in the hopes of the future, was pleased to forget the miseries of the present time. Rome was still the lawful mistress of the world: the pope and the emperor, the bishop and general, had abdicated their station by an inglorious retreat to the Rhône and the Danube; but if she could resume her virtue, the republic might again vindicate her liberty and dominion. Amidst the indulgence of enthusiasm and eloquence, Petrarch, Italy, and Europe, were astonished by a revolution which realized for a moment his most splendid visions. The rise and fall of the tribune Rienzi will occupy the following pages: the subject is interesting, the materials are rich, and the glance of a patriot bard will sometimes vivify the copious, but simple, narrative of the Florentine, and more especially of the Roman, historian.

In a quarter of the city which was inhabited only by mechanics and Jews, the marriage of an innkeeper and a washer woman produced the future deliverer of Rome. From such parents Nicholas Rienzi Gabrini could inherit neither dignity nor fortune; and the gift of a liberal education, which they painfully bestowed, was the cause of his glory and untimely end. The study of history and eloquence, the writings of Cicero, Seneca, Livy, Cæsar, and Valerius Maximus, elevated above his equals and contemporaries the genius of the young plebeian: he perused with indefatigable diligence the manuscripts and marbles of antiquity; loved to dispense his knowledge in familiar language; and was often provoked to exclaim, "Where are now these Romans? their virtue, their justice, their power? why was I not born in those happy times?" When the republic addressed to the throne of Avignon an embassy of the three orders, the spirit and eloquence of Rienzi recommended him to a place among the thirteen deputies of the commons. The orator had the honor of haranguing Pope Clement the Sixth, and the satisfaction of conversing with Petrarch, a congenial mind: but his aspiring hopes were chilled by disgrace and poverty and the patriot was reduced to a single garment and the charity of the hospital. From this misery he was relieved by the sense of merit or the smile of favor; and the employment of apostolic notary afforded him a daily stipend of five gold florins, a more honorable and extensive connection, and the right of contrasting, both in words and actions, his own integrity with the vices of the state. The eloquence of Rienzi was prompt and persuasive: the multitude is always prone to envy and censure: he was stimulated by the loss of a brother and the impunity of the assassins; nor was it possible to excuse or exaggerate the public calamities. The blessings of peace and justice, for which civil society has been instituted, were banished from Rome: the jealous citizens, who might have endured every personal or pecuniary injury, were most deeply wounded in the dishonor of their wives and daughters: they were equally oppressed by the arrogance of the nobles and the corruption of the magistrates; and the abuse of arms or of laws was the only circumstance that distinguished the lions from the dogs and serpents of the Capitol. These allegorical emblems were variously repeated in the pictures which Rienzi exhibited in the streets and churches; and while the spectators gazed with curious wonder, the bold and ready orator unfolded the meaning, applied the satire, inflamed their passions, and announced a distant hope of comfort and deliverance. The privileges of Rome, her eternal sovereignty over her princes and provinces, was the theme of his public and private discourse; and a monument of servitude became in his hands a title and incentive of liberty. The decree of the senate, which granted the most ample prerogatives to the emperor Vespasian, had been inscribed on a copper plate still extant in the choir of the church of St. John Lateran. A numerous assembly of nobles and plebeians was invited to this political lecture, and a convenient theatre was erected for their reception. The notary appeared in a magnificent and mysterious habit, explained the inscription by a version and commentary, and descanted with eloquence and zeal on the ancient glories of the senate and people, from whom all legal authority was derived. The supine ignorance of the nobles was incapable of discerning the serious tendency of such representations: they might sometimes chastise with words and blows the plebeian reformer; but he was often suffered in the Colonna palace to amuse the company with his threats and predictions; and the modern Brutus was concealed under the mask of folly and the character of a buffoon. While they indulged their contempt, the restoration of the *good estate*, his favorite expression, was entertained among the people as a desirable, a possible, and at length as an approaching, event; and while all had the disposition to applaud, some had the courage to assist, their promised deliverer.

A prophecy, or rather a summons, affixed on the church door of St. George, was the first public evidence of his designs; a nocturnal assembly of a hundred citizens on Mount Aventine, the first step to their execution. After an oath of secrecy and aid, he represented to the conspirators the importance and facility of their enterprise; that the nobles, without union or resources, were strong only in the fear nobles, of their imaginary strength; that all power, as well as right, was in the hands of the people; that the revenues of the apostolical chamber might relieve the public distress; and that the pope himself would approve their victory over the common enemies of government and freedom. After securing a faithful band to protect his first declaration, he proclaimed through the city, by sound of trumpet, that on the evening of the following day, all persons should assemble without arms before the church of St. Angelo, to provide for the reestablishment of the good estate. The whole night was employed in the celebration of thirty masses of the Holy Ghost; and in the morning, Rienzi, bareheaded, but in complete armor, issued from the church, encompassed by the hundred conspirators. The pope's vicar, the simple bishop of Orvieto, who had been persuaded to sustain a part in this singular ceremony, marched on his right hand; and three great standards were borne aloft as the emblems of their design. In the first, the banner of *liberty*, Rome was seated on two lions, with a palm in one hand and a globe in the other; St. Paul, with a drawn sword, was delineated in the banner of *justice*; and in the third, St. Peter held the keys of *concord* and *peace*. Rienzi was encouraged by the presence and applause of an innumerable crowd, who understood little, and hoped much; and the procession slowly rolled forwards from the castle of St. Angelo to the Capitol. His triumph was disturbed by some secret emotions which he labored to suppress: he ascended without opposition, and with seeming confidence, the citadel of the republic; harangued the people from the balcony; and received the most flattering confirmation of his acts and laws. The nobles, as if destitute of arms and counsels, beheld in silent consternation this strange revolution; and the moment had been prudently chosen, when the most formidable, Stephen Colonna, was absent from the city. On the first rumor, he returned to his palace, affected to despise this plebeian tumult, and declared to the messenger of Rienzi, that at his leisure he would cast the madman from the windows of the Capitol. The great bell instantly rang an alarm, and so rapid was the tide, so urgent was the danger, that Colonna escaped with precipitation to the suburb of St. Laurence: from thence, after a moment's refreshment, he continued the same speedy career till he reached in safety his castle of Palestrina; lamenting his own imprudence, which had not trampled the spark of this mighty conflagration. A general and peremptory order was issued from the Capitol to all the nobles, that they should peaceably retire to their estates: they obeyed; and their departure secured the tranquillity of the free and obedient citizens of Rome.

But such voluntary obedience evaporates with the first transports of zeal; and Rienzi felt the importance of justifying his usurpation by a regular form and a legal title. At his own choice, the Roman people would have displayed their attachment and authority, by lavishing on his head the names of senator or consul, of king or emperor: he preferred the ancient and modest appellation of tribune; the protection of the commons was the essence of that sacred office; and they were ignorant, that it had never been invested with any share in the legislative or executive powers of the republic. In this character, and with the consent of the Roman, the tribune enacted the most salutary laws for the restoration and maintenance of the good estate. By the first he fulfils the wish of honesty and inexperience, that no civil suit should be protracted beyond the term of fifteen days. The danger of frequent perjury might justify the pronouncing against a false accuser the same penalty which his evidence would have inflicted: the disorders of the times might compel the legislator to punish every homicide with death, and every injury with equal retaliation. But the execution of justice was hopeless till he had previously abolished the tyranny of the nobles. It was formally provided, that none, except the supreme magistrate, should possess or command the gates, bridges, or towers of the state; that no private garrisons should be introduced into the towns or castles of the Roman territory; that none should bear arms, or presume to fortify their houses in the city or country; that the barons should be responsible for the safety of the highways, and the free passage of provisions; and that the protection of malefactors and robbers should be expiated by a fine of a thousand marks of silver. But these regulations would have been impotent and nugatory, had not the licentious nobles been awed by the sword of the civil power. A sudden alarm from the bell of the Capitol could still summon to the standard above twenty thousand volunteers: the support of the tribune and the laws required a more regular and permanent force. In each harbor of the coast a vessel was stationed for the assurance of commerce; a standing militia of three hundred and sixty horse and thirteen hundred foot was levied, clothed, and paid in the thirteen quarters of the city: and the spirit of a commonwealth may be traced in the grateful allowance of one hundred florins, or pounds, to the heirs of every soldier who lost his life in the service of his country. For the maintenance of the public defence, for the establishment of granaries, for the relief of widows, orphans, and indigent convents, Rienzi applied, without fear of sacrilege, the revenues of the apostolic chamber: the three branches of hearth-money, the salt-duty, and the customs, were each of the annual produce of one hundred thousand florins; and scandalous were the abuses, if in four or five months the amount of the salt-duty could be trebled by his judicious economy. After thus restoring the forces and finances of the republic, the tribune recalled the nobles from their solitary independence; required their personal appearance in the Capitol; and imposed an oath of allegiance to the new government, and of submission to the laws of the good estate. Apprehensive for their safety, but still more apprehensive of the danger of a refusal, the princes and barons returned to their houses at Rome in the garb of simple and peaceful citizens: the Colonna and Ursini, the Savelli and Frangipani, were confounded before the tribunal of a plebeian, of the vile buffoon whom they had so often derided, and their disgrace was aggravated by the indignation which they vainly struggled to disguise. The same oath was successively pronounced by the several orders of society, the clergy and gentlemen, the judges and notaries, the merchants and artisans, and the gradual descent was marked by the increase of sincerity and zeal. They swore to live and die with the republic and the church, whose interest was artfully united by the nominal association of the bishop of Orvieto, the pope's vicar, to the office of tribune. It was the boast of Rienzi, that he had delivered the throne and patrimony of St. Peter from a rebellious aristocracy; and Clement the Sixth, who rejoiced in its fall, affected to believe the professions, to applaud the merits, and to confirm the title, of his trusty servant. The speech, perhaps the mind, of the tribune, was inspired with a lively regard for the purity of the faith: he insinuated his claim to a supernatural mission from the Holy Ghost; enforced by a heavy forfeiture the annual duty of confession and communion; and strictly guarded the spiritual as well as temporal welfare of his faithful people.

Final Settlement of the Ecclesiastical State. – Part Two

NEVER PERHAPS HAS THE energy and effect of a single mind been more remarkably felt than in the sudden, though transient, reformation of Rome by the tribune Rienzi. A den of robbers was converted to the discipline of a camp or convent: patient to hear, swift to redress, inexorable to punish, his tribunal was always accessible to the poor and stranger; nor could birth, or dignity, or the immunities of the church, protect the offender or his accomplices. The privileged houses, the private sanctuaries in Rome, on which no officer of justice would presume to trespass, were abolished; and he applied the timber and iron of their barricades in the fortifications of the Capitol. The venerable father of the Colonna was exposed in his own palace to the double shame of being desirous, and of being unable, to protect a criminal. A mule, with a jar of oil, had been stolen near Capranica; and the lord of the Ursini family was condemned to restore the damage, and to discharge a fine of four hundred florins for his negligence in guarding the highways. Nor were the persons of the barons more inviolate than their lands or houses; and, either from accident or design, the same impartial rigor was exercised against the heads of the adverse factions. Peter Agapet Colonna, who had himself been senator of Rome, was arrested in the street for injury or debt; and justice was appeased by the tardy execution of Martin Ursini, who, among his various acts of violence and rapine, had pillaged a shipwrecked vessel at the mouth of the Tyber. His name, the purple of two cardinals, his uncles, a recent marriage, and a mortal disease were disregarded by the inflexible tribune, who had chosen his victim. The public officers dragged him from his palace and nuptial bed: his trial was short and satisfactory: the bell of the Capitol convened the people: stripped of his mantle, on his knees, with his hands bound behind his back, he heard the sentence of death; and after a brief confession, Ursini was led away to the gallows. After such an example, none who were conscious of guilt could hope for impunity, and the flight of the wicked, the licentious, and the idle, soon purified the city and territory of Rome. In this time (says the historian,) the woods began to rejoice that they were no longer infested with robbers; the oxen began to plough; the pilgrims visited the sanctuaries; the roads and inns were replenished with travellers; trade, plenty, and good faith, were restored in the markets; and a purse of gold might be exposed without danger in the midst of the highway. As soon as the life and property of the subject are secure, the labors and rewards of industry spontaneously revive: Rome was still the metropolis of the Christian world; and the fame and fortunes of the tribune were diffused in every country by the strangers who had enjoyed the blessings of his government.

The deliverance of his country inspired Rienzi with a vast, and perhaps visionary, idea of uniting Italy in a great federative republic, of which Rome should be the ancient and lawful head, and the free cities and princes the members and associates. His pen was not less eloquent than his tongue; and his numerous epistles were delivered to swift and trusty messengers. On foot, with a white wand in their hand, they traversed the forests and mountains; enjoyed, in the most hostile states, the sacred security of ambassadors; and reported, in the style of flattery or truth, that the highways along their passage were lined with kneeling multitudes, who implored Heaven for the success of their undertaking. Could passion have listened to reason; could private interest have yielded to the public welfare; the supreme tribunal and confederate union of the Italian republic might have healed their intestine discord, and closed the Alps against the Barbarians of the North. But the propitious season had elapsed; and if Venice, Florence, Sienna, Perugia, and many inferior cities offered their lives and fortunes to the good estate, the tyrants of Lombardy and Tuscany must despise, or hate, the plebeian author of a free constitution. From them, however, and from every part of Italy, the tribune received the most friendly and respectful answers: they were followed by the ambassadors of the princes and republics; and in this foreign conflux, on all the occasions of pleasure or business, the low born notary could assume the familiar or majestic courtesy of a sovereign. The most glorious circumstance of his reign was an appeal to his justice from Lewis, king of Hungary, who complained, that his brother and her husband had been perfidiously strangled by Jane, queen of Naples: her guilt or innocence was pleaded in a solemn trial at Rome; but after hearing the advocates, the tribune adjourned this weighty and invidious cause, which was soon determined by the sword of the Hungarian. Beyond the Alps, more especially at Avignon, the revolution was the theme of curiosity, wonder, and applause. Petrarch had been the private friend, perhaps the secret counsellor, of Rienzi: his writings breathe the most ardent spirit of patriotism and joy; and all respect for the pope, all gratitude for the Colonna, was lost in the superior duties of a Roman citizen. The poet-laureate of the Capitol maintains the act, applauds the hero, and mingles with some apprehension and advice, the most lofty hopes of the permanent and rising greatness of the republic.

While Petrarch indulged these prophetic visions, the Roman hero was fast declining from the meridian of fame and power; and the people, who had gazed with astonishment on the ascending meteor, began to mark the irregularity of its course, and the vicissitudes of light and obscurity. More eloquent than judicious, more enterprising than resolute, the faculties of Rienzi were not balanced by cool and commanding reason: he magnified in a tenfold proportion the objects of hope and fear; and prudence, which could not have erected, did not presume to fortify, his throne. In the blaze of prosperity, his virtues were insensibly tinctured with the adjacent vices; justice with cruelty, liberality with profusion, and the desire of fame with puerile and ostentatious vanity. He might have learned, that the ancient tribunes, so strong and sacred in the public opinion, were not distinguished in style, habit, or appearance, from an ordinary plebeian; and that as often as they visited the city on foot, a single viator, or beadle, attended the exercise of their office. The Gracchi would have frowned or smiled, could they have read the sonorous titles and epithets of their successor, "Nicholas, severe and merciful; deliverer of Rome; defender of Italy; friend of mankind, and of liberty, peace, and justice; tribune august:" his theatrical pageants had prepared the revolution; but Rienzi abused, in luxury and pride, the political maxim of speaking to the eyes, as well as the understanding, of the multitude. From nature he had received the gift of a handsome person, till it was swelled and disfigured by intemperance: and his propensity to laughter was corrected in the magistrate by the affectation of gravity and sternness. He was clothed, at least on public occasions, in a party-colored robe of velvet or satin, lined with fur, and embroidered with gold: the rod of justice, which he carried in his hand, was a sceptre of polished steel, crowned with a globe and cross of gold, and enclosing a small fragment of the true and holy wood. In his civil and religious processions through the city, he rode on a white steed, the symbol of royalty: the great banner of the republic, a sun with a circle of stars, a dove with an olive branch, was displayed over his head; a shower of gold and silver was scattered among the populace, fifty guards with halberds encompassed his person; a troop of horse preceded his march; and their tymbals and trumpets were of massy silver.

The ambition of the honors of chivalry betrayed the meanness of his birth, and degraded the importance of his office; and the equestrian tribune was not less odious to the nobles, whom he adopted, than to the plebeians, whom he deserted. All that yet remained of treasure, or luxury, or art, was exhausted on that solemn day. Rienzi led the procession from the Capitol to the Lateran; the tediousness of the way was relieved with decorations and games; the ecclesiastical, civil, and military orders marched under their various banners; the Roman ladies attended his wife; and the ambassadors of Italy might loudly applaud or secretly deride the novelty of the pomp. In the evening, which they had reached the church and palace of Constantine, he thanked and dismissed the numerous assembly, with an invitation to the festival of the ensuing day. From the hands of a venerable knight he received the order of the Holy Ghost; the purification of the bath was a previous ceremony; but in no step of his life did Rienzi excite such scandal and censure as by the profane use of the porphyry vase, in which Constantine (a foolish legend) had been healed of his leprosy by Pope Sylvester. With equal presumption the tribune watched or reposed within the consecrated precincts of the baptistery; and the failure of his state-bed was interpreted as an omen of his approaching downfall. At the hour of worship, he showed himself to the returning crowds in a majestic attitude, with a robe of purple, his sword, and gilt spurs; but the holy rites were soon interrupted by his levity and insolence. Rising from his throne, and advancing towards the congregation, he proclaimed in a loud voice: "We summon to our tribunal Pope Clement: and command him to reside in his diocese of Rome: we also summon the sacred college of cardinals. We again summon the two pretenders, Charles of Bohemia and Lewis of Bavaria, who style themselves emperors: we likewise summon all the electors of Germany, to inform us on what pretence they have usurped the inalienable right of the Roman people, the ancient and lawful sovereigns of the empire." Unsheathing his maiden sword, he thrice brandished it to the three parts of the world, and thrice repeated the extravagant declaration, "And this too is mine!" The pope's vicar, the bishop of Orvieto, attempted to check this career of folly; but his feeble protest was silenced by martial music; and instead of withdrawing from the assembly, he consented to dine with his brother tribune, at a table which had hitherto been reserved for the supreme pontiff. A banquet, such as the Cæsars had given, was prepared for the Romans. The apartments, porticos, and courts of the Lateran were spread with innumerable tables for either sex, and every condition; a stream of wine flowed from the nostrils of Constantine's brazen horse; no complaint, except of the scarcity of water, could be heard; and the licentiousness of the multitude was curbed by discipline and fear. A subsequent day was appointed for the coronation of Rienzi; seven crowns of different leaves or metals were successively placed on his head by the most eminent of the Roman clergy; they represented the seven gifts of the Holy Ghost; and he still professed to imitate the example of the ancient tribunes. These extraordinary spectacles might deceive or flatter the people; and their own vanity was gratified in the vanity of their leader. But in his private life he soon deviated from the strict rule of frugality and abstinence; and the plebeians, who were awed by the splendor of the nobles, were provoked by the luxury of their equal. His wife, his son, his uncle, (a barber in name and profession,) exposed the contrast of vulgar manners and princely expense; and without acquiring the majesty, Rienzi degenerated into the vices, of a king.

A simple citizen describes with pity, or perhaps with pleasure, the humiliation of the barons of Rome. "Bareheaded, their hands crossed on their breast, they stood with downcast looks in the presence of the tribune; and they trembled, good God, how they trembled!" As long as the yoke of Rienzi was that of justice and their country, their conscience forced them to esteem the man, whom pride and interest provoked them to hate: his extravagant conduct soon fortified their hatred by contempt; and they conceived the hope of subverting a power which was no longer so deeply rooted in the public confidence. The old animosity of the Colonna and Ursini was suspended for a moment by their common disgrace: they associated their wishes, and perhaps their designs; an assassin was seized and tortured; he accused the nobles; and as soon as Rienzi deserved the fate, he adopted the suspicions and maxims, of a tyrant. On the same day, under various pretences, he invited to the Capitol his principal enemies, among whom were five members of the Ursini and three of the Colonna name. But instead of a council or a banquet, they found themselves prisoners under the sword of despotism or justice; and the consciousness of innocence or guilt might inspire them with equal apprehensions of danger. At the sound of the great bell the people assembled; they were arraigned for a conspiracy against the tribune's life; and though some might sympathize in their distress, not a hand, nor a voice, was raised to rescue the first of the nobility from their impending doom. Their apparent boldness was prompted by despair; they passed in separate chambers a sleepless and painful night; and the venerable hero, Stephen Colonna, striking against the door of his prison, repeatedly urged his guards to deliver him by a speedy death from such ignominious servitude. In the morning they understood their sentence from the visit of a confessor and the tolling of the bell. The great hall of the Capitol had been decorated for the bloody scene with red and white hangings: the countenance of the tribune was dark and severe; the swords of the executioners were unsheathed; and the barons were interrupted in their dying speeches by the sound of trumpets. But in this decisive moment, Rienzi was not less anxious or apprehensive than his captives: he dreaded the splendor of their names, their surviving kinsmen, the inconstancy of the people, the reproaches of the world, and, after rashly offering a mortal injury, he vainly presumed that, if he could forgive, he might himself be forgiven. His elaborate oration was that of a Christian and a suppliant; and, as the humble minister of the commons, he entreated his masters to pardon these noble criminals, for whose repentance and future service he pledged his faith and authority. "If you are spared," said the tribune, "by the mercy of the Romans, will you not promise to support the good estate with your lives and fortunes?" Astonished by this marvellous clemency, the barons bowed their heads; and while they devoutly repeated the oath of allegiance, might whisper a secret, and more sincere, assurance of revenge. A priest, in the name of the people, pronounced their absolution: they received the communion with the tribune, assisted at the banquet, followed the procession; and, after every spiritual and temporal sign of reconciliation, were dismissed in safety to their respective homes, with the new honors and titles of generals, consuls, and patricians.

During some weeks they were checked by the memory of their danger, rather than of their deliverance, till the most powerful of the Ursini, escaping with the Colonna from the city, erected at Marino the standard of rebellion. The fortifications of the castle were instantly restored; the vassals attended their lord; the outlaws armed against the magistrate; the flocks and herds, the harvests and vineyards, from Marino to the gates of Rome, were swept away or destroyed; and the people arraigned Rienzi as the author of the calamities which his government had taught them to forget. In the camp, Rienzi appeared to less advantage than in the rostrum; and he neglected the progress of the rebel barons till their numbers were strong, and their castles impregnable. From the pages of

Livy he had not imbibed the art, or even the courage, of a general: an army of twenty thousand Romans returned without honor or effect from the attack of Marino; and his vengeance was amused by painting his enemies, their heads downwards, and drowning two dogs (at least they should have been bears) as the representatives of the Ursini. The belief of his incapacity encouraged their operations: they were invited by their secret adherents; and the barons attempted, with four thousand foot, and sixteen hundred horse, to enter Rome by force or surprise. The city was prepared for their reception; the alarm-bell rung all night; the gates were strictly guarded, or insolently open; and after some hesitation they sounded a retreat. The two first divisions had passed along the walls, but the prospect of a free entrance tempted the headstrong valor of the nobles in the rear; and after a successful skirmish, they were overthrown and massacred without quarter by the crowds of the Roman people. Stephen Colonna the younger, the noble spirit to whom Petrarch ascribed the restoration of Italy, was preceded or accompanied in death by his son John, a gallant youth, by his brother Peter, who might regret the ease and honors of the church, by a nephew of legitimate birth, and by two bastards of the Colonna race; and the number of seven, the seven crowns, as Rienzi styled them, of the Holy Ghost, was completed by the agony of the deplorable parent, and the veteran chief, who had survived the hope and fortune of his house. The vision and prophecies of St. Martin and Pope Boniface had been used by the tribune to animate his troops: he displayed, at least in the pursuit, the spirit of a hero; but he forgot the maxims of the ancient Romans, who abhorred the triumphs of civil war. The conqueror ascended the Capitol; deposited his crown and sceptre on the altar; and boasted, with some truth, that he had cut off an ear, which neither pope nor emperor had been able to amputate. His base and implacable revenge denied the honors of burial; and the bodies of the Colonna, which he threatened to expose with those of the vilest malefactors, were secretly interred by the holy virgins of their name and family. The people sympathized in their grief, repented of their own fury, and detested the indecent joy of Rienzi, who visited the spot where these illustrious victims had fallen. It was on that fatal spot that he conferred on his son the honor of knighthood: and the ceremony was accomplished by a slight blow from each of the horsemen of the guard, and by a ridiculous and inhuman ablution from a pool of water, which was yet polluted with patrician blood.

A short delay would have saved the Colonna, the delay of a single month, which elapsed between the triumph and the exile of Rienzi. In the pride of victory, he forfeited what yet remained of his civil virtues, without acquiring the fame of military prowess. A free and vigorous opposition was formed in the city; and when the tribune proposed in the public council to impose a new tax, and to regulate the government of Perugia, thirty-nine members voted against his measures; repelled the injurious charge of treachery and corruption; and urged him to prove, by their forcible exclusion, that if the populace adhered to his cause, it was already disclaimed by the most respectable citizens. The pope and the sacred college had never been dazzled by his specious professions; they were justly offended by the insolence of his conduct; a cardinal legate was sent to Italy, and after some fruitless treaty, and two personal interviews, he fulminated a bull of excommunication, in which the tribune is degraded from his office, and branded with the guilt of rebellion, sacrilege, and heresy. The surviving barons of Rome were now humbled to a sense of allegiance; their interest and revenge engaged them in the service of the church; but as the fate of the Colonna was before their eyes, they abandoned to a private adventurer the peril and glory of the revolution. John Pepin, count of Minorbino, in the kingdom of Naples, had been condemned for his crimes, or his riches, to perpetual imprisonment; and Petrarch, by soliciting his release, indirectly contributed to the ruin of his friend. At the head of one hundred and fifty soldiers, the count of Minorbino introduced himself into Rome; barricaded the quarter of the Colonna: and found the enterprise as easy as it had seemed impossible. From the first alarm, the bell of the Capitol incessantly tolled; but, instead of repairing to the well-known sound, the people were silent and inactive; and the pusillanimous Rienzi, deploring their ingratitude with sighs and tears, abdicated the government and palace of the republic.

CHAPTER SEVENTY

Final Settlement of the Ecclesiastical State. – Part Three

WITHOUT DRAWING HIS SWORD, count Pepin restored the aristocracy and the church; three senators were chosen, and the legate, assuming the first rank, accepted his two colleagues from the rival families of Colonna and Ursini. The acts of the tribune were abolished, his head was proscribed; yet such was the terror of his name, that the barons hesitated three days before they would trust themselves in the city, and Rienzi was left above a month in the castle of St. Angelo, from whence he peaceably withdrew, after laboring, without effect, to revive the affection and courage of the Romans. The vision of freedom and empire had vanished: their fallen spirit would have acquiesced in servitude, had it been smoothed by tranquillity and order; and it was scarcely observed, that the new senators derived their authority from the Apostolic See; that four cardinals were appointed to reform, with dictatorial power, the state of the republic. Rome was again agitated by the bloody feuds of the barons, who detested each other, and despised the commons: their hostile fortresses, both in town and country, again rose, and were again demolished: and the peaceful citizens, a flock of sheep, were devoured, says the Florentine historian, by these rapacious wolves. But when their pride and avarice had exhausted the patience of the Romans, a confraternity of the Virgin Mary protected or avenged the republic: the bell of the Capitol was again tolled, the nobles in arms trembled in the presence of an unarmed multitude; and of the two senators, Colonna escaped from the window of the palace, and Ursini was stoned at the foot of the altar. The dangerous office of tribune was successively occupied by two plebeians, Cerroni and Baroncelli. The mildness of Cerroni was unequal to the times; and after a faint struggle, he retired with a fair reputation and a decent fortune to the comforts of rural life. Devoid of eloquence or genius, Baroncelli was distinguished by a resolute spirit: he spoke the language of a patriot, and trod in the footsteps of tyrants; his suspicion was a sentence of death, and his own death was the reward of his cruelties. Amidst the public misfortunes, the faults of Rienzi were forgotten; and the Romans sighed for the peace and prosperity of their good estate.

After an exile of seven years, the first deliverer was again restored to his country. In the disguise of a monk or a pilgrim, he escaped from the castle of St. Angelo, implored the friendship of the king of Hungary at Naples, tempted the ambition of every bold adventurer, mingled at Rome with the pilgrims of the jubilee, lay concealed among the hermits of the Apennine, and wandered through the cities of Italy, Germany, and Bohemia. His person was invisible, his name was yet formidable; and the anxiety of the court of Avignon supposes, and even magnifies, his personal merit. The emperor Charles the Fourth gave audience to a stranger, who frankly revealed himself as the tribune of the republic; and astonished an assembly of ambassadors and princes, by the eloquence of a patriot and the visions of a prophet, the downfall of tyranny and the kingdom of the Holy Ghost. Whatever had been his hopes, Rienzi found himself a captive; but he supported a character of independence and dignity, and obeyed, as his own choice, the irresistible summons of the supreme pontiff. The zeal of Petrarch, which had been cooled by the unworthy conduct, was rekindled by the sufferings and the presence, of his friend; and he boldly complains of the times, in which the savior of Rome was delivered by her emperor into the hands of her bishop. Rienzi was transported slowly, but in safe custody, from Prague to Avignon: his entrance into the city was that of a malefactor; in his prison he was chained by the leg; and four cardinals were named to inquire into the crimes of heresy and rebellion. But his trial and condemnation would have involved some questions, which it was more prudent to leave under the veil of mystery: the temporal supremacy of the popes; the duty of residence; the civil and ecclesiastical privileges of the clergy and people of Rome. The reigning pontiff well deserved the appellation of *Clement*: the strange vicissitudes and magnanimous spirit of the captive excited his pity and esteem; and Petrarch believes that he respected in the hero the name and sacred character of a poet. Rienzi was indulged with an easy confinement and the use of books; and in the assiduous study of Livy and the Bible, he sought the cause and the consolation of his misfortunes.

The succeeding pontificate of Innocent the Sixth opened a new prospect of his deliverance and restoration; and the court of Avignon was persuaded, that the successful rebel could alone appease and reform the anarchy of the metropolis. After a solemn profession of fidelity, the Roman tribune was sent into Italy, with the title of senator; but the death of Baroncelli appeared to supersede the use of his mission; and the legate, Cardinal Albornoz, a consummate statesman, allowed him with reluctance, and without aid, to undertake the perilous experiment. His first reception was equal to his wishes: the day of his entrance was a public festival; and his eloquence and authority revived the laws of the good estate. But this momentary sunshine was soon clouded by his own vices and those of the people: in the Capitol, he might often regret the prison of Avignon; and after a second administration of four months, Rienzi was massacred in a tumult which had been fomented by the Roman barons. In the society of the Germans and Bohemians, he is said to have contracted the habits of intemperance and cruelty: adversity had chilled his enthusiasm, without fortifying his reason or virtue; and that youthful hope, that lively assurance, which is the pledge of success, was now succeeded by the cold impotence of distrust and despair. The tribune had reigned with absolute dominion, by the choice, and in the hearts, of the Romans: the senator was the servile minister of a foreign court; and while he was suspected by the people, he was abandoned by the prince. The legate Albornoz, who seemed desirous of his ruin, inflexibly refused all supplies of men and money; a faithful subject could no longer presume to touch the revenues of the apostolical chamber; and the first idea of a tax was the signal of clamor and sedition. Even his justice was tainted with the guilt or reproach of selfish cruelty: the most virtuous citizen of Rome was sacrificed to his jealousy; and in the execution of a public robber, from whose purse he had been assisted, the magistrate too much forgot, or too much remembered, the obligations of the debtor. A civil war exhausted his treasures, and the patience of the city: the Colonna maintained their hostile station at Palestrina; and his mercenaries soon despised a leader whose ignorance and fear were envious of all subordinate merit. In the death, as in the life, of Rienzi, the hero and the coward were strangely mingled. When the Capitol was invested by a furious multitude, when he was basely deserted by his civil and military servants, the intrepid senator, waving the banner of liberty, presented himself on the balcony, addressed his eloquence to the various passions of the Romans, and labored to persuade them, that in the same cause himself and the republic must either stand or fall. His oration was interrupted by a volley of imprecations and stones; and after an arrow had transpierced his hand, he sunk into abject despair, and fled weeping to the inner chambers, from whence he was let down by a sheet before the windows of the prison. Destitute of aid or hope, he was besieged till the evening: the doors of the Capitol were destroyed with axes and fire; and while the senator attempted to escape in a plebeian habit, he was discovered and dragged to the platform of the palace, the fatal scene of his judgments and executions. A whole hour, without voice or motion, he stood amidst the multitude half naked and half dead: their rage was hushed into curiosity and wonder: the last feelings of reverence and compassion yet struggled in his favor; and they might have prevailed, if a bold assassin had not plunged a dagger in his breast. He fell senseless with the first stroke: the impotent revenge of his enemies inflicted a thousand wounds: and the senator's body was abandoned to the dogs, to the Jews, and to the flames. Posterity will compare the virtues and failings of this extraordinary man; but in a long period of anarchy and servitude, the name of Rienzi has often been celebrated as the deliverer of his country, and the last of the Roman patriots.

The first and most generous wish of Petrarch was the restoration of a free republic; but after the exile and death of his plebeian hero, he turned his eyes from the tribune, to the king, of the Romans. The Capitol was yet stained with the blood of Rienzi, when Charles the Fourth descended from the Alps to obtain the Italian and Imperial crowns. In his passage through Milan he received the visit, and repaid the flattery, of the poet-laureate; accepted a medal of Augustus; and promised, without a smile, to imitate the founder of the Roman monarchy. A false application of the name and maxims of antiquity was the source of the hopes and disappointments of Petrarch; yet he could not overlook the difference of times and characters; the immeasurable distance between the first Cæsars and a Bohemian prince, who by the favor of the clergy had been elected the titular head of the German aristocracy. Instead of restoring to Rome her glory and her provinces, he had bound himself by a secret treaty with the pope, to evacuate the city on the day of his coronation; and his shameful retreat was pursued by the reproaches of the patriot bard.

After the loss of liberty and empire, his third and more humble wish was to reconcile the shepherd with his flock; to recall the Roman bishop to his ancient and peculiar diocese. In the fervor of youth, with the authority of age, Petrarch addressed his exhortations to five successive popes, and his eloquence was always inspired by the enthusiasm of sentiment and the freedom of language. The son of a citizen of Florence invariably preferred the country of his birth to that of his education; and Italy, in his eyes, was the queen and garden of the world. Amidst her domestic factions, she was doubtless superior to France both in art and science, in wealth and politeness; but the difference could scarcely support the epithet of barbarous, which he promiscuously bestows on the countries beyond the Alps. Avignon, the mystic Babylon, the sink of vice and corruption, was the object of his hatred and contempt; but he forgets that her scandalous vices were not the growth of the soil, and that in every residence they would adhere to the power and luxury of the papal court. He confesses that the successor of St. Peter is the bishop of the universal church; yet it was not on the banks of the Rhône, but of the Tyber, that the apostle had fixed his everlasting throne; and while every city in the Christian world was blessed with a bishop, the metropolis alone was desolate and forlorn. Since the removal of the Holy See, the sacred buildings of the Lateran and the Vatican, their altars and their saints, were left in a state of poverty and decay; and Rome was often painted under the image of a disconsolate matron, as if the wandering husband could be reclaimed by the homely portrait of the age and infirmities of his weeping spouse. But the cloud which hung over the seven hills would be dispelled by the presence of their lawful sovereign: eternal fame, the prosperity of Rome, and the peace of Italy, would be the recompense of the pope who should dare to embrace this generous resolution. Of the five whom Petrarch exhorted, the three first, John the Twenty-second, Benedict the Twelfth, and Clement the Sixth, were importuned or amused by the boldness of the orator; but the memorable change which had been attempted by Urban the Fifth was finally accomplished by Gregory the Eleventh. The execution of their design was opposed by weighty and almost insuperable obstacles. A king of France, who has deserved the epithet of wise, was unwilling to release them from a local dependence: the cardinals, for the most part his subjects, were attached to the language, manners, and climate of Avignon; to their stately palaces; above all, to the wines of Burgundy. In their eyes, Italy was foreign or hostile; and they reluctantly embarked at Marseilles, as if they had been sold or banished into the land of the Saracens. Urban the Fifth resided three years in the Vatican with safety and honor: his sanctity was protected by a guard of two thousand horse; and the king of Cyprus, the queen of Naples, and the emperors of the East and West, devoutly saluted their common father in the chair of St. Peter. But the joy of Petrarch and the Italians was soon turned into grief and indignation. Some reasons of public or private moment, his own impatience or the prayers of the cardinals, recalled Urban to France; and the approaching election was saved from the tyrannic patriotism of the Romans. The powers of heaven were interested in their cause: Bridget of Sweden, a saint and pilgrim, disapproved the return, and foretold the death, of Urban the Fifth: the migration of Gregory the Eleventh was encouraged by St. Catharine of Sienna, the spouse of Christ and ambassadress of the Florentines; and the popes themselves, the great masters of human credulity, appear to have listened to these visionary females. Yet those celestial admonitions were supported by some arguments of temporal policy. The residents of Avignon had been invaded by hostile violence: at the head of thirty thousand robbers, a hero had extorted ransom and absolution from the vicar of Christ and the sacred college; and the maxim of the French warriors, to spare the people and plunder the church, was a new heresy of the most dangerous import. While the pope was driven from Avignon, he was strenuously invited to Rome. The senate and people acknowledged him as their lawful sovereign, and laid at his feet the keys of the gates, the bridges, and the fortresses; of the quarter at least beyond the Tyber. But this loyal offer was accompanied by a declaration, that they could no longer suffer the scandal and calamity of his absence; and that his obstinacy would finally provoke them to revive and assert the primitive right of election. The abbot of Mount Cassin had been consulted, whether he would accept the triple crown from the clergy and people: "I am a citizen of Rome," replied that venerable ecclesiastic, "and my first law is, the voice of my country."

> *Squalida sed quoniam facies, neglectaque cultû*
> *Cæsaries; multisque malis lassata senectus*
> *Eripuit solitam effigiem: vetus accipe nomen;*
> *Roma vocor. (Carm. l. 2, p. 77.)*

If superstition will interpret an untimely death, if the merit of counsels be judged from the event, the heavens may seem to frown on a measure of such apparent season and propriety. Gregory the Eleventh did not survive above fourteen months his return to the Vatican; and his decease was followed by the great schism of the West, which distracted the Latin church above forty years. The sacred college was then composed of twenty-two cardinals: six of these had remained at Avignon; eleven Frenchmen, one Spaniard, and four Italians, entered the conclave in the usual form. Their choice was not yet limited to the purple; and their unanimous votes acquiesced in the archbishop of

Bari, a subject of Naples, conspicuous for his zeal and learning, who ascended the throne of St. Peter under the name of Urban the Sixth. The epistle of the sacred college affirms his free, and regular, election; which had been inspired, as usual, by the Holy Ghost; he was adored, invested, and crowned, with the customary rites; his temporal authority was obeyed at Rome and Avignon, and his ecclesiastical supremacy was acknowledged in the Latin world. During several weeks, the cardinals attended their new master with the fairest professions of attachment and loyalty; till the summer heats permitted a decent escape from the city. But as soon as they were united at Anagni and Fundi, in a place of security, they cast aside the mask, accused their own falsehood and hypocrisy, excommunicated the apostate and antichrist of Rome, and proceeded to a new election of Robert of Geneva, Clement the Seventh, whom they announced to the nations as the true and rightful vicar of Christ. Their first choice, an involuntary and illegal act, was annulled by fear of death and the menaces of the Romans; and their complaint is justified by the strong evidence of probability and fact. The twelve French cardinals, above two thirds of the votes, were masters of the election; and whatever might be their provincial jealousies, it cannot fairly be presumed that they would have sacrificed their right and interest to a foreign candidate, who would never restore them to their native country. In the various, and often inconsistent, narratives, the shades of popular violence are more darkly or faintly colored: but the licentiousness of the seditious Romans was inflamed by a sense of their privileges, and the danger of a second emigration. The conclave was intimidated by the shouts, and encompassed by the arms, of thirty thousand rebels; the bells of the Capitol and St. Peter's rang an alarm: "Death, or an Italian pope!" was the universal cry; the same threat was repeated by the twelve bannerets or chiefs of the quarters, in the form of charitable advice; some preparations were made for burning the obstinate cardinals; and had they chosen a Transalpine subject, it is probable that they would never have departed alive from the Vatican. The same constraint imposed the necessity of dissembling in the eyes of Rome and of the world; the pride and cruelty of Urban presented a more inevitable danger; and they soon discovered the features of the tyrant, who could walk in his garden and recite his breviary, while he heard from an adjacent chamber six cardinals groaning on the rack. His inflexible zeal, which loudly censured their luxury and vice, would have attached them to the stations and duties of their parishes at Rome; and had he not fatally delayed a new promotion, the French cardinals would have been reduced to a helpless minority in the sacred college. For these reasons, and the hope of repassing the Alps, they rashly violated the peace and unity of the church; and the merits of their double choice are yet agitated in the Catholic schools. The vanity, rather than the interest, of the nation determined the court and clergy of France. The states of Savoy, Sicily, Cyprus, Arragon, Castille, Navarre, and Scotland were inclined by their example and authority to the obedience of Clement the Seventh, and after his decease, of Benedict the Thirteenth. Rome and the principal states of Italy, Germany, Portugal, England, the Low Countries, and the kingdoms of the North, adhered to the prior election of Urban the Sixth, who was succeeded by Boniface the Ninth, Innocent the Seventh, and Gregory the Twelfth.

From the banks of the Tyber and the Rhône, the hostile pontiffs encountered each other with the pen and the sword: the civil and ecclesiastical order of society was disturbed; and the Romans had their full share of the mischiefs of which they may be arraigned as the primary authors. They had vainly flattered themselves with the hope of restoring the seat of the ecclesiastical monarchy, and of relieving their poverty with the tributes and offerings of the nations; but the separation of France and Spain diverted the stream of lucrative devotion; nor could the loss be compensated by the two jubilees which were crowded into the space of ten years. By the avocations of the schism, by foreign arms, and popular tumults, Urban the Sixth and his three successors were often compelled to interrupt their residence in the Vatican. The Colonna and Ursini still exercised their deadly feuds: the bannerets of Rome asserted and abused the privileges of a republic: the vicars of Christ, who had levied a military force, chastised their rebellion with the gibbet, the sword, and the dagger; and, in a friendly conference, eleven deputies of the people were perfidiously murdered and cast into the street. Since the invasion of Robert the Norman, the Romans had pursued their domestic quarrels without the dangerous interposition of a stranger. But in the disorders of the schism, an aspiring neighbor, Ladislaus king of Naples, alternately supported and betrayed the pope and the people; by the former he was declared *gonfalonier*, or general, of the church, while the latter submitted to his choice the nomination of their magistrates. Besieging Rome by land and water, he thrice entered the gates as a Barbarian conqueror; profaned the altars, violated the virgins, pillaged the merchants, performed his devotions at St. Peter's, and left a garrison in the castle of St. Angelo. His arms were sometimes unfortunate, and to a delay of three days he was indebted for his life and crown: but Ladislaus triumphed in his turn; and it was only his premature death that could save the metropolis and the ecclesiastical state from the ambitious conqueror, who had assumed the title, or at least the powers, of king of Rome.

I have not undertaken the ecclesiastical history of the schism; but Rome, the object of these last chapters, is deeply interested in the disputed succession of her sovereigns. The first counsels for the peace and union of Christendom arose from the university of Paris, from the faculty of the Sorbonne, whose doctors were esteemed, at least in the Gallican church, as the most consummate masters of theological science. Prudently waiving all invidious inquiry into the origin and merits of the dispute, they proposed, as a healing measure, that the two pretenders of Rome and Avignon should abdicate at the same time, after qualifying the cardinals of the adverse factions to join in a legitimate election; and that the nations should *subtract* their obedience, if either of the competitor preferred his own interest to that of the public. At each vacancy, these physicians of the church deprecated the mischiefs of a hasty choice; but the policy of the conclave and the ambition of its members were deaf to reason and entreaties; and whatsoever promises were made, the pope could never be bound by the oaths of the cardinal. During fifteen years, the pacific designs of the university were eluded by the arts of the rival pontiffs, the scruples or passions of their adherents, and the vicissitudes of French factions, that ruled the insanity of Charles the Sixth. At length a vigorous resolution was embraced; and a solemn embassy, of the titular patriarch of Alexandria, two archbishops, five bishops, five abbots, three knights, and twenty doctors, was sent to the courts of Avignon and Rome, to require, in the name of the church and king, the abdication of the two pretenders, of Peter de Luna, who styled himself Benedict the Thirteenth, and of Angelo Corrario, who assumed the name of Gregory the Twelfth. For the ancient honor of Rome, and the success of their commission, the ambassadors solicited a conference with the magistrates of the city, whom they gratified by a positive declaration, that the most Christian king did not entertain a wish of transporting the holy see from the Vatican, which he considered as the genuine and proper seat of the successor of St. Peter. In the name of the senate and people, an eloquent Roman asserted their desire to cooperate in the union of the church, deplored the temporal and spiritual calamities of the long schism, and requested the protection of France against the arms of the king of Naples. The answers of Benedict and Gregory were alike edifying and alike deceitful; and, in evading the demand of their abdication, the two rivals were animated by a common spirit. They agreed on the necessity of a previous interview; but the time, the place, and the manner, could never be ascertained by mutual consent. "If the one advances," says a servant of Gregory, "the other retreats; the one appears an animal fearful of the land, the other a creature apprehensive of the water. And thus, for a short remnant of life and power, will these aged priests endanger the peace and salvation of the Christian world."

The Christian world was at length provoked by their obstinacy and fraud: they were deserted by their cardinals, who embraced each other as friends and colleagues; and their revolt was supported by a numerous assembly of prelates and ambassadors. With equal justice, the council of Pisa deposed the popes of Rome and Avignon; the conclave was unanimous in the choice of Alexander the Fifth, and his vacant seat was soon filled by a similar election of John the Twenty-third, the most profligate of mankind. But instead of extinguishing the schism, the rashness of the French and Italians had given a third pretender to the chair of St. Peter. Such new claims of the synod and conclave were disputed; three kings, of Germany, Hungary, and Naples, adhered to the cause of Gregory the Twelfth; and Benedict the Thirteenth, himself a Spaniard, was acknowledged by the devotion and patriotism of that powerful nation. The rash proceedings of Pisa were corrected by the council of Constance; the emperor Sigismond acted a conspicuous part as the advocate or protector of the Catholic church; and the number and weight of civil and ecclesiastical members might seem to constitute the states-general of Europe. Of the three popes, John the Twenty-third was the first victim: he fled and was brought back a prisoner: the most scandalous charges were suppressed; the vicar of Christ was only accused of piracy, murder, rape, sodomy, and incest; and after subscribing his own condemnation, he expiated in prison the imprudence of trusting his person to a free city beyond the Alps. Gregory the Twelfth, whose obedience was reduced to the narrow precincts of Rimini, descended with more honor from the throne; and his ambassador convened the session, in which he renounced the title and authority of lawful pope. To vanquish the obstinacy of Benedict the Thirteenth or his adherents, the emperor in person undertook a journey from Constance to Perpignan. The kings of Castile, Arragon, Navarre, and Scotland, obtained an equal and honorable treaty; with the concurrence of the Spaniards, Benedict was deposed by the council; but the harmless old man was left in a solitary castle to excommunicate twice each day the rebel kingdoms which had deserted his cause. After thus eradicating the remains of the schism, the synod of Constance proceeded with slow and cautious steps to elect the sovereign of Rome and the head of the church. On this momentous occasion, the college of twenty-three cardinals was fortified with thirty deputies; six of whom were chosen in each of the five great nations of Christendom, – the Italian, the German, the French, the Spanish, and the *English*: the interference of strangers was softened by their generous preference of an Italian and a Roman; and the hereditary, as well as personal, merit of Otho Colonna recommended him to the conclave. Rome accepted with joy and obedience the noblest of her sons; the ecclesiastical state was defended by his powerful family; and the elevation of Martin the Fifth is the æra of the restoration and establishment of the popes in the Vatican.

Final Settlement of the Ecclesiastical State. – Part Four

THE ROYAL PREROGATIVE OF coining money, which had been exercised near three hundred years by the senate, was *first* resumed by Martin the Fifth, and his image and superscription introduce the series of the papal medals. Of his two immediate successors, Eugenius the Fourth was the *last* pope expelled by the tumults of the Roman people, and Nicholas the Fifth, the *last* who was importuned by the presence of a Roman emperor. I. The conflict of Eugenius with the fathers of Basil, and the weight or apprehension of a new excise, emboldened and provoked the Romans to usurp the temporal government of the city. They rose in arms, elected seven governors of the republic, and a constable of the Capitol; imprisoned the pope's nephew; besieged his person in the palace; and shot volleys of arrows into his bark as he escaped down the Tyber in the habit of a monk. But he still possessed in the castle of St. Angelo a faithful garrison and a train of artillery: their batteries incessantly thundered on the city, and a bullet more dexterously pointed broke down the barricade of the bridge, and scattered with a single shot the heroes of the republic. Their constancy was exhausted by a rebellion of five months. Under the tyranny of the Ghibeline nobles, the wisest patriots regretted the dominion of the church; and their repentance was unanimous and effectual. The troops of St. Peter again occupied the Capitol; the magistrates departed to their homes; the most guilty were executed or exiled; and the legate, at the head of two thousand foot and four thousand horse, was saluted as the father of the city. The synods of Ferrara and Florence, the fear or resentment of Eugenius, prolonged his absence: he was received by a submissive people; but the pontiff understood from the acclamations of his triumphal entry, that to secure their loyalty and his own repose, he must grant without delay the abolition of the odious excise. II. Rome was restored, adorned, and enlightened, by the peaceful reign of Nicholas the Fifth. In the midst of these laudable occupations, the pope was alarmed by the approach of Frederic the Third of Austria; though his fears could not be justified by the character or the power of the Imperial candidate. After drawing his military force to the metropolis, and imposing the best security of oaths and treaties, Nicholas received with a smiling countenance the faithful advocate and vassal of the church. So tame were the times, so feeble was the Austrian, that the pomp of his coronation was accomplished with order and harmony: but the superfluous honor was so disgraceful to an independent nation, that his successors have excused themselves from the toilsome pilgrimage to the Vatican; and rest their Imperial title on the choice of the electors of Germany.

A citizen has remarked, with pride and pleasure, that the king of the Romans, after passing with a slight salute the cardinals and prelates who met him at the gate, distinguished the dress and person of the senator of Rome; and in this last farewell, the pageants of the empire and the republic were clasped in a friendly embrace. According to the laws of Rome, her first magistrate was required to be a doctor of laws, an alien, of a place at least forty miles from the city; with whose inhabitants he must not be connected in the third canonical degree of blood or alliance. The election was annual: a severe scrutiny was instituted into the conduct of the departing senator; nor could he be recalled to the same office till after the expiration of two years. A liberal salary of three thousand florins was assigned for his expense and reward; and his public appearance represented the majesty of the republic. His robes were of gold brocade or crimson velvet, or in the summer season of a lighter silk: he bore in his hand an ivory sceptre; the sound of trumpets announced his approach; and his solemn steps were preceded at least by four lictors or attendants, whose red wands were enveloped with bands or streamers of the golden color or livery of the city. His oath in the Capitol proclaims his right and duty to observe and assert the laws, to control the proud, to protect the poor, and to exercise justice and mercy within the extent of his jurisdiction. In these useful functions he was assisted by three learned strangers; the two *collaterals*, and the judge of criminal appeals: their frequent trials of robberies, rapes, and murders, are attested by the laws; and the weakness of these laws connives at the licentiousness of private feuds and armed associations for mutual defence. But the senator was confined to the administration of justice: the Capitol, the treasury, and the government of the city and its territory, were intrusted to the three *conservators*, who were changed four times in each year: the militia of the thirteen regions assembled under the banners of their respective chiefs, or *caporioni*; and the first of these was distinguished by the name and dignity of the *prior*. The popular legislature consisted of the secret and the common councils of the Romans. The former was composed of the magistrates and their immediate predecessors, with some fiscal and legal officers, and three classes of thirteen, twenty-six, and forty, counsellors: amounting in the whole to about one hundred and twenty persons. In the common council all male citizens had a right to vote; and the value of their privilege was enhanced by the care with which any foreigners were prevented from usurping the title and character of Romans. The tumult of a democracy was checked by wise and jealous precautions: except the magistrates, none could propose a question; none were permitted to speak, except from an open pulpit or tribunal; all disorderly acclamations were suppressed; the sense of the majority was decided by a secret ballot; and their decrees were promulgated in the venerable name of the Roman senate and people. It would not be easy to assign a period in which this theory of government has been reduced to accurate and constant practice, since the establishment of order has been gradually connected with the decay of liberty. But in the year one thousand five hundred and eighty the ancient statutes were collected, methodized in three books, and adapted to present use, under the pontificate, and with the approbation, of Gregory the Thirteenth: this civil and criminal code is the modern law of the city; and, if the popular assemblies have been abolished, a foreign senator, with the three conservators, still resides in the palace of the Capitol. The policy of the Cæsars has been repeated by the popes; and the bishop of Rome affected to maintain the form of a republic, while he reigned with the absolute powers of a temporal, as well as a spiritual, monarch.

It is an obvious truth, that the times must be suited to extraordinary characters, and that the genius of Cromwell or Retz might now expire in obscurity. The political enthusiasm of Rienzi had exalted him to a throne; the same enthusiasm, in the next century, conducted his imitator to the gallows. The birth of Stephen Porcaro was noble, his reputation spotless: his tongue was armed with eloquence, his mind was enlightened with learning; and he aspired, beyond the aim of vulgar ambition, to free his country and immortalize his name. The dominion of priests is most odious to a liberal spirit: every scruple was removed by the recent knowledge of the fable and forgery of Constantine's donation; Petrarch was now the oracle of the Italians; and as often as Porcaro revolved the ode which describes the patriot and hero of Rome, he applied to himself the visions of the prophetic bard. His first trial of the popular feelings was at the funeral of Eugenius the Fourth: in an elaborate speech he called the Romans to liberty and arms; and they listened with apparent pleasure, till Porcaro was interrupted and answered by a grave advocate, who pleaded for the church and state. By every law the seditious orator was guilty of treason; but the benevolence of the new pontiff, who viewed his character with pity and esteem, attempted by an honorable office to convert the patriot into a friend. The inflexible Roman returned from Anagni with an increase of reputation and zeal; and, on the first opportunity, the games of the place Navona, he tried to inflame the casual dispute of some boys and mechanics into a general rising of the people. Yet the humane Nicholas was still averse to accept the forfeit of his life; and the traitor was removed from the scene of temptation to Bologna, with a liberal allowance for his support, and the easy obligation of presenting himself each day before the governor of the city. But Porcaro had learned from the younger Brutus, that with tyrants no faith or gratitude should be observed: the exile declaimed against the arbitrary sentence; a party and a conspiracy were gradually formed: his nephew, a daring youth, assembled a band of volunteers; and on the appointed evening a feast was prepared at his house for the friends of the republic. Their leader, who had escaped from Bologna, appeared among them in a robe of purple and gold: his voice, his countenance, his gestures, bespoke the man who had devoted his life or death to the glorious cause. In a studied oration, he expiated on the motives and the means of their enterprise; the name and liberties of Rome; the sloth and pride of their ecclesiastical tyrants; the active or passive consent of their fellow-citizens; three hundred soldiers, and four hundred exiles, long exercised in arms or in wrongs; the license of revenge to edge their swords, and a million of ducats to reward their victory. It would be easy, (he said,) on the next day, the festival of the Epiphany, to seize the pope and his cardinals, before the doors, or at the altar, of St. Peter's; to lead them in chains under the walls of St. Angelo; to extort by the threat of their instant death a surrender of the castle; to ascend the vacant Capitol; to ring the alarm bell; and to restore in a popular assembly the ancient republic of Rome. While he triumphed, he was already betrayed. The senator, with a strong guard, invested the house: the nephew of

Porcaro cut his way through the crowd; but the unfortunate Stephen was drawn from a chest, lamenting that his enemies had anticipated by three hours the execution of his design. After such manifest and repeated guilt, even the mercy of Nicholas was silent. Porcaro, and nine of his accomplices, were hanged without the benefit of the sacraments; and, amidst the fears and invectives of the papal court, the Romans pitied, and almost applauded, these martyrs of their country. But their applause was mute, their pity ineffectual, their liberty forever extinct; and, if they have since risen in a vacancy of the throne or a scarcity of bread, such accidental tumults may be found in the bosom of the most abject servitude.

But the independence of the nobles, which was fomented by discord, survived the freedom of the commons, which must be founded in union. A privilege of rapine and oppression was long maintained by the barons of Rome; their houses were a fortress and a sanctuary: and the ferocious train of banditti and criminals whom they protected from the law repaid the hospitality with the service of their swords and daggers. The private interest of the pontiffs, or their nephews, sometimes involved them in these domestic feuds. Under the reign of Sixtus the Fourth, Rome was distracted by the battles and sieges of the rival houses: after the conflagration of his palace, the prothonotary Colonna was tortured and beheaded; and Savelli, his captive friend, was murdered on the spot, for refusing to join in the acclamations of the victorious Ursini. But the popes no longer trembled in the Vatican: they had strength to command, if they had resolution to claim, the obedience of their subjects; and the strangers, who observed these partial disorders, admired the easy taxes and wise administration of the ecclesiastical state.

The spiritual thunders of the Vatican depend on the force of opinion; and if that opinion be supplanted by reason or passion, the sound may idly waste itself in the air; and the helpless priest is exposed to the brutal violence of a noble or a plebeian adversary. But after their return from Avignon, the keys of St. Peter were guarded by the sword of St. Paul. Rome was commanded by an impregnable citadel: the use of cannon is a powerful engine against popular seditions: a regular force of cavalry and infantry was enlisted under the banners of the pope: his ample revenues supplied the resources of war: and, from the extent of his domain, he could bring down on a rebellious city an army of hostile neighbors and loyal subjects. Since the union of the duchies of Ferrara and Urbino, the ecclesiastical state extends from the Mediterranean to the Adriatic, and from the confines of Naples to the banks

of the Po; and as early as the sixteenth century, the greater part of
that spacious and fruitful country acknowledged the lawful claims and
temporal sovereignty of the Roman pontiffs. Their claims were readily
deduced from the genuine, or fabulous, donations of the darker ages:
the successive steps of their final settlement would engage us too far
in the transactions of Italy, and even of Europe; the crimes of Alexander the Sixth, the martial operations of Julius the Second, and the
liberal policy of Leo the Tenth, a theme which has been adorned by
the pens of the noblest historians of the times. In the first period of
their conquests, till the expedition of Charles the Eighth, the popes
might successfully wrestle with the adjacent princes and states, whose
military force was equal, or inferior, to their own. But as soon as the
monarchs of France, Germany and Spain, contended with gigantic
arms for the dominion of Italy, they supplied with art the deficiency
of strength; and concealed, in a labyrinth of wars and treaties, their
aspiring views, and the immortal hope of chasing the Barbarians beyond the Alps. The nice balance of the Vatican was often subverted by
the soldiers of the North and West, who were united under the standard of Charles the Fifth: the feeble and fluctuating policy of Clement
the Seventh exposed his person and dominions to the conqueror; and
Rome was abandoned seven months to a lawless army, more cruel and
rapacious than the Goths and Vandals. After this severe lesson, the
popes contracted their ambition, which was almost satisfied, resumed
the character of a common parent, and abstained from all offensive
hostilities, except in a hasty quarrel, when the vicar of Christ and the
Turkish sultan were armed at the same time against the kingdom of
Naples. The French and Germans at length withdrew from the field
of battle: Milan, Naples, Sicily, Sardinia, and the sea-coast of Tuscany,
were firmly possessed by the Spaniards; and it became their interest to
maintain the peace and dependence of Italy, which continued almost
without disturbance from the middle of the sixteenth to the opening
of the eighteenth century. The Vatican was swayed and protected by
the religious policy of the Catholic king: his prejudice and interest disposed him in every dispute to support the prince against the people;
and instead of the encouragement, the aid, and the asylum, which they
obtained from the adjacent states, the friends of liberty, or the enemies
of law, were enclosed on all sides within the iron circle of despotism.
The long habits of obedience and education subdued the turbulent
spirit of the nobles and commons of Rome. The barons forgot the arms
and factions of their ancestors, and insensibly became the servants of
luxury and government. Instead of maintaining a crowd of tenants and

followers, the produce of their estates was consumed in the private expenses which multiply the pleasures, and diminish the power, of the lord. The Colonna and Ursini vied with each other in the decoration of their palaces and chapels; and their antique splendor was rivalled or surpassed by the sudden opulence of the papal families. In Rome the voice of freedom and discord is no longer heard; and, instead of the foaming torrent, a smooth and stagnant lake reflects the image of idleness and servitude.

A Christian, a philosopher, and a patriot, will be equally scandalized by the temporal kingdom of the clergy; and the local majesty of Rome, the remembrance of her consuls and triumphs, may seem to imbitter the sense, and aggravate the shame, of her slavery. If we calmly weigh the merits and defects of the ecclesiastical government, it may be praised in its present state, as a mild, decent, and tranquil system, exempt from the dangers of a minority, the sallies of youth, the expenses of luxury, and the calamities of war. But these advantages are overbalanced by a frequent, perhaps a septennial, election of a sovereign, who is seldom a native of the country; the reign of a *young* statesman of threescore, in the decline of his life and abilities, without hope to accomplish, and without children to inherit, the labors of his transitory reign. The successful candidate is drawn from the church, and even the convent; from the mode of education and life the most adverse to reason, humanity, and freedom. In the trammels of servile faith, he has learned to believe because it is absurd, to revere all that is contemptible, and to despise whatever might deserve the esteem of a rational being; to punish error as a crime, to reward mortification and celibacy as the first of virtues; to place the saints of the calendar above the heroes of Rome and the sages of Athens; and to consider the missal, or the crucifix, as more useful instruments than the plough or the loom. In the office of nuncio, or the rank of cardinal, he may acquire some knowledge of the world, but the primitive stain will adhere to his mind and manners: from study and experience he may suspect the mystery of his profession; but the sacerdotal artist will imbibe some portion of the bigotry which he inculcates. The genius of Sixtus the Fifth burst from the gloom of a Franciscan cloister. In a reign of five years, he exterminated the outlaws and banditti, abolished the *profane* sanctuaries of Rome, formed a naval and military force, restored and emulated the monuments of antiquity, and after a liberal use and large increase of the revenue, left five millions of crowns in the castle of St. Angelo. But his justice was sullied with cruelty, his activity was prompted by the ambition of conquest: after his decease the abuses revived; the treasure was dissipated; he entailed on posterity thirty-five new taxes and the venality of offices; and, after his death, his statue was demolished by an ungrateful, or an injured, people. The wild and original character of Sixtus the Fifth stands alone in the series of the pontiffs; the maxims and effects of their temporal government may be collected from the positive and comparative view of the arts and philosophy, the agriculture and trade, the wealth and population, of the ecclesiastical state. For myself, it is my wish to depart in charity with all mankind, nor am I willing, in these last moments, to offend even the pope and clergy of Rome.

Prospect of the Ruins of Rome in the Fifteenth Century. – Part One

Prospect of the Ruins of Rome in the Fifteenth Century. – Four Causes of Decay and Destruction. – Example of the Coliseum. – Renovation of the City. – Conclusion of the Whole Work.

IN THE LAST DAYS of Pope Eugenius the Fourth, two of his servants, the learned Poggius and a friend, ascended the Capitoline hill; reposed themselves among the ruins of columns and temples; and viewed from that commanding spot the wide and various prospect of desolation. The place and the object gave ample scope for moralizing on the vicissitudes of fortune, which spares neither man nor the proudest of his works, which buries empires and cities in a common grave; and it was agreed, that in proportion to her former greatness, the fall of Rome was the more awful and deplorable. "Her primeval state, such as she might appear in a remote age, when Evander entertained the stranger of Troy, has been delineated by the fancy of Virgil. This Tarpeian rock was then a savage and solitary thicket: in the time of the poet, it was crowned with the golden roofs of a temple; the temple is overthrown, the gold has been pillaged, the wheel of fortune has accomplished her revolution, and the sacred ground is again disfigured with thorns and brambles. The hill of the Capitol, on which we sit, was formerly the head of the Roman empire, the citadel of the earth, the terror of kings; illustrated by the footsteps of so many triumphs, enriched with the spoils and tributes of so many nations. This spectacle of the world, how is it fallen! how changed! how defaced! The path of victory is obliterated by vines, and the benches of the senators are concealed by a dunghill. Cast your eyes on the Palatine hill, and seek among the shapeless and enormous fragments the marble theatre, the obelisks, the colossal statues, the porticos of Nero's palace: survey the other hills of the city, the vacant space is interrupted only by ruins and gardens. The forum of the Roman people, where they assembled to enact their laws and elect their magistrates, is now enclosed for the cultivation of pot-herbs, or thrown open for the reception of swine and buffaloes. The public and private edifices, that were founded for eternity, lie prostrate, naked, and broken, like the limbs of a mighty giant; and the ruin is the more visible, from the stupendous relics that have survived the injuries of time and fortune."

These relics are minutely described by Poggius, one of the first who raised his eyes from the monuments of legendary, to those of classic, superstition. .Besides a bridge, an arch, a sepulchre, and the pyramid of Cestius, he could discern, of the age of the republic, a double row of vaults, in the salt-office of the Capitol, which were inscribed with the name and munificence of Catulus. . Eleven temples were visible in some degree, from the perfect form of the Pantheon, to the three arches and a marble column of the temple of Peace, which Vespasian erected after the civil wars and the Jewish triumph. . Of the number, which he rashly defines, of seven *thermæ*, or public baths, none were sufficiently entire to represent the use and distribution of the several parts: but those of Diocletian and Antoninus Caracalla still retained the titles of the founders, and astonished the curious spectator, who, in observing their solidity and extent, the variety of marbles, the size and multitude of the columns, compared the labor and expense with the use and importance. Of the baths of Constantine, of Alexander, of Domitian, or rather of Titus, some vestige might yet be found. . The triumphal arches of Titus, Severus, and Constantine, were entire, both the structure and the inscriptions; a falling fragment was honored with the name of Trajan; and two arches, then extant, in the Flaminian way, have been ascribed to the baser memory of Faustina and Gallienus. . After the wonder of the Coliseum, Poggius might have overlooked small amphitheatre of brick, most probably for the use of the prætorian camp: the theatres of Marcellus and Pompey were occupied in a great measure by public and private buildings; and in the Circus, Agonalis and Maximus, little more than the situation and the form could be investigated. . The columns of Trajan and Antonine were still erect; but the Egyptian obelisks were broken or buried. A people of gods and heroes, the workmanship of art, was reduced to one equestrian figure of gilt brass, and to five marble statues, of which the most conspicuous were the two horses of Phidias and Praxiteles. . The two mausoleums or sepulchres of Augustus and Hadrian could not totally be lost: but the former was only visible as a mound of earth; and the latter, the castle of St. Angelo, had acquired the name and appearance of a modern fortress. With the addition of some separate and nameless columns, such were the remains of the ancient city; for the marks of a more recent structure might be detected in the walls, which formed a circumference of ten miles, included three hundred and seventy-nine turrets, and opened into the country by thirteen gates.

This melancholy picture was drawn above nine hundred years after the fall of the Western empire, and even of the Gothic kingdom of Italy. A long period of distress and anarchy, in which empire, and arts, and riches had migrated from the banks of the Tyber, was incapable of restoring or adorning the city; and, as all that is human must retrograde if it do not advance, every successive age must have hastened the ruin of the works of antiquity. To measure the progress of decay, and to ascertain, at each æra, the state of each edifice, would be an endless and a useless labor; and I shall content myself with two observations, which will introduce a short inquiry into the general causes and effects. . Two hundred years before the eloquent complaint of Poggius, an anonymous writer composed a description of Rome. His ignorance may repeat the same objects under strange and fabulous names. Yet this barbarous topographer had eyes and ears; he could observe the visible remains; he could listen to the tradition of the people; and he distinctly enumerates seven theatres, eleven baths, twelve arches, and eighteen palaces, of which many had disappeared before the time of Poggius. It is apparent, that many stately monuments of antiquity survived till a late period, and that the principles of destruction acted with vigorous and increasing energy in the thirteenth and fourteenth centuries. . The same reflection must be applied to the three last ages; and we should vainly seek the Septizonium of Severus; which is celebrated by Petrarch and the antiquarians of the sixteenth century. While the Roman edifices were still entire, the first blows, however weighty and impetuous, were resisted by the solidity of the mass and the harmony of the parts; but the slightest touch would precipitate the fragments of arches and columns, that already nodded to their fall.

After a diligent inquiry, I can discern four principal causes of the ruin of Rome, which continued to operate in a period of more than a thousand years. I. The injuries of time and nature. II. The hostile attacks of the Barbarians and Christians. III. The use and abuse of the materials. And,

IV. The domestic quarrels of the Romans.

I. The art of man is able to construct monuments far more permanent than the narrow span of his own existence; yet these monuments, like himself, are perishable and frail; and in the boundless annals of time, his life and his labors must equally be measured as a fleeting moment. Of a simple and solid edifice, it is not easy, however, to circumscribe the duration. As the wonders of ancient days, the pyramids attracted the curiosity of the ancients: a hundred generations, the leaves of autumn, have dropped into the grave; and after the fall of the Pharaohs and Ptolemies, the Cæsars and caliphs, the same pyramids stand erect and unshaken above the floods of the Nile. A complex figure of various and minute parts to more accessible to injury and decay; and the silent lapse of time is often accelerated by hurricanes and earthquakes, by fires and inundations. The air and earth have doubtless been shaken; and the lofty turrets of Rome have tottered from their foundations; but the seven hills do not appear to be placed on the great cavities of the globe; nor has the city, in any age, been exposed to the convulsions of nature, which, in the climate of Antioch, Lisbon, or Lima, have crumbled in a few moments the works of ages into dust. Fire is the most powerful agent of life and death: the rapid mischief may be kindled and propagated by the industry or negligence of mankind; and every period of the Roman annals is marked by the repetition of similar calamities. A memorable conflagration, the guilt or misfortune of Nero's reign, continued, though with unequal fury, either six or nine days. Innumerable buildings, crowded in close and crooked streets, supplied perpetual fuel for the flames; and when they ceased, four only of the fourteen regions were left entire; three were totally destroyed, and seven were deformed by the relics of smoking and lacerated edifices. In the full meridian of empire, the metropolis arose with fresh beauty from her ashes; yet the memory of the old deplored their irreparable losses, the arts of Greece, the trophies of victory, the monuments of primitive or fabulous antiquity. In the days of distress and anarchy, every wound is mortal, every fall irretrievable; nor can the damage be restored either by the public care of government, or the activity of private interest. Yet two causes may be alleged, which render the calamity of fire more destructive to a flourishing than a decayed city. . The more combustible materials of brick, timber, and metals, are first melted or consumed; but the flames may play without injury or effect on the naked walls, and massy arches, that have been despoiled of their ornaments. . It is among the common and plebeian habitations, that a mischievous spark is most easily blown to a conflagration; but as soon as they are devoured, the greater edifices, which have resisted or escaped, are left as so many islands in a state of solitude and safety. From her situation, Rome is exposed to the danger of frequent inundations. Without excepting the Tyber, the rivers that descend from either side of the Apennine have a short and irregular course; a shallow stream in the summer heats; an impetuous torrent, when it is swelled in the spring or winter, by the fall of rain, and the melting of the snows. When the current is repelled from the sea by adverse winds, when the ordinary bed is inadequate to the weight of waters, they rise above the banks, and overspread, without limits or control, the plains and cities of the adjacent country. Soon after the triumph of the first Punic war, the Tyber was increased by unusual rains; and the inundation, surpassing all former measure of time and place, destroyed all the buildings that were situated below the hills of Rome. According to the variety of ground, the same mischief was produced by different means; and the edifices were either swept away by the sudden impulse, or dissolved and undermined by the long continuance, of the flood. Under the reign of Augustus, the same calamity was renewed: the lawless river overturned the palaces and temples on its banks; and, after the labors of the emperor in cleansing and widening the bed that was encumbered with ruins, the vigilance of his successors was exercised by similar dangers and designs. The project of diverting into new channels the Tyber itself, or some of the dependent streams, was long opposed by superstition and local interests; nor did the use compensate the toil and cost of the tardy and imperfect execution. The servitude of rivers is the noblest and most important victory which man has obtained over the licentiousness of nature; and if such were the ravages of the Tyber under a firm and active government, what could oppose, or who can enumerate, the injuries of the city, after the fall of the Western empire? A remedy was at length produced by the evil itself: the accumulation of rubbish and the earth, that has been washed down from the hills, is supposed to have elevated the plain of Rome, fourteen or fifteen feet, perhaps, above the ancient level; and the modern city is less accessible to the attacks of the river.

Vidimus flavum Tiberim, retortis Littore Etrusco violenter undis, Ire dejectum monumenta Regis Templaque Vestæ. (Horat. Carm. I. 2.)

If the palace of Numa and temple of Vesta were thrown down in Horace's time, what was consumed of those buildings by Nero's fire could hardly deserve the epithets of vetustissima or incorrupta.]

II. The crowd of writers of every nation, who impute the destruction of the Roman monuments to the Goths and the Christians, have neglected to inquire how far they were animated by a hostile principle, and how far they possessed the means and the leisure to satiate their enmity. In the preceding volumes of this History, I have described the triumph of barbarism and religion; and I can only resume, in a few words, their real or imaginary connection with the ruin of ancient Rome. Our fancy may create, or adopt, a pleasing romance, that the Goths and Vandals sallied from Scandinavia, ardent to avenge the flight of Odin; to break the chains, and to chastise the oppressors, of mankind; that they wished to burn the records of classic literature, and to found their national architecture on the broken members of the Tuscan and Corinthian orders. But in simple truth, the northern conquerors were neither sufficiently savage, nor sufficiently refined, to entertain such aspiring ideas of destruction and revenge. The shepherds of Scythia and Germany had been educated in the armies of the empire, whose discipline they acquired, and whose weakness they invaded: with the familiar use of the Latin tongue, they had learned to reverence the name and titles of Rome; and, though incapable of emulating, they were more inclined to admire, than to abolish, the arts and studies of a brighter period. In the transient possession of a rich and unresisting capital, the soldiers of Alaric and Genseric were stimulated by the passions of a victorious army; amidst the wanton indulgence of lust or cruelty, portable wealth was the object of their search; nor could they derive either pride or pleasure from the unprofitable reflection, that they had battered to the ground the works of the consuls and Cæsars. Their moments were indeed precious; the Goths evacuated Rome on the sixth, the Vandals on the fifteenth, day: and, though it be far more difficult to build than to destroy, their hasty assault would have made a slight impression on the solid piles of antiquity. We may remember, that both Alaric and Genseric affected to spare the buildings of the city; that they subsisted in strength and beauty under the auspicious government of Theodoric; and that the momentary resentment of Totila was disarmed by his own temper and the advice of his friends and enemies. From these innocent Barbarians, the reproach may be transferred to the Catholics of Rome. The statues, altars, and houses, of the dæmons, were an abomination in their eyes; and in the absolute command of the city, they might labor with zeal and perseverance to erase the idolatry of their ancestors. The demolition of the temples in the East affords to *them* an example of conduct, and to *us* an argument of belief; and it is probable that a portion of guilt or merit may be imputed with justice to the Roman proselytes. Yet their abhorrence was confined to the monuments of heathen superstition; and the civil structures that were dedicated to the business or pleasure of society might be preserved without injury or scandal. The change of religion was accomplished, not by a popular tumult, but by the decrees of the emperors, of the senate, and of time. Of the Christian hierarchy, the bishops of Rome were commonly the most prudent and least fanatic; nor can any positive charge be opposed to the meritorious act of saving or converting the majestic structure of the Pantheon.

III. The value of any object that supplies the wants or pleasures of mankind is compounded of its substance and its form, of the materials and the manufacture. Its price must depend on the number of persons by whom it may be acquired and used; on the extent of the market; and consequently on the ease or difficulty of remote exportation, according to the nature of the commodity, its local situation, and the temporary circumstances of the world. The Barbarian conquerors of Rome usurped in a moment the toil and treasure of successive ages; but, except the luxuries of immediate consumption, they must view without desire all that could not be removed from the city in the Gothic wagons or the fleet of the Vandals. Gold and silver were the first objects of their avarice; as in every country, and in the smallest compass, they represent the most ample command of the industry and possessions of mankind. A vase or a statue of those precious metals might tempt the vanity of some Barbarian chief; but the grosser multitude, regardless of the form, was tenacious only of the substance; and the melted ingots might be readily divided and stamped into the current coin of the empire. The less active or less fortunate robbers were reduced to the baser plunder of brass, lead, iron, and copper: whatever had escaped the Goths and Vandals was pillaged by the Greek tyrants; and the emperor Constans, in his rapacious visit, stripped the bronze tiles from the roof of the Pantheon. The edifices of Rome might be considered as a vast and various mine; the first labor of extracting the materials was already performed; the metals were purified and cast; the marbles were hewn and polished; and after foreign and domestic rapine had been satiated, the remains of the city, could a purchaser have been found, were still venal. The monuments of antiquity had been left naked of their precious ornaments; but the Romans would demolish with their own hands the arches and walls, if the hope of profit could surpass the cost of the labor and exportation. If Charlemagne had fixed in Italy the seat of the Western empire, his genius would have aspired to restore, rather than to violate, the works of the Cæsars; but policy confined the French monarch to the forests of Germany; his taste could be gratified only by destruction; and the new palace of Aix la Chapelle was decorated with the marbles of Ravenna and Rome. Five hundred years after Charlemagne, a king of Sicily, Robert, the wisest and most liberal sovereign of the age, was supplied with the same materials by the easy navigation of the Tyber and the sea; and Petrarch sighs an indignant complaint, that the ancient capital of the world should adorn from her own bowels the slothful luxury of Naples. But these examples of plunder or purchase were rare in the darker ages; and the Romans, alone and unenvied, might have applied to their private or public use the remaining structures of antiquity, if in their present form and situation they had not been useless in a great measure to the city and its inhabitants. The walls still described the old circumference, but the city had descended from the seven hills into the Campus Martius; and some of the noblest monuments which had braved the injuries of time were left in a desert, far remote from the habitations of mankind. The palaces of the senators were no longer adapted to the manners or fortunes of their indigent successors: the use of baths and porticos was forgotten: in the sixth century, the games of the theatre, amphitheatre, and circus, had been interrupted: some temples were devoted to the prevailing worship; but the Christian churches preferred the holy figure of the cross; and fashion, or reason, had distributed after a peculiar model the cells and offices of the cloister. Under the ecclesiastical reign, the number of these pious foundations was enormously multiplied; and the city was crowded with forty monasteries of men, twenty of women, and sixty chapters and colleges of canons and priests, who aggravated, instead of relieving, the depopulation of the tenth century. But if the forms of ancient architecture were disregarded by a people insensible of their use and beauty, the plentiful materials were applied to every call of necessity or superstition; till the fairest columns of the Ionic and Corinthian orders, the richest marbles of Paros and Numidia, were degraded, perhaps to the support of a convent or a stable. The daily havoc which is perpetrated by the Turks in the cities of Greece and Asia may afford a melancholy example; and in the gradual destruction of the monuments of Rome, Sixtus the Fifth may alone be excused for employing the stones of the Septizonium in the glorious edifice of St. Peter's. A fragment, a ruin, howsoever mangled or profaned, may be viewed with pleasure and regret; but the greater part of the marble was deprived of substance, as well as of place and proportion; it was burnt to lime for the purpose of cement. Since the arrival of Poggius, the temple of Concord, and many capital structures, had vanished from his eyes; and an epigram of the same age expresses a just and pious fear, that the continuance of this practice would finally annihilate all the monuments of antiquity. The smallness of their numbers was the sole check on the demands and depredations of the Romans. The imagination of

Petrarch might create the presence of a mighty people; and I hesitate to believe, that, even in the fourteenth century, they could be reduced to a contemptible list of thirty-three thousand inhabitants. From that period to the reign of Leo the Tenth, if they multiplied to the amount of eighty-five thousand, the increase of citizens was in some degree pernicious to the ancient city.

> *Ad quæ marmoreas præstabat Roma columnas,*
> *Quasdam præcipuas pulchra Ravenna dedit.*
> *De tam longinquâ poterit regione vetustas*
> *Illius ornatum, Francia, ferre tibi.*
> *Oblectat me, Roma, tuas spectare ruinas:*
> *Ex cujus lapsû gloria prisca patet.*
> *Sed tuus hic populus muris defossa vetustis*
> *Calcis in obsequium marmora dura coquit.*
> *Impia tercentum si sic gens egerit annos*
> *Nullum hinc indicium nobilitatis erit.]*

IV. I have reserved for the last, the most potent and forcible cause of destruction, the domestic hostilities of the Romans themselves. Under the dominion of the Greek and French emperors, the peace of the city was disturbed by accidental, though frequent, seditions: it is from the decline of the latter, from the beginning of the tenth century, that we may date the licentiousness of private war, which violated with impunity the laws of the Code and the Gospel, without respecting the majesty of the absent sovereign, or the presence and person of the vicar of Christ. In a dark period of five hundred years, Rome was perpetually afflicted by the sanguinary quarrels of the nobles and the people, the Guelphs and Ghibelines, the Colonna and Ursini; and if much has escaped the knowledge, and much is unworthy of the notice, of history, I have exposed in the two preceding chapters the causes and effects of the public disorders. At such a time, when every quarrel was decided by the sword, and none could trust their lives or properties to the impotence of law, the powerful citizens were armed for safety, or offence, against the domestic enemies whom they feared or hated. Except Venice alone, the same dangers and designs were common to all the free republics of Italy; and the nobles usurped the prerogative of fortifying their houses, and erecting strong towers, that were capable of resisting a sudden attack. The cities were filled with these hostile edifices; and the example of Lucca, which contained three hundred towers; her law, which confined their height to the measure of fourscore feet, may be extended with suitable latitude to the more opulent and populous states. The first step of the senator Brancaleone in the establishment of peace and justice, was to demolish (as we have already seen) one hundred and forty of the towers of Rome; and, in the last days of anarchy and discord, as late as the reign of Martin the Fifth, forty-four still stood in one of the thirteen or fourteen regions of the city. To this mischievous purpose the remains of antiquity were most readily adapted: the temples and arches afforded a broad and solid basis for the new structures of brick and stone; and we can name the modern turrets that were raised on the triumphal monuments of Julius Cæsar, Titus, and the Antonines. With some slight alterations, a theatre, an amphitheatre, a mausoleum, was transformed into a strong and spacious citadel. I need not repeat, that the mole of Adrian has assumed the title and form of the castle of St. Angelo; the Septizonium of Severus was capable of standing against a royal army; the sepulchre of Metella has sunk under its outworks; the theatres of Pompey and Marcellus were occupied by the Savelli and Ursini families; and the rough fortress has been gradually softened to the splendor and elegance of an Italian palace. Even the churches were encompassed with arms and bulwarks, and the military engines on the roof of St. Peter's were the terror of the Vatican and the scandal of the Christian world. Whatever is fortified will be attacked; and whatever is attacked may be destroyed. Could the Romans have wrested from the popes the castle of St. Angelo, they had resolved by a public decree to annihilate that monument of servitude. Every building of defence was exposed to a siege; and in every siege the arts and engines of destruction were laboriously employed. After the death of Nicholas the Fourth, Rome, without a sovereign or a senate, was abandoned six months to the fury of civil war. "The houses," says a cardinal and poet of the times, "were crushed by the weight and velocity of enormous stones; the walls were perforated by the strokes of the battering-ram; the towers were involved in fire and smoke; and the assailants were stimulated by rapine and revenge." The work was consummated by the tyranny of the laws; and the factions of Italy alternately exercised a blind and thoughtless vengeance on their adversaries, whose houses and castles they razed to the ground. In comparing the *days* of foreign, with the *ages* of domestic, hostility, we must pronounce, that the latter have been far more ruinous to the city; and our opinion is confirmed by the evidence of Petrarch. "Behold," says the laureate, "the relics of Rome, the image of her pristine greatness! neither time nor the Barbarian can boast the merit of this stupendous destruction: it was perpetrated by her own citizens, by the most illustrious of her sons;

and your ancestors (he writes to a noble Annabaldi) have done with the battering-ram what the Punic hero could not accomplish with the sword." The influence of the two last principles of decay must in some degree be multiplied by each other; since the houses and towers, which were subverted by civil war, required by a new and perpetual supply from the monuments of antiquity.

Hoc dixisse sat est, Romam caruisee Senatû
Mensibus exactis heu sex; belloque vocatum (vocatos)
In scelus, in socios fraternaque vulnera patres;
Tormentis jecisse viros immania saxa;
Perfodisse domus trabibus, fecisse ruinas
Ignibus; incensas turres, obscuraque fumo
Lumina vicino, quo sit spoliata supellex.]
Nec te parva manet servatis fama ruinis
Quanta quod integræ fuit olim gloria Romæ
Reliquiæ testantur adhuc; quas longior ætas
Frangere non valuit; non vis aut ira cruenti Hostis,
ab egregiis franguntur civibus, heu! heu'
  – – – – Quod ille nequivit (Hannibal.)
Perficit hic aries.]

Prospect of the Ruins of Rome in the Fifteenth Century. – Part Two

THESE GENERAL OBSERVATIONS MAY be separately applied to the amphitheatre of Titus, which has obtained the name of the Coliseum, either from its magnitude, or from Nero's colossal statue; an edifice, had it been left to time and nature, which might perhaps have claimed an eternal duration. The curious antiquaries, who have computed the numbers and seats, are disposed to believe, that above the upper row of stone steps the amphitheatre was encircled and elevated with several stages of wooden galleries, which were repeatedly consumed by fire, and restored by the emperors. Whatever was precious, or portable, or profane, the statues of gods and heroes, and the costly ornaments of sculpture which were cast in brass, or overspread with leaves of silver and gold, became the first prey of conquest or fanaticism, of the avarice of the Barbarians or the Christians. In the massy stones of the Coliseum, many holes are discerned; and the two most probable conjectures represent the various accidents of its decay. These stones were connected by solid links of brass or iron, nor had the eye of rapine overlooked the value of the baser metals; the vacant space was converted into a fair or market; the artisans of the Coliseum are mentioned in an ancient survey; and the chasms were perforated or enlarged to receive the poles that supported the shops or tents of the mechanic trades. Reduced to its naked majesty, the Flavian amphitheatre was contemplated with awe and admiration by the pilgrims of the North; and their rude enthusiasm broke forth in a sublime proverbial expression, which is recorded in the eighth century, in the fragments of the venerable Bede: "As long as the Coliseum stands, Rome shall stand; when the Coliseum falls, Rome will fall; when

Rome falls, the world will fall." In the modern system of war, a situation commanded by three hills would not be chosen for a fortress; but the strength of the walls and arches could resist the engines of assault; a numerous garrison might be lodged in the enclosure; and while one faction occupied the Vatican and the Capitol, the other was intrenched in the Lateran and the Coliseum.

The abolition at Rome of the ancient games must be understood with some latitude; and the carnival sports, of the Testacean mount and the Circus Agonalis, were regulated by the law or custom of the city. The senator presided with dignity and pomp to adjudge and distribute the prizes, the gold ring, or the *pallium*, as it was styled, of cloth or silk. A tribute on the Jews supplied the annual expense; and the races, on foot, on horseback, or in chariots, were ennobled by a tilt and tournament of seventy-two of the Roman youth. In the year one thousand three hundred and thirty-two, a bull-feast, after the fashion of the Moors and Spaniards, was celebrated in the Coliseum itself; and the living manners are painted in a diary of the times. A convenient order of benches was restored; and a general proclamation, as far as Rimini and Ravenna, invited the nobles to exercise their skill and courage in this perilous adventure. The Roman ladies were marshalled in three squadrons, and seated in three balconies, which, on this day, the third of September, were lined with scarlet cloth. The fair Jacova di Rovere led the matrons from beyond the Tyber, a pure and native race, who still represent the features and character of antiquity. The remainder of the city was divided as usual between the Colonna and Ursini: the two factions were proud of the number and beauty of their female bands: the charms of Savella Ursini are mentioned with praise; and the Colonna regretted the absence of the youngest of their house, who had sprained her ankle in the garden of Nero's tower. The lots of the champions were drawn by an old and respectable citizen; and they descended into the arena, or pit, to encounter the wild bulls, on foot as it should seem, with a single spear. Amidst the crowd, our annalist has selected the names, colors, and devices, of twenty of the most conspicuous knights. Several of the names are the most illustrious of Rome and the ecclesiastical state: Malatesta, Polenta, della Valle, Cafarello, Savelli, Capoccio, Conti, Annibaldi, Altieri, Corsi: the colors were adapted to their taste and situation; the devices are expressive of hope or despair, and breathe the spirit of gallantry and arms. "I am alone, like the youngest of the Horatii," the confidence of an intrepid stranger: "I live disconsolate," a weeping widower: "I burn under the ashes," a discreet lover: "I adore Lavinia, or Lucretia," the ambiguous declaration of a modern passion: "My faith is as pure," the motto of a white livery: "Who is stronger than myself?" of a lion's hide: "If am drowned in blood, what a pleasant death!" the wish of ferocious courage. The pride or prudence of the Ursini restrained them from the field, which was occupied by three of their hereditary rivals, whose inscriptions denoted the lofty greatness of the Colonna name: "Though sad, I am strong:" "Strong as I am great:" "If I fall," addressing himself to the spectators, "you fall with me;" – intimating (says the contemporary writer) that while the other families were the subjects of the Vatican, they alone were the supporters of the Capitol. The combats of the amphitheatre were dangerous and bloody. Every champion successively encountered a wild bull; and the victory may be ascribed to the quadrupeds, since no more than eleven were left on the field, with the loss of nine wounded and eighteen killed on the side of their adversaries. Some of the noblest families might mourn, but the pomp of the funerals, in the churches of St. John Lateran and St. Maria Maggiore, afforded a second holiday to the people. Doubtless it was not in such conflicts that the blood of the Romans should have been shed; yet, in blaming their rashness, we are compelled to applaud their gallantry; and the noble volunteers, who display their magnificence, and risk their lives, under the balconies of the fair, excite a more generous sympathy than the thousands of captives and malefactors who were reluctantly dragged to the scene of slaughter.

This use of the amphitheatre was a rare, perhaps a singular, festival: the demand for the materials was a daily and continual want which the citizens could gratify without restraint or remorse. In the fourteenth century, a scandalous act of concord secured to both factions the privilege of extracting stones from the free and common quarry of the Coliseum; and Poggius laments, that the greater part of these stones had been burnt to lime by the folly of the Romans. To check this abuse, and to prevent the nocturnal crimes that might be perpetrated in the vast and gloomy recess, Eugenius the Fourth surrounded it with a wall; and, by a charter long extant, granted both the ground and edifice to the monks of an adjacent convent. After his death, the wall was overthrown in a tumult of the people; and had they themselves respected the noblest monument of their fathers, they might have justified the resolve that it should never be degraded to private property. The inside was damaged: but in the middle of the sixteenth century, an æra of taste and learning, the exterior circumference of one thousand six hundred and twelve feet was still entire and inviolate; a triple elevation of fourscore arches, which rose to the height of one hundred and eight feet. Of the present ruin, the nephews of Paul the Third are the guilty agents; and every traveller who views the Farnese palace may curse the sacrilege and luxury of these upstart princes. A similar reproach is applied to the Barberini; and the repetition of injury might be dreaded from every reign, till the Coliseum was placed under the safeguard of religion by the most liberal of the pontiffs, Benedict the Fourteenth, who consecrated a spot which persecution and fable had stained with the blood of so many Christian martyrs.

When Petrarch first gratified his eyes with a view of those monuments, whose scattered fragments so far surpass the most eloquent descriptions, he was astonished at the supine indifference of the Romans themselves; he was humbled rather than elated by the discovery, that, except his friend Rienzi, and one of the Colonna, a stranger of the Rhône was more conversant with these antiquities than the nobles and natives of the metropolis. The ignorance and credulity of the Romans are elaborately displayed in the old survey of the city which was composed about the beginning of the thirteenth century; and, without dwelling on the manifold errors of name and place, the legend of the Capitol may provoke a smile of contempt and indignation. "The Capitol," says the anonymous writer, "is so named as being the head of the world; where the consuls and senators formerly resided for the government of the city and the globe. The strong and lofty walls were covered with glass and gold, and crowned with a roof of the richest and most curious carving. Below the citadel stood a palace, of gold for the greatest part, decorated with precious stones, and whose value might be esteemed at one third of the world itself. The statues of all the provinces were arranged in order, each with a small bell suspended from its neck; and such was the contrivance of art magic, that if the province rebelled against Rome, the statue turned round to that quarter of the heavens, the bell rang, the prophet of the Capitol repeated the prodigy, and the senate was admonished of the impending danger." A second example, of less importance, though of equal absurdity, may be drawn from the two marble horses, led by two naked youths, who have since been transported from the baths of Constantine to the Quirinal hill. The groundless application of the names of Phidias and Praxiteles may perhaps be excused; but these Grecian sculptors should not have been removed above four hundred years from the age of Pericles to that of Tiberius; they should not have been transferred into two philosophers or magicians, whose nakedness was the symbol of truth or knowledge, who revealed to the emperor his most secret actions; and, after refusing all pecuniary recompense, solicited the honor of leaving this eternal monument of themselves. Thus awake to the power of magic, the Romans were insensible to the beauties of art: no more than five statues were visible to the eyes of Poggius; and of the multitudes which chance or design had buried under the ruins, the resurrection was fortunately delayed till a safer and more enlightened age. The Nile which now adorns the Vatican, had been explored by some laborers in digging a vineyard near the temple, or convent, of the Minerva; but the impatient proprietor, who was tormented by some visits of curiosity, restored the unprofitable marble to its former grave. The discovery of a statue of Pompey, ten feet in length, was the occasion of a lawsuit. It had been found under a partition wall: the equitable judge had pronounced, that the head should be separated from the body to satisfy the claims of the contiguous owners; and the sentence would have been executed, if the intercession of a cardinal, and the liberality of a pope, had not rescued the Roman hero from the hands of his barbarous countrymen.

But the clouds of barbarism were gradually dispelled; and the peaceful authority of Martin the Fifth and his successors restored the ornaments of the city as well as the order of the ecclesiastical state. The improvements of Rome, since the fifteenth century, have not been the spontaneous produce of freedom and industry. The first and most natural root of a great city is the labor and populousness of the adjacent country, which supplies the materials of subsistence, of manufactures, and of foreign trade. But the greater part of the Campagna of Rome is reduced to a dreary and desolate wilderness: the overgrown estates of the princes and the clergy are cultivated by the lazy hands of indigent and hopeless vassals; and the scanty harvests are confined or exported for the benefit of a monopoly. A second and more artificial cause of the growth of a metropolis is the residence of a monarch, the expense of a luxurious court, and the tributes of dependent provinces. Those provinces and tributes had been lost in the fall of the empire; and if some streams of the silver of Peru and the gold of Brazil have been attracted by the Vatican, the revenues of the cardinals, the fees of office, the oblations of pilgrims and clients, and the remnant of ecclesiastical taxes, afford a poor and precarious supply, which maintains, however, the idleness of the court and city. The population of Rome, far below the measure of the great capitals of Europe, does not exceed one hundred and seventy thousand inhabitants; and within the spacious enclosure of the walls, the largest portion of the seven hills is overspread with vineyards and ruins. The beauty and splendor of the modern city may be ascribed to the abuses of the government, to the influence of superstition. Each reign (the exceptions are rare) has been marked by the rapid elevation of a new family, enriched by the childish pontiff at the expense of the church and country. The palaces of these fortunate nephews are the most costly monuments of elegance and servitude: the perfect arts of architecture, sculpture, and painting, have been prostituted in their service; and their galleries and gardens are decorated with the most precious works of antiquity, which taste or vanity has prompted them to collect. The ecclesiastical revenues were more decently employed by the popes themselves in the pomp of the Catholic worship; but it is superfluous to enumerate their pious foundations of altars, chapels, and churches, since these lesser stars are eclipsed by the sun of the Vatican, by the dome of St. Peter, the most glorious structure that ever has been applied to the use of religion. The fame of Julius the Second, Leo the Tenth, and Sixtus the Fifth, is accompanied by the superior merit of Bramante and Fontana, of Raphael and Michael Angelo; and the same munificence which had been displayed in palaces and temples was directed with equal zeal to revive and emulate the labors of antiquity. Prostrate obelisks were raised from the ground, and erected in the most conspicuous places; of the eleven aqueducts of the Cæsars and consuls, three were restored; the artificial rivers were conducted over a long series of old, or of new arches, to discharge into marble basins a flood of salubrious and refreshing waters: and the spectator, impatient to ascend the steps of St. Peter's, is detained by a column of Egyptian granite, which rises between two lofty and perpetual fountains, to the height of one hundred and twenty feet. The map, the description, the monuments of ancient Rome, have been elucidated by the diligence of the antiquarian and the student: and the footsteps of heroes, the relics, not of superstition, but of empire, are devoutly visited by a new race of pilgrims from the remote, and once savage countries of the North.

Of these pilgrims, and of every reader, the attention will be excited by a History of the Decline and Fall of the Roman Empire; the greatest, perhaps, and most awful scene in the history of mankind. The various causes and progressive effects are connected with many of the events most interesting in human annals: the artful policy of the Cæsars, who long maintained the name and image of a free republic; the disorders of military despotism; the rise, establishment, and sects of Christianity; the foundation of Constantinople; the division of the monarchy; the invasion and settlements of the Barbarians of Germany and Scythia; the institutions of the civil law; the character and religion of Mahomet; the temporal sovereignty of the popes; the restoration and decay of the Western empire of Charlemagne; the crusades of the Latins in the East: the conquests of the Saracens and Turks; the ruin of the Greek empire; the state and revolutions of Rome in the middle age. The historian may applaud the importance and variety of his subject; but while he is conscious of his own imperfections, he must often accuse the deficiency of his materials. It was among the ruins of the Capitol that I first conceived the idea of a work which has amused and exercised near twenty years of my life, and which, however inadequate to my own wishes, I finally delivere to the curiosity and candor of the public.

Lausanne, June 27 1787

END OF VOL. SIX

ROYAL
CLASSICS

ROYAL
CLASSICS

ROYAL CLASSICS

ROYAL
CLASSICS